English Composition and Grammar

BENCHMARK EDITION

John E. Warriner

Second Course

Harcourt Brace Jovanovich, Publishers

Orlando San Diego Chicago Dallas

THE SERIES:

English Composition and Grammar: Introductory Course
English Composition and Grammar: First Course
English Composition and Grammar: Second Course
English Composition and Grammar: Third Course
English Composition and Grammar: Fourth Course
English Composition and Grammar: Fifth Course
English Composition and Grammar: Complete Course

Annotated Teacher's Edition and Teacher's Resource Book for each above title.

CORRELATED SERIES:

English Workshop: Introductory Course
English Workshop: First Course
English Workshop: Second Course
English Workshop: Third Course
English Workshop: Fourth Course
English Workshop: Fifth Course
English Workshop: Review Course

Composition: Models and Exercises, First Course
Composition: Models and Exercises, Second Course
Composition: Models and Exercises, Third Course
Composition: Models and Exercises, Fourth Course
Composition: Models and Exercises, Fifth Course
Advanced Composition: A Book of Models for Writing, Complete Course

Vocabulary Workshop: Introductory Course
Vocabulary Workshop: First Course
Vocabulary Workshop: Second Course
Vocabulary Workshop: Third Course
Vocabulary Workshop: Fourth Course
Vocabulary Workshop: Fifth Course
Vocabulary Workshop: Complete Course

John E. Warriner taught English for thirty-two years in junior and senior high schools and in college. He is chief author of the *English Composition and Grammar* series, coauthor of the *English Workshop* series, general editor of the *Composition: Models and Exercises* series, and editor of *Short Stories: Characters in Conflict*. His coauthors have all been active in English education.

For permission to reprint copyrighted material, grateful acknowledgment is made to the following sources:

Isaac Asimov: From *Asimov on Numbers* by Isaac Asimov. Copyright © 1977 by Isaac Asimov.

Atheneum Publishers, Inc.: From "Attitude" in *Happy to Be Here* by Garrison Keillor. Copyright © 1982 by Garrison Keillor.

Banyan Books, Inc.: From *Florida by Pack and Paddle* by Mike Toner and Pat Toner. Copyright © 1979 by Mike Toner and Pat Toner.

The Curtis Publishing Company: From "How to Make Champions" in *The Saturday Evening Post.* © 1956 by The Curtis Publishing Company.

Benjamin Franklin Literary & Medical Society, Inc.: From "Nature's Medicines: Spearmint" by Lois Wickstrom in *Child Life* Magazine. Copyright © 1981 by Benjamin Franklin Literary & Medical Society, Inc., Indianapolis, IN. From "Magnificent Failure—Or Was He?" by Eleanor Anderson in *Young World* Magazine. Copyright © 1978 by The Saturday Evening Post Company, Indianapolis, IN.

Friends of Animals, Inc.: From "Do You Really Want a Pet?" by Alice Herrington in *Family Circle* Magazine, January 25, 1983.

Harcourt Brace Jovanovich, Inc.: From *Concepts in Science,* Third Edition, Level Purple by Paul Brandwein, et al. From *American History* by John A. Garraty. Copyright © 1982 by Harcourt Brace Jovanovich, Inc. From *American Civics,* Fourth Edition by William H. Hartley and William S. Vincent. Copyright © 1967, 1970, 1974, 1979, 1983 by Harcourt Brace Jovanovich, Inc. From *Strategies in Reading C* by Ethel Grodzins Romm. Copyright © 1984 by Harcourt Brace Jovanovich, Inc. From Tests to accompany *AMERICA: Its People and Values,* Heritage Edition by Leonard C. Wood, Ralph C. Gabriel, and Edward L. Biller. Copyright © 1985 by Harcourt Brace Jovanovich, Inc. Graphics for the letter "M" from *HBJ School Dictionary.* Copyright © 1985 by Harcourt Brace Jovanovich, Inc. Entries "smart," "dexterous," and "lovely" from *The HBJ School Dictionary.* Copyright © 1977 by Harcourt Brace Jovanovich, Inc.

Harper & Row, Publishers, Inc.: Specified excerpt from p. 45 in *Weapons and Hope* by Freeman Dyson. Copyright © 1984 by Freeman J. Dyson. Originally published in *The New Yorker.*

Houghton Mifflin Company: Entries "offensive" and "credit" from the *American Heritage Student Dictionary.* © 1986 by Houghton Mifflin Company.

Jon R. Luoma: From "Troubled Skies, Troubled Waters" by Jon R. Luoma.

The Nature Conservancy News: Adapted from "Remembrances of a Rain Forest" by Paul Colinvaux in *The Nature Conservancy News,* Vol. 29, No. 4, July/August 1979.

The New York Times Company: From "7 Days on the Yangtze" by Barbara Goldsmith in *The New York Times,* March 17, 1985. Copyright © 1985 by The New York Times Company. From "What's New in Laser Technology" by Gordon Graff in *The New York Times,* April 7, 1985. Copyright © 1985 by The New York Times Company. From "Technology: Helping Driver Feel at Home" by John Holusha in *The New York Times,* February 28, 1985. Copyright © 1985 by The New York Times Company.

Outdoor Life Books: From *Bears* by Ben East. Published by Outdoor Life Books.

Prentice-Hall, Inc., Englewood Cliffs, NJ: From *The Amateur Naturalist's Handbook* by Vinson Brown. © 1980 by Prentice-Hall, Inc.

Random House, Inc.: From *Losing Battles* by Eudora Welty. Copyright © 1970 by Eudora Welty.

Russell & Volkening, Inc., as agents for Ann Petry: From *Harriet Tubman* (Titled: "They Called Her Moses") by Ann Petry. Copyright © 1955, renewed 1983 by Ann Petry.

Saturday Review: From "The Great American Barbe-Queue" by Charles Kuralt in *Saturday Review* Magazine, June 26, 1976. © 1976 by Saturday Review Magazine.

Scholastic Inc.: From "How Do They Make Snow?" by Brian McCallen in *Science World* Magazine, November 5, 1982. Copyright © 1982 by Scholastic Inc.

Simon & Schuster, Inc.: Entry for "Franklin Pierce" from *Webster's New World Dictionary of the American Language,* Second College Edition. Copyright 1970, 1972, 1974, 1976, 1978, 1979, 1980 by Simon & Schuster, Inc.

Smithsonian Institution Press: From "An old Africa hand fights to keep his lions wild and free" by Dick Houston in *Smithsonian* Magazine, July 1983.

PHOTO CREDITS

Key: T,Top; B,Bottom

Cover: HBJ Photo

Page 1,Ed Cooper; 2,Ed Cooper; IW1,Richard Howard; IW2,William Thompson; IW4T,HBJ Photo; IW4B,Ann Hagen Griffiths/Omni-Photo Communications; IW5,Clyde H. Smith from F/Stop Pictures; IW6T,Denver Public Library Western Collection; IW6B,William Thompson; IW8,George Ancona/International Stock Photo; IW9,Steve Elmore; IW10,General Biological Supply House, Inc.; IW12T,John R. McCauley/Photri; IW12B,Peter Fronk from Click/Chicago; IW13,John Moran; IW14,Frank Niemeir; IW16,Ed Cooper; 227,W. Metzen/H. Armstrong Roberts, Inc.; 228,Ed Cooper; 263,David Lissy from Click/Chicago; 264,Gianni Tortoli/Photo Researchers; 595,Phil Degginger/H. Armstrong Roberts, Inc.; 596,H. Armstrong Roberts, Inc.; 669,ZEFA/H. Armstrong Roberts, Inc.; 670,J. Smith/Leo De Wys, Inc.

Printed in the United States of America
ISBN 0–15–311732–X

To the Student

A long time ago when education did not have to be so complicated as it must be today, the main subjects in school were referred to as the three R's: reading, 'riting, and 'rithmetic. As a familiar song says, they were "taught to the tune of a hickory stick." The hickory stick, fortunately, is not much used any more, but the three R's remain. Two of them, reading and writing, make up a large part of the school subject called English.

If someone were to ask you the unlikely question, "What do you do in English?" your reply might be something like this: "In English we read stories and poems and stuff like that. We write our own stories and poems and themes. We learn about nouns and verbs and, well, subjects and predicates, I guess. And we give talks in front of the class." This answer is a fairly good account of what you do in English.

A teacher, however, would use different terms in answering the same question. Instead of mentioning just stories and poems, a teacher might say you study *literature.* Writing stories, poems, and themes is practicing written *composition.* Noun, verb, subject, and predicate are terms used in the study of *grammar.* Talks in front of the class are a means of improving your *speech.* The four main areas of English, then, are literature, composition, grammar, and speech.

This book deals mainly with the last three of the four areas, composition, grammar, and speech. To use a language well, you need to know how it works. By studying grammar, you learn how the language works. This knowledge will help you to improve both your writing and your speech.

Although you write much less often than you speak, written composition demands a large amount of English time because writing is hard to learn. Each year in school you will be expected to do more written work in most of your classes, but it is only in English class that you learn how to write.

By writing well, you communicate with others. By speaking (and listening) well, you also communicate with others. Speech skills are a vital part of your education because you spend so much of every day talking with others.

Mastering the three areas in this textbook—composition, grammar, and speech—is not an easy task. However, you can do it if you have sound guidance. Your teacher is your most helpful guide, but your textbook is also an important guide. Study it, follow the rules, do the practice exercises, and whenever you write or speak, put to use what you have learned. You will find your work will improve steadily.

J. W.

CONTENTS

Part Two: COMPOSITION: Writing and Revising Sentences

Part Three: TOOLS FOR WRITING AND REVISING

GRAMMAR

Part Five: SPEAKING AND LISTENING

PART ONE

COMPOSITION: The Writing Process

CHAPTER 1

Writing and Thinking

THE WRITING PROCESS

A *process* is a series of actions carried out to produce or create something. Writing is a process—it involves several stages of thinking and putting words on paper. Thinking, in fact, is a big part of the writer's job. In this chapter you will learn and practice all steps of the writing process, including the *critical thinking* that you must do at every stage.

THE WRITING PROCESS

The following list shows six stages in the writing process. Notice that the *prewriting* stage includes several steps.

PREWRITING

1. Deciding on a purpose, or reason, for writing
2. Thinking about the audience's needs and interests
3. Choosing a subject for writing
4. Limiting the subject to a suitable topic
5. Gathering information on the topic
6. Organizing the information

WRITING THE FIRST DRAFT

7. Expressing your ideas in sentences and paragraphs

EVALUATING

8. Reexamining the ideas, organization, and word choice in your first draft

REVISING

9. Making changes to improve the first draft

PROOFREADING

10. Checking for errors in grammar, usage, and mechanics
11. Correcting errors

MAKING THE FINAL COPY

12. Copying the final draft in a correct form
13. Correcting any copying errors

As you learn these steps, keep in mind that you will not always follow them in a rigid order. How you apply the process depends on what you are writing and on your habits as a writer. For example, if you are writing a quick note, you may spend only a minute or two planning your message. For an important report, you may spend several days in the prewriting stage. On some occasions, you may be revising a paper and find that you need to return to a prewriting step. Every time you write, you face a different situation and make different decisions.

EXERCISE 1. Understanding the Writing Process. The following entries from a writer's notebook show how one student used the writing process to prepare an article for the school newspaper. Use the list of writing stages on pages 3–4 to answer the questions following these entries.

Tuesday—I've spent an hour brainstorming subjects for my next article for the school newspaper. I think kids would be interested in the summer space-camp Brian attended. I can talk to Brian tomorrow and find out more about the camp.

Wednesday—Wow! Brian really had a lot to say about the model rockets they launched, their experiments with weightlessness, and the simulated space shuttle mission. I think I have plenty of information. All I have to do is write it up.

Thursday—I wrote half of my first draft, but when I read over it I wasn't thrilled. It's too disorganized. I thought I could tell what happened at camp day by day, but I got off the track. Maybe I should stop and organize my notes.

Friday—I finished writing my second draft and started revising. I decided I needed more details about the simulated space shuttle mission; I called Brian and got more information.

Saturday—Finished proofreading and correcting mistakes in the article. I can write the final copy.

1. What stage was the writer at on Tuesday? What step did the writer complete?
2. On what day did the writer move to the *writing* stage?
3. On Thursday the writer moved from the *writing* stage back to *prewriting*. Why?
4. Why did the writer move from *revising* back to *prewriting* on Friday?
5. What step in the process should the writer devote more time to when writing the next article?

PREWRITING

Prewriting includes all the thinking and planning that you do before you begin to write. What you put on paper during this stage will guide your writing.

Before You Write. Ask yourself:

- Why am I writing? (purpose)
- Who will read what I write? (audience)
- What will I write about? (topic)
- What will I say about the topic? (details)
- How will I organize my ideas? (order)

Understanding and making sound decisions about each of these questions will help you produce strong writing.

You do not have to answer these questions in the same particular order every time you prepare to write. Begin with what you know about the writing task. If your English teacher asks you to write a description that will interest your classmates, you know your purpose (to describe) and audience (your classmates). With these in mind, you can search for an appropriate topic and gather interesting details.

IDENTIFYING YOUR PURPOSE

1a. Determine your purpose for writing.

When you think about *why* you are writing, you think about your *purpose*. You will find that having a clear purpose in mind will help you decide what ideas to present to your readers.

Most writing has one of four basic purposes:

1. To tell a story, or what happened (*narrative* writing)

EXAMPLE We had just finished our picnic lunch when my uncle hollered, "Look at that!" Lumbering down the path toward us was an elephant. We thought the animal was loose until we saw one of the zookeepers walking beside her. The zookeeper explained that the elephant, named Tiny, was simply out for a stroll. As we talked, Tiny stood quietly waving her huge gray ears back and forth like fans, curling and uncurling her trunk. When the zookeeper tapped Tiny's front leg, she rose up on her hind legs and turned in a circle almost as if she were dancing.

2. To describe (*descriptive* writing)

EXAMPLE Tiny was at least three or four feet taller than the zookeeper. Her bulky gray body was covered with wrinkled, tough skin that hung in loose, baggy folds around her short, thick legs. In contrast, her ears were like two paper-thin palm leaves attached to each side of her head.

3. To explain or inform (*expository* writing)

EXAMPLE An elephant uses its trunk the way we use our hands. Because the trunk is strong and flexible, an elephant can lift and carry a six-hundred-pound log simply by curling its trunk around the log. Using the delicate knob at the end of its trunk, an elephant can locate and pick up an object as small as a dime. In the jungle heat an elephant cools off by filling its trunk with water and shooting the water across its back. An adult elephant can store a six-gallon shower in its trunk.

4. To persuade (*persuasive* writing)

EXAMPLE Many wildlife experts predict that the elephant —along with the cheetah, the Siberian tiger, and the rhinoceros—will disappear within the next twenty-five years. Few people realize that more than a thousand varieties of wild animals are threatened with extinction. The threats to these animals include the clearing of more than 100,000 acres of jungle every day, illegal hunting, and the poisoning of the environment with pesticides and powerful fertilizers. Unless people around the world support conservation groups such as the World Wildlife Fund and the zoo's Save the Animals program, seeing a live elephant or tiger may become as difficult as seeing a live dinosaur.

Occasionally, it may seem that the writing you are planning does not fit these four purposes. For example, you may decide to entertain your readers with humor. If you look closely at your plan, you will probably discover that you really have one of the four basic purposes. Perhaps you will entertain readers by *persuading* them to do something silly, by *telling a* funny *story,* or by *describing* an amusing scene.

Sometimes, part of a long piece of writing has a purpose separate from the basic purpose. For example, the main purpose of a newspaper article may be to persuade students to attend a workshop on bicycle safety. The reporter might begin by telling about a bicycle accident that happened because someone did not follow the safety rules. Most of the writing you do will have a single major purpose.

Before You Write. Decide whether your main purpose is to

- tell a story (tell what happened).
- describe.
- explain or inform.
- persuade.

Defining your purpose for writing will help you make decisions about the kinds of details you gather. Descriptive writing includes details about how something looks, tastes, smells, sounds, or feels when touched. Narrative writing emphasizes events and action. Expository writing gives readers new and specific information. In persuasive writing, you support an opinion with reasons and evidence.

Understanding your purpose can also help you decide on your topic. Some topics are more appropriate for one purpose than another. If you recently saw a magician's performance, you might describe the magician's appearance or tell what happened during the act. It would be more difficult, based only on your observations, to write a persuasive paper or to explain how each trick was performed.

EXERCISE 2. Identifying Purposes for Writing. Read each of the following paragraphs. Decide if the writer's purpose is to describe, to tell a story, to explain, or to persuade.

1. It was a perfect Halloween night. From behind the gray edges of the clouds, a round orange moon lit up a starless sky. The

moonlight outlined the bare twisted limbs of the apple tree in the yard. The wind whistled and moaned, scattering dead leaves and rattling in the dry weeds along the fence. Somewhere in the distance an owl hooted.

2. Several Halloween customs can be traced back to the Celts, who lived in England over a thousand years ago. The Celts believed dangerous spirits were allowed to roam the countryside on October 31, the night before their new year. To protect themselves from these wandering spirits, the Celts stayed at home and put good things to eat outside their doors. If they had to go out, they dressed up in unusual disguises, hoping any evil spirit they encountered would mistake them for other wandering spirits.

3. Some students and parents want to do away with trick-or-treating because candy or fruit can be tampered with—but marching around town in costumes is half the fun of Halloween! I think we should continue to trick-or-treat but accept only donations for UNICEF. We could all meet at school and divide into groups with one adult in each group. Later we could come back to the gym for a community Halloween party with games and refreshments. We could even turn the locker room into a "haunted house."

EXERCISE 3. Identifying Purposes for Writing. Imagine that you will write a one- or two-page paper about each of the following topics. For each one, tell what your major purpose for writing would be.

1. The sights and sounds of a hayride on a crisp autumn evening
2. Why your school needs a larger gymnasium
3. What happened at last Friday's pep rally
4. The training required to become a veterinarian
5. The time your aunt, a veterinarian, was knocked over by a cow

KNOWING YOUR AUDIENCE

1b. Always consider the needs and interests of your readers.

Another important step in prewriting is thinking about your *audience*—the person or persons who will read your writing. Good writers plan their writing to fit their audience's age, knowledge, interests, and opinions. Last week one student completed three pieces of writing:

A letter to Exotic Pets, Inc., about food for her new parrot
A one-page science report about the habits of tropical birds
A letter to her six-year-old cousin, who has the measles

When she wrote to her young cousin, she used simple words and short sentences that he could understand. To amuse him, she told a funny story about her new parrot. In her letter to Exotic Pets, Inc., she stated clearly what seeds and bird food she wanted. Because this was a business letter, she included only the information needed to fill her order. Since her teacher is interested in what she has learned about parrots, she wrote a report about their habits and behavior. She included scientific terms to show that she knew their meanings. In each situation, what she knew about her readers' age, education, interests, and opinions influenced how she handled her topic.

Before You Write. Consider your audience by asking yourself:

- Will the topic and details interest the readers?
- What background information do they need?
- How simple or complex should my language be?
- Do the readers have special feelings about the topic?

EXERCISE 4. Choosing Details to Fit the Audience. Imagine that the following items are details about your school and recent activities. Decide which details you would include in a letter to a new Japanese pen pal who has never been to the United States. Then decide which details you would include in a letter to a former classmate who has just moved away.

1. In winter I ride the bus, because we have a lot of snow and temperatures that are often below zero.

2. We watched the breakdancing on the river walk.
3. We took a field trip to the farm museum and watched a demonstration of plowing with horses.
4. The junior-high band will perform at the Spring Festival.
5. Saturday I played a new video game with Enrique and his sister at the arcade in the mall.
6. School starts at 7:30 in the morning and ends at 3:15.
7. Every day I have five classes, each taught by a different teacher.
8. Thursday there was a tornado warning. A siren went off, but nothing happened.
9. Our town has two high schools and three junior high schools.
10. In nice spring and fall weather, I ride my bicycle to school.

EXERCISE 5. Rewriting to Fit the Audience. The paragraph about Halloween customs on page 9 was written for an eighth-grade audience. Read it carefully; then rewrite it for an audience of third-grade students.

CHOOSING A SUBJECT

Do not overlook your own experiences when you search for a writing subject. Experienced writers know they often produce their best work when they write about what they know well. In the following paragraph, the writer used her experience with ice skating to explain how skates should fit.

> Beginners who wobble around the rink or can't balance on their blades often assume they have weak ankles. Actually, the problem is usually skates that are too big. When you rent skates, remember that skate sizes normally run larger than shoe sizes. Ask for skates that are a half size smaller than your shoe size. Lace the bottom two or three eyes of the skate loosely. Then lace the skate tightly up to your ankle and tie a half knot. Lace the rest of the skate loosely and stand up. You should be able to wiggle your toes, but if you can move your heels up and down inside your skates, your skates are too big.

Starting with Yourself

1c. Consider both direct and indirect experiences.

Direct experiences are those you experience yourself: places you visit, people you know, your hobbies, and sports you participate in. What interesting places could you describe? What is special about a person you know? What memorable events can you share with your readers?

EXAMPLES *Places:* sitting under the oak tree at the end of the cornfield, the waiting room at my dentist's office
People: how my cousin copes with her handicap
Hobbies: restoring a Model T Ford, raising rabbits as a 4-H project
Sports: tobogganing at the forest preserve, trying out for the swimming team
Work: stocking shelves at my aunt's hardware store

Indirect experiences are those you gain from reading, watching films or television, or listening to another person. If you have read several articles about experiments during flights of the space shuttle, you probably know enough to write about this subject. If your great-uncle has told you about the hardships his family faced during the Depression, you might write about his experiences.

EXAMPLES *Reading about the Loch Ness monster:* how scientists have searched for the monster
Tour of the local hospital: how a heart monitor works, why the community needs a trauma center
Nature program you heard on the radio: how animals communicate

Using Brainstorming

1d. Use brainstorming to discover ideas for writing.

Brainstorming encourages a free flow of thinking. It can help writers recall experiences they may have forgotten. When you brainstorm, you concentrate on a broad subject and record all the ideas that come into your mind, even those that seem far-fetched. A weak idea often leads to a good one. You can brainstorm alone or in a group. Find a quiet spot, write your subject at the top of a sheet of paper, and let your mind relax. Record all the ideas that occur to you. When you run out of ideas, go over your list. Circle any items that might be good writing subjects. If you have more ideas as you read through the list, add these.

Here are some of the notes one student made while brainstorming about his own experiences:

Places
- the tree house my sister and I built when I was six
- the hayloft of the farm

People
- canoeing with my grandfather
- my sister's struggle to make the gymnastics team

Part-time Work
- giving my aunt's terriers a bath
- the pros and cons of a paper route

Hobbies/Crafts
- how to do simple calligraphy
- collecting unusual bumper stickers
- making art objects out of old tin cans

Sports
- junior-high football—is it dangerous?
- skateboarding—picking the right skateboard

Clubs and Activities
- raising a seeing-eye dog as a 4-H project
- starting a music group with friends

EXERCISE 6. Using Brainstorming. Choose three of the following areas of experience. For each of these, spend at least five minutes brainstorming possible subjects for writing. When you have run out of ideas, exchange papers with at least two of your classmates. Ask them to tell you which subjects on your list interest them the most.

1. When I was seven . . .
2. Interesting places
3. People I know well
4. Sports and recreation
5. Chores and part-time jobs
6. Moments I'll never forget

Using a Writer's Notebook

1e. Keep ideas in a writer's notebook.

Many writers keep notes about their experiences in a special notebook, or journal. They express thoughts and feelings about people, events, and books or articles they have read. They may add newspaper clippings, quotations, cartoons, advertisements, or photographs that interest them. Some writers simply talk to themselves on paper or list questions for which they would like to find answers. Your writer's notebook can include anything that interests, puzzles, or impresses you—anything you want to remember or explore as a possible subject for writing and that you feel comfortable sharing with others. Here is an example entry from one student's journal.

> Jill is so funny. She's only three, but she tries so hard to be grown up. Yesterday in church she decided she should sing the hymns with everyone else. Of course, she can't read, so she just hums or goes "la-la-la-da." I couldn't help laughing. When she saw me, she got very serious, scowled and said, "Jimmy, I not funny." It's odd. Even when Jill messes up my room, I'm amused. When my nine-year-old sister does something silly or bothers me, I'm annoyed. I know I'm too hard on her. Maybe it's easier to understand brothers and sisters if they're much younger than you are. I wonder if other kids my age have the same feelings.

EXERCISE 7. Keeping a Writer's Notebook. For the next week, collect at least one item a day to put in a writer's notebook. (You may want to use a folder.) The daily entry might be a few sentences you write about an experience. It might also be a newspaper or magazine article, cartoon, comic strip, advertisement, picture, or a letter to an editor or advice columnist. Use your imagination in deciding what to include in your notebook.

Using Your Powers of Observation

1f. Use your powers of observation to find subjects.

Rather than waiting to be inspired, good writers use their powers of observation to discover subjects in the world around them. They train themselves to look closely, to notice details, and to explore the meaning of events and problems.

Here is a paragraph one student wrote about the school cafeteria. This writer not only used powers of observation to record a variety of details but also thought about the relationship of certain things in the scene.

> Twenty minutes after one. The last lunch hour ended fifteen minutes ago. Right now the only sound in the cafeteria is a muffled conversation coming from the kitchen. I'm sitting at a gray formica table near the door to the main hall. A pool of chocolate milk from an overturned carton has worked its way to the edge of the table, where it's dripping slowly to the floor. Under the table on the right, I can see three crumpled napkins, a plate smeared with half-eaten spaghetti and green beans, several forks, a spoon bent into a U, two grease-stained paper bags, and a half-eaten banana. This isn't unusual. All the tables are dotted with abandoned brown plastic trays, lunchbags, and spills. The Pep Club has taped "school spirit" posters on the walls around the room. Behind me a large orange-and-blue sign proclaims, "Be proud of your school." It's hard to be proud of this mess! Why can't school spirit include the lunchroom?

CRITICAL THINKING:
Observing and Interpreting Details

Writers train themselves to be observant. They begin by paying careful attention to the details that make up an experience. Often these are *sensory details*—ones that describe the sight, sound, feel, smell, or taste of something. Then they search for words and phrases that will help their readers understand what they have observed. A keen ability to observe and describe details takes practice. For that reason, writers make frequent sensory observations in their notebooks. One day they may record the posture and expressions of people waiting in a long line. Another day they might write about all the sounds they hear in a quiet library or about the taste of a spicy Mexican dinner.

EXERCISE 8. Observing Sensory Details. Choose two of the following experiences or images and describe each one in several sentences. Try to experience or observe directly each detail before you translate it into words.

1. The taste, smell, and feel of eating a spoonful of peanut butter
2. The expression on the face of someone who is angry
3. The look and sound of ice cubes in a glass of water
4. The inside of your school locker and the sounds of using it
5. The posture and expressions of two students waiting to catch the school bus

Considering Your Attitude

1g. Consider your attitude toward a subject.

Attitude is the feeling a writer has about a subject. This feeling is expressed in the *tone* of the writing: the kinds of words the writer chooses to talk about a subject. Good writers do not always search for unusual subjects. Instead, they may express a new or unusual attitude that makes even a common subject interesting. For example, probably thousands of writers have written about playing baseball. The following comments on this overworked subject are appealing because of the writer's amusing attitude. Rather than offering serious advice, he gives his readers some tips on how to act like a pro.

> 1. When going up to bat, don't step right into the batter's box as if it were an elevator. The box is your turf, your stage. Take possession of it slowly and deliberately, starting with a lot of back-bending, knee-stretching, and torso-revolving in

the on-deck circle. Then, approaching the box, stop outside it and tap the dirt off your spikes with your bat. You don't have spikes, you have sneakers, of course, but the significance of the tapping is the same. Then, upon entering the box, spit on the ground. It's a way of saying, "This here is mine. This is where I get my hits."

2. Spit frequently. Spit at all crucial moments. Spit correctly. Spit should be *blown,* not ptuied weakly with the lips, which often results in dribble. Spitting should convey forcefulness of purpose, concentration, pride. Spit down, not in the direction of others. Spit in the glove and on the fingers, especially after making a real knucklehead play; it's a way of saying, "I dropped the ball because my glove was dry."

3. At the bat and in the field, pick up dirt. Rub dirt in the fingers (especially after spitting on them). Toss dirt, as if testing the wind for velocity and direction. Smooth the dirt. Be involved with dirt. If no dirt is available (e.g., in the outfield), pluck tufts of grass. Fielders should be grooming their areas constantly between plays, flicking away tiny sticks and bits of gravel.

GARRISON KEILLOR

Before You Write. Choose a subject that

- is interesting to you.
- is interesting to your audience.
- draws on your experiences.

LIMITING THE SUBJECT

1h. Limit your subject to a topic that fits your writing task.

When you write, you are limited by space and time. You may have two hours and the space of a paragraph or a week and the space of a three-page report. Your writing will be easier, more enjoyable, and more interesting to readers if you make sensible decisions about how much of a subject you can cover.

A *subject* is a broad area of knowledge. The subject "science," for example, includes all kinds of science throughout history. Even in a very long book, it would be difficult to cover every aspect of this subject.

A *topic* is a limited subject. Working with a topic means that you can give readers the kind of specific information that makes writing interesting.

How much you need to limit a subject depends on the *form* of your writing. The form might be a paragraph, a two-page composition, or a ten-page report. Usually, shorter forms of writing require more limited subjects. If you are writing a paragraph, you will have to limit your subject to a topic that can be developed in several sentences. For a ten-page report you can select a topic that covers more information.

Before You Write. To limit your subject

- consider the *form* of your writing.
- choose a *topic* to fit the form.

CRITICAL THINKING:
Analyzing a Subject

To discover smaller parts of a subject, you can use the critical thinking skill of *analysis*. When you analyze something, you break it down into separate parts and think about how these parts are related. You can divide a subject into parts such as examples, features, time periods, places, events, causes, or uses; these divisions may be suitable topics for writing.

EXAMPLE *Subject:* Monsters

Places: Loch Ness (the monster), Frankenstein's castle, the Himalayas (the Yeti)

Time periods: Greek mythology (monsters in), the 1950's (monster movies of), the Middle Ages (dragons of), today's science fiction (monsters in)

Examples: sea monsters, vampires, King Kong, trolls

People: Mary Shelley (creator of Frankenstein), Dr. Seuss's Grinch, children and the monsters they imagine, scientists who have studied Loch Ness
Processes: how special effects are used to create film monsters, how to live in a house with a troll under the stairs

If your first analysis of a subject does not uncover topics that are limited enough, continue the process. Analyze, or break down, these topics into smaller and smaller parts.

EXAMPLE *Topic:* Movies about monsters
People: Bela Lugosi as Dracula, Boris Karloff as Frankenstein's monster, Steven Spielberg and monsters
Places: the planet of the apes, Transylvania, *Lost World*
Examples: silent films, slapstick monster films, 3-D films
Time periods: the Edison Company's first Frankenstein film, teen-oriented monster films of the 1950's, monster films of the 1980's
Processes: how special effects were used in *King Kong,* how makeup artists designed a face for Frankenstein's monster

EXERCISE 9. Recognizing Subjects and Topics. Number your paper 1–10. For each of the following items, write whether it is a subject or a topic suitable for a short composition.

1. Railroads
2. Caring for a gerbil
3. How a pencil is made
4. Famous Americans
5. Snoopy, the all-American dog
6. The development of the first railroad
7. Airplanes
8. How a small plane is checked for safety before takeoff
9. Stranded in a blizzard on Christmas Eve
10. Safety precautions for skateboarding

EXERCISE 10. Analyzing Subjects to Find Topics. Select one of the items in Exercise 9 that you recognized as a *subject.* List at least four divisions that you can break the subject into, such as time periods, events, and so on. Then write all the topics you can think of for each division. Underline answers that could be topics for a short composition.

GATHERING INFORMATION

Writers know they can write more effectively when they have many details to choose from. Before they write, they explore their topics thoroughly, gathering all the information they can.

Using Brainstorming and Clustering

1i. Use brainstorming or clustering to gather information.

Earlier in this chapter you used *brainstorming* to recall experiences that you could write about. You can also use brainstorming to remember details of an experience that lie buried in your memory. When you brainstorm, you relax and allow your mind to wander over the topic. One thought leads to another to unlock memory and flood the mind with once-forgotten details. For example, here are details the writer gathered for the paragraph about a school cafeteria on page 15:

varied sounds
muffled conversation
unusually quiet
mess
food
half-eaten banana
pool of chocolate milk
spaghetti and green beans
Trash spills over.
overturned milk cartons
crumpled napkins
list of spelling words
bent spoon
grease-stained paper bags
tables
formica tops
several forks
plastic trays

Notice that some details are words or phrases; one is a sentence. How you record your thoughts when you brainstorm is not important; you want to capture all ideas as they come to mind.

Clustering is another way to tap bits of information stored in your memory. To use clustering, write your topic in the center of a sheet of paper and draw a circle around it. Now let your mind wander freely over the topic. As details come to mind, write them down and circle them. Use lines or arrows to show how one detail is related to another. You will probably discover branches of related ideas growing out from the center. A cluster about the writer's school cafeteria might look like this:

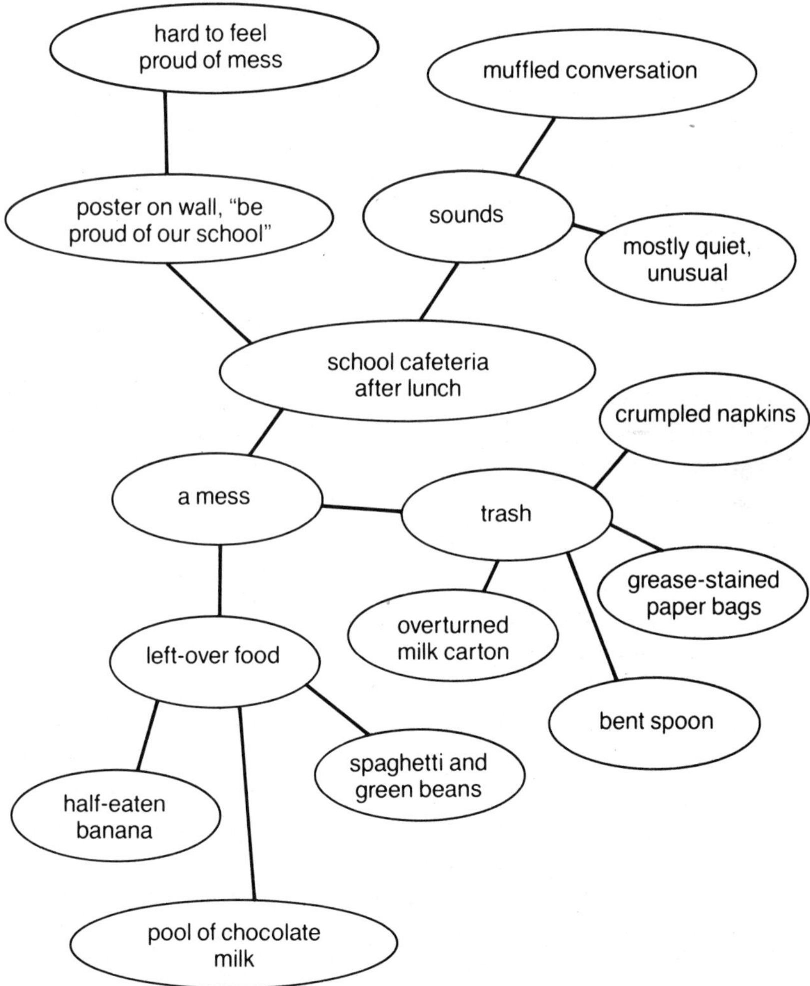

EXERCISE 11. Using Clustering. Choose a topic from the list in Exercise 12, or another topic. Write your topic in the center of a blank sheet of paper and circle it. Begin to add ideas around it as they come to mind. Continue to add, circle, and connect details until you are sure you have run out of ideas. Save your work.

Using the Library

1j. Use your library to gather information.

When you are interested in a topic but do not have much direct experience with it, you can use the library to find more information. Refer to Chapter 27 to review how to find information in magazines, newspapers, and reference books.

Asking the 5 *W-How?* Questions

1k. Use the *5 W-How?* questions to gather information.

To gather information for news stories, reporters use six basic questions: *Who? What? Where? When? Why?* and *How?* You can use this technique, too, when you want to gather details from the experiences of others or from your own experiences.

EXAMPLE *Topic:* Observing bald eagles
Who? I and my uncle, a photographer; plus about seven hundred other people
What? A field trip to observe bald eagles; almost three hundred live in the area
Where? On land owned by Nature Conservancy near Keokuk, Iowa; where Des Moines River joins the Mississippi River
When? Last weekend, at dawn, when birds are feeding on fish in the river
Why? To see and help photograph the eagles; carried some of my uncle's equipment
How? Used telephoto lens on camera; binoculars

You can gather even more information by asking additional questions. Notice in the next example how the writer used variations of the six basic questions to go further into the topic.

Where? On land owned by Nature Conservancy near Keokuk, Iowa
Why do the eagles come here? To escape the frozen rivers in Canada and to feed on the gizzard shad
What is the gizzard shad? Small boneless fish
How? Used a telephoto lens; binoculars
Why? It's difficult for a human to approach a bald eagle.
Why is it difficult? Eagles have keen eyesight and will leave an area if they sense anything out of the ordinary.

EXERCISE 12. Asking the *5 W-How?* Questions. Use the *5 W-How?* questions to gather information on one of the following topics or on another topic. Write down the questions you ask and your answers. (You may need to research some questions.)

1. An interesting relative
2. A special community event
3. An ideal weekend outing
4. A problem in your school
5. A hobby you enjoy
6. A childhood memory
7. A lesson from television
8. Your community in 1930
9. A recent teen fad
10. A violent storm

Asking Point-of-View Questions

1l. Use point-of-view questions to gather information.

Like a photographer, you can see a topic from different perspectives, or points of view. You can "zoom" in to look closely at special features. You can set a "time-lapse" view to reveal how something changes over time. Or you can step back for a "wide-angle" view to see how a topic fits into its natural background. To examine your topic from these three perspectives, you ask certain questions.

1. *What is it?*

From this point of view, you are looking closely at the topic, asking questions about its definition, appearance, and function.

EXAMPLE *Topic:* Statue of Liberty

How large is the statue? About 151 feet tall and weighs 225 tons

What is it made of? Iron framework covered with hundreds of copper plates; thickness of each plate about one-third inch

What does it look like? Tall woman in long gown with graceful folds, holding torch over her head

What is its function? Symbol of freedom, called "Liberty Enlightening the World"

2. *How does it change or vary?*

This point of view helps you focus on how your topic has changed or will change over a period of time.

EXAMPLE *Topic:* Statue of Liberty

When was the statue built? Built in France, then disassembled and shipped to New York in 214 boxes; arrived on June 19, 1885, but pedestal wasn't ready

What changes occurred? At first a bright copper; slowly acquired a green color (patina). Flame of the torch copper at first, then gold. In 1916, six hundred pieces of yellow glass installed to make light of torch brighter

Why did the statue need restoration? Torch in danger of collapse; much of the copper corroded. Braces inside the statue weakened; some parts of copper skin nearly worn through

How has restoration changed the statue? New double-decker glass elevator in base of statue. New railing on old circular stairway of 171 steps and a sturdier platform in the crown

3. *What are its relationships?*

This perspective reveals how the topic fits into a larger system and how parts of the topic relate to each other.

EXAMPLE *Topic:* Statue of Liberty

How does the statue relate to New York City? On Bedloe's Island (Liberty Island) at entrance to New York Harbor; tallest structure in the city in 1885

What meaning does the statue have for Americans today? Close to Ellis Island, where twelve million immigrants landed; first thing many of them saw from decks of the ships that brought them to America

EXERCISE 13. Asking Point-of-View Questions. Using the three different points of view, ask questions to gather information about one of the following topics. Write the questions you ask and your answers.

1. A job such as yardwork or baby-sitting
2. A room in your house or apartment
3. A kind of music
4. A nearby tourist attraction or park
5. An abstract concept such as teamwork or school spirit

ORGANIZING INFORMATION

Once you have gathered information about a topic, you must arrange your notes in an order that will be easy for readers to understand and follow. This prewriting step will give you a plan for your writing.

1m. Eliminate any notes not related to your purpose.

A first step in arranging information is to cross out any items that clearly do not relate to your purpose. Look at the following notes for a short paragraph. Its purpose is to inform readers about the man for whom Halley's Comet is named. Which item would you eliminate?

The comet was named after the astronomer Edmund Halley.
My great-grandfather, who is ninety, saw the comet in 1910.
Halley developed the theory that paths of comets are controlled by gravity.
He became interested in comets when he saw a brilliant one over England in 1682.
Halley also discovered the 75-year orbit of the comet that is named for him.

The second item should be crossed out because it does not give information about the astronomer Edmund Halley. Keep in mind that if you have gathered as much information as possible, you are likely to have more details than you need.

1n. Classify your notes by grouping related details.

The next step is to put related items into groups. Your purpose may suggest how to group your notes. For example, if you want to tell about amusing events at a wedding, you would probably group details by the time at which they happened: before the wedding, during the ceremony, and at the reception. If you want to describe three antique cars that a wedding party rode in, you would probably put details about each car in a separate group.

CRITICAL THINKING:
Classifying Information

When you *classify,* you identify items that have something in common. Then you group these items under a heading that explains how they are related. Here is how one writer classified notes about the Statue of Liberty:

Design of the Statue
- by French sculptor Bartholdi
- his wife posed as model, but statue has mother's face
- made four-foot clay model first, then larger models
- each model—more than 9000 measurements

Construction of Statue
- wooden molds built from pieces of full-size plaster model
- copper sheets hammered into shape over mold
- internal framework designed by Gustave Eiffel
- frame is four iron piers, ninety-seven feet tall with hundreds of struts and cross-braces

Transportation to New York
- statue presented to U.S. ambassador on July 4, 1884
- statue carefully taken apart and packed in boxes
- 214 boxes loaded aboard the *Isère*
- reached New York on June 19, 1885

EXERCISE 14. Classifying Information. Classify the items in the following list under these three main headings:

Facts about comets
The history of Halley's comet
The latest appearance of Halley's comet

comets only visible when they approach the sun
in November 1985, tail 50 million miles long
two kinds: those with straight, gaseous tails and those with curving, dusty tails
on latest orbit first visible to naked eye in November, 1985
1577—Queen Elizabeth I forbade anyone to look at comet
have a small nucleus, a coma, or head, and a tail
composed of icy particles
Halley's Comet—first observation recorded by Chinese in 240 B.C.
Middle Ages—thought Halley's comet would bring famine and plagues
1910—Earth passing through tail of Halley's comet; anti-comet pills taken for protection
usually look pink
comet at brightest from February to March 1986

1o. Arrange your notes in a logical order.

After you have sorted your notes into groups, the next step is to decide in what order you will present these details. Usually, your purpose will suggest an order. For example, the writer's purpose for using the following items is to tell what happened over a period of time. Such details are usually arranged chronologically—in the order in which they happened.

EXAMPLE *Topic:* How makeup artist turned Karloff into Frankenstein's monster

Details: a. Wax applied to eyelids
b. Invisible wire clamps to pull down corners of his mouth
c. Corners of forehead and brow built up with layers of cotton strips and adhesive

d. Gray-green makeup applied
e. Scar and fake metal clamps added to forehead
f. Took over three hours for whole process

The writer's purpose for the next group of details is to persuade readers by giving reasons. Details for persuasion are often arranged from least important to most important.

EXAMPLE *Topic:* Student council should volunteer to clean writing off lockers.

Details: a. If everyone helps, won't take long
b. Bring radios and have a party when finished
c. Graffiti unattractive; and suggest lack of concern about our school
d. If students know lockers are cleaned, may stay clean longer
e. Money saved in fund for another computer

Details that explain how to do or make something are usually arranged in the order in which they should be carried out. Details that describe are arranged to guide the reader's eye—from right to left, top to bottom, or near to far. If your purpose does not suggest an order, choose an arrangement that will be clear and easy for readers to follow. For example, you may decide that the notes under one heading should be presented first because your readers will need this information to understand the material under another heading.

Before You Write. To organize your notes,

- remove unrelated ideas.
- group related ideas.
- put ideas in a logical order.

EXERCISE 15. Arranging Details. Copy the following details, putting them in an order you think is logical. Be prepared to explain your arrangement.

1. At 5:13 A.M. on April 18, 1906, a severe earthquake struck the city of San Francisco.

2. In three days nearly five square miles of the city had been destroyed.
3. Rain fell on April 21 and extinguished the fires still smoldering in thousands of buildings.
4. The first severe shock was followed by two lesser earthquakes.
5. On April 19, the fire department had to dynamite buildings in the fire's path.
6. After the three earthquakes, fires broke out across the city.
7. On April 20, shifting winds pushed the fire into new areas, threatening the mansions on Nob Hill.
8. The city's six hundred firefighters sprang into action.
9. Broken water pipes throughout the city hampered the firefighters' efforts.
10. Within the week, the city started to rebuild.

REVIEW EXERCISE. Following the Steps for Prewriting. Plan a paragraph on a topic of your choice. Decide on your purpose and audience. Then choose a subject and limit it to a topic that can be covered in a single paragraph. Use at least one of the techniques for gathering information to make a list of specific details. Classify the details and arrange them in a logical order.

WRITING

The second stage of the writing process is writing a first *draft,* or first version, of your paper. Students sometimes think that good writers write exactly what they want to say the first time. Actually, most writers produce many drafts before they are completely satisfied.

WRITING A FIRST DRAFT

1p. Write a first draft based on your organized notes.

Before you begin your draft, take a few moments to review your organized notes. Then refer to them as you put your ideas into sentences and paragraphs. Remember that your first draft is only a beginning. You should have time later to make improvements.

Also, keep in mind that writing is a process of discovery. As your first draft takes shape, you may discover that you need more information, or you may decide that some details do not fit your topic. Perhaps the way you planned to present information is not as clear as you thought it would be. When these situations occur, remember that the writing process is flexible. You can always stop to gather more information or reorganize your ideas. You can even start over.

CRITICAL THINKING: Synthesis

Whenever you decide how to put together separate elements to create something new, you use the critical thinking skill called *synthesis*. Pioneer families used synthesis when they combined logs, clay, and straw to build frontier cabins. They used synthesis again when they collected scraps of fabric, cut them into interesting shapes, and fit them together to create patchwork quilts. Writers use synthesis when they collect and combine ideas or information to create paragraphs, compositions, letters, and stories.

When You Write. In a first draft, remember to

- use your prewriting plan as a guide.
- write freely.
- consider your purpose.
- keep your readers in mind.

EXERCISE 16. Writing a First Draft. Using the prewriting notes you developed for the Review Exercise (page 29), write a first draft of a paragraph.

EVALUATING

In any draft, there is room for improvement. To improve a draft, you first must *evaluate,* or make judgments about, the strengths and weaknesses of the draft.

EVALUATING YOUR WRITING

1q. Evaluate the content, organization, and style of your draft.

To judge your writing, consider three aspects: *content, organization,* and *style. Content* refers to what you have said. *Organization* concerns the way you have arranged your ideas. *Style* deals with your choice of words and sentences.

As you evaluate each aspect, you will be deciding what works and what does not work in your draft. You may realize that you do a little of this thinking while you are writing. Be careful not to let your judging block the free flow of your writing. Keep in mind that you will have this stage of the process in which to consider areas for improvement. Evaluation is often easier and more effective with a complete draft in hand.

When You Evaluate. Try these techniques:

- Set your draft aside for a while so you can come back to it with the fresh eye of a reader.
- Read the draft several times, considering just one aspect each time.
- Read your draft aloud, to hear any awkward language.
- Ask someone to read the draft and comment on its strengths and weaknesses.

Many professional writers ask someone to read their drafts and comment on them. Your teacher may occasionally ask you to exchange papers with one or more of your classmates and make comments about the writing. This exchange gives you a chance to learn how someone else handles a similar writing situation. Whenever you make suggestions about another person's writing, try to be specific and helpful. Before you say something, think about how you would feel if someone made the same comment about your writing. Would you understand what they meant? Would the comment help you improve your work or leave you feeling confused or discouraged?

CRITICAL THINKING:
Evaluation

When you evaluate your writing, you make judgments about it. To make good judgments, you need well-thought-out *standards,* or principles, by which to measure your writing.

The following guidelines can help you decide where your draft needs improvement. You can apply these standards to almost any form of writing. In other composition chapters, you will also find evaluation guidelines that apply to particular kinds of writing. Use those guidelines and always feel free to refer back to these guidelines when you judge your writing.

GUIDELINES FOR EVALUATING YOUR WRITING

Content

Purpose	1. Do all the ideas help to achieve a main purpose (explain or inform, tell a story, describe, or persuade)?
Topic	2. Is the topic suitably limited for the form of writing?
Audience	3. Are the topic and details suitable for the audience?
Topic Development	4. Is enough information given to understand the topic? Is too much given—does it all "belong"?

Organization

Order	5. Does the order of ideas fit the purpose? Will this order make sense to the reader?
Transitions	6. Are ideas clearly connected, with words such as *also, first, these, however,* and *therefore*?

Style

Word Choice	7. Are exact and vivid words used?
	8. Does the vocabulary fit the audience and purpose?
Sentence Structure	9. Do the sentences vary in length and how they begin?

EXERCISE 17. Evaluating a First Draft. Read the following first draft and answer the questions that follow it.

If it weren't for the whims of an Egyptian ruler, the figure we know as the Statue of Liberty might be standing on the banks of the Suez Canal. It's kind of a neat story; here's what happened. In 1867 Ismail Pasha, the khedive of Egypt, asked Frédéric Bartholdi, a French sculptor, to design a lighthouse to be built at the entrance to the Suez Canal. The canal was started in 1859 and finished in 1869. Impressed with the colossal Sphinx and obelisks he had seen on an earlier trip to Egypt, Bartholdi prepared drawings and architectural specifications for a lighthouse in the shape of a titanic human figure holding aloft a large torch. For unknown reasons, the khedive did not respond to Bartholdi's design. In 1869, Bartholdi abandoned the project, but he revived it in 1872 when he was asked to submit plans for a monument commemorating the ties between France and America.

1. Is the purpose of this paragraph (a) to persuade, (b) to describe, or (c) to tell what happened?
2. If this paragraph were intended for an audience of third-graders, what words would you change?
3. Is this topic limited enough for a paragraph?
4. Which sentence in this paragraph is not related to the topic?
5. Do you think the second sentence adds anything to the paragraph? Would you advise the writer to keep this sentence?

EXERCISE 18. Evaluating Your Draft. Using the guidelines on pages 32–33, evaluate the draft you wrote for Exercise 16. Read your draft several times. Consider carefully the answer to each guideline question.

REVISING

Once you have identified problems, experiment with changes that will improve your work. When you move around words, phrases, and ideas, you are *revising*—the next stage in the writing process.

REVISING YOUR FIRST DRAFT

1r. Revise your draft to improve its content, organization, and style.

Consider the aspects of content, organization, and style. Whichever aspect you want to work on, you can usually improve your writing with a combination of four basic techniques.

When You Revise. Use these techniques:

TECHNIQUE	EXAMPLE
• *Add* words, sentences, or even paragraphs that will make the meaning clearer.	The War of the Whiskers between France and England raged from 1152 to 1453.
• *Cut,* or remove, words, phrases, sentences, or paragraphs that are unnecessary or unrelated to the topic.	The successful Grand Prix race driver Jackie Stewart ~~speaks with a Scottish accent and~~ retired from racing at age thirty-four.
• *Reorder,* or rearrange, words, ideas, or paragraphs so that the flow of ideas is logical and easy to follow.	Our plans are to visit Vienna in September, London in November, ~~and~~ Lisbon in October.
• *Replace* words or details that do not work with wording or ideas that better fit the topic or audience.	The ~~really huge~~ carefully constructed Great Wall of China is the largest single structure of the ancient world.

The following chart gives examples of problems you might have found through your evaluation. It then shows how you use the four revision techniques to make improvements. Notice that these problems are the kind that might turn up in any kind of writing task. In other composition chapters, you will find revising charts for particular kinds of writing. Remember that you can refer to this chart anytime you are revising a draft.

REVISING A DRAFT

PROBLEM	TECHNIQUE	REVISION
The purpose is not clear.	Add/Cut	Make sure you know your purpose. Add details that fit it. Remove comments that do not fit it.
The ideas are too general.	Replace	Make general ideas more specific. Do more research, if needed. Be sure the topic is not too broad for the form of writing.
Some information is "extra" or not related to the main idea.	Cut	Remove "padding" and unrelated ideas. Keep only the background needed by the particular audience.
It is hard to follow the ideas.	Reorder/Add	Move sentences or paragraphs to fit what a reader needs to know first, second, and so on. Add linking words such as *this, when, then, these.*
Some terms are too complex or too simple for the audience.	Add/Replace	Add definitions to explain unfamiliar terms. Change the wording to fit the audience's age and background.

PROBLEM	TECHNIQUE	REVISION
The beginning is dull.	Add	Add examples, incidents, or other details that will interest the audience. Be sure the topic will interest the audience.
Some words are vague or overused.	Replace	Replace words that stand for a group of things with more exact words. Use exact, vivid adjectives, adverbs, and verbs.
Some wording seems very informal.	Cut/Replace	When light, informal expressions do not fit the purpose and audience, remove slang, contractions, and so on or replace them with standard formal words.
The sentences are monotonous.	Replace/ Reorder	Combine choppy sentences. Split rambling sentences. Change the word order so sentences begin in different ways.

EXERCISE 19. Analyzing a Writer's Revisions. Read the following first draft with the writer's revisions and answer the questions that follow it. If you are not sure what one of the revision symbols means, refer to the chart on pages 39–40.

For thirty dollars, car owners in our state can order ~~really neat~~ "prestige" license plates. Instead of a meaningless jumble ~~bunch~~ of letters and numbers ~~with no meaning~~, these plates carry a message of six or seven letters. ~~I kept a list of the messages I've seen on these special plates. The messages fall into several categories.~~ For convenience, ~~S~~some individuals, like my grandfather, simply have their initials and year of birth (HGD 1918) printed on their plates. ~~I guess that's convenient.~~ My aunt ~~who works as~~ a veterinarian has a plate that advertises her profession (DVM 146). I've also seen plates that read BARBER, THE DOC, TEACH, and PHOTOG, but I'm still wondering about a plate that read KGB SPY. A small group of friendly folks have plates with greetings ~~messages~~ like LOVE YA, SMILE, or HELLO. For sports fans, of course, a license plate is another way to show their team loyalty: GO SOX, ILLINI, and METS FAN are examples of this. I haven't figured out one thing is why Some drivers have plates that read A KLUTZ, DIZZY, or FAT BOY. Maybe they like to laugh at themselves. Maybe someone gave them the plate as a gag? My favorite plates are the ones that state the obvious. THE CAR, BACK END, BUMPER, VEHICLE, or MY AUTO fall into this category. Finally, one word of advice: watch out for the car with A GRUMP on the plate. That's my sister and she's not kidding.

1. What do you think is the writer's purpose?
2. Do you think this paragraph was written for an audience of young children, an audience of experts, or students your age? Explain your answer.
3. The writer crossed out three sentences. Why do you think these were taken out?
4. Where did the writer make a change to vary the beginning of a sentence? Is this change an improvement?
5. Where did the writer change a general word to a more specific word? How does this improve the draft?

EXERCISE 20. Revising a First Draft. Using the four revision techniques and the chart on pages 35–36, revise the first draft that you evaluated for Exercise 18.

PROOFREADING

The term *proofreading* comes from publishing. After the printer has made press plates for a book or article, a set of trial pages, called proofs, is run off. These proofs are checked carefully to correct all mistakes before thousands of copies roll off the press.

PROOFREADING YOUR WRITING

1s. Proofread your writing.

Proofreading is another important stage of the writing process. Errors in spelling, grammar, usage, or mechanics can distract the reader from the ideas in your paper.

When You Proofread. Use these techniques:

- Set your revised draft aside for a while so that it is easier to see mistakes.
- If you made any revisions, recopy the draft before you proofread.
- Cover with blank paper all lines except the one you are reading (to help you concentrate).
- Check all doubtful spellings in the dictionary.
- Look in the index of this book to find a point of grammar, usage, or mechanics that you want to review.

The chart on pages 39–40 shows common proofreading symbols. You can save time by learning to use these marks. Also, refer to the following Guidelines for Proofreading. The questions will help you identify common errors.

GUIDELINES FOR PROOFREADING

1. Does every verb agree in number with its subject? (pages 419–32)
2. Are verbs in the right form and tense? (pages 443–47, 457–58)
3. Are troublesome verbs such as *sit/set* and *rise/raise* used correctly? (pages 450–54)
4. Are all pronouns in the right form? (pages 465–71)
5. Are the comparative forms of adjectives and adverbs used correctly? (pages 479–84)
6. Are double negatives avoided? (pages 484–85)
7. Do all sentences and proper nouns and adjectives begin with a capital letter? (pages 512–21)
8. Are all words spelled correctly? (pages 572–93)
9. Is the punctuation correct at the end of sentences and within sentences? (pages 528–68)
10. Is every sentence a complete sentence? (pages 229–36)

EXERCISE 21. Proofreading a Revised Draft. Proofread the draft you revised for Exercise 20. Be sure to check each of the points in the Guidelines for Proofreading.

REVISING AND PROOFREADING SYMBOLS

Symbol	*Example*	*Meaning of Symbol*
≡	at Waukeshaw lake	Capitalize a lowercase letter.
/	a gift for my Uncle	Lowercase a capital letter.
∧	cost ∧ cents (fifty)	Insert a missing word, letter, or punctuation mark.
∧	ate two much (o)	Change a letter.
∧—	by their house (our)	Replace a word.
ℊ	What day is is it?	Leave out a word, letter, or punctuation mark.
ℊ͡	rakeing leaves	Leave out and close up.
⁀‿	any body	Close up space.
∿	recieved	Change the order of letters.

Symbol	Example	Meaning
(tr.)	The girl ^ with the dog (in the red dress)	Move the circled words to the place marked by the arrow. (Write (tr.) in nearby margin.)
¶	¶ The last step is	Begin a new paragraph.
⊙	Please be patient⊙	Add a period.
^,	Yes^, that's right.	Add a comma.
#	figure#skating	Add a space.
(:)	all of the following items(:)	Add a colon.
^;	It's not hard^; I'll help you.	Add a semicolon.
=	his great=grandfather	Add a hyphen.
’	Linda’s work	Add an apostrophe.
(stet)	a ~~bitterly~~ cold day	Keep the crossed out material. (Write (stet) in nearby margin.)

MAKING THE FINAL COPY

PREPARING A FINAL COPY

1t. Write your final version in standard manuscript form.

A manuscript is any handwritten or typed composition. Sometimes you can hand in a manuscript on which you have neatly made some corrections. Most of the time, however, you will want to prepare a clean, correct final copy. Certain rules for the form of a final version are widely used and accepted.

Using Correct Manuscript Form

Unless your teacher gives you other specific directions, follow these rules:

1. Use $8\frac{1}{2}$ x 11-inch paper, plain white for typed manuscripts or ruled white for handwritten ones.

2. Write only on one side of each sheet.

3. Write in blue or black ink, or type. If you type, double-space the lines.

4. On each page, leave one-inch margins at the top, the sides, and the bottom. Keep the left margin straight; make the right margin as straight as possible.

5. Indent the first line of each paragraph about one-half inch from the left margin.

6. Write your name, the class, and the date on the first page, as your teacher directs.

7. If your paper has a title, write it in the center of the first line. Do not enclose the title in quotation marks. Skip two lines between the title and the first line of your composition.

8. Number all pages. Place the number in the upper right corner, about one-half inch down from the top.

9. Write neatly, forming your letters carefully. Do not let *n*'s look like *u*'s, *a*'s like *o*'s, and so on; dot the *i*'s and cross the *t*'s. If you have to erase, do it neatly.

10. When you have finished preparing the final revision, proofread it again to correct any copying errors.

Using Abbreviations

In compositions, you rarely use abbreviations. Acceptable ones are *Mr., Mrs., Ms., Dr., Jr.,* and *Sr.,* when they are used with a name; *A.M.* (*ante meridiem*—before noon)—8:00 A.M., and *P.M.* (*post meridiem*—after noon)—3:00 P.M.; *A.D.* (*anno Domini* —in the year of our Lord)—A.D. 1986, and *B.C.* (before Christ) —200 B.C. (Note that A.D. precedes the number, but B.C. follows it.)

A few abbreviations for well-known organizations are also acceptable and may be used without periods. Examples are *YWCA, PTA, FBI,* and *UN.* If you are in doubt, spell it out.

Dividing Words

Follow these rules:

1. Divide a word only between syllables. (Thus, you can never divide a one-syllable word.) If you are unsure of the syllables, look up the word in the dictionary.
2. Never divide a word so that only one letter is left on a line.

Writing Numbers

In compositions, spell out numbers of one or two words; write longer numbers in numerals. If you write several numbers, some short and some long, write them all the same way. Always spell out a number that begins a sentence.

EXAMPLES **twenty-one, 201**
Karen had **90** baseball cards yesterday and now has **120.**
Two hundred and fifty-seven people were there.

Write out numbers like *seventh* and *fifty-third,* unless they stand for a day of the month, as in June **14.**

EXERCISE 22. Preparing a Final Copy. Prepare the final copy of the paragraph you proofread for Exercise 21.

CHAPTER 1 WRITING REVIEW

Applying Your Knowledge of the Writing Process. Write a one- or two-page composition on a topic of your choice. Use your knowledge of the writing process to complete the following steps:

1. Decide on a purpose, audience, and subject.
2. Limit the subject to a suitable topic.
3. Gather details and organize them.
4. Write a first draft.
5. Evaluate and revise the draft.
6. Proofread and prepare a final copy.
7. Correct any copying errors.

CHAPTER 2

Writing Paragraphs

STRUCTURE AND DEVELOPMENT

A *paragraph* is a group of closely related sentences. Together, the sentences make one main idea clear.

In this chapter you will study the structure and development of paragraphs. You will also learn to use the stages of the writing process to write your own paragraphs.

THE STRUCTURE OF A PARAGRAPH

Well-written paragraphs have certain common qualities. Learning to recognize these qualities will help you write effective paragraphs of your own.

THE MAIN IDEA

2a. A paragraph is a series of sentences that presents and develops one main idea about a topic.

The sentences in a well-written paragraph work together to make one main idea clear. Often, this main idea is stated in a single sentence. In the following paragraph, for example, the topic is dishonest sales practices. The main idea, that wise consumers learn to recognize such practices, is stated in the first sentence. Each of the other sentences helps make that idea clear by giving details (specific information). The details *develop,* or support, the main idea.

> **Wise consumers learn to recognize dishonest sales practices.** Store owners who offer large discounts such as "30 percent off," for example, may first have raised the original price of the merchandise. Another dishonest offer is called "bait and switch." A store advertises an item at a much lower price than usual (the bait). Customers asking for this item are told that it is inferior in quality and are pressured to buy another brand, one that costs more (the switch).

THE TOPIC SENTENCE

2b. The topic sentence states the main idea of a paragraph.

Often, as in the paragraph above, the topic sentence is the first sentence. In this position, it tells the reader immediately what the paragraph is about. It also helps the writer keep to the point.

The topic sentence may instead appear in the middle or at the end of a paragraph. In the following paragraph, for example, the details are given first, and the topic sentence concludes the paragraph.

> Coal miners once worked with pick and shovel and hand drill. Now they use power cutters, drilling machines, mechanical loaders, timbering machines, and roof bolters. Electric locomotives, which have replaced mules, pull larger cars that carry heavier loads. Conveyor belts, too, move coal in a continuous flow through mine tunnels to the cleaning, washing, and loading machines. **In every way, mechanization has vastly increased the efficiency of coal mining.**

In your reading, you will notice that some paragraphs do not have topic sentences. Until you have more writing experience, however, plan to begin your paragraphs with a topic sentence that states your main idea. This will give you valuable practice in identifying your main idea and developing it clearly.

EXERCISE 1. Identifying Topic Sentences. Identify the topic sentence in each of the following paragraphs. Be prepared to discuss how the other sentences develop the main idea.

1. Many people think that the rocket is a recent invention, but it was used as a primitive weapon many centuries ago. The Chinese had rockets in the thirteenth century and called them "arrows of fire." In the fifteenth century, the Italians used animal-shaped rockets that traveled over the ground on rollers. These Chinese and Italian rockets were probably not very destructive. They were designed to frighten enemies, not to kill them.

2. All lasers contain some material—a gas, crystal, or dye—that emits light waves when an electrical voltage or a light source is applied to them. These waves, unlike those in ordinary light, are perfectly aligned, resulting in a beam with such concentrated energy that it can cut through a 4-inch steel plate. Lasers are classified by the materials that emit the light—for example, carbon dioxide gas or yttrium-aluminum (YAG) crystal.

   GORDON GRAFF

3. Michigan was once called *Michigama,* an Algonquian name meaning "great water." Missouri comes from another Algonquian name for "people of the big canoes," and Wyoming comes from *Mecheweami-ing,* which means "large plains." Both North and South Dakota are named for a tribe, the Dakota, whose name means "to think of as a friend." Nearly half of the states have names based on words from Native American languages.

SUPPORTING SENTENCES

2c. Other sentences in a paragraph give specific information that supports the main idea in the topic sentence.

A paragraph should have enough specific information to make the main idea clear. Usually, three or more supporting details are necessary for an effective paragraph.

WEAK **Members of a group called the Animal Liberation Front "rescued" 260 animals in a middle-of-the-night raid on a university research center.** They claimed the animals were being mistreated. A university spokesman said they were not.

IMPROVED **Members of a group called the Animal Liberation Front "rescued" 260 animals in a middle-of-the-night raid on a university research center.** The group claimed that they had rescued 80 rats, 70 gerbils, 35 rabbits, 38 pigeons, 21 cats, 9 oppossums, and a baby primate from cruel experiments. Vicky Miller, the group's spokesperson, said that the animals were in "safe" shelters and homes. A university official denied that the animals had been mistreated and said that they were now in worse hands.

EXERCISE 2. Revising a Weak Paragraph. The following paragraph is weak in supporting details. Study the paragraph and answer the questions. Use your answers to revise the paragraph so that it has enough information to make the main idea clear. Write your revised paragraph on a separate sheet of paper.

Last night's crucial match between Fairview and Ridgemont was decided in the final thirty seconds of the game. The gym was very crowded, and the fans were excited. The score had been close all through the game, but in the last minute the home team pulled ahead by four points.

1. What kind of game was it?
2. Why was the game important? Which side was the home team?
3. What sounds could you hear?
4. Exactly what happened during the last thirty seconds of play? Who scored the winning points?
5. What did the players do when the game ended? The fans?

THE CLINCHER SENTENCE

2d. A paragraph may end with a clincher sentence.

A *clincher,* or *concluding, sentence* may be used to give a paragraph a sense of completeness. Such a sentence may emphasize the main idea by restating the idea in different words. It may instead summarize the details given or suggest a course of action.

In the following paragraph, notice how the concluding sentence summarizes the details given to support the topic sentence (the first sentence).

> **There is still some good outdoor cooking going on in this country, but none of it needs machinery.** The first meal that comes to mind is a clambake last summer in Maine. Here is the authentic recipe for a clambake: dig a big hole in a beach. If you have a Maine beach to dig your hole in, so much the better, but any beach will do. Line the hole with rocks. Build a big fire on the rocks and take a swim. When the fire is all gone, cover the hot rocks with seaweed. Add some potatoes just as they came from the ground; some corn just as it came from the stalk; then lobsters, then clams, then another layer of seaweed. Cover the whole thing with a tarp and go for another swim. Dinner will be ready in an hour. It will make you very happy. **No machine can make a clambake.**
>
> CHARLES KURALT

Not every paragraph needs a clincher sentence. Such a sentence is usually not needed in a short paragraph. Also, a clincher sentence should not just be tacked on to a paragraph that is effective without it.

EXERCISE 3. Writing Clincher Sentences. For each of the following paragraphs, write a clincher sentence. Try writing two or three versions for each paragraph, and tell which one you think is most effective.

1. Many movie stars changed their names when they went into show business. John Wayne's real name, for example, was

Marion Morrison, and Judy Garland's was Frances Gumm. Before he became Cary Grant, the dimpled movie star was Archibald Leach. Lauren Bacall was once Betty Perske, and Fred Astaire was Frederick Austerlitz. It's hard to tell where Woody Allen got "Woody"; his real name is Allen Stewart Konigsberg.

2. Surprisingly, in these days of ballpoint pens and computers, old-fashioned quill pens made from bird feathers are still in use. Lloyd's of London, which was founded in the eighteenth century to insure ships, uses swan quill pens for entering marine accidents into its record book. Lloyd's gets its swan quills from Abbotsbury, England, home of the largest swan flock in the world. During molting season each year, every one of the adult swans loses eleven quill feathers from each wing.

UNITY

2e. Every sentence in a paragraph should be directly related to the main idea.

All of the sentences in a paragraph should work together as a unit to make one main idea clear. Sentences that do not directly support the main idea confuse the reader; they should be removed. In the following paragraph, the crossed-out sentence is not directly related to the main idea in the topic sentence (the first sentence).

According to psychologists, certain adult personality traits are a result of a child's place in the family. Adults who were only children are likely to be high achievers, verbal, and self-confident. They like to work alone and tend to be perfectionists. Firstborn children have most of these same characteristics. ~~My sister Sheila, who is a firstborn, is finishing her second year in medical school.~~ Middle children must compete for their parents' attention, and as adults they are skilled in dealing with people. Adults who were youngest children tend not to be high achievers but work hard to be liked.

The best way to achieve unity in a paragraph is to check each supporting sentence against your topic sentence, as you draft your paragraph and again as you evaluate it.

EXERCISE 4. Identifying Sentences That Destroy Unity. Read each of the following paragraphs carefully. If all of the sentences in the paragraph are directly related to the main idea, write *U* (for unity) after the proper number. If the paragraph contains one or more sentences that destroy the paragraph's unity, write the sentence or sentences you think should be omitted.

1. Among the Chinese, there are surprisingly few last names. Almost all Chinese last names have only one syllable, and in Shanghai, China's largest city, only 408 one-syllable last names appear in the city's records. The most common are Zhang, Wang, Liu, and Li. Because there are so few last names, many people in China have exactly the same names. For example, almost 5,000 people in Shenyang, Manchuria, are named Li Shuzhen ("fair and precious"). In that same city, 4,300 people have the name Wang Yulan, and more than 3,000 are named Wang Wei. In the United States, the most common last names are Smith, Jones, and White. How many Robert Smiths can you find in your city's phone book?

2. Migrating birds travel at heights far above the 50 to 100 feet at which small birds usually fly. Flocks of thrushes and warblers have been sighted at heights of up to 20,000 feet. Bar-headed geese fly at almost 30,000 feet as they wing their way over Mount Everest, earth's highest mountain. Mount Everest is in the Himalayas on the border of Nepal and Tibet. Highest-flying of all is the Ruppell's griffon, a type of vulture, one of which collided with a plane at 37,000 feet over Africa. At this height, humans would die because of lack of oxygen, but birds have air sacs in addition to lungs. These air sacs enable them to get oxygen even at heights where there is very little oxygen.

3. A newly formed company is offering to broadcast messages into space. For a $30.00 fee, the company will send your message to any of the planets in our solar system. Just suppose

that you could actually broadcast your own message into space. What would you say? For an additional fee, the company will assist you in writing a message that is appropriate for the planet you have chosen. A brochure describing the service is available from Intraplanet, Inc., 4202 Woodlynne Avenue, Indianapolis, Indiana, 43201.

COHERENCE

2f. The ideas in a paragraph should be arranged in a clear order and connected smoothly.

A paragraph in which the ideas are easy to follow has *coherence;* its sentences flow smoothly and clearly from one to the next.

Order of Ideas

In this section you will learn four ways of arranging ideas in a clear order. The order you use for a particular paragraph will depend partly on your purpose and partly on your main idea.

Chronological Order

(1) Ideas may be arranged in chronological order.

Chronological, or *time, order* makes clear the order in which events happened. This order is usually used in paragraphs that tell a story or tell about a historical event. It is also used to make clear the order in which the steps in a process should be carried out. In the following paragraph, for example, the writer uses chronological order to tell how to ride a wave on a surfboard.

A new swell approaches, and you decide to ride it in. This is a much trickier feat. You turn your body toward shore and glance coolly over your shoulder to note how big the wave is, how fast it is coming and, most crucially of all, when it will break. Your judgment, let's say, is just right. You are already planing toward the beach when the wave reaches you. It bears you surgingly up and forward, and just then the threatening tracery along its crest breaks, not over you but under you.

You can feel its chaotic turbulence beating all along your body. It goes on and on, like some rolling hydraulic engine beneath you, shooting you wildly toward shore. At last it beaches you, with a certain grudging gentleness. Victory.

JOHN KNOWLES

EXERCISE 5. Writing a Paragraph Using Chronological Order. Arrange sentences a–h in chronological order. Then write the paragraph, beginning with the topic sentence given.

Topic sentence: In 1872 Susan B. Anthony led a group of women who challenged the laws that kept them from voting.

a. 1870—Fourteenth and Fifteenth Amendments added to the Constitution; gave black men the right to vote, but not women
b. After trial Anthony continued working for amendment giving women right to vote
c. 1920—Nineteenth Amendment ratified, giving women right to vote
d. At trial, Judge Ward Hunt told jury to find Anthony guilty; then dismissed jury before they could vote; trial helped movement for women's vote
e. October 1872—Anthony led group of fifteen women; registered to vote in Rochester, New York; insisted that wording in Fifteenth Amendment giving right to vote to "citizens of the United States" applied to women too
f. November 28, 1872—Anthony and other women arrested for having voted
g. U.S. government prosecuted only Anthony; trial began June 17, 1873
h. November 5, 1872—Anthony and other women cast their ballots in Rochester

Spatial Order

(2) Ideas may be arranged in spatial order.

Spatial order makes clear the location of the parts of a scene. Suppose you are describing a room. You might imagine yourself standing in the doorway and begin by mentioning the objects immediately to your left. You could then mention other objects in the order in which you see them as you move your eyes around the room from left to right. Other spatial orders include near to far, right to left, top to bottom, and inside to outside.

The following paragraph uses spatial order to describe the layers of the earth. Notice how the writer moves the reader's attention from the outer layers to the inner layers.

Earth scientists have discovered that the earth is composed of a number of layers. The outside layer, called the crust, is hard rock, which varies in thickness. In many places it is twenty or thirty miles thick, but beneath some parts of the sea it has a thickness of only three miles. Inside the crust, there is a layer about eighteen hundred miles deep called the mantle, which is composed of flowing rock. Beneath the mantle is the outer core, a layer about thirteen hundred miles thick and thought to be liquid iron. Finally, there is the inner core, which is a ball of hot, solid metal.

topic sentence

four layers described in spatial order (outside to inside)

EXERCISE 6. Writing a Paragraph Using Spatial Order. Use the following topic sentence and details to write a paragraph. Arrange the details in a spatial order from near to far.

Topic sentence: From where he sat on the beach, Sam had a clear view of the people and the ocean.
Details:

a. Directly in front of him—family with three young children, umbrella, portable crib, blankets
b. Far out at sea—two ships
c. Elderly couple on chairs reading magazines
d. At water's edge—children building sand castle
e. Close to shore—people bobbing in waves
f. Colorful sails of sailboats beyond the swimmers

Order of Importance

(3) Ideas may be arranged in order of importance.

In paragraphs that give information or persuade, ideas are often arranged in *order of importance.* Usually, the ideas are arranged from least important to most important. With this arrangement, the most important idea stays with the readers because it is the last thing they read. However, the opposite order may also sometimes be effective. In either case, the reader should be able to tell which of the ideas is the most important.

In the following paragraph the writer gives four reasons to explain why a school newspaper is needed. The reasons are arranged from least important to most important. What are the four reasons?

> **Our school needs a student newspaper.** A newspaper can entertain the school by printing interesting news about students. It can announce important events like a basketball game or a Halloween party. The money raised from sales can be donated to a worthy cause or used to buy a gift for the school. Most important, a student newspaper can provide valuable writing practice for students.

EXERCISE 7. Writing a Paragraph Using Order of Importance. Arrange sentences a–c in order of importance. You may use either most-to-least important or least-to-most important order, and you may add other related details. Then write the paragraph, beginning with the topic sentence given.

Topic Sentence: Every child over six should be responsible for a pet.

Reasons: a. teaches discipline
b. develops concern for other living things
c. provides companionship

Comparison or Contrast

(4) Ideas may be arranged in an order that shows comparison or contrast.

A *comparison* shows how two people, places, or things are alike. A *contrast* shows how they are different. Some paragraphs use both comparison and contrast.

In the following paragraph, the writer compares and contrasts ATBs (all-terrain bikes) with earlier models.

> Once, when Harry Truman was President and Joe Louis ruled the ring, bicycles were bicycles the way men were men—plain and strong. In those days, you could ride bikes over curbs. They had fat tires and wide, upright handlebars. So what if they only had one speed? Pushing 46 pounds of rubber and steel up a hill would have been very good exercise—if exercise had been invented yet. But then the '50s brought lighter, three-speed English bikes, and the '60s and '70s brought 21-pound ten-speeds, with downturned handlebars and skinny tires, bikes that could *go,* even up hills, but not over curbs. Then, as the '70s waned, there was another development. Out of California came all-terrain bikes. The ATBs have eighteen speeds, weigh 25 to 32 pounds, and are something of a throwback: they are plain and strong, with fat tires and upright handlebars, and you can ride them over curbs. But you can also ride them up hills, and they are light enough to carry up stairs.
>
> DAN LEVIN

EXERCISE 8. Analyzing a Paragraph of Comparison and Contrast. Answer these questions about the paragraph above.

1. Name two ways in which ATBs are different from bicycles of the '40s (when Truman was President). Name two ways in which ATBs are like bikes of the '40s.
2. Name three ways in which ATBs differ from bikes of the '60s and '70s. Name one way in which they are alike.

REVIEW EXERCISE A. Choosing an Order for Arranging Ideas. Number your paper 1–10. For each of the following topics, tell what kind of order you would use. Write *Chr* (chronological), *S* (spatial), *I* (order of importance), or *C-C* (comparison or contrast). Be prepared to explain your answers.

1. A typical Saturday morning in your home
2. How being in the eighth grade is different from being in the seventh grade
3. What the school cafeteria looks like after lunch
4. Your favorite pair of shoes
5. Why people should have hobbies
6. How mopeds are different from motorcycles
7. How to load a dishwasher
8. A time when you laughed a lot
9. Why everyone should wear a seat belt
10. Why you should be the first student to go on a space flight

Connections Between Ideas

To link the ideas within and between sentences, you can use *direct references* and *transitional expressions.*

Direct References

Direct references are words and phrases that remind the reader of something mentioned earlier in the paragraph. They may be pronouns, key words and phrases, or rewordings.

(1) Use pronouns to refer to nouns and ideas mentioned earlier.

Using pronouns lets you avoid repeating the same words over and over. Compare the following two examples.

UNNATURAL Jenny gets up at 6:00 A.M. every morning to shampoo and blow-dry Jenny's hair so that Jenny's hair looks shiny, soft, and clean.

NATURAL Jenny gets up at 6:00 A.M. every morning to shampoo and blow-dry *her* hair so that *her* hair will look shiny, soft, and clean.

(2) Repeat key words or phrases from earlier sentences.

A key word or phrase is one that is part of the main idea. For example, in the paragraph about Jenny, the key word *hair* is repeated. Repeating such terms not only links the sentences, it also emphasizes the main idea.

(3) Use words or phrases that mean the same thing as words or phrases in earlier sentences.

In the following paragraph, the boldfaced words or phrases are reworded in later sentences; the rewordings are underlined.

> Another project involving ergonomics (a word derived from the Greek "work" plus "law" or "customs") was conducted by the **design staff** of the General Motors Corporation. The designers studied **how a driver adjusts the seat** in response to various distances and angles between the steering wheel and foot pedals. With space at a premium in new, smaller cars, the designers hoped to be able to reduce the leeway of front-seat adjustment, thus providing more room for rear-seat passengers.
>
> JOHN HOLUSHA

Transitional Expressions

Words and phrases that show how ideas are related to one other are called *transitional expressions.* Notice how each underlined transitional expression in the following paragraph shows the relationship between the idea in the sentence and the idea in the preceding sentence.

> **The first plastic was invented as the result of a contest.** After the Civil War, the game of billiards became very popular. Billiard balls had always been made of ivory, but now there was not enough ivory to meet the demand. Consequently, one firm offered a prize of ten thousand dollars for a good substitute. Hoping to win this prize, John Wesley Hyatt mixed cellulose, nitric acid, and camphor to produce a substance called "celluloid." Since this new substance was not suitable for billiard balls, Hyatt did not win the prize. However, the invention turned out to be worth a great deal more than ten thousand dollars. Soon many articles were being made from this plastic. As a result, Hyatt became extremely wealthy.

Different transitional expressions show different kinds of relationships.

Transitional Expressions

To show chronological order

after	finally	next
afterward	first (second, etc.)	now
before	later	presently
eventually	meanwhile	soon

To show spatial order

above	below	in the distance
across	beyond	near
ahead	here	next to
around	in front of	outside
behind	inside	to the right (left)

To link similar ideas

again	for example	likewise
also	for instance	moreover
and	furthermore	of course
another	in addition	similarly
besides	in a like manner	too

To link ideas that are dissimilar or seem contradictory

although	in spite of	otherwise
as if	instead	provided that
but	nevertheless	still
even if	on the contrary	yet
however	on the other hand	

To indicate cause, purpose, or result

as	for	so
as a result	for this reason	then
because	hence	therefore
consequently	since	thus

Not every sentence requires a transitional expression. A paragraph that contains too many transitional expressions sounds awkward. Direct references, which are more natural, should be used whenever possible.

REVIEW EXERCISE B. Arranging Ideas in a Clear Order. On a separate sheet of paper, write the sentences a–g in an order that will make the main idea in the topic sentence clear. Save your paper.

Topic Sentence: Here are some ways to keep houseplants healthy.

a. Don't overwater.
b. Too much water causes root rot and kills houseplants.
c. Fertilize once a month from early spring through early fall.
d. You can test to see whether the soil is dry by pushing your finger into the top layer of soil.
e. Use the correct soil mixture so that plants have air and water around the roots.
f. Water thoroughly, but let the surface soil dry out thoroughly between waterings.
g. You can add one-third sand or perlite to a soil mixture.

REVIEW EXERCISE C. Writing a Coherent Paragraph. Using your paper from Review Exercise B, write a paragraph. Use direct references and transitional expressions to link the ideas in the paragraph.

THE DEVELOPMENT OF A PARAGRAPH

In Chapter 1 you learned about the writing process. Now you will learn how to use the writing process to write effective paragraphs.

PREWRITING

CHOOSING AND LIMITING A SUBJECT

2g. Choose a subject, and limit it to a topic that is suitable for a paragraph.

A *subject* is a broad area, one that has too many parts to cover in the 100–150 words in a paragraph. The subject "computers," for example, includes all of the different kinds of computers as well as their history, their uses, and so on. (See pages 11–17 for help with choosing a subject.)

To find a suitable *topic* for a paragraph, you begin by dividing the subject into its smaller, more specific parts. Three techniques for limiting a broad, or general, subject are brainstorming, clustering, and asking the *5 W-How?* questions.

Brainstorming

To brainstorm, begin by writing your subject at the top of a sheet of paper. Then jot down whatever ideas come to your mind, without stopping to judge them.

The following list shows the ideas one writer found by brainstorming on the subject "movies" for two minutes. Notice that the list is made up of narrower parts of the general subject.

Subject: Movies
Ideas: history of movies
silent films—silent film stars
how movies are made
my favorite movies—favorite movie stars
Oscars—history of Academy Awards
kinds of movies—Which are most popular?
movie classics—all-time great movies
rating systems for movies
watching movies at home with a VCR—pros and cons
special effects
movies of the future—What will they be like?

Although all of these topics are more limited than "movies," they are still too broad for a paragraph. The writer decided to use brainstorming to limit "history of movies" further, as follows:

Limited topics:
First motion picture
First movie theater
First sound film
First film in three colors

Clustering

Clustering produces a diagram instead of a list. First write your subject in the middle of a sheet of paper and circle it. Then, as you think of smaller parts of the subject, write each one down around the subject, circle it, and draw a line connecting it to the idea that made you think of it.

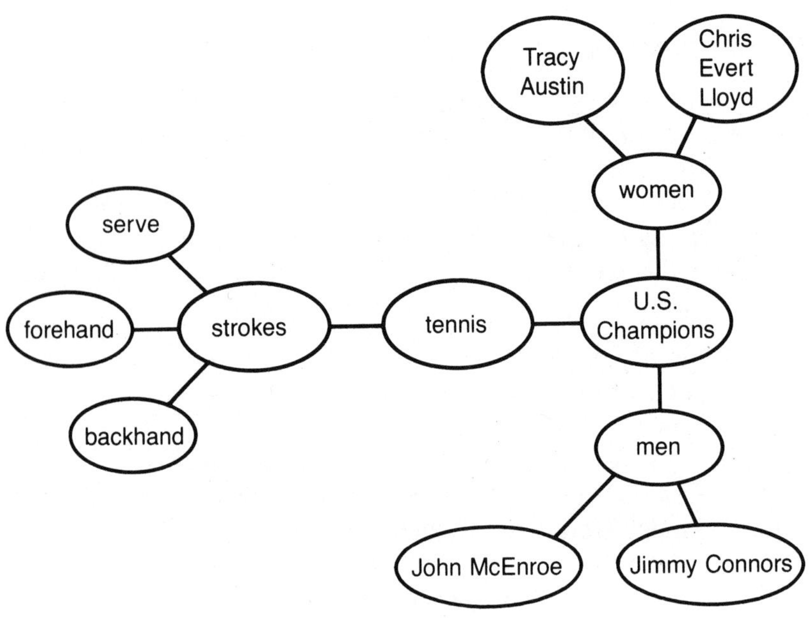

Asking the 5 *W-How?* Questions

The *5 W-How?* questions are *Who? What? When? Where? Why?* and *How?* The following example shows how one writer used these questions to limit the subject "kites."

General subject: Kites
5 W-How? questions: *What* is the history of kite flying?
Who invented kites? *Who* flies kites?
When were kites invented?
Where do people fly kites?

Why are kites so popular?
How do kites work? *How* do you build a kite? *How* do you fly a kite?

Changing the questions into phrases can help you decide whether the parts are limited enough for a paragraph. For example, you could change "Who invented kites?" to "The inventor of the kite," and "How do you build a kite?" into "How to build a kite." Either of these topics would be suitable for a paragraph.

If a part that you discover is too broad, you can use the *5 W-How?* questions to divide it further. "The history of kite flying," for example, is too broad for one paragraph because it covers hundreds of years and many countries. You could limit it further as follows.

General subject: The history of kite flying
5 W-How? questions: *What* is kite flying?
Who invented kites?
When were kites invented?

Before You Write. To limit a subject to a topic that is suitable for a paragraph:

- Use brainstorming, clustering, or the *5 W-How?* questions.
- Divide and subdivide the subject according to time periods, examples, features, places, uses, or causes.

EXERCISE 9. Choosing and Limiting a Subject. Choose one of the following subjects or a subject of your own. Limit the subject to find three topics that are suitable for a paragraph. Keep a record of the questions, lists, or diagrams that you use to limit the subject.

bicycling	drawing	gymnastics	raising livestock
camping	football	music	science fiction
cars	gardening	photography	skating

CONSIDERING PURPOSE

2h. Determine your purpose for writing.

Determining your purpose for writing will help you choose details to include in your paragraph. It will also help you set the *tone* of your writing—the attitude you reveal toward your subject and your audience. (See pages 6–9 for more information about purpose.)

EXAMPLES

Purpose: To persuade
Limited Topic: Why our state should pass a seat belt law
Details:
a. Wording of proposed bill
b. Reasons for passing bill
c. What citizens can do to support bill's passage

Purpose: To inform
Limited Topic: Results of seat belt law in one state
Details:
a. Statistics on deaths and serious injuries from automobile accidents during year *before* law went into effect
b. Statistics from same state during year *after* law went into effect
c. Conclusions based on two sets of statistics

Before You Write. Determine your purpose:

- to explain or inform
- to tell a story
- to persuade
- to describe

EXERCISE 10. Choosing a Purpose. Number your paper 1–5. For each of the following limited topics, write an appropriate purpose: to describe, to tell a story, to explain or inform, or to persuade. (For some topics, more than one purpose is appropriate.)

1. *Limited topic:* The launching of a rocket
2. *Limited topic:* Why every student should take a computer course

3. *Limited topic:* Your community's first settlers
4. *Limited topic:* What you like most about your best friend
5. *Limited topic:* Your favorite place outdoors

CONSIDERING AUDIENCE

2i. Consider how your audience will affect your writing.

Your *audience* (the people who read what you write) affects your writing in three ways:

1. *The topic you choose.* Your classmates, for example, would probably be more interested in the story of the curse written on the wall of the Egyptian King Tutankhamen's tomb than in an explanation of the king's foreign policy.

2. *The details you include.* For a class of fourth-graders, for example, you might tell when and why mockingbirds sing. For an older audience, you might include additional details such as the bird's scientific name and the results of a study on how females choose their mates.

3. *The language that you use.* You would need to use shorter, simpler sentences and easier words for a young audience than for adults. You would also need to avoid difficult concepts or explain them in simple terms.

> ***Before You Write.*** To consider how your audience will affect your writing, ask yourself:
>
> - What topic will my audience find most interesting?
> - What details about this topic will my audience find most interesting?
> - What ideas, words, and kinds of sentences will my audience be able to understand?

EXERCISE 11. Identifying Purpose and Audience. Bring to class three different paragraphs from newspapers, magazines, or books. Be prepared to identify the writer's purpose and audience.

GATHERING INFORMATION

2j. Gather information about your limited topic.

You can use a number of different techniques to gather information for a paragraph. If you are writing about a topic you know well, you can use brainstorming, clustering, or the *5 W-How?* questions to think of possible details to include. (See pages 20–25 for more information on these techniques.) If you are writing about an unfamiliar topic, you will need to do some research by interviewing someone who knows the topic well, or by using library sources. In any case, be sure to take detailed notes as you gather information, and save them to use as you organize and draft your paragraph.

EXERCISE 12. Gathering Information. Choose *one* of the limited topics you found for Exercise 9 (page 61). Using one or more of the techniques discussed above, gather information about your topic. Save your notes.

DEVELOPING A WORKING PLAN

2k. Develop a working plan for your paragraph.

A *working plan* for a paragraph is made up of a topic sentence and a list of supporting details arranged in a clear order.

EXAMPLE *Topic sentence:* Japanese folk tales include many stories of animals that help or reward people.

Details:

a. Kindness to animals; Japanese idea of divine spirit, *kami,* in all nature
b. Animals sometimes become human beings
c. Story of sparrow whose tongue was cut by washerwoman —punishment for eating woman's rice
d. Old couple (neighbors) found and cared for sparrow
e. Sparrow transformed to human—offered elderly couple two boxes; they chose small box that contained unending money

Writing an Effective Topic Sentence

An effective topic sentence states a single main idea clearly and precisely. It covers all of the supporting details and *only* those details. It also catches the readers' attention and makes them want to keep reading.

One writer gathered the following list of details about a computer game. Which of the suggested topic sentences would be most effective for a paragraph based on these details?

Details:

a. Computer software game—called "Synthetic Adventure —The Flask of Doom"
b. Created by chemistry professor, Fred D. Williams —teacher at Michigan Tech
c. Teaches organic chemistry
d. Player visits planet Organo—people who live there are organic compounds
e. Player's "mission" goal of game—finding a DNA molecule
f. DNA—basic material in all living matter; transmits inherited characteristics specific to each kind of plant or animal
g. Players, accompanied by chemicals (Organo residents), visit more than 50 locations; combinations of chemicals produce compounds to solve game's problems

Possible topic sentences:

a. Students can learn organic chemistry more easily.
b. A new computer game called "Synthetic Adventure—The Flask of Doom" helps make learning the chemical compounds of organic chemistry easier and more interesting.
c. "Synthetic Adventure—The Flask of Doom" is one of several new computer games.

Sentence b is the most effective. It covers all of the details, it is clear and precise, and it catches the readers' attention. Sentence a is not only too general—it does not mention the specific game that is the topic of the paragraph—it is dull. Sentence c is misleading because it suggests that the paragraph will be about more than one game.

Before You Write. As you write your topic sentence,

- Make sure that it covers all of the details you plan to include and *only* those details.
- State one main idea as clearly and precisely as you can.
- Try to catch the reader's attention.

EXERCISE 13. Writing Topic Sentences. Write a topic sentence for each of the following lists of details. (You may decide not to cover all of the details.) Try writing several different versions, and choose the one that you think is most effective.

1. a. More than one third of the approximately 60 million potential voters in the United States not registered
   b. About 80 percent of registered voters vote in Presidential elections
   c. Reasons people don't register: don't care; don't think a single vote can make a difference; don't want to be called to jury duty (voter registration rolls used for jury pool)
   d. Voting in elections a citizen's responsibility; can't vote if you're not registered
   e. Countries that have no free elections; many Americans take right to vote and other freedoms for granted
   f. Importance of registering to vote
   g. Necessity of making a special effort to get groups that traditionally have low voter-registration count to register
2. a. Mobile homes (trailers); way of life for many Americans
   b. Wyoming—18.3 percent of homes are mobile homes; Montana and Arizona—13 percent; Nevada—12.8 percent; New Mexico—12.5 percent
   c. National average—5.3 percent of all homes mobile homes
   d. More in Rocky Mountain states because of "boom and bust" jobs; temporary, immediate homes
   e. More trailers also in Sunbelt states; inexpensive and easily maintained homes
   f. Lowest percentage in Washington, D.C.—1 percent; low percentage of mobile homes in urban Northeast
   g. Feeling of rootlessness

CRITICAL THINKING:
Forming a Generalization

A *generalization* is a general conclusion about a group of people, events, objects, places, or ideas.

EXAMPLES Soccer is the most popular sport in the world.
Mammals give birth to live young.
Airplane travel is safer than automobile travel.

To be *valid* (reasonable), a generalization must be based on a fairly large number of facts or on many observations made without prejudice. A valid generalization suggests that additional facts or observations will probably also support the conclusion.

A *hasty generalization* is one that is based on too few facts or on prejudiced observations.

EXAMPLES Snakes are dangerous.
Athletes are poor students.

The topic sentence of a paragraph may state a generalization. The other sentences present evidence such as facts, examples, or reasons to support the generalization. In the following paragraphs from a handbook for foreigners who plan to study in the United States, for example, the boldfaced topic sentences are generalizations. What evidence is given to support each generalization?

> **Americans are very informal.** They like to dress informally, entertain informally, and they treat each other in a very informal way, even when there is a great difference in age or social standing. Foreign students may consider this informality disrespectful, even rude, but it is a part of U.S. culture.
>
> **Americans are achievers.** They are obsessed with records of achievement in sports, and they keep business achievement charts on their office walls and sports awards displayed in their homes.
>
> **Americans value punctuality.** They keep appointment calendars and live according to schedules. To foreign students, Americans seem "always in a hurry," and this often makes

them appear brusque. Americans are generally efficient and get a great many things done, simply by rushing around.

UNITED STATES INFORMATION AGENCY,
BUREAU OF EDUCATIONAL AND CULTURAL AFFAIRS

EXERCISE 14. Analyzing Paragraphs Based on Generalizations. Answer these questions about the paragraphs above about Americans.

1. Are these generalizations reasonable? Explain your answers.
2. What other valid generalizations can you make about Americans? List your generalizations and a sentence or two to support each one.

Choosing Details

Before you write your first draft, look again at your list of details. If any of them do not directly support your main idea, remove them. If you do not have enough details to make the main idea clear, either gather more information, revise your topic sentence, or select a new topic.

Once you have enough details to make your main idea clear, arrange them in the order in which you will present them. You may also want to give your paragraph a *title* that identifies your topic and catches the attention of your audience.

CRITICAL THINKING:
Deciding Which Details Support a Main Idea

To decide which details best support your main idea, you use the critical thinking skill of *analysis.* You decide how each detail is related to your main idea. Including only those details that are *directly* related to your main idea helps you write a unified paragraph.

EXAMPLE

Topic sentence: Too few American citizens take the privilege and responsibility of voting seriously.

Possible details:

a. More than one third (approximately 60 million) of those eligible to vote not registered
b. Only about 80 percent of registered voters vote in Presidential elections.
c. Can't vote if you're not registered
d. Many countries have no free elections
e. Where do you register to vote?
f. Everyone in my family registered to vote
g. Some people don't register because they don't think a single vote can make a difference; don't want to be called to jury duty (voter registration rolls used for jury pool)
h. Voter registration card—useful as identification
i. Registering to vote is not as complicated or as time consuming as many people think it is.

Details e, f, and h are not directly related to the paragraph's main idea. Therefore, these three details should not be included in the paragraph.

Before You Write. Use the following guidelines to decide which details to include and which ones to leave out.

- Is this detail *directly* related to the paragraph's main idea as it is stated in the topic sentence?
- How will this detail function within the paragraph? Is it an example?
- Will this detail help the reader understand the main idea, or will it confuse or distract the reader? Will the paragraph be easier to understand with the detail or without it?

EXERCISE 15. Analyzing Possible Details for a Paragraph. Decide which of the following details support the main idea in the topic sentence given, and write them on a separate sheet of paper. Be prepared to explain your choices.

Topic sentence: Running for office in a class election is a lot of work, but it can also be a lot of fun.

Possible details:

a. Qualifying for nomination—past grades and conduct examined
b. Writing campaign speeches—broadcast over radio
c. Candidates running for same office sometimes best friends: Pat and I both candidates for vice-president of Student Council
d. Fun preparing campaign posters, writing slogans, and handing out buttons
e. In city, state, and national elections, electioneering not permitted near polls
f. Suspense while votes counted
g. Day of elections—candidates exhausted, voters still trying to decide
h. Candidates talk to students: try to make themselves known, try to understand the concerns of their classmates
i. Responsibilities of class officer

REVIEW EXERCISE D. Developing a Working Plan. Develop a working plan for the topic on which you gathered information for Exercise 12. Write a topic sentence. Then list the details you have gathered, as well as any other details you can think of, and arrange them in a clear order. Save your paper.

WRITING

WRITING A FIRST DRAFT

2l. Write the first draft of your paragraph.

As you write your first draft, use your working plan that includes your topic sentence and list of supporting details as a guide. Keeping your purpose and audience in mind, begin with your topic sentence, and shape each of your supporting details into sentences. You may want to devote several sentences to one detail. You may combine several details into a single sentence, and you may include related details as you think of them.

Remember that you will have time later to improve your writing. Simply try to write your ideas down at this point.

When You Write. As you write your first draft:

- Use your working plan as a guide.
- Keep your purpose and audience in mind.
- Write freely, adding related ideas as you think of them.

EXERCISE 16. Writing a First Draft. Use the working plan you prepared for Review Exercise D (page 70) to write the first draft of your paragraph. Keep the above *When You Write* guidelines in mind as you write your draft. Remember that you will evaluate and revise your paragraph later. Save your paper.

EVALUATING

EVALUATING YOUR PARAGRAPH

2m. Evaluate the first draft of your paragraph.

When you *evaluate,* or judge, your paragraph, you read it carefully several times. You look for strengths and weaknesses in the content, organization, and style (word choice and sentence structure).

If possible, let some time pass between writing your first draft and evaluating it. You should try to read your draft as if you were seeing it for the first time. This will help you notice areas that need to be improved. You may also want to ask a classmate to evaluate your paragraph.

The following Guidelines for Evaluating Paragraphs will help you evaluate any paragraph you write. In Chapter 3 you will find specific guidelines for evaluating the four basic types of paragraphs (expository, persuasive, descriptive, and narrative).

GUIDELINES FOR EVALUATING PARAGRAPHS

Topic Sentence	1. Does the topic sentence identify a limited topic and clearly state one main idea?
Topic Development	2. Are enough supporting details and sentences given to make the main idea clear?
Unity	3. Does the paragraph have unity? Does each sentence directly support the main idea?
Concluding Sentence	4. Does the clincher sentence, if any, give the paragraph a strong ending?
Order of Ideas	5. Are the ideas arranged in a clear order? Does the order help make the main idea clear? Should any sentences or ideas be moved?
Relationships Between Ideas	6. Do the ideas flow smoothly from one sentence to the next? If appropriate, are transitional expressions used to show how ideas are related?
Word Choice	7. Is the language specific and vivid? Is it appropriate for the purpose and audience? Are difficult words defined or explained?
Sentence Variety	8. Do the sentences vary in structure and length? Are they appropriate for the audience?
Tone	9. Is the tone suitable for the purpose and the audience? Is the same tone used throughout the paragraph?

EXERCISE 17. Evaluating the First Draft of a Paragraph. Number your paper 1–9. Read the following first draft of a paragraph written for an eighth-grade audience. Then use the Guidelines for Evaluating Paragraphs on this page to evaluate it. Answer each question on the guidelines by writing *yes* or *no* after the appropriate number on your paper.

Japanese folk tales include many stories of animals that help or reward people. These stories increase the Japanese belief of kindness to animals, it is based on the believe that *kami* is found in all of nature. *Kami* is a divine presence. One story is about a sparrow, a washerwoman, and an old couple. The washerwoman cuts the sparrow's tongue because the sparrow ate some of her rice. The old couple found and cared for the sparrow. They had been kind to the sparrow even before this happened. The sparrow became a human being. The sparrow offered the couple a choice of two boxes. They chose the smallest box, they found in it unending money. In these folk tales the animals become human beings. I think everyone should be kind to animals.

EXERCISE 18. Evaluating Your Paragraph. Use the Guidelines for Evaluating Paragraphs on page 72 to judge the first draft of the paragraph you wrote for Exercise 16. Save your paper for later use.

REVISING

REVISING YOUR PARAGRAPH

2n. Revise the first draft of your paragraph.

Making changes to improve your writing is called *revising*. Four strategies for improving your writing are *adding, cutting, reordering,* and *replacing*. The following chart shows how you can use these four strategies to revise paragraphs.

REVISING PARAGRAPHS

PROBLEM	STRATEGY	REVISION
The paragraph does not have a topic sentence.	Add	Add a sentence that identifies the topic and clearly states the main idea.
The topic sentence is too broad.	Cut	Remove words, phrases, or clauses that do not keep to one main idea.
The topic sentence is too narrow.	Add	Add words, a phrase, or a clause that will make the sentence cover all the details in the paragraph.

PROBLEM	STRATEGY	REVISION
The topic sentence is dull.	Add/Replace	Add vivid details. Replace general words with specific ones.
One or more of the sentences are not directly related to the main idea.	Cut	Remove the sentence(s).
The paragraph does not contain enough details to make the main idea clear.	Add	Add facts, statistics, examples, reasons, concrete or sensory details, or an incident.
The paragraph trails off or ends abruptly.	Add	Add a clincher sentence: Restate the main idea, summarize the information given, or suggest a course of action.
The ideas are not arranged in a clear order.	Reorder	Rearrange the sentences to make the order of ideas clear.
The ideas do not flow smoothly.	Add/Replace	Add direct references and transitional expressions. Substitute more appropriate transitional expressions.
The language is dull.	Add/Replace	Add vivid nouns, verbs, adjectives, or adverbs. Replace general words with specific ones.
The language is too difficult for the audience.	Add/Replace	Add definitions and explanations. Substitute easier words.
The sentences are monotonous.	Replace	Combine sentences. Vary sentence beginnings. Vary sentence length.
The tone is not appropriate or does not stay the same throughout the paragraph.	Replace	Substitute words that are more formal/informal, serious/humorous, etc.

EXERCISE 19. Analyzing a Writer's Revisions. Study the following revised draft. (The notes in the margin show the revision strategies that the writer used.) Then answer the questions that follow the paragraph.

Japanese folk tales include many stories of
animals that help or reward people. These — add
stories ~~increase~~ the Japanese ~~belief~~ of kindness — replace
to animals, ~~it~~ is based on the ~~believe~~ that *kami* — replace; add; replace
is found in all of nature. ~~*Kami* is a divine~~ — add; cut
~~presence.~~ One story is about a sparrow, a — cut; add
washerwoman, and an old couple. The washerwoman cuts the sparrow's tongue because — add
~~the sparrow ate~~ some of her rice. ~~The~~ old — replace
couple found and cared for the sparrow. ~~They~~ — add; reorder
had been kind to the sparrow even before this
happened. The sparrow became a human
being. ~~The sparrow~~ offered the couple a — replace
choice of two boxes. They chose the smallest — replace
~~box, they~~ found in it ~~unending money~~. In these — replace; reorder
folk tales the animals ~~become~~ human beings. ~~I~~ — add; replace; cut
~~think everyone should be kind to animals.~~ — cut

1. Why did the writer add the word *grateful* and the clause *who are kind to them* to the topic sentence (the first sentence)?
2. What specific information did the writer add to the paragraph?
3. Find two places where the writer reordered information. Why do you think the writer made these changes?
4. How did the writer vary the sentence structure?
5. Why did the writer remove the last sentence?

EXERCISE 20. Evaluating and Revising a Paragraph. Use the Guidelines for Evaluating Paragraphs on page 72 to evaluate the following paragraph. Then revise the paragraph, using the paragraph revision chart on pages 73–74.

Jason is my best friend. He has been my best friend since he moved next door last summer. My family stayed home last summer because our car broke down and it cost a lot of money to get it fixed. Jason has a lot of talent. He plays the clarinet. He is in a youth symphony. He is also in the school band. Jason likes sports, too. He writes well, and he likes to tell jokes. He makes friends easily. Jason has a great sense of humor.

EXERCISE 21. Revising Your Paragraph. Using your answers for Exercise 18 and the chart on pages 73–74, revise the paragraph you wrote for Exercise 16. Save your paper.

PROOFREADING AND MAKING A FINAL COPY

PROOFREADING YOUR PARAGRAPH AND MAKING A FINAL COPY

2o. Proofread your revised paragraph and make a final copy. Then proofread again.

When you proofread, you read letter by letter to find and correct mistakes in usage, spelling, capitalization, and punctuation. You check for each kind of error separately, so that you do not overlook anything.

Once you have corrected such mistakes, recopy your paper neatly. Proofread this final copy also, to make sure you did not make any new errors in recopying.

EXERCISE 22. Proofreading a Paragraph. Using the Guidelines for Proofreading on page 39, proofread the following paragraph. Write the corrected version on a separate sheet of paper. You may need to reword the paragraph to correct run-on sentences and sentence fragments.

In the creation myth of the Iroquois tribe, the earth began when the mother of earth fell threw a hole in the sky. She fell into an endless lake but fortunately with her fell a cosmic tree, it had some magical earth around it's roots. The young woman who fell from the sky was saved from drowning by two swans. Then three animals—Otter, Beaver, Muskrat, and Toad—each dived to the bottom of the lake. To try to get some of the magical earth on the trees roots. Otter, Beaver, and Muskrat drownded; Toad was able to get a single mouthful of the earth, it grew first into an island for the mother of earth to stand on, and then it grew and grew and kept right on growing. Until it became the hole world.

EXERCISE 23. Proofreading Your Paragraph. Proofread the paragraph you revised for Exercise 21. Then make a final copy and proofread it.

CHAPTER 2 WRITING REVIEW

Writing an Effective Paragraph. For this assignment, your teacher may give you a topic. If not, you may choose and limit one of the following subjects or a subject of your own.

Athletes	Clothing
Dreams	Games
Science	Health

PREWRITING Make sure that your topic is limited enough to cover in one paragraph. After you have decided on your purpose and your audience, gather possible details to include. Then make a working plan: write a topic sentence, choose the details you will use to support it, and arrange the details in a clear order.

WRITING As you write your first draft, follow your working plan. Write freely, and be sure to keep your purpose and audience in mind.

EVALUATING AND REVISING Use the Guidelines for Evaluating Paragraphs (page 72) to judge your writing. Then use the paragraph revision chart (pages 73–74) as you revise your writing.

PROOFREADING AND MAKING A FINAL COPY Proofread your paragraph (see the Guidelines for Proofreading on page 39). Then make a clean copy and proofread it.

CHAPTER 3

Writing Paragraphs

FOUR TYPES OF PARAGRAPHS

Most paragraphs can be grouped into four types, according to the writer's main purpose, or reason, for writing.

TYPE OF PARAGRAPH	PURPOSE	EXAMPLE
Narrative	To tell a story	A paragraph telling what happened in the school cafeteria today
Descriptive	To describe	A paragraph describing what you had for lunch today
Expository	To explain or give information	A paragraph explaining how the cafeteria manager plans balanced meals
Persuasive	To persuade	A paragraph persuading students to keep the school cafeteria clean

In this chapter you will learn methods of developing these four types of paragraphs. Each method uses a different kind of *detail.*

THE NARRATIVE PARAGRAPH

A *narrative paragraph* tells a story or relates a series of events. It may illustrate a point, or it may simply entertain.

Developing a Narrative Paragraph

3a. Develop a narrative paragraph with the details of an incident.

An *incident* is an event that takes place in a short time. The following paragraph uses the details of an incident to develop the main idea in the topic sentence (the first sentence). Notice that the writer arranges the ideas in *chronological* (time) order. The italicized words help the reader keep track of the order of events.

> Not all of Adamson's encounters with his liberated lions have been so uneventful. *Several years ago,* he was out on patrol *when* he met up with two of his ex-charges, a male named Suleiman and his sister, Sheba. They playfully bounded straight at Adamson. Suleiman grabbed him from behind and the two of them crashed to the ground. *When* Adamson squeezed off a warning shot with his pistol, the animal—no longer playful—growled and bit deeply into his neck. Adamson *then* jammed the weapon into a fleshy area above the lion's shoulder and fired. *With that,* the lion retreated and Adamson hobbled off, bleeding profusely. He made it back to camp where doctors in Nairobi were radioed to fly up and repair the damage. "I worried *all night* about Suleiman," he recalled sheepishly. "I was relieved *the next morning when* he showed up looking little the worse for wear except for a bullet lodged under his skin."
>
> DICK HUSTON

Using Narrative Details

Narrative details are specific pieces of information—action verbs, specific nouns, and precise adjectives and adverbs. They help the reader picture the actions and answer the question *What happened?* Compare the following two versions of a paragraph.

WEAK The boy was riding a bicycle. He didn't see the barrier and hit it. He fell, and the bicycle fell on top of him. He picked himself up and rode away.

IMPROVED The sandy-haired boy in cutoff shorts and a yellow T-shirt was riding a rusty green Raleigh. As he rode across the narrow wooden footbridge, the boy turned to watch a tern dive-bomb into the water for a fish. Looking over his shoulder, he crashed into the metal barricade at the end of the bridge. For a moment he struggled to keep his balance. Then he fell beneath the bicycle, landing on his elbow and crashing against his funny bone. He looked around; no one had heard the crash or seen him fall. The boy rocked and moaned, cradling his elbow. As the terrible pain subsided, he picked up his bicycle and rode slowly away.

EXERCISE 1. Writing a Narrative Paragraph. Arrange the following details in order. Then write a narrative paragraph. You may add other related details.

Details:

a. Began to smell burning
b. Had to pay for repairing window
c. Nobody in family home, nobody could be reached
d. Left vegetables cooking on stove
e. Last summer—finally learned not to get locked out
f. Neighbor helped; broke bathroom window and climbed through
g. Went out of house for just a minute—left keys on kitchen table; door locked behind

Choosing a Point of View

In the *first-person point of view,* the storyteller (narrator) participates in the action. As you read the following paragraph from an article about a skiing trip through the Grand Canyon, notice that the writer uses the first-person pronouns *I, myself, my,* and *we* to show that he took part in the trip.

We clipped on our skis, slung on our packs, ducked under a gate and stepped onto the snow. It was ice. The morning was sunny, but there had been no fresh snow for more than a week, and the surface was solidly frozen. *We* set off at a modest pace, with Quiroz up front. *I* charged up a few hills to assure *myself I* could handle this, then dropped in behind Babbitt and Warner. *My* pack was already heavy.

KENNY MOORE

In the *third-person point of view,* the storyteller does not take part in the story. Instead, the writer uses the third-person pronouns *he, him, she, her, they,* and *them* to refer to the people in the story. The paragraphs about George Adamson (page 80) and about the boy on the bicycle (pages 80–81) are written from the third-person point of view.

Before beginning a narrative paragraph, decide which point of view you will use. Do not mix first- and third-person points of view in the same paragraph.

Before You Write. To develop a narrative paragraph:

- Select an incident that takes place in no more than a few hours.
- Use the *5 W-How?* questions to gather details.
- Arrange the important events in chronological order.
- Choose first-person or third-person point of view.
- Write a topic sentence that sums up the incident, tells how it came about, or states the general idea the incident illustrates.

EXERCISE 2. Writing a Narrative Paragraph. Write a narrative paragraph using the details of an incident. You may use one of the following ideas or one of your own.

1. An experiment that didn't work
2. Overcoming a fear
3. A time when I laughed a lot
4. A chore that turned out to be fun
5. A promise that was hard to keep

PREWRITING Use one or more of the techniques on pages 12–15 to find possible incidents to use. Select an incident that will interest your audience, and use the *5 W-How?* questions to gather details. Arrange the important events in chronological order. Then write a topic sentence that sums up the incident, tells how it came about, or states the general idea that the incident illustrates.

WRITING As you draft your paragraph, include only those details that will help the reader understand what happened. Try not to get sidetracked into details that are not needed and may confuse the reader.

EVALUATING AND REVISING Ask yourself: Have I arranged the events in the order in which they took place? Have I included only details that will help my readers understand what happened? Then use the Guidelines for Evaluating Narrative Paragraphs below and the paragraph revision chart on pages 73–74 to judge and improve your writing.

PROOFREADING AND MAKING A FINAL COPY After using the Guidelines for Proofreading on page 39 to correct your paper, make a final copy and proofread it.

Evaluating and Revising Narrative Paragraphs

You can use the following guidelines to evaluate, or judge, the narrative paragraphs you write. The paragraph revision chart on pages 73–74 will help you improve your writing.

GUIDELINES FOR EVALUATING NARRATIVE PARAGRAPHS

Topic Sentence	1. Does the topic sentence sum up the incident, tell how it came about, or state a general idea?
Topic Development	2. Are enough details included so that the audience can understand what happened?
Unity	3. Have unrelated details been left out?
Order of Ideas	4. Are the actions arranged in the order in which they took place?
Relationships Between Ideas	5. Do the ideas flow smoothly? Are they linked with direct references and with transitional expressions (*then, in the meantime,* etc.)?
Word Choice	6. Is the language specific rather than general? Is it appropriate for the audience?

EXERCISE 3. Evaluating and Revising a Narrative Paragraph. Number your paper 1–6. Use the guidelines on the previous page to evaluate the following first draft written for an eighth-grade audience. Answer each question. Then revise the paragraph on a separate sheet of paper, using the paragraph revision chart on pages 73–74. The questions following the paragraph may help you think of narrative details to add to the paragraph when you revise it.

When Amy was very little, she learned something important about driving a car. She got in her father's car. She locked the doors and released the emergency brake. The driveway was on a hill, so the car coasted backward down the hill. Amy cried. The car stopped moving. It was blocking the street. Amy's father came and got her out.

1. How old was Amy?
2. What did she learn from this experience?
3. How did Amy feel when the car began to move?
4. How did Amy's father find out what had happened?
5. How did he get Amy out of the car?

REVIEW EXERCISE A. Writing a Narrative Paragraph. Write a paragraph based on one of the following incidents or on an incident of your own choice.

1. You become lost on a wilderness hike.
2. You are taking your little sister for a walk when you meet a dangerous-looking dog.
3. You look out your window and see black smoke pouring from a neighbor's house (or apartment).
4. You help an elderly neighbor who lives alone.
5. You work very hard on a science project.

THE DESCRIPTIVE PARAGRAPH

A descriptive paragraph creates a picture in the reader's mind. It focuses on one person, place, or object. The details are usually arranged in spatial order.

Developing Descriptive Paragraphs

3b. Develop a descriptive paragraph with concrete and sensory details.

Concrete details mention specific objects, places, or people. *Sensory details* appeal directly to the senses: sight, hearing, taste, touch, and smell. Notice how the writer of the following paragraph uses concrete details and sensory details that appeal to smell, hearing, and sight to describe a place.

> I remember my first walk in a Nigerian rain forest. It is moist and the air is soft, a comforting warm smell actually made by the fungi underfoot. The trunks of the great trees rise straight up and tall, set out like pillars along the nave of a great Gothic cathedral. Clouds float between the branches, drifting patches of vapor that come and go. The trees branch out at about a hundred feet. Where there is a break in the canopy, light streams through against the rising mist in rays that you can see. I remember how an ugly dead growth on the branch of one tree suddenly opens in at the middle and says, "Gronk." It is a giant yellow casque hornbill. I remember, too, how the silence that makes me place my feet so carefully is broken as frogs begin to sing, then more frogs and more until the song sweeps into the distance and stops as suddenly as it began.
>
> PAUL COLINVAUX

EXERCISE 4. Gathering Sensory Details. Spend at least five minutes carefully observing each of the following objects. Write three sensory details that you could use to describe each object.

1. A green pepper
2. A penny
3. A toothbrush
4. A pencil
5. A shoe

Using Precise Language

A descriptive paragraph should be vivid. Specific nouns, action verbs, and carefully chosen adjectives and adverbs are needed to give the reader a clear picture.

The following paragraph is a character sketch of Julian Lennon, the rock musician whose father, John, was a member of the Beatles. Notice how the writer of the paragraph uses precise language to describe Julian.

> He is beginning to look more like his father. His pale face displays soft and sensuous features and sparkling eyes. His personality is an odd contradiction between depression and energy, self-doubt and triumph of spirit. Contemplating the demands of a new tour, he is extremely nervous. He sits for a while drumming his fingers, then jumps up and dashes around the room on a skateboard, then stops to fake a sob and moan, "I want me mommy!" But as rehearsals progress, the nervousness leaves him. He sings with abandon. His tentative movements on stage become a strut. In the first performance, the audience screams with delight. He is clearly in command of the stage and everyone on it, the hall and everyone in it.

EXERCISE 5. Making Descriptions Vivid. Revise each of the following sentences. Add specific nouns, action verbs, and precise modifiers to create a clear picture.

1. A woman answered the door.
2. The student sat at the desk.
3. Someone was using a machine that made a lot of noise.
4. The singer sang a sad song.
5. The audience applauded.
6. The basketball player scored two points.
7. The kitchen was filled with a good smell.
8. The baby cried loudly for a long time.
9. Lou felt bad about the news.
10. The driver got in the car and drove away quickly.

EXERCISE 6. Writing a Paragraph Describing a Person. Find a photograph in a newspaper or magazine that clearly shows a person's face and body. Observe the photograph carefully, and write a paragraph describing the person.

Using Comparisons and Figurative Language

Comparisons and figurative language help make a description vivid. In the following paragraph, Lewis Thomas compares the "dead" moon with the "living" earth. To say that the earth is alive is to use a figure of speech called a *metaphor*. Notice the other italicized figurative language.

> Viewed from the distance of the moon, the astonishing thing about the earth, catching the breath, is that it is alive. The photographs show the dry pounded surface of the moon in the foreground, *dead as an old bone.* Aloft, *floating free* beneath the moist, gleaming *membrane of bright blue sky,* is the rising earth, the only *exuberant thing* in this part of the cosmos. If you could look long enough, you would see the swirling of the great drifts of white cloud, covering and uncovering the half-hidden masses of land. If you had been looking for a very long, geologic time, you could have seen the continents themselves in motion, drifting apart on their crustal plates, *held afloat* by the fire beneath. It has the organized self-contained look of *a live creature, full of information, marvelously skilled in handling the sun.*
>
> LEWIS THOMAS

EXERCISE 7. Writing a Paragraph Describing an Object. Write a paragraph describing one of the objects in Exercise 4 or an object of your own choosing.

Creating a Main Impression

A descriptive paragraph may create a single main impression of a topic. Often, that main impression is revealed in the topic sentence. In the following paragraph, for example, the topic sentence gives the writer's main impression of the way she saw a harbor in China: as a speeded-up movie. Each supporting detail she includes helps reinforce that impression.

> As our bus draws up at the wharf in Chongqing, once known as Chungking, we seem to enter a speeded-up movie. Hordes of people scramble down a crazy-quilt pattern of steps that saw-tooth steeply in two opposing directions, criss-crossing

in the middle. It is low tide, and there are more than 300 steps swarming with men, women, and children all scampering down toward the river, carrying bamboo poles balancing baskets of cabbages, apples, mandarin oranges, tangerines, persimmons, radishes, grain, spices, chickens, ducks, fish. Children carry stoves, old men fishing poles and nets, Mao-suited businessmen briefcases. Beside a gangplank, people squat in small groups like coveys of birds, counting produce, rearranging cargo and finally funneling into a green, triple-decked ferryboat with a bright red star at the top. When the boat pulls away an hour later, we have observed more of life and human interaction than at any previous time in China.

BARBARA GOLDSMITH

EXERCISE 8. Writing a Paragraph Describing a Place. Write a paragraph describing one of the following places or a place of your own choosing.

1. The cafeteria during lunch hour
2. An empty football stadium
3. A park during a snowfall (or heavy rainstorm)
4. The street outside your home at 5:00 A.M.
5. A classroom during a test

Before You Write. To create a main impression in a descriptive paragraph:

- Use the *5 W-How?* questions to gather precise concrete and sensory details.
- Select only those details that will create a single impression.
- Arrange the details in spatial order.
- Write a topic sentence that gives the main impression you want to create.

Evaluating and Revising Descriptive Paragraphs

Use the guidelines on the next page to evaluate the descriptive paragraphs you write. Once you have decided which areas need to be improved, refer to the paragraph revision chart on pages 73–74 to revise your writing.

GUIDELINES FOR EVALUATING DESCRIPTIVE PARAGRAPHS

Topic Sentence	1. Does the topic sentence identify the topic? If it creates a main impression, does it do so clearly?
Topic Development	2. Are enough concrete and sensory details included to create a vivid picture of the topic?
Unity	3. Does each sentence reinforce the main impression?
Order of Ideas	4. Are the details arranged in spatial order?
Relationships Between Ideas	5. Do the ideas flow smoothly? Are they linked with direct references and with transitional expressions (*above, to the left,* etc.)?
Word Choice	6. Is the language specific rather than general? If figurative language is used, is it appropriate and effective?

REVIEW EXERCISE B. Evaluating and Revising a Descriptive Paragraph. Use the guidelines above to evaluate the following paragraph. Then revise the paragraph, adding specific details and replacing general words with specific ones. You may make up any additional information you need. The questions following the paragraph may help you think of details to add.

> The girl walked to the door of the house. She had long hair. She wore ordinary clothes. She looked worried and nervous. She carried something in her right hand. She waited next to the door.

1. What does the girl look like? How old is she? How tall? Is she slim or heavy? What color is her hair? How does she wear it?
2. What exactly is the girl wearing? What color are her clothes? Is the girl's appearance neat or sloppy?
3. How can an observer tell that she is worried and nervous? What is she carrying in her right hand? How does she move?
4. What does the house look like? Why is the girl waiting at the door? What does she do while she waits?
5. What sounds can the girl hear? What can she smell?

THE EXPOSITORY PARAGRAPH

The purpose of an expository paragraph is to give information or to explain. Expository paragraphs may be developed with facts and statistics, with examples, by definitions, with the details of a process, or by a combination of these methods.

The order in which you arrange the ideas in an expository paragraph depends on the specific purpose of the paragraph. A paragraph explaining how to do something, for example, uses chronological order to help the audience understand what to do first, second, and so on. (See pages 25–28 for more information.)

Developing with Facts and Statistics

3c. Develop an expository paragraph with facts and statistics.

A *fact* is information that can be proved to be true; a *statistic* is a numerical fact. The following paragraph uses facts and statistics to give information about a professional basketball player.

> Marques Haynes was on the road again, just as he has been every season since he left Langston nearly 40 years ago. He won't admit to his exact age—"I'm 37 $\frac{1}{2}$ and holding," the man says—but he figures to be 60 or thereabouts, assuming he was 21 when he graduated from Langston in '46. That was about 12,000 basketball games ago, Haynes estimates, played during an odyssey of more than four million miles with the Globetrotters (1947–'53); the original Harlem Magicians ('53–72); the Globetrotters again ('72–79); Meadowlark Lemon's Bucketeers ('79-81); the Harlem Wizards ('81–83); and finally his own Harlem Magicians again. It is an odyssey that has taken him to 97 countries and to so many American cities, towns, and hamlets that he is hard put, glancing at a map, to find a place he hasn't been.
>
> WILLIAM NACK

EXERCISE 9. Writing a Paragraph Using Facts and Statistics. Write an expository paragraph based on the following information. You need not use all of the information.

Details:

a. Roberto Clemente, one of baseball's all-time great outfielders and hitters
b. Tried to help others, especially young people in Puerto Rico, where he was born and grew up
c. Humanitarian—person who tried to help others
d. In 1972 after earthquake in Managua, Nicaragua, Clemente appealed to Puerto Ricans on radio and TV: contribute food and supplies for Managuans
e. Raised more than $150,000; 26 tons of supplies
f. New Year's Eve, 1972—Clemente on flight from San Juan, Puerto Rico, to Managua to deliver supplies
g. Plane took off at 9:00 P.M.; crashed at sea—no survivors
h. Clemente mourned as "*un gran hombre—un hombre de buen corazón*" (a great man—a man of good heart)

EXERCISE 10. Writing a Paragraph Using Facts and Statistics. Write an expository paragraph on one of the following topics or on a topic of your own.

1. Redwood trees
2. Blue whales
3. The Lincoln Memorial
4. The most recent Super Bowl
5. The Mississippi River

PREWRITING Use reliable reference works (See Chapter 27.) to gather accurate facts and statistics. As you select details to include, remember that too much information may confuse or bore your audience. Arrange your notes in an order that will be easy to follow, and then write a topic sentence stating your main idea.

WRITING Evaluate your choice of details as you write your draft. Remember to define unfamiliar terms for your audience.

EVALUATING AND REVISING Ask yourself: Does every piece of information directly support my main idea? Have I included neither too few details nor too many? Then use the evaluation guidelines on page 97 and the paragraph revision chart on pages 73–74 to judge and improve your writing.

PROOFREADING AND MAKING A FINAL COPY First make sure that you copied the information from your notes correctly. Then use the Guidelines for Proofreading on page 39. Remember to proofread your final copy as well.

Developing with Examples

3d. Develop an expository paragraph with examples.

An *example* is a person, thing, or event that stands for others of the same kind. Using examples that your audience is familiar with can help you make a general idea clear in the limited space of a paragraph. In the following paragraph, the writer uses examples to develop the main idea. What is that idea?

> The story of David with his slingshot slaying the clumsy giant has delighted children for at least three thousand years. David was an early example of a common type of folk hero—the one who fights with skill and daring against superior force and wins. Sometime before David's triumph in the valley of Elah, Odysseus was in Sicily winning his battle of wits against the Cyclops. Similar stories are found in the folklore of nations all over the world.
>
> FREEMAN DYSON

EXERCISE 11. Writing a Paragraph Using Examples. Write an expository paragraph developed with examples. You may use one of the following topics or a topic of your own.

1. Home accidents caused by carelessness
2. Ways of preserving foods
3. Skills needed to be an effective quarterback
4. The popularity of sports in America
5. Free or inexpensive spare-time activities

PREWRITING First decide how your topic can be explained through the use of examples. Then use an information-gathering technique (pages 20–25) to find examples that are familiar to your audience. Arrange the material in an easy-to-follow order, and write a topic sentence that states your main idea.

WRITING Keep your audience and purpose in mind as you write. Remember that you will have another chance to consider the examples when you evaluate your paragraph.

EVALUATING AND REVISING Ask yourself: Have I included enough examples to make my main idea clear? Will the examples be familiar to my audience? Then judge and improve your writing, using the evaluation guidelines on page 97 and the paragraph revision chart on pages 73–74.

PROOFREADING AND MAKING A FINAL COPY Proofread your paper, using the Guidelines for Proofreading on page 39. Then make a final copy and proofread it.

EXERCISE 12. Writing a Paragraph Using Examples. Write an expository paragraph developed with examples. You may use one of the following topics or a topic of your own.

1. Popular cartoon characters
2. Ways to keep healthy
3. Conveniences that were unknown fifty years ago
4. Words based on people's names
5. Study skills

Developing by Definition

3e. Develop an expository paragraph by definition.

A definition is a clear and detailed explanation of the meaning of a word. The first step in writing a definition is to identify the general class (group) to which the object or idea belongs.

EXAMPLE A *skunk* is a *mammal* of the weasel family.

The second step is to point out the characteristics that set the object or idea apart from all other members of its class.

EXAMPLE *Skunk*—bushy tail; small (about size of cat); black fur, generally with two white stripes down back; gives off foul-smelling liquid when attacked; nocturnal (active during night, sleeps during day)

The following paragraph defines the term *Impressionism* as it applies to painting. Notice that the topic sentence identifies the class and mentions two important characteristics (where Impressionism began and when). The supporting sentences list other characteristics and give examples and related information.

Impressionist painting began in France during the 1870's.	topic sentence
The Impressionists tried to capture the impression of an object in nature with short brush strokes of pure color. They were especially concerned with the effects of sunlight and often painted outdoors.	characteristics
Impressionist painters include Claude Monet, Camille Pissaro, Alfred Sisley, and Edgar Degas.	examples
Impressionism had a profound effect on painting. Before Impressionism, artists painted their subjects almost photographically. After Impressionism, artists felt free to express themselves however they wished.	importance of Impressionism

EXERCISE 13. Writing a Paragraph of Definition. Write a paragraph defining one of the following terms.

1. Bat (the animal)
2. Success
3. Diamond
4. Microwave oven
5. Responsibility

PREWRITING Identify the class to which the object or idea belongs and list as many distinctive characteristics as you can think of or find in reference books. You may also want to include several examples. Decide what information to use and how to arrange it. Then write a topic sentence that identifies the class and mentions one or two of the most important characteristics.

WRITING Write freely, adding transitions that will help your audience follow your ideas. Avoid using other terms for which you would need to provide definitions.

EVALUATING AND REVISING Ask yourself: Have I identified

the general class to which my topic belongs? Have I included enough details to show how it is different from other members of that class? Use the evaluation guidelines on page 97 and the revision chart on pages 73–74 to judge and improve your writing.

PROOFREADING AND MAKING A FINAL COPY Use the guidelines on page 39 to proofread your paragraph. Then make a final copy and proofread it.

Developing with Details of a Process

3f. Develop an expository paragraph with details of a process.

A *process paragraph* explains how to make or do something. The process should be limited enough to be explained fully in a paragraph. For example, "how to maintain a ten-speed bike" has too many parts to explain fully in one paragraph. You could, however, explain a limited topic such as "how to check the brakes on a ten-speed bicycle."

The details in a process paragraph are the supplies and equipment needed and the steps to be carried out. The steps are arranged in chronological order.

In the following paragraph, the writers explain how to do the basic forward stroke in paddling a canoe.

> In the flat waters of Florida, most of your effort will go into strokes designed to move the canoe forward in as straight a line as possible. **Even people who have never been in a canoe before seem to know instinctively how to execute the forward cruising stroke.** Bring the paddle forward, plant the entire blade in the water, and draw it back slightly past your shoulders. Simple. And by observing a few more points, it can become the kind of stroke you can repeat a thousand times a day without tiring. Be sure to reach forward slightly at the start of each stroke. The power comes when the blade is perpendicular to the surface, not at the end of the stroke as it flattens out in the water. And be sure to draw the paddle back parallel to the center line of the canoe, not the side. Otherwise, your partner will wind up fighting your efforts.
>
> MIKE TONER and PAT TONER

EXERCISE 14. Writing a Process Paragraph. Write a paragraph explaining how to make or do something. You may use one of the following topics or one of your own.

1. How to take a photograph
2. How to make a salad
3. How to study for a test
4. How to do a somersault
5. How to make a long-distance telephone call

PREWRITING To gather information, carry out the process yourself. Take notes on all of the details involved: materials, amounts, tools and equipment, time required, and the size, shape, texture, etc. of the end product. Then arrange the steps in chronological order, and write a topic sentence that identifies the process and catches the attention of your audience.

WRITING As you write your first draft, remember that your audience is probably not as familiar with the process as you are. Use specific words rather than general ones, and add transitions where they are needed.

EVALUATING AND REVISING Ask yourself: Have I included all of the necessary details? Have I arranged the steps in chronological order? Then use the Guidelines for Evaluating Expository Paragraphs on page 97, and refer to the paragraph revision chart on pages 73–74 as you improve your writing.

PROOFREADING AND MAKING A FINAL COPY Read your paragraph carefully, using the Guidelines for Proofreading on page 39. Proofread again after you make a final copy.

Before You Write. In planning an expository paragraph:

- Decide which method of development you will use: facts and statistics, examples, definition, details of a process, or a combination of methods.
- Arrange the information in an order that will be easy for your audience to follow.
- Write a topic sentence that identifies your topic and states your main idea clearly.

Evaluating and Revising Expository Paragraphs

The following guidelines will help you evaluate the expository paragraphs you write. Once you have found areas that need to be improved, you can use the paragraph revision chart on pages 73–74 to revise your writing.

GUIDELINES FOR EVALUATING EXPOSITORY PARAGRAPHS

Topic Sentence	1. Does the topic sentence identify a limited topic and clearly state one main idea?
Topic Development	2. Is the method of development (or combination of methods) appropriate for the main idea and for the audience? Are enough details given to make the main idea clear? Is the information accurate?
Unity	3. Is each sentence directly related to the main idea?
Conclusion	4. Does the clincher sentence, if any, provide a strong ending for the paragraph?
Order of Ideas	5. Are the ideas arranged in an order that will be easy for the audience to follow?
Relationships Between Ideas	6. Do the ideas flow smoothly? Are they linked with direct references and appropriate transitional expressions (*first, since, for example,* etc.)?
Word Choice	7. Is the language specific rather than general? Is it appropriate for the audience? Are technical terms and difficult words defined or explained?

REVIEW EXERCISE C. Writing an Expository Paragraph. Write an expository paragraph on one of the following topics or on a topic of your own.

1. Equipment and supplies for one-night campout
2. Mummies
3. How to save money on groceries
4. How to wash a car
5. What a termite is

THE PERSUASIVE PARAGRAPH

The purpose of a persuasive paragraph is to convince the reader to agree with an opinion, and, sometimes, to perform a certain action. The paragraph presents an *argument*, which is a well-thought-out explanation for the opinion. It uses language that creates a serious, unemotional *tone,* or expressed attitude.

Developing Persuasive Paragraphs

3g. Develop a persuasive paragraph with reasons.

In a persuasive paragraph, the topic sentence states the writer's opinion. The supporting sentences present *reasons,* statements that explain the opinion. Each reason is supported with *evidence* —details such as facts, statistics, or examples.

Distinguishing Fact from Opinion

The topic for a persuasive paragraph should be a debatable issue—one about which people can reach different conclusions. The topic sentence (sometimes called the *position statement*) states the writer's opinion on the issue. Statements of fact are not debatable because they can be proved to be true. Therefore they are not suitable topic sentences for persuasive paragraphs.

FACT Four out of ten high-school students in this country drop out of school without graduating.

OPINION To help keep students from dropping out of school, the school system should start a counseling program run by and for students.

The issue should also be one about which people have differing opinions, and it should not be just a personal preference.

NOT SUITABLE Students should learn to write well. [Most people would agree.]

SUITABLE Every eighth-grade student should be required to write two compositions a week.

NOT SUITABLE Pizza tastes best with mushrooms and onions. [personal preference]

SUITABLE The school cafeteria should not sell junk foods such as soda, candy, and other sweets.

The topic sentence for a persuasive paragraph should state the writer's opinion precisely and make a specific suggestion.

WEAK Something needs to be done about the long lines in the school cafeteria.

WEAK People have to wait too long to buy their lunches in the school cafeteria.

IMPROVED To relieve crowding in the cafeteria, students should be allowed to eat lunch outside of school.

Before You Write. In choosing a topic and writing a position statement for a persuasive paragraph:

- Make sure that the topic is a debatable issue that is not just a personal preference.
- State your opinion clearly and precisely.

EXERCISE 15. Identifying Effective Topic Sentences. Number your paper 1–10. If the topic sentence is suitable for a persuasive paragraph, write *S*. If it is not suitable, write *NS*. Be prepared to explain your answers.

1. Every eighth-grade student should be required to participate in at least one after-school activity.
2. Something should be done to reduce crime in this community.
3. Handicapped people should be treated fairly.
4. Living in the country is better than living in the city.
5. Automobile drivers and passengers should be required to wear seat belts.
6. The media should not be allowed to advertise alcoholic drinks.
7. Vandalism must be stopped.
8. Bicycling is better than jogging.

9. All students in physical education classes should do aerobic exercises three times a week.
10. Dog owners should be required to leash their dogs.

Building an Argument

Usually, at least three reasons are needed to explain an opinion in a persuasive paragraph. The reasons should be specific, and they should not simply repeat the opinion in different words.

Each reason should be supported with accurate details such as facts, statistics, or examples. For instance, statistics on successful student-run counseling programs would strengthen the argument for starting such a program in your school.

The reasons in a persuasive paragraph are usually arranged from least important to most important. Readers tend to remember best what they read last.

As you read the following paragraph, notice how the writer makes the argument build.

> All students who participate in extracurricular activities should be required to have grades of 70 or above in all of their academic subjects. First, many students devote so much time to extracurricular activities that they neglect their academic studies. Fifty-two percent of the freshmen at one high school are failing one or more courses. Second, academic subjects prepare students for jobs. Employers often examine school records to decide whom to hire. Most important, having to pass academic subjects will help students learn to balance work and leisure. People who can both work hard and play hard have skills for dealing with a rapidly changing world.

EXERCISE 16. Analyzing a Persuasive Paragraph. Use the paragraph above to answer the following questions in writing.

1. What is the issue? Is it suitable for a persuasive paragraph? Why or why not?
2. What is the writer's opinion?
3. How many reasons does the writer give to support the opinion in the position statement?

4. In what order does the writer give the reasons? Do you think the last reason is the most important? Why or why not?
5. What is your opinion on this issue? List your reasons briefly, in order from least important to most important.

Writing a Clincher Sentence

A *clincher* (concluding) *sentence* can provide a stong ending for a persuasive paragraph. It may (1) summarize the writer's argument or (2) suggest that the audience perform a specific action.

TO SUMMARIZE AN ARGUMENT	For these reasons, tobacco smoking should be banned in pubic places.
TO SUGGEST AN ACTION	To help defeat this proposal, attend the meeting of the city commission at 7:30 P.M.

Before You Write. To develop a persuasive paragraph:

- Give at least three reasons that explain your opinion.
- Gather details (facts, statistics, or examples) to support each reason.
- Arrange the reasons and supporting details from least important to most important.

REVIEW EXERCISE D. Writing a Persuasive Paragraph. Write a persuasive paragraph on one of the following topics or on a topic of your own.

1. An eleven-month school year for all students
2. An optional extra period at your school
3. A dress code for students at your school
4. A counseling program run by and for students at your school
5. A law banning tobacco smoking in public places

Evaluating and Revising Persuasive Paragraphs

You will find the following guidelines helpful for evaluating the persuasive paragraphs you write.

GUIDELINES FOR EVALUATING PERSUASIVE PARAGRAPHS

Topic Sentence	1. Is the topic a debatable issue that is not just a personal preference? Does the position statement present an opinion clearly and precisely?
Topic Development	2. Are at least three reasons given to explain the opinion? Is each reason supported by accurate details?
Unity	3. Is each sentence directly related to the opinion in the position statement?
Conclusion	4. Does the clincher sentence sum up the argument or suggest an action for the reader to take?
Order of Ideas	5. Are the reasons arranged from least important to most important?
Relationships Between Ideas	6. Are the ideas easy to follow? Are direct references and transitional expressions (*first, most importantly,* etc.) used to link the ideas?
Word Choice	7. Is the language specific rather than general?
Tone	8. Is the tone serious and unemotional?

Writing a Letter to the Editor

Letters to the editor appear on the editorial pages of newspapers and in special columns in magazines. The writer may comment on a debatable issue or on an earlier story or article. The writer may instead praise or criticize the work of a group or an individual.

A letter to the editor should be brief, but it should present enough reasons and supporting details to be convincing. It should be written in business letter form (see Chapter 7) and follow the publication's guidelines, which appear in the letters to the editor section.

Here is an example of a letter to the editor.

To the Editor:

This community should have middle schools for grades 6 through 8. Currently, students attend elementary schools from kindergarten through grade 6 and junior high schools from grades 7 through 9. Seventh- and eighth-grade students require the close supervision of the middle-school structure. These students are too big for elementary school but too young for the independence of junior high. In a middle school they would be less likely to be influenced by those older teen-agers who are trouble-makers. They would also be more likely to receive individual attention from teachers and administrators. Finally, teachers who know the specific needs of seventh- and eighth-graders would be better able to provide the leadership and guidance these students require.

A CONCERNED PARENT

EXERCISE 17. Writing a Letter to the Editor. Write a letter to the editor in which you agree or disagree with the opinion in the letter above. Give at least three reasons and details to support your opinion.

REVIEW EXERCISE E. Writing a Letter to the Editor. Write a letter to the editor of your local or school newspaper. You may use one of the topics in Review Exercise D or a topic of your own. Support your opinion with at least three reasons and specific information.

CHAPTER 3 WRITING REVIEW

Writing Different Types of Paragraphs. Write each of the following paragraphs:

1. A narrative paragraph about something funny that happened to you or to someone you know
2. A descriptive paragraph about a place (house, apartment, community) where you would like to live someday
3. An expository paragraph giving information about a topic you are interested in
4. A persuasive paragraph or letter to the editor suggesting a way to improve your school or community

CHAPTER 4

Writing Stories

USING NARRATION AND DESCRIPTION

Have you ever heard of a "natural storyteller"? This person can hold everyone's attention telling about a personal experience. The use of gestures, facial expressions, and tone of voice makes his or her stories vivid and interesting. Of course, the stories must also be organized so that they lead somewhere and end at a definite point. The "natural storyteller" is skilled in the art of *narration.*

Written narratives do not have the storyteller's facial expressions or personal contact. The words, alone, must create an interesting, funny, or thrilling story. It is therefore very important for the writer of narratives to have a plan and use effective devices. In this chapter, you will learn to plan a written story and use some devices to make it vivid and interesting.

PREWRITING

CHOOSING A SUBJECT FOR A STORY

4a. Choose a subject that is appropriate for your purpose.

The purpose of any narrative is to tell *what happened.* Whether the story is true or fictional, it usually begins with a problem or a conflict and then tells what happens as a result of that problem. The problem or conflict does not have to be serious nor does it have to be physical. It may be a humorous situation, such as being frightened by your younger brother looking for his pet hamster. It may be an internal problem, such as a teen-ager's embarrassment after doing poorly in class or on the soccer field. The subject for your story may be your own experience, one of someone you know, or the fictional experience of a person you create out of your imagination. Be sure the subject is one that you are willing to share with others.

Before You Write. To find a subject for a story,

- Look through your writer's notebook for exciting or moving experiences.
- Talk with friends or family members about experiences they have shared with you or events from the past.
- Brainstorm, searching your mind for events that stand out because of a problem or struggle and someone's attempt to solve it.
- Ask yourself questions: What was my most exciting day? What was the most serious problem I ever had to face? What was a hard decision for me? What was the best or worst thing that ever happened to me? What "firsts" —such as the first time I water-skied, snow-skied, gave a speech, performed in a play—would make an interesting story?

EXERCISE 1. Identifying Appropriate Subjects. Some of the following subjects are appropriate for a narrative purpose and some are not. Number your paper 1–10. For the appropriate subjects, write *A*. For the inappropriate ones, write *I*. Be prepared to discuss your answers.

1. How my illness spoiled our trip to Washington, D.C.
2. Finding your way around the Smithsonian Institution

3. The importance of participating in athletics
4. How I learned a lesson from a younger person
5. Why students should spend at least one hour studying each night
6. How to cook eggs sunny side up
7. My quarrel with Julian about the class party
8. The difference between reading a science fiction story and watching a science fiction movie
9. The time our car stalled in a blizzard
10. How I took the wrong plane and ended up in the Caribbean Islands

EXERCISE 2. **Searching for Story Subjects.** Using the suggestions in the preceding "Before You Write," make a list of at least ten problems or conflicts you could use as the basis for a story. Save your work.

EXERCISE 3. **Choosing a Subject for a Story.** From your list of problems or conflicts in Exercise 2, choose the one you think is the most interesting. If possible, talk over several choices with a small group to get their reactions.

LIMITING SUBJECTS TO MANAGEABLE TOPICS

4b. Limit your subject to a topic that is a specific problem or experience.

A topic for a brief story, one that can be handled in a few paragraphs or pages, must be limited. An appropriate topic for a short narrative is a *specific* problem or a *specific* conflict.

For example, a story about all the problems and conflicts you have faced with your best friend would be vague and unfocused. You would be forced to tell about several experiences—the time you were not invited to your friend's party, the time the two of you got into trouble for going to a movie after school, the time your friend loaned you a new tape player, and so forth. As a result, you would not be able to include any of the specific details that make a story interesting. If you limited your subject to one experience (the time your friend loaned you the new tape player), you could add precise details, developing your story in an interesting way.

EXERCISE 4. Limiting a Subject for a Brief Story. Some of the following subjects are too broad for a brief story. Others are suitably limited for a story of two or three pages. Number your paper 1–5. Write *B* if the subject is too broad and *L* if the subject is appropriately limited. Be prepared to discuss your answers.

1. The history of the English monarchy
2. An encounter with a runaway horse
3. Flying a balloon across the United States
4. How I lost a race and won a friend
5. My father's childhood in Maryland

EXERCISE 5. Limiting Your Subject for a Brief Story. Decide whether the subject you selected for Exercise 3 (or any other subject of your choice) is limited to a *specific* problem or experience. If it is not, rewrite it, making it suitable for a brief story that you will write later.

THINKING ABOUT PURPOSE AND AUDIENCE

4c. Think about the purpose and audience of your story.

Throughout the writing process—planning, writing, evaluating, revising—you should be aware of your purpose in writing and your audience. In a story, the purpose is to tell what happened in a way that will interest the reader (*audience*). Keeping that purpose in mind will help shape your story and make it more interesting.

Your audience may be your teacher and your classmates or another audience. All audiences, no matter who they are, have special needs and interests that you must identify and keep in mind to write effectively.

CRITICAL THINKING:
Analyzing the Needs and Interests of an Audience

Analysis is the critical thinking skill you use when you divide something into its parts and study the relationships among the parts. The needs and interests of your audience will affect what you can write. To analyze these needs and interests, ask yourself the following questions:

1. What background information does my audience already have?
2. What background information will my audience need to understand my story?
3. What kinds of problems and experiences will interest my audience?
4. What can I do to make the problem or experience interesting to my audience?
5. How will my audience's knowledge and background affect the words I use?

Suppose you are writing a story about an alligator climbing your back fence to chase your dog. Your readers will be your classmates in your new school in Minnesota. Using the five questions above, your analysis of your audience might be as follows:

1. They know that alligators live in warm climates and that they sometimes attack small animals and people.
2. They need to know that I used to live in Florida. They need to know that an alligator can move fast on land and can climb a wire fence.
3. They are interested in daring adventures of people their own age and in adventures with happy endings.
4. I need to get them interested in the danger to the dog and in the idea that an alligator can climb a fence. I should wait until the end of the story to let them know that the dog was saved.
5. They will understand almost any word I use. If I use difficult words such as "interceded" and "assault," they may be confused or think I am showing off.

EXERCISE 6. Analyzing an Audience. Choose one topic and one audience from the following lists. Write this topic and audience at the top of a sheet of paper. Using the five questions on page 108, analyze the audience. Number each item and write your answers. Be prepared to discuss your answers.

Topics	*Audiences*
1. The night we saw a spaceship over our house	a. readers of a local newspaper
2. Why I came in second in the contest	b. seven-year-old children in Japan
3. How I saved my cousin from the ocean's undertow	c. eighth-graders in your school

EXERCISE 7. Analyzing Your Audience. Using your topic from Exercise 5 (or any topic of your choice), answer the five questions on page 108. If your teacher has not assigned a specific audience, your readers will be your teacher and classmates. Save your work.

GATHERING INFORMATION FOR YOUR STORY

4d. Identify action details, and gather information for your story.

To gather information for a narrative, you must focus on the question *What happened?* The *5 W-How?* questions used by reporters will help you collect the details you need. In the following example, notice how a writer uses the *5 W-How?* questions to gather information.

Who was involved in this experience? My mother and I

What happened? Mother left me at home alone while she went to help a sick neighbor. I got scared. I hid under the bed and fell asleep. My mother couldn't find me and was afraid I had drowned in the well. She was angry when she found me.

Where did the experience take place? In our home

When did the actions occur? They started when my mother went to visit a sick friend. They ended when I woke up and crawled out from under the bed.

Why is this experience and its outcome interesting? I discovered how easily concern and relief can turn into anger.
How did I feel? I was afraid of being caught by a ghost or a kidnapper. I wondered why my mother was angry.

Before You Write. To gather information for a narrative, ask yourself:

- Am I writing about a problem or conflict of my own? (If so, review your writer's notebook, talk to friends or relatives, or brainstorm.)
- Am I writing about an experience or problem that is being faced by someone else? (If so, interview that person, if possible.)
- Am I writing about an imaginary event? (If so, allow your imagination to create what *might* have happened. Jot your ideas down; you can organize them later.)

EXERCISE 8. Gathering Information for a Narrative. Using your topic and audience analysis from Exercise 7 (or another topic of your choice), gather action details and information for your narrative. Refer to the *Before You Write* suggestions above, and use the *5 W-How?* questions. Write down the details you gather; you will use them later.

ARRANGING DETAILS AND DEVELOPING A STORY PLAN

4e. Arrange the information for your story.

The actions in a narrative are usually arranged in the order in which they happened (*chronological* order). Notice the chronological order of the action details below:

mother was called to take care of a sick person
left me at home alone

no problems before dark
sat outside
as darkness came, decided to go in house
felt sleepy
afraid to sleep on top of bed
crawled under the bed
fell asleep
awakened to sound of voices
heard them searching for me
crawled out from under bed and told them I was there
was surprised because my mother was angry with me rather than happy to see me

EXERCISE 9. Arranging Action Details for a Story. On a sheet of paper, list the following actions in the order you think they might have happened.

felt surprised
car suddenly started rolling
Aunt Ann left me in her car while she ran back into the house for something
went through a fence
pretended I was driving
sideswiped a tree
released the brake
smashed into neighbor's house
turned on the car radio

EXERCISE 10. Arranging Action Details for Your Story. Arrange the list of action details you gathered for Exercise 8 in chronological order. Save your list.

4f. Plan your story before you write it.

Before writing any narrative, work out a rough plan to guide your thinking. Your plan will help you to include all the necessary details. The information gathered with the *5 W-How?* questions can be used to create a story.

Before You Write. To create a story plan, include:

- *When* (My mother left me alone and went to visit a sick friend; I was a small child.)
- *Where* (I was at home.)
- *Who* (My mother and I)
- *What happened* (It became dark and I was afraid. I went into the house and crawled under the bed to hide. I fell asleep. Mother came home. She couldn't find me. She was afraid I was in the well. I woke up. I told her where I was. She was angry rather than happy.)
- *How I felt* (Puzzled that she was angry with me rather than happy to see me)

Read the following personal experience narrative taken from *Barrio Boy*. Does it tell *when, where, who, what happened,* and *how the writer felt*?

> A neighbor who lived at the other end of the block, across from the orchard, came to our cottage in distress. There was a sick person at their house and help was needed. It was a situation in which I would clearly be in the way. My mother did something unusual; she decided to leave me alone in the cottage. . . .
>
> While the twilight lasted I had no problems. I sat by the back door facing the orchard, thinking of many things, alert for the footsteps of Doña Henriqueta. But as night fell and the darkness deepened, I decided that since I was taking care of the house I might as well be inside of it. . . .
>
> My mother had said that if I felt sleepy I was to get into bed. That would have been very well if she had been there and it was still light outside. Now it was certainly the wrong thing to do. The back door would be open and I might be caught asleep on top of the bed by a ghost or a kidnapper.
>
> I crawled under the bed wrapped in my sarape and wedged myself on the floor as close to the door as possible. I intended to stay awake and crawl out as soon as my mother was home.

I was awakened by voices in the room. By the candlelight I could see feet shuffling by me. People were calling my name. I heard my mother say, "The well. Please look in the well again."

I wormed my way from under the bed, stuck out my head, and said, "Here I am."

I could not understand why a mother should not be overjoyed to find that her son had not fallen into the well and drowned but had only been asleep under the bed. She wanted to know since when I had forgotten that I was to answer instantly when I was called.

ERNESTO GALARZA

EXERCISE 11. Creating a Story Plan. Using the list of details you organized in Exercise 10 (or another topic and list of details), prepare a story plan. Save it for later use.

WRITING

CHOOSING DETAILS

4g. Choose specific details and specific verbs to make the action vivid.

The use of specific details makes a story vivid by telling the reader exactly what happened. If such details are missing, the reader may lose interest. Compare the following two paragraphs. Which is more interesting?

1. When the canoe touched the river bank, I told John to push us off. Instead he panicked. He got up, tried to climb to the shore, and overturned the canoe. I fell into the water.

2. The canoe glided toward the river bank. I felt a bump as it touched land. "Use your paddle. Push us away," I told John. He put his hand on the side of the canoe and pushed himself to

his feet. I yelled at him to sit down, but he wasn't listening. His hands trembled. Awkwardly he teetered on one foot as he reached out to grab a branch that was hanging over the bank. The canoe began to rock. "Sit down!" I yelled. The canoe rocked violently. Suddenly I was thrown from my seat and hit the water with a splash.

You will probably think that the second paragraph is more effective. The first paragraph gives only general information. The second paragraph tells how John used his hand to push himself up and how he looked (teetering awkwardly) as he tried to leave the canoe. Instead of the general statement *I fell into the water,* the second paragraph gives two specific details: being thrown from the seat and the splash of hitting the water. Also, the second paragraph does more than tell what happened; it *shows* what happened. Instead of directly stating *he panicked,* a detail, John's trembling hands, reveals his nervousness.

Specific verbs also make a story vivid. Some verbs describe actions more specifically than others. The verb *walk,* for example, gives a general idea of an action; the verbs *amble, stroll, swagger,* and *shuffle* give more specific impressions. Specific verbs can help the reader clearly picture the action. Of course, you should not try to use a vivid verb in *every* possible situation. If you are simply telling how you get to school in the morning, it would be better to use *walk* than *stroll* or *amble.* If the point is *how* you walk, a more specific verb may be better.

When You Write. To write an effective story,

- Give specific details to make the action vivid.
- Avoid general statements; instead let the readers draw their own conclusions from the details.
- Use enough specific details so that the readers feel they are participating in or witnessing the action.
- Use specific verbs.

EXERCISE 12. Identifying Specific Verbs. List the specific verbs in the following paragraph. Be prepared to explain how these verbs make the action vivid.

The circus was a blend of movement, color, and noise. In the center ring, a bareback rider performed. As her horse pranced around the ring, the rider tensed, whirled in the air, and landed neatly on the horse. In another ring, a seal held a large ball in its flippers. A clown dressed in orange, green, and purple tiptoed up and reached out for the ball. The seal yelped. The clown staggered back, threw up his hands, and flopped to the sawdust floor. Above the crowd, aerialists performed their dangerous work. A man swung out on a trapeze, holding a woman by the wrists. Suddenly he released her. As she plunged into space, a third aerialist swooped down just in time and caught her by the wrists.

EXERCISE 13. Using Specific Details. Using the suggestions above, rewrite one of the following paragraphs.

1. When the principal called on me, I was very nervous. I grew calmer as I explained why our class should be permitted to take a class trip out of town. At the end of my speech, my classmates applauded.

2. The two boys clenched their fists. Each wanted to appear brave but did not really want to fight. After the crowd watching them left, each muttered a final insult and left.

REVIEW EXERCISE. Writing a Paragraph Using Specific Details and Verbs. Write a paragraph of fifty to seventy-five words about one of the following situations. Include specific details and specific verbs.

1. Being caught in a violent storm
2. Winning (or losing) a race (for example, three-legged race at a picnic)
3. After riding for twenty minutes, discovering you are on the wrong bus
4. Trying to keep a young child from crossing the street against the traffic light
5. Making a report to the class

PREWRITING Draw on your experience or your imagination to plan your paragraph. Use the *5 W-How?* questions, brainstorming, or clustering to gather specific details about the situation. After you have identified several actions and specific details, arrange them in chronological order.

WRITING, EVALUATING, AND REVISING Review your plan and write a first draft that includes specific details and verbs showing how the actions occurred. Write freely without stopping to make corrections. Use the evaluation guidelines on page 127 to evaluate your work, and revise your paragraph by referring to the chart on page 73. Use the proofreading guidelines on page 39 as you proofread your paragraph and make a final copy.

USING DIALOGUE

4h. Use dialogue to make your story lively and convincing.

If you present the direct speech of people, your narrative will be more interesting and realistic than if you merely describe their thoughts and feelings indirectly. Dialogue helps to tell the story in a more exciting way. Using peoples' exact words also helps to reveal their personalities.

In the following passage, the characters are conversing, but what they say is described. The result is a dull, uninteresting paragraph.

> My friends Sue and Edie went abalone fishing at Hondo Beach. When I met them, I asked where they had been. They told me. I asked what an abalone was. Sue said it was a shellfish. I asked how they caught abalone. Sue said they waded out into the water and pried them off the rocks. Edie said the water was very cold.

In the following paragraphs, the conversation is written as dialogue. Notice how lively and convincing this second version is. Notice that the dialogue also indicates the distinct personalities of the speakers.

I ran into Sue and Edie on the street.

"Where'd you go yesterday?" I asked them.

"Abalone fishing at Hondo Beach," Sue said.

"What's abalone?" I wanted to know.

"A shellfish."

"Like oysters?"

"No more like oysters," Edie snorted, "than a wheelbarrow is like a motorcycle."

Sue explained, "An abalone has just one top shell, like a snail. It's open at the bottom."

"You fish for 'em with hook and line?"

"Gosh, are you ignorant!" Edie said.

"They stick to the rocks, underwater," Sue said, "and you wade out—"

"In water that's so cold you turn blue," Edie interrupted.

"—and you pry them off the rocks. It's easy."

"Sure," Edie said, "as easy as prying names off plaques."

One goal in writing conversation is to keep the reader aware of who is talking. How many different ways are shown in the passage above? Notice where the speaker is identified—at the beginning, at the end, or in the middle of the speech. With several speeches there is no identification, yet the author has made it clear.

When You Write. In writing dialogue,

- Make sure the dialogue has a purpose; that is, ask yourself if it reveals something about the characters or the action.
- Keep the reader aware of who is talking. Occasionally use the names of the speakers so the reader will not be confused.
- Place quotation marks around the words that are spoken.
- Use commas to separate a person's speech form the rest of the sentence. (See pages 555–60 for the rules on punctuating dialogue.)
- Start a new paragraph when the speaker changes.

EXERCISE 14. Writing Dialogue. Review the suggestions above. Select one of the following situations, and write a short conversation to fit it.

1. Two teen-agers are bragging about their athletic skills (or grades in school, etc.).
2. Two friends argue about a hero (from sports, television, movies, etc.).
3. A teen-ager insists that he or she is old enough and capable enough to have a part-time job.
4. An eighth-grader tries to convince his or her parents that an allowance must be increased.
5. A girl is helping a boy with his algebra, but he would rather talk about sports.

WRITING DESCRIPTION

4i. Use description to make your story vivid and convincing.

A good description makes the reader see, hear, or otherwise experience something. A description of a *scene* can help the reader visualize it. A description of a *person* can familiarize the reader with that person. Description can convince the reader that *what is happening* in a story is real. Even a sentence or two of vivid detail can make a story more effective. In this part of the chapter, you will learn how to use description to improve your stories.

(1) Use details that appeal to the senses.

To write a good description, you must be a keen observer. As you notice the sights, sounds, and smells around you, make a mental list of them. (For example, in the school halls, you might *see* the students milling around on their way to classes; you might *hear* them talking or shouting; finally, you might *feel* some of them jostling you.)

You can make a story lifelike by using these details that appeal to the senses. The senses you will use most often are *sight* and *hearing,* but many times you will also use *touch, taste,* and *smell.*

Notice where the writer appeals to various senses in the following description.

> I pushed up the high steps into the aisle of the bus. The shrill screaming, shouting, and laughing were a wall of noise in front of me. Because we had been waiting in the rain, the air in the bus was steamy and smelled of wet wool. As I tried to squeeze past the boy ahead of me, my books began to slide out of my arms. When I grabbed for them, my right hand struck a hockey stick and was twisted backward painfully. The books slipped away. I saw that every seat was taken, but nobody seemed to be sitting down. The aisle was jammed. Everywhere arms were waving and pushing.

EXERCISE 15. Observing Details. Test your powers of observation on your way home from school. How many details can you observe? To which senses do they appeal? List at least ten details and indicate the senses to which they appeal.

EXERCISE 16. Writing a Description. Organize the list of details you observed for Exercise 15 in chronological order (see the model above) or spatial order (pages 51–52). Using this list, write a one- or two-paragraph description of your trip home.

EXERCISE 17. Adding Descriptive Details. The addition of vivid details would improve the following paragraphs taken from stories. Revise two of the three paragraphs, using the directions in parentheses.

1. At the end of the debate an elderly man stood up. "I've attended many town meetings," he said, "and I've never heard such nonsense as I've heard tonight." Angrily he tore the meeting's agenda into pieces. (Insert two or three sentences to follow the first. Describe how the man looked and spoke.)

2. My sister had worked on the model boat for months. It had occupied most of her spare time. Carefully she had carved, sanded, and painted it. Now she displayed it to us proudly. (Write two or three sentences about the boat.)

3. It was a very unpleasant trip. I was relieved when the plane finally arrived at the airport in San Francisco. (Insert several sentences after the first. Show how the trip was unpleasant. Appeal to at least three of the senses.)

(2) Select adjectives and adverbs carefully, and use them sparingly.

You recall that an adjective describes a noun or a pronoun and tells *what kind, which one, how many,* or *how much.* An adverb describes a verb, an adjective, or another adverb and tells *when, where, how,* or *to what extent.* Adjectives and adverbs are called *modifiers.* (See pages 299 and 317.) Modifiers can be overused. Notice the dull, tired modifiers in the following example:

> We had a swell time, because the speaker was very interesting. He made some tremendously good remarks. After he finished, the applause was absolutely fabulous. We all agreed that he was a terrific speaker.

The speaker was *interesting* and *terrific,* but these overused words tell little about the speaker or his speech. Was he *stimulating? Thought-provoking? Witty? Persuasive?* Similarly, the applause is described as *absolutely fabulous,* a phrase that is vague. Was the applause *energetic? Deafening?* Avoid such words as *swell, terrible,* and *terrific.* When you evaluate and revise your own writing, replace them with more exact modifiers.

Some vague, overused adjectives and adverbs are

absolutely	grand	swell
awful	great	terrible
cool	horrible	terrific
cute	neat	tremendous
fabulous	nice	very
funny	really	wonderful

EXERCISE 18. Using Fresh, Exact Adjectives and Adverbs. Write the following sentences. In the first five, use fresh, exact *adjectives.* In the second five, use fresh, exact *adverbs.* If you wish, use a dictionary or a book of synonyms.

1. She refused to give him a(n) —— answer.
2. In spite of his —— suit, he looked well-dressed.
3. They ate an enormously —— dinner.
4. The actress had a strikingly —— hair style.
5. The general handled his troops with —— skill.
6. A frightened child —— asked a question.
7. My new sweater is —— scarlet.
8. After cleaning house, I flopped —— on the sofa.
9. It was chilly outside, but we sat —— around the fire.
10. Talking —— , I began to unwrap the presents.

(3) Use description to make characters seem real and interesting.

The people in a story are called *characters.* A writer usually focuses on a major character. Through description the character becomes more realistic. For example, the author focuses attention on one important character at the beginning of *Treasure Island.*

> I remember him as if it were yesterday, as he came plodding to the inn door, his sea chest following behind him in a handbarrow; a tall, strong, heavy, nut-brown man; his tarry pigtail falling over the shoulders of his soiled blue coat; his hands ragged and scarred, with black, broken nails; and the saber cut across one cheek, a dirty, livid white.
>
> ROBERT LOUIS STEVENSON

When You Write. To write a description of a character,

- Determine the interesting features of this character.
- Decide if anything about this character would affect the action of the story. (For example, is the character's quick temper important?)
- If the character is a real person, observe him or her. Take notes about appearance, mannerisms, etc.
- Use brainstorming or clustering to gather details.
- Select adjectives and adverbs that are fresh and exact.
- Use words that appeal to the reader's senses.
- Arrange details in a logical order.

EXERCISE 19. Writing a Description of a Character. Review the story plan you developed for Exercise 11. Select a character you plan to include in your story. Using the preceding suggestions, write a short description of the character.

(4) Use description to make the setting vivid.

The *setting* is where a story happens. If you were writing about a night spent in a supposedly haunted house, a specific description of the house (setting) would make your story more effective. In the following description from the novel *Losing Battles,* the description of dawn suggests the importance of the rural setting.

> When the rooster crowed, the moon had still not left the world but was going down on flushed cheek, one day short of the full. A long thin cloud crossed it slowly, drawing itself out like a name being called. The air changed, as if a mile or so away a wooden door had swung open, and a smell, more of warmth than wet, from a river at low stage, moved upward into the clay hills that stood in darkness.
>
> Then a house appeared on its ridge, like an old man's silver watch pulled once more out of its pocket. A dog leaped up from where he'd lain like a stone and began barking for today as if he meant never to stop.
>
> EUDORA WELTY

When You Write. To write the description of a setting,

- Brainstorm for details. (See page 20.)
- If your setting is a real place you can visit, go there and observe as many details as you can.
- Try to recall or observe specific sights, sounds, smells, tastes, and feelings related to the setting.
- Select details that reflect the *mood* of the setting —mysterious, dreary, pleasant, etc.
- List the details, using vivid, fresh adjectives and adverbs.
- Arrange the details in a logical order. (Review spatial order, pages 51–52.)

EXERCISE 20. Writing a Description of a Setting. Review the story plan you developed for Exercise 11. Using the suggestions above, write one or two paragraphs describing the setting of your narrative.

WRITING A FIRST DRAFT

4j. Write a first draft of your story.

Most good narratives include five basic story elements: interesting start, beginning explanation, action, climax, and ending. Many good stories may omit one or more of the five elements. Keeping them in mind, however, will help you organize your story.

Interesting Start and Beginning Explanation

If you do not interest your readers in the first one or two sentences, they may stop reading—and never discover the rest of your story. Note the beginning of the following narrative.

> Some years ago my friend Chip and I tried to go to the moon, but some apples and pears got in our way. Both Chip and I had seen a television program about reaching the moon. When we talked about the program, we agreed that the important thing was to get up enough speed to overcome the earth's gravity. The rest would be easy. We decided to try an experiment. There was a long block in our neighborhood that ran downhill and then uphill. If we took Chip's wagon and got up enough speed going downhill, we might be able to leave the earth going uphill.

The first sentence contains an *interesting start* because it arouses the reader's curiosity. It also introduces the subject and the characters in addition to telling when ("some time ago").

The rest of the paragraph is the *beginning explanation.* Notice that the paragraph does not supply unnecessary information (for example, how Chip and the writer became friends). It does, however, include an important description of the setting, "There was a long block in our neighborhood that ran downhill and then uphill."

This paragraph avoids a common problem in story writing: beginning in the wrong place. The writer should not begin the story with getting up that morning or going to school or even with meeting Chip. The real beginning of the story is the decision by Chip and the writer to make the trip.

When You Write. In writing the beginning of your story,

- Make the start interesting; make your reader want to keep reading.
- Identify the time, place, and people, if this information is important.
- Include any background information the reader will need to understand the action of the narrative.

EXERCISE 21. Writing the Beginning of Your Story. Using your topic and the plan you developed for Exercise 11, write a story beginning.

Action and Climax

The middle of a narrative is made up of the action and the climax. The *action* is the series of step-by-step events that happen after the beginning explanation, and the *climax* is the high point of the story. In the story about the trip to the moon, the second paragraph gives the step-by-step account of the action. Notice how it tells specifically what happened the morning of the attempted trip.

> The next morning we got up very early. We wanted to reach the block before people started coming out of their apartment houses to go to work. I sat in the front of the wagon. Chip gave a push and jumped on behind me. The wagon went faster and faster. Chip and I cheered. We were sure that we would leave the earth's gravity and would be on our way to the moon. I began to daydream about newspaper headlines and being interviewed on television.

In this story the climax, in the third paragraph, is the wagon crashing into Mrs. Clark's fruit stand. Notice the way in which this climax is made vivid by the use of specific details and effective verbs.

> Suddenly Chip yelled, "Watch out!" Going uphill had made our wagon change direction. We were headed straight for Mrs. Clark's fruit stand. I grabbed the handle of the wagon to steer, but it was too late. We crashed into the fruit stand and almost hit Mrs. Clark. Mrs. Clark shouted, as the fruit spilled in all directions.

When You Write. In writing the middle of your story,

- Allow enough time to write the entire middle section in one sitting.
- Keep your story plan nearby. Make any necessary changes as you write.
- Let your thoughts flow freely, concentrating on actions that build toward the climax, the high point of the story.
- Use chronological order.
- Include dialogue if it is appropriate.
- Use vivid, specific details that appeal to the reader's senses.

EXERCISE 22. **Writing the Middle of Your Story.** Using the suggestions above, write the middle section of the story you started to write in Exercise 21.

Ending

The ending of a story ties up the loose ends. The ending may state how the writer felt about the events of the story, or it may merely suggest the writer's feelings. In this story, the ending tells what happened after the wagon hit the fruit stand. Although we are not told directly, the details about the dented wagon, being grounded, and paying for the damaged fruit give us a good idea of how Chip and the writer must have felt. We are not surprised that they did not plan another trip to the moon for a while.

> The story has a sad ending. Out of our allowances we paid \$3.40 for the fresh fruit that Mrs. Clark lost. Chip's wagon had a big dent in it. I was grounded for sneaking out of the house in the early morning. Chip and I postponed our plans for the next moonshot indefinitely.

What happened in this ending? Can you tell how the writer felt? What clues are given to tell you the writer's feelings?

When You Write. To write the ending of your story, ask yourself:

- What has happened so far in the opening and the middle?
- What is the outcome of these events?
- How can I tie up all the loose ends?
- What are my feelings about the story? Should I state these feelings directly or just suggest them?
- Will my ending satisfy my reader that the story is over? (Some stories are *open-ended;* that is, they do not tell the reader what finally happens.)

EXERCISE 23. Writing the Ending for Your Story. Using the questions above as a guide, write an ending for the story you began in Exercises 21 and 22.

EVALUATING

EVALUATING A NARRATIVE

4k. Evaluate the first draft of your story.

Many writers feel that the evaluation stage is the most important part of the writing process. Here, once the first draft is on paper, the writer can decide which changes would shape and polish the story. Try to set your draft aside. Then, when you evaluate, carefully consider content, organization, and style. Use the following guidelines to evaluate your draft.

GUIDELINES FOR EVALUATING NARRATIVES

Start	1. Does the start grab the audience's attention immediately?
Beginning Explanation	2. Are the characters and setting introduced in the beginning explanation? Is necessary background information included?
Action	3. Do specific details make the action vivid? Are any important actions missing? Should any actions be omitted because they could distract the reader by not being directly related to the story?
Climax	4. Is the story's high point obvious?
Ending	5. Does the ending tie up the loose ends? Are the writer's feelings about the story expressed or suggested?
Order	6. Are the actions arranged in chronological order?
Characters	7. Are the characters' most important features or traits obvious? Are details arranged to emphasize these features?
Dialogue	8. Is the dialogue lively and natural-sounding? Are sentences fairly short, as they are in normal conversation? Does the dialogue tell something about the characters or action?
Setting	9. Do details of setting reflect the right mood for the story? Are they arranged in spatial order?
Word Choice	10. Are words and sentences appropriate for the audience? Are specific nouns, verbs, adjectives, and adverbs used to create vivid pictures? Are there any unnecessary adjectives and adverbs? (Remember that too many could spoil your descriptions.)

EXERCISE 24. Evaluating Your Story. Using the preceding guidelines, evaluate your first draft. Make notes on the draft to remind you where to revise. If possible, have another reader help you evaluate. Perhaps you can read your story to a small group and then discuss whether it follows each guideline.

REVISING

REVISING A NARRATIVE

4l. Revise the first draft of your story.

After you evaluate your draft, you are ready to revise those areas that need improving. Very few writers are satisfied with their first effort, so they evaluate and revise with care. To revise, you can cut out words or sentences. You can add new ideas and details, or you can reorder what you have already written. You can also replace one word or sentence with another. The following chart suggests how to use these techniques to revise your story.

REVISING STORIES

PROBLEM	TECHNIQUE	REVISION
The start is not interesting.	Replace	Replace the beginning with an opening situation or dialogue that will grab the reader's attention or arouse curiosity.
The characters are not introduced clearly.	Add	At an appropriate place in the beginning explanation, add more details about the characters. Use vivid, lively language.
The setting is vague or missing.	Add	If the setting is important, add descriptive details early in the story. Use details that reflect the mood of your story (exciting, mysterious, etc.).

PROBLEM	TECHNIQUE	REVISION
Specific details about what happened are missing.	Add	Review your story plan; then add missing details to the first draft.
Some actions or details are not directly related to the story.	Cut/Replace	Cut any details that are not related to the story or the characters. Replace unrelated details with ones that will make the story's events clear.
The climax is lost.	Add	Add details that will make the climax stand out or that will make it more exciting, vivid, etc.
The ending is not satisfying.	Replace/Add	Replace the ending with one that is more interesting, logical, or realistic. Add your feelings about the story either directly or indirectly to the ending of your story.
The order of the events is not clear.	Reorder	Reorder details or actions that are confusing, out of order or are not clear to the reader.
The characters' personality traits are not clear.	Add/Reorder	Add details that emphasize the characters' most important features. Rearrange details so that the most important ones stand out.
The dialogue is not natural-sounding.	Replace	Ask someone to read the dialogue aloud. Replace any dialogue that does not sound natural. Remember that people usually speak in very short sentences or even parts of sentences.

PROBLEM	TECHNIQUE	REVISION
Some dialogue does not reveal anything about the characters or the action.	Cut/Add	Cut dialogue that fails to tell something about events or characters. Add dialogue about important actions or people.
The setting doesn't seem to fit the story.	Replace/ Reorder	Replace details of setting that do not reflect the right mood. Reorder details so they help to tell the story.
Some words are not appropriate for the audience.	Replace	Review the characteristics of your audience; then replace the inappropriate words.
There are too many adjectives and adverbs.	Cut/ Replace/ Add	Cut unnecessary adjectives and adverbs. Replace them with comparisons (something is *like* something else) or reword sentences to make nouns and verbs do the work of describing. (*He darted,* for example, instead of *He suddenly ran.*) Add specific, exact words.

EXERCISE 25. Analyzing a Writer's Revisions. Read the following revised draft of two paragraphs from the personal experience narrative on pages 123–26. Then answer the questions that follow the paragraphs.

The next morning we got up very early. We wanted to reach the block before people started coming out of their apartment houses to go

to work. ~~My dad always leaves early, too~~. I sat — cut
in the front of the wagon. Chip gave a push
and jumped on behind me. The wagon went
faster and faster. Chip and I cheered. We were
sure that we would leave the earth's gravity
and would be on our way to the moon. I began to daydream about newspaper headlines and being interviewed on television. — add
We were headed straight for Mrs. Clark's — reorder
fruit stand. Suddenly Chip yelled, "Watch
out!" Going uphill had made our wagon
change direction. I grabbed the handle of the
wagon to steer, but it was too late. We ~~ran~~ crashed into — replace
the fruit stand and almost hit Mrs. Clark. Mrs.
Clark ~~was angry~~ shouted. The fruit spilled in all di- — replace
rections.

1. Why did the writer add a sentence to the first paragraph?
2. Why did the writer cut one sentence?
3. Why did the writer reorder some sentences?
4. Why did the writer replace "ran" with "crashed" and "was angry" with "shouted"?
5. What other changes should the writer make? Why do you think so?

EXERCISE 26. Replacing Overused Adjectives and Adverbs. Number your paper 1–10. For each item, replace the overused adjectives and adverbs in italics with words that are fresher and more exact.

EXAMPLE 1. I wanted to paint the room purple, but Geraldo thought it would look *funny*.
1. *peculiar*

1. Sabrena, your birthday party was *nice.*
2. I had an *absolutely terrible* time at the dentist's.
3. It is a *cute* little puppy that often does *cute* tricks.
4. Paul Simon has recorded a *terrific* new song.
5. Just as we ran out of ideas, Wanetta made a *neat* suggestion.
6. Kim gave a *swell* performance in the class play.
7. Margie's hair looks *horrible* this morning.
8. The homework Mr. Rubin assigned is *really* difficult.
9. Jonathan plays the clarinet *awfully* well.
10. We had an *awfully wonderful* weekend at your home.

EXERCISE 27. Omitting Unnecessary Adjectives and Adverbs. The following paragraph has too many adjectives and adverbs. Rewrite it by eliminating unnecessary modifiers, by using comparisons, and by replacing a verb and an adverb with an exact verb.

> The shabby, pathetic-looking little man shuffled timidly and fearfully along the dingy, cracked, uneven sidewalk. His old, battered hat jiggled precariously on his head. When he saw Mr. Abercrombie, the banker, coming up the street, he cautiously sidled up to him. Mr. Abercrombie walked haughtily past.

EXERCISE 28. Revising Your Own Story. Using the revising chart on pages 128–30, revise the draft of the narrative you evaluated in Exercise 24.

PROOFREADING

PROOFREADING YOUR STORY AND MAKING A FINAL COPY

4m. Proofread your story and make a final copy.

If possible, put your paper away for a few days and come back to it with a fresh eye. The Guidelines for Proofreading (page 39) will remind you of the things to look for. If you have used dialogue in your narrative, pay particular attention to the punctuation and paragraphing of each speaker's words.

Remember that your aim is to have people enjoy what you have written. Readers may be unable or unwilling to read a paper that does not follow correct manuscript form. Review those standards (page 41) or your teacher's directions before making your final copy.

EXERCISE 29. **Proofreading and Making a Final Copy of Your Narrative.** Using the Guidelines for Proofreading on page 39, proofread the narrative you revised for Exercise 28. Then make your final copy. Proofread it again to check for any mistakes made in recopying.

CHAPTER 4 WRITING REVIEW

Writing a Story About an Imaginary Experience. Write a story about an imaginary experience, such as your or someone else's first day in a new school or first attempt at some athletic or artistic task. Using the process you practiced in this chapter to choose a subject, consider your purpose and audience, gather and arrange information, write, evaluate, revise, proofread, and make a final copy of your narrative.

CHAPTER 5

Writing Exposition

THE WHOLE COMPOSITION

In this chapter you will use the steps in the writing process to write expository compositions—compositions whose purpose it is to explain or inform. A composition is a group of closely related paragraphs that, together, present a single main idea about a topic. Most compositions can be divided into three main sections—the introduction, the body, and the conclusion.

PREWRITING

SEARCHING FOR SUBJECTS

5a. Search for subjects for your expository compositions.

Many of the compositions you write this year will be on subjects assigned by your teachers. Sometimes, however, you may have to find a subject of your own. For example, your teacher might ask you to write one of the following expository compositions:

A composition explaining how to make *something* or how to do *something*

A composition giving directions to *some place*
A composition giving information about *someone, something,* or *some place*

To find a subject for an expository composition, begin by examining your personal resources—your interests, your knowledge, and your experiences. In your search, you can use any of the methods described below.

(1) In your search for subjects, consider what you know about and what you like to do.

Perhaps you know a great deal about collecting stamps or coins: how to start a collection, where to obtain specimens, what pleasures and advantages this hobby offers. You may like to hike on nearby nature trails or play tournament chess. These are all possible subjects for an expository composition.

Before You Write. To examine your personal resources for an expository composition, ask yourself:

- What are my interests? What do I especially look forward to doing in my free time?
- What do I know about through my hobbies, reading, participation in sports and other after-school activities, TV viewing, and movie-going?
- What experiences have I had that might interest someone else?

EXERCISE 1. Examining Your Personal Resources. Using the questions in Before You Write (above), examine your interests, knowledge, and experiences. Save your answers for use later in this chapter.

(2) In your search for subjects, observe the world around you.

Suppose that you have been asked to write a composition explaining how to do something. To find a subject to write about, you can observe the world around you. For example, you may have noticed how a neighbor plants a vegetable garden, how a friend strings her guitar, and how a relative uses a computer. Thinking about your own resources, you may realize that using a computer interests you more than planting a garden or stringing a guitar. You have discovered a possible subject for your expository composition.

Before You Write. To find possible subjects for an expository composition by observing, ask yourself:

- What have I observed in the world around me—at home, in my neighborhood, in school, on a trip, etc.?
- Which of these observations are of interest to me?

EXERCISE 2. Using Your Observations to Search for Subjects. Using your observations of the world around you, list at least three broad subjects for each of the following expository writing assignments. For example, for a composition giving information about something, three broad subjects that might grow out of your observations are "sea creatures," "repairing a broken sidewalk," and "trees in my neighborhood."

1. Giving information about an event
2. Explaining how to do something
3. Giving information about a person
4. Explaining how to make something
5. Giving information about a place

(3) Use a writer's journal as a source of possible subjects.

Keep a writer's journal in which you record your feelings, thoughts, and experiences. Later, when you want to find something to write about, you can look through your journal for a possible subject.

For example, here is a sample entry from one student's journal:

> We had a speaker at school today—a stockbroker from New York. She explained how stocks are traded at the New

York Stock Exchange on Wall Street. In some ways it's much simpler than I expected. If I wanted to buy some stock in a company, I would call my personal stockbroker. This person would place my order with a telephone clerk at the stock exchange in New York. The clerk would talk to a broker there. This broker, who is on the floor of the stock exchange, would actually bargain with other brokers to get the amount of stock I want to buy at the best possible price. After the deal is made, the broker would tell the telephone clerk, who would call my personal broker. I would have to pay for the stock five days later.

If you read this entry in your writer's journal, it might suggest "buying stock" as a broad subject for an expository composition. Thinking about this entry might also lead you to other possible broad subjects such as "becoming a stockbroker" or "the New York Stock Exchange." Keeping a writer's journal not only lets you record things you can refer to later, but also suggests subjects for compositions.

EXERCISE 3. Keeping a Writer's Journal. Keep a writer's journal for three to five days. This journal can be a notebook or a file folder. In your journal, record the thoughts, feelings, and experiences you want to share with other people. Then, using your writer's journal as a source, list at least five broad subjects for an expository composition. (Remember that the purpose of exposition is to inform or to explain.) If you already keep a journal regularly, you may refer to any entries you wish.

(4) Use brainstorming in your search for subjects.

You can also use brainstorming to search for subjects to write about. When you brainstorm for subjects, you write down as many ideas as you can think of all at once. Your aim is to list as many subjects as possible, without stopping to judge their suitability. Deciding which subjects you can actually write about comes later in the writing process.

Suppose, for example, that your English teacher has asked you to write a composition giving information about someone or something. To search for subjects, you might brainstorm for ideas by using the question "Who or what do I know about?" The list you come up with might look like this:

playing the piano	waltzing on ice skates
planting a vegetable garden	understanding my brother
the local recreation program	snorkeling
being a day-camp counselor	types of cameras
my uncle's trip to Alaska	

After you brainstorm, you can select a subject from those on your list. These subjects are still too broad or general to be suitable for an expository composition, but you have discovered several possible subjects to write about.

EXERCISE 4. Using Brainstorming to Search for Subjects. Use brainstorming to search for at least ten subjects for an expository composition. Focus on your own knowledge. Think up as many answers as possible to the question "Who or what do I know about?" Keep your list of possible subjects. You may want to refer to this list later in the chapter.

(5) Use clustering in your search for subjects.

You can also use clustering to search for subjects to write about. When clustering, you make a diagram instead of a list. You begin by writing a word or a phrase in the center of a sheet of paper. Then you write down as many ideas related to that word or phrase as you can. As you add each idea, circle it and connect these circled words and phrases with lines. Each line should connect an idea with the idea it came from. As in brainstorming, you do not take time to judge your ideas.

As with the other methods of searching for subjects, any one of the circled words or phrases can be a broad subject for an expository composition.

Suppose, for example, that your teacher has asked you to write a composition explaining how to make or do something. Your clustering diagram might look like this:

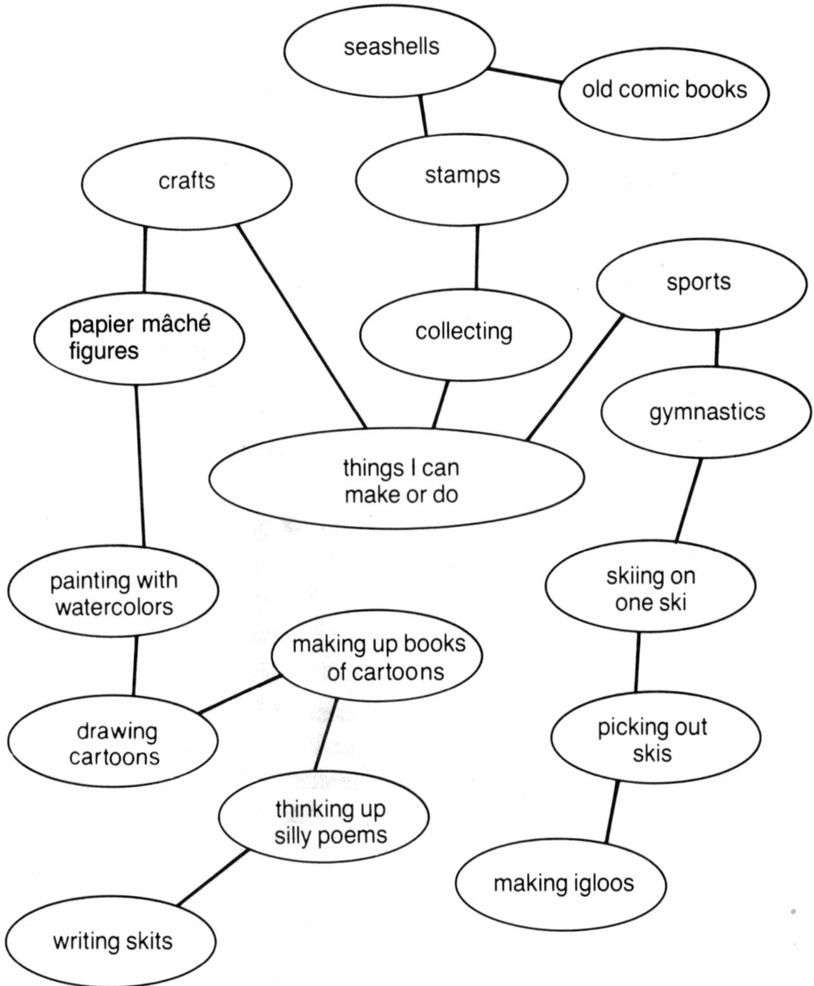

EXERCISE 5. Using Clustering to Search for Subjects. Use clustering to search for possible subjects for an expository composition. Use one of the following ideas to start your cluster diagram:

Things I am interested in	Things I know about
Things I can make or do	Things I have experienced

Circle and connect the words or phrases you think of. Keep your work in your notebook for use later in this chapter.

CHOOSING A SUBJECT

5b. From your list of possible subjects, choose one to write about.

To choose a subject, review the subjects you discovered in Exercises 1–5 on pages 135–39. The subject you choose should be one you understand well enough to explain to someone else.

Before You Write. When choosing a subject, ask yourself the following questions:

- What subject interests me enough to want to explain it to someone else?
- What subject do I know enough about to explain it clearly to someone else?
- What subject do I have enough experience with to explain it to someone else?

Usually subjects that you understand well enough to explain to someone else will appear in your answers to at least two of these three questions.

EXERCISE 6. Choosing a Subject for Your Composition. Review the lists of possible subjects you made for Exercises 1–5. Using the questions above, choose one subject for an expository composition.

THINKING ABOUT YOUR AUDIENCE

5c. Think about the audience for your expository composition.

Your audience is the person or people for whom you write. In expository writing the audience is especially important because the purpose of exposition is to inform *someone* about something or to explain something to *someone*.

Suppose, for example, that you chose "science-fiction movies" as a subject for your composition. How you explain this broad subject will depend on who your audience is. If you are writing for fourth-graders, you might want to explain why certain movies are called science fiction. For an audience made up of your classmates, you might explain the differences between the special effects in two science-fiction movies. For an audience of parents, you might explain why science-fiction movies are good entertainment for people your age.

Your audience will also affect how you write your composition. For an audience of fourth-graders, for example, you will have to use simple vocabulary and easy-to-understand sentences. For an audience of parents, on the other hand, you can use more technical terms and more difficult sentences.

Before You Write. To think about your audience, ask yourself these questions:

- How can I best describe my audience? Is it made up of children? Adults? Classmates?
- Is this particular subject suitable for this audience?
- What does my audience already know about this subject?
- What does my audience want to know or need to know about this subject?

EXERCISE 7. Thinking About Audiences. Following are five audiences paired with five subjects. Answer the question about the audience that follows each pair.

1. *Subject:* Microcomputers in math class
   Audience: Members of an eighth-grade class
   How can you describe this audience?
2. *Subject:* Safety with strangers
   Audience: First-graders
   What does this audience want to know or need to know about this subject?
3. *Subject:* William Shakespeare
   Audience: Eighth-grade English teachers
   What does this audience already know about the subject?

4. *Subject:* Summer arts festivals
   Audience: Readers of the local newspaper
   How can you describe this audience?
5. *Subject:* Local elementary schools
   Audience: Tenth-graders
   Is this subject suitable for this audience? Why or why not?

EXERCISE 8. Thinking About Your Audience. Using the four questions in Before You Write on page 141, think about the audience for your expository composition. Write a brief answer for each question.

LIMITING YOUR SUBJECT

5d. Limit your subject to a manageable topic.

A subject is a broad area with many different parts. Suppose, for example, you chose the subject "stamp collecting." To explain the different parts of this subject, you would have to write a long report. For a short expository composition, "stamp collecting" should be limited to one of its smaller parts, called a "topic." The limited topic "beginning a stamp collection" is an example of a manageable topic for a short expository composition.

CRITICAL THINKING:
Analyzing a Broad Subject

To limit your broad subject to a manageable topic, analyze your subject by dividing it into its smaller parts. The following questions will help you analyze your subject:

1. What are *examples* of the subject?
2. What are *uses* of the subject?
3. What are *types* of the subject?
4. What are *activities* involving the subject?
5. What *time periods* does the subject include?
6. What *places, people,* or *events* does the subject include?

As you answer these questions about your subject, you will be dividing it into smaller, more limited, topics for your composition. Keep in mind, however, that you will probably not be able to use each question with every subject. The broad subject "stamp collecting," for example, can be limited by using questions 3 and 4:

Subject: Stamp collecting
Types: rare stamps, first day covers, commemorative stamps, specialized stamps (railroads, birds, ships, paintings, etc.)
Activities: trading with other collectors, joining stamp clubs or societies, attending exhibitions, beginning to collect and display stamps

Any one of the limited topics listed above could be a manageable topic for an expository composition.

EXERCISE 9. Identifying Limited Topics. Four of the subjects listed below are too broad to be manageable composition topics. Four are limited enough to be suitable topics. Number your paper 1–8. Write *S* after the number of each suitably limited topic. Write *NS* after the number of each subject that is not suitably limited.

1. The youth of an American President
2. Mystery stories
3. Profile of a local disc jockey
4. Pioneer life
5. Environmental pollution
6. Starting a vegetable garden
7. Hunting for snakes
8. The women's rights movement

EXERCISE 10. Developing Limited Topics. For each of the four broad subjects identified in Exercise 9, develop at least two limited topics. Remember to use the questions in Critical Thinking on page 142 to divide each broad subject into its smaller parts.

EXERCISE 11. Developing Your Own Limited Topic. Using the broad subject you chose for Exercise 6, develop a topic that is limited enough for a composition. Use the Critical Thinking questions to divide your subject into its smaller parts. Be sure to limit, or narrow, your subject enough so that it can be clearly explained in a short composition.

STATING YOUR PURPOSE

5e. State the purpose of your expository composition.

The purpose of an expository composition is to explain or inform. For your statement of purpose, however, you should focus specifically on *what* your composition will explain to your audience, or *what* you will inform your audience about. To do so, use phrases such as *to explain, to inform, to show, to indicate,* or *to discuss* in your statement of purpose. For example, for the topic "beginning a stamp collection," the statement of purpose might read: *to explain how a beginner can collect and display stamps.*

Focusing on your topic in this way will help you later in the writing process. By clearly stating the purpose of your composition, you will know what kind of information you should gather for your composition. This statement of purpose can also be included in the introductory paragraph you write for your composition.

EXERCISE 12. Stating a Purpose. For each limited topic listed below, write a statement of purpose for an expository composition.

1. Muhammad Ali's prizefighting record
2. How Manhattan got its name
3. Making toothpick sculptures
4. Space achievements of the 1980's

EXERCISE 13. Stating a Purpose for Your Own Composition. Write a statement of purpose for the limited topic you have chosen for your expository composition. Save this statement of purpose in your notebook for possible use in the introductory paragraph of your expository composition.

GATHERING INFORMATION

5f. Gather information for your expository composition.

The three strategies that follow will help you gather information for your expository composition.

(1) List ideas and details for your expository composition.

Listing ideas and details is very much like brainstorming and clustering. Your purpose is to jot down as many ideas and details as possible. Later you will decide which ones you should include in your composition and how they should be organized.

Study the following sample list of ideas and details for the topic "beginning a stamp collection." Notice that the information is listed as it occurred to the writer, rather than in an organized plan. Keep in mind that there may be some ideas and details the writer might eventually decide not to use in an expository composition on this topic.

Topic: Beginning a stamp collection
Purpose: To explain how a beginner can collect and display stamps
Ideas and details:

family mail
hobby stores
removing stamps from envelopes
fun of watching collection grow
learning locations of countries
appreciating beauty of stamps
stamp dealers
history of postage stamps
learning about people and customs of foreign lands
mounting stamps in album
supplies: tongs, hinges, album
post office
stamp packets
approval sheets
valuable stamps

EXERCISE 14. Listing Ideas and Details. For each limited topic that follows, list at least five ideas and details. (Your teacher may instead want you to select only one topic and list as many ideas as you can about it.)

1. Differences between concerts and record albums
2. How to ride a bicycle safely
3. Why I watch television
4. The care and feeding of small animals

(2) Use your writer's journal as a source of information about your topic.

On pages 136–37 you learned about using a writer's journal to search for subjects for a composition. A writer's journal can also be a source of ideas and details about your topic.

The sample entry on page 136, for example, contains ideas and details about how stocks are traded. If you were writing a composition on this topic, you could use this particular journal entry as a source of information on how a stockbroker goes about buying stocks.

EXERCISE 15. Gathering Information from a Writer's Journal. If you keep a writer's journal, review it for any ideas and details related to the limited topic you developed in Exercise 11. Write these ideas and details in your notebook.

(3) Ask the *5 W-How?* questions to gather information on your topic.

Asking questions is often a useful way to find information about a topic. Newspaper writers ask the *5 W-How?* questions: *Who? What? When? Where? Why? How?* The answer to each of these questions will give you a piece of information—an idea or a detail—about your topic.

For example, study how one student used the *5 W-How?* questions to gather information on the topic "being a day-camp counselor."

Who? Who can be a day-camp counselor?
Young people with day-camp experience, good personal reputations, and some outdoor camping and crafts skills

What? What do day-camp counselors do?
Supervise children in day camps, give classes in craft projects and outdoor skills, assist the camp directors

When? When are jobs available for day-camp counselors?
Every summer, usually in one-week sessions in June, July, and August

Where? Where are jobs available for day-camp counselors?
Local communities, religious groups, community organizations, and groups like the Boy Scouts, Girl Scouts, and Camp Fire Girls sponsor day camps.

Why? Why would someone want to be a counselor at a day camp?
To work with young people, to make some money, and to spend the summer outdoors in an interesting environment

How? How can someone get a job as a day-camp counselor?
Call local religious groups, ask the local parks and recreation department, contact groups such as the Boy Scouts and Girl Scouts. See what jobs they have and what kind of people they like to fill them with.

EXERCISE 16. Asking the 5 W-How? Questions. Select a topic from the following list. Then ask the *5 W-How?* questions to gather information on the topic. For each question, write at least one answer.

1. My favorite team's greatest accomplishment
2. What I really want to do this summer
3. Recreational opportunities in our community

EXERCISE 17. Gathering Information on Your Topic. Using one or more of the methods described on pages 145–47, gather information on the limited topic you have chosen for your expository composition. Keep the information you gather for use later in this chapter.

GROUPING IDEAS AND DETAILS

5g. Group the related ideas and details you have gathered.

You are now ready to begin grouping, or classifying, the information you have gathered for your expository composition.

To classify information, you identify and group together closely related ideas and details. Then you give each group a heading that shows how the items are related. For example, the ideas and details listed for the topic "beginning a stamp collection" (page 145) can be classified into the following groups under four headings:

GROUP 1: Pleasure of collecting stamps
fun of watching collection grow
appreciating beauty of stamps

GROUP 2: Educational value
learning about people and customs of foreign lands
learning locations of countries

GROUP 3: Sources of stamps
family mail
hobby stores
post office
dealers: packets, approval sheets

GROUP 4: Displaying stamps
removing stamps from envelopes
supplies: tongs, hinges, album
mounting stamps in album

When you attempt to group the ideas and details you have gathered, you may find that some items do not fit anywhere. For example, two ideas in the list on page 145 have been eliminated from the above groupings.

history of postage stamps [eliminated because it does not contribute to purpose of composition]
valuable stamps [eliminated because a beginning collector would not ordinarily try to collect valuable stamps]

Remember that in exposition, as in most other kinds of writing, what you leave out can be as important as what you put in. By omitting an unrelated idea or detail from your list, you can often improve your composition.

Before You Write. To group ideas and details, ask yourself these questions:

- Which of my ideas and details are closely related?
- Which heading will show how each group of ideas and details is related?
- Which, if any, ideas and details should be eliminated because they do not fit anywhere?

EXERCISE 18. Eliminating Ideas and Details. The following list contains several ideas or details that do not fit the topic "repairing a bicycle." Decide which items do not fit and copy them on your paper. Be prepared to explain your choices.

Topic: Repairing a bicycle
Purpose: To show how to make simple repairs on a bicycle
Ideas and details:

adjusting the handlebars	safety helmets
long-distance bicycling	selecting a bicycle
streets vs. dirt roads	locking the bicycle
removing the chain	measuring the height of the seat
locating a tire puncture	

EXERCISE 19. Grouping Ideas and Details. The ideas for each of the following topics can be grouped under two separate headings. First write down the topic. Then supply appropriate headings and list related ideas and details under each heading.

EXAMPLE 1. Baking bread
Mixing ingredients; flour; shortening; kneading dough; setting oven; yeast; salt; forming loaves; water; letting dough rise

1. *Baking bread*

Ingredients	*Procedure*
flour	*mixing ingredients*
shortening	*kneading dough*
yeast	*forming loaves*
salt	*letting dough rise*
water	*setting oven*

1. School activities
   Glee club; football; baseball; science club; drama club; gymnastics
2. Model planes
   Balsa wood; sharp knife; cutting out parts; gluing parts together; blueprints; paint; painting; glue

EXERCISE 20. Grouping Your Own Information. Sort into groups the ideas and details you gathered for a topic of your own in Exercise 17. First give each group a heading; then list related ideas and details under the headings.

ARRANGING YOUR IDEAS AND DETAILS

5h. Arrange your ideas and details in logical order.

Often the ideas and details you have listed for your composition suggest the most logical arrangement. For example, the details for a composition about producing a play might follow the order of time: choosing the play, casting the play, and rehearsing the play. A composition on "our responsibilities," on the other hand, might call for an arrangement that builds from the most general to the most specific: responsibilities to our country, responsibilities to our community, responsibilities to our family, and responsibilities to ourselves.

As you arrange your ideas, experiment with the order until you find the arrangement that will present your ideas in the clearest possible way and will make the most sense to your audience.

Before You Write. To arrange your ideas in order, ask yourself:

- Does my list of ideas and details suggest the use of time order or of another order?
- Does the arrangement present my ideas in the clearest possible way?
- Will the arrangement make sense to my audience?

EXERCISE 21. Deciding on Order of Arrangement. For each of the following topics, indicate the order you would use to arrange the headings for a composition: order of time, general to specific, or specific to general.

1. How to assemble a telescope
2. The importance of being familiar with microcomputers
3. How to prepare for a math test
4. Directions to the Bijou Theater from Edgewater High School
5. The ambitions of my generation

EXERCISE 22. Arranging Your Own Ideas and Details. Arrange the ideas and details you grouped in Exercise 20 into the order most logical for your composition.

MAKING AN OUTLINE

5i. Make a topic outline for your expository composition.

By organizing and grouping your ideas and details, you have developed an informal plan for your composition. You are now ready to make a topic outline—a formal plan prepared according to a specific set of rules.

A topic outline is made up of main headings—the most important ideas—and subheadings. Subheadings are the details that support the idea expressed in a main heading. Each heading in a topic outline is expressed in a word or a phrase.

A topic outline should include a title. Although you may change the title later, be sure that it indicates your topic and appeals to the interest of your audience. Including your statement of purpose will help you keep that purpose in mind.

As you study the rules for outlining on pages 152–53, refer to the following topic outline for the composition about beginning a stamp collection.

Title: Beginning a Stamp Collection [title not part of outline]
Purpose: To explain how a beginner can collect and display stamps

I. Reasons for collecting stamps — main heading
   A. Pleasure — subheading
      1. Fun of watching collection grow
      2. Appreciating beauty of stamps — subheadings
   B. Educational value
      1. Learning about people and customs of foreign lands
      2. Learning locations of countries — subheadings
II. Sources for the collector
   A. Family mail
   B. Post office
   C. Hobby stores
   D. Stamp dealers
      1. Packets
      2. Approval sheets
III. Stamp display
   A. Supplies
      1. Album
      2. Hinges
      3. Tongs
   B. Procedure
      1. Removing from envelopes
      2. Mounting in album
IV. Specialization

Notice that a fourth main idea has been added to provide a conclusion for the composition.

Rules for Outlining

Observe the following rules when you make a topic outline:

(1) First, write the title and the purpose of your composition.

(2) Use a Roman numeral and a period before each main heading. Before each subheading under a main heading, use a capital letter and a period. Before each subheading under another

subheading, use an Arabic numeral and a period. For most short compositions, these levels of headings and subheadings are sufficient, as shown in the sample outline on page 152.

(3) Do not include a single subheading under a main heading or under another subheading. You cannot divide a heading into fewer than two subheadings.

(4) Indent subheadings so that all capital letters and numerals of the same kind are lined up directly under one another.

(5) Begin each main heading and subheading with a capital letter. Since the headings in a topic outline are not complete sentences, they should not be followed by periods.

EXERCISE 23. Completing a Topic Outline. Copy the incomplete outline given at the left. Then fill in the blanks with the appropriate items listed at the right.

Title: Our Science Club
Purpose: To explain how our science club began and to show its activities

I. Formation of club
  A. ——
  B. ——
  C. ——
    1. Campaigning for office
    2. ——
  D. Writing the club constitution
II. ——
  A. ——
    1. Government laboratories
    2. ——
  B. Projects
    1. ——
    2. ——
  C. Talks by eminent speakers
  D. ——

Holding elections
Tours of laboratories
Recruiting members
Discussions of current scientific developments
Raising an ant colony
Choosing a name
Industrial laboratories
Electing officers
Club activities
Studying a bacterial mold

EXERCISE 24. Developing a Topic Outline. Arrange the following ideas and details into a topic outline. Include a statement of purpose. The completed outline, like the one on page 152, should have three levels: Roman numerals, capital letters, and Arabic numerals.

Title: Taking a Camping Trip
Major ideas:
Camp health and safety
Planning
Setting up camp
Supporting ideas and details:

Selecting equipment	Dry ground
Making a fire	Safety when hiking
Safety tips	Arranging the wood
Setting up tents	Tents
Presence of fuel	Purifying water
Knives, hatchets, and axes	Safety in the water
Chopping wood	Choosing a campground
Selecting clothing	Bedding
Personal health	Food, pans, plates, spoons, etc.

EXERCISE 25. Developing a Topic Outline for Your Own Composition. Prepare an outline for the information you grouped and arranged in Exercises 20 and 22. Remember that this outline will guide you when you write your composition. Make certain, therefore, that it includes all the ideas you want to explain in your composition.

WRITING

WRITING A FIRST DRAFT

5j. Write a draft of your expository composition. Include an introduction, a body, and a conclusion.

In Chapter 4 you learned that a narrative has a beginning, a middle, and an end. In the same way, a composition has three main parts: an introduction (the beginning); a body (the middle); and a conclusion (the end). Each of these parts has its own purpose in presenting your topic to your audience.

As you write the first draft of your expository composition, allow your writing to flow freely. Concentrate on putting down your ideas about your topic. Later you will be able to revise and proofread. Right now you should simply focus on writing down your thoughts about your topic.

Use your outline as a guide, but if new ideas about your topic occur to you, include them in your draft even though they do not appear in your outline. Later in the writing process, you will be able to decide which ideas to keep.

Writing the Introduction

The *introduction* to an expository composition should arouse the interest of your audience and indicate the purpose and topic of your composition. For example, the first sentence in the introduction to the sample composition on page 158 arouses interest by asking a question which is then answered. The introductory paragraph goes on to suggest the topic and the purpose of the composition—to explain how to begin a stamp collection. You may, if you wish, make your statement of purpose the last sentence in the introduction.

EXERCISE 26. Writing an Introductory Paragraph. Write an introduction for your expository composition. Be sure you include a sentence that states your composition's general purpose and topic; in this way, your audience will know what to expect when they read your composition.

Writing the Body

The body is the longest part of a composition. In it, you develop the main ideas and supporting details shown in your topic outline. As a general rule, write at least one paragraph for each main heading. Sometimes, however, you may need more than one paragraph to explain an idea clearly and fully. In the sample composition on pages 158–60, for example, section II in the outline (page 152) is developed in three paragraphs; section III is developed in two paragraphs.

Using Transitional Words and Phrases

To help your audience follow the ideas developed in the body of your composition, use transitional words and phrases. In Chapter 2 you studied one use of transitional words and phrases—to connect *ideas* within a paragraph. In a composition, transitional words and phrases are also used to make smooth connections between *paragraphs*. By showing how one idea relates to another, transitional words and phrases enable your audience to follow your train of thought from sentence to sentence and from paragraph to paragraph.

Here are some commonly used transitional words and phrases.

next	moreover	furthermore	at the same time
then	besides	nevertheless	first (second, third)
thus	therefore	for example	on the other hand
in fact	finally	in addition	

Keep in mind that it is especially important to use transitional words and phrases in expository writing. When you are writing to inform or explain, you need to be sure your audience is following each point you make. This is particularly true of compositions that explain how to make or do something and of compositions that give directions. For each of these expository compositions, success depends on understanding how each step relates to the next. For example, if you were explaining how to make toast, you would probably use words or phrases that show time order: "*First* place the slice of bread in the toaster, *then* push the handle down, and *finally* remove the toast when it pops up."

EXERCISE 27. Identifying Transitional Words and Phrases. Find an expository paragraph in an encyclopedia, newspaper article, magazine article, how-to manual, cookbook, or textbook.

If you are permitted to cut the paragraph out, paste it to a sheet of paper; then circle all the transitional words and phrases in the paragraph. If you cannot cut the paragraph out, simply write down all the transitional words and phrases it contains. How do they help you follow the writer's train of thought? Be prepared to explain why these transitions are or are not effective.

When You Write. When you write the body of your composition

- use your topic outline as a guide.
- write at least one paragraph for each of the main headings in your outline.
- use transitional words and phrases to help your audience follow your ideas from sentence to sentence and from paragraph to paragraph.

EXERCISE 28. **Writing the Body of Your Expository Composition.** Using the topic outline you developed for Exercise 25, write the body of your expository composition.

Writing the Conclusion

The *conclusion* should bring your composition to a definite close. One way of concluding a composition is to sum up some of the points you made earlier in the composition. For example, notice that the last sentence of the sample composition on page 160 restates the main idea of the first paragraph. In a short composition, the conclusion can be only one or two sentences long.

When You Write. When you write your conclusion

- bring your composition to a definite close.
- leave your audience with something to think about.

EXERCISE 29. **Writing the Conclusion.** Think about the preceding *When You Write* as you write the conclusion for your expository composition.

Studying a Sample Composition

The sample composition that follows was developed from the topic outline on page 152. The notes in the margin show how the outline and the composition are related. Notice how the introduction arouses interest and suggests the purpose of the composition. Each paragraph in the body then explains the main headings in the outline. Finally, notice that the conclusion brings the composition to a definite end.

BEGINNING A STAMP COLLECTION

introduction (reasons for collecting stamps—I, A-B in outline)

Have you ever wondered why people collect stamps? Stamp collecting is a popular hobby for several reasons. Collectors gain pleasure from the varied colors and designs of the stamps, while enjoying the fun of watching their collections grow. In addition, stamp collecting has educational value. Stamps often tell the collector a great deal about the customs, events, and famous citizens of a country. Furthermore, collectors soon learn to find out the exact location of a country and often become interested enough to find out other important facts about that country. Now that you know how interesting stamp collecting can be, you may want to begin a collection of your own.

transition (In addition); transition (Furthermore)

body (acquiring stamps—II, A in outline)

Beginning collectors can start with family mail. A variety of stamps can be collected from the letters and packages the average family receives. If a relative or family friend happens to be living overseas, another valuable source is available.

(II, B-C in outline; transition)

In addition, the collector can buy domestic stamps at the post office. Some large post offices have special windows for new stamps, and all local post offices sell the new stamps when they are first issued. Foreign stamps can be bought in hobby stores or ordered from stamp dealers.

In fact, stamp dealers who advertise in magazines (often in magazines popular with young people) are an important source of stamps for all collectors. Most dealers offer beginners a packet of assorted stamps at a low price. After collectors have acquired many common stamps, they may be interested in dealers' approval sheets. Stamps on an approval sheet are usually less common than those in the packets; each is mounted and priced separately. Collectors keep any stamp they want and send their money and the remaining stamps back to the dealer. (II, D in outline; transition)

Most collectors display their stamps in albums. Albums for beginners usually have pictures of some of the stamps and sections for the different countries. Besides an album, a collector needs stamp tongs—a sort of tweezers—and hinges—small bits of gummed paper that attach the stamp to the album page. (displaying stamps—III, A in outline)

Stamps taken from the family mail, as well as some stamps included in the packets that come from dealers, have to be removed from the envelope to which they are still sticking. To remove a stamp, the collector first places it face down on a blotter and moistens the envelope paper with warm water. After the paper is thoroughly soaked, the stamp can (III, B in outline) (transition) (transition) usually be removed easily. By working slowly and carefully with the tongs, the collector can avoid tearing or otherwise damaging the stamp. To mount the stamp in an album, the collector allows it to dry, then folds a hinge with the gummed side out, moistens it, and attaches the stamp to the page. — transition

After beginners have had a taste of the pleasure of collecting, they are likely to want to specialize. For example, they may wish to concentrate on stamps of a particular country, or on those that have ships or certain animals on them. Whether they specialize or not, however, they are certain to gain much enjoyment and knowledge from their hobby.

conclusion (specializing—IV in outline)

restates first sentence

EXERCISE 30. Studying an Expository Composition. Answer each of the following questions about the sample composition on pages 158–60. Be prepared to explain your answers.

1. Who is the audience? Why do you think so?
2. If you were writing this composition, what information would you add? What information would you omit? Why?
3. How could the writer of this composition form paragraphs differently and still explain the topic clearly?
4. Select any one paragraph in the composition. Write down its topic sentence, and then list all the ideas and details that support this topic sentence. Also, compare these ideas and details to those listed in the outline. How are the composition and outline similar or different?
5. Do you think the writer successfully explained how to begin a stamp collection? Why or why not?

REVIEW EXERCISE. Writing an Expository Composition. Following the Guidelines for Writing Expository Compositions at the end of this chapter (pages 168–69) and the steps in the writing process, write a composition on a topic of your own.

EVALUATING

EVALUATING YOUR DRAFT

5k. Evaluate the draft of your composition for content, organization, and style.

When you evaluate something, you judge whether it measures up to certain standards. The standards you use to evaluate your draft are a measure of its content, its organization, and its style.

Content is what you say about your topic—the ideas and details you use to develop the major ideas about your topic. *Organization* is the arrangement of those ideas and details. *Style* concerns the words you use and the kinds of sentences you write; for example, short and simple or long and complicated.

The following Guidelines for Evaluating Expository Compositions provide standards for judging the content, organization, and style of your draft. These guidelines will help you identify the parts of your draft that should be changed to achieve the basic purpose of an expository composition: to explain something to a particular audience or to inform an audience about something. Read each guideline question and answer it honestly. When you answer no, you have identified something that needs to be changed. The labels at the left will help you focus not only on the part of your composition that should be changed but also on the particular writing skill that should be improved.

GUIDELINES FOR EVALUATING EXPOSITORY COMPOSITIONS

Introduction	1. Does the introduction attract the attention of the audience?
Purpose	2. Does the introduction tell the audience what the composition will be about?
Development	3. Do the paragraphs in the body develop the main ideas and supporting details in the topic outline? Is there at least one paragraph for each main heading?

	4. Are enough details included to make the topic clear to the reader? Are there any details that should be omitted because they are not related to the topic?
Arrangement	5. Are the paragraphs in the body arranged in an order that will be clear to the reader and easy to follow?
Transitions	6. Do transitional words and phrases help the reader follow ideas from sentence to sentence and from paragraph to paragraph?
Conclusion	7. Does the conclusion bring the composition to a definite close?
Word Choice	8. Will the audience understand the language used in the composition? Are any unusual words defined or explained?

EXERCISE 31. Using the Guidelines for Evaluating Expository Compositions. Following is a draft of the third paragraph in the sample composition on pages 158–60. Read the draft and reread the guidelines. Then answer each question that follows the draft. Be prepared to give reasons for your answers. Not all the guidelines apply to the draft.

> The collector can also get local stamps at the post office. Foreign stamps can be bought or ordered. Some really large post offices have places to buy new stamps, and all post offices have these stamps when they first come out. Some of the foreign stamps are unusual.

1. Is there a transition between this paragraph and the paragraph that precedes it?
2. Does the paragraph help develop one of the main headings in the topic outline on page 152?
3. Are enough details included to make the explanation clear to the reader? Should any details be omitted?
4. Are the details arranged in an order that is easy to follow?
5. Are the words and sentences appropriate for the topic?
6. Based on your answers to these questions, what specific changes do you think the writer should make in the draft?

EXERCISE 32. Evaluating Your Own Composition. Evaluate the draft you wrote for the Review Exercise on page 160 by applying each of the Guidelines for Evaluating Expository Compositions. Mark places in your draft where you should make changes and keep the marked draft for use later in the chapter.

REVISING

REVISING YOUR DRAFT

5l. Revise your draft, making any necessary changes to improve the content, organization, and style.

By evaluating your draft, you have identified those parts that should be changed. Using this information, you are now ready to revise your draft, making the changes that will improve it.

You can use four strategies to revise your draft:

1. You can cut—or omit—words, phrases, and sentences.
2. You can add ideas and details.
3. You can reorder—or rearrange—words, sentences, and paragraphs.
4. You can replace one thing with another.

The following chart shows how you can use these strategies to revise your expository composition.

REVISING EXPOSITORY COMPOSITIONS

PROBLEM	TECHNIQUE	REVISION
The introduction does not tell what the composition will be about.	Add	Include the statement of purpose or another sentence that suggests the purpose.

PROBLEM	TECHNIQUE	REVISION
The introduction does not arouse interest.	Add	Begin with an appropriate question or with another means of attracting interest.
A paragraph discusses more than one main idea.	Cut/Add	Omit details that are not related to a single main idea. Make a new paragraph with these details, or add them to an existing paragraph on the same idea.
The order of ideas is not easy to follow.	Reorder	Find the sentence or paragraph where the flow of ideas is interrupted; then move it so that the order of ideas is clear to the reader.
It is difficult to follow ideas from sentence to sentence (or from paragraph to paragraph).	Add	Add transitional words or phrases to connect ideas (or paragraphs); for example, *besides, finally, on the other hand, thus.*
Some of the words are not appropriate to the topic (or the audience).	Add/Replace	Add definitions or explanations as needed. As appropriate, replace informal words with more formal vocabulary.
The composition does not come to a definite close.	Add	Add a summary of points made in the body of the composition, or restate the main idea indicated in the introduction.

Following is a revised draft of the paragraph you evaluated in Exercise 31. As you study the revisions, refer to the notes in the margin. They indicate the revision strategies used by the writer.

In addition, *buy domestic*	
The collector can ~~also get local~~ stamps at	add; replace
the post office. Foreign stamps can be	reorder
in hobby stores *from stamp dealers*	
bought, or ordered. Some ~~really~~ large post	add; cut
special windows for	
offices have ~~places to buy~~ new stamps, and	replace
local *sell the new*	
all post offices ~~have these~~ stamps when they	add; replace
are *issued.*	
first ~~come out~~. ~~Some of the foreign stamps~~	add; replace; cut
~~are unusual.~~	cut

EXERCISE 33. Studying a Revised Paragraph. Answer each of the following questions by referring to the preceding paragraph.

1. In line 1 the writer added *In addition* to the first sentence in the paragraph. Why do you think the writer added this phrase?
2. In lines 1, 4, 5, and 6, the writer replaced certain words and phrases. Why do you think the writer made each of these changes in the paragraph? (In your answer consider clarity, accuracy, appropriateness.)
3. In lines 3 and 5 the writer added words and phrases. How do these additions help the reader?
4. In line 3 the writer omitted a word. In lines 6–7 the writer omitted a sentence. Why do you think these cuts were made?
5. The writer moved a sentence in line 2 to the end of the paragraph. Why do you think this change was made?
6. Does the revision correct the problems you identified in Exercise 31? Do you think the revision is better than the first draft? Why or why not?

EXERCISE 34. Revising Your Own Composition. Using the revision chart on pages 163–64, decide what strategies to use when revising your own composition. Then make the necessary revisions. For help with correcting monotonous or rambling sentences, refer to Chapter 9.

PROOFREADING

PROOFREADING YOUR EXPOSITORY COMPOSITION

5m. Proofread your expository composition.

After you revise your draft, check your composition for any mistakes in spelling, grammar, usage, and mechanics. By correcting these mistakes, you will make it easier for your audience to understand the ideas you are trying to communicate about your topic.

To proofread effectively, read over your composition several times, concentrating on a different item each time. In one reading, check for correct spelling and proper capitalization; in another check for correct punctuation; in another check for correct verb form and tenses, and so on. By focusing on one item at a time, you will notice errors more easily.

While you are proofreading, refer to the Guidelines for Proofreading on page 39 and the Revising and Proofreading Symbols on pages 39–40.

EXERCISE 35. Proofreading Your Expository Composition. Proofread the composition you revised in Exercise 34. Then exchange compositions with a classmate to double-check one another's proofreading skills.

WRITING THE FINAL VERSION

MAKING THE FINAL COPY

5n. Make the final copy of your expository composition.

You are now ready to make the final copy of your composition. This is the version that you will pass along for your audience to read. When you prepare this copy, use correct manuscript form (see Chapter 1) or follow any special instructions your teacher may give you.

After you make this final copy of your composition, proofread it again. It is easy to omit words or to make accidental errors as you recopy your draft. Proofreading one more time will help you catch these mistakes before your audience reads your composition.

EXERCISE 36. **Preparing a Final Copy.** Prepare a final copy of any expository composition you have written, evaluated, and revised in this chapter. Proofread your final copy for mistakes in spelling, grammar, usage, punctuation, and capitalization before your audience reads it.

CHAPTER 5 WRITING REVIEW 1

Writing an Expository Composition. Following the steps of the writing process, write an expository composition on a topic of your choice. As you plan, write, and revise your composition, be sure to refer to the Guidelines for Writing Expository Compositions at the end of this Review. Also refer to the Guidelines for Evaluating Expository Compositions (pages 161–62), to the revision chart (pages 163–64), and to the Guidelines for Proofreading (page 39). If your teacher allows, you may also want to share your composition with your classmates after you have revised and proofread.

CHAPTER 5 WRITING REVIEW 2

Studying Your Expository Writing. What you have learned about writing exposition in this chapter applies to the expository writing you do in all your school subjects. Select and read over an expository paragraph or composition you have written for one of your other classes, such as a paper for a science or social studies class. Then answer the following questions:

1. Who is your audience for this paper?
2. What did you do to adjust to your audience's needs when you wrote this paper?
3. Did you follow the steps in the writing process when you wrote this paper? Why or why not?
4. What part of the writing process would you use differently to improve your paper? Why?
5. How do you think knowing about the writing process can help you improve your writing in your other classes?

GUIDELINES FOR WRITING EXPOSITORY COMPOSITIONS

Prewriting

1. Select a topic you are interested in and understand well enough to explain to someone else.
2. Limit your topic so that you can discuss it clearly and thoroughly in a few paragraphs.
3. Ask yourself what someone unfamiliar with your topic might want or need to know about your topic. Then gather information for your composition with your audience in mind.
4. Determine whether you have used any technical or unusual words which need to be defined.
5. Group and arrange ideas and details so that your topic will make sense to your audience. Use this arrangement to help you prepare a topic outline for your composition.

Writing

6. Write an introduction that includes a statement indicating the general purpose and topic of your composition.
7. Use your topic outline as a guide when you draft the body of your composition. Be sure to connect your ideas by using transitional words and phrases.
8. Write a conclusion that brings your composition to a definite close.

Evaluating and Revising

9. After you write a draft of your composition, evaluate it for content, organization, and style. Make certain that you have included enough information to explain the topic to your audience. Ask yourself if you have presented ideas

and details in an order that will be clear to your audience. Check that the words and sentences you have used fit your audience. Then revise your draft, making necessary changes.

Proofreading and Preparing a Final Copy

10. Proofread your composition for mistakes in spelling, grammar, usage, punctuation, and capitalization *before* and *after* you prepare a final copy for your intended audience.

CHAPTER 6

Writing Exposition

SUMMARIES AND REPORTS

All through school, you will be asked to find information and to report on it in your own words. This is one of the most useful skills that you will study this year—not just in English class, but in your other courses as well.

WRITING SUMMARIES

The simplest kind of report is the *summary,* an account in your own words of a longer piece of writing. As with other forms of writing, preparing a summary involves using the writing process.

PREWRITING

CONSIDERING PURPOSE AND AUDIENCE

6a. Consider the purpose and the audience for a summary.

The *purpose* of a summary is to provide a short account of a longer piece of writing while retaining its essential meaning. To accomplish this purpose, include the main ideas of the original article. Leave out unimportant details, examples, and so on.

Your audience will affect the way in which you write the summary. If your summary is for a younger audience than the original audience, you may have to use shorter sentences and less difficult vocabulary. For some audiences, you may also need to define terms and to give some background information. For example, if you are summarizing an article on dangerous insects for students in your science class, you can assume they know what an insect is. For a class of second-graders, you might need to explain that an insect is "a small animal with three pairs of legs, such as a fly or mosquito."

EXERCISE 1. Deciding on Main Ideas. Read the following article carefully to decide which main ideas should be included in a summary. Then answer the question that follows the paragraphs.

> To get the full picture of what a swarm of army ants looks like, imagine a tide of them up to 33 yards (30 m) wide moving through the jungle at speeds up to 38 yards (35 m) an hour. A swarm this big makes a crackling and hissing sound in the jungle somewhat like rain coming through the trees.
>
> The eerieness of a swarm of army ants is increased by the fact that, en masse, they have—just as their name suggests—a distinctly military appearance. In fact, many species of army ants travel in a classic pincher formation that is shaped something like a *V*. This pincher formation allows an army—of people or ants—to encircle an enemy and fall upon it suddenly from all sides.
>
> A feature of army ants that makes them so dangerous is their constant hunger for fresh, live food. Unlike ordinary ants, which usually scurry about looking for bits of dead food, grains of sugar, fresh leaves, and so forth, army ants kill what they eat. Their diet includes anything that comes in their path—grasshoppers, baby birds in a low-hanging nest, lizards, snakes, and rats. There have even been reports of army ants attacking penned livestock and, within minutes, tearing whole cows to pieces.
>
> DONALD CAUSEY

Each of the following notes is from the article on army ants. Which of them should be included in a summary?

Notes:

1. Army ants can travel up to 35 meters an hour.
2. The swarm sounds like rain coming through the jungle.
3. Many army ants travel, like a military formation, in a *V*.
4. One reason army ants are so dangerous is that they are always searching for fresh, live food.
5. Examples of the kinds of food regular ants eat are grains of sugar and fresh leaves.

GATHERING INFORMATION

6b. Gather information for the summary by taking notes.

To write a summary, first read through the article carefully, looking for main ideas. During this first reading, do not take notes. Instead, concentrate on understanding what you read. Then read over the article again, this time jotting down the main ideas. In taking notes, be certain that you use your own words.

EXAMPLE

Original:

> **Halley's comet,** *HAL eez,* is a brilliant comet named for the English astronomer Edmund Halley. Before Halley made his investigations, most people believed that comets appeared by chance and traveled through space in no set path. But Halley believed that comets belonged to the solar system and took definite paths around the sun at regular intervals. He found that the paths taken by certain comets in 1531 and 1607 were identical with the path of a comet observed in 1682. He decided that the same comet made all these paths. He predicted that it would reappear in 1758 and at fairly regular intervals thereafter. The comet was seen in 1758 and made its closest approach to the sun in 1759. It appears an average of every 77 years and was seen as long ago as 240 B.C.
>
> JOSEPH ASHBROOK

Notes:

1. Comet named for English astronomer Edmund Halley
2. Before Halley's study, comets thought to appear by chance
3. Halley believed comets followed paths, appeared regularly
4. Proved comet named after him reappears every 77 years

Notice how the writer of these notes concentrates on what Halley learned about comets. The notes do not include details such as exact years.

Before You Write. To gather information for a summary:

- Think about these questions:
  1. What general topic is the article about? (*Hint:* Look carefully at the first and last paragraphs, which often introduce and sum up the general topic.)
  2. What are the most important ideas about this topic? (*Hint:* Subtitles or headings within the article often identify main ideas.)
  3. What supporting details (specific dates, examples, or descriptions) can be left out without changing the essential meaning?
- Use a dictionary to look up unfamiliar words or phrases.
- As you take notes, remember to
  1. Follow the pattern of organization used in the article.
  2. Put ideas into your own words, or paraphrase.
  3. Copy the writer's exact words, if you use a direct quotation. Enclose the writer's words in quotation marks, and give the page number on which the quotation appears.

EXERCISE 2. Taking Notes. The following paragraphs are from an article about people who worked to improve the lives of others. First, read the article carefully, looking for main ideas. Then read the article again, making notes on the main ideas.

HELPING THE DISADVANTAGED

Many people were unwilling to live in isolated communities and abandon all the customs and patterns of ordinary life.

They were nonetheless sincerely interested in improving society. Some devoted their energies to helping people in need. Samuel Gridley Howe, a Boston doctor, specialized in the education of the blind. In the 1830s he founded a school, the **Perkins Institution.** He developed a method for printing books with raised type so that blind people could learn to "read" with their fingertips. Howe's greatest achievement was teaching Laura Bridgman, a child who was both blind and deaf, to read in this way and to communicate with others through signs called a manual alphabet. Another of his pupils, Anne Sullivan, learned the manual alphabet to communicate with Laura. She later became the teacher of Helen Keller, a remarkable woman who lost her sight and hearing as an infant.

Another Massachusetts reformer, Dorothea Dix, practically revolutionized the treatment of the mentally ill. Dix was a schoolteacher. One day in 1841 she was asked to teach a Sunday school class in a jail in Cambridge, Massachusetts. When she went to the jail, she discovered to her horror that insane and feeble-minded people were being kept there and treated like ordinary criminals.

Thereafter, Dix devoted her life to improving the care of the insane. She visited prisons all over the country and wrote reports describing conditions and exposing their faults. Dix insisted that insanity should be treated as a disease and that it could be cured. Through her efforts many states set up asylums for the care of the mentally ill.

JOHN A. GARRATY

WRITING

WRITING THE FIRST DRAFT

6c. Write the first draft of a summary.

Rely primarily on your notes to write the first draft of your summary. The summary must be in your own words, and should follow the organization of ideas in the original.

EXAMPLE

Original: AMERICAN ECONOMIC SUCCESS

The United States is one of the richest nations in the world. Most Americans enjoy a high standard of living. A nation's **standard of living** is the well-being of its population based on the amount of goods and services they can afford. On the average, we have more money to spend, and more goods to buy, than the people of most other nations. Our economic system produces more goods and services than any other in the world.

What makes all this possible? There are a number of reasons for our economic success. First of all, the United States is a land of great natural resources. We have timber, minerals, energy resources, a good climate, and fertile soil in abundance. In addition, we always have had energetic and inventive people. They have taken our resources and turned them into needed and desirable products.

Furthermore, our system of government has ensured the right of private enterprise—that is, the owning and operating of businesses by individuals rather than by the government. It has protected the right of individuals to own property and make a profit. Finally, the United States has developed an economic system in which most of its people can find work and earn financial success.

WILLIAM H. HARTLEY *and* WILLIAM S. VINCENT

Summary:

The United States is one of the wealthiest nations on earth. Americans, who provide more goods and services than any other people, have a high standard of living. They can afford to buy many goods and services. America is economically successful because it is rich both in natural resources and in industrious people. Our system of government, which ensures the individual's right to own businesses and to make a profit, also contributes to our economic success.

When You Write. To write your summary

- State the main ideas clearly and briefly.
- Present ideas in the same order used in the original article.
- Keep your summary to one fourth or one third the length of the original article.
- Include all important ideas, but do not add ideas that are not in the article.

EXERCISE 3. Writing a First Draft of a Summary. Using your notes from Exercise 2, write a first draft of a summary. Your teacher may ask you to turn in your notes with the first draft of your summary.

EVALUATING AND REVISING

EVALUATING AND REVISING THE SUMMARY

6d. Evaluate and revise the first draft of your summary.

Like any other first draft, the first draft of your summary can probably be improved. When you examine a first draft to locate its strong points and weak points, you are evaluating your work. If possible, put your first draft aside for several hours or a day before you evaluate it. Then reread your first draft and answer each of the questions in the Guidelines for Evaluating a Summary.

GUIDELINES FOR EVALUATING A SUMMARY

Main Ideas	1. Are only the main ideas of the original article included in the summary?
Audience	2. Is the summary suitable for the audience?

Paraphrasing	3. Is the summary written in the writer's own words?
Order	4. Does the organization of ideas in the summary follow that of the original?
Length	5. Is the summary one third or less the length of the original?

After you have evaluated your summary, revise it by using the four revising techniques: adding, cutting, reordering, and replacing. The chart below suggests how you can use these techniques to improve your draft. Keep the original article until you have completed your revision, as you may need to check details.

REVISING SUMMARIES

PROBLEM	TECHNIQUE	REVISION
The wrong details are included.	Cut/Add	Cut unimportant details that are not main ideas. Add important ideas.
The summary doesn't seem right for the audience.	Replace	Replace words and sentences to make them more suitable for the audience.
The summary is not written in your own words.	Replace/Add	Replace the author's words with your own. Add quotation marks to show where the author's exact words are used.
The order of ideas isn't the same as the original article.	Reorder	Reorder sentences or ideas until the organization follows the original.
The summary is too long.	Cut/Replace	Cut unimportant details in the summary. Replace long discussions with shorter ones.

EXERCISE 4. Evaluating and Revising a Summary. Using your work from Exercise 3, evaluate and revise the first draft of your summary. Then recopy the summary. Before handing in your final draft, proofread it for errors. (See the Guidelines for Proofreading on page 39.)

REVIEW EXERCISE. Writing a Summary. Using what you have learned in this chapter, prepare a summary of one of the selections listed below. Follow these steps:

(a) Read the article, looking for main ideas.
(b) Read the article again, taking notes on the main ideas.
(c) Use your notes to write a first draft.
(d) Evaluate your first draft using the guidelines on pages 176–77.
(e) Revise, using the chart on page 177 to make necessary changes.
(f) Proofread the draft for errors.
(g) Make a final copy, proofreading again to catch any mistakes.

1. An article in a magazine or newspaper
2. An encyclopedia article
3. A magazine profile of a historical figure or a famous person
4. An editorial from your school or local newspaper
5. Part of a chapter in your science or social studies book

WRITING LONGER REPORTS

A more challenging kind of report, which you will often be asked to write, requires that you gather and organize information from a number of sources. To write this kind of report, you follow these basic steps:

1. Develop a limited topic
2. Gather information
3. Organize the information
4. Write a first draft
5. Evaluate and revise the report

PREWRITING

DEVELOPING A LIMITED TOPIC

6e. Develop a limited topic, keeping in mind your purpose, audience, and library sources.

Sometimes your teacher will assign a report topic; at other times you may be asked to develop your own topic. If you begin with a broad subject, such as "animals," "astronomy," or "computers," you must limit it in the same way you would a composition topic (see pages 142–43). Your factual report will probably be a short one, perhaps only several paragraphs long. The topic should be one about which you can give detailed information in that amount of space.

Before You Write. Use your library as a source for subject ideas.

- To gather subject ideas, skim articles in current magazines and newspapers, thumb through the subject cards in the library card catalog, or look at articles and pamphlets in the library's vertical file.
- Before you make a final decision about a subject, check your library to learn what sources are available. You will probably need at least four books, articles from magazines and newspapers, or pamphlets for your report. If your subject is very new or very technical, you may not find the information you need.

The purpose of a factual report is to present factual information. Select a topic about which you can find information in sources such as books and encyclopedias, not a topic based on personal experience. For example, you may have had an exciting experience participating in a bike-a-thon to support diabetes research. Your experience riding in the bike-a-thon is a personal one; you will not find information about it in your library. However, you could write a factual report about some aspect of diabetes—its causes, effects, and possible cures. You would be able to find the needed information in the library.

The topic you develop should also be interesting to your audience. Most audiences are interested in new or unusual topics or in fresh information on well-known topics. For example, most eighth-graders have learned something about when, where, and how dinosaurs lived, but they may not know why skeletons of dinosaurs that lived in swampy marshlands are found today in dry, desert climates.

Before You Write. To develop a limited topic for a factual report:

- See pages 142–43 for more information on ways to limit a subject.
- Think about your audience and their interests when you develop a limited topic: What do they already know about the subject? What aspect, or part, of the subject will be new to them?
- Keep in mind both the number of available sources and the length of your report. A short report on a subject with many sources means limiting your subject more than you would for a longer report or a report based on fewer sources.
- Remember that the main purpose of a report is to present information you have gathered. Avoid limited topics for which you would rely on your own experiences or opinions: "why we need more computers in our school," "what it was like to be hypnotized."

EXERCISE 5. Choosing Report Topics. Some of the following topics are suitable for a factual report; others are not.

Number your paper 1–10. Write *S* for topics that are suitable and *U* for ones that are unsuitable. (Unsuitable topics may be based on personal experience or they may be uninteresting to the audience. They may also be too broad for a short report or too technical for available sources.) Be prepared to explain your answers.

1. How computers are used to help paralyzed people walk
2. The role of women in the settlement of the West
3. The first walk on the moon
4. Unicorns and other mythical animals
5. How and why hypnotism works
6. Why the class-sponsored carwash was a failure
7. UFO's
8. The feeding habits of the male strap-toothed whale
9. What I learned about crazy diets
10. Magnetic resonance readings for medical diagnosis

EXERCISE 6. Developing a Limited Topic. Develop a limited topic for your factual report. You may use a topic already mentioned in this chapter or a topic of your own. Review the *Before You Write* suggestions on pages 179 and 180 as you develop your topic. Save your work.

GATHERING INFORMATION

6f. Find sources of information about your topic.

The reference section of your library is the best place to begin gathering information. An encyclopedia or other general reference work will usually provide you with a good introduction to your topic. However, this introduction is usually only a general one. Depending on your subject, you may also find additional information in more specialized reference books (pages 618–23). For more detail, you must find books and magazine or newspaper articles about your topic.

Before You Write. To locate sources of information on your topic:

- Write down the titles of any sources listed at the end of encyclopedia articles about your topic. Look for these sources in your library.
- Look under all possible subject headings in the card catalog and the *Readers' Guide to Periodical Literature.* Sources with information on the lost colony of Roanoke, for example, might be found under "Roanoke," "United States History," or "North Carolina—History."
- Check the bibliography (an alphabetical list of sources the author used) of any useful book you find to identify other possible sources.
- Examine both the index (an alphabetical list of topics covered in that book) and the table of contents (a list of chapter titles) to find how much information that source has about your topic.

6g. Record information about the sources from which you gather information.

Your readers will want to know where you found the facts used in your report. They may want to read more about your topic or check that you reported facts accurately. When you take notes from a source, prepare a separate card, called a *source card,* that gives information about the source.

Use 3 x 5-inch note cards or slips of paper as source cards. The source cards you prepare for books, magazine articles, and encyclopedia entries will be slightly different. On the source card for each, record the following information.

An encyclopedia source card:

1. The name of the author of the article, if there is one
2. The name of the article (in quotation marks)
3. The name of the encyclopedia (underlined)
4. The year of the edition

EXAMPLE

> Smelser, Marshall. ①
> "Lost Colony." World Book Encyclopedia. 1985 ed.

Notice the punctuation on the card. A period comes at the end of the article's title, before the quotation marks. A period also follows the name of the encyclopedia. Note that *edition* is abbreviated as *ed.*

A book source card:

1. The name of the author (last name first)
2. The title of the book (underlined)
3. The place of publication
4. The name of the publishing company and the year of publication

EXAMPLE

> ②
> Kupperman, Karen Ordahl.
> Roanoke: The Abandoned Colony. Totowa: Rowman & Allanheld, 1984.

Place a comma between the author's first and last names. A period comes after both the author's name and the book's title. Notice the colon after the place of publication and the comma between the name of the publishing company and the year of publication.

A magazine or newspaper source card:

1. The name of the author, if there is one
2. The name of the article (in quotation marks)
3. The name of the magazine or newspaper (underlined)
4. The date of the magazine or newspaper
5. The page numbers of the article

EXAMPLE

(3)

"Lost Colony: A Mystery Now Solved?" U.S. News & World Report, 9 July 1984: 61.

If the article begins on one page and then continues later in the magazine, put a comma between page numbers. A hyphen between page numbers means that the article is on all pages between the numbers. Notice how the date is written: day, month, year, with a colon following the year. Also notice that neither the word *page* nor its abbreviation *p.* is used, and that a period follows the page number.

Note that each source card has a circled number in its upper right-hand corner. As you fill out each source card, assign a number in this way to each source. Later, when you begin taking notes, you can mark each note card with this number, instead of writing out the name of the source on each note card.

EXERCISE 7. Gathering Information. Using your school library, locate four sources of information about the limited topic you developed for Exercise 6. Find at least one encyclopedia article, one book, and one magazine or newspaper article about your topic.

EXERCISE 8. Preparing Source Cards. Using 3 x 5-inch note cards or slips of paper, prepare a source card for each source you found for Exercise 7, in the correct format. Give each source card a number, beginning with 1.

DEVELOPING A WORKING OUTLINE

6h. As you read about your topic, develop a working outline.

Suppose you are preparing a report on the "lost colony," a settlement on Roanoke Island off the coast of North Carolina. Established by English settlers in the sixteenth century, the colony simply disappeared.

In the library, you have found an encyclopedia article, two books, and a magazine article about your topic. After reading the encyclopedia article, you decide that you will deal with three main points or ideas in your report:

I. Departure of colonists from England
II. Arrival of colonists on Roanoke Island
III. Disappearance of colonists

These points, or topics, are the beginning of a working outline that can guide your research. You now know, for example, that you need to find information on each of these three topics. You may discover other topics as your research continues. If a new topic seems important to your report, add it to your rough outline. If you are gathering many notes on one topic, consider breaking that heading down into two or more subdivisions. (For more information on outlining, see pages 151–53.)

EXERCISE 9. Developing a Working Outline. First, read one of the sources from Exercise 7 that gives general information for your report. Then write down three topics that you think you will cover. Use your working outline to guide your research.

TAKING NOTES

6i. Take notes on your reading.

Your reading will include encyclopedia articles, parts of books, and magazine articles. You cannot hope to remember all of the details of information that you collect. Consequently, you will need to take notes.

The best way to take notes is to write them on note cards or slips of paper, using a different card for each note. Early in your reading, you will find that information for your report falls into a number of general divisions or topics. Once you have three or four divisions, you can use them as headings for your note cards. When you find information that relates to one of these headings, write the heading at the top of the card and underline it. Then write your notes under the heading. Underneath the note, write the page number(s) on which you found the information.

EXAMPLE

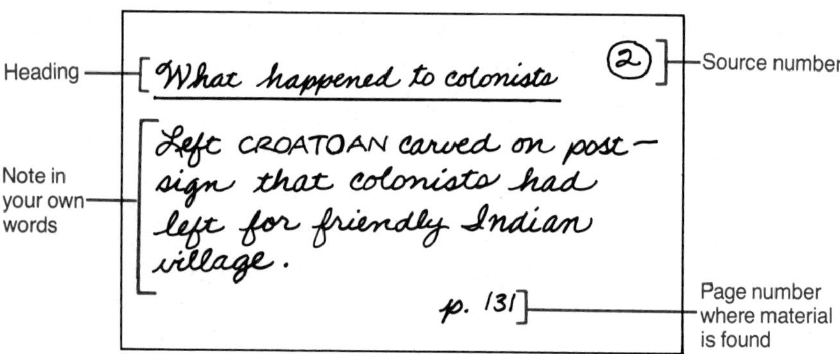

The number in the upper right-hand corner means this note is from source card 2 (*Roanoke: The Abandoned Colony*). Use separate note cards for each heading and for each source. For example, the note above is about what happened to the Roanoke colonists. You might also find information on that topic in an encyclopedia and a magazine article. You would then have three note cards with the same heading but different source numbers.

Before you begin taking notes, read over your source material, looking for main ideas. Then, as you read back over your material, jot down notes. There are three ways that you can take notes, illustrated in the following example.

1. You can *paraphrase,* putting material in your own words.
2. You can *summarize* by giving only the main ideas.
3. You can combine paraphrasing with direct quotation from the material.

Original:

If they did indeed go to Croatoan, the mist of history closes over them there. They may have stayed and intermarried with the Indians. Over a century later the explorer John Lawson, writing in 1709, said he saw the ruins of the fort on Roanoke and found some guns and coins there. And he said the surviving Indians of the Hatteras area claimed to have white ancestors.

DAN LACY

Paraphrase of information:

If colonists went to Croatoan, they were lost to history —may have intermarried with Indians there. One hundred years later, explorer named John Lawson saw ruins of fort on Roanoke, also guns and coins. Lawson said Hatteras Indians believed they had white ancestors.

Summary of information:

If colonists went to Croatoan, they were lost to history. Explorer later found evidence of colonists of Roanoke. Hatteras Indians believed they had white ancestors.

Paraphrase of information, with quotation:

If colonists went to Croatoan, "the mist of history closes over them there"—may have intermarried with Indians. One hundred years later, explorer named John Lawson saw ruins of fort of Roanoke, also guns and coins. Lawson said Hatteras Indians believed they had white ancestors.

EXERCISE 10. Taking Notes. Using your sources from Exercise 7, prepare at least ten note cards. On each note card, tell whether your note is a paraphrase, a summary, a quotation, or a combination of these.

ORGANIZING THE REPORT

6j. Organize your notes according to their headings, and make a final outline.

Now you must prepare to use the notes for your report. Eliminate notes that contain duplicate information or facts that do not fit your limited topic. Next sort the cards in piles according to their headings. Each pile will contain all the information on one main idea or topic. Review each pile to decide if you have enough notes to explain each heading, or if you should gather more. Also decide if a large number of notes should be divided into two headings.

After eliminating and sorting, you are ready to shape your final outline. Put your headings and subheadings in a logical order that will make sense to your audience. Then prepare a final outline, using correct outline form (see pages 151–53). Study this final outline for the report on the lost colony.

I. Departure of colonists from England
    A. Purpose of colonists
    B. Purpose of earlier explorers
II. Arrival of colonists on Roanoke Island
    A. Disappearance of earlier explorers
    B. Beginning of colony
        1. Need for food and supplies
        2. Return of leader to England
III. Disappearance of settlers
    A. John White's return to Roanoke
    B. Absence of settlers
        1. Missing houses and household goods
        2. Carved sign
    C. Ideas about disappearance
        1. Spanish ships
        2. Hostile Indians
        3. New life with friendly Indians

EXERCISE 11. Preparing an Outline. Using the note cards you made for Exercise 10, prepare an outline for your report.

WRITING

WRITING THE FIRST DRAFT

6k. Using your final outline and your notes, write the first draft of your report.

As you write the first draft of your report, consider the following suggestions.

1. Remember that a factual report is a kind of expository composition. As such, it has the same basic parts: *introduction, body, conclusion.* It should have an interesting, limited topic sufficiently developed with specific details. (See Chapter 5.)
2. Be certain that you understand all the terms you use. Look up difficult or unfamiliar words in the dictionary.
3. Use your own words in writing the report. Introduce quotations only when they are particularly apt or striking, and use them correctly.
4. Put every necessary detail into your report, and omit unnecessary items. Stick to your topic.
5. Using your outline as a guide, present information in a logical order, one that is easy for readers to follow.

6l. On a separate sheet of paper, list the works cited in your material.

Study the list of sources, the *bibliography,* at the end of the model report (page 192). Notice that sources are listed alphabetically by the last name of the author; when an author is not given, the source is listed alphabetically by the first word in the title ("'Lost Colony': A Mystery Now Solved?").

If you filled out your source cards correctly, making a list of your sources is easy. You can copy information directly from these source cards. However, before you begin, check each source card to be sure you have (a) included all the required information for that source, (b) recorded information in the right order, and (c) used punctuation correctly.

CRITICAL THINKING:
Analyzing a Model

You use the critical thinking skill of *analysis* when you look closely at something to understand what its parts are and how they are put together. Carefully examining the parts and organization of a model report will help you write your own factual report. As you read the following model, notice how the writer introduces the topic and develops it further in each paragraph. Think about the writer's plan of organization, whether paragraphs are arranged in a logical order, and look for topic sentences in each paragraph.

ROANOKE: THE LOST COLONY

1 In May 1587 a group of 117 men, women, and children sailed from England, headed for the part of the New World they called Virginia. As the travelers said goodbye to their native land, they never expected to return home. Their purpose was to begin a new life across the ocean—to build houses and to plant crops. They were to be the first English settlers in that vast new land.

2 Although these settlers were the first English people who intended to make their homes in Virginia, they were not the first to reach the land. In both 1584 and 1585 groups of Englishmen had landed in the New World. These groups, however, had come for a much different reason. Their purpose was to find a base for English ships in the New World. From the base, English ships could easily attack the ships of England's great enemy, Spain, sailing in the nearby Caribbean. Both groups of explorers landed on Roanoke Island, off the coast of present-day North Carolina. To their disappointment, the early explorers found that the waters there were too shallow to be used as ports for their ships. All but fifteen of the men in these two groups returned to England.

3 On July 22 the ships carrying the third group of English people—the settlers—anchored off Roanoke Island. On the island, they found that the fifteen men left behind from the earlier group had disappeared. All that remained was the skeleton of one sailor lying across the path. The few huts that the men had built stood in ruins, overgrown with twisted vines. These new settlers would have to begin again.

4 The Roanoke colonists set to work to build new houses. By August 18, less than a month after they landed, they must have already felt a tie to their new home. On that day Virginia Dare became the first English child born in the New World. The colonists intended to plant crops and to learn to hunt and fish, but it would be a long time before they could take care of themselves. At the end of the year, they would need more supplies. John White, a leader of the expedition and the grandfather of Virginia Dare, agreed to return to England with a group of sailors. There he hoped to gather more supplies and to return to Roanoke Island before the year was out.

5 John White never saw his new granddaughter or the other settlers again. On his return to England, he found that England's enemy, Spain, was gathering a vast fleet of ships. With these ships, called the Armada, Spain intended to gain control of the seas and, in this way, to dominate England. To defend England, Queen Elizabeth ordered all ships to remain at home. It was not until three years later that John White was able to return to Roanoke with the promised supplies.

6 As White finally approached the shore of Roanoke, one day before his granddaughter's third birthday, he called out to the colonists through the dark night. There was no answer. The sailors landed and crossed the island looking for the colonists. In the sand were footprints that the sailors knew must have been made by Indians. The English colonists would have worn shoes. The colonists' houses had been torn down, the planks taken away. All of the colonists' clothes and household goods were gone also. Near the huts, carved in the bark of a tree, were the letters CRO. Nearby, on a post, the word CROATOAN had been carved.

7 Now, John White thought he knew where the colonists

might have gone. Before he had left three years earlier, he and the colonists agreed on some signs. If the colonists had to leave Roanoke for some reason, they were to carve the name of the place where they were going. Croatoan was a village of friendly Indians on an island fifty miles away. White thought that the colonists, probably near starvation after three years with no supplies, had gone there for help. White was comforted that there was no cross carved in the tree above CROATOAN. A cross was the colonists' signal that they were in danger.

8 The next day, White planned to sail from Roanoke to Croatoan to search for the colonists. Because of violent storms, however, the ships had no choice but to sail for England. John White never again returned to Roanoke.

9 What happened to the settlers on Roanoke Island remains a mystery. Some historians believe that Spanish ships may have landed and carried them away. Others believe that the settlers were captured and killed by hostile Indians. There is, however, another possible solution. In southeastern North Carolina, not far from the original Roanoke, live the descendants of a group of Indians called the Lumbees. Unlike most brown-eyed descendants of Native Americans, many of the present-day Lumbees have blue eyes. Many of them also have the English names of some of the English settlers, names like Bailey, Dale, and Cooper. Perhaps the colonists, in the three years of their isolation, began a new life with their Indian neighbors.

10 The next group of settlers to the New World came to Jamestown, Virginia. With them they brought records kept by John White about the experiences of the Roanoke colonists. Those records helped the new colony to succeed. That is why, even though Jamestown is recognized as the first English settlement in the New World, the Roanoke settlers will always be remembered for their important role in America's history.

Works Cited

Kupperman, Karen Ordahl. Roanoke: The Abandoned Colony. Totowa : Rowman & Allanheld, 1984.

Lacy, Dan. The Lost Colony. New York: Franklin Watts, 1972.

"'Lost Colony': A Mystery Now Solved?" U.S. News & World Report 9 July 1984: 61.

Smelser, Marshall. "Lost Colony." World Book Encyclopedia. 1985 ed.

EXERCISE 12. Analyzing a Model Report. Write your answers to the following questions about the model report.

1. What is the limited topic for this report? Is it a suitable topic for a short factual report?
2. How does the writer catch the audience's attention in the introductory first paragraph?
3. The conclusion does not simply repeat the ideas in the report. What does it do instead?
4. What is the topic sentence of paragraph 2? What details develop this main idea?
5. What is the topic sentence of paragraph 7? What details develop this main idea?
6. This report has unity because each paragraph develops the topic. What does paragraph 4 tell you about the topic?
7. What information does paragraph 9 give you about the topic?
8. This report has coherence because its ideas are arranged in a logical order. In paragraph 1, the English settlers leave England for the New World. What happens to the settlers in paragraph 3? In paragraph 6?
9. What transition word connects the last sentence in paragraph 1 with the first sentence in paragraph 2?
10. How does the writer connect the last sentence in paragraph 6 with the first sentence in paragraph 7?

EXERCISE 13. Writing a First Draft. Using your outline and your notes, write a first draft of your report.

EVALUATING AND REVISING

EVALUATING AND REVISING YOUR REPORT

6m. Evaluate and revise your report.

If possible, put your first draft aside for a few days. This time away from your writing will help you look at it more objectively. To evaluate your report, either alone or in a small group carefully examine your first draft. Decide how well it meets the guidelines for a factual report. As you reread your first draft, ask yourself each of the questions in the following Guidelines for Evaluating Factual Reports. Your answers to these questions will help you decide where you need to make changes in, or revise, your first draft.

You can revise your report by adding, cutting, replacing, or reordering. The chart on page 177 will help you decide which technique you should use to improve a particular part of your writing.

GUIDELINES FOR EVALUATING FACTUAL REPORTS

Topic	1. Does the report have a suitably limited topic? Is it suitable for the audience?
Introduction	2. Does the introduction catch the audience's attention?
Paragraph Development	3. Does each paragraph have a main idea expressed in a topic sentence? Is this main idea developed with details?
Conclusion	4. Does the conclusion signal that the report is ending, without repeating ideas in the body?
Unity	5. Are all details in the report related to the topic?
Coherence	6. Are details given in a logical order?
Topic Development	7. Does the report include enough factual information to develop the topic?
Source Material	8. Is the report written in the writer's own words? Is the material paraphrased or summarized as appropriate? Does quoted material use quotation marks for the writer's exact words?
Sources	9. Are sources listed at the end of the report?

EXERCISE 14. Evaluating and Revising Your Report. Use the guidelines on page 194 to evaluate the first draft of your report. Then revise it, referring to the chart on page 177. Proofread your paper, using the guidelines on page 39. Recopy

your report, and proofread it carefully before you hand it in. Your teacher might ask you to hand in your source and note cards, your outline, and your first draft, as well as your final draft.

WRITING A BOOK REPORT

A book report gives two kinds of information: what the book is about and what you think of it.

PREWRITING

6n. Think about the purpose and audience for your book report. Think also about gathering specific information from your book.

Prewriting Hints for Writing a Book Report

1. *The purpose for writing a book report is to inform your audience about the book's content and about your opinion of the book.* In the first part of a book report, you usually tell what the book is about, identify the title and author, and explain whether the book is fiction or nonfiction. If you are reporting on a novel, indicate the background of the story—time, place, main characters, and conflict. For a nonfiction book, summarize the important information given. If you are reporting on a biography, indicate why the person written about is important, and mention chief incidents in that person's life.

In the second part of a book report, you usually explain your reaction to the book. This part of the report is important because it shows how carefully and thoughtfully you have read the book.

2. *Use specific details or examples from the book.* Whether you are telling about the book's content or your reaction to it, support what you say with specific details or examples from the book. You may want to quote words or sentences from the book. For example, notice the first paragraph of the sample book report (page 197). The writer says that the book is about eight people

who have made important contributions to other people's lives. Then the writer mentions the specific contributions of two people. In the second paragraph of the report (page 197), the writer gives one reason for liking the book. In the rest of the paragraph, the writer gives details to support the reason.

In preparing a book report, use your note-taking skills (see pages 172–73). After you read the book, jot down notes about its content and your reaction. Look up details that you may have forgotten about the plot and the characters.

3. *Summarize information about the book.* Avoid getting bogged down in too many details. You cannot possibly give every detail of plot in a novel or every piece of information in a nonfiction book. Instead, concentrate on selecting important details about the plot and the main characters, or discuss the main ideas in a nonfiction book.

EXERCISE 15. Preparing a Book Report. Select a book for your report. Read the book and make notes about its content and your reaction to it. List specific details from the book. For a novel, jot down details about plot, setting, and main characters. For a nonfiction book, make notes about important information. For both types, note specific details to support your reaction to the book.

WRITING

6o. Write a first draft of your book report.

In preparation for writing your own report, read the following sample report. As you read, ask yourself these questions:

1. What is the book about?
2. What specific details does the writer give about its content?
3. What is the writer's reaction to the book?
4. What specific details are included to support the writer's reaction?

A Report on *Shortchanged by History: America's Neglected Innovators,* by Vernon Pizer

1 *Shortchanged by History: America's Neglected Innovators,* by Vernon Pizer, is the story of eight Americans who have "fallen through the cracks of history." Each of these people has made an important contribution to the lives, health, and safety of millions of people, but each has been forgotten. Among these people is the man who designed and built the first flour mill. This same man also built, in the early 1800's, a steampowered vehicle that actually moved across roads under its own power and then left behind its land wheels to become a boat. Another one of these people discovered the process for separating red and white blood cells to make plasma. The plasma, which could be dried and safely stored, has saved the lives of countless burn and wound victims.

identifies title, author, and subject of the book

example helps reader understand content of book

second example

2 I like this book because each of the eight accounts reads like an exciting adventure story. James Eads, for example, worked on a Mississippi riverboat during the mid-1800's. Underneath the treacherous waters of the Mississippi, all up and down the river, were wrecks of riverboats. James Eads thought there should be a way to recover the cargo and the engines of the wrecks lying at the river's bottom. While in his early twenties, Eads invented a diving

writer's reaction and first reason for this opinion

specific example supports writer's opinion

bell that, carrying two men, could be lowered through the heavy currents. Through the open bottom of the diving bell, the men could attach lines to the submerged cargo. Air pumped from the salvage boat above kept water out of the bell. Before his first bell was ready, Eads was asked to recover a cargo of gold ingots. Unable to refuse the challenge, Eads fitted a huge wooden barrel with weights and descended through the raging current. Much to everyone's astonishment, the twenty-two-year-old Eads rescued the entire cargo.

3 Another reason I like *Shortchanged by History* is that each of the people described in the book had great moral courage. Sara Josephine Baker, for example, became a physician in 1898, a time when most people did not approve of women doctors. Because she wanted so much to help people, Dr. Baker became a health inspector for New York City. In her job, she was sent to the place with the worst living conditions in the city—a place called "Hell's Kitchen." Going by herself from tenement to tenement, Dr. Baker worked especially to improve the health of infants. When she began her work, as many as fifteen hundred babies were dying in New York City each week. Battling the constant prejudice against women doctors, she trained a team of nurses to go into the slums to teach health education. She established free clinics throughout the city for mothers and

second reason for writer's opinion

specific example supports writer's reaction

their babies. Before her work ended, she was responsible for reducing the death rate of infants in New York City by 50 percent.

4 In the world today, names like Alexander Graham Bell, Thomas Edison, and Wilbur Wright are remembered. The author of *Shortchanged by History* helps us recognize the important contributions of eight other Americans.

brief conclusion emphasizes book's value

EXERCISE 16. Writing the First Draft of a Book Report. Using your notes from Exercise 15, write the first draft of your book report.

EVALUATING AND REVISING

6p. Evaluate and revise the first draft of your book report.

The following guidelines will help you evaluate the draft of your book report. Revise your report by referring to the chart on page 177. You should proofread your report, make a final copy, and then proofread again to catch any accidental errors. (See the guidelines on page 39.)

GUIDELINES FOR EVALUATING A BOOK REPORT

Title, Author	1. Are the book's title (underlined) and author mentioned early in the report? Is the title of the book underlined when it is mentioned?
Content and Reaction	2. Does the report give information about both the book's content and the writer's reaction to the book?
Development	3. Do specific details and examples support the writer's statements about the book? Do specific reasons explain the writer's reaction to the book?

Novel — 4. For a novel, are the setting and main characters discussed? Is enough of the plot revealed to give readers a general idea of the story?

Nonfiction — 5. For a nonfiction book, does the report summarize important information?

EXERCISE 17. Evaluating and Revising a Book Report. Evaluate the first draft of your book report from Exercise 16. Revise to make changes that improve the first draft, using the chart on page 177. Using the guidelines on page 39, proofread your report. Then recopy your paper and proofread again.

CHAPTER 6 WRITING REVIEW

Applying Your Knowledge of Summaries, Reports, and Book Reports. Complete one or more of the following activities.

1. Following the procedure you learned in this chapter, write a summary of the model report on the lost colony of Roanoke Island (pages 190–93). Remember that your summary should be no more than one third the length of the original report.
2. Develop another limited topic for a factual report. Using this new topic, follow the steps of the writing process to develop another report.
3. Choose a different type of book from the one you reported on in this chapter. For example, if you have already reported on a nonfiction book, choose a novel. Then follow the steps in the writing process to write a book report.

CHAPTER 7

Writing Letters and Completing Forms

SOCIAL LETTERS, BUSINESS LETTERS, AND FORMS

Letters from friends are enjoyable. It is interesting to learn about their experiences and thoughts, about general news of other friends. However, you will not receive many letters unless you write letters.

SOCIAL LETTERS AND NOTES

PREWRITING

DECIDING WHAT TO SAY

7a. In a friendly letter, write about the things that interest you and the person to whom you are writing.

Before you write, jot down your ideas. Include news that will interest your friend. Think of your friend's letter to you. Reply to questions or comments. As you write, keep in mind your audience—the receiver of your letter. You would not send the same kind of letter to a friend as you would send to a parent.

Study the following example of a friendly letter. Would you say that Bill is thinking of his friend Tom as he writes? Would this letter be different if it were written to Bill's grandmother?

1849 West Sixth Street
Los Angeles, California 90014
April 14, 1988

Dear Tom,

You asked what Carl and I have been up to lately. Well, Carl is taking care of a horse for friends of his parents, but he's afraid to ride it. I said I'd ride it. You know me—no brains.

That horse jumped suddenly high into the air and tried to throw me off. I stayed on, though, until it reared straight up and fell over backwards. Carl's dad ran over to me. He was mad, but all he said was that maybe we'd better put the horse back in the stable.

You asked what I'm doing for the Science Fair at school. Carl and I have taken photographs of cloud formations. We are mounting these photographs for an exhibit on weather forecasting.

How about letting me know what you're doing?

Sincerely,
Bill

A Friendly Letter

WRITING

WRITING A FRIENDLY LETTER

7b. Choose stationery and ink that are suitable for a friendly letter.

Use letter stationery. White is always appropriate, though other colors may be used.

Write in ink, never in pencil. (If you can type *well,* type your letters.) Avoid ink blots and erasures. Keep your writing neatly spaced and properly aligned; crowded lines that climb, stagger, or droop give a bad impression. Keep your margins wide and equal on the top and bottom as well as on the sides.

7c. Follow generally accepted rules for the form of a friendly letter.

The form of a friendly letter is easy to master. Study the following instructions and sample letter.

The Heading

The *heading* tells when and where the letter was written. It consists of three lines, placed at the upper right corner of the page. The writer's address is written on the first two lines, and the date of the letter is written on the third. A comma is used between city and state and between the day of the month and the year. The ZIP code number appears several spaces after the state and on the same line. There is no punctuation at the ends of the lines.

Two kinds of headings are appropriate in a friendly letter. The example on this page is in *block style.* All lines of the heading begin directly below the beginning of the first line. Another form often used for friendly letters is *indented style,* in which the heading looks like this:

2534 Polk Place
Portland, Oregon 97235
May 6, 1988

18 Prince Street
Houston, Texas 77008
April 14, 1988

Dear Bob,

Sincerely yours,
Jim

Form of a Friendly Letter

The Salutation

The *salutation* begins at the left-hand margin, is placed a short distance below the heading, and is followed by a comma.

The Body

The *body* of a friendly letter is the message, what you have to say. The first line of the first paragraph should be indented about an inch from the left margin. The first line of other paragraphs must be indented the same way.

The Closing

The *closing* for a friendly letter may be *Your friend, Sincerely, Sincerely yours,* or any similar phrase, except *Yours truly* and *Very truly yours,* which are used in business letters. The closing is placed below the last line of the letter, begins to the right of the middle of the page, and is followed by a comma. Only the first word of the closing is capitalized.

The Signature

The *signature* in a friendly letter is usually your first name. Center it under the closing and write it by hand, even if you have typed the entire letter.

EXERCISE 1. **Writing a Friendly Letter.** Write a letter to a friend your own age about the experiences you have had in the last few days. Remember to use the correct form.

EXERCISE 2. **Writing a Friendly Letter.** Write a letter to a relative or an adult about the same experience you used in Exercise 1. Keep in mind the receiver, or audience, of your letter. Be prepared to discuss how your two letters differ.

Addressing the Envelope

The envelope of a letter should be addressed carefully, for the letter may not be delivered if the address is carelessly written. Always include the ZIP code number and a return address (so that the letter may be returned if your correspondent has moved).

Susan Froelich
597 Spruce Street
Kansas City, Kansas 66143

Miss Astrid Addison
89 Kirkland Street
Cambridge,
Massachusetts 02127

A Model Envelope

Study the example above and the following instructions.

1. Place the return address (your address) in the upper left corner of the envelope.

2. Place the address of the receiver just below the middle and to the left of the center of the envelope.

3. If the letter is going to an adult, write a title before the name: *Mr., Mrs., Ms., Dr.,* etc. Do not use a title in the return address.

4. Write the state on the same line as the city, with a comma after the city. Place the ZIP code number several spaces after the state.

5. If you use *Post Office Box, Rural Free Delivery,* or *Rural Route* in the address, you may use abbreviations: *P.O. Box, R.F.D.,* or *R.R.*

EXERCISE 3. Addressing Envelopes. Using your ruler, draw the outlines of two envelopes. Address each, using your own return address.

1. Ms. Ellen Craig 111 Orchid Way
   Butte, Montana 59601
2. Dr. N. T. Bain P.O. Box 753
   Winamac, Indiana 46996

EXERCISE 4. Writing a Friendly Letter. Write a letter for one of the following situations, or for a situation of your own. Also address an envelope for your letter.

1. You are visiting relatives in another city, and they have taken you to a World Series game. Write to your parents.
2. A next-door neighbor has moved away. Give her news about your neighborhood and ask questions about her new neighborhood.
3. You are a ham radio operator, and you have been exchanging messages with another ham radio hobbyist. Invite him or her to visit you. Tell him or her what to expect during the visit.

Folding the Letter

If your letter stationery is a folded page, fold it in half and insert it, fold first, into the envelope. If the stationery is a single sheet as wide as the envelope, fold it into thirds and insert it into the envelope, with the last fold first, as on page 216.

WRITING SOCIAL NOTES

7d. Write prompt, courteous social notes.

Social notes are written to extend or accept an invitation or to thank someone for a gift or favor. They follow the form of a friendly letter and are written on personal stationery, or if they are brief, on correspondence cards.

The Bread-and-Butter Note

Occasionally you visit friends or relatives who live out of town. After your visit, you should write a note to your host or your friend's parents to thank them for their kindness. This note, called a "bread-and-butter" note, should be written promptly. Tell your hosts how much you appreciated their efforts to make your visit pleasant. Mention some of the things they did for you. Your hosts may be interested, too, in your trip home, so you may also mention it briefly.

Study the sample bread-and-butter note. Notice that it follows the form of a friendly letter.

34 Casa Grande Drive
Berkeley, California 94713
August 6, 1988

Dear Mr. and Mrs. De Stefano,

Ever since I got home, I've been thinking about the wonderful week I spent with your family in Yosemite Park. The park had always been a sort of picture album place to me, and now I've got my own snapshots of it! But the outdoor scenery was only part of the pleasure of camping with your family. Waking up in the morning to the smell of frying bacon and eggs, hiking up the steep trails and coming back to cool off with a swim in the river, sitting around the campfire singing and telling stories — I'll remember these things for a long time. Thanks ever so much for having me as a guest.

Please tell Helen I'll send her some of my snapshots as soon as they are ready.

Sincerely yours,
Nora Davis

A Bread-and-Butter Note

The Thank-You Note

After receiving a gift or favor from someone you cannot thank in person, you should write a thank-you note. Always write promptly. A delay suggests that you do not appreciate the gift. A thank-you note will seem less like a duty if you also write about something else and give specific reasons for your gratitude. Notice how Tony thanks his uncle in the thank-you note below.

641 Ardmore Avenue
Philadelphia, Pennsylvania 19153
June 3, 1988

Dear Uncle Harry,

Thanks ever so much for the model plane engine. I'm having a lot of fun with it. The other boys tell me that a Junior Wasp model like this is very dependable. It starts easily and runs with no trouble. I've been running it on a breaking-in block. It's surprising how much roar such a tiny engine has! I'm eager to finish building my model. I know this engine will really make it zoom.

The folks gave me some fine birthday presents too; but I suspect that I'll remember this birthday most of all because of your wonderful gift.

Your nephew,
Tony

A Thank-You Note

EXERCISE 5. Writing a Bread-and-Butter Note. Write a bread-and-butter note for one of the following situations, or for a situation of your own.

1. A friend's family has taken you on a camping trip.
2. You stayed for a week on your grandparents' farm.

3. An uncle has taken you on a trip to New York City, where you visited the Empire State Building and the Statue of Liberty.

EXERCISE 6. Writing a Thank-You Note. Write a thank-you note and address an envelope for one of the following situations, or for a situation of your own.

1. An aunt, who owns her own company, has sent you a share of her company's stock for graduation.
2. Your grandfather, who lives in another town, has sent you ten dollars for your birthday.
3. An older cousin lives in Europe. He knows you have been collecting stamps since you were seven. He has sent you proof sets of stamps from various countries.

EVALUATING AND REVISING

EVALUATING AND REVISING SOCIAL LETTERS

7e. Evaluate your social letter; then revise it by making necessary changes.

To evaluate, read your letter several times to locate strengths and weaknesses in its content, organization, appearance, and form. Locate any items which need more explanation and any unnecessary points. You may want to make notes in pencil on your first draft. Use the following guidelines to evaluate your social letters.

GUIDELINES FOR EVALUATING SOCIAL LETTERS

Content	1. In a friendly letter, is there news the reader would like to know or find interesting? Are questions answered that may have been asked in the friend's last letter? In a note of thanks, is it clear what the writer appreciates?

Coherence	2. Is the letter organized so the reader can follow it easily?
Appearance	3. Is the letter neatly written in pen or typed?
Form	4. Is the form correct, with each of the parts complete and correctly placed? Are the address and date in the heading? Is the salutation suitable? Does a comma follow the salutation? Are the first line of the body and the first lines of any other paragraphs indented? Is the closing appropriate? Is the first word in the closing capitalized? Does a comma come at the end of the closing?
Envelope	5. Is the address on the envelope complete? Is it correctly placed?

You should revise your social letters to improve their content, organization, appearance, and form. Use the four revising techniques: cutting, adding, replacing, and reordering. Use the suggestions in the chart on page 222 to revise your social letters. Proofread your letters by referring to the Guidelines for Proofreading on page 39. Be sure to proofread again after you recopy your letters.

BUSINESS LETTERS AND FORMS

Business letters and forms are important in our daily lives. You may have already written to order merchandise or to request information. Later you may write business letters to apply for a job or a school. You will have to know how to complete forms correctly as you go through school and get a job.

PREWRITING

PLANNING A BUSINESS LETTER

When you plan your business letters, use the following steps.

1. *Consider your purpose.* Think about why you are writing the letter. Are you ordering something? Are you asking for information?
2. *Consider your audience.* Keep in mind your audience. What do they already know? What do they need to know?
3. *Consider your tone.* A business letter should sound courteous. If you must make a complaint in a letter, do so politely.
4. *Gather your ideas.* Jot down exactly what you want to say or whatever information you intend to convey. Include as much information as necessary to explain the situation fully.
5. *Be brief.* Check to see that you have not included any unnecessary information. However, do not leave out any important details; if you do, the reader of the letter will not be able to respond promptly.

WRITING

WRITING A BUSINESS LETTER

7f. Follow generally accepted rules for the form of a business letter.

You should use unruled white paper that is $8\frac{1}{2}$ x 11 inches. If you type well, it is always good to type your business letters. If you do not type well, it is acceptable to write carefully in black or blue ink.

Make your letter neat and attractive. Center it on the page, leaving equal margins on the right and left sides and on the top and bottom. Avoid ink blots, erasures, and crossed-out words. Write only on one side of the page.

The form of a business letter is somewhat different from that of a personal letter. A business letter always includes an *inside address,* as in the following example:

567 Hardwood Street
San Diego, California 92128
December 10, 1988

Mr. John Anders
Acme Sporting Goods Company
33 Norton Avenue
Cleveland, Ohio 44105

Dear Mr. Anders:

Very truly yours,

Donald Hayes

Donald Hayes

Form for a Business Letter

The Heading

A business letter always requires a complete heading: street address on the first line; city, state, and ZIP code number on the second line, with a comma between the city and state; date on the third line, with a comma between the day and the year. Block style, not indented style, should be used in the heading of a business letter. The two-letter state codes recommended by the postal service are used by many businesses in both the heading and the inside address.

The Inside Address

A business letter includes an inside address, which gives the name and the address of the person or the firm (sometimes both) to whom you are writing. A comma is used between the city and state, and the ZIP code number appears several spaces, or about one-quarter inch, after the state. Place the inside address four typewriter lines below the heading and on the other side of the page, flush with the left-hand margin.

The Salutation

The salutation is placed two typewriter lines below the inside address, flush with the left-hand margin. It is followed by a colon, not a comma as in a friendly letter. Salutations will vary. If you are writing to a person whose name you have used in the inside address, you say *Dear Mr.——:* (or *Dear Miss——:* or *Dear Mrs.——:* or *Dear Ms.——:*).

EXAMPLE Ms. S. E. Sorenson, Circulation Manager
Astronomy Magazine
67 East Eighth Street
New York, New York 10003

Dear Ms. Sorenson:

If you are writing to a person whose name you do not know, but whose official position you do know, say *Dear Sir:* or *Dear Madam:*

EXAMPLE Public Relations Director
State Oil Company
317 Bush Street
Dallas, Texas 75243

Dear Sir: (or Dear Madam:)

If, however, you are writing to a group or a company, you may use an impersonal salutation (*Customer Service:, Editors:, Personnel:*).

EXAMPLE Bradley Electronics Corp.
56 La Mesa Drive
Lafayette, California 94549

Mail Order Department:

The Body

The first sentence of the body begins two lines below the salutation. This first line should be indented and the first lines of all other paragraphs should be indented the same distance. (If you are using a typewriter, indent five spaces.) Keep the left-hand margin straight; keep the right-hand margin as straight as possible.

The Closing

The correct closing for a business letter is *Yours truly* or *Very truly yours* or *Sincerely yours.* The closing should begin a little to the right of the middle of the page. Only the first word is capitalized. A comma follows the closing.

The Signature

In line with and directly below the closing, sign your full name in ink. If you are typing the letter, type your name below your written signature. Do not put a title (Mr., Mrs., Miss, etc.) before your handwritten signature.

Yours truly,
Margaret Nolan

Very truly yours,
John Anderson
John Anderson

The Envelope

The return address and the address on the envelope of a business letter are written and placed exactly as they are on the envelope of a friendly letter. The "outside" address should be the same as the inside address.

Folding the Letter

If the letter is written on $8\frac{1}{2} \times 11$-inch paper and is to be put into a long envelope, fold the sheet up a third of the way from the bottom, then fold the top third down over it.

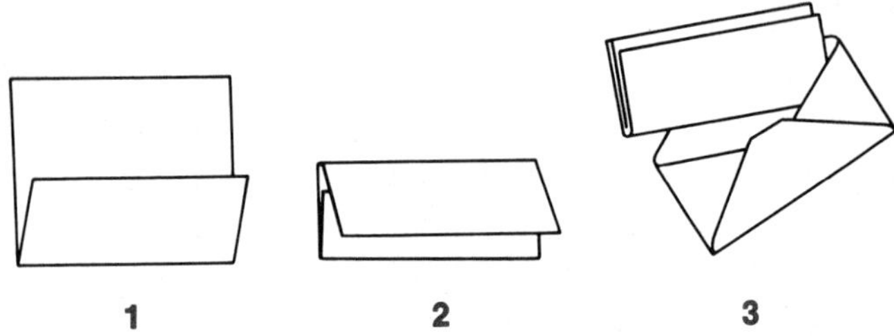

If the sheet is to go into a small envelope, fold the page up from the bottom to within a quarter of an inch of the top; then fold the right side over a third of the way, and fold the left side over it. Insert the letter into the envelope with the last fold at the bottom of the envelope.

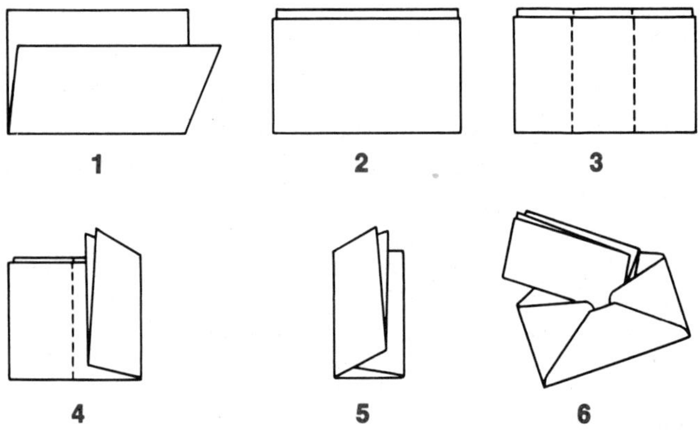

EXERCISE 7. Writing a Business Letter; Addressing an Envelope. The information needed for a business letter follows. Write the letter in correct form on a sheet of unruled white paper and address an envelope for it.

32 Brenda drive, Flagstaff, Arizona 86001 december 2 1988 Acme outfitting company inc p.o. box 289 milwaukee wisconsin 53248 customer service department kindly send me your mail order catalog on sporting goods and hunting and fishing equipment thank you yours truly judy muller

Writing the Order Letter and the Request Letter

7g. Become familiar with the two common kinds of business letters: the *order* letter and the *request* letter.

The Order Letter

In an order letter, identify the merchandise you want by catalog number, by the place you saw it advertised, and by price. State how you are paying for the merchandise (cash, check, money order, C.O.D., or charge).

89 East First Street
Kankakee, Illinois 60901
March 10, 1988

Standard Equipment Company
448 Westwood Boulevard
St. Louis, Missouri 63107

Mail Order Department:

Please send me the field glasses, No. 791, which you advertised for $11.98, postpaid, in the February 17 issue of the Farm Gazette.

I am enclosing a money order for $11.98.

Very truly yours,

Rachel Beam

Rachel Beam

Model Order Letter

Sometimes you may need to return merchandise that was not exactly what you ordered. In your letter, indicate what merchandise you wanted. Be sure to use a polite tone.

NOTE You will order many items of merchandise not by letter, but by order blank. When you use an order blank, follow the directions carefully and fill in all the blanks. No cover letter is necessary.

EXERCISE 8. Evaluating an Order Letter. Select an item you would like to order from the advertisements in a catalog, newspaper, or magazine, and write a letter ordering it. Exchange letters with a classmate to evaluate each other's letter. Check to see whether (1) it follows correct form; (2) it identifies the item wanted; (3) it states how the item is being paid for.

EXERCISE 9. Writing a Business Letter. Write a letter for one of the following situations. Also address an envelope for the letter.

1. You ordered a pair of rabbits, New Zealand Giants, from Beyer's Mail Order Mart, 88 Hemingway Street, Augusta, Georgia 30915. Instead of live rabbits, you received a set of "rabbit ears" antennae for a television set. You enclosed full payment.
2. You ordered a cotton sweater from the Chic Shop, 49 Sierra Road, Philadelphia, Pennsylvania 19154. You received the wrong size and color.
3. For your mother's birthday, you ordered a sweater from Gifts Galore, 819 West Drive, Dubuque, Iowa 52018. In your letter you enclosed a money order. Your mother's birthday is a week away, and the sweater has not yet arrived.
4. You ordered (enclosing full payment) a pair of work gloves from Mercantile Mail Order Company, 97 West Ivy Street, Akron, Ohio 44153. You received twelve pairs of mittens.

The Request Letter

Occasionally you have to write a letter requesting information or sample materials. In such a letter you are asking a favor. Be brief, clear, and courteous.

34 Addison Place
Boise, Idaho 83742
December 2, 1988

Air-Industry, Inc.
10 West Norton Avenue
Los Angeles, California 90037

Publicity Department:

Our eighth-grade class at Brice Junior High School is studying the use of helicopters in farming operations. If you have a free brochure describing your helicopters and how they are used on farms, we would appreciate receiving ten copies.

Yours truly,

Martha Ames

Martha Ames

Model Request Letter

EXERCISE 10. Writing a Request Letter. Write to a government department, asking for free pamphlets about the duties and services of the department. Address an envelope for your letter, but do not mail the letter.

EXERCISE 11. Writing a Business Letter. Write a letter for one of the following situations. Address an envelope, but do not mail the letter.

1. Your class has been studying wildlife conservation. You would like some maps showing the great "flyways" on the North America continent used by migrating birds. Write to the Fish and Wildlife Service, United States Department of the Interior, Washington, D.C.

2. Your class wants to visit a famous museum in your area (or in another city). Write for information about visiting hours and fees. Ask whether a reduced rate is possible for your group. Inform the management of your purpose for making the visit.
3. Write to the United States Government Printing Office, Washington, D.C. Ask for publications on a particular subject and tell why you are interested in this subject.

COMPLETING FORMS

7h. Complete forms accurately and thoroughly.

Forms are an important source of information, used when you order magazines, join clubs, or apply for jobs or to schools. Knowing how to complete forms accurately and thoroughly is an important skill that can save you time and lessen certain errors.

STUDENT INFORMATION FORM

Pinewood Junior High School

(No Nicknames)
Name *Zurich, Karen Lee*
Last First Middle

Age *13* Male ____ Female *X*
Date of Birth *6/4/74*
Place of Birth *Tampa, Florida*
City State
Home Address *111 Tice Place*
Lakeland, Florida 33805
Phone# *(813) 858-5040*

Transported by bus Yes *X* No ____
Bus # *309*

Last School Attended *Lowery Elementary*
Where *Tampa, Florida*
City State

Date Withdrew or Graduated *6/85*

With whom do you live *Jean & Phil Zurich*
Relationship *mother & father*

Father
Zurich, Philip Mark
Last First Middle
Address *111 Tice Pl. Lakeland, Fl.*
Place of Employment *Cli Electric*
Occupation *Sales Manager*

Mother
Zurich, Jean Mary
Last First Middle
Address *111 Tice Place*
Place of Employment *Cob Real Estate*
Occupation *Real Estate Consultant*

NAME OF FAMILY DOCTOR *Dr. M.H. Marte*

Model Student Information Form

For any form, supply all the information requested and answer accurately. If you do not have the information requested, do not make up anything; do some research to locate the correct details. Study the sample form on page 220 and notice the type of information that forms usually require.

EXERCISE 12. Completing a Form. Supply the information needed to complete each blank in a form provided by your teacher.

EVALUATING AND REVISING

EVALUATING AND REVISING BUSINESS LETTERS AND FORMS

7i. Evaluate and revise your business letters and forms.

Use the following guidelines to evaluate your business letters and forms for clarity and appearance. Use the revising chart on page 222 to make changes which will improve your work. Be sure to proofread your work, using the Guidelines for Proofreading on page 39. Also proofread again after you recopy your letter or form.

GUIDELINES FOR EVALUATING BUSINESS LETTERS AND FORMS

Content	1. Is the letter's purpose clear? Is all necessary information included?
Order Letter	2. In an order letter, is the letter brief and to the point?
Request Letter	3. In a request letter, is the request made courteously?
Form	4. Is the letter neat? Does the heading give the complete address and the full date? Is the inside address accurate, complete, and properly spaced? Is the salutation appropriate? Are the first lines of the body and other paragraphs

	indented? Is the closing appropriate? Is the form correct, with each of the parts correctly placed and punctuated?
Style	5. Is block style used correctly in the letter?
Envelope	6. Is the address on the envelope accurate, complete, correctly placed, and identical to the inside address? Has the letter been folded to fit the envelope? Is the return address on the envelope?
Forms	7. Is all the requested information supplied? Is it accurate?

REVISING SOCIAL LETTERS, BUSINESS LETTERS, AND FORMS

PROBLEM	TECHNIQUE	REVISION
The content is not clear, or information is missing.	Add	Add details that make your message clear. Add a concluding sentence that sums up the letter. Add details that answer questions or provide requested information.
The order of ideas doesn't make sense.	Reorder	Rearrange sentences and paragraphs in a logical order that makes your point clear.
The letter or form looks messy.	Replace	Rewrite or retype the letter or form so that there are no messy corrections.
The heading or inside address is not complete, or is incorrectly placed.	Add/Reorder	Add missing details about addresses or the date. Move heading or address to the correct position.
The salutation or closing doesn't sound right.	Replace	Use a salutation or closing that fits the purpose of the letter and the receiver.

PROBLEM	TECHNIQUE	REVISION
The body is not indented correctly.	Replace	Indent all paragraphs the same way.
The address on the envelope is incomplete.	Add	Add the return address and ZIP code numbers. Add missing items to the address.

CHAPTER 7 WRITING REVIEW 1

Writing a Friendly Letter. Write the letter for one of the following situations, or for a situation of your own. Evaluate, revise, and proofread your draft.

1. You are a 4-H Club member. At a recent convention you made friends with another 4-H member. Write a letter to your new friend, telling about club activities and your exhibit for the 4-H Club county fair.
2. You have been elected secretary of your club. Write to a friend or relative, describing the club, its purpose, and its members.
3. Write to an older brother or sister at college or an out-of-town relative. Tell about your own progress at school, and ask questions about that person's life.

CHAPTER 7 WRITING REVIEW 2

Writing Business Letters. Write a letter for each of the following situations. Evaluate, revise, and proofread your letters, and address an envelope for each.

1. Write an order letter to Travis Novelty Company, 18 Meadow Street, St. Louis, Missouri 63128, for the following merchan-

dise: 2 giant balloons, at $.85 each; 18 pencils, with the name "Pat" printed in silver, at $.35 each; and 1 box of birthday candles, at $1.35. You are enclosing a money order to cover the total cost.

2. Write a request letter asking for the summer schedule of plays at the Beacon Summer Theater, Portsmouth, Rhode Island 02871; inform the theater that you represent a group and need information on group ticket rates.

☞ **NOTE** The United States Postal Service recommends using two-letter codes for states, the District of Columbia, and Puerto Rico. The service also recommends using nine-digit ZIP codes. When you use these codes, the address should look like this:

EXAMPLE Ms. Linda Ramos
6 Northside Dr.
St. Joseph, MO 64506–1212

The two-letter code is in capital letters and is never followed by a period. The following is a list of two-letter codes for states, the District of Columbia, and Puerto Rico.

Alabama AL
Alaska AK
Arizona AZ
Arkansas AR
California CA
Colorado CO
Connecticut CT
Delaware DE
District of Columbia DC
Florida FL
Georgia GA
Hawaii HI
Idaho ID
Illinois IL
Indiana IN
Iowa IA
Kansas KS
Kentucky KY
Louisiana LA
Maine ME
Maryland MD
Massachusetts MA
Michigan MI
Minnesota MN
Mississippi MS
Missouri MO
Montana MT
Nebraska NE

Nevada NV
New Hampshire NH
New Jersey NJ
New Mexico NM
New York NY
North Carolina NC
North Dakota ND
Ohio OH
Oklahoma OK
Oregon OR
Pennsylania PA
Puerto Rico PR
Rhode Island RI
South Carolina SC
South Dakota SD
Tennessee TN
Texas TX
Utah UT
Vermont VT
Virginia VA
Washington WA
West Virginia WV
Wisconsin WI
Wyoming WY

PICTURE THE POSSIBILITIES: IDEAS FOR WRITING

Pictures can bring back memories, awaken strong feelings, and spark the imagination. In this section you will learn how to use pictures to discover ideas for writing.

262
261

Probing the Picture

One way to use this picture would be to write a **dialogue** between the two girls. To create an interesting situation, you could brainstorm to develop questions such as *Who are the girls? How old are they? What part of the country do they live in? Why are they in the arena? Do the girls own the horses? Do they live on farms, or are they from the city? Why is the girl on the left smiling?* Your answers to these questions would help you create lively, natural-sounding conversation.

A second way to use the picture would be to write a **story**. If you have ever ridden a horse, you could brainstorm to discover a personal experience to write about. If not, you could use the *5 W-How?* questions to make up a story in which the girls are the main characters. For example, *What problem do the girls face? Where and when does the action take place? Who else takes part in or witnesses the events? How is the problem worked out?* Using your imagination to answer these questions would help you develop a plan for your story.

Writing Activities

Using the steps of the writing process, complete one of the following activities.

- Create a situation and write a short dialogue that shows the personalities of the girls in the picture.
- Use the picture to write either a personal experience narrative or a made–up story.

PURPLE
P
U
PURPLE
R
P

Probing the Pictures

This combination of pictures could serve as the basis for an **expository** paragraph of comparison or contrast. One approach would be to study both pictures carefully in order to develop a list of details showing how the scenes are similar and how they are different. To do this, you could make a chart with two columns at the top, one labeled "Similar" and the other labeled "Different." Then you could list the features of the pictures (rides, hair styles, clothing, etc.) down the left side of the chart. Once you had filled in the chart, you could decide whether to use comparison, contrast, or both. Another approach would be to use library sources to find out what free-time activities young people enjoyed in the 1900's and compare or contrast them with the ones you and your friends enjoy.

You could instead use the picture to write a **persuasive** paragraph. To find possible debatable issues, you could brainstorm on the subject "rides," developing questions such as *Should children under twelve be forbidden to go on certain rides without an adult? Should people who do not follow safety precautions on rides be required to leave the grounds? Should people be required to wear shoulder harnesses on certain rides? Should local inspectors make sure that rides are safe before the public is allowed to use them?*

Writing Activities

Using the steps of the writing process, complete one of the following activities.

- Write an expository paragraph comparing or contrasting the pictures.
- Write a persuasive paragraph on one of the issues suggested above or on another issue the pictures suggest.

PARK ON
SOUTH

Probing the Picture

You could use this picture to write a **descriptive** paragraph. To create a main impression, you could focus on the picture's strongest features: the detailed circular pattern within the triangle and the reflection of light from the web's strands. You could instead imagine yourself observing the web in person and gather concrete and sensory details by asking questions such as *What other patterns do I see in the web? In the surrounding branches? What odors do I smell in this part of the woods? How does the web feel against my skin when I accidentally brush against it?*

Another possibility would be to use the picture to write an **expository** composition. You could begin by dividing the subject "spiders" into smaller parts to find possible topics. Then you could use the *point-of-view questions* to gather information from library sources. For the topic "tarantula," for example, you might ask questions such as *What other names are these spiders known by? Where do they live? What do they eat? How are they like other kinds of spiders? How are they different?* For the topic "spider webs," you might ask, *Do all spiders build webs? What function does a spider web serve? What material is it made of? What are the features (size, shape, strength, etc.) of a spider web?*

Writing Activities

Using the steps of the writing process, complete one of the following activities.

- Write a paragraph describing the picture.
- Write an expository composition on a topic you find by dividing the subject "spiders" into smaller parts.

Probing Pictures to Discover Writing Ideas

The following questions will help you use any picture to discover ideas for writing.

1. What about this picture do I find most interesting? What idea does it suggest?
2. For what purpose could I use this idea?
3. What are the picture's strongest features? How could I use those features to achieve my purpose?
4. Would using the *5 W-How?* questions help me gather information to use?
5. What might have happened just before or just after the picture was taken? What might the person(s) have said?
6. What main impression do I get from this picture?
7. What concrete and sensory details do I observe as I study the picture? What details do I imagine when I think of myself as being in the scene?
8. Could I explain how to make or do what the picture shows?
9. Could I give information about what the picture shows by telling who or what the subject is, what its history is, or how it is similar to and different from others of the same kind?
10. What debatable issues does the picture suggest to me?

On Your Own

Write a paper for your classmates on any of the pictures you have not written about. You may choose the form (paragraph, report, story, letter-to-the-editor) and the purpose (to tell a story, to describe, to explain or inform, or to persuade). Follow the steps of the writing process.

PART TWO

COMPOSITION: Writing and Revising Sentences

NO VEHICLES
ALLOWED

CHAPTER 8

Writing Complete Sentences

SENTENCE FRAGMENTS AND RUN-ON SENTENCES

When you speak, you signal the end of a sentence by making your voice rise or fall and by pausing. When you write, the signals you use are end marks: periods, question marks, and exclamation points. If you use these marks incorrectly, you give your reader the wrong signals. You can eliminate many punctuation problems by reading aloud what you have written, listening for the signals your voice gives. In this chapter you will learn to identify and avoid two frequent errors that occur in written composition: the *sentence fragment* and the *run-on sentence*.

FRAGMENTS

A sentence expresses a complete thought. When only a part of a sentence is punctuated as though it were a complete sentence, the resulting error is a *sentence fragment*. A fragment often belongs with the sentence that precedes it.

8a. A *fragment* is a separated sentence part that does not express a complete thought.

To decide whether or not a group of words is a sentence, ask yourself these two questions: (1) Does it have a verb and its subject? (2) Does it express a complete thought? If the answer to either question is "no," the group of words is not a sentence but a sentence fragment.

Each of the following examples contains a sentence and a fragment, which is printed in italics.

> The newspaper staff worked late. *Putting out a special edition.* [The fragment contains no main verb or subject.]
>
> We look forward to meeting Ms. Cox. *Our new teacher.* [The fragment contains no verb or subject.]
>
> *As the horses neared the gate.* The excitement increased. [The fragment contains a verb and a subject, but it does not express a complete thought. It leaves the reader wondering what happened *as the horses neared the gate.*]

Since these fragments belong with the sentences they precede or follow, you can correct them by joining them to the sentences.

> The newspaper staff worked late **putting out a special edition.**
>
> We looked forward to meeting Ms. Cox, **our new teacher.**
>
> **As the horses neared the gate,** the excitement increased.

EXERCISE 1. Identifying Sentences and Fragments; Correcting Fragments. Seven of the italicized groups of words that follow are fragments, while three are complete sentences. Indicate a complete sentence by placing a *C* after the proper number. Correct each fragment by writing the entire item and making the fragment part of the sentence.

EXAMPLES
1. Dolphins are intelligent animals. *That are being closely studied today.*
1. *Dolphins are intelligent animals that are being closely studied today.*
2. The study of this aquatic mammal has already shown surprising results. *The dolphin has been trained as a diver's seagoing partner.*
2. *C*

1. The man who has done the most research on the dolphin is Dr. John C. Lilly. *Who is attempting to devise a method of communication between humans and dolphins.*
2. *By putting a partially paralyzed dolphin into a tank with other dolphins.* Dr. Lilly discovered the dolphin's distress call.
3. The dolphin emitted its distress call. *When it began to sink.*
4. It was immediately assisted by two other dolphins. *They lifted it to the surface for air.*
5. Dolphins usually stay in groups. *Helping each other out in times of trouble.*
6. A baby dolphin is looked after by two adults. *Its mother and an assistant mother serve as nurses.*
7. Even a deadly shark is no match for two angry mother dolphins. *Striking at their foe with their beaklike noses.*
8. *In addition to having unusual ability to mimic the human voice.* The dolphin is of extreme interest because of its streamlined body and its amazing built-in sonar system.
9. Nuclear-powered submarines have been designed in the same general shape as the dolphin. *It is the most perfectly streamlined animal known.*
10. The dolphin possesses a built-in sonar apparatus. *Which is as accurate as sonar equipment used by scientists.*

Three Kinds of Fragments

The *subordinate clause,* the *verbal phrase,* and the *appositive phrase* are three common kinds of fragments.

The Subordinate Clause

8b. A subordinate clause must not be written as a sentence.

A subordinate clause is a group of words that contains a verb and its subject but does not express a complete thought (see page 384). It cannot stand by itself but must always be attached to an independent clause (a group of words that contains a subject, a verb and does express a complete thought). *As she turned the corner* is a subordinate clause. If you read this word group aloud, you will hear at once that it is not a complete sentence. Read the following subordinate clauses aloud. Do they sound like complete sentences? Then notice the difference when they are joined to independent clauses.

When it rains during a football game [What happens then?]

Who directed us to our seats [If a question is intended, the word group is a sentence. If not, it is a fragment.]

When it rains during a football game, the stadium looks like a patchwork quilt of umbrellas.

We found an usher, **who directed us to our seats.**

Relative pronouns (*who, whom, whose, which, that*) or subordinating conjunctions (see the list on page 392) introduce subordinate clauses. These are very important words, for they can change a sentence into a fragment.

SENTENCE It rains during a football game.
FRAGMENT **When** it rains during a football game.
SENTENCE An usher directed us to our seats.
FRAGMENT An usher **who** directed us to our seats.

EXERCISE 2. Correcting Sentence Fragments. The following paragraphs contain ten fragments. Write the paragraphs, attaching the fragments to the related independent clauses.

Fifteen very young dinosaurs were waiting in a nest. While their mother went looking for food. Before the adult dinosaur could return. Disaster struck. The small prehistoric creatures all perished. When a volcano buried the nest in debris.

Scientists recently uncovered the fossils of these small dinosaurs. Which lived 70 million years ago. After they studied the remaining fragments of bones. Scientists reconstructed the appearance of the dinosaurs. The name given to these extinct lizards was *hadrosaur*. Which means "duck-billed lizard." Adult hadrosaurs were plant eaters. That could scoop up vegetation from watery swamps.

The discovery of these fossils was important. Because it shed light on one of the mysteries about dinosaurs. Before this recent discovery was made. Scientists debated whether dinosaurs were coldblooded or warmblooded. Fossil evidence shows these tiny hadrosaurs were living in a nest. They were likely warmblooded. Because few coldblooded animals are fed by their parents or protected in nests.

EXERCISE 3. Correcting Sentence Fragments. Make each of the following fragments into a complete sentence by adding an independent clause. Write each sentence on your paper, using punctuation and capital letters correctly.

EXAMPLE 1. Because I missed the bus by seconds.
1. *I was twenty minutes late to school because I missed the bus by seconds.*

1. Who broke her glasses.
2. That are working on a clean-up campaign for the school.
3. If you want to own a pet.
4. Because the library closes at six o'clock.
5. Whom I met at your party.

The Verbal Phrase

8c. A verbal phrase must not be written as a sentence.

A verbal is a word that is formed from a verb but that is used as another part of speech. Present participles and gerunds are verbals that usually end in *-ing* (*coming, working, being*). Past participles are verbals that usually end in *-d, -ed, -t, -n,* or *-en* (*looked, slept, broken*). Infinitives are verbals that usually consist of *to* plus the verb (*to go, to play*).

A verbal phrase is a phrase (group of words working together as a part of speech) containing a verbal. It is often mistaken for a sentence because the verbal is often mistaken for a main verb. However, a phrase does not have both a subject and a verb and, therefore, cannot express a complete thought. By itself, a verbal phrase is a fragment.

FRAGMENTS Lying lazily on the beach
Built of bamboo
Waiting at the doctor's office
To see a movie

Like subordinate clauses, verbals depend on independent clauses to make their meaning complete.

SENTENCES **Lying lazily on the beach,** I fell asleep.
A house **built of bamboo** cannot withstand a heavy wind.
Waiting at the doctor's office is difficult for me.
They wanted **to see a movie.**

EXERCISE 4. Correcting Sentence Fragments. The following paragraphs contain ten verbal phrases incorrectly used as sentences. Revise the paragraphs, joining the fragments to the proper independent clauses.

Alice's Adventures in Wonderland is a literary classic. Read by college students as well as elementary-school students. Every child enjoys this story. Missing some of the fun but laughing at many of the comic incidents. When children grow up, they read the story again. Finding more humor in it.

In one of the most famous episodes in the book, Alice finds herself at an unusual tea party. Given by the Hatter. Being very lazy. The Hatter and his companions, the March Hare and the Dormouse, have allowed dirty dishes to pile up all over. The Dormouse tells a long story. Falling asleep in the middle. The March Hare offers Alice wine. Alice is told that there is no wine. After accepting the offer. For a while the three creatures ask her riddles. Having no answers. Then they ignore her. Carrying on a ridiculous conversation among themselves. Finally, Alice manages to escape. Thoroughly exhausted.

The Appositive Phrase

8d. An appositive phrase must not be written as a sentence.

An appositive identifies or explains the noun or pronoun it follows (see pages 375–76). An appositive phrase is an appositive with its modifiers. Neither an appositive nor an appositive phrase can stand alone; it should be set off from the rest of the sentence by a comma or commas.

FRAGMENT The eighteen sailors rowed 3,618 miles to Timor. *An island near Java.*

SENTENCE The eighteen sailors rowed 3,618 miles to Timor, **an island near Java.** [*An island near Java* is an appositive phrase explaining *Timor* and should be joined to the preceding sentence.]

FRAGMENT We had dinner at the Banana Tree. *A restaurant near Key West.*

SENTENCE We had dinner at the Banana Tree, **a restaurant near Key West.** [*A restaurant near Key West* is an appositive phrase explaining *Banana Tree.*]

EXERCISE 5. Correcting Sentence Fragments. Revise the following items, attaching the appositive phrases to the independent clauses from which they have been separated. Change punctuation and capital letters wherever necessary. Some of the appositive phrases belong in the middle of sentences.

1. Rachel and I enjoy playing *Parcheesi.* A game from India.
2. We saw two movies. A science fiction thriller and a western.
3. In 1818 Mary Wollstonecraft Shelley wrote *Frankenstein.* The famous horror novel.
4. The Battle of Marathon was won by the Greeks. One of the most famous battles in the history of the world.
5. Coretta King has become as well known as her husband for the advocacy of civil rights. The widow of Dr. Martin Luther King, Jr.

REVIEW EXERCISE A. Correcting Fragments. Revise the following items, eliminating fragments by attaching them to independent clauses.

1. As I was driving home. I saw a turtle on the highway.
2. It had been rolled over on its back by a car. While trying to cross the road.
3. Now it was lying there in the middle of the highway. Helplessly moving its feet back and forth.
4. Because I remembered that a turtle cannot get off its back on a smooth surface. I stopped the car and picked the animal up.
5. It immediately drew its feet and head under its shell. So that I could see nothing more than two eyes. Staring at me from inside the shell.
6. The turtle was a box turtle. A very shy land dweller.
7. I took it to Tall Oaks. My parents' cottage in the mountains. Because I wanted to observe it for a while.
8. Arriving there, I put the turtle down on a rug. Which covers most of the living room floor.
9. The turtle slowly began to stick its feet and head out from its shell. After being still for almost ten minutes.
10. As soon as it felt safe, it crawled very awkwardly but quickly across the rug. Heading for a corner of the room.

RUN-ON SENTENCES

Another common writing fault is the *run-on sentence.* Run-on sentences occur when the writer fails to recognize the end of a sentence and runs on into the next sentence without proper punctuation or, sometimes, without any punctuation at all.

8e. A *run-on sentence* consists of two or more sentences separated only by a comma or by no mark of punctuation.

RUN-ON Romare Bearden is a prominent artist his collage is in the museum.

CORRECTED Romare Bearden is a prominent artist**. H**is collage is in the museum.

RUN-ON Lee Trevino was playing in the golf tournament, I hoped I could go.

CORRECTED Lee Trevino was playing in the golf tournament**.** **I** hoped I could go.

A comma marks a pause in a sentence, not the end of the sentence, and thus should not be used between two sentences.

EXERCISE 6. Revising Run-on Sentences. Revise the following run-ons. Number your paper 1–10. After the proper number, write the last word in the first sentence and place a period after it; then write the first word of the next sentence, beginning it with a capital letter.

EXAMPLE 1. The Virgin Islands' weather is perfect, daytime temperatures are in the 80's year round.
1. *perfect. Daytime*

1. In nineteenth-century England there were two types of English pepper moths one type was all black, and the other had gray and white speckles.
2. The black variety was extremely rare, most people had only seen speckled pepper moths.
3. The moths lived on the bark of surrounding trees, most trees in England had a gray moss covering them.
4. The speckled moths blended into this background the birds that ate pepper moths could not see them against the moss.
5. The black moths could be easily seen they were frequently killed by birds.
6. The Industrial Revolution in England produced many factories, when the smoke and soot created by the factories filled the air, it covered the neighboring trees.
7. The amount of soot, two tons per square mile, was enough to color the trees black, the speckled moths could now be easily seen by birds searching for food.
8. The black moths blended into the background of the black trees, the birds began to dine on the speckled variety.
9. Within fifty years, the black variety outnumbered the speckled moths 99 to 1, the advantage of a particular color for protection had completely reversed.

10. Other animals use protective coloration certain kinds of fish have the same color as their surroundings and can blend with the background to escape enemies.

EXERCISE 7. Revising Run-on Sentences. Each of the following passages contains several run-on sentences. You will find the passages hard to read because run-on sentences interfere with the clear expression of ideas. After you have decided where each sentence should end, write the last word of each complete sentence on your paper. Place the appropriate end mark after the word; then write the first word of the next sentence, beginning it with a capital letter.

EXAMPLE 1. *Jest* once had a different meaning than it does today, in medieval times the English used the word to refer to a brave act or the story of such a deed, by the sixteenth century it meant "to jeer or mock" now, of course, a *jest* is a joke.

1. *today. In*
deed. By
mock." Now

1. Our word *humor* has an interesting history, it comes from the Latin word for liquid, in the Middle Ages people believed that four liquids in the body made up one's character, thus a person with too much of one humor might be quite odd or eccentric.
2. Our word *paper* comes from the French word *papier,* this word can be traced back to the Greek *papyros,* which is the name of an Egyptian plant, part of this plant was sliced into strips and then soaked in water, finally, it was pressed and pasted into a writing material that was used by the Egyptians, Greeks, and Romans.
3. The comma can be traced back to the Greek language, our word *comma* comes from the Greek word *komma,* which means "a piece cut off" when you use a comma, you cut off an expression from the rest of the sentence.
4. The word *rigmarole* came from a group of documents called *ragman roll* written in 1291, Scottish lords signed these

documents to prove their loyalty to King Edward I of England since many of the documents were so full of signatures that they were confusing and hard to read, the word *rigmarole* came to mean "a series of confused or foolish statements."

5. Have you ever wondered about the origin of the word *sandwich*, it came into use during the eighteenth century, John Montagu, the Earl of Sandwich, was addicted to gambling, so addicted that he often would not stop for his meals, during one of his twenty-four-hour gambling sessions, he instructed someone to bring him slices of bread with roast beef inserted between them because the Earl of Sandwich did not want to stop gambling long enough to go to dinner, the world gained the sandwich.

REVIEW EXERCISE B. Identifying Sentences, Fragments, and Run-ons. Some of the following expressions are sentences. Others are fragments or run-ons. Number your paper 1–20. After the proper number, write *S* (sentence), *F* (fragment), or *R* (run-on). Be prepared to tell how you would correct the fragments and run-ons.

1. Medusa and her two sisters were three horrible monsters who had at one time been beautiful women.
2. The most beautiful of the three, Medusa, was very proud, she boasted that she was even more beautiful than the goddess Athena.
3. Because of her pride, she and her two sisters were turned into monsters.
4. Who had hissing serpents for hair.
5. No one dared look upon Medusa and her sisters.
6. Because anyone who did turned to stone.
7. Lying all about them were stones that had once been men.
8. Medusa and her two sisters menaced the land for years finally they were challenged by Perseus.
9. A young, handsome warrior.
10. Having been given magic weapons by the gods.

11. Perseus set out to kill Medusa.
12. The only mortal one of the three sisters.
13. When he approached the area in which the monsters lived.
14. Perseus put on a magic cap that made him invisible, he held up a shield that had been given to him by Athena.
15. Studying the reflection of Medusa and her sisters in his shield.
16. Perseus slowly approached the monsters.
17. Luckily, they were sleeping.
18. Still using the shield as a mirror, he cut off Medusa's head with a single stroke he put the head into a special pouch.
19. Which had also been given to him by Athena.
20. The other sisters awoke but could not see him, therefore he escaped with the head of Medusa.

REVIEW EXERCISE C. Revising Fragments and Run-ons in Your Own Writing. Pretend that you are writing to a person who has never seen a comic strip. Write a paragraph in which you describe one of the main characters in your favorite comic strip. After you have finished writing the paragraph, read your sentences aloud, one by one, to be sure that you have not carelessly written a fragment or a run-on. Make any necessary corrections.

CHAPTER 9

Writing Effective Sentences

SENTENCE COMBINING AND REVISING

As your writing assignments become more demanding, you should develop the habit of writing at least two drafts of a composition. In the first draft, express what you have to say. In the revised draft, concentrate on writing clearly and on eliminating faults in style. Watch especially for groups of choppy, abrupt sentences and for rambling sentences held together by a string of conjunctions. Such sentences, while occasionally effective, become tiresome if used too often. This chapter will show how to recognize such poorly written sentences and how to revise them.

CORRECTING A CHOPPY STYLE BY COMBINING SENTENCES

Short sentences are often effective in a composition, but a long series of short sentences tends to irritate readers. They slow the reader down and make it difficult to focus on what is being said. Such choppy sentences are often similar in construction and thus are monotonous in their effect. The following passage of choppy sentences would irritate most readers.

> Victor visited Williamsburg, Virginia. Marsha also went. The visit took place during the summer. They both visited for the first time. They toured the buildings together. Marsha was studying the antiques collection. Victor was examining the architecture. They began to share each other's interest. The architecture was from the colonial period. The antiques were from the colonial period.

By combining sentences that are closely related, the passage could be revised as follows:

> During the summer, Victor and Marsha visited Williamsburg, Virginia, for the first time. As they toured the buildings together, Marsha was studying the antiques collection, but Victor was examining the architecture. They began to share each other's interest because both the architecture and the antiques were from the colonial period.

Several methods have been used in revising the passage. For example, the first four sentences in the original version have been combined into one sentence containing a compound subject and two prepositional phrases. You should be familiar with ways to combine short, related sentences.

9a. Combine short, related sentences by inserting adjectives, adverbs, or prepositional phrases.[1]

WEAK At half time, the coach gave the players confidence in themselves.
The players had been discouraged.

BETTER At half time, the coach gave the discouraged players confidence in themselves. [The adjective *discouraged* in the second sentence is inserted into the first sentence.]

WEAK In the second half, the team improved. They improved rapidly.

BETTER In the second half, the team improved rapidly. [The adverb *rapidly* in the second sentence is inserted into the first sentence.]

[1] If you need to review adjectives, adverbs, and prepositional phrases, see Chapters 11 and 12.

WEAK The solar-energy panels were installed yesterday.
They are on the garage roof.

BETTER The solar-energy panels were installed yesterday on the garage roof. [The prepositional phrase *on the garage roof* in the second sentence is inserted into the first sentence.]

When you join short sentences by inserting adjectives, adverbs, or prepositional phrases, be sure the new sentence reads smoothly. (Review the rule concerning commas separating adjectives on page 533.)

EXERCISE 1. Combining Sentences by Inserting Adjectives, Adverbs, or Prepositional Phrases. Combine each group of short, related sentences into one sentence by inserting adjectives, adverbs, or prepositional phrases. There may be more than one correct way to combine the sentences. Add commas where they are necessary.

EXAMPLE 1. The bird sings in the cage.
The bird is yellow.
It sings sweetly.
The cage is by the window.
1. *The yellow bird sings sweetly in the cage by the window.*

1. Conservation laws protect wildlife.
   The laws are strong.
   They protect wildlife inside state parks.
2. We will make the decorations.
   We will do this shortly.
   The decorations are for Flag Day.
3. Miguel wrote his letter.
   He wrote it on Saturday.
   It was a letter to the mayor.
4. Poland has one of the tallest structures.
   It is one of the tallest structures on earth.
   Poland is in northeastern Europe.

5. The two parties argued their cases.
   The parties were angry.
   They argued in front of the judge.

9b. Combine closely related sentences by using participial phrases.

A participle is a verb form that acts as an adjective, modifying a noun or a pronoun. A participial phrase (see page 363) is a group of related words that contains a participle. In the following examples, all the words in boldfaced type are part of the participial phrase.

EXAMPLES **Grinning from ear to ear,** Michelle trotted off the stage. [*Grinning* is a present participle.]

Battered by the high seas, the small ship limped into port. [*Battered* is a past participle.]

Two closely related sentences can be combined by making one of the sentences a participial phrase.

EXAMPLE The librarian answered our question.
He was whispering in low tones.

Whispering in low tones, the librarian answered our question.

A participial phrase must be placed close to the noun or pronoun it modifies. Otherwise, the phrase may confuse the reader.

MISPLACED Caught in the chicken coop, the farmer cornered the fox.

IMPROVED The farmer cornered the fox caught in the chicken coop.

> ☞ **NOTE** Use a comma after a participial phrase that begins a sentence.

EXAMPLE Embarrassed by our loss, our team sat in the locker room.

EXERCISE 2. Combining Sentences by Using a Participial Phrase. Combine each of the following groups of sentences into one sentence by using a participial phrase. Insert the participial phrase in the correct place and add commas where they are necessary.

EXAMPLE 1. The class worked quickly.
They divided up the job.
1. *Dividing up the job, the class worked quickly.* or *Working quickly, the class divided up the job.*

1. The referee signaled a score.
   She was standing beneath the basket.
2. The secretary called a meeting.
   He was troubled by the press reports.
3. The audience applauded loudly.
   They were interrupting the singer.
4. The town is safe and secure.
   It nestles beneath two mountains.
5. I was puzzled by the rules of the game.
   I decided not to play.

9c. Combine short, related sentences by using appositive phrases.

Appositive phrases (see page 376) are useful for explaining or identifying nouns or pronouns. The following sentence contains an appositive phrase in boldfaced type.

EXAMPLE At the movie theater I saw Mrs. Jacovina, **our next-door neighbor.**

Two related sentences can be combined by using an appositive phrase.

TWO SENTENCES Marlene won the competition.
She is an excellent tennis player.
ONE SENTENCE Marlene, an excellent tennis player, won the competition.

EXERCISE 3. Combining Sentences by Using an Appositive Phrase. Combine each group of sentences by using an appositive phrase. Place the phrase next to the noun or pronoun it explains or modifies. Put commas at the beginning and end of each appositive phrase to set it off from the rest of the sentence.

EXAMPLE 1. Karen bought me a sweater.
She is my good friend.
1. *Karen, my good friend, bought me a sweater.*

1. Lena Jackson lived in Japan before moving here.
   She is our new doctor.
2. I finally spoke to Mr. Powell.
   He is the store manager.
3. Joan made the lasagna.
   It was the most popular dish at the picnic.
4. Bob was at the last baseball game.
   He is the sportswriter for our newspaper.
5. *Carnival of Autumn* is in the Museum of Fine Arts in Boston.
   It is a painting by Marsden Hartley.

Another method of combining short, related sentences is to join the subjects to make a compound subject or to join the verbs to make a compound verb.

9d. Combine short, related sentences by using compound subjects.

A compound subject (see page 278) consists of two or more simple subjects joined by a conjunction and having the same verb.

EXAMPLE This **table** and that **chair** are ready for the movers.

Often two short sentences may contain similar verbs but different subjects.

EXAMPLE The radio report predicted rain.
The television news also predicted it.

You can combine these short sentences by writing a single sentence with a compound subject.

EXAMPLE **Both the radio report and the television news** predicted rain.

Words that connect (called *conjunctions*) a compound subject are *and, or, both—and, either—or,* and *neither—nor.* The choice of the conjunction depends on the meaning of the sentence.

Compound subjects must agree with the verb in the sentence.

EXAMPLES Paul has missed the bus.
His sister has missed it also.

Paul **and** his sister have missed the bus. [Subjects joined by *and* or *both—and* take a plural verb.]

An almanac gives the answer.
An atlas gives the answer.

Either an almanac **or** an atlas gives the answer. [Singular subjects joined by *or, either—or,* or *neither—nor* take a singular verb.]

EXERCISE 4. Combining Sentences by Using a Compound Subject. Combine each pair of sentences by writing one sentence with a compound subject. Be sure the subject and the verb agree in number.

EXAMPLE 1. Arlene will not be at the party tomorrow.
Margery will not be there either.
1. *Neither Arlene nor Margery will be at the party tomorrow.*

1. Rugby is played in England.
Soccer is played there also.
2. My sister went to the zoo.
I went there with her.
3. The sun is a reliable source of energy.
Coal is another reliable source.
4. Engineering might be Teng's career choice.
Medicine might be his career choice instead.
5. Cheating is not allowed in class.
Whispering is not allowed either.

9e. Combine short, related sentences by using compound verbs.

A compound verb (see page 278) consists of two or more verbs that have the same subject and are joined by a connecting word. In the following example, the compound verb is printed in boldface.

EXAMPLE The senator **voted** for the conservation law but **lost** the election.

You can combine two sentences by writing one sentence with a compound verb.

EXAMPLE He backed the car down the driveway.
He lurched to a stop in the street.

He **backed** the car down the driveway and **lurched** to a stop in the street.

The connecting words used most frequently to join compound verbs are *and, but, or, either—or, neither—nor,* and *both—and.* The choice of the conjunction (or connecting word) depends on the sentence meaning.

EXERCISE 5. Combining Sentences by Using a Compound Verb. Combine each pair of short sentences into a single sentence with one subject and a compound verb. Use appropriate connecting words to clearly express the meaning.

EXAMPLE 1. In February Teresa visited her grandparents in Puerto Rico.
She also toured Everglades Park in Florida.

1. *In February Teresa both visited her grandparents in Puerto Rico and toured Everglades Park in Florida.*

1. He repaired the bicycle yesterday.
He raced with it today.
2. I had heard of polecats.
I had never seen one before.
3. The guard did not hear the car approaching.
She was taken completely by surprise.

4. The train was late leaving the station.
   It still arrived on time.
5. Mr. Verris casually crossed the hall.
   He entered the room and quietly handed out the tests.

REVIEW EXERCISE A. Revising a Passage by Combining Sentences. The following passage contains several short, related sentences. Revise the passage, combining the sentences by the methods you have learned thus far. Do not change the meaning of the original. Add commas where they are necessary.

The Majestic River runs between the mountains. It is a deep river. It runs swiftly. The mountains are high. Lush, green vegetation crowds the river's shores. The vegetation also grows up the mountain slopes. Campers fish in the river's pools. Day hikers also fish there. The pools are clear. The pools are beneath the rapids. Canoes can navigate the river. Rafts can also do this. The rafts are rubber. Canoes and rafts can navigate the river from High Falls to Bolt's Landing.

9f. Combine short, related sentences by making them into a compound sentence.

A compound sentence is really two or more simple sentences joined together. When simple sentences are joined together in a compound sentence, they are called independent clauses. (See pages 404–406 for more information on independent clauses and compound sentences.) The following sentence has two independent clauses.

EXAMPLE Tractor drivers [S] bulldozed [V] a barrier around the forest fire, and helicopter crews [S] drenched [V] the fire with chemicals.

Two simple sentences closely related in meaning may be joined into one compound sentence.

EXAMPLE The quarterback threw a long pass.
A defender intercepted the ball.

The quarterback threw a long pass, but a defender intercepted the ball.

The conjunctions (connecting words) used to join the parts of a compound sentence are usually *and, but, or,* or *nor.* The choice of the conjunction depends on the meaning of the sentence.

Be sure that the ideas you connect in the compound sentence are closely related and equal in importance. If you attempt to correct a choppy passage by connecting unrelated ideas, the result will be even worse than the original choppy version.

UNRELATED IDEAS	I read the entire television schedule. I like to watch news documentaries.
RELATED IDEAS	I read the entire television schedule. I could not find even one interesting program.
UNEQUAL IDEAS	Lynn was elected class president. Cara didn't vote.
EQUAL IDEAS	Lynn was elected class president. Peter became secretary.

☞ **NOTE** Remember to put a comma before *and, but, or,* and *nor* when they join independent clauses (see page 534).

EXAMPLE Alice brought her new water skis, and Tina borrowed her parents' ski boat.

EXERCISE 6. Combining Sentences by Making Them into a Compound Sentence. Most of the following items consist of two or more closely related ideas. Combine these ideas into a single compound sentence, using *and, but,* or *or* as the connecting word. Add commas where they are necessary. A few items contain unrelated or unequal ideas. In such cases, write *U* after the proper number on your paper to show that the ideas are better expressed in two separate sentences.

1. Other nations use the metric system.
   The United States has decided to use the same system.

2. International trade depends on a uniform system of weights and measures.
   The United States leads the world in scientific research.
3. The United States is slowly converting to the metric system.
   This process is called metrification.
4. We can resist the change in systems until the last possible moment.
   We can learn to use the metric system now.
5. The metric system is actually very easy to use.
   A decimeter is one tenth of a meter.
6. Metric weights are based on the kilogram.
   Metric lengths use the meter as the basic unit.
7. Many citizens of the United States still use the old system of measurement.
   Many professions and corporations have switched to the metric system.
8. All metric measurements are based on the number 10.
   Some baseball parks measure their distances in meters.
9. Counting by tens is second nature to most people.
   The metric system still seems complicated to many.
10. Metrification will be a difficult process.
    Careful planning will help.

Compound sentences can combine equal items from two separate sentences. When combining unequal ideas, however, it is best to use complex sentences.

9g. Combine short, choppy sentences into a complex sentence. Put one idea into a subordinate clause.

A complex sentence (see page 408) has an independent clause and at least one subordinate clause.

(1) Use an adjective clause to combine sentences.

An adjective clause (see page 386) is a group of words containing a subject and verb that, like an adjective, modifies a noun or a pronoun. In the following example, the adjective clause is in boldfaced type.

EXAMPLE The girl **who just waved to me** is my first cousin. [The adjective clause modifies *girl.*]

Adjective clauses begin with one of the relative pronouns —*who, whom, whose, which,* or *that* (see page 387). Study the following examples of the relative pronoun used in a sentence.

EXAMPLES Mr. Allen praised Tom, **who** had written an excellent paper.
Mr. Bingley gave a slide show, **which** the entire class enjoyed.
The answer **that** she gave was an abrupt "no."

When two sentences are closely related, the second sentence may help to modify a noun, pronoun, or adjective in the first sentence.

EXAMPLE Nora played her favorite record.
I had given it to her. [This sentence modifies *record* in the first sentence.]

You can combine these two sentences by turning the second sentence into an adjective clause and inserting it into the first sentence.

Nora played her favorite record, **which I had given to her.**

> ☞ **NOTE** Use commas to set off adjective clauses that are not essential to the basic meaning of the sentence. Do not use commas with clauses that are essential to the meaning. (See page 536.)

EXAMPLES This is my favorite coin, **which I bought four years ago.** [nonessential clause]
This is the coin **that I told you about.** [essential clause]

EXERCISE 7. Combining Sentences by Using an Adjective Clause. Combine each of the following groups of sentences into a single sentence by putting one of the ideas into an adjective clause. Use commas where they are necessary.

EXAMPLE 1. Wendy Quon won the championship.
She is a great athlete.
1. *Wendy Quon, who is a great athlete, won the championship.*

1. The motion was passed by the Student Council.
   I had stated it.
2. Julie dived in to help Jan.
   Julie is the best swimmer in our crowd.
3. I helped with the campaign of Senator Blake.
   He was the best candidate for the office.
4. "The Tell-Tale Heart" is my favorite story.
   It was written by Edgar Allan Poe.
5. She gave us some advice.
   It hindered more than it helped.

(2) Use an adverb clause to combine sentences.

An adverb clause (see page 390) is a group of words containing a subject and verb that, like an adverb, modifies a verb, an adjective, or an adverb.

EXAMPLE She sings **whenever she is alone.**

Adverb clauses, like adverbs, may tell *how, when, where, why, to what extent,* or *under what condition* an action is done. They begin with a subordinating conjunction. In the example, *whenever* is a subordinating conjunction. Study the following list:

Subordinating Conjunctions

after	before	than	whenever
although	if	unless	where
as	since	until	wherever
because	so that	when	while

Examine these two sentences:

The conductor stopped the orchestra.
The violins were not in tune.

You can combine these two sentences by turning the second sentence into an adverb clause and inserting it into the first sentence.

The conductor stopped the orchestra because the violins were not in tune.

When you combine two short sentences by turning one of them into an adverb clause, be careful to choose the correct subordinating conjunction. A poorly chosen conjunction will show a false or meaningless relationship between clauses. For example, a number of subordinating conjunctions could be used to join the following two sentences, but not all of them would show a relationship that makes sense.

EXAMPLE Mario is industrious.
He receives high grades.
UNCLEAR Unless Mario is industrious, he receives high grades.
CLEAR **Since** Mario is industrious, he receives high grades.

> ☞ **NOTE** A comma is used after an adverb clause placed at the beginning of a sentence.

EXAMPLE Although her head ached, she continued dancing.

EXERCISE 8. Combining Sentences by Using an Adverb Clause. Combine each of the following groups of sentences into a single sentence by putting one idea into an adverb clause. Refer to the subordinating conjunctions on pages 253 and 392.

EXAMPLE 1. Rosa saw the fox near the tree.
She photographed it.
1. *When Rosa saw the fox near the tree, she photographed it.*

1. Her ankle pained her sharply.
   She kept on playing.
2. He saw the truck rolling down the hill toward him.
   He jumped onto the curb.
3. Jane's mother motioned to us.
   We walked across the street.
4. Cathy held the tent up straight.
   Jeannette hammered down the stakes.
5. Norm forgot the time of the party.
   We were late.

REVIEW EXERCISE B. Using Sentence-Combining Methods. Combine each of the following groups of sentences into one smooth, clear sentence by using the sentence-combining methods you have learned. Do not change the meaning of the sentences you combine. Add commas where they are necessary.

1. No one has ever solved the mystery.
   It is the mystery of the ship *Mary Celeste.*
   It set sail in 1872 bound for Europe.
   It set sail from New York.
2. The ship was found.
   It was floating in the Atlantic Ocean.
   It was found without a crew.
3. The crew may have been murdered.
   The crew may have deserted.
   No sign of a struggle was found.
4. A child's toys lay undisturbed.
   They lay on the bed.
   It was the captain's bed.
   The toys suggest that the child left suddenly.
5. People still look for clues.
   These people are curious.
   The clues may explain the crew's disappearance.

REVIEW EXERCISE C. Revising a Paragraph by Eliminating Choppy Sentences. Revise the following paragraph to eliminate choppy sentences, but be careful not to change the meaning of the original paragraph. Use the sentence-combining methods you have learned. Add commas as necessary.

> Robert Frost wrote many poems. Frost grew up in New England. Many of his poems are about the countryside in winter. One poem has been popular with students. It is titled "Stopping by Woods on a Snowy Evening." In this poem a traveler pauses on a journey. The traveler pauses for a moment. The journey is by horse and wagon. The traveler watches the snow. It is falling in the woods. The woods are far from the nearest village. People disagree about the poem's meaning. They enjoy it immensely. It seems to touch on a deep truth about life. It describes a common experience.

CORRECTING A MONOTONOUS STYLE

If you look at the first passage on page 242, you will notice that each sentence in the paragraph begins in the same way, with a subject followed by a verb. In the revised passage, however, each sentence begins differently. The first sentence begins with a prepositional phrase, the second sentence begins with a subordinate clause, and so on. This was done to avoid monotony.

9h. Correct a monotonous style by varying the beginnings of sentences.

Young writers often write a paragraph of sentences all of which begin with the subject. To avoid such monotony, you can revise some sentences to begin with a modifier: an adverb, an adverb clause, a prepositional phrase, or a participial phrase. You will not need to revise them all, however. If all the sentences were changed to begin with an adverb, for example, the passage would be as monotonous as before. Moreover, you should never write an unclear or awkward sentence merely for the sake of variety. If a sentence sounds best with the subject first, you should leave it that way and try to revise some of the sentences near it, if necessary.

(1) Vary sentences by beginning them with adverbs.

EXAMPLES She paid her debts willingly.
Willingly she paid her debts.

She said sorrowfully, "We're leaving."
Sorrowfully she said, "We're leaving."

(2) Vary sentences by beginning them with adverb clauses.[1]

EXAMPLES The pain eased after the tooth was pulled.
After the tooth was pulled, the pain eased.

He was not afraid to fight, although he was small.
Although he was small, he was not afraid to fight.

EXERCISE 9. Beginning Sentences with an Adverb or Adverb Clause. Revise the following sentences by beginning them with either an adverb or an adverb clause.

1. She agreed to his proposal reluctantly.
2. She lived in Mexico before she moved here.
3. Tim was polite although they had angered him.
4. She will wash the car if you wish.
5. She wisely pretended not to hear.

(3) Vary sentences by beginning them with prepositional phrases.[2]

EXAMPLES A portrait of our mother hung on the wall.
On the wall hung a portrait of our mother.

A police officer sat in the car.
In the car sat a police officer.

Sometimes when you move a prepositional phrase, you may want to change the position of the verb also.

EXAMPLE A kettle hung above the fire.
Above the fire hung a kettle.

[1] See pages 390–92 for an explanation of adverb clauses.
[2] See page 354 for an explanation of the prepositional phrase.

(4) Vary sentences by beginning with participial phrases.[1]

A participial phrase is usually separated from the rest of the sentence by a comma.

EXAMPLES The fielder, **leaping up,** caught the ball.
Leaping up, the fielder caught the ball.

They stared at each other in bewilderment, **stunned by the news.**
Stunned by the news, they stared at each other in bewilderment.

(5) Vary sentences by beginning them with infinitive phrases.[2]

EXAMPLES **To get to Homer's Fish Market,** turn left at the next corner.
To stay on the team, you must attend every game.

EXERCISE 10. Writing Sentences with Introductory Phrases. Use the following prepositional and participial phrases to begin sentences of your own.

1. On her day off,
2. Resisting temptation,
3. In shocked surprise,
4. Inside the old valise,
5. Delighted with the new coat,

EXERCISE 11. Beginning Sentences with an Adverb, a Phrase, or a Clause. All of the following sentences begin with the subject. For the sake of variety, revise them with an adverb, a phrase, or a clause at the beginning.

1. Alice practices the piano after she finishes her homework.
2. She sang in her shrill voice to annoy me.
3. The rainmaker, jumping from his chair, smiled with satisfaction as he pointed at the dark clouds massing overhead.
4. The general wore a Medal of Honor around his neck.
5. Her parents said, finally, that she could go hiking on Saturday afternoon if she finished painting the fence.

[1] See page 363 for an explanation of the participial phrase.
[2] See page 371 for an explanation of infinitive phrases.

REVIEW EXERCISE D. Combining Sentences; Varying Sentence Beginnings. Revise choppy and monotonous sentences in the following paragraphs by combining short sentences into longer sentences and by varying the beginnings of sentences. It may not be necessary to revise every sentence. Your aim should be a series of sentences that are clear, show variety, and are pleasing to read.

A lens is different from an ordinary pane of glass. A pane of glass has a flat surface. A lens is curved. Rays of light go through a pane of glass without much change. Rays of light are bent, or refracted, in a lens. This refraction may change both the shape and the size of an image. The curve of the lens determines the size of the image. A concave lens curves inward. It is called a reducing glass. A convex lens curves outward. It is a magnifying glass. Lenses often combine the qualities of a concave and a convex lens. Lenses may be concave on one side and convex on the other. A lens may also have one flat surface. A planoconcave lens is flat on one side and concave on the other, for example.

An optical lens must be made from glass of high quality. It must be manufactured by highly trained experts. Optical glass is first tested for flaws. It is then molded into discs. A disc is first ground roughly, then precisely, to give it the correct shape. It is finally polished with ferric oxide. This substance is called rouge by glassmakers.

Two or more lenses are combined in a microscope so that we can see very small objects. One lens is called the objective. It produces the primary image. The second lens is the eyepiece, or ocular. It magnifies the primary image. A microscope is judged not only by its magnifying power. It is also judged by its resolving power. This is its power to show separation between things that are very close together.

CORRECTING RAMBLING SENTENCES

Sometimes you may try to avoid a choppy style by stringing many short sentences together, using the conjunctions *and, but,* and *so* to join them. Such rambling sentences are just as irritating and monotonous to read as short, choppy sentences. Learn to avoid them in your writing.

9i. Correct rambling sentences by combining ideas and avoiding the overuse of *and, but,* and *so.*

Since rambling sentences are usually choppy sentences joined by conjunctions, the methods of correcting choppy sentences may also be applied to rambling sentences. Some of the clauses can be combined into compound or complex sentences. Study the following rambling sentence to see how it was revised.

RAMBLING I saw a television program last night, and it was about invaders from another planet and my little brother Ted became frightened so Mom calmed him down and told him that there is little evidence of life on other planets but that there may be life on Mars but few people believe that life exists there either.

REVISED Last night I saw a television program which was about invaders from another planet. When my younger brother Ted became frightened, Mom calmed him down. She told Ted that there is little evidence of life on other planets. Mom added that there may be life on Mars but few people believe that life exists there either.

As with choppy sentences, the first step in revising a rambling sentence is to recognize it as bad writing. When you review your compositions, watch for long sentences in which the conjunctions *and, but,* or *so* are used a great deal. Usually you will find that the independent clauses are not very closely related. These clauses should be rewritten to show a closer relationship, or, sometimes, they should be allowed to stand as complete sentences. The final step in revising rambling (or choppy) sentences is to read aloud what you have written. If the passage does not sound right, you have more revising to do.

EXERCISE 12. Revising a Rambling Style. Revise the rambling style of the following passages. Break the sentences down into clauses, and combine some clauses into compound or complex sentences. Let other clauses stand as complete sentences. To avoid a monotonous style, vary the beginnings of some sentences. Then read the passages aloud to see if the sentences flow smoothly and have variety.

1. Paul bought some skis, and he decided he must systematically learn to ski, and so he asked himself what to do first. The answer was to consult an instructor, and the instructor pointed out that it was dangerous to ski if you didn't know how to fall down properly, and so Paul thanked her, and he went home, and he dressed in his new ski clothes, and he went down the slopes and practiced falling down all day. He sprained his wrist at 3:00, and he twisted his leg at 4:36, and he left the slopes at 4:38, and now the skis are mine. I bought them from Paul for a song, and so tomorrow I plan to take my first fall at 9:30 sharp.

2. Joan thinks she can speak French, but she made a funny mistake the other day when Lisa came limping into class with a bandage on her ankle, and she had sprained it while playing hockey, so Joan thought she would show off her French. She meant to say, "*C'est dommage,*" and it means "That's too bad," but she said, "*C'est fromage*" instead, and it means "That's cheese," but Joan was quite proud of herself until Mrs. Stevens pointed out the mistake.

REVIEW EXERCISE E. Revising a Passage by Eliminating Choppy and Rambling Sentences. There are both choppy and rambling sentences in the following passage. Revise it so that the sentences are clear, well written, and varied. Read your revised version aloud to see if the sentences flow smoothly.

The dam is not a modern invention. It was used in ancient times. It was used very early in Egypt. It was used to dam the Nile River. The first dam recorded in history was built about 2600 B.C. It was a large stone dam. It was located about eighteen miles south of Memphis. This dam was an engineering failure. Other Egyptian kings built other dams to store water. Their dams created Lake Moeris.

The Babylonians also built dams to control the Tigris and Euphrates rivers, and the Romans built dams, and the dams lasted for centuries. Emperor Nero directed the building of a dam, and it lasted for 1,300 years, but the Arabians built a dam that lasted more than 1,000 years, and it was two miles long and 120 feet high so it was the greatest dam ever built.

Two of the largest dams in the world today are in the United States. One is the Hoover Dam, and it is near Las Vegas, Nevada. The other is the Grand Coulee Dam, and it is in the state of Washington. Each dam is an important source of electrical power. Both serve American cities. They produce over 10,000 megawatts of power each year.

PART THREE

TOOLS FOR WRITING AND REVISING:

Grammar ▪ Usage ▪ Mechanics

CHAPTER 10

The Sentence

SUBJECT AND PREDICATE, KINDS OF SENTENCES

Suppose that you began to read a story that opened as follows:

> Awakened in study hall John leaped from his seat into the balcony above him came the marching band led by the drum major playing "The Star-Spangled Banner" on his hat a tall plume nodded to John it was a rude awakening.

This story is difficult to understand because it is not clear where one thought ends and a new one begins. When you communicate by speaking, you raise and lower your voice and you use pauses to help your listener understand your meaning. When you write, you have only words and punctuation as your means of communication. You need to use these in patterns that are familiar to your readers—in complete sentences that are set off clearly by punctuation.

DIAGNOSTIC TEST

A. Identifying Subjects and Predicates. Write each italicized group of words, and indicate whether it is the subject or the predicate of the sentence. Underline the simple subject or the simple predicate (verb) in each.

EXAMPLES 1. *The mean dog next door* barks fiercely.
1. *The mean dog next door—subject*
2. The mean dog next door *barks fiercely.*
2. *barks fiercely—predicate*

1. Mr. Adams *gave me his old croquet set.*
2. Why did *that large new boat* sink on such a clear day?
3. *Trees and bushes all over the neighborhood* had been torn out by the storm.
4. On his way to school, Bill *was splashed by a passing car.*
5. *My old bicycle with the ape-hanger handlebars* is rusting away in the garage now.
6. *The creek behind my house* rises during the summer rains.
7. Sandy's little sister *bravely dived off the high board at the community pool.*
8. *Does* Max *want another serving of pie*?
9. My cousins and I *played basketball and walked over to the mall yesterday.*
10. *Fridays and other test days* always seem longer than regular school days.

B. Identifying Sentences by Purpose. Number your paper 11–20. After the proper number, identify each sentence as *declarative, interrogative, imperative,* or *exclamatory.*

EXAMPLE 1. What did you say?
1. *interrogative*

11. That may have been the longest string of train cars I have ever seen.
12. Follow these directions exactly.
13. No, I haven't seen Jenny all day.
14. Run for it—Tommy just knocked down a wasp's nest!
15. What's wrong with the television set?
16. I don't care.
17. Take this book down to Mrs. Esteva's office.
18. Mai Lin and her family suffered many hardships at sea.

GRAMMAR

19. Ouch, that hurts!
20. May my dog have the rest of your sandwich?

THE SENTENCE

10a. A *sentence* is a group of words expressing a complete thought.

A sentence begins with a capital letter and concludes with an end mark: a period or a question mark or an exclamation point. Sometimes a group of words looks like a sentence when it is not. You must examine the group of words closely to be sure that it expresses a complete thought. Reading it aloud will help you.

NOT A SENTENCE	The music of Scott Joplin. [This is not a complete thought. What about the music of Scott Joplin?]
SENTENCE	The music of Scott Joplin is popular again.
NOT A SENTENCE	Upon hearing Jose Feliciano. [The thought is not complete. Who heard Feliciano? What was the response?]
SENTENCE	Upon hearing Jose Feliciano, the audience applauded.
NOT A SENTENCE	After she had worked a long time. [The thought is not complete. What happened after she had worked a long time?]
SENTENCE	After she had worked a long time, Louise Nevelson completed the sculpture.

EXERCISE 1. Identifying and Writing Sentences. Capital letters and end marks have been omitted from the following groups of words. If a group of words is a sentence, write it after the proper number, using a capital letter and end punctuation. If the group of words is not a sentence, write *NS*. Then write the group of words, adding words to complete the thought and make it a sentence.

GRAMMAR

EXAMPLES
1. living alone in the mountains
1. *NS—Living alone in the mountains, the couple make their own furniture and clothes.*
2. classes in mountain climbing will begin soon
2. *Classes in mountain climbing will begin soon.*

1. catching the baseball with both hands
2. in the back of the room stands a tall pile of boxes
3. a long narrow passage with a trapdoor at each end
4. after waiting for six hours
5. the gymnasium is open
6. last night there were six television commercials every half hour
7. instead of calling the doctor about her sore throat
8. beneath the tall ceiling of the church
9. are you careless about shutting off unnecessary lights
10. doing the multiplication tables

EXERCISE 2. Identifying Sentences. Number your paper 1–20. After each number on your paper, write *S* if the group of words is a sentence and *NS* if it is not a sentence.

1. One of the best-known women in our history is Sacajawea. **2.** A member of the Lemhi band of the Shoshoni Indians. **3.** She is famous for her role as interpreter for the Lewis and Clark expedition. **4.** Which was seeking the Northwest Passage.

5. In 1800 the Lemhis had encountered a war party of the Hidatsa. **6.** Who captured some of the Lemhis, including Sacajawea. **7.** Later, with Charbonneau, her French-Canadian husband, and their two-month old son. **8.** Sacajawea joined the Lewis and Clark expedition in what is now North Dakota. **9.** Her knowledge of Indian languages enabled the explorers to communicate with various tribes. **10.** Sacajawea also searched for eatable plants. **11.** And once saved valuable instruments during a storm. **12.** As they traveled further. **13.** The explorers came across the Lemhis. **14.** From whom Sacajawea had been separated years before. **15.** The Lemhis helped the explorers. **16.** By giving them guidance.

17. After they returned from the expedition. **18.** Clark tried to establish Sacajawea and Charbonneau in St. Louis. **19.** However, the couple moved back to Sacajawea's native land. **20.** Where this famous woman died in 1812.

EXERCISE 3. Writing Interesting Sentences. The following groups of words are not sentences. On your paper, add words to make interesting sentences.

EXAMPLE 1. at the last minute
1. *At the last minute they remembered the secret message.*

1. on the last day of summer
2. found only in the country
3. a graceful ballerina
4. burning out of control
5. the old building by the lake

THE SUBJECT

You have learned that a sentence is a group of words expressing a complete thought. In order to express a complete thought, a sentence must have a subject and a predicate.

10b. The *subject* of a sentence is the part about which something is being said.

EXAMPLES A line of people | waited to see the movie. (subject: *A line of people*)

Standing in line were | several sailors. (subject: *several sailors*)

Since the subject is that part of the sentence about which something is being said, you can usually locate it by asking yourself *Who?* or *What? Who* waited to see that movie? *Who* was standing in line? Notice that the subject comes at the beginning of the first example and at the end of the second.

In the subject part of each of these sentences, one word stands out as essential: in the first sentence, *line;* in the second sentence, *sailors*. These two words, which cannot be removed from the subject part of the sentences, are called *simple subjects*. The simple subject and the other words that belong with it, taken together, are called the *complete subject.*

10c. The *simple subject* is the main word in the complete subject.

The simple subjects in the following sentences are printed in boldface (heavy type).

complete subject
My **date** for the dance | arrived late.

complete subject
The long, hard **trip** across the desert | was finally over.

complete subject
Pacing back and forth in the cage was | a hungry **tiger.**

When the subject is only one word or one name, the complete subject and the simple subject are the same.

complete subject
EXAMPLES **Patsy Mink** | was elected to office in Hawaii.
She | was chosen congresswoman.

EXERCISE 4. Identifying Complete Subjects and Simple Subjects. Write the complete subject in each sentence. Then underline the simple subject.

EXAMPLE 1. The day of the performance arrived.
1. *The day of the performance*

1. A tense excitement filled the air.
2. Several students had been nervous all day.
3. The crew in charge of sets got ready for the first act.
4. The director of the play told everyone to "break a leg."
5. The curtain inched slowly upward.
6. Everyone in the audience stopped talking.

7. The lights flooded the stage.
8. On the stage stood the actors.
9. They said their lines with confidence.
10. The first performance of the play was a great success.

From now on in this book, the word *subject* will refer to the simple subject.

EXERCISE 5. Identifying the Subject. Number your paper 1–20. After the proper number, write the subject (simple subject) of each sentence. Ask yourself what or whom the sentence says something about.

1. Mark Twain wrote many entertaining stories. **2.** Among them is "The Celebrated Jumping Frog of Calaveras County." **3.** One of the characters in this story will apparently believe anything. **4.** In a broken-down mining camp, this character meets Mr. Simon Wheeler. **5.** He asks the kindly old man a simple question. **6.** Instead of a simple answer, Mr. Wheeler gives a long, fantastic, and funny reply. **7.** This reply is in the form of a humorous tall tale. **8.** The tale features Jim Smiley, the owner of a very athletic frog. **9.** Mr. Smiley trained this frog for jumping contests. **10.** Confidently, Mr. Smiley bragged about his frog's leaping ability. **11.** Soon someone challenged Smiley's frog. **12.** The challenger, however, did not have a jumping frog for the contest. **13.** To Smiley, this was no problem. **14.** In a nearby swamp he found a frog for the challenger. **15.** Each creature was held on the starting line. **16.** Then, with a shout, each man released his frog. **17.** But Smiley's famous frog never jumped. **18.** The ordinary frog from the swamp easily won the contest. **19.** Smiley had been fooled by a trick. **20.** You will enjoy reading this story.

THE PREDICATE

The subject is one of the two essential parts of a sentence; the other essential part is the predicate.

GRAMMAR

10d. The *predicate* of a sentence is the part that says something about the subject.

EXAMPLES N. Scott Momaday | wrote several books. (*predicate*)

My whole family | heard Marian Anderson sing. (*predicate*)

On either side of me were | my two friends. (*predicate*)

To find the predicate in a sentence, ask, *What is being said about the subject?* or *What happened?* In the normal order of an English sentence, the predicate follows the subject, but in some sentences the predicate comes before the subject. (See the sentence above.)

The Simple Predicate, or Verb

Just as the simple subject is the most important part of the complete subject, so the simple predicate is the most important part of the complete predicate. The simple predicate is usually called the *verb* of the sentence.

10e. The *simple predicate,* or *verb,* is the main word or group of words in the predicate.

In each of the following sentences the simple predicate, or verb, is in boldface.

complete subject / *complete predicate*
The movie star | **signed** autographs for hours.

complete subject / *complete predicate*
The trees | **sagged** beneath the weight of the ice.

The simple predicate may be a one-word verb, or it may be a verb of more than one word, such as *has signed* or *will be sagging*. A simple predicate of two or more words is called a *verb phrase*. Note the verb phrases in boldface in the following sentences:

The famous novel *Frankenstein* **was written** by Mary Wollstonecraft Shelley.
After the concert the guitarist **will sign** autographs.
Your vocabulary **can be increased** by the study of the origins of words.

The *complete predicate,* which consists of the verb or verb phrase and the other words that belong to it, usually comes after the subject, but it sometimes can appear at the beginning of a sentence, as in the following sentences.

complete predicate | *complete subject*
There on its back **was** | a large **tortoise.**

complete predicate | *complete subject*
At the top of the tree **sat** | a bird's **nest.**

The subject may come in the middle of the predicate so that part of the predicate is on one side of the subject and the rest is on the other side. In the following examples, the complete predicate is in boldface.

During the winter many birds **fly south.**
Do sparrows **fly south**?

The words *not* and *never,* which are frequently used with verbs, are not verbs. They may be part of the predicate, but they are never part of a verb or a verb phrase.

EXAMPLES She **did** not **believe** me.
We **had** never **met.**

From now on in this book, the simple predicate will be called the verb.

EXERCISE 6. Identifying Complete Predicates. Write the complete predicate from each of the following sentences. Then underline the verb or verb phrase twice.

EXAMPLE 1. A ton and a half of groceries may seem like a big order for a family of five.
1. *may seem like a big order for a family of five*

1. Such a big order is possible in the village of Pang.
2. This small village is located near the Arctic Circle.
3. The people of Pang receive their groceries once a year.
4. A supply ship can visit Pang only during a short time each year.
5. In spring, families order their year's supply of groceries by mail.
6. The huge order is delivered to Pang a few months later.
7. The people store the groceries in their homes.
8. Frozen food is kept outdoors.
9. Too costly for most residents is the air-freight charge of two dollars a kilogram.
10. Villagers also fish in the icy water or hunt for wild game.

EXERCISE 7. Identifying Verbs and Verb Phrases. Number your paper 1–10. After the proper number, write the verb or verb phrase of the sentence.

1. For many years the diary had been written in a secret shorthand.
2. This secret shorthand was decoded after much hard work.
3. Samuel Pepys had kept this diary between 1660 and 1669.
4. A personal look at life in England during the seventeenth century is given in his diary.
5. Some of the entries tell about funny incidents of daily life.
6. Other entries are very serious.
7. In fact, in entries during 1666, Pepys described the great London fire.
8. What have accounts of the fire told us about this tragedy?
9. Pepys contributed his diaries and other works to Cambridge University.
10. These works are still read by people today.

WRITING APPLICATION A:
Expressing Your Ideas in Complete Sentences

Did anyone ever hold out two closed fists for you to choose the one that contained a surprise? When you communicate your thoughts to others, you offer them a surprise. You are sharing a thought that is unique and special. In conversations, you can tell by your listener's expression whether or not your message is clear. In writing, however, you cannot see your reader's expression. Therefore, when you communicate your thoughts in writing, you should use complete sentences to express your thoughts completely.

EXAMPLES *Groups of Words:* She'd been gone. Black-and-white. Missing for several days. Boy across the street. There on the side of the road. ASPCA

Sentences: Boots, our black-and-white cat, had been missing for days. Then, Monday morning, the boy who lived across the street knocked on our door. He said he had seen Boots. She had been found on the side of the road and taken to the ASPCA. We could claim her there.

Writing Assignment

You don't always know how you feel about something until you put your thoughts into words. Writing your ideas in complete sentences helps you organize your thinking. You may even discover thoughts you did not know you had. Discover what you think about the following subjects by making a complete sentence out of each group of words. Some groups are subjects and some are predicates.

1. the way to beat feeling lonely
2. always makes a class more interesting
3. dark, rainy days
4. really gets on my nerves
5. is a game that appeals to me

EXERCISE 8. Identifying Subjects and Verbs. Find the subject and the verb in each sentence and write them on your paper after the proper number.

1. Carla's mother drove us to the theater.
2. The bumblebee carries pollen from one plant to another.
3. A strong, gusty wind is blowing out to sea this morning.
4. My sister accidentally locked her keys inside the car.
5. From Maine to California the bicyclists made a cross-country journey.
6. The Medusa of Greek mythology was one of the three Gorgons, terrible in appearance.
7. For centuries she has been pictured with a head of snakes.
8. The picture of Medusa with her snaky hair appears in many books on mythology.
9. According to myth, a glance at the Medusa would turn a mortal to stone.
10. She was slain by Perseus with the aid of the goddess Athena.

EXERCISE 9. Writing Complete Sentences. Some of the following word groups are complete subjects and some are complete predicates. Write each group of words on your paper, adding whatever part is needed to make it a sentence. Then underline the subject once and the verb twice.

EXAMPLE 1. marched for five hours
1. *The members of the band marched for five hours.*

1. should not be left alone
2. the vacant lot down the street
3. danced across the floor
4. looked mysteriously at us
5. their best player

THE SENTENCE BASE

You have been studying the two most important parts of the sentence: the subject and the verb. Because these two parts are essential to the sentence, they are called the *sentence base.* All other parts of the sentence are attached to the sentence base.

Sentence base: **Dogs play.**

Sentence base with other parts attached: Every day two frisky **dogs** named Bison and Stark **play** for hours on our lawn.

The parts that were added give additional information, but they would be meaningless without the sentence base.

EXERCISE 10. Using the Sentence Base. The following subjects and verbs are sentence bases that state complete thoughts. Add other parts to each of them to create more interesting sentences.

EXAMPLE 1. Balloons floated.
1. *At dawn, fifty hot-air balloons floated over Nashville.*

1. Sparks flashed.
2. Car swerved.
3. Lion roars.
4. Band played.
5. Runner was sprinting.
6. Flower bloomed.
7. Girl laughed.
8. Child jumped.
9. Riders were sitting.
10. Years have passed.

COMPOUND SUBJECTS AND COMPOUND VERBS

Some sentences have more than one subject.

ONE SUBJECT **Alicia** carried her book.
THREE SUBJECTS **Alicia, Joy,** and **Carmen** carried their books.

ONE SUBJECT **New York City** is our destination.
TWO SUBJECTS Either **New York City** or **Niagara Falls** is our destination.

Notice that when two or more subjects have the same verb, a connecting word—usually *and* or *or*—is used between them. The connected subjects are referred to as a *compound subject.*

GRAMMAR

10f. A *compound subject* consists of two or more connected subjects that have the same verb. The usual connecting words are *and* and *or*.

COMPOUND SUBJECT The **Senate** and the **House** are in session. [There are two subjects—*Senate* and *House*. They are joined by a connector word—*and*—and have the same verb —*are*.]

EXERCISE 11. Identifying Compound Subjects. Write the compound subject, including the connecting word, from each of the following sentences. Then write the verb or verb phrase.

EXAMPLE 1. Cicely Tyson and Paul Winfield starred in a film together.
1. *Cicely Tyson and Paul Winfield—starred*

1. Florida and California have world-famous amusement parks.
2. Records and tapes were sold at a discount.
3. The Aztecs, the Mayas, and the Incas developed impressive cultures in Central and South America.
4. Garlic or oregano may be used in the recipe.
5. Scarlett O'Hara and Melanie Wilkes are characters created by Margaret Mitchell.
6. The mayor and the governor were at the conference.
7. Suddenly, the sleet and the hail poured from the dark clouds.
8. Jim or Carol must take notes for me.
9. In the center ring were ten clowns, five acrobats, and three elephants.
10. Hawaii, Maui, and Oahu are three of the Hawaiian Islands.

Just as a sentence may have a compound subject, so it may have a compound verb.

10g. A *compound verb* consists of two or more connected verbs that have the same subject.

ONE VERB Surfing **has become** a very popular sport.

COMPOUND VERB The dog **barked** and **growled** at the thief. [There are two verbs—*barked* and *growled* —joined by *and*. Both verbs have the same subject—*dog*.]

COMPOUND VERB The man **was convicted** but later **was found** innocent of the crime. [There are two verb phrases—*was convicted* and *was found* —joined by *but*. Both verb phrases have the same subject—*man*.]

EXERCISE 12. Identifying Compound Verbs. Write the compound verb, together with the connecting word(s), from each of the following sentences. Then write the subject of the verb.

EXAMPLE 1. The hikers loaded their backpacks and studied the map of the mountain trails.
1. *loaded and studied—hikers*

1. Linda wrote her essay and practiced the piano last night.
2. Miami is the largest city in southern Florida and has been a popular resort area since the 1920's.
3. According to Greek mythology, Arachne angered Athena and was changed into a spider.
4. Martina Arroyo has sung in major American opera halls and has made appearances abroad.
5. Chip was bothered by the cold and was having a bad day.
6. During special sales, shoppers arrive early at the mall and search for bargains.
7. Maria Montessori studied medicine in Italy and developed new methods for teaching children.
8. Jim Rice autographed baseballs and made a short speech.
9. General Lee won many battles but lost the war.
10. In the summer many students go to music camps and improve their skills.

Sometimes you will see a sentence that has a compound subject and a compound verb. In such a sentence, both of the subjects go with both of the verbs.

S S V
EXAMPLE The **captain** and the **crew** **battled** the storm
V
and **prayed** for better weather. [Both *captain* and *crew* performed both actions—*battled* and *prayed*.]

EXERCISE 13. Identifying Compound Subjects and Compound Verbs. Write the following sentences on your paper, underlining the subjects once and the verbs or verb phrases twice.

EXAMPLE 1. Several fine poems and novels were written by the Brontë sisters.
1. *Several fine poems and novels were written by the Brontë sisters.*

1. Charlotte and Emily are the most famous Brontë sisters.
2. Originally, they wrote and published under pen names.
3. *Jane Eyre* and *Wuthering Heights* are their well-known books.
4. In Charlotte Brontë's novel, Jane Eyre endured and overcame many hardships.
5. Emily Brontë's *Wuthering Heights* saddens me and makes me tearful.
6. Catherine Earnshaw and Heathcliff stand as unforgettable characters.
7. As children they wandered and explored the moor.
8. Catherine loved Heathcliff but married Edgar.
9. *Jane Eyre* and *Wuthering Heights* became movies.
10. I watched the movies and then read the books again.

EXERCISE 14. Writing Sentences with Compound Subjects and Compound Predicates. Using titles, words, and characters of songs, books, and poems, write ten sentences—five with compound subjects and five with compound predicates. Underline subjects once and verbs twice.

EXAMPLE 1. *Tom Sawyer and Becky Thatcher were childhood sweethearts.*

WRITING APPLICATION B:
Adding Variety to Your Sentences by Placing the Subject in New Positions

Have you really looked at your room lately? You probably haven't unless something has been changed. When you see the same items in the same places over and over, you usually stop paying attention to them. This reaction holds true for writing: if you start every sentence with the subject, your reader may lose interest. In other words, you need to liven up your writing to hold your reader's interest. One way to do this is to place the subject of your sentence in a new place, perhaps in the middle or at the end of the sentence.

EXAMPLES In spite of everything, **I** still believe that people are really good at heart.—ANNE FRANK
Across the bottom of the television picture came the **words** *tornado watch.*

Writing Assignment

The lives of other people—even ordinary people—are often a source of entertainment and sometimes of inspiration, too. Write a mini-biography of a friend or relative. Add variety by occasionally placing the subject in the middle or at the end of your sentences.

CLASSIFYING SENTENCES BY PURPOSE

10h. Sentences may be classified according to purpose. There are four kinds of sentences.[1]

(1) A *declarative sentence* makes a statement. It is followed by a period.

EXAMPLES Miriam Colon founded the Puerto Rican Traveling Theater**.**

[1] The classification of sentences according to structure (simple, compound, complex, compound-complex) is taught in Chapter 16.

Curiosity is the beginning of knowledge.

(2) An *interrogative sentence* asks a question. It is followed by a question mark.

EXAMPLES What do you know about glaciers?
Why do we see only one side of the moon?
Was the game exciting?

(3) An *imperative sentence* gives a command or makes a request. It is followed by a period. Strong commands are followed by exclamation points.

EXAMPLES Do your homework each night.
Watch out!
Please close the door, John.

At first glance, none of these sentences seems to have any subject. Actually, the person or persons addressed in each case is the subject. The subject *you* is said to be "understood" in such sentences.

(You) Do your homework each night.
(You) Watch out!
John, (you) please close the door.

(4) An *exclamatory sentence* shows excitement or expresses strong feeling. It is followed by an exclamation point.

EXAMPLES What a sight the sunset is!
They're off!
Sarah won the videotape player!

Many students overuse the exclamatory sentence. Save your exclamation points for sentences that really do show strong emotion. If overused, the exclamatory sentence loses its impact.

EXERCISE 15. Classifying Sentences. Number your paper 1–10. Write the kind of sentence each quotation is and give the punctuation mark that should follow the sentence.

EXAMPLE 1. The only thing we have to fear is fear itself —FRANKLIN D. ROOSEVELT

1. *declarative* **.**

1. Shall I compare thee to a summer's day —WILLIAM SHAKESPEARE
2. Tact is after all a kind of mind-reading —SARAH ORNE JEWETT
3. Sail on, O Ship of State—HENRY WADSWORTH LONGFELLOW
4. The history of every country begins in the heart of a man or woman—WILLA CATHER
5. What happiness is there which is not purchased with more or less of pain—MARGARET OLIPHANT
6. Bring me my bow of burning gold—WILLIAM BLAKE
7. No one can make you feel inferior without your consent —ELEANOR ROOSEVELT
8. Since when was genius found respectable —ELIZABETH BARRETT BROWNING
9. Speak softly and carry a big stick—THEODORE ROOSEVELT
10. An expert is one who knows more and more about less and less—NICHOLAS MURRAY BUTLER

DIAGRAMING THE SUBJECT AND VERB

A diagram shows the structure of a sentence as a kind of picture. Making a diagram of the subject and the verb is a way of showing that you understand these two parts of the sentence.

PATTERN

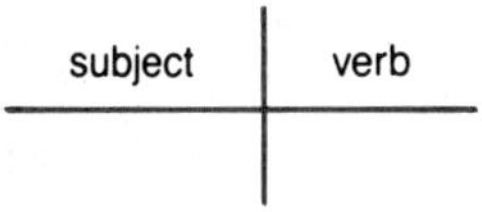

subject | verb

EXAMPLES Lions roar.

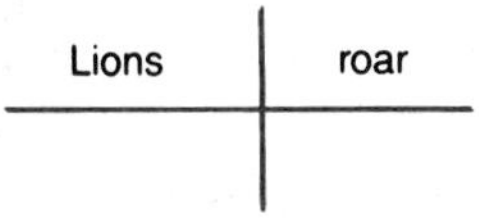

Lions | roar

People speak.

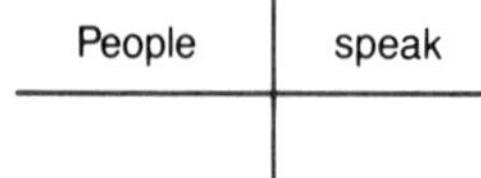

Notice that the parts of the sentence base—the subject and the verb—are placed on a horizontal line with a vertical line separating the subject from the verb. The capital marking the beginning of the sentence is used, but not the punctuation.

To diagram a sentence, you first pick out the subject and the verb and then write them on the horizontal line, separated by a crossing vertical line.

EXAMPLES The energetic reporter dashed to the fire.

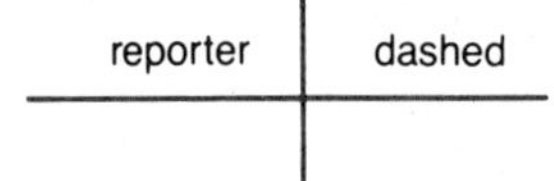

Have you been studying for the final test?

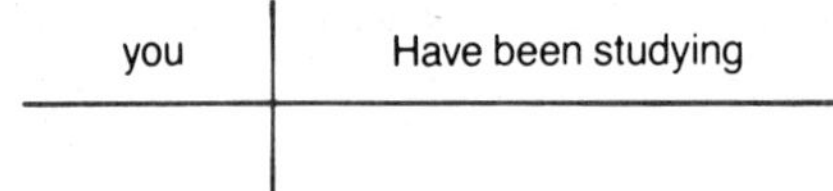

Listen to the beautiful music.

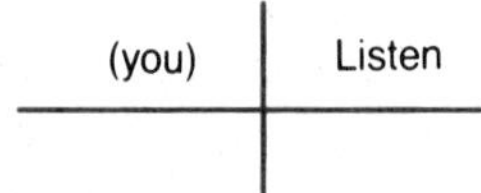

EXERCISE 16. Diagraming Simple Subjects and Verbs. Diagram only the simple subjects and verbs in the following sentences. Draw your diagrams with a ruler, leaving plenty of space between them.

1. Midas is a character in Greek mythology.
2. He was the king of Phrygia.
3. One of the gods gave Midas a magic power.
4. With this power, Midas could turn anything into gold.
5. This could be done with a simple touch of Midas's hand.

6. For a while, this gift pleased Midas.
7. Soon it became a curse.
8. Do you know why?
9. Read the story of King Midas in a mythology book.
10. Today, people with "the Midas touch" can make money in any project at all.

The following example shows how to diagram a sentence with a compound subject. Notice the position of the connecting word *and.*

EXAMPLE Vines and weeds grew over the old well.

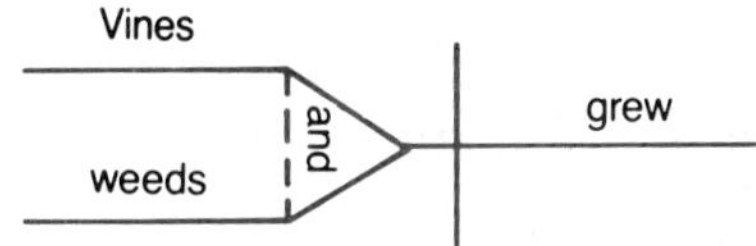

To diagram a sentence with a compound verb, you follow a similar pattern.

EXAMPLE The model walked across the platform and turned around.

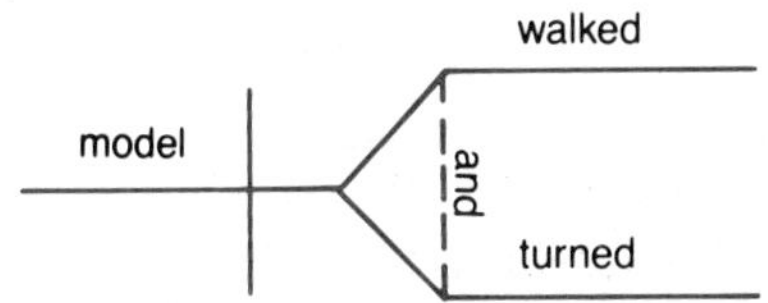

If the sentence has both a compound subject and a compound verb, it is diagramed this way:

EXAMPLE Ken and Marti dived into the water and swam across the pool.

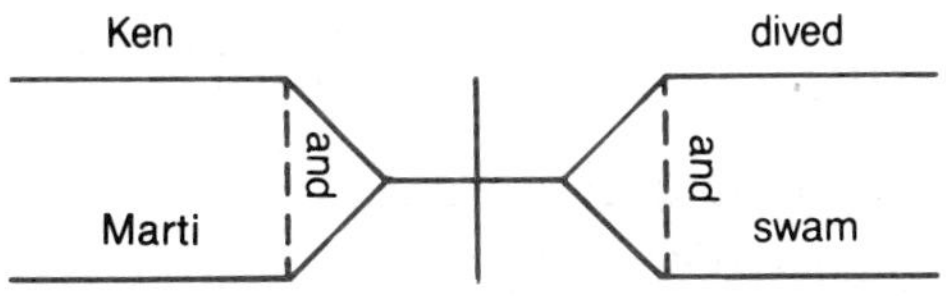

EXERCISE 17. Diagraming Subject and Verbs. Diagram the simple subjects and the verbs or verb phrases in the following sentences.

1. We ran to the railroad station and barely caught the train.
2. The students and the faculty combined their efforts and defeated the proposal.
3. The plane circled above the landing field but did not descend.
4. Pencil and paper are needed for tomorrow's assignment.
5. The actress and her costar prepared for the scene.

REVIEW EXERCISE A. Identifying Complete Subjects and Predicates. Write the following sentences on your paper. Separate the complete subject from the complete predicate with a vertical line. Then underline the simple subject once and the verb twice.

EXAMPLE 1. Legends and folk tales have been repeated and enjoyed throughout the Americas.

1. *Legends and folk tales have been repeated and enjoyed throughout the Americas.*

1. The Chorotega people lived in Nicoya, Costa Rica, hundreds of years ago.
2. One Chorotega folk tale tells the story of Nicoya's treasure and praises Princess Nosara for her protection of it from the enemy.
3. The warriors of the Chirenos landed on the Nicoyan peninsula and attacked the Chorotegas.
4. The Indians of Nicoya were surprised and could not react quickly.
5. Nosara grabbed the treasure in her father's house.
6. Nosara and her suitor took a bow and arrow and fled into the woods.
7. The two ran from the enemy all night and at last reached a river.
8. The brave girl dashed into the mountains, hid the treasure, and returned to the river.
9. The enemy killed the princess and her friend.
10. The murderous tribe never found the gold.

REVIEW EXERCISE B. Classifying Sentences. Write each sentence, adding the correct end punctuation. Then write what kind of sentence it is.

EXAMPLE 1. Turn left at the corner
1. *(you) Turn left at the corner.—imperative*

1. Several recent movies have shown the problems of life on a farm
2. How many times have they tried to win the championship
3. Imagine a ride in the space shuttle
4. Because of its funny appearance, the frilled lizard looks like a comical monster
5. Can you give me directions to the post office
6. How fresh the air feels after a storm
7. Think about both sides of the problem
8. Many large museums in America have pottery from New Mexico by Maria Martinez
9. What teams are playing in the World Series
10. What a fantastic world lies beneath the waves

CHAPTER 10 REVIEW: POSTTEST 1

A. Identifying Subjects and Predicates. Write each italicized group of words and indicate whether it is the subject or the predicate of the sentence. Underline the simple subject or the verb in each word group you write.

EXAMPLES 1. *My aunt in Florida* took us to Sea World.
1. *My aunt in Florida—subject*
2. My aunt in Florida *took us to Sea World.*
2. *took us to Sea World—predicate*

Our whole family (1) *drove down to my aunt's house in Florida last summer.* (2) *The long drive and the steamy heat, especially in the southern states,* wore out all of us.

The first two days at my aunt's house, (3) *my mother and father and my brother and I* spent almost all of our time in my aunt's air-conditioned back room. Lounging on the couch, we (4) *could look out the picture windows at the lake and palm trees in the back yard.* My brother, (5) *naturally, was bored and pestered everyone.* (6) *Does* your little brother *always act that way, too*?

On the third day there, (7) *all of us* rode up to Sea World. (8) *The various exhibits and shows* featured all kinds of strange and wonderful animals. Many animals, particularly dolphins and killer whales, (9) *performed tricks and seemed very intelligent.*

In one huge tank swam (10) *scary-looking sharks.* A clear glass or plastic tunnel (11) *went right through the middle of the shark tank.* My mother and my brother (12) *did not like the tunnel.*

(13) *My brother's favorite part of Sea World* was the pirate ship. He (14) *ran and played all over the ship with a bunch of other children his age.* Even after a whole day there, (15) *none of us* wanted to leave.

B. Identifying Sentences by Purpose. Write the last word of each of the following sentences, and then add the correct mark of punctuation. Identify each sentence as *declarative, interrogative, imperative,* or *exclamatory.*

EXAMPLE 1. Write your name at the top of your paper
1. paper. *imperative*

16. Maria plans to study architecture at the state university
17. This isn't the right answer, is it
18. No, it definitely is not
19. Clean up your room this instant, and don't make up any excuses or try to get out of it
20. I can't right now, Mom; everybody's waiting for me down at Andy's house

---

CHAPTER 10 REVIEW: POSTTEST 2

Writing a Variety of Sentences. Write ten sentences of your own according to the guidelines given. Make the subjects and predicates different for each sentence.

1. A declarative sentence with a compound subject
2. An imperative sentence with a compound predicate
3. A declarative sentence with a single subject and a single predicate
4. An interrogative sentence with a compound subject
5. An interrogative sentence with a compound predicate
6. An exclamatory sentence with a single subject and a single predicate
7. An imperative sentence with a single subject and a single predicate
8. A declarative sentence with a compound predicate
9. An exclamatory sentence with a compound predicate
10. A declarative sentence with a compound subject and a compound predicate

GRAMMAR

CHAPTER 11

The Parts of Speech

NOUN, PRONOUN, ADJECTIVE

There are many thousands of different words in the English language, but there are only eight different *kinds* of words. These eight kinds, which are called "parts of speech," are the *noun,* the *pronoun,* the *adjective,* the *verb,* the *adverb,* the *preposition,* the *conjunction,* and the *interjection.* In this chapter you will study three of these eight parts of speech: the *noun,* the *pronoun,* and the *adjective.*

DIAGNOSTIC TEST

Identifying Nouns, Pronouns, and Adjectives. Number your paper 1–20. After the proper number, write each italicized word in the following sentences and indicate whether it is a noun (*n.*), a pronoun (*pron.*), or an adjective (*adj.*).

EXAMPLE 1. The biplane had four *wings* and a *wooden* propeller.
1. *wings—n., wooden—adj.*

1. Sometimes I don't feel well when *it* gets cloudy and the *dark* sky threatens rain.

2. My little sister, *afraid* of thunder and *lightning,* hid under the bed.
3. Inger's mother gave *each* of us a tall glass of *cold* milk.
4. One by one, *each* husky ventured out into the *cold.*
5. *Who* went to church *Sunday* morning?
6. While the *Wilsons* were on vacation, Julio fed *their* dog.
7. The house across the street has been up for *sale* again since *Tuesday*.
8. Under the *rotten* pine flooring my *brother-in-law* found a small tin canister.
9. *That* rifle doesn't belong to *anyone*.
10. *That* is a *Persian* cat.
11. Give me *some* iced *tea,* please.
12. *Somebody* said that there would be no more *discount* movie tickets.
13. I got a *discount* on *our* tickets, though.
14. *Mr. Taylor* donated the *sports* equipment.
15. Barney is going to try out for *track* and several *other* sports.
16. *Everyone* liked one painting or the *other*.
17. June went to the *mall* by *herself*.
18. Hobbies take up so *much* time that they often become *work*.
19. My father's *work* schedule often takes *him* out of town.
20. *This* parakeet screeches if you don't give him *enough* seed.

THE NOUN

If you were to travel to a foreign country where a language other than English is spoken, you would soon find yourself asking, "What's that called?" Knowing the names of things is basic to communication. A word that names something is called a *noun.*

11a. A *noun* is a word used to name a person, place, thing, or idea.

Persons Helen Hayes, Dr. Lacy, child, architect
Places Wyoming, Mexico, Europe, home, city

Things money, shell, wind, worm, desk
Ideas courage, love, freedom, sorrow, luck

Some nouns name things that you can see, while others do not. The nouns that name unseen things, like ideas, can be more difficult to identify.

EXERCISE 1. Identifying Nouns. Number your paper 1–10. Pick out fifty nouns from the following sentences. (*Which, they,* and *all* are not nouns.)

EXAMPLE 1. Both children and adults enjoyed the comedy.
1. *children, adults, comedy*

1. Rods, reels, and lines are called tackle.
2. Mines are important to the economy and industry of Utah.
3. Hobbies teach many people new skills and provide hours of entertainment.
4. During the war, women in our country worked in hospitals, factories, and offices.
5. The pollution of the air and water has been a serious problem for many years.
6. Computers have become a part of the daily lives of both children and adults.
7. Huge crowds of people attended the Olympics in summer.
8. All responsible citizens in a democracy should exercise the right to vote in elections.
9. Armadillos have an excellent sense of smell, which they use in their daily searches for food such as insects, lizards, and other small creatures.
10. A person never knows when courage will be needed in the face of danger or of a personal problem.

Compound Nouns

Sometimes a single noun is made up of two or more words. These words may be written as a single word (redwood), as two words (red pepper), or with a hyphen (self-esteem). Nouns that are names of particular people or things also often consist of more than one word: Rose Fitzgerald Kennedy, Buckingham Palace, *The Adventures of Huckleberry Finn* (the name of a book). Nouns such as these are called *compound nouns.* To be sure how a compound noun is written, look it up in your dictionary.

Proper Nouns and Common Nouns

There are two main classes of nouns: common nouns and proper nouns. While the *common noun* names a class or a group of persons, places, or things, the *proper noun* names a particular person, place, or thing. The proper noun begins with a capital letter. If it consists of more than one word, each important word is capitalized *(Declaration of Independence).*

COMMON NOUNS	PROPER NOUNS
poem	"To a Skylark"
country	Kenya
man	Roberto Clemente
ship	*Mayflower*
newspaper	*New York Times*
ocean	Pacific Ocean
street	Market Street
date	November 6, 1987
city	Los Angeles

EXERCISE 2. Identifying Nouns. Number your paper 1–10. After each number, list the nouns you find in the corresponding sentence. (*Note: One* and *their* are not nouns.)

EXAMPLE 1. Forests come in many different shapes, kinds, and sizes.
1. *forests, shapes, kinds, sizes*

1. Trees in a tropical jungle have an ample supply of water.
2. Rain forests are usually located in tropical regions.
3. However, one rain forest is on a peninsula in the northwestern state of Washington.
4. Along the coast of California grow the famous redwoods, the tallest trees in the world.

5. The forests in Canada contain mostly evergreens, which adapt well to a cold climate.
6. Forests in the temperate zones have evergreens and also trees that shed leaves, such as oaks, beeches, and maples.
7. The giant Douglas fir, an evergreen tree, is a valuable source of lumber.
8. Many other types of plants are dependent on trees for their life.
9. Forests swarm with insects, mammals, birds, and reptiles.
10. A national park such as Sequoia National Park protects large areas of forest.

REVIEW EXERCISE A. **Classifying Nouns.** Make two columns on your paper. Label one column *Proper Nouns* and the other column *Common Nouns.* Under the appropriate heading, list the nouns from the following paragraph.

Each day several thousand people visit the Lincoln Memorial in Washington. The monument was designed by Henry Bacon and was dedicated on Memorial Day. Located in West Potomac Park, the Lincoln Memorial consists of a large marble hall that encloses a lifelike statue of Abraham Lincoln. The figure, which was made from blocks of white marble by Daniel Chester French, a distinguished sculptor, is sitting in a large armchair as if in deep meditation. On the north wall is found a famous passage from an inaugural address by Lincoln, and on the south wall is inscribed the Gettysburg Address.

THE PRONOUN

Once you can recognize nouns, you can learn to identify pronouns. A *pronoun* is a word that stands for a noun. Without pronouns we would be forced to repeat the same nouns again and again.

EXAMPLE When Kelly saw the signal, Kelly pointed the signal out to Teresa.
When Kelly saw the signal, **she** pointed **it** out to Teresa.

11b. A *pronoun* is a word used in place of one or of more than one noun.

Name the nouns that the pronouns in the following sentences stand for.

1. Gail read the book and returned **it** to the library.
2. The models bought **themselves** new dresses.
3. "Sam," the teacher said, "**you** will be the discussion leader tomorrow."
4. Sharon and Pat went fishing. **Both** caught six bass.

The noun that a pronoun stands for is called the *antecedent.* Sometimes the antecedent is not stated.

EXAMPLES **Catherine** (*antecedent*) told **her** (*pron.*) father **she** (*pron.*) would be late.

You (*pron.*) can't sleep now. [no antecedent stated]

There are several kinds of pronouns. The following pronouns are the *personal pronouns:*

I, me, mine, my, myself
you, your, yours, yourself, yourselves
he, him, his, himself
she, her, hers, herself
it, its, itself
we, us, our, ours, ourselves
they, them, their, theirs, themselves

In this book, pronouns that come directly before nouns and show possession (*my, his, her, its, your, their*) are called *possessive pronouns.* Your teacher may prefer that you call them *possessive adjectives.*

Make sure that you learn the differences between *its* and *it's* and between *their, they're,* and *there.* Avoid using *hisself* and *theirselves,* which are not standard English.[1]

Other common pronouns are

[1] *Standard* and *nonstandard* are the terms used in this book to describe kinds of usage. See pages 497–98 for a discussion of standard and nonstandard English.

who, whom, whoever, whomever
everybody, everyone, someone, somebody
no one, nobody, none, others

The following words are pronouns when they are used in the place of nouns:

what, which, whatever, whichever, whose
this, that, these, those
one, each, some, any, other, another
many, more, much, most
both, several, few, all, either, neither

EXERCISE 3. Identifying Pronouns. List the pronouns in each of the following sentences after the proper number. After each pronoun, write the noun or nouns that the pronoun refers to.

EXAMPLE 1. Beth saw the kittens in the snow, and she decided to bring them inside.
1. *she—Beth*
them—kittens

1. When the luggage cart fell on its side, the bags and their contents scattered everywhere.
2. The passengers scrambled to find their luggage; they even got down on their hands and knees to pick up the belongings.
3. One salesperson shouted, "This bag belongs to me! It has my name on it."
4. "Are you sure these socks are yours?" asked another traveler. "I have a pair just like them."
5. One couple asked, "Who owns a pink-and-yellow shirt? This isn't ours."
6. As a crowd of people gathered, many just laughed, but several offered to help.
7. The travelers found themselves quibbling over toothbrushes, combs, and magazines.
8. "I lost my comb!" exclaimed one annoyed person. "Who has it?"

9. One worried traveler asked, "Where are the birthday presents for my cousin? He will be disappointed if I lose them."
10. Finally, the problem was resolved, and no one was unhappy.

WRITING APPLICATION A:
Using Pronouns to Avoid Unnecessary Repetition

Sometimes adults don't realize that they are telling you the same things over and over. At times they even repeat the exact words. How do you feel when this happens? You probably get irritated and impatient. In your writing, you can use pronouns to avoid irritating your reader with unnecessary repetition of nouns. You can see in the following example that the use of pronouns would make the information on Poe read much more smoothly.

> Edgar Allan Poe had a sad life. Edgar Allan Poe was the son of professional actors. Edgar Allan Poe was an orphan at age three. Edgar Allan Poe was raised and educated by a wealthy couple in Virginia. Edgar Allan Poe could not get along with Edgar Allan Poe's foster father. Edgar Allan Poe's young wife died of tuberculosis. Edgar Allan Poe did not take good care of Edgar Allan Poe, and Edgar Allan Poe survived Edgar Allan Poe's wife by only two years.

Writing Assignment

Select a well-known person from public life, the entertainment field, or sports. Describe this person without revealing his or her name until the end of your paragraph. Have the class guess who the person is.

EXERCISE 4. Writing Pronouns in Sentences. Rewrite the following paragraphs by filling in the blanks with appropriate pronouns. If necessary, refer to the lists of pronouns on pages 295–96.

GRAMMAR

Let —— tell —— about the experience that —— of my friends, Mary Tam, had on vacation. —— was taking a group tour through the dense Australian forests. After traveling for hours at night through wilderness, —— in the group wanted to make camp, but the guide insisted that —— continue. Finally, —— agreed to travel for just one more hour.

Soon —— were rewarded for the trip. At the edge of the forest, the guide pointed to the top of a large tree where several koalas were feeding. —— of the animals swung from one tree to —— .

The group watched —— from the ground. —— dared to speak a word. The koalas munched happily on the leaves of the trees. —— held onto branches with their sharp claws. —— of the animals carried a cub on her back. —— was feeding the cub while she also fed —— .

Although —— of the koalas have been hunted ruthlessly, a —— of the animals thrive within remote Australian forests. —— of the tour members marveled at the unique appearance of the koalas. —— look different from any other animal in the world.

REVIEW EXERCISE B. Identifying Pronouns. Number your paper 1–10. Write the pronouns from each sentence after the corresponding number. Circle all possessive pronouns.

1. All of us saw Rosemary Casals play in the tennis tournament.
2. Many of the spectators watching in the stands played tennis themselves.
3. Who would not like to be on the court playing during one of the sets?
4. Casals began to play, and the crowd was awed by the strength of her serve.
5. People were amazed that anyone could play with that much stamina.
6. Casals played such a strong game that she seemed to be rewarding us for our support.
7. Did you know that Rosemary Casals has played in many tennis tournaments?

8. I remembered that Casals had won my admiration by fighting for equal rights for women in professional tennis.
9. Several people in the audience showed by their enthusiasm that they had enjoyed watching the matches.
10. We met them for dinner after the tournament.

THE ADJECTIVE

Allen and Sonia have just finished the final exam for the history course they are taking. Neither of them will be satisfied with saying merely that it was a test. Rather, they will describe the test as being *long* or *difficult* or even *unfair.*

Not satisfied with just naming things, we often like to make a noun more definite by describing it in some way. The words that we use to make a noun more definite are called *adjectives.* When a noun is described by an adjective, it is said to be *modified.* Since a pronoun may be used in place of a noun, it too may be modified by an adjective.

11c. An *adjective* is a word used to modify a noun or a pronoun.

An adjective often answers one of these questions: *What kind? Which one? How much?* or *How many?*

WHAT KIND?	WHICH ONE?	HOW MUCH? or HOW MANY?
a *tall* woman	the *other* one	*five* times
a *steep* mountain	*this* year	*many* mistakes
a *long* hike	the *last* answer	*several* others
an *eager* clerk	*those* people	*no* supplies
a *tired* dog	*that* dress	*few* marbles

The most frequently used adjectives are *a, an,* and *the.* These adjectives are called *articles.*

EXERCISE 5. Writing Appropriate Adjectives. Rewrite the following sentences, replacing the italicized questions with adjectives that answer them.

EXAMPLE 1. They sold *how many?* tickets for the *which one?* show and *how many?* tickets for the *which one?* one.

1. *They sold fifty tickets for the first show and seventy-five tickets for the last one.*

1. Even though we had run *how many?* laps around the track, we still had to run *how many?* others.
2. *Which one?* weekend, *how many?* hikers went on a *what kind?* trip to the *what kind?* park.
3. We rode in a *what kind?* van that carried *how many?* people and went *how many?* miles to the basketball game.
4. There was *how much?* time left when I started to answer the *which one?* question on the test.
5. During the *what kind?* afternoon we washed more than *how many?* cars and earned *how many?* dollars.

An adjective sometimes follows the word it modifies. Note the position of the adjectives in the following sentences.

Each one of the students brought **used books** for the auction.

The **books,** although **old** and **worn,** were quickly bought.

EXERCISE 6. Identifying Adjectives and the Words They Modify. Write the following sentences, underlining the adjectives. Then draw an arrow from each adjective to the noun it modifies. Do not underline the articles *a, an,* and *the.*

EXAMPLE 1. It was a stormy night by the time the weary hikers reached the campground.

1. *It was a stormy night by the time the weary hikers reached the campground.*

1. Melville described whaling in his famous novel *Moby Dick.*
2. Whaling used to be considered a romantic adventure.
3. Whalers took long voyages on sailing ships with tall masts.
4. Modern whaling is a different kind of adventure.
5. Today, ships that hunt for whales are huge floating factories.

6. Sharp harpoons are shot from guns and carry explosive tips.
7. In the nineteenth century, the products of whaling had great value, but today the products are not in much demand.
8. Some types of whales are becoming a rare sight.
9. Of the nine species of whales, six are now on the list of endangered species.
10. Citizens, both young and old, have been working for a long time to protect whales.

WRITING APPLICATION B: Making Writing More Exact Through the Careful Use of Adjectives

Some words, especially adjectives, have been used so many times that they no longer carry much meaning. If you describe a friend with words like *nice,* or *great,* and other common adjectives, you are not saying much. Keep a notebook of new adjectives and use them in your writing and speaking. You will be able to communicate more information, and you will be more exact.

EXAMPLE The people of Florida raised money to restore the interior of the old capitol to the way it had been in 1845. Red, white, and blue were the original colors, but they had been natural colors and soft pastels. The ceiling over the entry hall has been painted in a *terra-cotta* red.

Do you know what *terra cotta* is? Other specific color adjectives include *azure, mauve, cerise, taupe* and *scarlet.*

Writing Assignment

Make up a new product that would be a magnificent discovery. Write a sales pitch or some other kind of advertisement for this product. Use at least three lively, exact adjectives describing your new product. Underline these adjectives.

EXERCISE 7. Writing Sentences with Adjectives. Except for *a, an,* and *the,* the following sentences contain no adjectives. Rewrite each sentence and, wherever possible, add interesting adjectives to modify the nouns and pronouns.

EXAMPLE 1. The children took a nap.
1. *The five grumpy children took a long nap.*

1. Carolyn gave a cat to her aunt.
2. Luis donated books and jeans for the sale.
3. We watched the parade pass under our window.
4. The fielder caught the ball and made a throw to the catcher.
5. The dancer leaped across the stage.

Proper Adjectives

A *proper adjective* is formed from a proper noun, and like a proper noun, it begins with a capital letter.

PROPER NOUN	PROPER ADJECTIVE
Africa	**African** nations
China	**Chinese** calendar
Shakespeare	**Shakespearean** drama
Islam	**Islamic** law

EXERCISE 8. Identifying Proper Nouns and Proper Adjectives. Number your paper 1–10. Write each proper noun and proper adjective after its sentence number. Next to each proper adjective, write the noun it modifies.

EXAMPLE 1. In recent years many American tourists have visited the Great Wall in China.
1. *American—tourists, Great Wall, China*

1. The Colorado beetle has destroyed many potato crops in the United States.
2. The professor of African literature gave a lecture on the novels of Camara Laye, a writer who was born in Guinea.
3. Marian McPartland, a jazz pianist from New York City, played several songs that Scott Joplin wrote.

4. The program about the Egyptian ruins was narrated by an English scientist and a French anthropologist.
5. The exchange students from Europe were fascinated by the video games in America.
6. The society of Victorian England was the subject of many British novels in the late 1800's.
7. During the press conference the President commented on the Congressional vote.
8. My friend from Tokyo gave me a Japanese kimono.
9. We saw a display of Appalachian crafts in the public library.
10. Which Arthurian legend have you chosen for your report?

Changing Parts of Speech

Sometimes nouns are used as adjectives: *library* book, *airplane* ride, *school* mascot. *Library, airplane,* and *school* are nouns, but they act as adjectives when they are put in front of nouns. The way that a word is used in a sentence determines what part of speech it is.

Words such as *each, some,* and *whose* are sometimes pronouns and sometimes adjectives, depending on their use in a sentence. When they are used in place of nouns, they are pronouns; when they modify nouns, they are adjectives. When they are adjectives, they always precede a noun.

PRONOUN **Each** did the assignment.
ADJECTIVE **Each** person did the assignment.

PRONOUN **Some** have gone to their dressing rooms.
ADJECTIVE **Some** actors have gone to their dressing rooms.

PRONOUN **Whose** are these?
ADJECTIVE **Whose** gloves are these?

EXERCISE 9. Identifying Adjectives and Pronouns. Label the italicized word in each sentence as an adjective (*adj.*) or pronoun (*pron.*).

EXAMPLE 1. Say *whatever* you think.
1. *pron.*

1. *Both* passed the test.
2. At the tryouts *each* one of the students recited the lines from the first act.
3. *Many* high schools offer driver training.
4. It's hard to know what *one* should do in this situation.
5. *Some* twins do not look exactly alike.
6. After several days in Paris, *each* of the tourists flew to London.
7. They took *both* bicycles to be repaired.
8. Sally asked *another* friend to the party.
9. *Many* of us volunteered to help the teacher.
10. A unicycle has only *one* wheel, making it difficult to ride.

REVIEW EXERCISE C. Identifying Adjectives. There are twenty-five adjectives in the following paragraph. Make a list of them as they appear. Do not list articles.

1. The ancient Greeks and Romans worshiped twelve major gods. **2.** The one with the most power was Zeus, or Jupiter, who lived on a high mountain, Mount Olympus. **3.** From the cloudy peak he surveyed the various affairs of the world. **4.** He rode in a great chariot that was drawn by four white horses. **5.** Whenever he liked, he called for a great assembly of the gods. **6.** At the huge assembly would be Poseidon, or Neptune, the god of the sea; Hades, or Pluto, the god of the shadowy land of the dead; Hera, or Juno, the handsome but quarrelsome wife of Zeus; Apollo, the shining god of the sun; Artemis, or Diana, the swift goddess of the hunt, who in time became known as the goddess of the moon; Hermes, or Mercury, the swift messenger of the gods; Hestia, or Vesta, the goddess of the hearth, who became a special protector of the home; Ares, or Mars, the dreadful god of war; Athena, or Minerva, the favorite daughter of Zeus, who was noted for her great wisdom; Hephaestus, or Vulcan, the ugly but useful god of fire and of the forge; and Aphrodite, or Venus, the lovely goddess of beauty.

DIAGRAMING NOUNS AND ADJECTIVES

Diagraming, as you recall from Chapter 10, is a way of seeing the relationships between words and groups of words. When you first studied the adjective, you drew an arrow from the adjective to the noun that it modified. This relationship can also be expressed in a diagram.

PATTERN

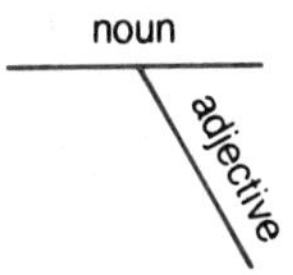

EXAMPLES bright star a special person

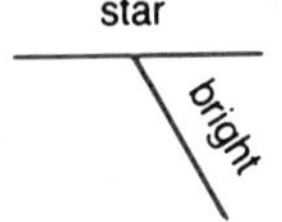

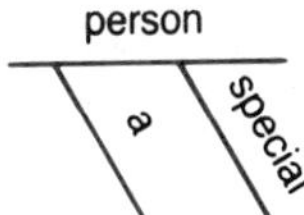

Two or more adjectives joined by a connecting word are diagramed this way.

PATTERN

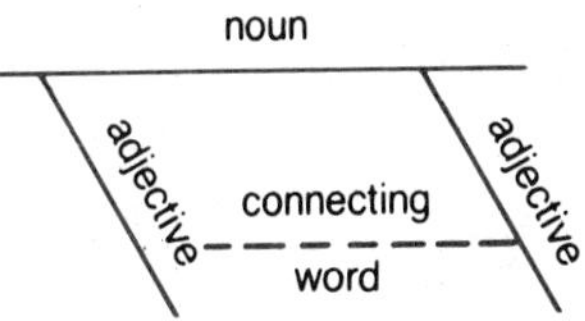

EXAMPLE a lovely and quiet place

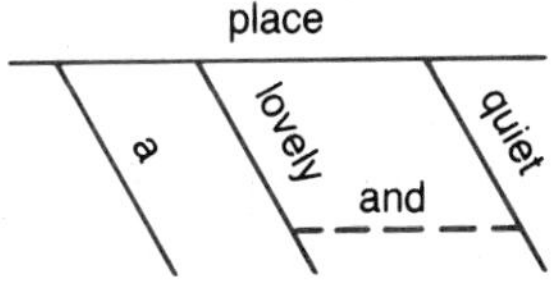

Possessive pronouns are diagramed in the same way adjectives are.

EXERCISE 10. Diagraming Nouns and Adjectives. Diagram the following items. Draw your diagrams with a ruler and allow plenty of space between diagrams.

1. mighty warrior
2. big blue ox
3. a narrow path
4. long, exciting movie
5. his one purpose
6. the last one
7. short and funny story
8. many others
9. my final offer
10. the slow but persistent turtle

EXERCISE 11. Diagraming Sentences. Diagram the following sentences.

EXAMPLE 1. A funny clown performed.

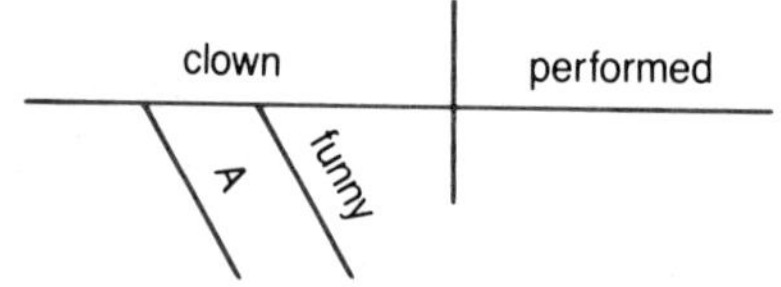

1. Our Swedish visitor arrived.
2. Several answers were given.
3. The small, shy boy won.
4. The poor but generous woman helped.
5. A house and a large barn have burned.

REVIEW EXERCISE D. Identifying Nouns, Pronouns, and Adjectives. Write the following paragraph on your paper, leaving an extra line of space between lines of writing. Over each noun, write *n.;* over each pronoun, write *pron.;* and over each adjective, write *adj.* Disregard the articles *a, an,* and *the.*

Charles Drew developed techniques that are used in the separation and preservation of blood. His research saved numerous lives during World War II. After he received his medical degrees, he taught at Howard University in Washington, D.C. He set up centers in which blood could be stored. The British government asked him to develop a storage system in England. During the war, Dr. Drew was director of an important effort for the American Red Cross that involved the donation of blood. Dr. Drew was also chief surgeon at Freedman's Hospital. We are indebted to this scientist for his great contributions. Many people who have needed blood owe their lives to his methods.

REVIEW EXERCISE E. Diagraming Sentences. Diagram the following sentences:

1. Every minute counts.
2. Five days and five nights passed.
3. The powerful motor shook and roared.
4. The ventriloquist and the dummy talked and sang.
5. Black and gray ties have been sold.

CHAPTER 11 REVIEW: POSTTEST 1

Identifying Nouns, Pronouns, and Adjectives. Number your paper 1–25. After the proper number, write each italicized word in the following sentences, and indicate whether it is a noun, a pronoun, or an adjective. Use the abbreviations *n.* (noun), *pron.* (pronoun), and *adj.* (adjective).

1. Jenna prepared supper *herself* this *morning.*
2. *Everybody* says that *high school* will be more work, but more fun, too.
3. *This* is the biggest mistake *they* ever made.
4. Jackie became a *high-school* senior *last* year.
5. Does *anybody* know *whose* bicycle this is?
6. *Mr. Lander* owns a grove of *citrus* trees.
7. That German shepherd *dog* is a *lively* animal.
8. The lady across the street owns a *Swiss* clock that has *ivory* numbers.
9. Vincent lived in *Los Angeles* before *his* family moved here.
10. This is *their* fault because they ignored all the *danger* signals.
11. I'm telling you, *you* are in *danger.*

12. *It* seemed that *whatever* happened always turned out all right.
13. The answer, *plain* and simple, is that *somebody* needs to do more work.
14. Give me *some* candy out of that *old* jar, will you?
15. The *football* player had to retire after his third knee *injury.*
16. Are you going to *the* dance *Saturday* night?
17. I told him to give you *something* for *your* stomachache.
18. The dogcatcher picked up *my* dog last *Saturday.*
19. *Each* student is required to take *English.*
20. *Each* of them believed that the *best* response would be no response at all.
21. *No one* gave Ms. Lucas *any* trouble.
22. *That* drummer is the *best.*
23. The *waiter* brought dessert even though Richard had said that he didn't want *any.*
24. *Mama* said to turn off the *television,* Billy.
25. I learned a new *dance* step from that *television* show.

CHAPTER 11 REVIEW: POSTTEST 2

Writing Sentences with Nouns, Pronouns, and Adjectives. Write two sentences with each of the following words. Use each one as two different parts of speech—noun and adjective or pronoun and adjective. Write the part of speech of the word after each sentence.

EXAMPLE 1. this
1. *This bicycle is mine. adjective*
1. *This cannot be the right answer. pronoun*

1. game
2. their
3. American
4. right
5. whose
6. that
7. green
8. school
9. mine
10. yours
11. Greek
12. paper
13. lake
14. square
15. bicycle
16. one
17. many
18. money
19. date
20. government

CHAPTER 12

GRAMMAR

The Parts of Speech

VERB, ADVERB, PREPOSITION, CONJUNCTION, INTERJECTION

In Chapter 11 you studied two of the workhorses of the sentence, the *noun* and the *pronoun;* and the part of speech that makes the noun or pronoun more definite, the *adjective.* In this chapter you will learn about the other workhorse of the sentence—the *verb*—and the remaining four parts of speech—*adverb, preposition, conjunction,* and *interjection.*

DIAGNOSTIC TEST

Identifying Verbs, Adverbs, Prepositions, Conjunctions, and Interjections. Number your paper 1–20. After the proper number, write the italicized word or word group in each of the following sentences and label it as an action verb (*a.v.*), a linking verb (*l.v.*), a helping verb (*h.v.*), an adverb (*adv.*), a preposition (*prep.*), a conjunction (*conj.*), or an interjection (*interj.*).

EXAMPLE 1. That girl has *traveled* widely with her family.
1. *traveled—a.v.*

1. Rosie *hit* a home run and tied up the score.

2. *Wow,* that's the best meal I've eaten in a long time!
3. School can *be* fun sometimes.
4. Neither Carlos nor Jan wanted to go *very* far out into the water.
5. That dog looks mean *in spite of* his wagging tail.
6. *Have* you ever seen any wild animals around here?
7. If Ken will *not* help us, then he cannot share in the rewards.
8. My older sister was a cheerleader *during* her senior year.
9. The road that runs *close* to the railroad tracks is usually crowded.
10. Several of my friends *enjoy* working at the mall.
11. No one could do much to help, *for* the damage had already been done.
12. *Where* have you been putting the corrected papers?
13. *Oh,* I didn't know he had already volunteered.
14. Jodie *was* taking in the wash for her mother.
15. Surely Ms. Johnson doesn't *expect* us to finish by tomorrow.
16. May I have a glass of milk and a combination sandwich *without* onions?
17. James *became* impatient, but he waited quietly.
18. My uncle almost always *brings* us something when he visits during the holidays.
19. The car swerved suddenly, *yet* the driver remained in control.
20. The rose *smells* lovely.

THE VERB

You know that the verb is one of the parts of the sentence base. It helps to make a statement about its subject. Some verbs do this by expressing the action of the subject: girl *ran;* monkeys *chatter;* sun *sets.* Other verbs help to make a statement without expressing action: I *am* an eighth-grader; this *is* good; they *seem* happy.

12a. A *verb* is a word that expresses action or otherwise helps to make a statement.

Action Verbs

The action expressed by a verb may be physical action or mental action.

PHYSICAL ACTION jump, shout, search, carry, run
MENTAL ACTION worry, think, believe, imagine

The action verbs in the following sentences are in boldfaced type.

Langston Hughes **wrote** volumes of poetry.
Julia Child **makes** gourmet cooking fun.
We **listened** to the *Jupiter* Symphony by Mozart.

EXERCISE 1. Identifying Action Verbs. Number your paper 1–11. After the proper number, write the verb or verbs in each sentence. There are twenty action verbs in the passage.

1. In the winter our house makes strange noises. **2.** Doors on old brass hinges creak as they open and close. **3.** Pipes in the basement shudder when the water heater starts up. **4.** Loose floorboards crack from the weight of footsteps. **5.** The window curtains rustle softly when the winds blow outside. **6.** The old china cabinet clatters each time a truck passes by. **7.** Beams and rafters in the attic strain and groan during the cold, windy nights.

8. Often members of my family sit silently and listen for these noises of the house. **9.** We disconnect the television and the appliances. **10.** We count the different kinds of noises. **11.** Sometimes we pretend that ghosts lurk upstairs and cause the eerie noises.

Linking Verbs

Many verbs do not express action. Instead, they help to make a statement by acting as links between a subject, which normally comes before the verb, and a word in the predicate, which usually follows the verb. Such verbs are called *linking verbs* because they link their subjects with nouns or adjectives in the predicate.

GRAMMAR

EXAMPLES The star's name **is** Ruby Dee. [name = Ruby Dee]

Marie Curie **became** a famous scientist. [Marie Curie = scientist]

Wild animals **remain** free on the great animal reserves in Africa. [free animals]

The watermelon **looks** ripe. [ripe watermelon]

The verb most commonly used as a linking verb is the verb *be.* You should memorize its various forms.

***Forms of the Verb* Be**

am, is, are, was, were, be, being, been

Any verb ending in *be* or *been* is a form of *be: shall be, will be, can be, might be, has been, have been, had been, would have been, might have been,* etc.

In addition to *be,* there are several other verbs that are often used as linking verbs:

appear, look, seem	feel, smell, sound, taste
become, grow	remain, stay

EXERCISE 2. Writing Linking Verbs. Write the following sentences, inserting a different linking verb in each blank. Be prepared to tell which word each verb links to its subject.

EXAMPLE 1. Judith Jamison —— calm during the premiere of the dance.

1. *Judith Jamison remained calm during the premiere of the dance.* [*Remained* links *Jamison* and *calm.*]

1. The first day —— long.
2. Your suggestion —— good to me.
3. Our room —— festive after we decorated it for the party.
4. The orange —— a little too sweet.
5. In the novel the main character —— a doctor, and he returns home to set up a clinic.
6. Before a storm the air —— wet and heavy.
7. Did she —— happy living in Florida?
8. The diver —— more confident with each dive she made.

9. They —— interested in the guest speaker.
10. The lilacs —— lovely.

Most linking verbs may also be used as action verbs. Whether a verb is used to express action or to link words depends on its meaning in a given sentence.

LINKING The tiger **looked** tame.
ACTION The tiger **looked** for something to eat.

LINKING The soup **tasted** good.
ACTION I **tasted** the soup.

LINKING She **grew** tired of playing.
ACTION She **grew** into a fine woman.

EXERCISE 3. Identifying Action Verbs and Linking Verbs. Number your paper 1–10. In the following sentences, when the verb is used as an action verb, write the verb and its subject beside the appropriate number. When the verb is used as a linking verb, write the verb, its subject, and the word or words that the verb links to its subject.

EXAMPLES 1. Ms. Brody appeared suddenly in the classroom.
1. *appeared, Ms. Brody*
2. Ms. Brody appeared quite cheerful.
2. *appeared, Ms. Brody—cheerful*

1. At Marla's request, we tasted the chili.
2. The chili tasted very spicy.
3. The cook looked unhappy about our comments.
4. She looked at her sister Joan suspiciously.
5. Yesterday the chili in the school cafeteria looked good.
6. Marla looked at Joan then, too.
7. Joan felt mischievous.
8. She felt a laugh in the back of her throat.
9. The doorbell sounded down the hall.
10. Marla's voice, usually pleasant, sounded angry.

EXERCISE 4. Identifying Verbs. Number your paper 1–14. After the proper number, list the verb or verbs that appear on that line. If the verb is a linking verb, list also the subject and the word or words that the verb links to its subject.

Matt is a young musician who loves all kinds of music. According to his parents, he practices the piano every day. No one knows how many hours he plays each week, although many people guess at least twenty. His parents worry about him. They think he remains indoors too much. Still, Matt seems happy.

One day Matt becomes restless. The notes sound wrong, and everything appears impossible. However, Matt seems confident. He grabs some sheets of music paper and then writes down some notes. After some careful revisions Matt forms the notes into an original harmony.

That night he performs his song for his parents. They exclaim, "Matt, we are so proud of our son, the pianist and composer!"

WRITING APPLICATION A:
Using Verbs That Make Your Writing Fresh and Lively

Verbs are vital to communication. To make your writing lively and original, try to use verbs that catch your reader's attention. Sportswriters often vary their verbs to give their reports more action and excitement.

EXAMPLE Celtics **rip** Lakers
Mississippi State **bashes** Michigan

Writing Assignment

When you use chronological order, you place events in the order in which they occurred. Write a summary of an incident from a book, a movie, or a television show that you consider to be exciting. Present the incident in chronological order, using verbs that are fresh and lively. Underline these verbs.

Helping Verbs

So far in this chapter you have been studying one-word verbs, sometimes called *main verbs*. Frequently, though, the main verb is accompanied by other verbs called *helping verbs*. The main verb and the helping verbs together make up a *verb phrase*. Notice in the following examples that the main verb may change its form when a helping verb is added.

MAIN VERB crawl
VERB PHRASE will crawl

MAIN VERB listen
VERB PHRASE have been listening

MAIN VERB find
VERB PHRASE would have been found

Here is a list of the most commonly used helping verbs.

Commonly Used Helping Verbs

be (am, is, are, etc.)	shall	should	must
has	will	would	do
have	can	may	did
had	could	might	does

The verb *be* in its various forms is the most frequently used helping verb. *Be* used as a helping verb is very easy to distinguish from *be* used as a linking verb. When *be* is used as a helping verb, there is always a main verb used with it; but when *be* is used as a linking verb, it is itself the main verb.

HELPING VERB These books **have been read** many times.
LINKING VERB The children **have been** good today.

The following sentences contain verb phrases. The verbs are in boldface, and the main verbs are also underlined.

Seiji Ozawa **has been <u>praised</u>** for his fine conducting.
His recordings **should be <u>heard</u>** by anyone interested in classical music.
He **will <u>conduct</u>** many outstanding orchestras.

EXERCISE 5. Identifying Verb Phrases. Number your paper 1–10. Write the verb phrases in the order in which they appear in the following paragraph:

Many people are earning their livings at unusual jobs. Even today people can find positions as shepherds, inventors, and candlestick makers. It may seem strange, but these people have decided that ordinary jobs can become too tedious for them. Some people have been working as messengers. You may have seen them when they were wearing costumes such as gorilla suits. Other people have been finding work as mimes. With a little imagination, anyone can find an unusual job.

Sometimes the verb phrase is interrupted by other parts of speech, as in the following examples:

Because of the fog, we **could** not **see** the road.
People **may** someday **communicate** with dolphins.
How much **do** you **know** about Lucy Stone, the suffragist?

REVIEW EXERCISE A. Labeling Linking Verbs and Action Verbs. Number your paper 1–20. List the verbs and the verb phrases that appear in the following paragraph. After each action verb or verb phrase, write *a.v.;* after each linking verb or verb phrase, write *l.v.*

The term *Viking* was used for all sailors of the North, whether they were Norwegians, Swedes, or Danes. The Vikings were a fierce people who roamed the seas for about three hundred years. For several centuries people considered the Vikings the scourge of Europe because they invaded and pillaged other countries. They worshiped such fierce gods as Thor and Odin, and they hoped that they would die in battle. The Vikings believed that when they died in battle, they went to Valhalla, where they could eternally enjoy battles and banquets. The Vikings thought that each day the warriors in Valhalla would go out to the battlefield and would receive wounds time and time again. Then, in spite of their injuries, at the end of each day they would all meet back at the banquet hall, where their wounds would promptly heal and they could boast about their great bravery in battle.

REVIEW EXERCISE B. Labeling Parts of Speech. Write the following sentences using every other line of your paper. Underline the italicized words, and over each of these, write an abbreviation to show its part of speech: *n.* for noun, *pron.* for pronoun, *adj.* for adjective, *a.v.* for action verb, and *l.v.* for linking verb. Treat proper names and verb phrases as single words.

EXAMPLE 1. *Mary McLeod Bethune* is a *major* figure in American history.

n. *adj.*

1. *Mary McLeod Bethune is a major figure in American history.*

1. *She* dedicated her *life* to helping young people.
2. In her *early* years she *began* a teaching career.
3. In 1904 she moved to Florida and *opened* a school of *her* own.
4. The school eventually *became* the Bethune-Cookman College, and Bethune served as its *president.*
5. In 1930 Bethune *was invited* to a *Presidential* conference on child health and protection.
6. Then, during Roosevelt's administration, *she* helped in the establishment of the *National Youth Administration.*
7. Her outstanding efforts *impressed* Roosevelt, and *he* established an important office on minority affairs.
8. This office granted funds to *serious* students so that *they* could continue their education.
9. In 1945 she *was* an observer at the conference that organized the *United Nations.*
10. Bethune *remained* interested in education, and her *notable* efforts earned her national recognition.

THE ADVERB

12b. An *adverb* is a word used to modify a verb, an adjective, or another adverb.

An *adverb* usually answers one of these questions: *Where? When? How? To what extent (how much* or *how long)?*

WHERE?

The fire started **here.**
The couple was married **nearby.**

WHEN?

The police arrived **promptly.**
Then the suspects were questioned.

HOW?

The accident occurred **suddenly.**
The Prime Minister spoke **carefully.**

TO WHAT EXTENT (HOW MUCH or HOW LONG)?

We should **never** deceive our friends.
She has **scarcely** begun the lesson.

(1) An adverb modifies a verb more often than it modifies an adjective or an adverb.

Notice how an adverb makes the meaning of the verb more definite.

EXAMPLES The man crawled **down**. [The adverb tells *where* the man crawled.]
He halted **abruptly.** [The adverb tells *how* he halted.]
Now we are busy. [The adverb tells *when* we are busy.]
The speaker droned on **endlessly**. [The adverb tells *to what extent* the speaker droned.]

Adverbs are sometimes used to ask questions.

EXAMPLES **Where** are you going?
How did you do on the test?

EXERCISE 6. Identifying Adverbs That Modify Verbs. The following sentences contain twenty adverbs, all modifying verbs. Number your paper 1–9. After the proper number, write the adverbs in that sentence.

1. The snowstorm has completely blocked traffic and has temporarily grounded airplanes today.
2. How can you develop into a strong runner now?
3. Yesterday three police officers secretly followed the suspect.
4. The doctor came immediately, but the patient had already recovered.
5. Gymnastics has recently attracted many students, and the equipment is always in use.
6. The coach argued violently, but the umpire calmly ignored him.
7. February is never a warm month in Maine.
8. Her luncheon was well attended, and her speech was applauded loudly afterward.
9. Today astronomers can accurately chart the courses of planets, yet the motions of some celestial bodies are still a mystery.

GRAMMAR

(2) An adverb sometimes modifies an adjective.

An adverb is sometimes needed to make the meaning of an adjective more definite. An *extremely* good dancer is quite different from a *fairly* good dancer.

EXAMPLES An **unusually** fast starter, Karen easily won the hurdles event. [The adjective *fast* modifies the noun *starter*; the adverb tells *how fast* the starter was.]

Our committee is **especially** busy at this time of year. [The adjective *busy* modifies the noun *committee;* the adverb tells *how busy* the committee is.]

EXERCISE 7. Identifying Adverbs That Modify Adjectives. Number your paper 1–10. After the proper number, write the adverbs that modify adjectives in each sentence. After each adverb, write the adjective that it modifies.

EXAMPLE 1. Because so many bicycles have been stolen, the principal hired a guard.
1. *so, many*

1. The team is extremely proud of its record.
2. All frogs may look quite harmless, but some are poisonous.
3. The class was unusually quiet today.
4. Newborn animals are very clumsy at first.
5. The coach said we were too careless when we made the routine plays.
6. The situation seemed utterly futile.
7. When kittens are with their mother, they look thoroughly contented.
8. Weekends are especially hectic for me when all of my teachers assign homework.
9. The lecture seemed much longer than one hour.
10. The new exchange student who comes from Norway is surprisingly fluent in English.

EXERCISE 8. Writing Adverbs to Modify Adjectives. The adverb *very* is used far too often to modify adjectives. Write an adverb to modify each adjective below. Do not use *very*.

EXAMPLE 1. strong
1. *incredibly strong*

1. cheerful	6. timid
2. sour	7. heavy
3. wide	8. long
4. messy	9. calm
5. honest	10. graceful

(3) An adverb occasionally modifies another adverb.

EXAMPLES Elena finished the problem **more** quickly than I did. [The adverb *quickly* modifies the verb *finished* and is, in turn, modified by the adverb *more,* which tells *how quickly* Elena finished the problem.]

Our guest left **quite** abruptly. [The adverb *abruptly* modifies the verb *left* and is modified by *quite,* which tells *how abruptly* our guest left.]

EXERCISE 9. Identifying Adverbs That Modify Other Adverbs. Number your paper 1–5. Beside the appropriate number, list each adverb that modifies another adverb. Then write the adverb that it modifies.

EXAMPLE 1. The new swimming pool is most certainly an improvement over the old one.
1. *most, certainly*

1. Condors are almost entirely extinct in the United States.
2. They are more frequently seen soaring over the Andes Mountains in South America.
3. Condors are the largest living birds, and some people think that they are most assuredly the ugliest.
4. Even though condors have not been welcomed too enthusiastically into the hearts of people, they still need protection.
5. The balance of nature quite definitely depends on all kinds of animals, even on the ones that are not cute and cuddly.

REVIEW EXERCISE C. Identifying Adverbs. Number your paper 1–10. Beside the appropriate number, list the adverbs in the order that they appear in each of the following sentences. After each adverb, write the word or expression that the adverb modifies. Some sentences have more than one adverb.

EXAMPLE 1. The movie ended too quickly.
1. *too—quickly; quickly—ended*

1. I have been a fan of mystery stories since I was very young.
2. My favorite stories are about detectives who cleverly match wits with equally clever villains.
3. Some stories are incredibly exciting from start to finish, but others slowly build suspense.
4. If I like a story, I can hardly put it down until I finish it.
5. I should never become involved in a story if I have tons of homework to do, because then I am too tempted to read.
6. If I am not able to guess the ending, I can scarcely prevent myself from peeking at the last chapter.

7. I restrain myself unusually well when I am tempted.
8. I wonder if I would have the nerve to creep around and look for clues in a terribly dark, spooky basement.
9. Clues are often found in carefully guarded places.
10. How do the mystery detectives find the answers to some of the most complicated cases?

DIAGRAMING VERBS AND ADVERBS

The verb, like the noun and pronoun, always appears on a horizontal line. The adverb is diagramed on a slanting line under the word it modifies.

1. An adverb modifying a verb:

EXAMPLES studies hard does not exercise daily

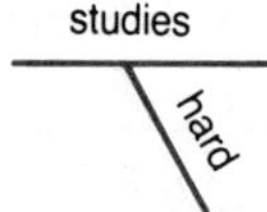

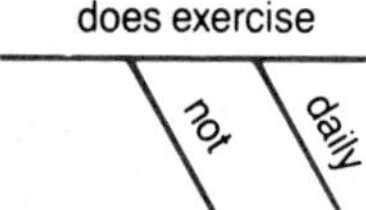

2. An adverb modifying an adjective:

EXAMPLES extremely strong wind much better swimmer

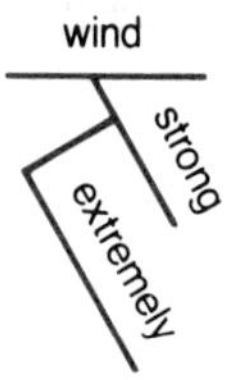

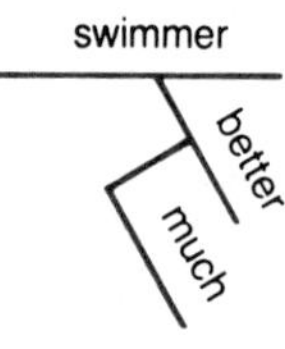

3. An adverb modifying another adverb:

EXAMPLES tried rather hard flew almost too high

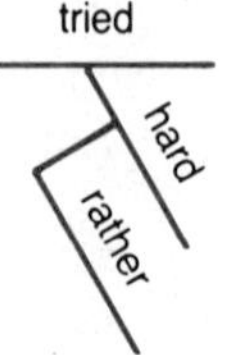

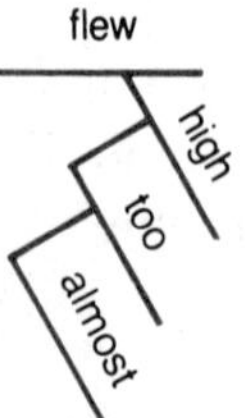

EXERCISE 10. Diagraming Verbs and Adverbs. Diagram the following groups of words. Use a ruler and leave plenty of space between diagrams.

1. answered quickly
2. badly worn sail
3. listened quite intently
4. worked very late
5. dangerously sharp curve
6. never plans very carefully
7. walked proudly away
8. somewhat rickety bridge
9. may possibly happen
10. drove rather slowly

EXERCISE 11. Diagraming Sentences. Diagram the following sentences. Use a ruler and leave plenty of space between diagrams.

1. The plane landed smoothly.
2. The shutters rattled quite noisily.
3. We are definitely leaving tomorrow.
4. The anxious motorist drove much too far.
5. The unbelievably slow turtle got there first.
6. The guide limped noticeably.
7. The extremely nervous passenger collapsed.
8. Our turn finally came.
9. They tried very hard.
10. The new car had been slightly damaged.

THE PREPOSITION

12c. A *preposition* is a word used to show the relationship of a noun or a pronoun to some other word in the sentence.

Notice how a change in the preposition changes the relationship between *package* and *tree* in each of the following sentences.

The package **under** the tree is mine.
The package **in** the tree is mine.
The package **near** the tree is mine.
The package **behind** the tree is mine.
The package **beside** the tree is mine.

Learn to recognize the following words, which are commonly used as prepositions.

Commonly Used Prepositions

aboard	behind	from	throughout
about	below	in	to
above	beneath	into	toward
across	beside	like	under
after	between	near	underneath
against	beyond	of	until
along	but (except)	off	unto
amid	by	on	up
among	down	over	upon
around	during	past	with
at	except	since	within
before	for	through	without

Occasionally you will find compound prepositions—prepositions of more than one word. A compound preposition may be considered as one word.

Compound Prepositions

because of	in spite of	instead of
on account of	according to	out of

EXERCISE 12. Identifying Prepositions. Number your paper 1–10. List the prepositions in order beside the appropriate number. Include all parts of any compound prepositions you find.

EXAMPLE 1. Many Roman myths were adaptations of Greek myths.
1. *of*

1. Mars, the god of war, is perhaps the most Roman god in Roman mythology.
2. Many Roman gods were borrowed from Greek mythology.
3. According to legend, Mars was the father of Romulus and Remus, twin brothers.
4. When the twins were babies, an evil ruler threw them into the Tiber River.

5. Romulus and Remus were rescued from the river, then were fed by a wolf, and were raised under the care of a shepherd.
6. These twins fought against each other in a deadly rivalry.
7. Instead of working with his brother, Romulus killed Remus.
8. It is said that Romulus founded the city of Rome around 753 B.C.
9. Throughout the centuries people have read about the legend of Romulus and Remus.
10. Out of hundreds of legends, this one has remained among the best known.

A preposition is always followed by a noun or a pronoun that the preposition relates to another word in the sentence. The noun or the pronoun following the preposition is called the *object* of the preposition. Words that modify the object may come between the preposition and the object. Taken together, the preposition, its object, and the modifiers of the object are called a *prepositional phrase*.

EXAMPLE **across** the dusty **prairie** [The entire prepositional phrase includes the preposition *across*, its object *prairie*, and two adjectives modifying the object—*the* and *dusty*.]

EXERCISE 13. Identifying Prepositional Phrases. Number your paper 1–10, and, after the proper number, write the prepositional phrase in each sentence. Underline each preposition.

EXAMPLE 1. Walt Whitman wrote a very moving poem, "O Captain! My Captain!", about Abraham Lincoln.
1. *about Abraham Lincoln*

1. In this poem the ship's captain represents Abraham Lincoln.
2. The ship has just completed a voyage through rough weather.
3. On the shore, people celebrate the ship's safe arrival.
4. One member of the ship's crew addresses his captain.
5. "For you they call, the swaying mass, their eager faces turning. . . ."

6. Everyone except the captain can hear the rejoicing.
7. He has died during the voyage.
8. The ship represents the ship of state.
9. The ship's voyage across rough seas symbolizes the Civil War.
10. Lincoln, the captain, directed his ship toward a safe harbor.

WRITING APPLICATION B: Using Prepositional Phrases To Create Vivid Similes

Color can add considerable appeal and interest to a picture. You know that you can use specific describing words to create the same kind of vivid impression in your writing. You can also try experimenting with *similes*. To form a simile, use *like* or *as* to show how one thing is similar to another thing, even though the two items are basically different. Notice how the following similes are expressed in prepositional phrases beginning with *like*.

EXAMPLES Her coat was red and silky, and there was a blaze of white down her chest and a circle of white around her throat. Her face was wrinkled and sad, **like a wise old man's.**

JAMES STREET

For nearly a year, I sopped around the house, the Store, the school and the church, **like an old biscuit.**

MAYA ANGELOU

Writing Assignment

A *tall tale* is a highly improbable humorous story that stretches the facts beyond any hope of belief. Tall tales include people as tall as mountains, woodsmen who use trees as toothpicks, and other impossible situations. Write a tall tale in which you use at least three similes that are expressed in prepositional phrases beginning with *like* or *as*. Underline these similes.

Sometimes the same word may be used either as a preposition or as an adverb. To tell an adverb from a preposition, remember that a preposition is always followed by a noun or pronoun object.

ADVERB The plane circled above.
PREPOSITION The plane circled above the field. [Note the object of the preposition—*field*.]

ADVERB We remained within.
PREPOSITION We remained within the shelter. [Note the object of the preposition—*shelter*.]

EXERCISE 14. Writing Sentences with Adverbs and Prepositions. Use each of the following words in two sentences, first as an adverb and then as a preposition. Underline the designated word.

EXAMPLE 1. along
1. *"Why can't I go along?" asked the child.*
1. *Wildflowers were blooming along the riverbank.*

1. off 2. across 3. below 4. above 5. down

You must also be careful not to confuse a prepositional phrase beginning with *to* (*to town, to her club*) with a verb form beginning with *to* (*to run, to be seen*). Again, remember that a prepositional phrase always ends with a noun or pronoun.

THE CONJUNCTION

12d. A *conjunction* is a word that joins words or groups of words.

Conjunctions joining single words:

hot **or** cold
small **but** comfortable

Conjunctions joining groups of words:

through a forest **and** across a river
wanted to notify **but** not to alarm

Conjunctions joining groups of words that are sentences:

The stars seem motionless, **but** actually they are moving rapidly through space.
One leader was very powerful, **and** the other was very weak.

Conjunctions are of three kinds: *coordinating, correlative,* and *subordinating.*

The *coordinating conjunctions* are *and, but, or, nor, for, so,* and *yet.*

EXAMPLES The water was cold, **yet** refreshing.
You may take the test now, **or** you may wait until later.
I didn't like him, **nor** did he like me.

When *for* is used as a conjunction, it connects groups of words that are sentences. On all other occasions, *for* is used as a preposition.

CONJUNCTION We wrote to the tourist bureau, **for** we wanted information on places to visit.
PREPOSITION We waited patiently **for** a reply.

Correlative conjunctions are always found in pairs that have other words dividing them: *either . . . or, neither . . . nor, both . . . and, not only . . . but also.*

EXAMPLES Our class will furnish **either** the punch **or** the cookies for the party.
Both cats **and** dogs make good pets.
Clare Boothe Luce was **not only** a playwright **but also** an ambassador.

Subordinating conjunctions occur in complex sentences and are explained on pages 391–92.

EXERCISE 15. Identifying Coordinating and Correlative Conjunctions. Number your paper 1–20. After the proper number, write the coordinating or correlative conjunctions in each sentence. Be prepared to tell what words or groups of words each conjunction joins. Treat a pair of correlative conjunctions as one conjunction.

EXAMPLE 1. Our teacher bought either a jeep or a pickup truck.
1. *either—or*

1. The disc jockey played records and tapes for us.
2. We were afraid that neither the Ferris wheel nor the roller coaster was safe.
3. Some people like checkers, but others prefer chess.
4. We are working hard on the project, for the science fair starts tomorrow.
5. The players practiced hard and yet did not win the regional title.
6. Our club members will either make the decorations or bring refreshments.
7. Many players and coaches would like to change the rules of the game.
8. Ms. Whiting is both a teacher and a writer.
9. The girls' basketball team not only won the game but also scored the most points in our school's history.
10. If the girls rehearse, they will perform at the game and at the dance on Saturday.
11. Sarah speaks French or German.
12. I hope I improve my grades, for I have been studying hard this term.
13. They must practice fielding and batting.
14. We will be working on the balance beam or the trampoline this week in gym class.
15. I didn't receive a letter from my cousin today, nor did I really expect one.
16. The drivers braked and swerved to avoid the dog.
17. Either you or I should send the invitations.
18. The people waited patiently for the bus, but it never came.
19. The artist used neither oils nor acrylics to paint this picture.
20. The principal was excited, for the school board had approved his plan for a new cafeteria.

THE INTERJECTION

12e. An *interjection* is a word that expresses emotion and that is not related grammatically to other words in the sentence.

EXAMPLES **Oh!** You surprised me.
Wow! Am I tired!
Well, I did my best.

DETERMINING PARTS OF SPEECH

You have now finished a study of the eight parts of speech. On page 334 is a chart that briefly summarizes what you have learned.

12f. A word's use determines its part of speech.

Although words are given as examples of particular parts of speech in the chart that follows, you cannot really tell what part of speech a word is until you know how the word is used in a sentence. For example, the same word can be used as a pronoun or an adjective or as an adverb or a preposition.

EXAMPLES **Each** did his part. [pronoun]
Each student baked a cake. [adjective]

The tired shoppers sat **down** for a while. [adverb]
The ball rolled **down** the hill. [preposition]

A member of the crew has spotted **land.** [noun]
The pilot can **land** here safely. [verb]

We didn't find her, **for** she had left. [conjunction]
Everybody searched **for** the lost child. [preposition]

Well, he seems to have recovered. [interjection]
He doesn't look **well** to me. [adjective]

REVIEW EXERCISE D. Identifying Parts of Speech. Number your paper 1–20. After each number, write the italicized word from the corresponding sentence. Then write the part of speech of the word. Be prepared to explain your answer.

EXAMPLES 1. The *ship* entered the harbor slowly.
1. *ship—noun*
2. Did they *ship* the package to Dee and Tom?
2. *ship—verb*

1. The English test was easy *for* him.
2. He didn't go to the movies, *for* he wanted to practice on the drums.
3. It was a steep *climb,* but we finally made it to the top of the hill.
4. Instead of riding the elevator, June and I *climb* the stairs for exercise.
5. *Some* volunteered to sell tickets.
6. We donated *some* clothes to the rummage sale.
7. Looking for shells, the girl strolled *along* the shore.
8. When we went sailing, Raul and Manuel came *along*.
9. I lost *my* book report!
10. *My!* This is not a good day!
11. No one *but* Jill saw it.
12. I play guitar, *but* Julianne sings.
13. Most club members voted in favor of the hayride, but *many* voted against it.
14. Christie has *many* lovely quilts in her room.
15. The *plan* for the trip has been confirmed.
16. My parents *plan* to attend the school play.
17. The hospital is located *nearby*.
18. After the movie we went to a *nearby* restaurant.
19. When the batter hit the ball, it popped *up*.
20. The neighbor's dog chased Fluffy *up* the crabapple tree.

REVIEW EXERCISE E. Identifying Different Parts of Speech. Number your paper 1–50. After the proper number, write each of the italicized words or groups of words in the following paragraphs. After each, write what part of speech it is, using these abbreviations: *n.* (noun), *pron.* (pronoun), *v.* (verb), *adj.* (adjective), *adv.* (adverb), *prep.* (preposition), *conj.* (conjunction), *interj.* (interjection).

Dancing may be (1) *easy* for (2) *some,* but I have (3) *always* had (4) *two* left (5) *feet.* (6) *Yesterday* after (7) *school,* one of my friends (8) *tried* to teach (9) *me* the latest dance. (10) *Well!* I was (11) *so* embarrassed I could have hidden (12) *in* the (13) *closet.* My feet (14) *have* (15) *minds* of (16) *their* own, (17) *and* they do (18) *not* behave well.

Today I (19) *thought* (20) *about* this (21) *problem* (22) *throughout* lunch. (23) *Later* I thought about it (24) *during* math class. I have considered every (25) *possible* solution. I have (26) *even* wanted to put (27) *down* cutouts of (28) *paper* feet (29) *with* numbers on them.

My (30) *mother* (31) *has shown* me (32) *some* dances that (33) *were* popular when (34) *she* was my age. I've tried (35) *hard* (36) *many* times to follow the (37) *steps,* (38) *but* all my efforts (39) *have seemed* (40) *useless.*

"Either you are (41) *too* tense when you dance, (42) *or* you are trying too hard. (43) *You* should (44) *relax* more," people say to me.

(45) "*What!* (46) *How* can I relax?" I groan. (47) "*No one* can relax when the body goes (48) *left* and the feet go right!" At that point, I usually (49) *decide* to give up, but I always try (50) *again* the next day.

CHAPTER 12 REVIEW: POSTTEST 1

Identifying Verbs, Adverbs, Prepositions, Conjunctions, and Interjections. Number your paper 1–25. After the proper number, write each italicized word or word group in the following sentences, and indicate whether it is a verb, an adverb, a preposition, a conjunction, or an interjection. Use the abbreviations *v.* (verb), *adv.* (adverb), *prep.* (preposition), *conj.* (conjunction), and *interj.* (interjection). For each verb, indicate whether it is an action verb, a helping verb, or a linking verb.

EXAMPLE 1. I *am reading* a book *about* dinosaurs.
1. *am reading—v. (action), about—prep.*

1. We *watched* the skywriter spell out the letters *carefully*.
2. *Both* the dog *and* the cat *are* dirty and need baths.
3. His cousins don't *know* much *about* sports.
4. When the horse reared *back,* the girl held *onto* its mane.
5. She *would have been* on time if the bell had *not* rung early.
6. Clever replies *never* occur to me until the situation is *long* past.
7. If I *had known* how to identify verbs, I would have gotten a better grade *on* that test.
8. *When* do you usually feel your best and why *do* you *feel* that way then?
9. He won't go, *nor* will he *willingly* cooperate.
10. Juan exercised *daily* for twenty minutes *before* breakfast.
11. One of the runners *almost* tripped over the hurdle, *yet* he still placed third.
12. There are times when Jill *thinks* that she cares *almost* too much about making the team.
13. *Whoops*! I dropped my ring, and it rolled *under* the counter.
14. My scout leader said that she *had* never tasted stew like mine *before*.
15. Although *not* many people *like* the heat, the desert can be beautiful.
16. Be sure that you *sharpen* your pencil *now* because you won't be allowed to leave your seat after the test begins.
17. *Did* you *bring* a note *from* your parents?
18. The girl *tried* again *in spite of* her previous difficulty.
19. My mom took me *aboard* the ship where she once *worked*.
20. Nguyen *does* not *wish* to intrude, *nor* does he feel fully at ease in such situations.
21. Jill *cares* almost *too* much about making the team.
22. *Well,* I plan to help Andrea, for I believe in her cause.
23. The fish quickly darted *under* a rock.
24. Jeff loaned Anne a dollar and *then* found out that he didn't have *quite* enough money for his own lunch.
25. I don't know *very* much *about* my great-grandparents.

GRAMMAR

CHAPTER 12 REVIEW: POSTTEST 2

Writing Sentences Using Different Parts of Speech. Write two sentences using each of the following words as the parts of speech given in parentheses. Underline the word in the sentence, and write its part of speech after the sentence.

EXAMPLE 1. over (*adv.* and *prep.*)
1. *The skies began to clear when the storm was* *over*. (*adverb*)
2. *The horse jumped* *over* *the fence.* (*preposition*)

1. but (*conj.* and *prep.*)
2. like (*v.* and *prep.*)
3. run (*n.* and *v.*)
4. well (*adv.* and *interj.*)
5. that (*pron.* and *adj.*)
6. more (*adj.* and *adv.*)
7. last (*v.* and *adj.*)
8. one (*adj.* and *pron.*)
9. near (*v.* and *prep.*)
10. around (*prep.* and *adv.*)
11. all (*pron.* and *adj.*)
12. past (*n.* and *prep.*)
13. so (*interj.* and *adv.*)
14. for (*conj.* and *prep.*)
15. fight (*n.* and *v.*)
16. even (*v.* and *adv.*)
17. since (*prep.* and *adv.*)
18. taste (*n.* and *v.*)
19. boy (*n.* and *interj.*)
20. any (*pron.* and *adj.*)

SUMMARY OF PARTS OF SPEECH

Rule	*Part of Speech*	*Use*	*Examples*
11a	noun	names a person, a place, a thing, or an idea	Wilma, cave, Asia, freedom, honesty
11b	pronoun	takes the place of a noun	she, ourselves, who, anyone
11c	adjective	modifies a noun or pronoun	sick, tiny, purple, smooth
12a	verb	shows action or helps to make a statement	play, study, were, become
12b	adverb	modifies a verb, an adjective, or another adverb	very, too, usually, quickly, not

12c	preposition	relates a noun or a pronoun to another word; begins a prepositional phrase	beside [her], to [town], for [John], with [them]
12d	conjunction	joins words or groups of words	and, but, either . . . or
12e	interjection	shows strong feeling	Well! Wow! Oh!

CHAPTER 13

Complements

DIRECT AND INDIRECT OBJECTS, SUBJECT COMPLEMENTS

Every sentence has a sentence base, which consists of, at the least, a verb and its subject.

S V
John shouted.

S V
The squirrels scampered across the campus.

The sentence base often has another part, in addition to the subject and verb, called a *complement.* The word *complement* means "completer." A complement completes the meaning begun by the subject and verb. The following word groups are not complete, even though they have subjects and verbs.

S V
Marlene brought [what?]

S V
I met [whom?]

S V
Her friend is [what?]

Here a complement completes the meaning of each.

S V C
Marlene brought a cake.

S V C
I met Carlos.

S V C
Her friend is a painter.

DIAGNOSTIC TEST

Identifying Direct Objects, Indirect Objects, and Subject Complements. Number your paper 1–20. After the proper number, write the italicized word or word group in the following sentences. Correctly identify each, using these abbreviations: *d.o.* (direct object), *i.o.* (indirect object), *p.n.* (predicate nominative), and *p.a.* (predicate adjective).

EXAMPLES 1. The rancher raised prize-winning *cattle.*
1. *cattle—d.o.*
2. The rancher became a rich *man.*
2. *man—p.n.*

1. Brenda caught the *ball* and threw it to first base.
2. Your cousin seems *nice.*
3. I'm not the *one* who did that.
4. The sun grew *hotter* as the day went on.
5. Mrs. Ford gave *me* ride to the Special Olympics.
6. That hamburger meat smells *bad* to me.
7. Jane's father and mother are both *truck drivers.*
8. Have you bought your *tickets* yet?
9. My mother won't buy me a *trail bike.*
10. The irate customer sent the *store manager* a letter of complaint.
11. The nurse gave *Virgil* a flu shot.
12. Earl often looks *tired* on Monday mornings.
13. With his calloused hands he cannot feel the *texture* of velvet.
14. Her grades are always *higher* than mine.
15. Heather, who is new at our school, is the nicest *girl* I know.

16. Overhead, the vultures circled the injured *gazelle.*
17. Throw *Eric* a screen pass.
18. When left to dry in the sun, plums become *prunes.*
19. Why did Mr. Santos loan *Arnie* five dollars?
20. Ms. Rossetti will be our Spanish *teacher* this fall.

13a. A *complement* is a word or a group of words that completes the meaning begun by the subject and verb.

Jody redecorated her **room.** [*Room* completes the meaning by telling *what* Jody redecorated.]

My aunt sent **me** a **postcard** from Amsterdam. [*Me* and *postcard* complete the meaning by telling *what* was sent and *to whom* it was sent.]

The Ephron sisters are humorous **writers.** [*Writers* completes the meaning by telling something about the subject *sisters.*]

The *Mona Lisa* is very **famous.** [*Famous* completes the meaning by describing the subject *Mona Lisa.*]

In these four sentences, you see two kinds of complements. The first two sentences have complements that are affected by the action of the verb. The third and fourth have complements that refer to the subject. A noun, a pronoun, or an adjective can serve as a complement, but an adverb can never be a complement.

The bus is **here.** [*Here* is an adverb, not a complement.]

A complement, like a subject, is never in a prepositional phrase.

Sarah is reading the **dictionary**. [*Dictionary* is a complement; it completes the meaning begun by the subject and verb.]

Sarah is thumbing through the dictionary. [*Dictionary* is in the phrase *through the dictionary;* it is not a complement.]

Helen is an expert **skier** and **skater.** [*Skier* and *skater* are complements.]

Helen is in Colorado. [*Colorado* is in the phrase *in Colorado*; it is not a complement.]

EXERCISE 1. Identifying Subjects, Verbs, and Complements. Make three columns labeled *Subject, Verb,* and *Complement.* Enter the parts of the base of each of the following sentences in the appropriate columns. Remember that a complement is never in a prepositional phrase.

1. In Shakespeare's time, plays were very popular in England.
2. Many people watched plays at the Globe Theater in London.
3. William Shakespeare was one of the owners of the Globe.
4. The playhouse looked quite different from most of our modern theaters.
5. It was a building with eight sides.
6. The building contained an inner courtyard.
7. The stage was a platform at one end of the courtyard.
8. Many playgoers did not have seats during a performance.
9. The people without seats filled the courtyard in front of the stage.
10. Many of them watched the action of the play from a position next to the stage.

EXERCISE 2. Writing Sentences with Subjects, Verbs, and Complements. Write five sentences using the following sentence bases. Add enough words to make *interesting* sentences.

SUBJECT	VERB	COMPLEMENT
girl	delivered	telegram
days	are	long
Pam	won	contest
runner	appeared	tired
Venus	is	planet

DIRECT AND INDIRECT OBJECTS

There are two kinds of complements that are affected by the action of the verb: the *direct object* and the *indirect object.*

13b. The *direct object* receives the action expressed by the verb or names the result of the action.

Dorothea Lange photographed **farmers** in the Midwest during the Depression. [*Farmers* is the direct object; it receives the action of the verb *photographed.*]

Lange built an impressive **collection.** [*Collection* is the direct object; it names the result of the action *built.*]

Direct objects follow action verbs only. They answer the question *What?* or *Whom?* after an action verb. Lange, in the first sentence, photographed *whom*? She photographed *farmers;* therefore, *farmers* is the direct object. In the second sentence, Lang built *what*? She built a *collection;* therefore, *collection* is the direct object.

EXERCISE 3. Identifying Direct Objects. Number your paper 1–10. Write the action verb and its object in each sentence. Say the verb to yourself and ask *What?* or *Whom?* Remember that objects are never in a prepositional phrase.

EXAMPLE 1. Volunteers distributed food to the flood victims.
1. *distributed—food*

1. On the plains the Cheyenne hunted buffalo for food and clothing.
2. We watched a performance of Lorraine Hansberry's *A Raisin in the Sun.*
3. During most of its history the United States has welcomed refugees from other countries.
4. The leading man wore a hat with a large plume.
5. Are you preserving the environment?
6. After the game the coach answered questions from the sports reporters.
7. Did you see her performance on television?
8. The researchers followed the birds' migration from Mexico to Canada.
9. Mayor Fiorello La Guardia governed New York City during the Depression.
10. Have the movie theaters announced the special discount for teen-agers yet?

13c. The *indirect object* of the verb precedes the direct object and tells *to whom* or *what* or *for whom* or *what* the action of the verb is done.

Sarita bought **us** a chess set. [*Us* is the indirect object because it tells *for whom* Sarita bought a chess set.]

Dad gave the **car** a coat of paint. [*Car* is the indirect object because it tells *to what* Dad gave a coat of paint.]

Notice that these two sentences contain direct objects as well as indirect objects. The indirect object is always used with a direct object and normally precedes the direct object.

The guide gave **me** clear **directions.** [*Me* is the indirect object; *directions* is the direct object.]

The indirect object, like the direct object, is never in a prepositional phrase.

She sent her **mother** some of her earnings. [*Mother* is an indirect object, telling *to whom* she sent some of her earnings.]

She sent some of her earnings to her mother. [*Mother* is not an indirect object; it is the object of the preposition *to*.]

EXERCISE 4. Identifying Direct Objects and Indirect Objects. Number your paper 1–10. Write the direct objects and the indirect objects from the following sentences and label each (*d.o.* or *i.o.*). Not every sentence has an indirect object.

EXAMPLE 1. They gave us their solemn promise.
1. *us, i.o.; promise, d.o.*

1. Sue's parents shipped her the books she had forgotten.
2. They sent me on a wild-goose chase.
3. Gloria mailed the company a check yesterday.
4. The speaker showed the audience the slides of Niagara Falls.
5. Juan would not deliberately tell you a lie.
6. Luckily, we had asked three of our friends to help.
7. I sent my cousins some embroidered pillows for their new apartment.

8. Several sports magazines have sent me subscription order blanks lately.
9. Carly and Doreen taught themselves the importance of hard work.
10. In European countries, Americans must carry their passports for identification.

REVIEW EXERCISE A. Identifying Direct and Indirect Objects. The following sentences contain ten direct objects and five indirect objects. Number your paper 1–10. After the proper number, write the object or objects in the sentence. Label direct objects *d.o.* and indirect objects *i.o.*

1. Mr. Luis told us many interesting stories about his childhood in Puerto Rico.
2. No one in the class finished yesterday's math assignment.
3. Allow yourselves more time for your homework assignments.
4. Television viewers in our country can watch events as they happen in any part of the world.
5. Who told you that ridiculous story about the gorilla in the gymnasium?
6. A permanent member of the United Nations Security Council can veto any resolution.
7. The Panama Canal greatly shortened the trip by boat between Europe and Japan.
8. Rudolf Diesel's first motor exploded during his experiments and nearly killed him.
9. The jeweler, Mrs. Adams, offered me a hundred dollars for my pearl necklace.
10. I brought her my antique silver bracelet, but she was not interested in it.

Diagraming Direct and Indirect Objects

All complements except the indirect object are diagramed on the main horizontal line, with the subject and the verb, as part of the sentence base. The direct object is diagramed on the horizontal line with a vertical line preceding it. The vertical line stops at the horizontal line to distinguish it from the line separating the subject and the verb.

PATTERNS

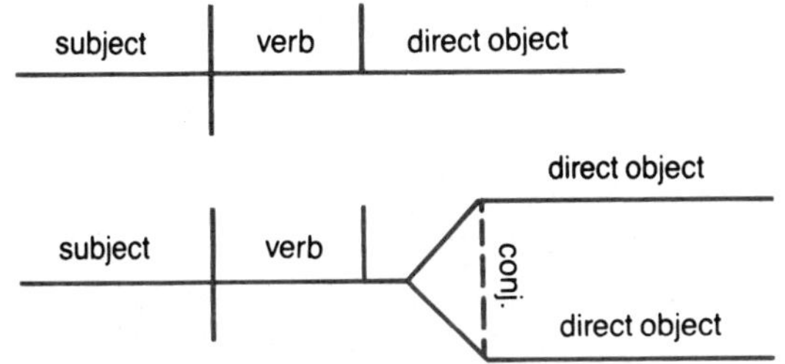

EXAMPLES The rain cleaned the street.

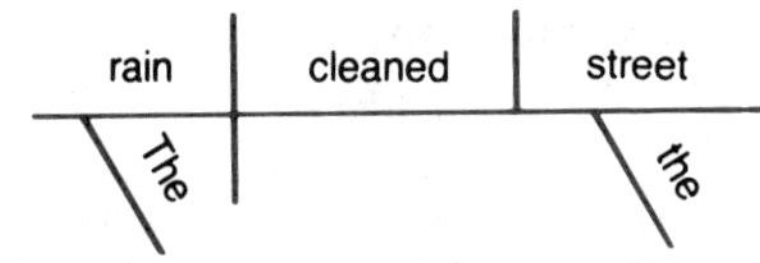

We sold lemonade and oranges.

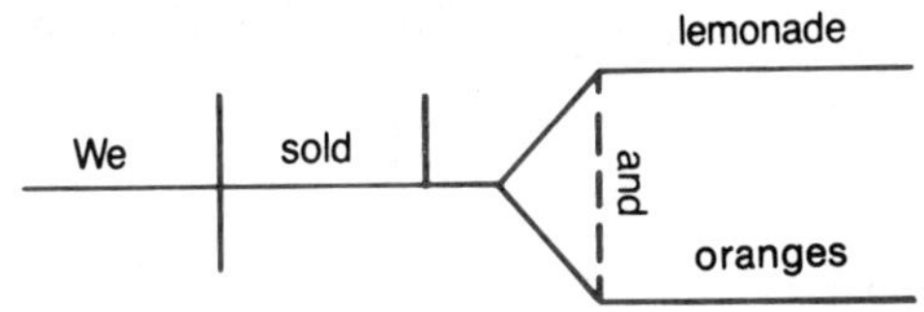

EXERCISE 5. Diagraming Sentences with Direct Objects. Diagram the following sentences, which contain direct objects. Use a ruler and leave plenty of space between diagrams.

1. The quarterback made the touchdown.
2. The famous conductor directed his own composition.
3. Our class collects leaves and rocks.
4. The audience saw a serious one-act play and two comical skits.
5. We grow orchids and ferns.

GRAMMAR

To diagram an indirect object, write it on a short horizontal line below the verb. Connect it to the verb by a slanted line.

PATTERNS

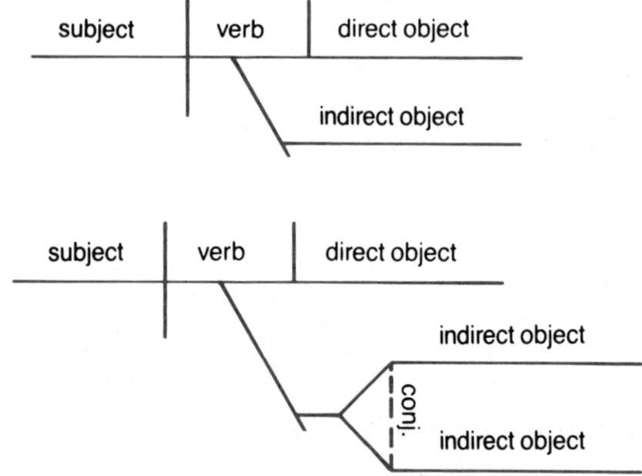

EXAMPLES The artist showed me his painting.

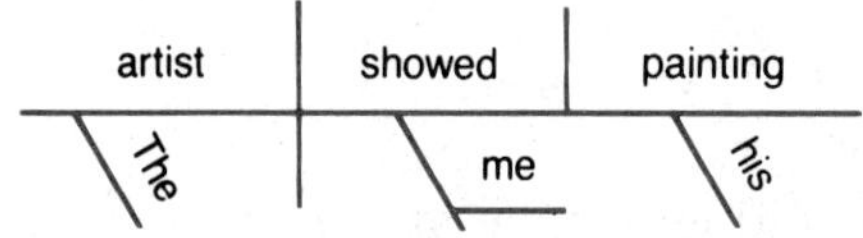

The company gave Jan and John summer jobs.

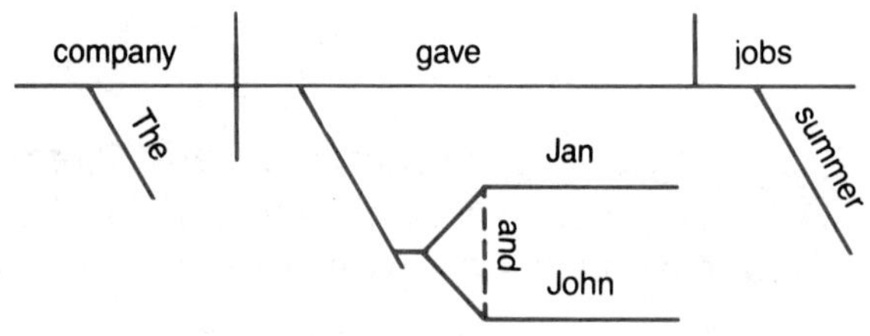

EXERCISE 6. Diagraming Sentences with Direct and Indirect Objects. Diagram the following sentences.

1. The lifeguard gave us lessons.

2. Cara's sister taught her the rules.
3. The cashier handed the children balloons.
4. The judges awarded Jean and Rae the prizes.
5. Snow gives motorists and pedestrians trouble.

SUBJECT COMPLEMENTS

Sometimes a complement completes the meaning of a sentence by explaining or describing the subject. Such a complement is called a *subject complement.* While the direct and the indirect object follow action verbs only, the subject complement follows linking verbs only. (See page 312 for the list of linking verbs.)

13d. A *subject complement* is a word which follows a linking verb and refers to (explains or describes) the subject.

Alice Eng is a **teacher.** [*Teacher* follows the linking verb *is,* and explains something about *Alice Eng.*]

We are the **ones.** [*Ones* follows the linking verb *are* and refers to the subject *we.*]

A lemon tastes **sour.** [*Sour* follows the linking verb *tastes* and describes *lemon*—sour lemon.]

Nouns, pronouns, and adjectives can serve as subject complements.

Predicate Nominatives and Predicate Adjectives

There are two kinds of subject complements—*predicate nominatives* and *predicate adjectives.*

(1) If the subject complement is a noun or a pronoun, it is called a *predicate nominative.*

EXAMPLES Tuesday is my **birthday.** [*Birthday* is a predicate nominative. It is a noun referring to the subject *Tuesday.*]

He is **one** of the members. [*One* is a predicate nominative. It is a pronoun referring to the subject *he.*]

Like subjects and objects, predicate nominatives never appear in prepositional phrases.

The result was a **declaration** of war.

The predicate nominative is *declaration,* not *war.* Not only is *war* part of a prepositional phrase, but the *result* was just a *declaration,* not the war itself.

(2) If the subject complement is an adjective, it is called a *predicate adjective.* A predicate adjective modifies the subject.

EXAMPLES An atomic reactor is very **powerful.** [*Powerful* is a predicate adjective modifying the subject *reactor.*]

This ground looks **swampy.** [*Swampy* is a predicate adjective modifying the subject *ground.*]

EXERCISE 7. Identifying Predicate Nominatives and Predicate Adjectives. Write the linking verb and the subject complement from each of the following sentences. Label each complement *p.n.* (predicate nominative) or *p.a.* (predicate adjective).

EXAMPLE 1. The raincoat looked too short for me.
1. *looked, short—p.a.*

1. My dog is playful.
2. I am the one who called you yesterday.
3. Many public buildings in the East are proof of I. M. Pei's architectural skill.
4. The downtown mall appeared especially busy today.
5. Sally Ride sounded confident during the television interview.
6. The package felt too light to be a book.
7. These questions seem easy to me.
8. The singer's clothing became a symbol that her fans imitated.
9. Some poems, such as "The Bells" and "The Raven," are delightfully rhythmical.
10. While the mountain lion looked around for food, the fawn remained perfectly still.

Some verbs, such as *look, grow,* and *feel,* may be used as either linking verbs or action verbs. They are followed by predicate nominatives or predicate adjectives only when the nouns or adjectives that follow them refer back to the subject. They are followed by objects when the nouns that follow them receive the action of the verb or name the result of the action.

LINKING VERB The sailor **felt happy.** [*Happy* is a predicate adjective after the linking verb *felt. Happy* refers back to sailor.]

ACTION VERB The sailor **felt** the **breeze.** [*Breeze* is a direct object after the action verb *felt*, and names what the sailor felt.]

WRITING APPLICATION: Using Predicate Adjectives to Help Organize a Description

A good way to organize a paragraph is to start with a topic sentence that states three things about your topic. The pattern you would use would be subject—linking verb —predicate adjectives.

EXAMPLE A computer can be fascinating, challenging, and occasionally frustrating.

Using this pattern for the beginning sentence of your paragraph, you then could supply facts, reasons, or details that develop the adjectives into an organized description.

Writing Assignment

Describe a favorite spare-time activity in a paragraph that begins with a sentence containing a compound predicate adjective with three adjectives. Underline the predicate adjectives in your beginning sentence, and in your paragraph tell why or how each adjective describes the activity you are writing about.

GRAMMAR

REVIEW EXERCISE B. Identifying Subject Complements. Number your paper 1–10. After the appropriate number, write the subject complement or complements in each of the following sentences, identifying each one as a predicate nominative (*p.n.*) or predicate adjective (*p.a.*).

EXAMPLE 1. The child was very restless.
1. *restless, p.a.*

1. Some varieties of apples taste tart.
2. Some dishes are spicy, while others seem bland.
3. Exotic orchids can be surprisingly easy to grow.
4. Cheese is a valuable source of protein.
5. After connecting the batteries to the engine, we will see whether our machine is a success.
6. If the sky is clear and the water is warm enough, we will go.
7. It could be worse.
8. The saxophone is a popular instrument in the jazz band.
9. Silver dollars have long been favorite collector's items.
10. According to some, the new style looks ugly.

Diagraming Subject Complements

A subject complement is diagramed somewhat like a direct object. But the short vertical line separating it from the verb is slanted toward the subject to show that the complement refers to the subject.

PATTERNS

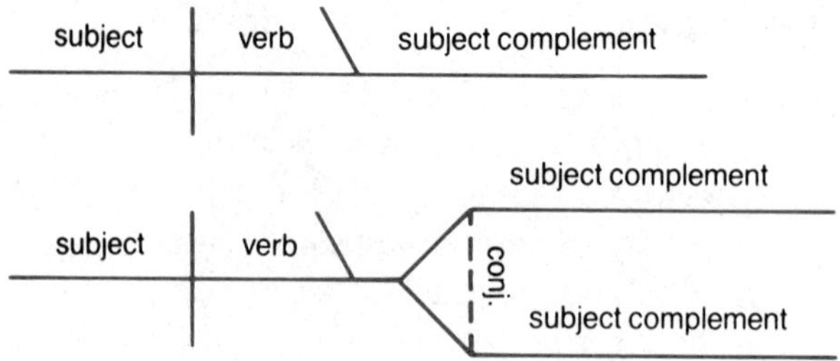

EXAMPLES The dancers are graceful.

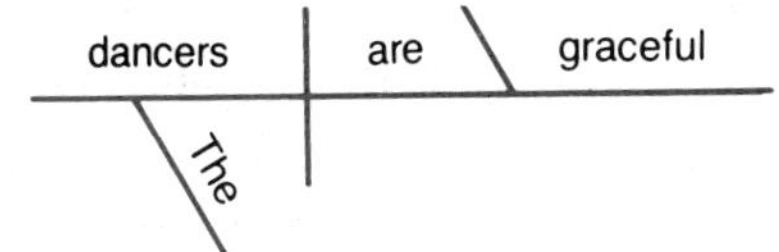

The contestants are Joan and Dean.

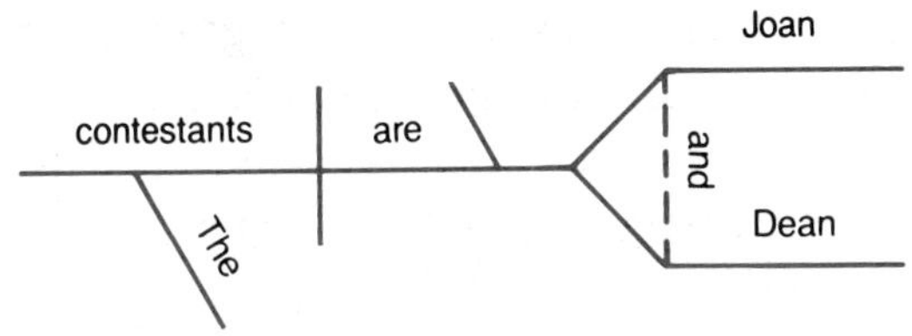

EXERCISE 8. Diagraming Subject Complements. Diagram the following sentences.

1. Is Michael Jackson your favorite singer?
2. The cave was cold and damp.
3. Sir Francis Drake was a brave explorer.
4. The chimpanzees seemed tired but happy.
5. My shoes looked worn and dusty after the long walk.

REVIEW EXERCISE C. Identifying Verbs and Their Objects or Subject Complements. Number your paper 1–10. After the proper number, write the verb or verbs in the sentence. If a verb has one or more objects, write each object after it. If a verb is a linking verb, write the subject complement after it. Then identify each object or complement as direct object (*d.o.*), indirect object (*i.o.*), predicate adjective (*p.a.*), or predicate nominative (*p.n.*).

EXAMPLE 1. I have never seen a live manatee, but in pictures they look gentle.
1. *have seen, manatee—d.o.; look, gentle—p.a.*

1. The embarrassed guest accidentally broke the antique Chinese vase.
2. The symphony conductor is the speaker for today.

3. After thieves had stolen his money, the store owner installed a burglar alarm.
4. Five of my relatives are politicians, but I would never cast my vote for any of them.
5. The ladder by the doorway looks sturdier than the one in the corner.
6. The book club sent me the wrong selection this month.
7. These are only some of the popular songs from ten years ago.
8. The performing seals gave us a good laugh.
9. White gloves were once common in stylish circles.
10. Whenever something is beautiful, some people will feel a need to destroy it.

REVIEW EXERCISE D. Diagraming Complete Sentences. Diagram these sentences:

1. Her mother was an important ballerina with a famous ballet troupe.
2. Don and Maria acted the parts of Romeo and Juliet.
3. The origin of the Gypsies remains mysterious and strange.
4. The girls made themselves bracelets and necklaces.
5. Two world-famous canals are the Suez Canal and the Panama Canal.

CHAPTER 13 REVIEW: POSTTEST 1

Identifying Direct Objects, Indirect Objects, Predicate Nominatives, and Predicate Adjectives. Number your paper 1–20. After the proper number, write each italicized word and indicate whether it is a direct object (*d.o.*), an indirect object (*i.o.*), a predicate nominative (*p.n.*), or a predicate adjective (*p.a.*).

Girls aren't the only (1) *ones* who know how to cook. My mom got a (2) *job* last summer, so she gave (3) *me* cooking lessons before school began this year. At first, I felt (4) *reluctant* about learning what I considered a "girl's job." However, Dad reminded me that he makes a (5) *number* of specialties, and he said that cooking lessons would be a good (6) *idea* for me. Boy, was he ever (7) *right!*

When I began, I could hardly boil (8) *water* without fouling up, but my mom remained (9) *patient* and showed me the correct and easiest ways to do things. For example, did you know that water will boil faster if it has a little (10) *salt* in it or that cornstarch makes an excellent thickening (11) *agent* in everything from batter to gravy?

My first attempts tasted (12) *awful,* but gradually I've become a fairly good (13) *cook.* Probably my best complete meal is beef (14) *stew.* Although stew doesn't require the highest (15) *grade* of beef, a good cut of chuck roast will give (16) *it* a much better taste. I am always very (17) *careful* about picking out the vegetables too. Our grocer probably thinks I am too (18) *picky* when I demand the best (19) *ingredients.* I don't care, though, because when I serve my (20) *family* my stew, they say it is their favorite dish.

CHAPTER 13 REVIEW: POSTTEST 2

Writing Sentences with Direct Objects, Indirect Objects, and Subject Complements. Write sentences according to the following guidelines. Underline the direct object, the indirect object, or the subject complement in each sentence.

1. a declarative sentence with a direct object
2. a declarative sentence with a predicate nominative
3. an interrogative sentence with a predicate adjective
4. an imperative sentence with an indirect object
5. an exclamatory sentence with a predicate adjective

GRAMMAR

CHAPTER 14

The Phrase

PREPOSITIONAL, VERBAL, AND APPOSITIVE PHRASES

In Chapters 11 and 12, you studied single-word modifiers: the adjective and the adverb. Whole groups of words also may act as modifiers. Just as a verb phrase acts as a single verb, so an adjective or adverb phrase acts as a single adjective or adverb. An entire phrase may also serve as a noun. This chapter will focus on how to identify and use phrases in writing.

DIAGNOSTIC TEST

Classifying Phrases. Number your paper 1–20. After the proper number, write each italicized phrase and indicate what kind of phrase it is. Use the abbreviations *prep.* (prepositional phrase), *part.* (participial phrase), *inf.* (infinitive phrase), *ger.* (gerund phrase), and *app.* (appositive phrase). Do not separately identify a prepositional phrase that is part of a larger phrase.

EXAMPLE 1. He tried *to do his best.*
1. *to do his best—inf.*

1. *Fishing for bass* is my father's favorite pastime.
2. The seagulls *gliding through the air* looked like pieces of paper caught in the wind.

3. The school bus was on time *in spite of the traffic jam.*
4. Ms. Hoban, *my science teacher,* got married last week.
5. There is no time left *to answer your questions.*
6. *Under a white flag* of truce, the defeated soldiers glumly emerged from the fort.
7. My brother plans *to marry Maureen in June.*
8. Nobody seems to be interested in *going to the fireworks display.*
9. Have you seen my cat, *a striped Persian with yellow eyes*?
10. Joel said that he can go *to the dance or the movies* on Friday.
11. *Hoping for a new bicycle and a toy robot,* my brother couldn't sleep at all on Christmas Eve.
12. Tom Sawyer tricked his friends into *painting the fence for him.*
13. In America, citizens have the right *to speak their minds.*
14. My aunt's car, *an old crate with a beat-up interior and a rattly engine,* used to belong to my grandfather.
15. Debbie's sister denied *taking the cookies.*
16. Last Sunday, we all piled in the car and went *to the beach, the bowling alley, and the mall.*
17. The shark *chasing the school of fish* looked like a hammerhead.
18. Nobody wanted to read the book, *a thick hardback with a faded cover.*
19. All of the invitations *sent to the club members* had the wrong date on them.
20. Buddy's cousin ran off *to join the circus.*

14a. A *phrase* is a group of related words that is used as a single part of speech and does not contain a verb and its subject.

You have already studied the *verb phrase,* which is introduced by a helping verb (*have* bought). You have also been introduced to the *prepositional phrase.* In this chapter you will learn more about the prepositional phrase, and you will meet several new kinds of phrases—the *participial phrase,* the *infinitive phrase,* the *gerund phrase,* and the *appositive phrase.*

THE PREPOSITIONAL PHRASE

14b. A *prepositional phrase* is a group of words that begins with a preposition and usually ends with a noun or pronoun.

In the following examples, the prepositional phrases are in boldface.

> **During the night** the horse ran off.
> Marian operates her computer **from her wheelchair.**

A single prepositional phrase may contain two or more objects.

> The dish is filled **with crackers and rice cookies.**
> The group traveled **through Spain and Italy.**

EXERCISE 1. Identifying Prepositional Phrases. Number your paper 1–10, using every other line. After the appropriate number, write the prepositional phrases in each sentence.

1. The daily schedule prepared by the camp directors was followed from dawn until late evening.
2. We were awakened at six by a bugle, played with cold fingers by a sleepy camper.
3. Standing attentively outside our cabins, we shivered in the early morning breeze coming across the lake.
4. After exercises, everyone swam in the icy water.
5. Fearing death from freezing, we raced back and dressed for breakfast.
6. Activity period included classes in painting, crafts, music, drama, and folklore.
7. The rest of the morning was devoted to sports.
8. After lunch, we spent an hour in our cabins.

9. Then we had two hours of water sports.
10. At night, talented campers and counselors entertained us.

The Adjective Phrase

14c. An *adjective phrase* is a prepositional phrase that modifies a noun or a pronoun.

Notice that the adjectives and the adjective phrases in boldface in the following sentences do the same work: they modify a noun.

ADJECTIVE The **lighthouse** beacon stayed on all night.

ADJECTIVE PHRASE The beacon **from the lighthouse** stayed on all night.

ADJECTIVE Their **varsity** players are bigger than our players.

ADJECTIVE PHRASE The players **on their varsity** are bigger than our players.

Like the adjective, an adjective phrase is usually located next to the word it modifies. But while the adjective generally precedes the word it modifies, the adjective phrase usually follows the word it modifies.

EXERCISE 2. Identifying Adjective Phrases. Number your paper 1–10. After the proper number, write the adjective phrase in each sentence and the noun or pronoun it modifies.

EXAMPLE 1. The dancers on the stage were thrilling.
1. *on the stage—dancers*

1. The strait between the Pacific Ocean and San Francisco Bay is called the Golden Gate.
2. The Golden Gate Bridge spans this narrow body of water.
3. San Francisco was once a small village on the bay but is now a busy metropolitan center.

4. The California gold rush of 1849 swelled San Francisco's population.
5. The 1906 earthquake destroyed the homes of many people.
6. Today sightseers from many different nations crowd San Francisco's streets.
7. Some of the streets are very steep.
8. Chinatown in San Francisco attracts many visitors.
9. This city beside the bay has many charms.
10. Do you know any songs about San Francisco?

Sometimes one adjective phrase follows another. The second phrase usually modifies the object in the first phrase.

EXAMPLE Sicily is an island **off the coast of Italy.**

EXERCISE 3. Identifying Adjective Phrases. Each of the following sentences contains two adjective phrases. Write each adjective phrase and the word it modifies after the appropriate number.

EXAMPLE 1. Sharon read a book on the origins of words.
1. *on the origins, book; of words, origins*

1. My sister Connie, a real terror with a whale of a temper, shouts "Beans!" when something goes wrong.
2. Some terms for the expression of anger were originally Latin or Greek words.
3. Many of us in English class wanted to discuss how people express their annoyance.
4. Imagine what would happen if everybody in every house in the city had a bad day.
5. We agreed that the best thing to do is to avoid people with chips on their shoulders.

The Adverb Phrase

When a prepositional phrase is used as an adverb to modify a verb, adjective, or adverb, it is called an *adverb phrase.* Like a single-word adverb, the adverb phrase answers the question *How? When? Where?* or *To what extent?*

14d. An *adverb phrase* is a prepositional phrase that modifies a verb, an adjective, or an adverb.

EXAMPLES The snow fell **like feathers.** [The adverb phrase modifies the verb *fell,* telling *how* the snow fell.]

Her dress is too long **in the back.** [The adverb phrase modifies the adjective *long,* telling *where* the dress is too long.]

We arrived early **in the morning.** [The adverb phrase modifies the adverb *early,* telling *when* we were early.]

EXERCISE 4. Identifying Adverb Phrases. Number your paper 1–10. After the appropriate number, write the adverb phrase from each sentence. Then write the verb, adjective, or adverb that the phrase modifies.

EXAMPLE 1. Our town was built over a river.
1. *over a river—was built*

1. The Cheery Oh Restaurant has opened across the road.
2. The food is fantastic beyond belief.
3. Almost everyone has gone to the new place.
4. At the Cheery Oh you can eat exotic food.
5. People sit late into the night drinking tropical fruit juices and chatting.
6. They enjoy themselves in the friendly atmosphere.
7. People appear happy with the service.
8. For three weeks the Cheery Oh has been crowded.
9. Some say in all seriousness that it resembles an English coffeehouse.
10. If the famous writers John Dryden and Joseph Addison were alive today, they could probably be found at this charming restaurant.

GRAMMAR

Unlike an adjective phrase, an adverb phrase may be separated from the word it modifies by other words. Adverb phrases may be moved about in the sentence.

EXAMPLES **For many centuries** people searched **for a way** to make gold.

People searched **for many centuries for a way** to make gold.

EXERCISE 5. Identifying Adverb Phrases. Number your paper 1–5. After the proper number, write the adverb phrase or phrases in each sentence. After each adverb phrase, write the word or phrase it modifies.

EXAMPLE 1. I am going to camp during vacation.
1. *to camp—am going; during vacation—am going*

1. Mount Vernon is interesting for its history.
2. The house was named Mount Vernon by Lawrence Washington, who lived there for many years.
3. Somewhat later, George and Martha Washington moved to Mount Vernon.
4. After Washington's death the house was owned by a series of people.
5. In 1858, it was bought by the Mount Vernon Ladies' Association, which restored it.

EXERCISE 6. Writing Sentences with Prepositional Phrases. Write sentences of your own in which you use the following phrases as adjective or adverb phrases. In each sentence, underline the word or word group that the phrase modifies and label the phrase as *adj. phr.* (adjective phrase) or *adv. phr.* (adverb phrase).

1. under the bridge
2. for our kitchen
3. outside the cabin
4. without any help
5. down the river
6. with bright lights
7. through the hallway
8. beside the path
9. in the laundry
10. through our efforts

Diagraming Adjective and Adverb Phrases

An adjective or adverb phrase is diagramed below the word it modifies. Write the preposition on a line slanting down from the modified word. Then write the object of the preposition (the noun or pronoun following the preposition) on a horizontal line extending from the slanting line.

PATTERNS

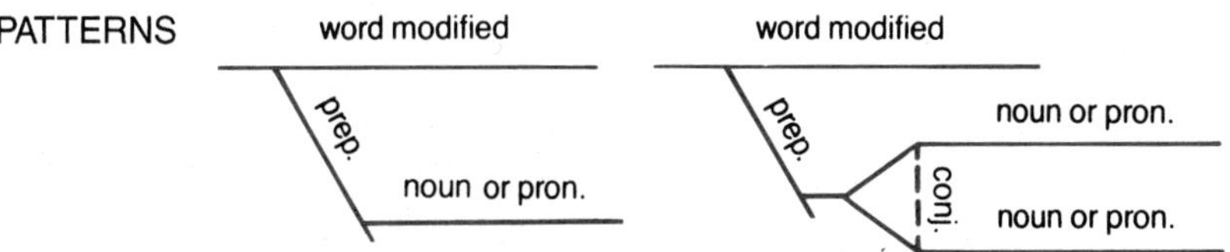

EXAMPLES walked along the road

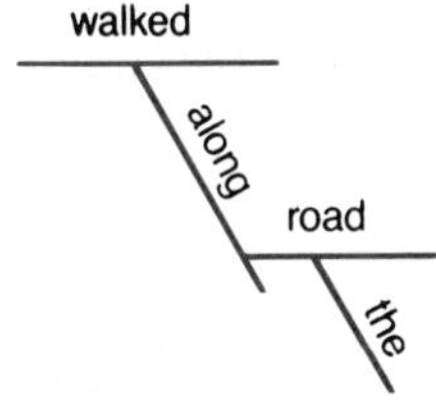

paintings by famous artists

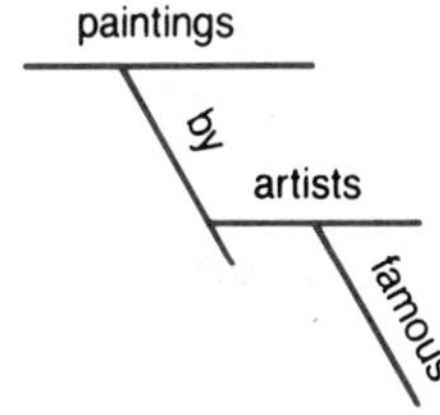

went with Hollis and Dave

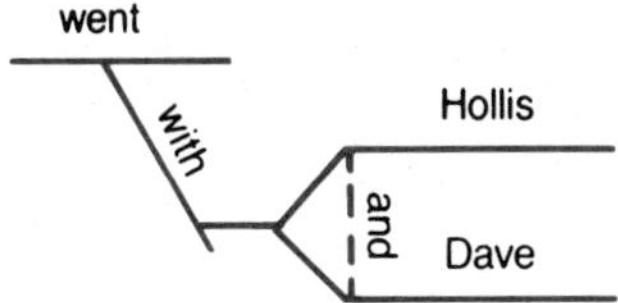

GRAMMAR

When a prepositional phrase modifies the object of another prepositional phrase, the diagram looks like this:

EXAMPLE camped on the side of a mountain

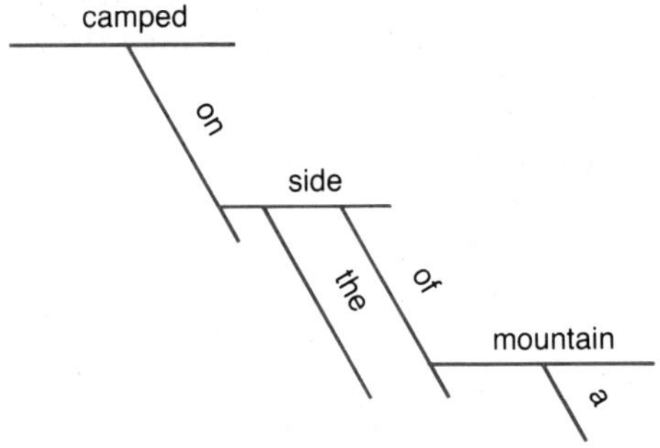

EXERCISE 7. Diagraming Prepositional Phrases. Diagram the following word groups, which contain prepositional phrases. Use a ruler, and leave plenty of space between diagrams.

1. invited to the celebrations
2. a glimpse of the famous ruler
3. one of the people in the room
4. read about King Midas and his golden touch
5. drove to a village near Paris

EXERCISE 8. Diagraming Sentences with Adjective Phrases and Adverb Phrases. Diagram the following sentences, each of which contains an adjective phrase or an adverb phrase or both.

EXAMPLE The company of actors performed for an audience of children.

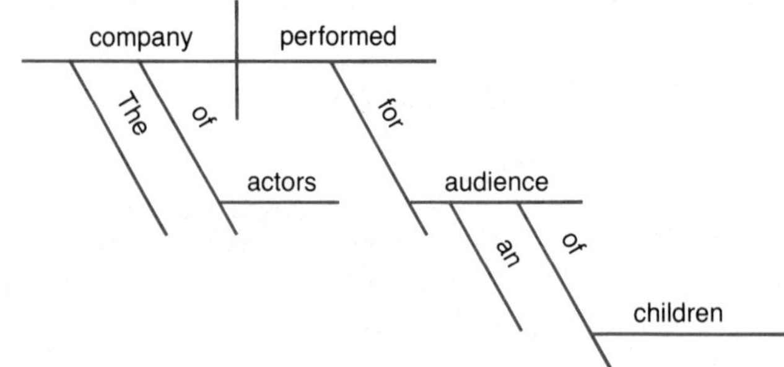

1. The number of whales is decreasing.
2. Some familiar animals can be found only in zoos.
3. Hundreds of species have vanished from the earth.
4. Citrus fruits are grown in California and Florida.
5. Many historic events have been decided by sudden changes in the weather.
6. The defeat of the Spanish Armada resulted from a violent ocean storm.

REVIEW EXERCISE A. Identifying Adjective Phrases and Adverb Phrases. After the proper number, list in order each adjective and adverb phrase in the following sentences. After each phrase, write the word or expression it modifies. Be ready to tell whether it is an adjective phrase or an adverb phrase.

EXAMPLE 1. Through old journals, our understanding of the pioneers has increased.
1. *Through old journals—has increased; of the pioneers—understanding*

1. Few of us appreciate the determination and courage of the pioneers who traveled west.
2. The word *travel* comes from the French word *travailler,* which means "to work hard."
3. On the trip westward only small children rode in the wagons.
4. Everyone else traveled on foot over the mountains.
5. Sometimes a wagon train would stop in a valley and then spend the winter in houses that were built quickly.
6. In one account of a harsh winter, a pioneer recorded an incident of a roof collapsed under the weight of the snow.
7. Food was often scarce, and hundreds never recovered from the hardships.
8. A typical day's chores began long before dawn.
9. The pioneers who did survive by sheer determination often continued their journey.
10. At their western destination, many families often shared the same cabin.

VERBALS AND VERBAL PHRASES

A *verbal* is a word that is formed from a verb but is used in a sentence as a noun, an adjective, or an adverb. There are three kinds of verbals: the *participle,* the *gerund,* and the *infinitive.*

The Participle

14e. A *participle* is a verb form that can be used as an adjective.

There are two kinds of participles—present participles and past participles. Present participles end in *-ing.* Past participles often end in *-ed, -d,* or *-t.*

EXAMPLES The horses **trotting** past were not frightened by the crowd. [*Trotting* (a form of the verb *trot*) modifies the noun *horses—trotting horses.*]

Buried by pirates, the treasure lay undiscovered for centuries. [*Buried* (a form of the verb *bury*) modifies the noun *treasure—buried treasure.*]

Do not confuse participles used as in the examples above with participles used in a verb phrase.

PARTICIPLE **Broken,** the toy still ran.
VERB PHRASE The toy **was broken** by Tim, but it still ran.

PARTICIPLE **Planning** their trip, the class learned some geography.
VERB PHRASE While they **were planning** their trip, the class learned some geography.

The participle in a verb phrase is part of a verb and does not act as an adjective.

EXERCISE 9. Identifying Participles. Number your paper 1–10. After the proper number, write the participle from each sentence, then the noun or pronoun it modifies. Be prepared to identify the participle as a present participle or a past participle.

EXAMPLE 1. We heard the train whistling and chugging in the distance.
1. *whistling—train; chugging—train*

1. Records, cracked and warped, were in the old trunk in the attic.
2. Shouting loudly, Becky warned the pedestrian to look out for the car.
3. The sparkling water splashed in our faces.
4. The papers, aged and yellowed, are kept in the file.
5. For centuries the ruins remained there, still undiscovered.
6. Smiling politely, she gave directions to the post office.
7. The charging bull thundered across the field.
8. Cheering and clapping, the spectators greeted their team.
9. The children, fidgeting noisily, waited eagerly for recess.
10. Recently released, the movie has not yet come to our local theaters.

The Participial Phrase

When a participle introduces a group of related words that act together as an adjective, this word group is called a *participial phrase.*

14f. A *participial phrase* is a group of related words that contains a participle and that acts as an adjective.

A prepositional phrase often follows the participle. When it does, it is considered a part of the participial phrase. In the following examples, an arrow is drawn from each participial phrase (shown in boldface) to the word that it modifies.

Seeing itself in the mirror, the duck seemed bewildered.

It stood in front of the mirror, **watching its image closely.**

Then, **disgusted with the other duck,** it began to peck the mirror.

GRAMMAR

EXERCISE 10. Identifying Participial Phrases. Number your paper 1–10. After the appropriate number, write the participial phrase in each sentence. After the phrase, write the word or words that it modifies.

1. Noted for her beauty, Venus was sought by all the gods as a wife.
2. Bathed in radiant light, Venus brought love and joy wherever she went.
3. Jupiter, knowing her charms, nevertheless married her to Vulcan, the ugliest of the gods.
4. Mars, known to the Greeks as Ares, was the god of war.
5. Terrified by Ares' power, many Greeks did not like to worship him.
6. They saw both land and people destroyed by him.
7. Observing his path, they said that Ares left blood, devastation, and grief behind him.
8. The Romans, having great respect for Mars, made him one of their three chief deities.
9. They imagined him dressed in shining armor.
10. Mars, supposed to be the father of the founders of Rome, has a month named after him.

EXERCISE 11. Writing Sentences with Participial Phrases. Use the following participial phrases in sentences of your own. Place each phrase as close as possible to the noun or pronoun that it modifies. If you use a participial phrase to begin a sentence, put a comma after the phrase.

EXAMPLE 1. standing in line
1. *Standing in line, we waited twenty minutes for the store to open.*

1. waiting for the bus in the rain
2. passing the store window
3. planning the escape
4. jumping from stone to stone
5. hearing the whistle blow and feeling the train lurch forward

WRITING APPLICATION A:
Using Participial Phrases to Combine Closely Related Sentences

When you were younger, you probably wrote mostly short, choppy sentences that contained simple ideas. As you have grown older, you have learned to combine ideas to pack more information into your sentences. One way you do this is by using participles.

EXAMPLE I sat down at the table. Mother was at the table. I took out my class schedule for next year. Mother and I discussed my classes. These classes were offered for ninth-graders. [The style of this example is short and choppy.]

Sitting down at the table, I took out my class schedule to show Mother. She and I discussed the classes **offered for ninth-graders next year.** [This is one way to improve the short, choppy sentences. Notice the participial phrases in boldface.]

Writing Assignment

Before people begin activities of various kinds, they often have warm-ups. This is true whether they are getting ready to swim in a race, play in a band concert, or perform in a dance recital. Describe either a person or a group of persons warming up. Use at least three participial phrases, and underline these phrases.

The Gerund

Besides acting as participial modifiers, verbs ending in *-ing* can also be another kind of verbal called a *gerund.* Gerunds function as nouns in sentences.

14g. A *gerund* is a verb form ending in *-ing* that is used as a noun.

GRAMMAR

EXAMPLES **Jogging** can be good exercise. [subject]
My favorite hobby is **fishing.** [predicate nominative]
Lock the door before **leaving.** [object of preposition]
Did they go **hiking?** [direct object]

Because the gerund acts as a noun, it can be modified by adjectives and adjective phrases.

EXAMPLE The **quiet** gurgling **of the water** was restful. [The adjective *quiet* and the adjective phrase *of the water* both modify the gerund *gurgling.*]

Because gerunds are also verb forms, they can be modified by adverbs and adverb phrases, too.

EXAMPLE We crossed the stream by stepping **carefully from stone to stone.** [The adverb *carefully* and the adverb phrase *from stone to stone* both modify the gerund *stepping.*]

Remember that gerunds are nouns. Do not confuse a gerund with a participle used as part of a verb or as an adjective.

EXAMPLE **Pausing,** [PART.] the deer **was sniffing** [V.] the wind before **stepping** [GER.] into the open meadow.

Pausing is a participle modifying *deer*, and *sniffing* is part of the verb phrase *was sniffing. Stepping* is a gerund, serving as the object of the preposition *before.*

EXERCISE 12. Identifying Gerunds. Number your paper 1–10. After the appropriate number, write the gerund in each sentence. If there is no gerund in the sentence, write *none.*

EXAMPLE 1. Typing is a useful skill.
1. *Typing*

1. Their singing caused the dogs to howl.
2. Jerry has been practicing pole vaulting every day after school.
3. My sister has always enjoyed horseback riding.

4. In the past, working took up most people's time six days a week.
5. I look forward to resting after this tiring job is done.
6. Uncle Eli's specialty is barbecuing on the outdoor grill.
7. Nobody could stand the child's unceasing whine.
8. The colonel will be commending the scout for volunteering for the dangerous mission.
9. Studying usually pays off in higher scores.
10. Considering the other choices, Melinda decided on walking.

The Gerund Phrase

A gerund may be accompanied by modifiers and complements, which together with the gerund form a *gerund phrase.*

14h. A *gerund phrase* includes the gerund and all the words related to the gerund.

A gerund is formed from a verb. It may be modified by an adverb and may also have a complement, usually a direct object. Since a gerund functions as a noun, it may be modified by an adjective. A gerund phrase includes the gerund and all of its modifiers and complements.

EXAMPLE **Shouting at people** does not make them understand you better.

In the above example, *shouting* is a gerund, and *at people* is a prepositional phrase acting as an adverb that modifies *shouting.* Together, *shouting at people* is a gerund phrase that acts as the subject of the sentence.

EXAMPLE Most of the players obeyed **the stern warning from the coach.**

In the preceding example, the gerund *warning* is modified by the article *the,* the adjective *stern,* and the prepositional phrase *from the coach.* The word group *the stern warning from the coach* is a gerund phrase that serves as object of the verb *obeyed.*

EXAMPLE The child spelled her name by **carefully printing each letter.**

Here the gerund *printing* is modified by the adverb *carefully* and takes a direct object, *each letter.* The phrase as a whole, *carefully printing each letter,* is the object of the preposition *by.*

> ☞ **NOTE** Since a gerund acts as a noun, any noun or pronoun that comes immediately before it should be in the possessive case.

EXAMPLES **Michael's** cooking is the best I've ever tasted.
The vultures didn't let anything disturb **their** feeding.

EXERCISE 13. Identifying Gerund Phrases. After the appropriate number, write the gerund phrase in each of the following sentences.

EXAMPLE 1. The rain interrupted their building of the bonfire.
1. *their building of the bonfire*

1. Vincent's pleading did not influence his mother's decision.
2. The man was given a ticket for driving the wrong way on a one-way street.
3. We sat back and enjoyed the slow rocking of the boat.
4. The blue jay's screeching at the cat woke us up at dawn.
5. Give practicing the piano a chance.
6. When did that piercing clanging begin?
7. The frantic darting of the fish indicated that a shark was nearby.
8. She is considering running for class president.
9. Ants try to protect their colonies from storms by piling up sand against the wind.
10. The wading egret was intently searching for frogs and other small animals during its early-morning feeding.

EXERCISE 14. Writing Sentences with Gerund Phrases. Use each of the following gerund phrases in a sentence of your own. Underline the gerund phrase and identify it as subject, predicate nominative, direct object, indirect object, or the object of a preposition.

EXAMPLE 1. Hiking up the hill
1. *Hiking up the hill took us all morning.* *subject*

1. getting up in the morning
2. arguing among themselves
3. refusing any help with the job
4. sharpening my pencil
5. peeling carrots carefully

WRITING APPLICATION B:
Using Gerunds to Explain Activities Involving Action

The versatile paper clip can be used to fasten together pieces of paper, to hang up lightweight pictures, and to perform a number of other tasks. The gerund is the paper clip of the English language. It can be subject, direct object, predicate nominative, or anything else a noun can be. When you need a noun that expresses action, a gerund can be very helpful.

EXAMPLES **Learning to play a violin** is harder than I thought it would be. [gerund phrase used as subject.]
My brother dislikes **taking out the trash.** [gerund phrase used as object of the verb.]

Writing Assignment

If you could have any job you wanted, what would it be? Write a paragraph telling about this job and why you would choose it. Use three gerund phrases, and underline these phrases.

GRAMMAR

The Infinitive

Besides the participle and the gerund, there is a third kind of verbal called the *infinitive.* An infinitive can act as an adjective, a noun, or an adverb.

14i. An *infinitive* is a verb form that can be used as a noun, an adjective, or an adverb.

An infinitive has the word *to* directly before the plain form of the verb, as in *to win, to go,* and *to consider.*

To determine what part of speech an infinitive is, look at how the infinitive is used in the sentence.

Infinitives used as nouns: She expected **to finish** the race, but not **to win.** [*To finish* and *to win* are objects of the verb *expected.*

To forgive does not always mean **to forget.** [*To forgive* is the subject of the sentence; *to forget* is the predicate nominative.]

Infinitives used as adjectives: The best time **to visit** Florida is December through April. [*To visit* modifies *time.*]

If you want information about computers, that is the magazine **to read.** [*To read* modifies *magazine.*]

Infinitives used as adverbs: They were eager **to try.** [*To try* modifies the adjective *eager.*]

The caravan stopped at the oasis **to rest.** [*To rest* modifies the verb *stopped.*]

> ☞ USAGE NOTE *To* plus a noun or a pronoun (*to class, to them, to the dance*) is a prepositional phrase, not an infinitive. Be careful not to confuse infinitives with prepositional phrases beginning with *to.*

INFINITIVE I want **to go.**
PREPOSITIONAL PHRASE I want to go **to town.**

EXERCISE 15. Identifying Infinitives. Number your paper 1–10. After the appropriate number, write the infinitive in each sentence. If a sentence contains no infinitive, write *none.*

EXAMPLE 1. June doesn't know how to dance.
1. *to dance*

1. After school June and I like to walk home together.
2. Usually, we go to my house or her house to listen to tapes.
3. Sometimes I get up to move with the music, but June never does.
4. One day I asked her to join me.
5. She said that she had never been to dancing school or learned any steps.
6. "Do you want me to show you some?" I asked.
7. "I'm ready to try," she answered.
8. I didn't know which steps to start with.
9. After doing my best to teach her for three weeks, I gave up.
10. It's a good thing that June doesn't plan to become a dancer.

The Infinitive Phrase

An infinitive may be followed by a group of related words, which together with the infinitive form an *infinitive phrase.*

14j. An *infinitive phrase* consists of an infinitive together with its complements and modifiers.

An infinitive may be modified by an adjective or an adverb; it may also have a complement. Together, an infinitive and its modifiers and complements make up an infinitive phrase. The entire phrase may act as an adjective, an adverb, or a noun.

EXAMPLE **To lift those weights** takes a lot of strength.

The infinitive phrase *to lift those weights* is used as a noun that is the subject of the sentence. The infinitive *to lift* has an object, *weights,* which is modified by *those.*

EXAMPLE Peanuts and raisins are good snacks **to take on a camping trip.**

The infinitive phrase *to take on a camping trip* is used as an adjective modifying *snacks*. The infinitive *to take* is modified by the prepositional phrase *on a camping trip*.

EXAMPLE The crowd grew quiet **to hear the speaker.**

The infinitive phrase *to hear the speaker* is used as an adverb modifying the adjective *quiet*. The infinitive *to hear* has the complement *the speaker*.

EXERCISE 16. Identifying Infinitive Phrases. After the appropriate number, write the infinitive phrase in each sentence, and identify it as a noun, an adjective, or an adverb. If there is no infinitive phrase in the sentence, write *none*.

EXAMPLE 1. My uncle taught me to take care of my bicycle.
1. *to take care of my bicycle—noun*

1. Taking care of your bicycle will help to make it last longer.
2. We used machine oil to lubricate the chain.
3. He said to place a drop of oil on each link.
4. Then he showed me the valve to fill the inner tube.
5. Using a hand pump, we added air to the back tire.
6. We were careful not to put in too much air.
7. Next, we got out wrenches to tighten several bolts.
8. My uncle warned me not to pull on the wrench too hard.
9. Overtightening can cause as much damage to a bolt as not tightening it enough can.
10. I thanked my uncle for taking the time to give me tips about taking care of my bicycle.

EXERCISE 17. Writing Sentences with Infinitives. Use each of the following infinitive phrases in a sentence of your own. Underline the infinitive phrase and identify it as a noun, an adjective, or an adverb.

EXAMPLE 1. to leave school early on Tuesday
1. *The principal gave me permission to leave school early on Tuesday.—adj.*

1. to give the right answers
2. to go home after school
3. to run after the bus
4. to read the entire book
5. to spend the night

REVIEW EXERCISE B. Identifying and Classifying Verbals and Verbal Phrases. After the appropriate number, write the verbal or verbal phrase in each of the following sentences. Identify each verbal or verbal phrase as a *gerund, gerund phrase, infinitive, infinitive phrase, participle,* or *participial phrase.*

EXAMPLE 1. Raising his head, the steer eyed us lazily.
1. *Raising his head—participial phrase*

1. Even the people in charge didn't know what to do.
2. The "flying fox" is actually a bat.
3. Bo was commended for organizing the clean-up campaign.
4. What did you say to her to make her so mad?
5. According to experts, swimming is the best form of exercise.
6. One of the women taking tickets at the door gave us directions to our seats.
7. The old hermit preferred living alone in the forest.
8. The tourist looked exhausted, but he didn't stop for a rest.
9. One solution may be to offer them more money.
10. His constant complaining grated on everyone's nerves.

Diagraming Verbals and Verbal Phrases

Participles alone are diagramed like any other adjective. Participial phrases are diagramed as follows:

EXAMPLE **Shaking her head,** my older sister winked at me.

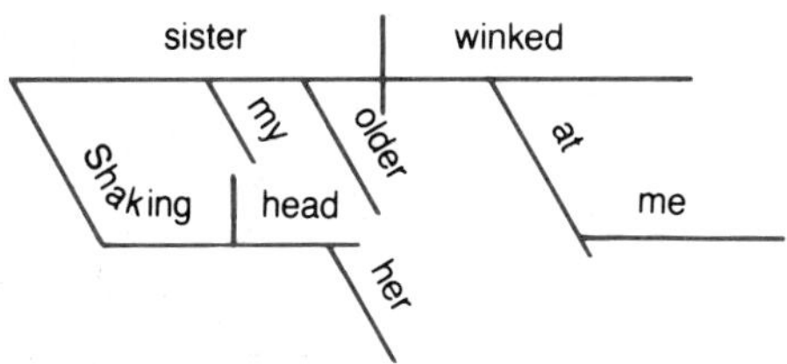

Gerunds and gerund phrases are diagramed as follows:

EXAMPLE **Being slightly ill** is no excuse for **missing two days of baseball practice.** [Gerund phrases used as subject and as object of preposition. The first gerund has a subject complement (*ill*); the second gerund has a direct object (*days*).]

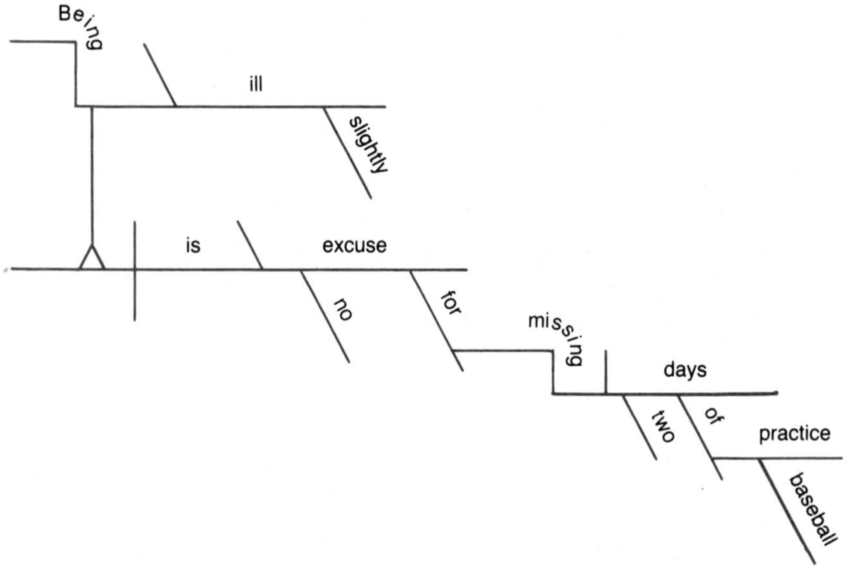

Infinitives and infinitive phrases used as modifiers are diagramed like prepositional phrases.

EXAMPLE He was the first one **to solve that tricky problem.**

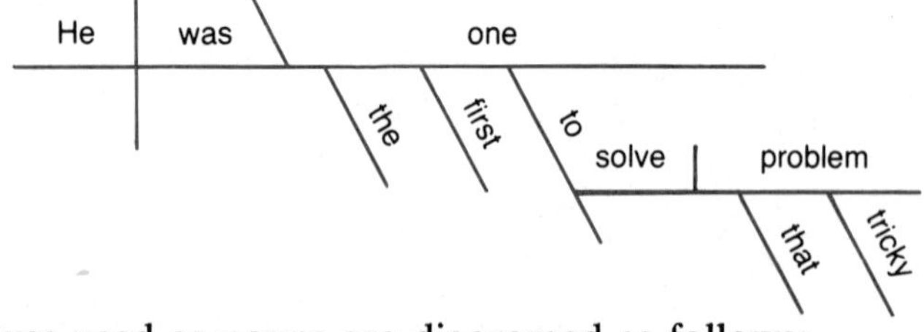

Infinitives used as nouns are diagramed as follows:

EXAMPLE Marge was hoping **to go with us.**

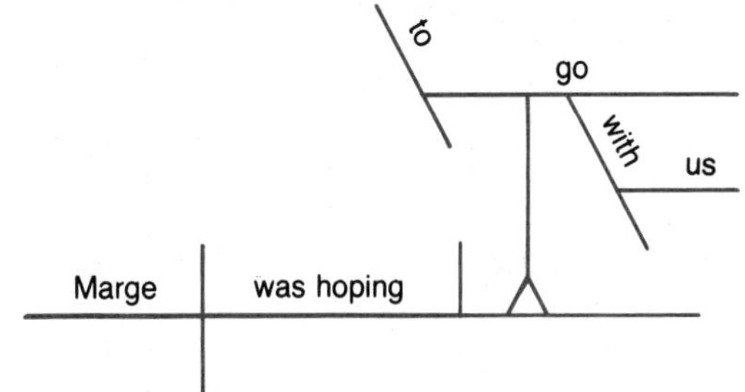

EXERCISE 18. Diagraming Sentences with Verbal Phrases. Diagram the following sentences:

1. Taking that shortcut will cut several minutes off the trip.
2. I want to watch that program tonight.
3. That is my cat licking its paws.
4. Did they say what to do about this?
5. Checking the time, Wynetta rushed to the gym.

APPOSITIVES AND APPOSITIVE PHRASES

When you want to explain more exactly who or what you are talking about, you usually give additional information. You have already learned to add information by using complements. Another way is to use an *appositive* or an *appositive phrase.* Study these two ways to add information:

COMPLEMENT Mrs. Collins is **my English teacher.**
APPOSITIVE Mrs. Collins, **my English teacher,** went to school with my mother.

Notice that the sentence using the appositive gives more information about the subject than is possible with the complement alone.

14k. An *appositive* is a noun or a pronoun that explains the noun or pronoun it follows.

Appositives are often set off from the rest of the sentence by commas. However, when an appositive is necessary to the meaning of the sentence or is closely related to the word it follows, no commas are necessary.

EXAMPLES Troy, **a good friend of mine,** is camping with us.
The book ***Island of the Blue Dolphins*** is one of my favorites.

Sometimes you include modifiers in your appositive. When words are added to describe an appositive, an *appositive phrase* is created.

14l. An *appositive phrase* is made up of an appositive and its modifiers.

EXAMPLE The Newbery Medal, **an award for outstanding children's books,** was named for a man who sold children's books in the 1700's.

Diagraming Appositives and Appositive Phrases

To diagram an appositive, write it in parentheses after the word it explains. The modifiers in an appositive phrase are diagramed in the usual way beneath the appositive.

EXAMPLE Bill Cosby, **the popular TV star,** is now the author of a best-seller.

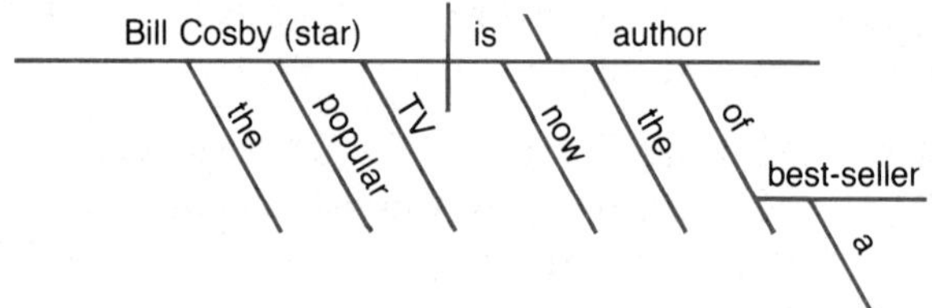

EXERCISE 19. Identifying Appositives and Appositive Phrases. After the appropriate number, write the appositive or appositive phrase in each of the following sentences. If a sentence has no appositive or appositive phrase, write *none.*

EXAMPLE 1. My dog, the mutt with floppy ears, can do tricks.
1. *the mutt with floppy ears*

1. Don't lock that door, the exit out the back of the gym.
2. This color, midnight blue, is just what I've been looking for.
3. Two men, a truck driver and a fisherman, helped my father push the car off the road.
4. I'll have a sandwich, tuna salad on rye bread, please.
5. Ollie has the same class, American history, this afternoon.
6. My sister's friend forgot her sweater and her books.
7. Dee wondered where her friend Bonnie had gone.
8. Somebody reported the hazard, a pile of trash containing broken bottles, to the police.
9. Be sure to bring the exact change, fifty cents.
10. We sang the song "I've Been Working on the Railroad" over and over all the way down the path.

REVIEW EXERCISE C. Identifying Verbals and Appositives. Number your paper 1–10. After the appropriate number, write all verbals and appositives that appear in the following sentences. Write only the appositive or the verbal, not its modifiers or complements. In parentheses after each word, identify it as *appositive, infinitive, gerund,* or *participle.*

EXAMPLE 1. Skating on the sidewalk, my little brother Shawn tried to do some acrobatics, and that put an end to his playing for a while.
1. *Skating (participle), Shawn (appositive), to do (infinitive), playing (gerund)*

1. Instead of falling on the soft ground, Shawn managed to hit right on the concrete.
2. The concrete, broken and crumbling, cut him in several places, mostly his knees and elbows.
3. We heard his piercing wail all the way up at our house, and my mother and I rushed to see what had happened.
4. By the time we got to him, all the cuts had started bleeding, and he was struggling to get his skates off.
5. Bending down, my mother pulled the skates off and dabbed at the seeping red cuts and scrapes.

6. Shawn, a brave little boy usually, could not control his crying.
7. Mom carried Shawn to the house, and I followed with the new skates, bent and ruined on the first day he used them.
8. After cleaning Shawn's cuts, Mom decided to take him to the emergency clinic.
9. The doctor, an Indian lady, said that she would have to close two of the cuts with stitches.
10. When we got home, Mom told Shawn that she wasn't going to get him another pair of skates until he was old enough to pay his own doctor bills.

CHAPTER 14 REVIEW: POSTTEST 1

Identifying Prepositional, Verbal, and Appositive Phrases. After the proper number, write each italicized phrase in the following paragraphs, and indicate what kind of phrase it is. Use the abbreviations *prep.* (prepositional phrase), *part.* (participial phrase), *ger.* (gerund phrase), *inf.* (infinitive phrase), and *app.* (appositive phrase). Do not separately identify a prepositional phrase that is part of a larger phrase.

EXAMPLES After (1) *driving past the intersection,* my father had (2) *to drive over a mile farther before the next turn.*

1. *driving past the intersection—ger.*
2. *to drive over a mile before the next turn—inf.*

Jill, (1) *my best friend since elementary school,* and I decided (2) *to go to the mall after school yesterday*. Jill suggested (3) *taking the back way* so that we could jog, but I was wearing sandals (4) *instead of my track shoes,* so we just walked. Along the way we saw Cathy (5) *sitting on her front porch* and asked her if she wanted (6) *to join us*. She was earning a little spending money by (7) *baby-sitting her neighbor's children,* though, and couldn't leave.

(8) *Walking up to the wide glass doors at the mall,* Jill and I looked in our purses. We both had a few dollars and our student passes, so we stopped (9) *to get a glass of orange juice* while we checked what movies were playing. None of the four features looked (10) *interesting to us*. However, John Bowers, (11) *a friend from school and an usher at the theater,* said that there would be a sneak preview (12) *of a new adventure film* later, and we told him we'd be back then.

Since most stores do not allow customers food or drinks inside, Jill and I gulped down our orange juice before (13) *going into our favorite dress shop*. We looked (14) *through the sale racks,* but none of the dresses, (15) *all of them formal or evening gowns,* appealed to us. A salesclerk asked if we were shopping (16) *for something special*. After (17) *checking with Jill,* I told the clerk we were just looking, and we left.

We walked past a couple of shops— (18) *the health food store and a toy store*—and went into Record World. (19) *Seeing several cassettes of my favorite group,* I picked out one. By the time we walked out of Record World, I'd spent all my money. We never did get (20) *to go to the movie that day.*

GRAMMAR

CHAPTER 14 REVIEW: POSTTEST 2

Writing Sentences with Prepositional, Verbal, and Appositive Phrases. Write ten sentences using the following phrases. Follow the directions in parentheses.

1. after the game (*use as an adverb phrase*)
2. instead of your good shoes (*use as an adjective phrase*)
3. in one of Shakespeare's plays (*use as an adjective phrase*)
4. going to school every day (*use as a gerund phrase, as the subject of the sentence*)
5. living in a small town (*use as a gerund phrase, as the object of a preposition*)
6. walking through the empty lot (*use as a participial phrase*)

7. dressed in authentic costumes (*use as a participial phrase*)
8. to drive a car for the first time (*use as an infinitive phrase, as the direct object of the sentence*)
9. the best athlete in our school (*use as an appositive phrase*)
10. my favorite pastime (*use as an appositive phrase*)

GRAMMAR

CHAPTER 15

The Clause

INDEPENDENT AND SUBORDINATE CLAUSES

A phrase is a group of related words without a verb and its subject. In a sentence there may also be other groups of related words called *clauses,* which do contain both a verb and its subject.

PHRASES **on the tugboat** [no subject or verb]
have been laughing [no subject]

CLAUSES **as the tugboat crossed the river** [a verb—*crossed* —and its subject—*tugboat*]
who have been laughing [a verb—*have been laughing* —and its subject—*who*]

In this chapter you will learn about independent and subordinate clauses.

DIAGNOSTIC TEST

Identifying Independent and Subordinate Clauses; Classifying Subordinate Clauses. Number your paper 1–20. After the proper number, identify each of the italicized clauses in the following sentences as an independent clause or a subordinate clause. Classify each italicized subordinate clause as an *adj. cl.*

(adjective clause), *adv. cl.* (adverb clause), or *n. cl.* (noun clause) to show how it functions in the sentence.

EXAMPLES
1. The customer thumbed through the book, but *it didn't seem to interest her.*
1. *independent clause*
2. Anyone *who gets a high score on this test* will not have to take the final exam.
2. *subordinate clause, adj. cl.*

1. *After it had been snowing for several hours,* we took our sleds out to Sentry Hill.
2. The ring *that I lost at the beach last summer* had belonged to my great-grandmother.
3. If he doesn't get here soon, *I'm leaving.*
4. Do you know *who she is?*
5. Nobody has seen Shawn *since the football game ended.*
6. *In the morning they gathered their belongings and left* before the sun rose.
7. Nobody knew *that John had worked out the solution.*
8. *The dogs chased the deer onto the ice,* which was more than two feet thick.
9. My dad says not to trust strangers *who seem too friendly.*
10. *That he had been right* became obvious as the problem grew worse.
11. Julio knew the right answer *because he looked it up in the dictionary.*
12. Do you know *how a bill becomes a law?*
13. On our vacation we visited my dad's old neighborhood, *which is now an industrial park.*
14. *It just doesn't seem right* that I have to do all this work without getting paid.
15. Did you get the message *that your mother called?*
16. Andy raked up the leaves *while his father stuffed them into plastic bags.*
17. Before the program began, *the band tuned their instruments,* and the audience got refreshments.

18. We will be over *as soon as Sandy finishes his lunch.*
19. That is the man *whose dog rescued my sister.*
20. Free samples were given to *whoever asked for them.*

15a. A *clause* is a group of words that contains a verb and its subject and is used as a part of a sentence.

Every clause, like every sentence, has a subject and a verb; however, not every clause expresses a complete thought, as all sentences do. Clauses that express a complete thought are called *independent clauses.* Clauses that do not express a complete thought by themselves are called *subordinate clauses.* Subordinate clauses, like phrases, can serve as nouns, adjectives, and adverbs.

THE INDEPENDENT CLAUSE

15b. An *independent* (or *main*) *clause* expresses a complete thought and can stand by itself as a sentence.

If you can recognize a sentence, you will be able to recognize independent clauses. Independent clauses can stand alone as sentences. They are usually called independent clauses only when they are part of a more complex sentence.

SENTENCE **I baked her a cake.**

INDEPENDENT CLAUSE Since it was my mother's birthday, **I baked her a cake.**

In the following sentences, the independent clauses are in boldface. Notice that the third sentence has more than one independent clause.

If you have worked with the soil, **you are familiar with *humus*.**
***Humus* comes from a Latin word** that means "earth."
***Humilis* means "on the ground,"** and **from this Latin word we derive the word "humility."**

THE SUBORDINATE CLAUSE

Although an independent clause can stand alone as a complete thought, a subordinate clause cannot stand alone.

SENTENCE	Writers gathered at the home of Gertrude Stein when she lived in Paris.
INDEPENDENT CLAUSE	Writers gathered at the home of Gertrude Stein. [can stand alone]
SUBORDINATE CLAUSE	when she lived in Paris [cannot stand alone]

15c. A *subordinate* (or *dependent*) *clause* does not express a complete thought and cannot stand alone.

Subordinate means "lesser in rank or importance." Since a subordinate clause cannot stand by itself, it is considered "below the rank" of an independent clause.

Study the following sentences, which contain subordinate clauses set in boldface. Notice that the subordinate clauses all contain verbs and their subjects. Some subordinate clauses begin with words such as *since, when, if,* or *as.*

S V
As the monster appeared from beneath a huge rock, all of us in the movie theater held our breath.

S V
Since most plants die without light, we moved our house plants closer to the window.

Some subordinate clauses begin with words such as *who, which,* or *that.*

S V
The animals **that I saw in the game preserve** were protected from hunters.

S V
Michelle, **who was on the debating team last year,** won her argument with the teacher.

In the last example, notice that the word *who* is both the introductory word in the clause and the subject of the clause.

EXERCISE 1. Identifying Independent Clauses, Subordinate Clauses, and Phrases. Some of the following expressions are sentences, some are subordinate clauses, and some are phrases. Number your paper 1–10. If the expression is a sentence, write *S* after the proper number; if it is a subordinate clause, write *C;* if it is a phrase, write *P.*

EXAMPLE 1. as I answered the telephone
1. *C*

1. we memorized the lyrics
2. by the back porch
3. if no one is coming
4. who was born on Valentine's Day
5. which everyone enjoyed
6. after last year's flood
7. the singer wore a silk scarf
8. when the lights were flickering
9. since the first time we talked
10. beside the lion's cage

EXERCISE 2. Identifying Subordinate Clauses and Their Subjects and Verbs. After the proper number, write the subordinate clause from each of the following sentences. Underline the subject of the clause once and the verb twice.

EXAMPLE 1. In history class we learned about the plague that spread across Europe in the fourteenth century.
1. *that spread across Europe in the fourteenth century*

1. In 1347, trading ships arrived on the Mediterranean island of Sicily from Caffa, which was a port city on the Black Sea.
2. As they emerged from the boats, many of the sailors carried a strange illness.
3. No medicine could save the sailors, who died quickly and painfully.

4. In the same year, many other people became sick and died as the plague spread across Sicily and Europe.
5. Even doctors caught the illness when they hurried to the bedsides of sick patients.
6. If a person traveled to another city in Europe, the disease probably traveled too.
7. The fast-spreading, deadly plague terrified the survivors, who thought the world was coming to an end.
8. Since it originated in the Black Sea area, the plague was called the Black Death.
9. No one is sure of the total number of people who died.
10. Since medicine offers new ways for controlling plague, the spread of this disease is unlikely today.

GRAMMAR

EXERCISE 3. Writing Sentences with Independent and Subordinate Clauses. Add an independent clause to each subordinate clause, and write the whole sentence. Draw one line under the subject and two lines under the verb of each clause.

EXAMPLE 1. who came late
1. *Susie is the volunteer who came late.*

1. when the ice melts
2. if my teacher approves
3. since you insist
4. when they act silly
5. who borrowed my notes
6. as she began to shout
7. when we danced on stage
8. who gave the report
9. since I sleep soundly
10. that I bought yesterday

THE ADJECTIVE CLAUSE

Like an adjective or an adjective phrase, a clause may modify a noun or a pronoun. In the following word groups, you see first an adjective phrase, then an adjective clause.

ADJECTIVE PHRASE the woman **in the car**
ADJECTIVE CLAUSE the woman **who is in the car**

ADJECTIVE PHRASE a tree **with red blossoms**
ADJECTIVE CLAUSE a tree **that has red blossoms**

15d. An *adjective clause* is a subordinate clause used as an adjective to modify a noun or a pronoun.

Observe how the adjective clauses in the following sentences modify nouns or pronouns. Notice that adjective clauses usually follow immediately after the words that they modify.

> Helen Keller was a remarkable woman **who overcame blindness and deafness.**
>
> Ms. Jackson showed slides **that she had taken in Egypt.**
>
> The ones **whose flight was delayed** spent the night in Detroit.

The Relative Pronoun

Adjective clauses are easy to identify because they are almost always introduced by a *relative pronoun. Who, whom, whose, which,* and *that* are called *relative* pronouns because they *relate* to another word or idea in the sentence.

EXAMPLES Leonardo da Vinci was the artist **who painted the Mona Lisa.** [The relative pronoun *who* begins the clause and relates to the noun *artist.*]

Everything **that could be done** was done. [The relative pronoun *that* begins the clause and relates to the pronoun *everything.*]

EXERCISE 4. Identifying Adjective Clauses. After the proper number, write each adjective clause, circling the relative pronoun. Then write the word that the pronoun refers to.

EXAMPLE 1. Our friends have a canary that is named Neptune.
1. *(that) is named Neptune—canary*

1. Proverbs are sayings that usually give advice.
2. Trivia questions have been organized into games that have become quite popular.
3. A black hole, which results after a star has collapsed, can trap energy and matter.

4. A special award was given to the student whose work had improved most.
5. Frances Perkins, who served as Secretary of Labor, was the first woman to hold a Cabinet position.
6. The problem that worries us now is the pollution of underground sources of water.
7. We enjoyed the poems of Gwendolyn Brooks, who for years has been poet laureate of Illinois.
8. In *Walden,* Thoreau shared ideas that have influenced many.
9. Athena, who ranked as an important Greek goddess, protected the city of Athens.
10. A friend is a person whom you can trust.

WRITING APPLICATION A: Using Adjective Clauses to Make Your Writing Specific

Improvements in technology have allowed us to store larger and larger amounts of information in smaller and smaller spaces. As you become more experienced in writing, you too learn how to pack more information into smaller spaces. Specific facts, for example, can sometimes be compressed into adjective clauses.

EXAMPLE The first library, *which contained a dining room, private studies, laboratories, and a walkway for strolling,* was located in Alexandria, Egypt.

Writing Assignment

In some cases people misunderstand each other because they do not have in mind the same meanings for words. For example, what *you* think is a "good" report card may not be the same as what your *parents* think is a "good" report card. Write a paragraph defining one of the following terms. Use at least two adjective clauses, and underline these clauses.

a clean room	a loyal friend	a fun weekend
a good teacher	an ideal pet	a good-looking outfit

Sometimes the relative pronoun is preceded by a preposition. Traditionally, this is the correct position when a relative pronoun is the object of a preposition; but nowadays you will often see the preposition at the end of the clause.

the day **which we looked forward to**
the day **to which we looked forward**
my friend, **whom I would do anything for**
my friend, **for whom I would do anything**

EXERCISE 5. Identifying Adjective Clauses. Write the adjective clause from each of the following sentences. Circle the relative pronoun. Remember that a relative pronoun may sometimes be preceded by a preposition.

1. Coco Chanel is the woman for whom the perfume is named.
2. Darth Vader, the enemy that Luke Skywalker fought, was an evil villain in *Star Wars.*
3. The cello, when played by Pablo Casals, is an instrument to which I could listen for hours.
4. Ella Fitzgerald, who started singing in New York City, is famous throughout the world.
5. Christopher Marlowe wrote of Helen of Troy, "Was this the face that launched a thousand ships?"
6. Anita was one of the sopranos who sang in the chorus.
7. In the play *My Fair Lady,* Eliza Doolittle, a poor flower merchant, becomes a woman whom everyone admires.
8. The Kinderhook was the creek in which we found the shells.
9. Janet Flanner, who wrote dispatches from Paris, used the pen name Genêt.
10. The astronauts, to whom travel in the space shuttle is routine, must always keep in shape.

EXERCISE 6. Writing Adjective Clauses in Sentences. Supply an adjective clause for each blank. Write the complete sentence on your paper. Circle each relative pronoun.

EXAMPLE 1. Pineapples —— thrive in Hawaii.
1. *Pineapples, (which) do not grow in many parts of the United States, thrive in Hawaii.*

1. Our club sponsored a dance —— .
2. The car —— is the sportiest one on the block.
3. The young paramedic quickly gave first aid to the motorist —— .
4. Suits of armor —— weigh hundreds of pounds.
5. Rita and Jon met the professional football player —— .

THE ADVERB CLAUSE

Like an adverb or an adverb phrase, a subordinate clause may modify a verb, an adjective, or an adverb. Such a clause is called an *adverb clause.*

ADVERB PHRASE **During the winter** many animals hibernate.
ADVERB CLAUSE **When winter sets in,** many animals hibernate.

15e. An *adverb clause* is a subordinate clause used as an adverb.

An adverb clause may modify a verb, an adjective, or an adverb by telling *how, when, where, why, to what extent* (*how much* or *how long*), or *under what conditions.*

There was a great sea wave **when the volcano erupted.** [The adverb clause tells *when* there *was* a great sea wave.]

Because the day was very hot, the cool water felt good. [The adverb clause tells *why* the water *felt* good.]

If it does not rain tomorrow, we will go to see Crater Lake. [The adverb clause tells *under what conditions* we *will go* to see Crater Lake.]

As these examples show, the adverb clause may be placed at various places in the sentence. When it begins the sentence, an adverb clause is usually followed by a comma.

WRITING APPLICATION B:
Using Adverb Clauses to Explain a Process

It's fun to browse in bookstores. In the self-help section, you can find books on how to build things, how to cook, how to study, and even how to get over a broken heart! Adverb clauses are useful in explaining how to do something. They help a reader understand exactly how one thing is related to another in an explanation. Notice in the following example how the subordinating conjunction *if* helps relate the information in the adverb clause to information in the rest of the sentence.

EXAMPLE *If you want a tasty, nourishing dessert,* you should try combining an orange, an apple, and some pecans.

Writing Assignment

Write a paragraph explaining a process that you have used. List any equipment needed to complete the process, and include all of the steps. Use at least three adverb clauses. Underline these clauses, and circle the subordinating conjunctions that introduce them. Here are some ideas:

How to clean a trumpet
How to pack for a beach trip
How to study for a test

The Subordinating Conjunction

Chapter 12 discusses two kinds of conjunctions: coordinating conjunctions, such as *and* and *but;* and correlative conjunctions, such as *either . . . or* and *neither . . . nor.* A third kind, called a *subordinating conjunction,* introduces an adverb clause.

The following words are commonly used to begin adverb clauses. Remember that *after, before, since, until, as,* and many other subordinating conjunctions may also be used as prepositions or other parts of speech.

Subordinating Conjunctions

after	as though	so that	whenever
although	because	than	where
as	before	though	wherever
as if	if	unless	while
long as	in order that	until	
as soon as	since	when	

EXERCISE 7. Identifying Adverb Clauses. There are ten adverb clauses in the following paragraph. Write the number of the line on which the clause begins. Then write the clause. In each clause, circle the subordinating conjunction, and underline the subject once and the verb twice.

EXAMPLE While we were listening to the radio, we heard the news bulletin.

1. *While we were listening to the radio*

What countries would you visit if you could travel anywhere in the world? After you had thought about all the possibilities for a few minutes, you would probably list some of the countries in Europe. Of course, England, France, Spain, Germany, or Italy would likely be on your list, since you have heard much about them. As you studied a map of Europe, you might also notice Liechtenstein and Andorra. Although you might need a magnifying glass to see them, these two European countries could go on your list. When you search for places to visit, you can often overlook some of the less famous areas. However, there are many charming spots in the world. Give some consideration to these whenever you make your travel plans. Because the world is so vast and full of interesting people and lands, it is worthwhile to search for different possibilities so that you can have a choice. When you are planning which places to visit, look beyond the obvious ones and consider some of the many small treats hidden away all over the world.

EXERCISE 8. Writing Adverb Clauses in Sentences. Add an adverb clause to each of the following sentences. Write the entire sentence; then circle the subordinating conjunctions, and underline the subject of each adverb clause once and the verb twice.

EXAMPLE 1. The movie finally ended.
1. *(After) we spent three hours in the theater, the movie finally ended.*

1. Members of the Drama Club auditioned.
2. Erica speaks three languages.
3. We prepared *moussaka,* a dish with lamb and eggplant, for our Cooking Club's international supper.
4. The Goldmans had flown to Acapulco many times.
5. Jill daydreams in class.

THE NOUN CLAUSE

In addition to acting as modifiers, subordinate clauses may also serve as nouns. A subordinate clause that acts as a subject, a predicate nominative, a direct object, an indirect object, or the object of a preposition in a sentence is called a *noun clause.*

15f. A *noun clause* is a subordinate clause used as a noun.

Like a noun, a noun clause can be used as a subject, a complement (predicate nominative, direct object, indirect object), or an object of a preposition.

NOUNS	NOUN CLAUSES
Subject Ann's **anger** was obvious.	**That Ann was angry** was obvious.
Predicate nominative Three dollars is their **offer.**	Three dollars is **what they offered.**
Direct object The judges determined the **winner.**	The judges determined **who won.**
Indirect object The sheriff gave each **volunteer** a flashlight.	The sheriff gave **whoever volunteered** a flashlight.

NOUNS	NOUN CLAUSES
Object of preposition They agreed with his **statements.**	They agreed with **whatever he said.**

Most noun clauses are introduced by *that, what, whatever, who, whom, whoever,* and *whomever.* The introductory word sometimes has a function within the clause; at other times its only function is to introduce the clause.

EXAMPLES They told him **what he should do.** [The introductory word *what* is the direct object of the noun clause —*he should do what.* The entire noun clause *what he should do* is the direct object of the verb *told.*]

Give a free pass to **whoever asks for one.** [The introductory word *whoever* is the subject of the noun clause—*whoever asks for one.* The entire noun clause *whoever asks for one* is the object of the preposition *to.*]

Their complaint was **that the milk smelled sour.** [The introductory word *that* simply introduces the noun clause and has no other function in the clause. The noun clause *that the milk smelled sour* is the predicate nominative, referring to the subject of the sentence—*complaint.*]

EXERCISE 9. Identifying and Classifying Noun Clauses. After the proper number, write the noun clause in each of the following sentences. Then tell how the entire noun clause is used in the sentence: as *subject, predicate nominative, direct object, indirect object,* or *object of the preposition.*

EXAMPLE 1. We couldn't find what was making the noise in the car.
1. *what was making the noise in the car—direct object*

1. Whatever you decide will be fine with us.
2. Whoever takes us to the beach is my friend for life.
3. Do you know what happened to the rest of my tuna fish sandwich?

4. Stu is looking for whoever owns that red bicycle.
5. Checking our supplies, we discovered that we had forgotten the flour.
6. The worst flaw in the story is that it doesn't have a carefully developed plot.
7. Unfortunately, these results are not what we had planned.
8. The painter gave whatever spots had dried another coat of enamel.
9. At lunch, my friends and I talked about what we should do as our service project.
10. That anyone could doubt their story seemed to amaze the children.

GRAMMAR

Diagraming Subordinate Clauses

Diagram an adjective clause by connecting it with a broken line to the word it modifies. Draw the broken line between the relative pronoun and the word that it relates to. The relative pronoun is either the subject or the object in the adjective clause.

EXAMPLE The grades that I got last term pleased my father.

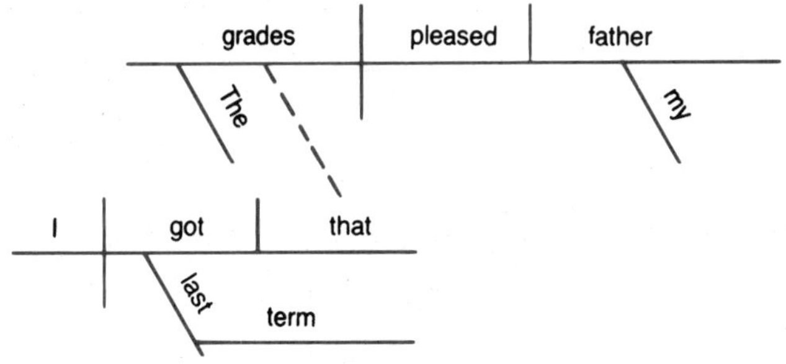

Diagram an adverb clause by using a broken line to connect the adverb clause to the word it modifies. Place the subordinating conjunction that introduces the adverb clause on the broken line.

EXAMPLE When I come home from school, I usually eat a sandwich.

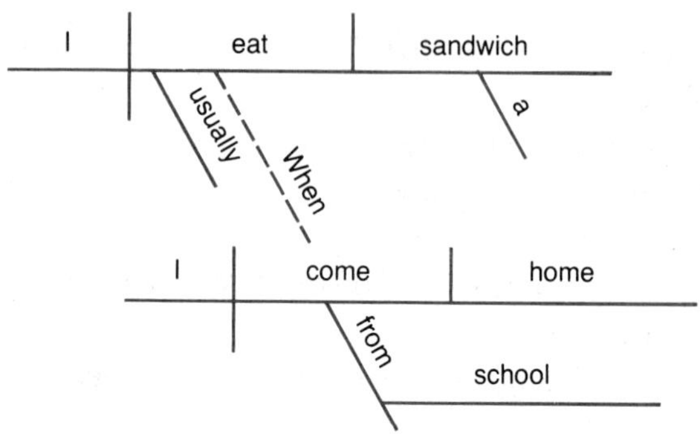

Diagram a noun clause according to how it is used in the sentence. Connect the noun clause to the independent clause with a solid line, as shown in the following two examples.

EXAMPLE Olive knew what she wanted. [The noun clause *what she wanted* is the direct object of the independent clause. The word *what* is the direct object in the noun clause.]

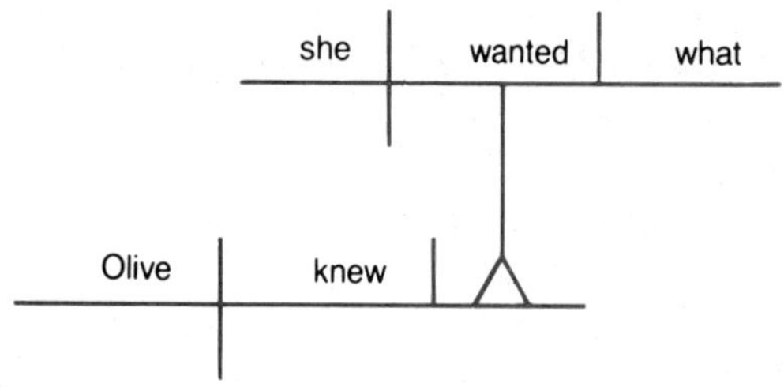

When the introductory word of the noun clause does not have a specific function in the noun clause, the sentence is diagramed in this way:

EXAMPLE The problem is that they lost the map. [The noun clause *that they lost the map* is the predicate nominative of the independent clause. The word *that* has no function in the noun clause except as an introductory word.]

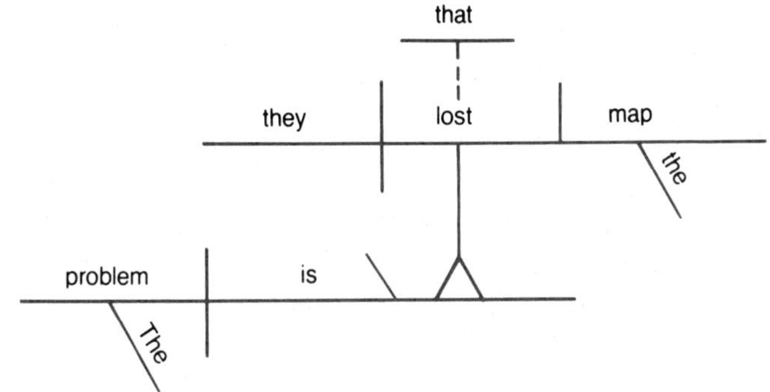

EXERCISE 10. Diagraming Sentences with Subordinate Clauses. Diagram the following sentences.

1. The test that we took on Friday was hard.
2. If I had not studied Thursday night, I could not have answered half the questions.
3. Our teacher announced what would be on the test.
4. Several friends of mine were not paying attention when the teacher gave the assignment.
5. My friends who did not know what to study are worried now about their grades.

REVIEW EXERCISE A. Identifying Adjective, Adverb, and Noun Clauses. Each of the following quotations contains at least one adjective clause, adverb clause, or noun clause. Write the clause or clauses after the proper number. Write *adj. cl., adv. cl.,* or *n. cl.* where appropriate.

1. It's no use shutting the barn door after the horse is gone.
—OLD PROVERB
2. They also serve who only stand and wait.—JOHN MILTON
3. You gain strength, courage and confidence by every experience in which you really stop to look fear in the face.
—ELEANOR ROOSEVELT
4. Let me not criticize any man until I have walked a mile in his moccasins.—OLD INDIAN PROVERB

5. I believe that man will not merely endure: he will prevail.

—WILLIAM FAULKNER

REVIEW EXERCISE B. Identifying Subordinate Clauses. There are ten subordinate clauses in the following paragraphs. Write the number of the line in which the first word of the clause appears. Then write the clause. Write *adj. cl.* after each adjective clause, *adv. cl.* after each adverb clause, and *n. cl.* after each noun clause.

Robert Browning, who was a poet of the Victorian period, wrote a poem about Childe Roland, a daring knight who set out on a dangerous quest for the Dark Tower. Many brave knights had been killed searching for the tower, but Roland was determined that he would find it.

After Roland had searched for years, he came upon an old man who pointed the way to the tower. Following the old man's directions, Roland came to what he had been seeking. As he gazed upon the structure, he remembered the tales about all of the knights who had died in their searching. He knew that he must fulfill the quest for all of them. As he moved toward the tower, Roland raised his horn to his lips and blew: "*Childe Roland to the Dark Tower came.*"

CHAPTER 15 REVIEW: POSTTEST 1

Identifying Independent and Subordinate Clauses; Classifying Subordinate Clauses. After the proper number, identify each of the italicized clauses in the following paragraphs as an independent clause or a subordinate clause. Tell whether each italicized subordinate clause is a noun clause (*n. cl.*), adjective clause (*adj. cl.*), or an adverb clause (*adv. cl.*)

EXAMPLES When my father got a new job, (1) *we had to move to another town.*

1. *independent clause*

(2) *When my father got a new job,* we had to move to another town.
2. *subordinate clause-adv. cl.*

Earlier this year I had to transfer to another school (1) *because my father got a new job*. This is the fourth time (2) *that I have had to change schools,* and every time I've wished (3) *that I could just stay at my old school.* (4) *As soon as I make friends in a new place,* I have to move again and leave them behind. Then at the new school (5) *I am a stranger all over again.*

We lived in our last house for three years, (6) *which is the longest time we've spent in any one place* (7) *since I was little.* Living there so long, (8) *I had a chance to meet several people* (9) *who became good friends of mine.* My two best friends, Chris and Marty, said (10) *that they would write to me,* and I promised to write to them, too. However, the friends (11) *that I had before* always promised to write, but (12) *after a letter or two we lost touch.* (13) *Why this happens* is a mystery to me, but it has happened every time.

I dreaded registering at my new school two months (14) *after the school year had begun.* By then, everyone else would already have made friends, and (15) *I would be an outsider,* (16) *as I knew from past experience.* There are always some students who bully and tease (17) *whoever is new at school* or anyone else (18) *who is different.* Back in elementary school I would get angry and upset (19) *when people would pick on me.* Since then, I've learned how to fit in and make friends (20) *in spite of whatever anyone does to hassle me or make me feel uncomfortable.*

Everywhere (21) *that I've gone to school,* some students always are friendly and offer to show me around. (22) *I used to be shy,* and I wouldn't take them up on their invitations. Since they didn't know (23) *whether I was being shy or unfriendly,* they soon left me alone. Now (24) *whenever someone is friendly to me at a new school or in a new neighborhood,* I fight down my shyness and act friendly myself. It's still hard to get used to new people and places, but (25) *it's a lot easier with help from new friends.*

CHAPTER 15 REVIEW: POSTTEST 2

Writing Sentences with Independent and Subordinate Clauses. Write your own sentences according to each of the following instructions. Underline the subordinate clauses.

EXAMPLE 1. A sentence with an independent clause and an adjective clause
1. I am going to the game with Jim, *who is my best friend.*

1. A sentence with an independent clause and no subordinate clauses
2. A sentence with an independent clause and one subordinate clause
3. A sentence with an adjective clause that begins with a relative pronoun
4. A sentence with an adjective clause in which a preposition precedes the relative pronoun
5. A sentence with an introductory adverb clause
6. A sentence with an adverb clause and an adjective clause
7. A sentence with a noun clause used as a direct object
8. A sentence with a noun clause used as a subject
9. A sentence with a noun clause used as the object of a preposition
10. A sentence with a noun clause and either an adjective clause or an adverb clause

GRAMMAR

CHAPTER 16

The Kinds of Sentence Structure

THE FOUR BASIC SENTENCE STRUCTURES

Chapter 10 explains how sentences may be classified according to their purpose: *declarative, interrogative, imperative,* and *exclamatory.* Another way to classify sentences is according to their construction—the kind and number of clauses they contain. In this chapter you will study the four kinds of sentence structure: *simple, compound, complex,* and *compound-complex.*

DIAGNOSTIC TEST

Identifying the Four Kinds of Sentence Structure. Number your paper 1–20. Identify each of the following sentences as simple, compound, complex, or compound-complex.

EXAMPLE 1. We bought a new computer program that helps with spelling and grammar.
1. *complex*

1. Nancy wanted to go to the dance, but she had to baby-sit.
2. When the rabbit saw us, it ran into the bushes.

3. Beyond that building and around the corner, the line stretched all the way down the block to the movie theater.
4. You should either buy a new bicycle or fix your old one.
5. Judy said that this was the shortest route, but I disagree.
6. There was no way to tell what had really happened.
7. Yes, that seems like the right answer to me.
8. The steer broke out of its pen and trampled the roses.
9. Do you know who wrote this?
10. I'm not sure what you said, but I think I agree.
11. Nobody is worried about that, for it will never happen.
12. Whatever you decide will be fine with me.
13. Is the movie that we wanted to see playing at the drive-in, or do we have to go to the theater in the mall?
14. Leroy knew the plan, and he assigned us each a part.
15. Amphibians and some insects can live both on the land and in the water.
16. The detective searched for the man who had been wearing a beret, but there weren't many clues.
17. The tornado cut across the edge of the housing development, and seven homes were destroyed.
18. Until then, everyone had agreed with his main argument.
19. Before the game started, all the football players ran out onto the field, and everyone cheered.
20. My father stopped to help the family whose car had broken down on the highway.

THE SIMPLE SENTENCE

Remember that a clause is a sentence part that contains a verb and its subject. An independent clause expresses a complete thought and may stand alone. A subordinate clause does not express a complete thought and cannot stand alone. When an independent clause stands alone with no other clauses attached to it, it is called a *simple sentence.*

16a. A *simple sentence* has one independent clause and no subordinate clauses.

In the following examples, the subjects and verbs are printed in boldface. Notice that a simple sentence may have a compound subject (second sentence), a compound verb (third sentence), or both (fourth sentence).

EXAMPLES The **hair stylist gave** John a new look.

Beth Heiden and **Sheila Young won** Olympic medals. [compound subject: *Beth Heiden* and *Sheila Young*]

Lawrence caught the ball but then **dropped** it. [compound verb: *caught* but *dropped*]

The **astronomer** and her **assistant studied** the heavens and **wrote** reports on their findings. [compound subject: *astronomer* and *assistant*; compound verb: *studied* and *wrote*]

EXERCISE 1. Identifying Subjects and Verbs in Simple Sentences. Number your paper 1–10. After the proper number, write the subjects and the verbs of the following sentences. Some sentences have compound subjects and verbs.

EXAMPLE 1. The first combustion engines were quite different from those of today.
1. *engines—were*

1. No kitten or puppy compares to my pet boa constrictor.
2. Officers in uniform boarded the ship in the harbor.
3. We gave apples to the trick-or-treaters.
4. Often juniors or seniors serve as tutors.
5. The amount of food will depend on the number of guests.
6. The first mayor of our town was elected in 1854 and won by a unanimous vote.
7. The accident occurred during the late-afternoon rush hour.
8. The Olympic Games inspired pride in our athletes and renewed interest in the support and training of amateur

athletes in the United States.

9. Soldiers waiting for orders and volunteers waiting for supplies organized a system to help the flood victims.
10. After the dance the students, remembering their manners, thanked the chaperons.

GRAMMAR

THE COMPOUND SENTENCE

Sometimes two or more independent clauses appear in the same sentence without any subordinate clauses. Such a sentence is called a *compound sentence.*

16b. A *compound sentence* has two or more independent clauses but no subordinate clauses.

The independent clauses are usually joined by the coordinating conjunctions *yet, and, but, or, nor, for,* or *so.*

EXAMPLES **According to legend, Betsy Ross made our first flag,** but **there is little evidence.** [two independent clauses joined by the conjunction *but*]

The whistle blew, the drums rolled, and **the crowd cheered.** [three independent clauses, the last two joined by the conjunction *and*]

EXERCISE 2. Identifying Subjects, Verbs, and Conjunctions in Compound Sentences. For each sentence, write the subject and verb of the first independent clause, the coordinating conjunction that joins the independent clauses, and the subject and verb of the next clause. Insert a comma before the conjunction. Underline subjects once and verbs twice.

EXAMPLE 1. A director of a theater-in-the-round visited our class, and we listened to his humorous stories for almost an hour.

1. *director visited*, and *we listened*

1. Many strange things happen backstage during a performance, but the audience usually does not know about them.
2. Audiences at theaters-in-the-round add to the director's problems, for they sit very close to the stage.
3. Members of the audience sometimes use stage ashtrays, or they hang their coats on the actors' coat racks.
4. Sometimes these actions are overlooked by the stagehands, and the results can be very challenging for the actors.
5. The main clue in a certain mystery play depended on a scarf left lying on the stage floor, but the audience had gathered on the stage during intermission.
6. During the scene after the intermission, the detective in the play counted three scarves instead of one, but the actor showed no surprise.
7. Directors cannot always predict the reactions of the audience, nor can they always control the audience.
8. During the performance of another mystery drama, a spectator in the front row became too excited about the action of the play, for at one point, leaping up on the stage, the spectator tackled the killer.
9. The workers in charge of properties are usually alert and efficient, but they do sometimes make mistakes.
10. In one production of *Romeo and Juliet,* the character Juliet prepared to kill herself with a dagger, but unfortunately there was no dagger on the stage.

Sentences with Compound Parts

Although it consists of two or more subjects joined by a conjunction, a compound subject is still regarded as one subject. Similarly, a compound verb is still regarded as one verb. A simple sentence, which has only one subject and one verb, is still a simple sentence even when its subject or verb is compound. Do not confuse a simple sentence containing a compound subject or a compound verb with a compound sentence, which has a subject and a verb in each of its independent clauses.

SIMPLE SENTENCE Bill and Joe increased their speed and passed the other runners. [compound subject and compound verb]

COMPOUND SENTENCE Bill led half the way, and then Joe took the lead.

If a subject is repeated, then the sentence is considered compound.

SIMPLE SENTENCE I ran to the window and looked out at the snow.

COMPOUND SENTENCE I ran to the window, and I looked out at the snow.

EXERCISE 3. Distinguishing Between Compound Sentences and Compound Subjects and Verbs. After the proper number, write each subject and verb in the following sentences. Underline the subjects once and the verbs twice. Then write *S.* for each simple sentence and *Cd.* for each compound sentence.

EXAMPLES 1. David Attenborough has studied unusual creatures around the world and has photographed their habitats and behavior.

1. *David Attenborough has studied, has photographed—S.*
2. He always manages to find unique animals, and he rarely misses a chance to observe them in their natural habitats.
2. *He manages, he misses—Cd.*

1. He has boundless curiosity about living creatures and treats them with respect.
2. Many of his television programs focus on animal life, but several include information about plants and geology.
3. Some prefer the program *Life on Earth,* but I like *The Living Planet* better.
4. David Attenborough has also written books and has contributed many of the outstanding photos in them.
5. Someday everyone might have the same enthusiasm for life on this planet, and then people will take care of the environment.

Diagraming Compound Sentences

The independent clauses in a compound sentence are diagramed like simple sentences. The second clause is diagramed below the first and is joined to it by a coordinating conjunction diagramed as shown.

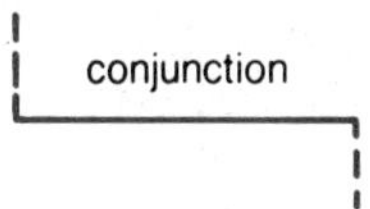

EXAMPLE The quarterback threw a good pass, but the end did not catch it.

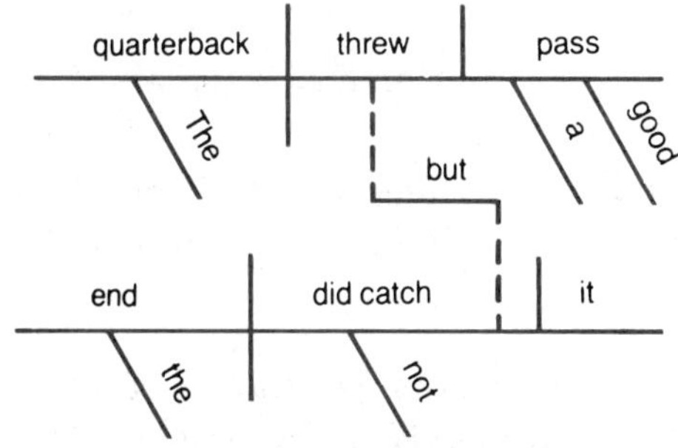

EXERCISE 4. Diagraming Compound Sentences. Diagram the following compound sentences.

1. I want a motorboat, but Jan prefers a sailboat.
2. The bus stopped at the restaurant, and everyone got off.
3. Our club is very small, but it is growing.
4. Shall we meet you at the station, or will you take a taxi?
5. In Arizona the temperature is often high, but the humidity always remains low.

THE COMPLEX SENTENCE

Like a compound sentence, a complex sentence contains more than one clause. However, unlike the compound sentence, the complex sentence has at least one subordinate clause.

16c. A *complex sentence* has one independent clause and at least one subordinate clause.

A subordinate clause may be an adjective clause (pages 386–90), an adverb clause (pages 390–93), or a noun clause (pages 393–95).

Adjective clauses usually begin with a relative pronoun: *who, whom, whose, which,* or *that.* Adverb clauses usually begin with a subordinating conjunction such as *after, although, because, if, until, when,* or *where.* Noun clauses usually begin with *that, what, whatever, who, whoever, whom,* or *whomever.*

In the following examples, the subordinate clauses are printed in boldface.

EXAMPLE **When I watch Martha Graham's dances,** I feel like studying dance.

One independent clause	I feel like studying dance
Subordinate clause	When I watch Martha Graham's dances

EXAMPLE Some of the sailors **who took part in the mutiny on the British ship *Bounty*** settled Pitcairn Island.

One independent clause	Some of the sailors settled Pitcairn Island
Subordinate clause	who took part in the mutiny on the British ship *Bounty*

EXAMPLE In *Gone with the Wind,* **when she is faced with near-starvation,** Scarlett vows **that she will never be hungry again.**

One independent clause	In *Gone with the Wind,* Scarlett vows
Two subordinate clauses	when she is faced with near-starvation
	that she will never be hungry again

EXERCISE 5. Identifying Independent and Subordinate Clauses in Complex Sentences. Write the following complex sentences. Draw one line under each independent clause and two

lines under each subordinate clause. Circle subordinating conjunctions and relative pronouns. Be prepared to identify the subject and the verb in each clause. A sentence may have more than one subordinate clause.

EXAMPLES
1. China is a largely agricultural country that has a population of more than one billion people.
1. *China is a largely agricultural country that has a population of more than one billion people.*
2. Although my brother bought one of those coins for his collection, it was nearly worthless.
2. *Although my brother bought one of those coins for his collection, it was nearly worthless.*

1. The detective show appeared on television for several weeks before it became popular with viewers.
2. Most of the albums that we have from the 1960's are sitting in the corner of the basement behind the broken refrigerator.
3. Richard E. Byrd is but one of the explorers who made expeditions to Antarctica.
4. As studies continued, many important facts about nutrition were discovered.
5. A group of popular singers, who donated their time, recorded a song that made people aware of the problems in Ethiopia.
6. The players who were sent back to the minor leagues received a chance to improve their skills.
7. After we have written our report on the history of computers, we may be able to go to the picnic.
8. Although few students or teachers knew about it, a group of sociologists visited our school to study the relationship between the classroom environment and students' grades.
9. While the stage crew was constructing the sets, the performers continued their rehearsal, which went on into the night.
10. Because the park is maintained by the city, the citizens have complained to the mayor about vandalism.

GRAMMAR

Diagraming Complex Sentences

Since a complex sentence has at least one subordinate clause, in order to diagram a complex sentence you need to know how to diagram subordinate clauses. The methods for diagraming subordinate clauses—adjective clauses, adverb clauses, and noun clauses—have been covered on pages 395–97.

Here is how to diagram each of the three kinds of subordinate clauses in a complex sentence:

EXAMPLES We had lunch in the student cafeteria when we visited the college. [complex sentence containing an adverb clause]

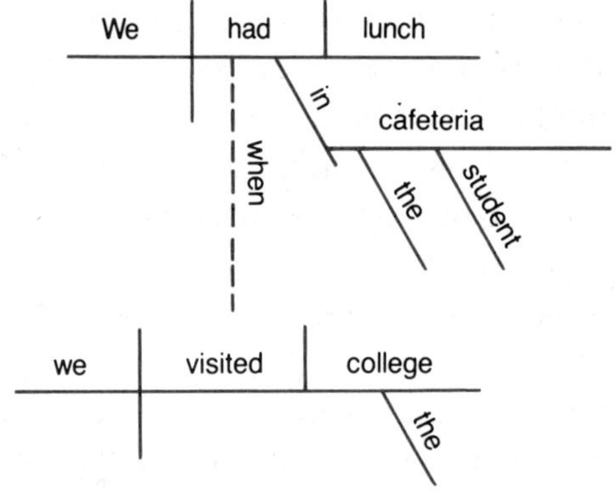

Blair has a ring that belonged to her great-grandmother. [complex sentence containing an adjective clause]

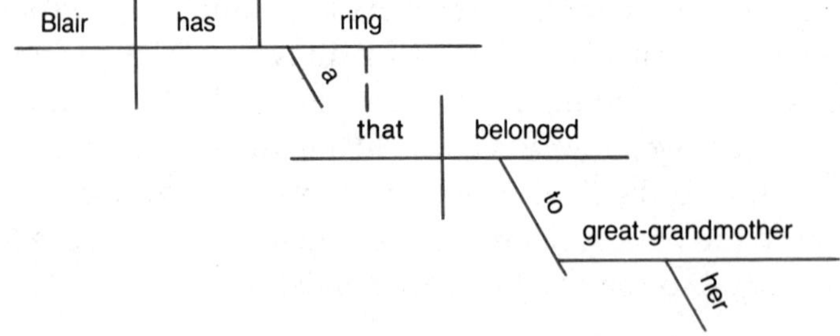

All of the children believed that they had actually seen Santa Claus. [complex sentence containing a noun clause]

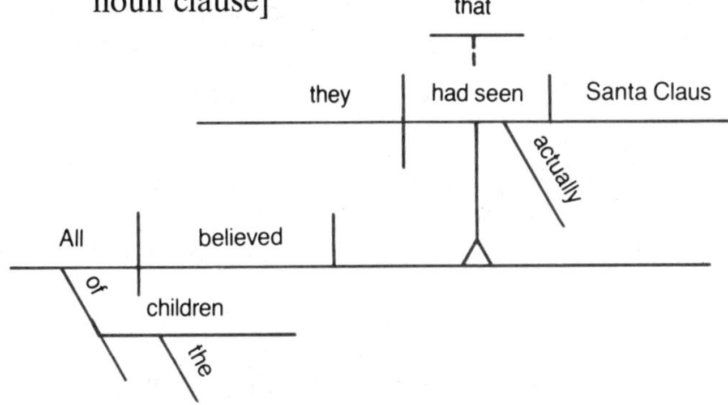

EXERCISE 6. Diagraming Complex Sentences. Diagram the following complex sentences.

1. We felt sorry for the cub that had caught its leg in a trap.
2. Invite whomever you want.
3. The satellite will be launched if the weather remains good.
4. The knight in black armor fought whoever would challenge him.
5. Alexander the Great, who conquered most of the known world, died at the age of thirty-three.

THE COMPOUND-COMPLEX SENTENCE

A compound-complex sentence is a combination of the compound sentence and the complex sentence. Like a compound sentence, it has at least two independent clauses; like a complex sentence, it has at least one subordinate clause.

16d. A *compound-complex sentence* has two or more independent clauses and at least one subordinate clause.

EXAMPLE Isabel began painting only two years ago, but she has already been asked to hang one of her paintings at the art exhibit that is scheduled for next month.

Two independent clauses	Isabel began painting only two years ago
	she has already been asked to hang one of her paintings at the art exhibit
Subordinate clause	that is scheduled for next month

GRAMMAR

EXERCISE 7. Identifying Clauses in Compound-Complex Sentences. The following sentences are compound-complex. Write each clause separately, and identify it as *independent* or *subordinate.*

EXAMPLE 1. The little-theater group was happy with the performances, and everyone immediately set to work to find new plays so that next season would be successful, too.

1. *The little-theater group was happy with the performances—independent*
1. *everyone immediately set to work to find new plays—independent*
1. *so that next season would be successful, too —subordinate*

1. Before we conducted the experiment, we asked for permission to use the science lab, but the principal insisted on teacher supervision of our work.
2. Inside the old trunk up in the attic, which is filled with boxes and toys, we found some dusty photo albums, and one of them contained pictures from the early 1900's.
3. We told them that their plan wouldn't work, but they wouldn't listen to us.
4. Every expedition that had attempted to explore that region had vanished without a trace, yet the young adventurer was determined to map the uncharted jungle because he couldn't resist the challenge.
5. The smoke, which grew steadily thicker and darker, billowed through the dry forest, and the animals ran ahead of it as the fire spread quickly.

WRITING APPLICATION:
Using Different Kinds of Sentences to Achieve Variety

Wouldn't it be boring to wear the same clothes every day? Your writing can be just as boring if you always use the same kind of sentence. You can learn to include all four kinds of sentences in your writing, as in the following example.

EXAMPLE O. Henry had an unusual life. He grew up in North Carolina. He became a pharmacist's apprentice. He moved to Texas and became a rancher, a bank teller, and a newspaper writer. He was accused of embezzlement. He fled to Honduras. He returned to Texas. His wife was dying. He went to prison. He wrote short stories there. He wrote more than two hundred short stories. They became very popular. [The paragraph uses all simple sentences.]

O. Henry had an unusual life. [simple] He grew up in North Carolina, and he became a pharmacist's apprentice. [compound] After moving to Texas, he became a rancher, a bank teller, and a newspaper writer before he was accused of embezzlement. [complex] He fled to Honduras, but he returned to Texas because his wife was dying. [compound-complex] While he was in prison, he wrote short stories. [complex] His stories—more than two hundred—became very popular. [simple]

Writing Assignment

Write a summary of the life of an American author. Include all four kinds of sentences. At the end of each sentence, write in parentheses the kind of sentence it is. Here are some ideas for a subject:

John Steinbeck	Mark Twain	Robert Frost
Edgar Allan Poe	Emily Dickinson	Gwendolyn Brooks

REVIEW EXERCISE. Identifying Simple, Compound, Complex, and Compound-Complex Sentences. Number your paper 1–10. Identify the kinds of sentences—simple (*S.*), compound (*Cd.*), complex (*Cx.*), or compound-complex (*Cd.–Cx.*) —in the following paragraphs.

1. People who are learning a new sport begin by mastering basic skills, and they usually are very enthusiastic. **2.** After people have been practicing the basic skills for several weeks or months, they usually progress to more difficult moves. **3.** At this point a beginner is likely to become discouraged, and the temptation to quit grows strong.

4. One of the most common problems that beginners face is coordination, and another is muscular aches and pains. **5.** If the student is not careful, the muscles can be injured, but the strenuous activity usually strengthens the muscle tissues. **6.** However, when enough oxygen reaches the warmed-up muscles, the danger of injury is lessened, and the muscles grow in size. **7.** At the same time, coordination grows, along with confidence.

8. The hours of practice that a beginner puts in often result in noticeable improvements. **9.** Obviously, learning something new takes time and work, or it would not be worthwhile. **10.** In sports, as in most activities, persistence and patience can earn rewards.

CHAPTER 16 REVIEW: POSTTEST 1

Identifying the Four Kinds of Sentence Structure. Number your paper 1–20. After the proper number, identify each of the following sentences as simple, compound, complex, or compound-complex.

EXAMPLE 1. When my grandmother came to visit at Christmas time, we decided to make our own ornaments for the Christmas tree.

1. *complex*

1. Last year my grandmother came to stay with us from the middle of December until my brother's birthday in January. **2.** While we were getting out the holiday decorations, Grandma told us all about how she and her family used to make their own decorations when my mother was a girl. **3.** Mom said that she remembered making splendid decorations and that it used to be fun, so we decided to try making some.

4. My dad, my brother, and I drove out to the woods to gather pine cones. **5.** We had forgotten to ask Grandma what size pine cones to get, and since Dad had never made decorations in his family, he didn't know. **6.** We decided to play it safe and get all different sizes, which was easy to do because there were pine cones everywhere. **7.** My brother picked up all the hard little ones, and my dad and I threw about a hundred medium and big ones into the trunk of the car. **8.** When Mom and Grandma saw how many we had, they laughed and said there were enough for decorating ten houses.

9. First we sorted the cones; the little hard ones went into one pile, and the bigger ones into another. **10.** Dad and I painted the little ones silver, and Mom and Grandma painted stripes, dots, and all sorts of designs on them. **11.** Then we tied strings to the tops of them, and later, when we put them up, they made great ornaments.

12. We painted the bigger pine cones all different colors and glued on cranberries and beads, which made each cone look like a miniature fir tree. **13.** We saved some of the smaller ones for the dining room table, and we put most of the others around on the windowsills and all over the house. **14.** My brother took some to school, too.

15. Besides the pine-cone decorations, we made some strings to decorate the mantel. **16.** My mom got some needles and a spool of heavy thread out of her sewing basket, and we all strung the rest of the cranberries on six-foot lengths of the thread.

17. Mom and Grandma cut off more pieces of thread, and we made strings of popcorn, just like our strings of cranberries.

18. We left some of the strings white and painted the others different colors.

19. Decorating our tree was even more fun than usual, and I think that the tree looked prettier, too, with all our homemade ornaments. **20.** From now on, we're going to make decorations every year.

CHAPTER 16 REVIEW: POSTTEST 2

Writing a Variety of Sentence Structures. Write your own sentences according to the following instructions:

1. A simple sentence with a compound subject
2. A simple sentence with a compound predicate
3. A compound sentence with two independent clauses joined by *but*
4. A compound sentence with two independent clauses joined by *or*
5. A complex sentence with an adjective clause beginning with the relative pronoun *that*
6. A complex sentence with an adjective clause beginning with the relative pronoun *who*
7. A complex sentence with an adverb clause at the beginning of the sentence
8. A complex sentence with an adverb clause at the end of the sentence
9. A complex sentence with a noun clause
10. A compound-complex sentence

CHAPTER 17

Agreement

SUBJECT AND VERB, PRONOUN AND ANTECEDENT

USAGE

Certain words in a sentence are closely related. The verb is closely related to its subject. A pronoun is closely related to the noun it stands for. Such closely related words have matching forms. When the related words are correctly matched, we say that they *agree.*

DIAGNOSTIC TEST

A. Identifying Verbs That Agree with Their Subjects. Number your paper 1–10. In each of the following sentences, if the italicized verb agrees with its subject, write *C* after the proper number. If the italicized verb does not agree with its subject, write the correct form of the verb.

EXAMPLES
1. Ms. Suarez, our gym teacher, *don't* know what happened.
1. *doesn't*
2. The answers to that question *don't* make sense.
2. *C*

1. Neither of the plants *need* water yet.
2. Everyone who wears eyeglasses *is* having vision tests today.
3. Two minutes *are* long enough to boil an egg.
4. Mr. Adams said that it *don't* look like rain today.
5. My baseball and my catcher's mitt *is* back in my room.
6. Neither Esteban nor Tina *have* tried out yet for the play.
7. All of the programs *have* been on television before.
8. *Don't* the team captain plan to put her into the game?
9. One of the men *have* decided to get his car washed.
10. The Bill of Rights *give* American citizens the right to worship where they please.

B. Identifying Pronouns That Agree with Their Antecedents. Number your paper 11–20. In each of the following sentences, if an italicized pronoun agrees with its antecedent, write *C* after the proper number. If an italicized pronoun does not agree with its antecedent, write the correct pronoun.

EXAMPLES 1. Each of the boys brought *their* permission slips.
1. *his*
2. One of the does was accompanied by *her* fawn.
2. *C*

11. Have all the girls taken *their* projects home?
12. Paul, Mike, and Chip each sent in *their* application.
13. Many of the trees had lost *its* leaves.
14. Neither Sally nor Marilyn had worn *their* gym suit.
15. Every dog had a tag hanging from *their* collar.
16. Someone in the Boy Scout troop camped near poison ivy and has gotten it all over *themselves.*
17. A few of the carpenters had brought tools with *them.*
18. My dog was among the winners in the show that had *its* picture taken.
19. According to the teacher, both of those titles should have lines drawn underneath *it.*
20. No one was sure which of the streets had *its* names changed.

AGREEMENT OF SUBJECT AND VERB

Singular and Plural Number

17a. When a word refers to one person, place, thing, or idea, it is *singular* in number. When a word refers to more than one, it is *plural* in number.

SINGULAR book, woman, fox, one, I, he
PLURAL books, women, foxes, many, we, they

EXERCISE 1. Classifying Nouns and Pronouns According to Number. Number your paper 1–10. After each number, write *S* if the word is singular and *P* if it is plural.

EXAMPLE 1. cat
1. *S*

1. tomatoes
2. coach
3. they
4. I
5. many
6. basis
7. mice
8. we
9. parents
10. it

EXERCISE 2. *Oral Drill.* Classifying Nouns and Pronouns by Number. Read the following expressions aloud. Tell whether each is singular or plural.

1. The lion yawns.
2. The cubs play.
3. No one stays.
4. The refugees arrive.
5. She wins.
6. They have.
7. The actors rehearse.
8. The play opens.
9. Everyone goes.
10. All applaud.

17b. A verb agrees with its subject in number.

(1) Singular subjects take singular verbs.

EXAMPLES The **car comes** to a sudden stop.
On that route **the plane flies** at a low altitude.
[The singular subjects *car* and *plane* take the singular verbs *comes* and *flies.*]

(2) Plural subjects take plural verbs.

EXAMPLES The **prisoners walk** in the exercise yard.
Again and again the **dolphins leap** playfully.
[The plural subjects *prisoners* and *dolphins* take the plural verbs *walk* and *leap.*]

Generally, subjects ending in *s* are plural (*candles, prisoners, dolphins*), and verbs ending in *s* are singular (*burns, comes, flies*). The verb *be* is a special case.

SINGULAR	PLURAL	SINGULAR	PLURAL
I am	we are	I was	we were
you are	you are	you were	you were
he is	they are	she was	they were
Luis is	the boys are	Linda was	the girls were

EXERCISE 3. Identifying the Correct Number of Verbs. Number your paper 1–10. After the proper number, write the word in parentheses that agrees with the given subject.

EXAMPLE 1. it (is, are)
1. *is*

1. this (costs, cost)
2. plants (grows, grow)
3. the batter (swings, swing)
4. we (considers, consider)
5. the men (was, were)
6. she (asks, ask)
7. these (needs, need)
8. those colors (seems, seem)
9. that ink (lasts, last)
10. days (passes, pass)

Prepositional Phrases Between Subject and Verb

Errors in agreement often occur because words in prepositional phrases are mistaken for the subjects of verbs.

NONSTANDARD[1] The many lights on the Christmas tree makes it look very festive. [*Lights,* not *tree,* is the subject.]

STANDARD The many **lights** on the Christmas tree *make* it look very festive.

17c. The number of a subject is not changed by a prepositional phrase following the subject.

Remember that a word in a prepositional phrase can never be the subject of a verb. If a sentence confuses you, imagine that the prepositional phrase is enclosed by parentheses, and go directly from the subject to the verb.

EXAMPLE The **silence** (in the halls) is unusual.

EXERCISE 4. Identifying Subjects and Verbs That Agree in Number in Sentences with Phrases Following the Subjects. Number your paper 1–10. After the proper number, write the subject and then the correct form of the verb. Remember that the subject is never part of a prepositional phrase.

EXAMPLE 1. The houses on my block (has, have) two stories.
1. *houses, have*

1. The launch of a space shuttle (attracts, attract) the interest of people throughout the world.
2. The thermos bottle in the picnic basket (is, are) filled with apple juice.
3. My favorite collection of poems (is, are) *Where the Sidewalk Ends.*
4. The chimes in the tower (plays, play) every hour.
5. The starving children of the world (needs, need) food and medicine.
6. The cucumbers in my garden (grows, grow) very quickly.
7. The koalas of Australia (eats, eat) eucalyptus leaves.

[1] For explanation of nonstandard and standard, see pages 497–98.

8. The principal of each school (awards, award) certificates to honor students.
9. Ceramic tiles from Mexico (makes, make) a beautiful trivet for a Mother's Day gift.
10. The house beside the city park (is, are) where my grandfather was born.

Indefinite Pronouns

Certain pronouns do not refer to a definite person, place, thing, or idea and are therefore called *indefinite* pronouns.

You should learn the number of all the indefinite pronouns so that you will not make an error in agreement when an indefinite pronoun is the subject of the sentence.

USAGE

17d. The following common pronouns are singular and take singular verbs: *each, either, neither, one, everyone, everybody, no one, nobody, anyone, anybody, someone, somebody.*

Pronouns like *each* and *one* are frequently followed by prepositional phrases. Remember that the verb agrees with the subject of the sentence, not with a word in a prepositional phrase.

EXAMPLES **One** of the chairs **looks** comfortable.
Either of the answers **is** correct.
Everyone with passports **was** accepted.
Someone in the stands **has been waving** at us.

17e. The following common pronouns are plural and take plural verbs: *both, few, several, many.*

EXAMPLES **Many** of the students **walk** to school.
Both of the apples **are** good.
Few of the guests **know** of the robbery.

17f. The words *some, any, none, all,* and *most* may be either singular or plural.

This rule is an exception to rule 17c because the number of the subjects *some, any, none, all,* and *most* is determined by a word in the prepositional phrase that follows the subject. If the word the subject refers to is singular, the subject is singular; if the word is plural, the subject is plural.

EXAMPLES **All** of the fans **rush** home. [*All* refers to plural *fans.*]

All of my work **is** finished. [*All* refers to singular *work.*]

Some of the birds **have** gone south.

Some of the glare **has** disappeared.

EXERCISE 5. Identifying Verbs That Agree with Indefinite Pronouns Used as Subjects. Number your paper 1–10. After the proper number, write the subject and then the correct one of the verbs in parentheses.

1. All of my friends (has, have) had the chicken pox.
2. Everyone at the party (likes, like) the cottage cheese and vegetable dip.
3. Both of Fred's brothers (celebrates, celebrate) their birthdays in July.
4. Some of my classmates (takes, take) tennis lessons after school.
5. None of the rosebushes in front of the house (blooms, bloom) in February.
6. Several of those colors (appeals, appeal) to me.
7. Many of Mrs. Taniguchi's students (speaks, speak) fluent Japanese.
8. Nobody in the beginning painting class (displays, display) work in the annual art show.
9. Most of the appetizers on the restaurant menu (tastes, taste) delicious.
10. One of Georgia O'Keeffe's paintings (shows, show) an animal's skull.

WRITING APPLICATION A: Using Indefinite Pronouns Correctly in Narration

Sometimes when you write, you may not want to use specific names because names are not important in what you are writing or because so many people are involved that using all their names would be confusing. In these cases, you probably will use indefinite pronouns, which do not refer to a particular person, place, thing, or idea. When you use these pronouns, be sure to proofread carefully to make certain that your pronouns match their verbs in number.

EXAMPLE Many of the students enjoys the water slide. [The indefinite pronoun *many* does not agree with the singular verb *enjoys*.]

Many of the students **enjoy** the water slide. [The plural pronoun *many* agrees with the plural verb *enjoy*.]

USAGE

Writing Assignment

Write a narrative in the present tense telling about a real or imaginary class or club trip. In your paragraph, use at least four indefinite pronouns, such as *many, few, several, either, all,* and *some.* Here is an idea about how you can begin your narrative:

Every year, at the end of May, my chorus class takes a trip to the beach. *Some* students bring fishing gear. *Many* bring inflatable rafts to float on. A *few* pack lotion to help prevent bad sunburns.

REVIEW EXERCISE A. Proofreading Sentences for Subject-Verb Agreement. Number your paper 1–10. Read each sentence aloud. If the verb agrees with the subject, write *C*. If the verb does not agree with the subject, write the correct form of the verb. Some sentences have more than one verb for you to consider.

EXAMPLES 1. One of the women practice medicine.
1. *practices*
2. Both of them work hard.
2. *C*

1. All of the concert chorus members harmonize very well with each other.
2. Several of the eighth-grade track stars also compete in the swimming meets.
3. Britain's prehistoric monument Stonehenge challenges tourists to uncover its mysteries.
4. Everybody want to know who erected the massive stones.
5. Most of the visitors assumes that the ancient Druids built Stonehenge.
6. Many of the archaeologists studying Stonehenge believe that it was built before the time of the Druids.
7. None of the tour guides at Stonehenge explain the secrets of the monument.
8. All of the tourists wonders why the structure was built.
9. One of Justin's grandmothers visit Stonehenge once a year.
10. The stones in Stonehenge weighs as much as fifty tons.

Compound Subjects

Most compound subjects that are joined by *and* name more than one person or thing; therefore, they are plural and require a plural verb.

17g. Subjects joined by *and* are plural and take a plural verb.

EXAMPLES **Antonia Brico** and **Sarah Caldwell are** famous conductors. [Two people are conductors.]

Last year a **library** and a **museum were** built in our town. [Two things were built.]

If the items in a compound subject actually refer to only one person or are thought of as one thing, the verb is singular.

EXAMPLES The **captain** and **quarterback** of the team is the speaker. [One person is both the captain and the quarterback.]

Chicken and dumplings is a favorite southern dish. [Chicken and dumplings is one dish.]

EXERCISE 6. Choosing Verbs That Agree in Number with Compound Subjects. Number your paper 1–10. Decide whether the compound subject of each sentence is singular or plural. Choose the correct verb form in parentheses, and write it after the proper number.

EXAMPLE 1. Cleon and Pam (is, are) here.
1. *are*

USAGE

1. March and April (is, are) windy months.
2. My mother and the mechanic (is, are) discussing the bill.
3. Virginia Wade and Tracy Austin (plays, play) today.
4. Steak and eggs (is, are) my favorite breakfast.
5. (Does, Do) Carla and Jean take dancing lessons?
6. (Is, Are) the knives and forks in the drawer?
7. English and science (requires, require) hours of study.
8. (Here's, Here are) our star and winner of the meet.
9. Where (is, are) the bread and the honey?
10. (Does, Do) an Austrian and a German speak the same language?

17h. Singular subjects joined by *or* or *nor* take a singular verb.

EXAMPLES A **pen or** a **pencil** is needed for this test. [Either one is needed.]

Neither Miami nor Jacksonville is the capital of Florida. [Neither one is the capital.]

EXERCISE 7. Choosing Verbs That Agree in Number with Compound Subjects. Number your paper 1–10. From each pair of verbs in parentheses, choose the one that agrees with the subject.

EXAMPLE 1. Either tea or coffee (is, are) fine with me.
1. *is*

1. Either Mrs. Gomez or Mr. Ming (delivers, deliver) the welcome speech on the first day of school.
2. Our guava tree and our fig tree (bears, bear) more fruit than our entire neighborhood can eat.
3. Tuskegee Institute or Harvard University (offers, offer) the best courses in Chester's field.
4. Armadillos and anteaters (has, have) tubular mouths and long sticky tongues for catching insects.
5. Either the president or the vice-president of the class (calls, call) roll every morning.
6. Georgia's frog and Sam's frog often (jumps, jump) out of the aquarium.
7. Red and royal blue (looks, look) nice in this bedroom.
8. Bridge or canasta (is, are) my favorite card game.
9. Neither my sister nor I (mows, mow) the lawn without protesting.
10. The tulips and the daffodils (blooms, bloom) every April.

17i. When a singular subject and a plural subject are joined by *or* or *nor,* the verb agrees with the nearer subject.

EXAMPLES Either Joan or her **friends are** mistaken. [The verb agrees with the nearer subject, *friends.*]

Neither the players nor the **director was** on time for rehearsal. [The verb agrees with the nearer subject, *director.*]

Whenever possible, avoid this kind of construction. The second sentence can be rewritten to read: *Both the players and the director were late for rehearsal.*

EXERCISE 8. Choosing Verbs That Agree with Singular and Plural Compound Subjects. Number your paper 1–5. From each pair of verbs in parentheses, choose the one that agrees with the subject, and write it after the proper number.

1. Either Sylvia or her brothers (washes, wash) the kitchen floor each Saturday morning.
2. This bread and this cereal (contains, contain) no preservatives or dyes.
3. Either the students or the teacher (reads, read) aloud during the last ten minutes of each class period.
4. The heavy rainclouds and the powerful winds (indicates, indicate) that a hurricane is approaching.
5. Neither the seal nor the clowns (catches, catch) the ball that the monkey throws into the circus ring.

REVIEW EXERCISE B. Choosing Verbs That Agree with Singular and Plural Subjects. Number your paper 1–10. Then choose from the words in parentheses the verb that agrees with the subject, and write it after the proper number.

1. Either the squirrels or the dog (digs, dig) a new hole in the yard at least once a day.
2. Jeffrey and his dad (builds, build) fireplaces for clients throughout the summer months.
3. Someone (places, place) the bricks around the inside of each of the fireplaces.
4. None of the bricks (cracks, crack) if they are installed very carefully.
5. Yellowstone National Park in Wyoming (fascinates, fascinate) many people.
6. The grizzly bears and coyotes (terrifies, terrify) would-be hikers.
7. A car or camper (provides, provide) protection from animals.
8. Some of the tourists foolishly (approaches, approach) the wild bears to give them food.
9. Unfortunately, several of these generous people (has, have) been killed or maimed by the bears.
10. Most of the park's visitors now (realizes, realize) that wild bears are truly wild.

Other Problems in Agreement

17j. Collective nouns may be either singular or plural.

A collective noun names a group of persons or things and is singular in form.

Common Collective Nouns

army	club	family	squadron
assembly	crowd	group	swarm
audience	fleet	herd	team
class	flock	public	troop

A collective noun takes a plural verb when the noun refers to the individual parts or members of the group. A collective noun takes a singular verb when the noun refers to the group as a unit.

EXAMPLES The **family were arguing** about where to spend the next vacation. [*Family* here refers to individuals acting separately.]

The **family was** calmed down by the grandparents. [*Family* here refers to a group considered as a unit.]

The **crowd are straining** to see the balloon. [The sentence leads you to picture the effort of individuals in the crowd.]

The **crowd is** gone. [The whole group is gone.]

EXERCISE 9. Writing Sentences with Collective Nouns. Select five collective nouns. Use each noun as the subject of two sentences. In the first, make the subject singular in meaning so that it calls for a singular verb. In the second, make the subject plural in meaning so that it takes a plural verb.

17k. A verb agrees with its subject, not with its predicate nominative.

Sometimes the subject and the predicate nominative of a sentence are different in number. In this case the verb agrees with the subject, not with the predicate nominative. The subject usually comes *before* the linking verb and the predicate nominative *after*.

EXAMPLES The happiest **time** of my life **was** my childhood days.
My childhood **days were** the happiest time of my life.

17l. When the subject follows the verb, as in sentences beginning with *there* and *here* and in questions, find the subject and make sure that the verb agrees with it.

EXAMPLES Here **is** my **seat.**
Here **are** our **seats.**
There **is** an exciting **ride** at the fair.
There **are** exciting **rides** at the fair.
Where **are** the programs?

Be especially careful when you use the contractions *here's* and *there's*. These contain the verb *is* and should be used only with singular subjects.

NONSTANDARD There's the books.
STANDARD There **are** the **books.**

EXERCISE 10. Choosing Verbs That Agree in Number with Singular and Plural Subjects. Number your paper 1–10. Write the correct verb for each sentence.

1. The audience (loves, love) the mime performance.
2. (Here's, Here are) the answers to Chapter 8.
3. The club (sponsors, sponsor) a carwash each September.
4. Andy's gift to Jynelle (was, were) two roses.
5. (Here's, Here are) the letters I have been expecting.
6. The public (differs, differ) in their opinions on the referendum.
7. (There's, There are) only three people in the contest.
8. The tennis team (plays, play) every Saturday morning.
9. His legacy to us (was, were) words of wisdom.
10. (Where's, Where are) the bell peppers for the salad?

WRITING APPLICATION B:
Checking for Correct Agreement When the Subject Follows the Verb

One of the reasons that people from foreign countries sometimes have difficulty learning English is that the word order, or syntax, of English sentences can vary. The subject, the verb, and any modifiers may appear at the beginning, in the middle, or at the end of a sentence. For example, in sentences that begin with *here* or *there,* the subject usually follows the verb. In your writing, you need to proofread to make certain that each verb agrees with its subject in number, particularly when the verb comes *before* the subject.

INCORRECT There has been many exciting TV shows lately about historical figures. [The subject *shows* is plural; it does not agree in number with the singular verb *has been.*]

CORRECT There **have been** many exciting TV **shows** lately about historical figures. [The plural verb *have been* agrees with the plural subject *shows.*]

Writing Assignment

Pretend that you are welcoming a group of people to a new time or a new place. Explain to them the strange new things they will encounter. Start at least four sentences with *here* or *there.* Be sure to proofread carefully for agreement errors. Here are several ideas for new times and places for your explanation:

1. A new, previously unknown planet
2. A spaceship from another planet
3. Your home when you are twenty-five years old
4. The school your children attend in the year 2010

17m. *Don't* and *doesn't* must agree with their subjects.

Use *don't* with plural subjects and with the pronouns *I* and *you*.

EXAMPLES These gloves **don't** fit.
You **don't** speak clearly.
I **don't** like that record.

Use *doesn't* with other subjects.

EXAMPLES The **music box doesn't** play.
She doesn't like cold weather.
It doesn't matter.

The most frequent errors in using *don't* and *doesn't* are made when *don't* is incorrectly used with *he, she,* or *it.* Remember always to use *doesn't* with these singular subjects: *he doesn't, she doesn't, it doesn't.*

USAGE

EXERCISE 11. *Oral Drill.* Using *Doesn't* with Singular Subjects. Read the following sentences aloud. By getting accustomed to hearing the correct use of *doesn't* and *don't,* you will get into the habit of using these two words correctly.

1. It doesn't look like a serious wound.
2. She doesn't call meetings often.
3. One doesn't interrupt a speaker.
4. He doesn't play records loudly.
5. Doesn't the television set work?

EXERCISE 12. Writing *Doesn't* and *Don't* with Subjects. Number your paper 1–10. Write the subject of each sentence and then the correct verb, *doesn't* or *don't.*

EXAMPLE 1. —— they go to our school?
1. *they, Don't*

1. —— anyone in the class know about Susan B. Anthony?
2. My three-year-old sister —— use good table manners.
3. They —— have enough people to form a softball team.
4. Pearl and Marshall —— need to change their schedules.
5. It —— hurt to practice the piano an hour a day.

6. —— you think that the music is too loud?
7. Those snow peas —— look crisp.
8. Hector —— win every track meet, but he often places second.
9. —— anyone know the time?
10. He —— know the shortest route from Dallas to Peoria.

REVIEW EXERCISE C. Proofreading Sentences for Subject-Verb Agreement. Number your paper 1–20. If a sentence is correct, write *C* after the proper number. If a sentence contains an error in agreement, write the correct form of the incorrect verb.

EXAMPLE 1. There is a man and a woman here to see you.
1. *are*

1. Walter or one of his assistants replaces the bald tires.
2. Leilani and Yoshi doesn't know how to swim.
3. Either Maribeth or Wade are expected to win the speech contest.
4. The flock of geese flies over the lake at dawn.
5. The Seminole Indians of Florida sews beautifully designed quilts.
6. Here's the sweaters I knitted for you.
7. Neither Frank nor his classmates thinks the test is fair.
8. The windmill generates power.
9. Each of the ten-speed bicycles cost over a hundred dollars.
10. Few of the boxers leave the ring without some bruises.
11. Most of the puddle disappear after the sun comes out from behind the clouds.
12. Somebody in this room know where the car keys are hidden.
13. The soccer team celebrate each victory with a pizza party.
14. The wheelchair division of the six-mile race was won by Randy Nowell.
15. The caribou and the reindeer is closely related.
16. Don't you think three hours of homework is enough?
17. Both of the doctors agrees that she must have her tonsils removed.

18. Any of those dresses look nice on you.
19. All of those books smells musty from being stored in the basement.
20. Where's the bus schedule for downtown routes?

AGREEMENT OF PRONOUN AND ANTECEDENT

Every pronoun refers to another word, called its *antecedent.* For example, in the phrase *the car with its windows open,* the pronoun *its* refers to the antecedent *car.* Whenever you use a pronoun, make sure that it agrees with its antecedent.

17n. A pronoun agrees with its antecedent in number and gender.

Some singular personal pronouns have forms that indicate gender. *He, him,* and *his* refer to masculine antecedents, while *she, her,* and *hers* refer to feminine antecedents. *It* and *its* refer to antecedents that are neither masculine nor feminine.

Here are several sentences containing pronouns that agree with their antecedents in both number and gender:

EXAMPLES **Bryan** lost **his** book.
Dawn loaned **her** book to Bryan.
The **book** had Dawn's name written inside **its** cover.

The antecedent of a personal pronoun can be another kind of pronoun, such as *each, either,* or *one.* To determine the gender of a personal pronoun that refers to one of these other pronouns, you may need to look in a phrase that follows the antecedent pronoun.

EXAMPLE **Each** of the men put on **his** hard hat.
Neither of those women got what **she** wanted.

Some antecedents may be either masculine or feminine, while others may be both. When referring to such antecedents, the masculine form of the personal pronoun may be used, or both the masculine and the feminine may be used.

EXAMPLES **No one** on the committee gave **his** approval.
or **No one** on the committee gave **his or her** approval.

Everyone in the class wanted to know **his grade.**
or **Everyone** in the class wanted to know **his or her** grade.

In conversation, you may be more accustomed to using a plural pronoun to stand for a singular antecedent that may be either masculine or feminine. Such usage is becoming more acceptable in writing, too, and may someday be considered acceptable in standard written English.

EXAMPLES **Everybody** rode **their** bicycle.
Each student paid for **their** ticket.

(1) Use a singular pronoun to refer to *each, either, neither, one, everyone, everybody, no one, nobody, anyone, anybody, someone,* or *somebody.*

EXAMPLES **Nobody** in the three classes would admit **his** (*or* **his or her**) guilt.

Each of the birds built **its** own nest.

A prepositional phrase does not affect the number of the antecedent. In both examples, the antecedent is singular and, therefore, takes a singular pronoun to agree with it.

(2) Two or more singular antecedents joined by *or* or *nor* should be referred to by a singular pronoun.

EXAMPLES **Julio or Van** will bring **his** football.
Neither **the mother nor the daughter** had forgotten **her** umbrella.

USAGE NOTE Rules (1) and (2) are often disregarded in conversation; however, they should be followed in writing.

(3) Two or more antecedents joined by *and* should be referred to by a plural pronoun.

EXAMPLES My **mother and father** send **their** regards.
My **dog and cat** never share **their** food.

EXERCISE 13. Proofreading Sentences for Pronoun-Antecedent Agreement. Number your paper 1–10. After the proper number, write *C* if the sentence is correct. If the sentence contains an error in agreement, write the antecedent, then the correct form of the pronoun. Follow the rules for standard written English.

EXAMPLE 1. Everyone in my English class has to give their oral report on Friday.
1. *Everyone—his* (or *his or her*)

1. Either Robert or Buddy will be the first to give their oral report.
2. Several others, including me, volunteered to give mine first.
3. Everybody else in class wanted to put off giving their report as long as possible.
4. Last year my best friend Sandy and I figured out that waiting to give our reports was worse than actually giving them.
5. I am surprised that more people didn't volunteer to give his or her reports first.
6. Someone else will be third to give their report; then I will give mine.
7. A few others in my class are going to try to get out of giving his or her reports at all.
8. However, my teacher, Mrs. Murray, said that anyone who does not give an oral report will get an "incomplete" as their course grade.
9. Most of us wish that he or she did not have to give an oral report at all.
10. Since no one can get out of giving their report, though, I'd rather get it over with as soon as possible.

EXERCISE 14. Identifying Antecedents and Writing Pronouns That Agree with Them. Number your paper 1–10. After the proper number, write a pronoun that will complete the meaning of the sentence. Then, write the antecedent for that pronoun. Follow the rules for standard written English.

EXAMPLE 1. Ann and Margaret wore —— cheerleader uniforms.
1. *their, Ann and Margaret*

1. The trees lost several of —— branches in the thunderstorm last night.
2. Each of these magazines has had the President's picture on —— cover.
3. Has anyone turned in —— paper yet?
4. The mob raised —— voices in protest.
5. The creek and the pond lost much of —— water during the drought.
6. One of my uncles always wears —— belt buckle off to one side.
7. No person should be made to feel that —— is worth less than someone else.
8. None of the dogs had eaten all of —— food.
9. A few of my neighbors have fenced —— backyards.
10. The fire engine and the police car went rushing by with —— lights flashing.

USAGE

REVIEW EXERCISE D. Proofreading Sentences for Pronoun-Antecedent Agreement. Number your paper 1–10. After the proper number, write *C* if the sentence is correct. If the sentence contains an error in agreement, write the antecedent, then the correct form of the pronoun. Follow the rules for standard written English.

1. Each member of the President's Cabinet gave their advice about what to do.
2. Nearly every one of the girls in our class had their hair cut short.

3. Was Mr. Avery or Mr. Jones going to show their classes that film today?
4. The guard said that anybody who didn't have their pass could not get in.
5. Some of the Boy Scouts had built an authentic Indian wigwam for their shelter.
6. Neither of those trees needs their limbs trimmed.
7. Every one of the soldiers carried extra rations in their pack.
8. Andrea, Tammy, and Laura trade outfits so that she can always have something different to wear.
9. All of the volunteers quickly went to work at his or her jobs.
10. A person should weigh their words carefully before criticizing someone else.

CHAPTER 17 REVIEW: POSTTEST

A. Identifying Verbs That Agree with Their Subjects. Number your paper 1–15. If the italicized verb in a sentence agrees with its subject, write *C*. If an italicized verb does not agree with its subject, write the correct form of the verb.

EXAMPLES
1. The people on the bus have all been seated.
1. *C*
2. The fish, bass and perch mostly, *has* started feeding.
2. *have*

1. Pencil and paper *is* needed for this test.
2. Either Sol or Anthony *have* been assigned to give a report.
3. *Doesn't* any of the children ride the bus?
4. Mrs. Holmes and Mr. Davis *assigns* homework almost every night.
5. Nearly every cat, no matter what breed, *go* crazy for catnip.
6. James Fenimore Cooper's *Leatherstocking Tales is* a famous collection of stories about the early American wilderness.

7. None of the answers you gave *was* correct.
8. Up until recently hardly anyone *have* been able to own a personal computer.
9. The club often *argues* among themselves about finances and activities.
10. Every player on the varsity teams *go* to daily exercise.
11. Somebody said that he, of course, *don't* approve.
12. There *is* probably a few children who don't like strawberries.
13. My spelling lessons and science homework sometimes *takes* me hours to finish.
14. The mice or the cat *has* eaten the cheese that was left out.
15. The swarm of bees *have* deserted its hive.

B. Identifying Pronouns That Agree with Their Antecedents. Number your paper 16–25. If the italicized pronoun in a sentence agrees with its antecedent, write *C*. If it does not agree with its antecedent, write the correct pronoun.

EXAMPLES 1. Either of the men could have offered *their* help.
1. *his*
2. Both of the flowers had spread *their* petals.
2. *C*

16. Why doesn't somebody raise *their* hand and ask for directions?
17. In most cases, a dog or a cat that gets lost in the woods can take care of *themselves.*
18. One of the birds had lost most of *their* tail feathers.
19. By the end of the day, all of the streets in our neighborhood had new yellow lines painted along *its* edges.
20. Everyone who will be going will need to bring a note from *their* mother.
21. I don't understand how chameleons sitting on a green leaf or a bush change *their* color.
22. Each of these tests has *their* own answer key.
23. Please ask some of these girls to pick up *her* own materials from the supply room.

24. The air conditioner and the refrigerator have switches that turn *it* off and on automatically.
25. The audience clapped *its* hands in approval.

CHAPTER 18

Using Verbs Correctly

PRINCIPAL PARTS, REGULAR AND IRREGULAR VERBS

USAGE

Few errors in speaking or writing are more obvious than verb errors. Students who write *she done it, he begun, they drownded,* or *it bursted* immediately tag themselves as people who do not know the standard usages of their language.

DIAGNOSTIC TEST

A. Writing the Past and Past Participle Forms of Verbs. Number your paper 1–15. After the proper number, write the past or past participle of the verb given before the sentence.

EXAMPLES 1. *take* *We don't know why it —— them so long.*
1. *took*
2. *take* We don't know why it has —— them so long.
2. *taken*

1. *lie* The cat —— down in front of the warm fire.
2. *raise* Since the storm began, the river has —— four feet.
3. *go* Did you see which way they —— ?

4. *write* I should have —— you sooner.
5. *break* Two runners on our track team have —— the school record for the mile run.
6. *burst* When the manager unlocked the door, a mob of shoppers —— into the store to take advantage of the sale.
7. *shrink* Larry washed his wool sweater in hot water, and it —— .
8. *see* The witness said that she —— the blue car run through the red light.
9. *rise* Look in the oven to see if the cake has —— yet.
10. *ring* Everyone should be in class after the bell has —— .
11. *know* You have all —— for a week that we were going to have a test today.
12. *lay* Jeanette carefully —— her coat across the back of the chair.
13. *freeze* Usually, by January the lake has —— hard enough to skate on.
14. *choose* No one could understand why Terry —— the striped one instead of the others.
15. *swim* So far, Dena has —— fifteen laps around the pool.

B. Correcting Verbs in the Wrong Tense. Number your paper 16–20. After the proper number, write the italicized verb in the correct tense.

EXAMPLE 1. He looked out the window and *sees* the storm approaching.
1. *saw*

16. Jan was late, so she *decides* to run the rest of the way.
17. The man at the gate *takes* our tickets and said that we were just in time.
18. My uncle often travels in the Far East and *brought* me some fascinating souvenirs.
19. When his mother told the little boy it was his bedtime, he *throws* a temper tantrum.

20. The waitress brought my order and *asks* me if I wanted anything else.

THE PRINCIPAL PARTS OF A VERB

Besides naming an action, a verb also shows its time. This expression of time by the verb is called *tense.* To express different times, a verb has different tenses. These tenses are formed from four *principal parts* of the verb.

18a. The principal parts of a verb are the *infinitive,* the *present participle,* the *past,* and the *past participle.*

From these four principal parts all the tenses of our language are formed. The four principal parts of *sing* are *sing* (infinitive), *singing* (present participle), *sang* (past), and *sung* (past participle). Notice in the following sentences how the four principal parts are used to express time.

I **sing** in the school glee club.
We **are singing** at the music festival tonight.
Mahalia Jackson **sang** gospels at Carnegie Hall.
We **have sung** all over the state.

Here are the principal parts of two familiar verbs:

INFINITIVE	PRESENT PARTICIPLE	PAST	PAST PARTICIPLE
work	working	worked	(have) worked
eat	eating	ate	(have) eaten

Notice that the present participle always ends in *-ing.* The past participle is the form used with *has, have,* or *had.*

THE SIX TENSES

By using the four principal parts of the verb, along with various helping verbs, you can form six tenses for every verb. When you give the forms for the six tenses of a verb, you are *conjugating* that verb.

Conjugation of Write

Principal parts: write, writing, wrote, (have) written.

Present Tense

Singular	*Plural*
I write	we write
you write	you write
he, she, *or* it writes	they write

Past Tense

Singular	*Plural*
I wrote	we wrote
you wrote	you wrote
he, she, *or* it wrote	they wrote

Future Tense

Singular	*Plural*
I will (shall) write	we will (shall) write
you will write	you will write
he, she, *or* it will write	they will write

Present Perfect Tense

Singular	*Plural*
I have written	we have written
you have written	you have written
he, she, *or* it has written	they have written

Past Perfect Tense

Singular	*Plural*
I had written	we had written
you had written	you had written
he, she, *or* it had written	they had written

Future Perfect Tense

Singular	*Plural*
I will (shall) have written	we will (shall) have written
you will have written	you will have written
he, she, *or* it will have written	they will have written

REGULAR VERBS

18b. A regular verb forms its past and past participle by adding *-ed* or *-d* to the present form.

INFINITIVE	PRESENT PARTICIPLE	PAST	PAST PARTICIPLE
follow	following	followed	(have) followed
date	dating	dated	(have) dated
miss	missing	missed	(have) missed

Pay careful attention to pronunciation of the past and past participle. Avoid nonstandard pronunciation, which usually follows two patterns: (1) adding an extra syllable—*drownded* for *drowned, attackted* for *attacked;* (2) not pronouncing the *-ed* ending—*ask* for *asked, suppose* for *supposed.*

EXERCISE 1. *Oral Drill.* Forming the Past and Past Participle Forms of Regular Verbs. Use the following verbs in sentences. Put each verb in the past tense, or use the past participle and the helping verb *have* or *has.*

1. hope
2. talk
3. call
4. gallop
5. walk
6. own
7. decide
8. finish
9. support
10. love

IRREGULAR VERBS

18c. An *irregular verb* forms its past and past participle in a different way than a regular verb does.

Irregular verbs form their past and past participle in several ways:

1. by a vowel change: *ring, rang,* (have) *rung*
2. by a consonant change: *make, made,* (have) *made*
3. by a vowel and consonant change: *bring, brought,* (have) *brought*
4. by no change: *burst, burst,* (have) *burst*

If you do not know the principal parts of irregular verbs, you may make errors like this:

NONSTANDARD She has drank all her milk. [*Drunk,* not *drank,* is the past participle.]

To avoid errors, memorize the principal parts of irregular verbs. Include *have* with the past participle.

Irregular Verbs Frequently Misused

INFINITIVE	PRESENT PARTICIPLE	PAST	PAST PARTICIPLE
begin	beginning	began	(have) begun
blow	blowing	blew	(have) blown
break	breaking	broke	(have) broken
bring	bringing	brought	(have) brought
burst	bursting	burst	(have) burst
choose	choosing	chose	(have) chosen
come	coming	came	(have) come
do	doing	did	(have) done
drink	drinking	drank	(have) drunk
drive	driving	drove	(have) driven
eat	eating	ate	(have) eaten
fall	falling	fell	(have) fallen
freeze	freezing	froze	(have) frozen
give	giving	gave	(have) given
go	going	went	(have) gone
know	knowing	knew	(have) known
lie	lying	lay	(have) lain
ride	riding	rode	(have) ridden
ring	ringing	rang	(have) rung
rise	rising	rose	(have) risen
run	running	ran	(have) run
see	seeing	saw	(have) seen
set	setting	set	(have) set
shrink	shrinking	shrank	(have) shrunk
sing	singing	sang	(have) sung

sit	sitting	sat	(have) sat
speak	speaking	spoke	(have) spoken
steal	stealing	stole	(have) stolen
swim	swimming	swam	(have) swum
take	taking	took	(have) taken
throw	throwing	threw	(have) thrown
write	writing	wrote	(have) written

Caution: Be careful not to confuse irregular verbs with regular ones. Never say *knowed, throwed, shrinked,* or *bursted.*

EXERCISE 2. Writing the Past and Past Participle Forms of Irregular Verbs. As your teacher or a classmate reads aloud to you the infinitive forms of the thirty-two irregular verbs just listed, write the past and the past participle forms on your paper.

Merely knowing the principal parts of irregular verbs is not enough. You need to practice using them in sentence patterns. Use the following example to help you practice usage of irregular verbs.

Today I **bring** lunch.
Yesterday I **brought** lunch.
Often I **have brought** lunch.

EXERCISE 3. Identifying the Correct Forms of Irregular Verbs. Number your paper 1–10. Choose the correct one of the two verbs in parentheses, and write it after the proper number. After your paper has been corrected, read each sentence *aloud* several times.

EXAMPLE 1. The bread (rised, rose) as it cooked.
1. *rose*

1. Ray Charles, a blind musician, has (wrote, written) many beautiful songs.
2. Olympic champion Mary Lou Retton (began, begun) her gymnastics training when she was eight years old.
3. Leigh (did, done) everything the instructions said.
4. She (knew, knowed) we had planned a busy day.

USAGE

5. Maria Tallchief (chose, choosed) a career as a dancer.
6. My woolen socks (shrinked, shrank) when I washed them in hot water.
7. He (eat, ate) chicken salad on whole-wheat bread for lunch.
8. The monkey had (stole, stolen) the food from its brother.
9. Henry and Tonya (sang, sung) a duet in the talent show.
10. The shy turtle (came, come) closer to me to reach the lettuce I was holding.

EXERCISE 4. Writing the Past and Past Participle Forms of Verbs. Number your paper 1–20. After the proper number, write the past or the past participle of the verb given before each sentence to complete the sentence correctly.

EXAMPLE 1. *do* Nobody knew why he —— that.
1. *did*

1. *ring* The telephone —— while I was in the shower.
2. *throw* The outfielder —— the ball to home plate.
3. *swim* Diana Nyad —— sixty miles from the Bahama Islands to Florida.
4. *choose* Did he say why he had —— that one?
5. *drive* We have —— all night to attend my sister's college graduation exercises.
6. *write* I have —— a letter of complaint to the manufacturer.
7. *drown* He would have —— if the lifeguard hadn't noticed the splashing in the waves.
8. *give* Kay —— her dog a reward after each trick.
9. *know* She —— that she could run the three-mile race.
10. *run* On the day of the race, she —— the course in less than twenty minutes.
11. *drink* After she finished the race, she —— three glasses of water.
12. *break* He —— his arm when he fell on the pavement.
13. *burst* The balloon —— when it strayed too near the flame.

14. *freeze* The catfish —— in the pond last winter.
15. *go* I have —— from one room to another looking for my lost shoe.
16. *blow* The siren —— long and loud to warn the residents of danger.
17. *ride* Uncle Olaf —— his snowmobile up to the remote mountain cabin.
18. *sit* Peter —— quietly throughout the entire discussion.
19. *see* Marianne —— that he disagreed with her.
20. *steal* Our dog had —— a steak from the grill while we were inside.

REVIEW EXERCISE A. Proofreading Sentences for Correct Verb Forms. Number your paper 1–20. Write *C* after the number of each correct sentence. Write the correct form of the verb after the number of each incorrect sentence.

EXAMPLES 1. I broke a water glass.
1. *C*
2. We rung the door bell.
2. *rang*

1. Sally give me a menu from the new downtown restaurant.
2. I had spoke to my parents last week about trying this restaurant.
3. We had never went there before.
4. My big brother Mark drived us there in Mom's car.
5. We had almost reached the restaurant when Mark hit a curb.
6. We falled off the curb with a big bounce.
7. We all seen that he was very embarrassed.
8. I shrinked down in the back seat so he wouldn't notice that I was laughing.
9. When we arrived at the restaurant, I runned ahead of everyone to tell the hostess we needed five seats.
10. The waiter had brought our menus before we all sit down.
11. We drunk water with lemon slices in the glasses.
12. Have you ever ate spaghetti with clam sauce?

13. Dad chose the ravioli.
14. My little sister Emily taked two helpings of salad.
15. The waiter bringed out our dinners on a huge platter as soon as we finished our salads.
16. Mark give me a taste of his eggplant parmigiana.
17. Emily stealed a bite of my lasagna.
18. Mom breaked the last breadstick in half so that Emily and I could share it.
19. Dad writed on the bill that the food was delicious and the service was excellent.
20. We had made a good decision to try that new restaurant.

SPECIAL PROBLEMS WITH VERBS

Sit and *Set*

Study the principal parts of the verbs *sit* and *set.* Notice that *sit* changes to form the past tense, but *set* remains the same in the past and the past participle.

INFINITIVE	PRESENT PARTICIPLE	PAST	PAST PARTICIPLE
sit (to rest)	sitting	sat	(have) sat
set (to place)	setting	set	(have) set

Sit and *set* are often confused. You will not make mistakes with these two verbs if you remember two facts about them:

(1) *Sit* means "to rest in an upright, seated position," while *set* means "to put or place (something)."

Let's **sit** under the tree.
Let's **set** the bookcase here.

The tourists **sat** on benches.
The children **set** the dishes on the table.

We **had sat** down to eat when the telephone rang.
We **have set** the reading lamp beside the couch.

(2) *Sit* is almost never followed by an object, but *set* often does take an object.

My aunt **sits** in the large chair. [no object]
She **sets** the chair in the corner. [Sets what? *Chair* is the object.]

The audience **sat** near the stage. [no object]
The stagehand **set** a microphone near the Judds. [Set what? *Microphone* is the object.]

EXERCISE 5. *Oral Drill.* Using the Forms of *Sit* and *Set* Correctly. Read each sentence aloud, paying close attention to the meaning of *sit* and *set.* Pronounce each verb distinctly.

1. Let's sit down here.
2. Look at the dog sitting on the porch.
3. Our teacher set a deadline for our term projects.
4. Have you set the clock?
5. I have always sat in the front row.
6. Please set the carton down inside the doorway.
7. She has set a high standard for her work.
8. After I set the mop in the closet, I sat down to rest.

USAGE

EXERCISE 6. Using the Correct Forms of *Sit* and *Set.* Number your paper 1–10. After the proper number, write the correct one of the two words in parentheses. If the verb you choose is a form of *set,* write its object after it.

EXAMPLE 1. Please (sit, set) the serving platter on the table.
1. *set, platter*

1. Will you (sit, set) down here?
2. It's Aaron's turn to (sit, set) the table for dinner.
3. Carolyn (sat, set) her notebook on the kitchen counter.
4. I have been (sitting, setting) here all day.
5. (Sit, Set) the fine crystal in the china cabinet.
6. The referee is (sitting, setting) the ball on the fifty-yard line.
7. The cat cautiously (sat, set) beside the Great Dane.

8. Zachary (sits, sets) up in bed at night while he reads another chapter from his library book.
9. Let's (sit, set) that aside until later.
10. They have been (sitting, setting) there for fifteen minutes without saying a word to each other.

Lie and *Lay*

Study the principal parts of *lie* and *lay*.

INFINITIVE	PRESENT PARTICIPLE	PAST	PAST PARTICIPLE
lie (to recline)	lying	lay	(have) lain
lay (to put)	laying	laid	(have) laid

Like *sit, lie*[1] has to do with resting, and it has no object. *Lay* is like *set* because it means "to put (something) down" and because it may have an object.

USAGE

The cows **are lying** in the shade. [no object]
The workers **are laying** the foundation for the building. [*Are laying* what? *Foundation* is the object.]

The soldiers **lay** very still while the enemy passed by. [No object—*lay* here is the past tense of *lie.*]
The soldiers **laid** a trap for the enemy. [*Laid* what? *Trap* is the object.]

The injured man **had lain** in the cave for weeks. [no object]
The lawyer **had laid** the newspaper next to her briefcase. [*Had laid* what? *Newspaper* is the object.]

EXERCISE 7. *Oral Drill.* Using the Forms of *Lie* and *Lay* Correctly. Read each of the following sentences aloud several times. Be able to explain why the verb is correct.

1. The delegates laid the groundwork for future conferences.
2. Don't lie in the sun too long!
3. You shouldn't lay your papers on the couch.

[1] The verb *lie* meaning "to tell a falsehood" is a different word. Its past forms are regular: *lie, lying, lied, lied.*

4. The lion had been lying in wait for an hour.
5. The senator laid her notes aside after her speech.
6. He had lain still for a few minutes.
7. He has laid his books on his desk.
8. Our cat lies on the radiator.
9. She lays the sharp knives on the top shelf.
10. The exhausted swimmer lay helpless on the sand.

EXERCISE 8. Writing the Correct Forms of *Lie* and *Lay*. Number your paper 1–10. After the proper number, write the correct form of *lie* or *lay* for each of these sentences.

1. The television journalist —— aside her career while her children were young.
2. My dad was —— down when I asked for my allowance.
3. We need to —— down some club rules.
4. Have you ever —— on a water bed?
5. Andrew had —— his keys beside his wallet.
6. My cat loves to —— in the tall grass behind our house.
7. My brother left his clothes —— on the floor until they began to smell.
8. Yesterday that alligator —— in the sun all day.
9. The groundskeeper has —— new sod on the golf course.
10. The newspaper had —— in the yard until the sun faded it.

EXERCISE 9. Writing Sentences Using Forms of *Lie* and *Lay*. Use each of the following verbs or verb phrases correctly in a sentence of your own.

1. lies
2. laid
3. was laying
4. has lain
5. lays
6. has been lying
7. lay (past tense of *lie*)
8. have laid
9. will lie
10. are lying

Rise and *Raise*

Study the principal parts of *rise* and *raise*.

USAGE

INFINITIVE	PRESENT PARTICIPLE	PAST	PAST PARTICIPLE
rise (to go up)	rising	rose	(have) risen
raise (to lift up)	raising	raised	(have) raised

The verb *rise* means "to go up" or "to get up." Rise, like *lie,* never has an object. *Raise,* which means "to lift up" or "to cause to rise," usually, like *lay,* has an object.

My neighbors **rise** very early in the morning. [no object]
Every morning they **raise** their shades to let the sunlight in. [*Raise* what? *Shades* is the object.]

The moon **rose** slowly last night. [no object]
Last year Ana and Bill **raised** corn and tomatoes in their garden. [*Raised* what? *Corn* and *tomatoes* are the objects.]

The senators **have risen** from their seats to show respect for the Chief Justice. [no object]
The wind **has raised** a cloud of dust. [*Has raised* what? *Cloud* is the object.]

USAGE

EXERCISE 10. *Oral Drill.* Using the Correct Forms of *Rise* and *Raise.* Repeat each of the following correct sentences aloud several times, stressing the italicized verbs and thinking of the meanings of the verbs.

1. The reporters *rise* when the President enters the room.
2. The reporters *raise* their hands to be recognized.
3. The reporter who was recognized *rose* to her feet.
4. She *has raised* an interesting question.
5. Another reporter *was rising.*
6. Several reporters *rose* at the same time.
7. Who *had risen* first?
8. Will Congress *raise* taxes this year?

EXERCISE 11. Writing the Correct Forms of *Rise* and *Raise.* Number your paper 1–10. After the proper number, write the correct one of the two verbs in parentheses. If the verb you choose is a form of *raise,* write its object after it.

1. The steam was (rising, raising) from the pot of hot chicken soup on the stove.
2. That comment (rises, raises) a very good question.
3. The child's fever (rose, raised) during the night; she seems much better this morning.
4. The sun (rises, raises) later each morning.
5. The teacher will call only on students who (rise, raise) their hands.
6. We must (rise, raise) the flag in the courtyard each morning before school begins.
7. The student body's interest in this subject has (risen, raised) to new heights.
8. The kite has (risen, raised) above the power lines.
9. My father promised to (rise, raise) my allowance if I pull the weeds.
10. The department store (rose, raised) the price on that clock radio last week.

EXERCISE 12. Writing the Correct Forms of *Rise* and *Raise*. Number your paper 1–10. After the proper number, write the correct form of *rise* or *raise* in each blank in the following paragraphs.

We girls —— early to start our hike to Lookout Mountain. From our position at the foot of the mountain, it looked as though it —— straight up to the heavens.

But we had not —— at daybreak just to look at the high peak. We —— our supply packs to our backs and started the long climb up the mountain. With every step we took, the mountain seemed to —— that much higher. Finally, after several hours, we reached the summit and —— a special flag that we had brought for the occasion. When our friends at the foot of the mountain saw the flag —— , they knew that we had reached the top safely. They —— their arms and shouted.

Our friends' shouts were like an applause that seemed to —— from the valley below. Then we felt glad that we had —— early enough to climb to the top of Lookout Mountain.

WRITING APPLICATION A: Using Irregular Verbs Correctly When Writing About Experiences in the Past

When you talk with other people and when you write, you often deal with past personal experiences. One of the most common errors in English usage is misuse of the past and past participle forms of irregular verbs. Since these verbs do not add a simple *-ed* for the past tense, you have to memorize their correct forms.

INCORRECT Drivers in England *have* always *drove* on the left side of the street. [The past participle *driven* should be used with the helping verb *have.*]

CORRECT Drivers in England *have* always *driven* on the left side of the street. [The error in agreement is corrected.]

Writing Assignment

Select several of the irregular verbs discussed in this chapter. Using their correct forms, write a paragraph about a personal experience. Following are some ideas.

Learning to Swim
Making Ice Cream
A Horseback Ride
The Time I Ate Too Much

USAGE

REVIEW EXERCISE B. Using the Correct Forms of *Sit* and *Set*, *Lie* and *Lay*, and *Rise* and *Raise*. Number your paper 1–25. Choose the correct verb from the two in parentheses, and write it after the proper number. If a sentence has two verbs, write both of them on the same line in the order in which they occur. Be prepared to explain your choices in class.

1. The sun has (risen, raised), and you are still (lying, laying) in bed.
2. While their grandmother (sat, set) in the shade, Marilyn and Ed (sat, set) the table for the picnic.

3. The water level has not (risen, raised) since last summer.
4. Cooks often (lie, lay) their spoons in special spoon rests.
5. Key West (lies, lays) off the southwestern coast of Florida.
6. To study how solar energy works, our class (sit, set) a solar panel outside the window of our classroom.
7. The golfer carefully (sits, sets) the ball on the tee.
8. Since I have gotten taller, I have (rose, raised) the seat on my bicycle.
9. We all (sit, set) in alphabetical order in algebra class.
10. (Lie, Lay) the grass mats on the sand so that we can (lie, lay) on them.
11. (Sit, Set) the groceries on the table while I start dinner.
12. The squirrels (rose, raised) their heads when they heard me tapping on the window.
13. (Rise, Raise) the car higher so that we can change the tire.
14. When the sun (rises, raises), I sometimes have difficulty (sitting, setting) aside my covers and getting up.
15. When the sun had (sit, set), I wearily (lay, laid) on the hard earth in my tent.
16. I (lay, laid) my flashlight beside my sleeping bag.
17. My dog Beau (lay, laid) just outside the tent.
18. We (sat, set) under a beach umbrella.
19. Mr. DeLemos (lay, laid) the foundation for our new patio.
20. Your grades must (rise, raise), or you will not make the honor roll this term.
21. Would you please (sit, set) the sofa down here?
22. The people in front of me (raised, rose) up in their seats.
23. You'd better (sit, set) down while I tell you this.
24. He left his books (lying, laying) on the table.
25. The crane (rose, raised) the steel beam into place.

CONSISTENCY OF TENSE

You should never shift tenses needlessly. When you are writing about events in the past tense, you should use the past tense consistently unless there is a reason to change tenses. You should not shift without reason to the present tense.

18d. Do not change needlessly from one tense to another.

NONSTANDARD After we were comfortable, we begin to do our homework. [*Were* is past tense and *begin* is present.]

STANDARD After we **were** comfortable, we **began** to do our homework. [Both *were* and *began* are in the past tense.]

NONSTANDARD Suddenly the great door opened, and an uninvited guest comes into the dining hall. [*Opened* is past tense and *comes* is present.]

STANDARD Suddenly the great door **opens,** and an uninvited guest **comes** into the dining hall. [Both *opens* and *comes* are in the present tense.]

STANDARD Suddenly the great door **opened,** and an uninvited guest **came** into the dining hall. [Both *opened* and *came* are in the past tense.]

EXERCISE 13. Proofreading a Paragraph to Make the Tenses of the Verbs Consistent. Read the following paragraph, and decide what tense you should use to tell about the events. Prepare to read the paragraph aloud, making the verb tense consistent throughout.

At my grandparents' house that morning, I wake up before anyone else and quietly grabbed the fishing pole and head for the pond. Across the water, I saw ripples. "I have to catch the fish," I say to myself. I threw my lure near where I see the ripples and reeled in the line. The fish don't seem interested. I saw more ripples and throw the line in the water again. "I've got a strike!" I shout to the trees around me. As I reeled in the line, a beautiful trout jumps out of the water and spit out the hook. Discouraged, I go back to the house. Grandpa was sitting at the table with a bowl of hot oatmeal for me. I say, "Maybe tomorrow we'll have trout for breakfast."

WRITING APPLICATION B:
Being Consistent in Using Verb Tenses

Every day you encounter many things that indicate the time, such as sunrise, bells, and alarm clocks. The way you signal the time to your readers is through the use of *tense*. Avoid shifting tenses unless you have a good reason. An important rule to remember is *be consistent.*

EXAMPLE In *The Secret Life of Walter Mitty,* by James Thurber, the main character *was henpecked* by his wife. [past tense] When she *fusses* at him, [present tense] he *will dream* about being some famous person. [future tense]

In this example, the tenses are not consistent. They switch from past to present to future. The example could be corrected by writing all three verbs in either the present or the past tense to make them consistent.

Writing Assignment

Select a story or book that you have read recently. Write a paragraph summarizing the plot. Proofread your paragraph to make sure that you have used verb tense consistently.

REVIEW EXERCISE C. **Using the Correct Verb and the Correct Verb Form.** Number your paper 1–20. Write the correct one of the verb forms in parentheses from each sentence. Some sentences have more than one verb.

1. He (knew, knowed) he would not get his wish even though he (blew, blowed) out all his birthday candles.
2. Buffy Sainte-Marie has (sang, sung) professionally for more than twenty years.
3. Have you (began, begun) your homework yet?
4. Cindy Nicholas was the first woman who (swam, swum) the English Channel both ways.

5. I'm glad you (come, came) with us to the lake.
6. When the baby sitter (rose, raised) her voice, the children (knew, knowed) it was time to behave.
7. After we had (saw, seen) all the exhibits at the county fair, we (ate, eat) a snack and then (went, go) home.
8. The egg (burst, bursted) in the microwave oven.
9. I was very nervous when I (go, went) on the ski lift for the first time.
10. He (lay, laid) his lunch money on his desk.
11. When he tried to claim the money later, he found that it had been (stole, stolen).
12. The loud noise (breaked, broke) my concentration.
13. Grandma (give, gave) me a belt for my birthday.
14. For the creative writing assignment, I had (wrote, written) a story about my deep-sea fishing trip.
15. Robbie had (chose, chosen) to take band this year.
16. The thirsty plants (drank, drunk) all the rainwater.
17. The truck has (rode, ridden) over the rough country road with ease.
18. We had (rode, ridden) halfway across the desert when I began to wish I had (brought, brung) more water.
19. The oranges and grapefruit had (froze, frozen) on the trees last winter.
20. We liked that movie so much that we (sat, set) through it three times on Saturday.

USAGE

REVIEW EXERCISE D. Using the Correct Verb and the Correct Verb Form. Number your paper 1–10. After the proper number, write the form of the verb at the left that correctly fills the blank in each sentence.

1. *sing* Stevie Wonder —— at the concert hall here last week.
2. *run* Have you ever —— in a race with Alberto Salazar?
3. *break* Pearl Moore —— a record in basketball by scoring 4,061 points during her college career.

4. *fall* The newly hatched sparrow —— from its nest.
5. *steal* The bandits —— over seven million dollars in cash.
6. *shrink* The meat patties —— while they were being cooked.
7. *ring* The child cried each time a Halloween goblin —— the doorbell.
8. *speak* Have you —— to the counselor about your schedule for next year?
9. *take* Who —— a bite from my blueberry muffin?
10. *do* He —— the best he could on the paper but received only a B for his efforts.

CHAPTER 18 REVIEW: POSTTEST

A. Writing the Past and Past Participle Forms of Verbs. Number your paper 1–15. After the proper number, write the past or past participle of the verb given before the sentence.

EXAMPLES
1. *run* The deer —— across the road in front of our car.
1. *ran*
2. *run* Her dog has —— away from home.
2. *run*

1. *shrink* The older girl —— from the responsibility of caring for her younger brothers and sister.
2. *write* Have you —— your history report yet?
3. *eat* I don't think I should have —— that last handful of sunflower seeds.
4. *sit* The blue jay that —— on the telephone wire called to its mate.
5. *know* She is the nicest person I have ever —— .
6. *break* When the medicine finally began to work, his fever —— .
7. *ring* That phone has —— every five minutes since I got home.

8. *come* Earl thought and thought, but the answer never —— to him.
9. *freeze* If that had happened to me, I would have —— with fear.
10. *sing* Through the murky depths the whales —— to one another.
11. *give* The coach —— us all a pep talk before the game.
12. *begin* We knew that it would rain soon because the crickets had —— chirping.
13. *take* That job shouldn't have —— you all day.
14. *bring* Everyone else had —— along a warm sweater.
15. *fall* Though he had —— from the top of the tree, the baby squirrel was all right.

B. Writing the Correct Forms of *Lie–Lay, Sit–Set,* and *Rise–Raise* in Sentences. Number your paper 16–20. Choose the correct verb from the two verbs given in parentheses, and write it after the proper number on your paper.

EXAMPLE 1. My cat (lies, lays) around the house all day.
1. *lies*

16. We had to wait for the drawbridge to (rise, raise) before we could sail out to the bay.
17. (Sit, Set) that down in the chair, will you?
18. The treasure had (lay, lain) at the bottom of the ocean for more than four hundred years.
19. My grandfather and grandmother like to (sit, set) on the porch and talk.
20. Look on the other side of any logs (lying, laying) in the path to avoid stepping on a snake.

C. Correcting Verbs in the Wrong Tense. Number your paper 21–25. In each of the following sentences, the italicized verb is in the wrong tense. After the proper number, write the italicized verb in the correct tense.

EXAMPLE 1. My father looked at his watch and *decides* that it was time to leave.
1. *decided*

21. Marjorie's sister refused to give us a ride in her car, and then she *asks* us to loan her some money for gas.
22. He says he's sorry, but he *didn't* mean it.
23. The trees grow close together and *had* straight trunks.
24. When the show ended, we *get* up to leave, but a crowd had already gathered.
25. Several mechanics worked on my aunt's car before one of them finally *finds* the problem.

USAGE

CHAPTER 19

Using Pronouns Correctly

NOMINATIVE AND OBJECTIVE CASE FORMS

The case of a noun or a pronoun depends on how the noun or pronoun is used in the sentence. A word used as a subject is in the *nominative* case; a word used as an object is in the *objective* case; and a word used to show ownership or relationship is in the *possessive* case.

The case of nouns presents no problem because a noun has the same form in the nominative and objective cases.

> The **woman** [nominative] said she saw another **woman** [objective] in the park.

The possessive case of a noun usually requires only the addition of an apostrophe and an *s*.

> The **woman's** friend has arrived.

Personal pronouns, however, change form in the different cases.

DIAGNOSTIC TEST

Using Pronouns Correctly in Sentences. Number your paper 1–20. Write the correct one of the two pronouns in parentheses.

EXAMPLE 1. Just between you and (I, me), I think he's wrong.
1. *me*

1. When I got home, a package was waiting for (I, me).
2. Everyone thought that (she, her) was very intelligent.
3. We saw (they, them) riding their bikes to school.
4. The winners in the contest turned out to be Jill and (I, me).
5. The wasp flew in the window and bit (he, him) on the arm.
6. Elton and (she, her) will give reports this morning.
7. The two scouts who have earned the most merit badges are Angelo and (he, him).
8. Several people in my neighborhood helped (we, us) boys clear the empty lot and measure out a baseball diamond.
9. Nina has promised to give Ralph and (I, me) some help with our music lessons.
10. My father and (he, him) are planning to go into business together.
11. We thought that we'd be facing (they, them) in the finals.
12. May I sit next to Marvin and (he, him)?
13. After class the teacher asked Kim and (she, her) to help erase the chalkboard.
14. My little sister always gives (me, I) a lot of trouble.
15. Did you know that it was (I, me) who called?
16. Corey's mother and my father said that (we, us) could go on the field trip.
17. The bears wanted (we, us) to feed them our sandwiches.
18. Invite (she, her) and the new girl in class to the party.
19. We hoped that the job would fall to Leon and Greg instead of (we, us).
20. The best soloists in the band are (they, them), apparently.

THE CASE FORMS OF PERSONAL PRONOUNS

Study the following list of pronouns to see how their forms differ in the three cases.

Personal Pronouns

NOMINATIVE CASE	OBJECTIVE CASE	POSSESSIVE CASE
	Singular	
I	me	my, mine
you	you	your, yours
he, she, it	him, her, it	his, her, hers, its
	Plural	
we	us	our, ours
you	you	your, yours
they	them	their, theirs

The pronouns *you* and *it* cause few usage problems because their forms remain unchanged in the nominative and objective cases. The possessive case forms, which show ownership or relationship, need care in spelling. (See pages 562–63.) Omitting *you* and *it* and the possessive pronouns from the above list leaves the following pronouns, which have different forms in the nominative and objective cases. Memorize the list for each case.

NOMINATIVE CASE	OBJECTIVE CASE
I	me
he	him
she	her
we	us
they	them

THE NOMINATIVE CASE

19a. The subject of a verb is in the nominative case.

EXAMPLES **I** like music. [*I* is the subject of the verb *like.*]

He and **she** sold tickets. [*He* and *she* are the subjects of the verb *sold.*]

They called while **we** were away. [*They* is the subject of *called; we* is the subject of *were.*]

Pronoun usage errors occur most frequently when the subject is compound. It is easy to say, "Lois and me study together" when you should say, "Lois and I study together." "Lois and I" is a compound subject. If you test the pronoun by itself with the verb, you can tell which form is correct.

EXAMPLE Lois and me study together. [me study—nonstandard]
Lois and **I** study together. [I study—standard]

Use the same test in sentences such as "We girls work together" and "Us girls work together." Use the pronouns alone before the verb. "Us work together" is incorrect. "We work together" is correct; consequently, "We girls work together" is correct.

EXERCISE 1. *Oral Drill.* Practicing Correct Pronoun Usage. Read the following sentences aloud, stressing the italicized pronouns.

1. *He* and *she* collect seashells.
2. My grandmother and *I* are painting the boat.
3. Both *they* and *we* were frightened.
4. Did Sally or *she* answer the phone?
5. *We* girls are giving a fashion show.
6. *You* and *I* will stay behind.
7. Where are *he* and *she*?
8. My parents and *they* are good friends.

EXERCISE 2. Writing Pronouns in Sentences. Number your paper 1–10. Beside the proper number, write a pronoun that will correctly fill each blank. Use a variety of pronouns. Don't use *you* or *it.*

EXAMPLE 1. —— and —— will have a debate.
1. *We, they*

1. Yesterday she and —— went shopping.
2. Our cousins and —— are ready for the race.
3. Neither —— nor Kathy was nominated.
4. —— and Margie have copies of the book.
5. When are —— and —— coming?

USAGE

6. Everyone remembers when —— won the big game.
7. Someone said that —— and —— are finalists.
8. Did you or —— ride in the hot-air balloon?
9. Both —— and —— gave excellent speeches.
10. Has —— or Eduardo seen that movie?

19b. A predicate nominative is in the nominative case.

A *predicate nominative* is a noun or a pronoun that completes the meaning of a linking verb. A pronoun used as a predicate nominative usually follows a form of the verb *be* (*am, is, are, was, were*) or a verb phrase ending in *be* or *been,* such as *will be* or *has been.*

Read these examples aloud; stress the boldfaced words.

The speakers are **she** and **I.** [*She* and *I* are predicate nominatives following the linking verb *are.*]

Do you think it was **they**? [*They* is a predicate nominative following the linking verb *was.*]

EXERCISE 3. Identifying Correct Pronoun Usage for Predicate Nominatives. Number your paper 1–10. Write the linking verb in each sentence; then write the correct pronoun.

EXAMPLE 1. It was (I, me) at the door.
1. *was, I*

1. We hoped it was (her, she).
2. That stranger thinks I am (she, her).
3. Luckily, it was not (them, they) in the accident.
4. It could have been (she, her) that he called.
5. Everyone believed it was (we, us) students.
6. It might have been (him, he), but I'm not sure.
7. Our opponents could have been (them, they).
8. I thought it was (they, them) to whom he spoke.
9. If the singer had been (her, she), I would have listened.
10. Was that Claudia or (she, her)?

☞ **USAGE NOTE** You should understand two facts about English usage. First, some usages are acceptable in conversational English, but not in written English. Second, from time to time usage changes, so that expressions that were once considered nonstandard may become standard. The application of rule 19b provides examples of both these facts. The expressions *It's me, That's her, It was them,* etc., although they violate the rule, have now become acceptable spoken English. In writing, however, standard usage still follows the rule.

SPOKEN No one would believe it was her. (him, etc.)
WRITTEN No one would believe it was she. (he, etc.)

Of course, it would be correct to use *she* in speaking, even though *her* is acceptable.

In doing the exercises in this book, base your answers on the usage of written English.

THE OBJECTIVE CASE

19c. Direct and indirect objects of a verb are in the objective case.

EXAMPLES You surprised **us.** [*Us* is the object of the verb *surprised.*]

Our neighbor gave **her** and **me** a job. [*Her* and *me* are indirect objects; they tell *to whom* our neighbor gave a job.]

The ranger guided **us** boys to the camp. [*Us* is the object of the verb *guided.* Using the pronoun alone after the verb shows that the ranger guided *us* (not *we*) to the camp.]

Most errors in the use of the objective case occur when the object is compound. You can often avoid making an error with a compound object by trying each pronoun separately with the verb, as in the following example.

The representative met (she, her) and (he, him).

NONSTANDARD The representative met she.
The representative met he.

STANDARD The representative met **her.**
The representative met **him.**
The representative met **her** and **him.**

EXERCISE 4. *Oral Drill.* Practicing Correct Pronoun Usage for Objects. Read the following sentences aloud at least twice, stressing the italicized pronouns.

1. The hot soup burned Gail and *me.*
2. Karen showed *her* and Allen her houseplants.
3. The dog followed *her* and *him* to school.
4. Did you expect *us* or *them*?
5. The doctor gave *her* and *me* flu shots.
6. Let's help Sarah and *him* with their chores.
7. Have you seen the Romanos or *them*?

EXERCISE 5. Writing Pronouns as Direct and Indirect Objects. Number your paper 1–10. Write a correct pronoun for each blank. Use a variety of pronouns, but do not use *you* and *it.* When your answers have been checked, read aloud at least three times the corrected form of each sentence you missed.

EXAMPLE 1. The teacher asked —— some hard questions.
1. *us*

1. The judges picked —— and —— as the winners.
2. They asked —— and Ms. Shore for permission.
3. Rita can usually find Alberto and —— at our house.
4. Did you know Jarvis and —— ?
5. My grandmother helped —— girls make homemade bread.
6. Aunt Aggie took —— and —— to the zoo.
7. The driver left my sister and —— at the corner.
8. Should we call Mark and —— ?
9. Do you remember —— and —— ?
10. The dog chased Adam and —— .

WRITING APPLICATION:
Using Pronouns Correctly in Compound Subjects and Objects

Have you ever seen someone whose socks didn't match? When you are in a hurry, sometimes it's easy to make a mistake. Pronoun usage errors often occur when writers are in too much of a hurry. These mistakes are particularly easy to make when a subject or an object is compound.

EXAMPLE Me and Jana waited for a tennis court so that we could play. [The pronoun *me* should not be used as the subject of a verb.]

Jana and I waited for a tennis court so that we could play. [The nominative case pronoun *I* is correct as the subject of the verb *waited.*]

Writing Assignment

Write a paragraph about an incident that involved you and a friend. Supply details that make this incident memorable. Include two compound subjects and two compound objects. Underline these constructions. Be sure to use nominative case pronouns for subjects and objective case pronouns for objects.

19d. The object of a preposition is in the objective case.

A prepositional phrase begins with a preposition and ends with an object, which is always a noun or a pronoun. When the object is a pronoun, you must be careful to use the objective case. Note the case of the objects in the following prepositional phrases.

with **me**	near **her**	except **them**
to **him**	by **us**	for **us**

Most errors in usage occur when the object of the preposition is compound. Notice that in the prepositional phrases in the following exercise all pronouns are in the objective case.

EXERCISE 6. *Oral Drill.* Practicing Correct Pronoun Usage. Read each of the following sentences several times, stressing the correct, italicized pronouns.

1. The safari continued without *her* and *me.*
2. Everyone except *us* counselors had left the camp.
3. We stood beside their families and *them* during the ceremony.
4. Do you have any suggestions for Jane or *me*?
5. The clowns talked to Claire and *him.*
6. Give this to either your father or *her.*
7. With the help of Juan and *her,* we built a fire.
8. There was a spelling bee between *us* and *them.*

EXERCISE 7. Writing Pronouns as Objects of Prepositions in Sentences. Write the prepositional phrase in each sentence, adding a pronoun that will complete the phrase correctly. Use a variety of pronouns, but do not use *you* or *it.*

EXAMPLE 1. We could not find all of —— .
1. *of them*

1. You always give advice to Bob and —— .
2. I made an appointment for —— and you.
3. There are some seats behind Jenny and —— .
4. No one except —— and Beth was studying.
5. I couldn't have done it without you and —— .
6. Why didn't you speak to —— and Christie?
7. Our team has played soccer against the Jets and —— .
8. I was near you and —— during the parade.
9. Just between you and —— , I think our chances are good.
10. About your cousin and —— , there is no doubt.

REVIEW EXERCISE A. Identifying Correct Pronoun Usage in Sentences. Number your paper 1–20. After the proper number, write the correct pronoun of the two in parentheses. After each answer, write an abbreviation showing how the pronoun is used: *subj., p.n., d.o., i.o., obj. prep.*

EXAMPLE 1. Say hello to (she, her) and Ann.
1. *her, obj. prep.*

1. The mayor congratulated (we, us) volunteers for our effort.
2. The election resulted in a tie between Diane and (he, him).
3. Last year's winner was (she, her).
4. Where should you and (I, me) meet after school?
5. The audience clapped for (he, him) and Ned.
6. (We, Us) sisters should help Dad with the lawn.
7. The best singer in the choir is (she, her).
8. We beat Betty and (they, them) at tennis.
9. The poet dedicated the book to Greg and (she, her).
10. The film editor showed the visitors and (we, us) students around the television station.
11. Deborah and (he, him) will recite next.
12. Have you given Arlene and (they, them) directions?
13. Please invite your cousin and (they, them) to the horse show this Saturday.
14. She sewed Aunt Elsie and (I, me) matching vests.
15. The one by the yellow car is (he, him).
16. The officer gave (we, us) girls a ride to the gas station.
17. The oldest members are Jerry and (she, her).
18. Tomorrow you and (they, them) can distribute posters.
19. I was standing by Consuelo and (she, her).
20. I wrote a story about my great-grandmother and (he, him).

REVIEW EXERCISE B. Identifying Correct Pronoun Usage. Number your paper 1–10. After the proper number, write the correct one of the two pronouns in parentheses.

EXAMPLE 1. It was news to (I, me).
1. *me*

1. Craig and (he, him) are washing the car.
2. Honorable mention was given to Mary and (I, me).
3. The first speakers will be you and (she, her).
4. Members of the decorating committee for the dance include four juniors and (we, us).

5. Everyone except Steve and (I, me) will be at the game.
6. Did you get these books from Cindy or (she, her)?
7. She will tell (we, us) runners when to line up.
8. It was (they, them) who rescued you.
9. That could have been (they, them) at the store.
10. The Jensens and (we, us) watched the fireworks display.

CHAPTER 19 REVIEW: POSTTEST

Determining the Proper Case of Pronouns in Sentences. Number your paper 1–20. After the proper number, write any incorrect pronoun and then its correct form. If the sentence is correct, write *C*.

EXAMPLE 1. The teacher told Jim and I to stop talking.
1. *I—me*

1. Several people have asked if you and me are related.
2. The winning science project was entered by Carol and he.
3. That announcer always irritates my father and I.
4. Did you give she the answer?
5. The last person I would have suspected was him.
6. Let's ask Neil and him for help.
7. The coach taught we linemen not to budge an inch.
8. We split the pie between him and I.
9. Shirley and him generously donated their time to the fund drive.
10. The ones who deserve a reward are the Thompsons and them.
11. After reading the inscription, they awarded she the plaque.
12. Us teammates have to stick together, right?
13. When my mother finally found me sitting on the curb, she was mad at me.
14. Would they suggest what Irene and me should make for dinner?

15. The shop teacher said he was pleased with Ling and I.
16. Why don't they give we girls a chance?
17. At the movies we met Julia and she while buying popcorn.
18. The strongest discus thrower we have is him.
19. Was that Hank or him?
20. My mother never tires of telling Mary Anne and I what it was like when she was our age.

USAGE

CHAPTER 20

Using Modifiers Correctly

COMPARISON AND PLACEMENT

A *modifier* describes or makes more definite the meaning of another word. Adjectives modify nouns or pronouns, and adverbs modify verbs, adjectives, or other adverbs. Phrases and clauses may also be used as modifiers. This chapter will help you learn to use modifiers correctly and more effectively.

DIAGNOSTIC TEST

A. Using the Correct Comparative, Superlative, and Negative Forms. The following sentences contain errors in the use of comparison modifiers and negatives. After the proper number, write the incorrect words from each sentence. Then write the correct form, adding or omitting words if necessary. In some cases you may need to write the entire sentence.

EXAMPLES
1. Sara is more neater than her sister is.
1. *more neater—neater*
2. I never get to have no fun.
2. *never, no—I never get to have fun.*

1. Of all the rides, the roller coaster was the most funnest.
2. Alan thinks that this pie tastes gooder than the others.

3. I couldn't hardly believe she said that.
4. Yoshi is the tallest of the twins.
5. The detective kept getting curiouser about the suspect's alibi.
6. The movie doesn't cost much, but I don't have no money.
7. They offer so many combinations that I don't know which one I like more.
8. The house on Drury Avenue is the one we like the bestest.
9. There's nothing I like more better than barbecued ribs.
10. Why doesn't the teacher give us questions that are more easier?

B. Revising Sentences by Correcting Misplaced and Dangling Modifiers. Each of the following sentences contains a dangling or misplaced modifier in italics. After the proper number, revise each sentence by placing the italicized modifier where it will make the meaning of the sentence logical and clear. In some cases you will need to add or omit words.

EXAMPLE 1. *Waiting at the curb for the bus,* a car splashed water on me.

1. *Waiting at the curb for the bus, I had water splashed on me by a car.*

or

1. *A car splashed water on me while I was waiting at the curb for a bus.*

11. *Under the doormat,* I looked for the key.
12. The library has several books about dinosaurs *in our school.*
13. *Sleeping soundly,* Howard woke his father when supper was ready.
14. The book is not in the library *that I wanted to read.*
15. Aunt Joan sent away a coupon for a free recipe book *in a magazine.*
16. The band is my favorite *that will perform next week.*
17. *Left alone for the first time in his life,* strange sounds in the night scared my little brother.
18. *After eating all their food,* we put the cats outside.

19. *Often slaughtered only for their tusks,* many African nations prohibit the hunting of elephants.
20. *Sitting in the bleachers,* the outfielder caught the ball right in front of us.

GOOD AND *WELL*

20a. Distinguish between *good* and *well* as modifiers.

Use *good* to modify a noun or a pronoun, never use *good* to modify a verb. Use *well* to modify a verb.

NONSTANDARD Doris bowls good.
STANDARD Doris bowls **well.**

NONSTANDARD The orchestra played very good.
STANDARD The orchestra played very **well.**

In the following examples, *good* is correct because it is a predicate adjective modifying the subject. Like all predicate adjectives, it follows a linking verb.

STANDARD The pie tastes especially **good.** [good pie]
STANDARD Over the microphone her voice sounds **good.** [good voice]

Well can also be used as an adjective when it refers to a person's health or appearance.

EXAMPLES Doug feels **well** today. [*Well* is a predicate adjective modifying the subject *Doug.*]
You look **well** in red. [*Well* is a predicate adjective modifying the subject *you.*]

EXERCISE 1. *Oral Drill.* Practicing the Correct Use of the Modifier *Well.* Read aloud each of the following sentences, stressing the italicized words.

1. Everyone did *well* on the test.
2. We work *well* together.

3. Do you sing as *well* as your sister does?
4. I can't water-ski very *well.*
5. How *well* can you write?
6. All went *well* until the actor forgot his lines.
7. Our class pictures turned out *well.*
8. The freshman quarterback can pass as *well* as the senior.

EXERCISE 2. Identifying the Correct Use of *Good* and *Well.* Number your paper 1–10. If *good* or *well* is correctly used in a sentence, write *C* after the corresponding number. If *good* or *well* is not correctly used, write the correct word.

EXAMPLE 1. We danced good at the recital.
1. *well*

1. Peg did not run as good during the second race.
2. The casserole tasted good to us.
3. How good does she play the part?
4. I didn't answer the questions very well.
5. He certainly looks well in spite of his illness.
6. I gave them directions as well as I could.
7. The children behaved very good.
8. Spinach salad always tastes good to them.
9. The debate did not go as good as we had hoped.
10. How good the pool looks on such a hot day!

COMPARISON OF MODIFIERS

Adjectives and adverbs may be used in comparing two or more things. When adjectives and adverbs are used to make comparisons, they express degrees of comparison. *Degrees of comparison* show the degree to which one word states a quality, as compared with another word that states the same quality.

This building is **tall.**
This building is **taller** than that one.
This building is the **tallest** one in the world.

I ski **frequently.**
I ski **more frequently** than she does.
Of the three of us, I ski **most frequently.**

20b. There are three degrees of comparison of modifiers: ***positive, comparative,*** **and** ***superlative.***

POSITIVE	COMPARATIVE	SUPERLATIVE
weak	weaker	weakest
ancient	more ancient	most ancient
loud	louder	loudest
loudly	more loudly	most loudly
good	better	best
bad	worse	worst

USAGE

There are two regular ways to compare modifiers. To form the comparative degree, the letters *-er* may be added to the end of a word, or the word *more* may precede it. To form the superlative, the letters *-est* may be added to the end of a word, or the word *most* may precede it.

(1) Most one-syllable modifiers form their comparative and superlative degrees by adding ***-er*** **and** ***-est.***

POSITIVE	COMPARATIVE	SUPERLATIVE
near	nearer	nearest
meek	meeker	meekest

(2) Some two-syllable modifiers form their comparative and superlative degrees by adding ***-er*** **and** ***-est,*** **but most two-syllable modifiers form their comparative and superlative degrees by means of** ***more*** **and** ***most.***

POSITIVE	COMPARATIVE	SUPERLATIVE
simple	simpler	simplest
drowsy	drowsier	drowsiest
modern	more modern	most modern
pleasant	more pleasant	most pleasant

When you are in doubt about which way a modifier forms its degrees of comparison, consult a dictionary.

(3) Modifiers having three or more syllables form their comparative and superlative degrees by means of *more* and *most*.

POSITIVE	COMPARATIVE	SUPERLATIVE
ignorant	more ignorant	most ignorant
happily	more happily	most happily

EXERCISE 3. Forming the Degrees of Comparison of Modifiers. Write the forms for the comparative and superlative degrees of the following modifiers:

EXAMPLE 1. long
1. *longer, longest*

1. slow
2. cautious
3. agilely
4. thankful
5. possible
6. short
7. easy
8. confident
9. forcefully
10. plain

(4) Comparisons to indicate *less* and *least* of a quality are accomplished by using the words *less* and *least* before the modifier.

POSITIVE	COMPARATIVE	SUPERLATIVE
skillful	less skillful	least skillful
delicate	less delicate	least delicate

Irregular Comparison

When adjectives and adverbs do not follow the regular methods of forming their comparative and superlative degrees, they are said to be compared irregularly. You should learn the comparative and superlative degrees of these five modifiers:

POSITIVE	COMPARATIVE	SUPERLATIVE
bad	worse	worst
good	better	best
well	better	best
many	more	most
much	more	most

REVIEW EXERCISE A. Writing the Comparative and Superlative Degrees of Modifiers. Write the comparative and superlative degrees of the following modifiers. When in doubt about words of two syllables, consult a dictionary.

EXAMPLE 1. wasteful
1. *more wasteful, most wasteful*

1. sheepish
2. simply
3. much
4. surely
5. gracious
6. quick
7. weary
8. suddenly
9. many
10. frequently
11. furious
12. enthusiastic
13. easily
14. tasty
15. generous
16. hot
17. good
18. well
19. near
20. old

USAGE

Use of Comparative and Superlative Forms

20c. Use the *comparative* degree when comparing two things; use the *superlative* when comparing three or more.

Comparing two things:

The second problem is **harder** than the first.
This blouse is **larger** than the other one.
She is **more studious** than her sister.
This book is **more carefully** written than that one.

Comparing three or more things:

This road is the **narrowest** of the three we've traveled.
Of all the performers, she was the **best.**
This is the **simplest** recipe for bread that I've seen.
Monday is the **worst** day of the week.

Most mistakes in the use of modifiers are made when two things are being compared. Remember that the comparative degree should be used when two things are compared.

NONSTANDARD Of the two soups, this is the best one.
STANDARD Of the two soups, this is the **better** one.

NONSTANDARD Marie is the youngest of the two girls.
STANDARD Marie is the **younger** of the two girls.

When comparing one thing with a group to which it belongs, do not omit the word *other.*

NONSTANDARD She is taller than any girl on her team. [She is a member of her team, and she obviously cannot be taller than herself.]

STANDARD She is taller than any **other** girl on her team.

WRITING APPLICATION A:
Using Modifiers Correctly When Comparing Two Things

It's fun to have a pet. If you could have any pet you wished, what kind would you choose? Would you like an unusual pet such as a seal or a chimpanzee, or would you prefer a more common pet such as a cat or dog? You would probably narrow your decision down to two kinds of pets before selecting one. When you make comparisons between two things, you use the comparative degree of a modifier. To form the comparative degree, you add *-er* to the end of the word or use the word *more* before it.

EXAMPLES A snake would be *more amusing* than a tropical fish.
An elephant would be *harder* to feed than a parrot.

Writing Assignment

Select two books, two movies, or two TV shows that interest you. Write a comparison of the two. Use comparative forms to give specific reasons why you prefer one to the other. Proofread for inaccuracies in the use of modifiers.

20d. Avoid the double comparison.

A *double comparison* occurs when *-er* or *-est* is added to a modifier and, at the same time, the modifier is preceded by *more* or *most.* Words should be compared in only one of these two ways; you should never use both ways at the same time.

NONSTANDARD Our dog is more smaller than yours.
STANDARD Our dog is **smaller** than yours.

NONSTANDARD It was the most beautifulest waterfall I had ever seen.
STANDARD It was the **most beautiful** waterfall I had ever seen.

EXERCISE 4. Identifying Correct Usage of Degrees of Comparison. Write *C* after the number of each correct sentence. After the number of each incorrect sentence, revise the sentence, using the correct form of comparison.

EXAMPLE 1. It's the most homeliest dog in the world.
1. *It's the homeliest dog in the world.*

1. The rehearsals are getting more longer every day.
2. Judith, the pitcher, is worse at bat than any member of the team.
3. That modern sculpture is the most strangest I've ever seen.
4. After watching the two kittens for a few minutes, Rudy chose the most playful one.
5. This morning was more sunnier than this afternoon.
6. Your cough sounds worser today.
7. The music on this album is better for dancing than the music on that one.
8. New York City has a larger population than any city in the United States.
9. I can see more better with my new glasses.
10. She was the most talented singer in the show.

THE DOUBLE NEGATIVE

Words like the following ones are called negatives: *no, not, none, never, no one, nothing, hardly, scarcely.* (Notice that many negatives begin with the letter *n.*) When such a word is used in a sentence, it makes an important change in the meaning.

I have found the wallet that I lost.
I have **never** found the wallet that I lost.

20e. Avoid the use of double negatives.

We often make negative statements such as "I never ran in a marathon." Negative statements in standard English require only one negative word. Use of more than one negative word is called a *double negative.* For example, the sentence "I never ran in no marathon" contains a double negative. Double negatives are considered nonstandard English.

NONSTANDARD We don't have no extra chairs.
STANDARD We have **no** extra chairs.
STANDARD We do**n't** have any extra chairs.

NONSTANDARD He couldn't hardly talk.
STANDARD He **could hardly** talk.

EXERCISE 5. Correcting Sentences with Double Negatives. Revise the following sentences, eliminating the double negatives.

EXAMPLE 1. We don't hardly have time to relax.
1. *We hardly have time to relax.*
or *We don't have time to relax.*

1. Josie hasn't never been to Tennessee.
2. Because of the heavy rain, we couldn't scarcely find our way home.
3. He never had no problem with public speaking.
4. The athletes don't hardly have a break between events.
5. Don't use no forks to get toast out of the toaster.
6. By the time I had made sandwiches for everyone else, I didn't have nothing left for me.
7. I never hardly listen to gossip.
8. Your answer doesn't make no difference to me.
9. Don't never say *not* and *scarcely* together.
10. The goalie doesn't have no excuse.

WRITING APPLICATION B: Using Modifiers Correctly When Comparing More Than Two Things

All through your life you are faced with decisions. Some are just small decisions, such as whether to order chicken, beef, or fish. Other decisions, however, such as whether to go to college, get a job, or volunteer for military service, are much more serious. You must make many comparisons in order to come to a decision. When you are describing a decision involving more than two options, use the superlative degree of modifiers instead of the comparative degree.

EXAMPLE I plan to work with children. Of the three activities, teacher helper, candy striper, and camp assistant, I think being a teacher helper will best prepare me for my career. [The use of the superlative modifier *best* is correct because more than two things are being compared.]

Writing Assignment

Even though graduation is a long way off, you may have given some thought to what you would like to do after you graduate. Sometimes your goal can affect what subjects you take in high school. Select three possible career choices. Write a paragraph comparing these three. Based on this comparison, indicate which job you think would suit you best. Remember to use the superlative degree for your modifiers.

USAGE

REVIEW EXERCISE B. **Correcting Improperly Used Modifiers.** Revise each incorrect sentence, eliminating errors in the use of modifiers. If a sentence is correct, write *C* after its number.

EXAMPLE 1. We don't never stay after school.
1. *We never stay after school.*

1. Which did you like best—the book or the movie?
2. Gina has more ideas for the festival than anyone.
3. Since the defeat, we have worked more harder.
4. I can't hardly reason with her.
5. Jean and Frank work good as a team.
6. Lana's bruise looks worse today than it did yesterday.
7. They haven't said nothing to us about it.
8. Of the two singers, Rose has the best voice.
9. Which has better sound, your stereo or mine?
10. The cast performed extremely well.

PLACEMENT OF MODIFIERS

Notice how the meaning of the following sentence changes when the phrase *from Canada* is moved about in the sentence.

> The professor **from Canada** gave a televised lecture on famous writers.
> The professor gave a televised lecture on famous writers **from Canada.**
> The professor gave a televised lecture **from Canada** on famous writers.

The first of the three sentences above says that the *professor* was from Canada; the second sentence, that the *famous writers* were from Canada; the third, that the *televised lecture* came from Canada. As you can see, shifting the position of the modifying phrase has resulted in important changes in meaning.

20f. Place modifying phrases and clauses so that they clearly and sensibly modify a word in the sentence.

Prepositional Phrases

You know that prepositional phrases are used as adjectives and adverbs. To make a sentence clear and sensible, you should place a prepositional phrase near the word it modifies.

> ☞ **NOTE** As was said on page 358, adverb phrases are more flexible than adjective phrases and do not have to come immediately after the modified word. However, to avoid confusion, an adverb phrase should be placed near the modified word. Often, as in the standard sentence in the following example, it precedes the modified word.

NONSTANDARD I read about the lost puppy that was found in today's newspaper. [The puppy was not found in the newspaper.]

STANDARD **In today's newspaper** I read about the lost puppy that was found.

Be careful to avoid having a prepositional phrase come between two words that it might modify. Instead, place it next to the *one* word that you intend it to modify.

UNCLEAR She said in the morning she was going to Chicago.

CLEAR She said she was going to Chicago **in the morning.**

CLEAR **In the morning** she said she was going to Chicago.

EXERCISE 6. Identifying the Appropriate Placement of Modifiers. The meaning of each of the following sentences is not clear and sensible, because the modifying phrase is in the wrong place. Decide where the phrase belongs; then revise the sentence.

EXAMPLE 1. I read about the satellite that was launched in the news today.

1. *I read in the news today about the satellite that was launched.*

1. The nature photographer told us about filming a herd of water buffalo in class today.
2. Inside the ring we watched the antics of a dancing bear.
3. The mannequins drew a huge crowd in the window display.
4. Hundreds of people were watching the show in their cars.

5. The assignment required three articles from magazines on the Statue of Liberty.
6. My aunt promised me on Saturday she would take me to the symphony.
7. There is one gymnast who can tumble as well as vault on the gymnastics team.
8. The marathon runner twisted his ankle with the blue T-shirt.
9. The model posed gracefully in front of the statue in the designer gown.
10. We saw the trapeze artist swinging dangerously through our field binoculars.

USAGE

Participial Phrases

A participial phrase modifies a noun or pronoun. When a participial phrase begins the sentence, it modifies the noun or pronoun immediately following it. Notice that the participial phrases below are separated from the other parts of the sentences by commas. (For a review of participles, see page 362.)

EXAMPLES **Screaming wildly,** the bandits chased the stagecoach.

Arriving after the others, we waited until intermission to be seated.

When you begin a sentence with a participial phrase, you should be sure that it modifies the noun or pronoun that immediately follows it; otherwise, your sentence will have a *dangling participle.* A dangling participle is a participle that is not closely connected to the noun or pronoun it modifies. The following examples show the methods of correcting dangling participles.

DANGLING Coming in for a landing, the tower radioed the plane. [The participial phrase dangles because the *tower* was not coming in for a landing.]

CORRECTED **Coming in for a landing,** the plane was radioed by the tower.

CORRECTED The tower radioed the plane **coming in for a landing.**

DANGLING Broken in many pieces, I saw my watch lying on the floor. [The participial phrase dangles because *I* was not broken in many pieces.]

CORRECTED **Broken in many pieces,** my watch was lying on the floor.

DANGLING Jogging down the sidewalk, my dog followed me. [The dog was not jogging.]

CORRECTED My dog followed me **as I jogged down the sidewalk.**

EXERCISE 7. Identifying the Correct Placement of Participial Phrases in Sentences. Some of the following sentences are nonsensical or awkward because they contain dangling participial phrases. If a sentence is correct, write *C* after its number. Revise all incorrect sentences. (You may have to supply some words.) Set off a participial phrase beginning a sentence with a comma.

EXAMPLE 1. Dressed in our costumes, the police officer waved to us clowns.

1. *The police officer waved to us clowns dressed in our costumes.*

1. Standing on the dock, a boat almost sank right in front of us.
2. Exploring the old house, Janet and Patty found a secret passageway.
3. Having bolted the cabin door, the hungry bear never really frightened us.
4. Punctured by a nail, I had to repair my bicycle tire.
5. Surrounded by reporters, many questions were asked of the governor.
6. Suffering from blisters, the race was lost by last year's winner.
7. Reading a book, my cat crawled into my lap.
8. The old suit hanging in the closet would make the perfect costume for the play.
9. Balancing precariously on the wire, the tightrope walker performed amazing tricks.
10. Exhausted after our exercises, a tall, cool glass of water was what we craved.

EXERCISE 8. Writing Sentences with Introductory Participial Phrases. Use correctly the following introductory participial phrases in sentences of your own.

EXAMPLE 1. Sitting near the stage,
1. *Sitting near the stage, I was able to see the dancers clearly.*

1. Locked in the old trunk,
2. Hanging from the ceiling,
3. Expecting a phone call from her boyfriend,
4. Almost lost in the confusion,
5. Looking toward the sunset,

Clauses

Like modifying phrases, adjective clauses should be placed as close as possible to the words they modify. Notice in the following examples how the confusion resulting from misplaced clauses is cleared up when the clauses are placed near the words they modify.

MISPLACED My parents traded an old television for a new tape recorder that they no longer wanted. [The parents no longer wanted the new tape recorder?]

CORRECTED My parents traded an old television **that they no longer wanted** for a new tape recorder.

MISPLACED The book was about insects that we read. [Did you read the insects?]

CORRECTED The book **that we read** was about insects.

EXERCISE 9. Correcting the Placement of Clauses in Sentences. Decide which word each misplaced clause should modify. Write the sentence, placing the clause near the right word.

EXAMPLE 1. I retyped the first draft on clean paper which I had corrected.
1. *I retyped the first draft, which I had corrected, on clean paper.*

USAGE

1. The soldiers were far from their base camp who had volunteered for the mission.
2. We tiptoed over the ice in our heavy boots, which had begun to crack.
3. The spaniel belongs to Bernie that won the dog show.
4. Several gospel songs were presented at yesterday's assembly that were often sung by Mary Lou Williams.
5. The telethon had achieved its goal that ran for thirty-six hours.
6. The game was canceled by the two schools that was scheduled for tomorrow.
7. The strange messenger gave Mr. Johnson a dozen balloons who was dressed as a chicken.
8. The sweater belongs to my best friend that I have lost.
9. My married sister Becky came for the weekend to see me who lives in Michigan.
10. The documentary was filmed at several locations which will be broadcast in the fall.

REVIEW EXERCISE C. Identifying the Correct Use of Modifiers in Sentences. In each of the following sentences, a modifier is used incorrectly. The mistake may result from (1) a confusion of *good* and *well,* (2) incorrect comparison, (3) the use of a double negative, or (4) a dangling or misplaced modifier. Revise the sentences, correcting the mistakes.

EXAMPLE 1. This is the most interesting of the two articles.
1. *This is the more interesting of the two articles.*

1. During last night's concert, the singing group was protected from being swarmed by guards.
2. Attempting to raise money for the homeless, many sad songs were sung by the group.
3. Years ago the singers wore strange costumes and makeup so that fans couldn't hardly tell what their faces looked like.
4. When the fans began to tire of these gimmicks, the singers tried out a new look who were also tired of gimmickry.

5. They finally chose the most simply tailored look of the two they had considered.
6. Warned about the fickleness of fans, a different style of singing was also practiced by the group.
7. Few fans could tell the first time they appeared in public after changing their style how nervous the singers were.
8. "That was the most scariest performance of my career," one singer remarked.
9. Cheering heartily, the singers' fears were relieved.
10. Both the concert and the fund raising ended exceptionally good.

CHAPTER 20 REVIEW: POSTTEST

A. Using the Correct Comparative and Superlative Forms. Number your paper 1–15. The sentences in the following paragraphs contain double negatives and errors in the use of comparative and superlative modifiers. After the proper number, write the incorrect word or words. Then write the correct form, adding or omitting words if necessary.

EXAMPLES
1. We don't want none of that food.
1. *don't, none—We don't want any of that food.*
2. Gail was even more later than I was.
2. *more later—later*

(1) The wonderfullest place in the whole world is my grandmother's house. (2) We used to live there when we didn't have no apartment of our own. (3) Since her house is bigger than any house in the neighborhood, we all had plenty of room. (4) My grandmother was glad to have us stay because my dad can fix things so that they're gooder than new. (5) He plastered and painted the walls in one bedroom so that I wouldn't have to share a room no more with my sister. (6) I don't know which was best—having so much space of my own or having privacy from my sister.

(7) My grandmother can sew better than anybody can. (8) She taught my sister and me how to make the beautifullest clothes. (9) She has three sewing machines and my mother has one, but I like Grandma's older one better. (10) We started with the more simpler kinds of stitches. (11) After my sister and I could do those, Grandma showed us elaborater stitches and sewing tricks. (12) For instance, she taught us to wrap thread behind buttons we sew on so that they will be more easier to button. (13) We learned how to make dresses, skirts, blouses, and all sorts of things, until now there isn't hardly nothing we can't make.

(14) I was sad when we left Grandma's house, but I like our new apartment more better than I thought I would. (15) Luckily, we moved to a place near my grandmother's, and after school I can go over there or go home—whichever I want to do most.

USAGE

B. Revising Sentences by Correcting Misplaced and Dangling Modifiers. After the proper number, revise each sentence by correcting the misplaced or dangling modifier. In some cases you will need to add or omit words.

EXAMPLE 1. Tearing away his umbrella, Mr. Perez became drenched in the storm.
1. *Tearing away his umbrella, the storm drenched Mr. Perez.*

16. Our teacher told us that she had been a nurse in class today.
17. The woman helped us who runs the store.
18. Destroyed by the fire, the man looked sadly at the charred house.
19. After missing the bus, my mother gave me a ride in the car.
20. The fox escaped from the hounds pursuing it with a crafty maneuver.
21. Walking through the park, the squirrels chattered at me.
22. My uncle lives in Germany who is in the Army.
23. The squid fascinated the students preserved in formaldehyde.
24. Keeping track of the race with binoculars, the blue car with a yellow roof pulled into the lead.
25. We watched the snow pile up in drifts inside our warm house.

CHAPTER 21

Glossary of Usage

COMMON USAGE PROBLEMS

USAGE

This chapter contains a short glossary of English usage for you to use as a reference when you are uncertain about a question of usage.

Several kinds of usage problems are treated in this glossary. Some require the writer or speaker to choose between two words, according to the meaning intended. Others involve a choice between two words in which one word is less acceptable than the other. A few of the words and expressions discussed here should be avoided altogether. (Spelling problems arising from the confusion of similar words are treated in Chapter 25.)

DIAGNOSTIC TEST

Revising Sentences by Correcting Errors in Usage. One sentence in each of the following sets contains an error in usage. After the proper number, write the letter of the sentence that contains an error, and revise the sentence to agree with standard formal usage.

EXAMPLE 1. (a) I rode a unicycle. (b) Everyone came except Michael. (c) The side affects of the medicine are well known.

1. *(c) The side effects of the medicine are well known.*

1. (a) They bought themselves new pens. (b) The balloon busted. (c) Use less flour.
2. (a) She did not feel well. (b) Jack ought to help us. (c) John hisself bought that.
3. (a) Tom could of come. (b) This book has fewer pages. (c) He sang well.
4. (a) We had already been there. (b) She feels alright now. (c) We looked everywhere for him.
5. (a) He behaved badly. (b) She felt badly about being late. (c) There is no talking between classes.
6. (a) We saved ten dollars between the four of us. (b) Bring a salad when you come. (c) The chair broke.
7. (a) She set down. (b) This news may affect his decision. (c) They left less milk for me.
8. (a) I cannot go unless I finish my work first. (b) Your my friend. (c) She laid the packages on the table.
9. (a) My father use to play the piano. (b) We have a long way to go. (c) Yesterday I read in the newspaper that the governor is in town.
10. (a) I know how come she left. (b) It's windy. (c) He likes this kind of movie.
11. (a) I am somewhat hungry. (b) Will you learn me how to ski? (c) Do as the leader does.
12. (a) She looks as though she is exhausted. (b) Meet me outside of the building. (c) He wrote the letter and mailed it.
13. (a) The reason why he works is that he wants to save money for a trip. (b) Your backhand has improved somewhat. (c) There are not enough chairs.
14. (a) I just bought those shoes. (b) This here ride is broken. (c) Try to relax.
15. (a) I am real happy. (b) Study now. Then go outside. (c) They're new in school.
16. (a) Take the report when you go. (b) She might have gone. (c) Mr. Bennigan he is my English teacher.

USAGE

17. (a) We worked for a hour. (b) She accepted your invitation. (c) They can hardly see the sign.
18. (a) Where do you study? (b) Divide the tasks among the two of us. (c) If he had been there, I would have seen him.
19. (a) You should have come. (b) Less sugar is needed. (c) It's pedal is stuck.
20. (a) He likes these kinds of ties. (b) It looks like a rabbit. (c) She raised up on her tiptoes.

LEVELS OF USAGE

To use the glossary properly, you will need to be familiar with the terms *standard English, formal English, informal English,* and *nonstandard English*. To identify special uses of English, you need to know the terms *slang, colloquialisms,* and *jargon.*

USAGE

Standard English

Standard English is the form of English most widely accepted by educated people. It conforms to the rules and conventions given throughout this textbook, such as those concerning subject-verb agreement, pronoun-antecedent agreement, and pronoun usage.

Formal English is the standard English used most often in formal writing or speaking situations, such as in formal reports that have footnotes and bibliographies, formal essays, and speeches given on serious occasions. Formal English avoids contractions and slang. Presidential State of the Union speeches are examples of formal English.

Informal English is the standard English that most of us use every day in our conversation and in much of our personal writing. It is used in many newspapers, magazines, and books; on radio and television; by professional and business people; and by students. Informal English is not appropriate for formal occasions.

Nonstandard English

Nonstandard English is the form of language that does not conform to the rules and conventions discussed in this textbook.

EXAMPLE My hands are more smaller than his. [nonstandard]
My hands are **smaller** than his. [standard]

Special Uses of English

Slang and colloquialisms are most often found in informal spoken English. **Jargon** may be found in formal or informal English.

Slang consists of new words, or old words in new uses, that are adopted because they seem colorful and clever and they show that the user is up to date. Slang is often found in the speech of young people and those who belong to groups set apart from the community.

EXAMPLE My older brother always **hassles** me.

Colloquialisms are words or phrases usually found in the speech, but not in the writing, of educated speakers. Colloquialisms are more widespread than slang.

EXAMPLE Let's **put our heads together** to solve this problem.

Jargon consists of words and phrases used in a particular activity, such as a sport, hobby, or field of study, or by people engaged in a particular occupation. Often jargon assigns a specified meaning to a word already in common use.

EXAMPLE The base runner tried to **steal** second base.

In most of the writing that you do for school, you should use standard formal English. Sometimes a writing assignment may use informal English. When choosing your words, always keep your purpose and audience in mind.

USAGE GLOSSARY

a, an Use *a* before words beginning with consonant sounds; use *an* before words beginning with vowel sounds.

EXAMPLES Mike will stay at **a** hotel.
I live on **a** one-way street.
Susan is **an** honest person.
My older sister gave me **an** orange sweater.

accept, except *Accept* is a verb; it means "to receive." *Except* may be either a verb or a preposition. As a verb, it means "to leave out" or "to omit"; as a preposition, it means "excluding."

EXAMPLES I **accept** your apology.
Some students will be **excepted** from this assignment.
Mark has written all his friends **except** John.

affect, effect *Affect* is a verb meaning "to influence." *Effect* used as a verb means "to accomplish." Used as a noun, *effect* means "the result of some action."

EXAMPLES His score on this test will **affect** his final grade.
Bo and Alice's hard work **effected** a solution to the problem.
The **effects** of the medicine were immediate.

ain't Avoid this word in speaking or writing; it is nonstandard English.

all ready, already *All ready* means "completely prepared" or "in readiness." *Already* means "previously."

EXAMPLES We had **already** seen that film.
The soup is **all ready** to be served.

all right Used as an adjective, *all right* means "satisfactory" or "unhurt." Used as an adverb *all right* means "satisfactory." *All right* is always two words. *Alright* is not an acceptable spelling.

EXAMPLES Your work is **all right.** [adjective]
Maria fell, but she is **all right.** [adjective]
You did **all right** at the track meet. [adverb]

anywheres, everywheres, nowheres, somewheres Use these words without the final *s.*

EXAMPLE I didn't go **anywhere** [not *anywheres*] yesterday.

as See **like, as.**

as if See **like, as if.**

at Do not use *at* after *where.*

NONSTANDARD Where will you be at?
STANDARD Where will you be?

bad, badly *Bad* is an adjective; in most uses, *badly* is an adverb. The distinction between the two forms should be observed in standard formal usage.

EXAMPLES The fish tastes **bad.** [The adjective *bad* modifies *fish.*]
The boy's wrist was sprained **badly**. [The adverb *badly* modifies *was sprained.*]

In informal usage, however, the expression "feel badly" has become acceptable, though ungrammatical, English.

INFORMAL Marcia felt badly about her low grade.
FORMAL Marcia felt **bad** about her low grade.

because See **reason . . . because.**

between, among Use *between* when you are thinking of two things at a time, even though they may be part of a group consisting of more than two.

EXAMPLES In English, Marc sits **between** Bob and me.

Some players practice **between** innings. [Although there are more than two innings, the practice occurs only *between* any two of them.]

Next year we will study the War **Between** the States. [Although thirty-five states were involved, the war was *between* two sides.]

USAGE

Use *among* when you are thinking of a group rather than of separate individuals.

EXAMPLES There was disagreement **among** the players about the coach's decision. [The players are thought of as a group.]

We saved twenty dollars **among** the three of us. [Three people together saved twenty dollars.]

bring, take *Bring* means "to come carrying something." *Take* means "to go carrying something." Think of *bring* as related to *come* and of *take* as related to *go*.

EXAMPLES Please **bring** my book when you come.
Take this dish when you go.

bust, busted Avoid using these words as verbs. Use a form of either *burst* or *break*.

EXAMPLES The balloon **burst** [not *busted*] when June sat on it.
The dish **broke** [not *busted*] when I dropped it.

can't hardly, can't scarcely The negative words *hardly* and *scarcely* should never be used with another negative word.

EXAMPLES I **can** [not *can't*] **hardly** read Jack's handwriting.
We **had** [not *hadn't*] **scarcely** enough food for everyone.

could of *Could have* sometimes sounds like *could of* when spoken. Do not write *of* with the helping verb *could*. Write *could have*. Also avoid *ought to of, should of, would of, might of,* and *must of*.

EXAMPLE Sally **could have** [not *of*] played the piano for the reception.

effect See **affect, effect.**

everywheres See **anywheres,** etc.

USAGE

fewer, less *Fewer* is used with plural words, *less* with singular words; *fewer* tells "how many," *less* "how much."

EXAMPLES We have **fewer** balloons than we need.
This recipe calls for **less** flour.

good, well *Good* is always an adjective. Never use *good* to modify a verb; use *well,* which is an adverb.

NONSTANDARD Nancy sang *good* at the audition.
STANDARD Nancy sang **well** at the audition.

Although it is usually an adverb, *well* is used as an adjective to mean "healthy."

> ☞ **USAGE NOTE** *Feel good* and *feel well* mean different things. *Feel good* means "to feel happy or pleased." *Feel well* means "to feel healthy."

EXAMPLES He did not feel **well** yesterday. [predicate adjective meaning "healthy"]
I felt **good** when I received an A in English.

had of See **of.**

had ought, hadn't ought Unlike other verbs, *ought* is not used with *had.*

NONSTANDARD Gary had ought to help us; he hadn't ought to have missed our meeting yesterday.
STANDARD Gary **ought to** help us; he **oughtn't to have** missed our meeting yesterday.

or

Gary **should** help us; he **shouldn't have** missed our meeting yesterday.

he, she, they In writing, do not use an unnecessary pronoun after a noun. This error is called the *double subject.*

NONSTANDARD Mrs. Pine she is my mother's friend.
STANDARD Mrs. Pine is my mother's friend.

hisself *Hisself* is nonstandard English. Use *himself.*

EXAMPLE Ira bought **himself** [not *hisself*] a yellow tie.

how come In informal English, *how come* is often used instead of *why;* but in formal English, *why* is always preferable.

INFORMAL I don't know how come she's not here.
FORMAL I don't know **why** she is not here.

its, it's *Its* is a personal pronoun in the possessive form. *It's* is a contraction of *it is* or *it has.*

EXAMPLES **Its** window is broken. [*Its* is a possessive pronoun.]
It's a hot day. [*It's* means "it is."]
It's been a good trip. [*It's* means "it has."]

USAGE

kind, sort, type In writing, the demonstrative words *this, that, these,* and *those* must agree in number with the words *kind, sort,* and *type.*

EXAMPLE Maria likes **this kind** of book better than any of **those** other **kinds.**

kind of, sort of In informal English, *kind of* and *sort of* are used to mean "somewhat" or "rather"; but in formal situations, *somewhat* or *rather* is always preferable.

INFORMAL It was kind of embarrassing.
FORMAL It was **somewhat** embarrassing.

learn, teach *Learn* means "to acquire knowledge." *Teach* means "to instruct" or "to show how."

EXAMPLES I am **learning** how to use this computer.
My father is **teaching** me how.

less See **fewer, less.**

WRITING APPLICATION:
Using *Kind of* Correctly in Writing Definitions

If you are not a basketball fan, you might not know what a *slam-dunk* is. If you are not a climber, you have probably never heard of *chimneying.* Sometimes words are familiar only to people who have a special interest in a particular subject. Your reader might be eager to learn about a new subject that you know much about. To explain a particular subject, you would give a definition of it. Definitions often include the phrase *kind of,* which should not be followed by *a.*

EXAMPLE A piranha is a **kind of** tropical fish with very sharp teeth that attacks and destroys its prey. [Notice that *kind of* is not followed by *a.*]

Writing Assignment

Write a paragraph in which you define a term that is familiar to you but may not be well known to other people. Here are some ideas:

woofer *or* tweeter Siamese cat word processor ceramics

Use the phrase *kind of* at least twice, and underline it each time you use it.

lie, lay See pages 452–53.

like, as *Like* is a preposition, introducing a prepositional phrase. In informal English, *like* is often used as a conjunction meaning "as"; but in formal English, *as* is always preferable.

EXAMPLES This tastes **like** pineapple juice. [Like is a preposition introducing the phrase *like pineapple juice*.]

Please do **as** he suggests. [*He suggests* is a clause

and needs the conjunction *as* (not the preposition *like*) to introduce it.]

like, as if In formal English, *like* should not be used for the compound conjunctions *as if* or *as though.*

EXAMPLE You looked **as though** [not *like*] you knew the answer.

might of, must of See **could of.**

nowheres See **anywheres,** etc.

of Do not use *of* with prepositions such as *inside, off,* and *outside.*

EXAMPLE He quickly walked **off** [not *off of*] the stage and left the theater.
She waited **outside** [not *outside of*] the school.
What is **inside** [not *inside of*] this large box?

Of is also unnecessary with *had.*

EXAMPLE If I **had** [not *had of*] seen her, I would have said hello.

ought to of See **could of.**

real In informal English, *real* is often used as an adverb meaning "very" or "extremely"; but in formal English, *very* or *extremely* is preferable.

INFORMAL I am real tired.
FORMAL I am **very** tired.

reason . . . because In informal English, *reason . . . because* is often used instead of *reason . . . that.* In formal English, use *reason . . . that,* or revise your sentence.

INFORMAL The reason I did well on the test was because I had studied hard.

FORMAL The **reason** I did well on the test was **that** I had studied hard.

or

I did well on the test **because** I had studied hard.

rise, raise See pages 453–54.

shall, will Some people prefer to use *shall* with first person pronouns and *will* with second and third person in the future and future perfect tenses. Nowadays, most Americans do not make this distinction. *Will* is acceptable in the first person as well as in the other two.

sit, set See pages 450–51.

so Because this word is usually overworked, avoid it in your writing whenever you can.

INFORMAL I want to get a good grade, so I will study tonight.
FORMAL Because I want to get a good grade, I will study tonight.

or

I want to get a good grade; therefore, I will study tonight.

some, somewhat In writing, do not use *some* for *somewhat* as an adverb.

NONSTANDARD My math has improved some.
STANDARD My math has improved **somewhat.**

than, then Do not confuse these words. *Than* is a conjunction; *then* is an adverb.

EXAMPLES Margo is a faster runner **than** I am.
First we went to the department store; **then** we went to the library.

their, there, they're *Their* is the possessive form of *they*. *There* is used to mean "at that place" or to begin a sentence. *They're* is a contraction of *they are*.

EXAMPLES **Their** team won the game.
We will go **there** in the spring.
There were twenty people at the party.
They're the best players on the team.

theirself, theirselves *Theirself* and *theirselves* are nonstandard English. Use *themselves.*

EXAMPLE They bought **themselves** [not *theirself* or *theirselves*] new basketballs.

them *Them* should not be used as an adjective. Use *these* or *those.*

EXAMPLE I gave you **those** [not *them*] records yesterday.

this here, that there The *here* and the *there* are unnecessary.

EXAMPLE Do you like **this** [not *this here*] shirt or **that** [not *that there*] one?

this kind, sort, type See **kind,** etc.

try and In informal English *try and* is often used for *try to;* but in formal English *try to* is always preferable.

INFORMAL Try and be early.
FORMAL **Try to** be early.

use to, used to Be sure to add the *d* to *use. Used to* is the past form.

EXAMPLE We **used to** [not *use to*] own a dog.

very Avoid overusing this word. Try to use more precise words in its place.

EXAMPLES I was **trembling** [instead of *very* afraid].
He was **delighted** [instead of *very* happy] with his gift.

way, ways Use *way,* not *ways,* in referring to a distance.

EXAMPLE They still had a long **way** [not *ways*] to go before reaching the town.
We took the short **way** [not *ways*] home.

when, where Do not use *when* or *where* incorrectly in writing a definition.

NONSTANDARD Listening is when a person pays close attention to what the other person is saying.
STANDARD Listening is paying close attention to what the other person is saying.

where Do not use *where* for *that.*

EXAMPLE I read in our newspaper **that** [not *where*] John will be the new sportswriter.

which, that, who Remember that the relative pronoun *who* refers to people only; *which* refers to things only; *that* refers to either people or things.

EXAMPLES She is the student **who** had the lead in the school play. [person]
I rode my bike, **which** is blue and has ten speeds. [thing]
This is the pen **that** I want to buy. [thing]
He is the person **that** can help you. [person]

without, unless Do not use the preposition *without* in place of the conjunction *unless*.

EXAMPLE I will not be able to go to the party **unless** [not without] I finish my homework first.

would of See **could of.**

your, you're *Your* is the possessive form of *you. You're* is the contraction of *you are.*

EXAMPLES **Your** dinner is on the table.
You're one of my closest friends.

CHAPTER 21 REVIEW: POSTTEST

Revising Sentences by Correcting Errors in Usage. After the proper number, write the letter of the sentence in each set that contains an error in usage. Then revise the sentence, following standard formal usage.

EXAMPLE 1. (a) The chicken tastes bad. (b) Where is the book at? (c) There was agreement among the five dancers.
1. *(b) Where is the book?*

1. (a) Bring your notes when you come. (b) The dish busted. (c) He could have danced.
2. (a) I drew an apple. (b) The cold affects the plant. (c) We are already to go.
3. (a) Mike feels alright today. (b) She went everywhere. (c) We have fewer chairs than we need.
4. (a) They danced good at the party. (b) If I had sung, you would have laughed. (c) You ought to help.
5. (a) It's cold. (b) He made it hisself. (c) Its knob is broken.
6. (a) Teach me the song. (b) That story is kind of funny. (c) The dog lay down.
7. (a) Mr. Barnes is here. (b) I know why he left. (c) This kinds of bikes are expensive.
8. (a) These taste like oranges. (b) Sing as she does. (c) She might of moved.
9. (a) Please come inside the house. (b) I am real happy. (c) The reason she laughed was that your dog looked funny.
10. (a) I wanted the telephone but its broken. (b) Your forehand has improved somewhat. (c) He sings better than I do.
11. (a) Your coat is beautiful. (b) You're a fast runner. (c) I cannot leave without I wash the dishes first.
12. (a) She is the student which plays the violin. (b) We only

USAGE

have a short way to go. (c) We read in our newspaper that a new store is opening in town.

13. (a) I use to read mysteries. (b) Set that crate down here. (c) This hat is old.
14. (a) I gave you them books. (b) They bought themselves new shirts. (c) There is the cat.
15. (a) Sit down. (b) They're smiling. (c) There team is good.
16. (a) Gail did not feel well. (b) Have a orange. (c) You invited everyone except Sue.
17. (a) I raised at 8:00 this morning. (b) Have you read about the effects of the sun's rays? (c) We already read the book in class.
18. (a) You did all right. (b) They went nowheres. (c) He looks as if he is sad.
19. (a) Nancy's ankle was hurt bad. (b) We listened to the discussion among the three governors. (c) The pipe burst.
20. (a) I cannot hardly dance. (b) Warm days make me feel good. (c) It's pretty.
21. (a) He must be somewhere. (b) I can scarcely ride this bike. (c) The reason why I like him is because he is kind.
22. (a) We have fewer shelves than we need. (b) Those kinds of shirts are warm. (c) This morning I laid in bed too long.
23. (a) Pat always lays her books on the couch. (b) Learn how to play this game. (c) Do like he does.
24. (a) They are inside of the house. (b) I will have a sandwich. (c) He set the chair down.
25. (a) Their my cats. (b) Do you need those books? (c) This house has fourteen rooms.

CHAPTER 22

Capital Letters

RULES FOR CAPITALIZATION

Capital letters indicate important words—the beginnings of sentences and quotations, titles, and other words that deserve special attention. You have probably already mastered most of the rules for capitalization. Perhaps there are some that you still find troublesome. In this chapter you will review the rules for using capital letters correctly.

DIAGNOSTIC TEST

Correcting Sentences by Using Capitalization Correctly. Number your paper 1–20. Each of the following sentences contains incorrect capitalization. After the proper number, write the word or words correctly, supplying capitals where they are necessary and omitting capitals where they are unnecessary.

EXAMPLE 1. The Maxwells enjoyed visiting the southwest, particularly the Alamo in San Antonio.
1. *Southwest*

1. Dr. Powell's office is at Twenty-first street and Oak Drive.
2. On labor day we always go to Three Trees State Park.
3. We invited aunt Mae and her two children to go with us.
4. Our junior high school had a much more successful carnival than Lakeside junior high school did.

MECHANICS

5. When our class read *a Tale of two Cities,* we also studied the French Revolution.
6. My cousin joined the Peace corps and lived in a small village on the west coast of Africa for a year.
7. No fish live in the Great salt lake in Utah.
8. One famous hero of World War I is sergeant Alvin York.
9. We have studied Japanese culture and the shinto religion.
10. This year I have English, American History, Spanish, and shop in the afternoon.
11. On sunday my mother and I are going to an antique car show.
12. The Robinsons live near route 41 just off the Memorial Parkway on the south side of town.
13. At our Wednesday night meeting, the reverend Terry Witt gave a short talk on the beliefs of Lutherans.
14. We salute you, o Caesar!
15. Thursday was named after the Norse God Thor.
16. An icy gust of Winter air chilled the scouts to the bone.
17. Dale Evans and Roy Rogers always sang "Happy trails to you" at the end of their television programs.
18. Ms. Morelli's class has studied the Supreme court.
19. My uncle served in the U.S. Army during the War in Vietnam.
20. The American revolution took place toward the end of the Age of Enlightenment in the eighteenth century.

MECHANICS

22a. Capitalize the first word in every sentence.

To capitalize the first word in a sentence, you must be able to identify the beginning of a sentence. The section on run-on sentences (pages 236–37) will help you.

INCORRECT More and more people are discovering the benefits of exercise daily workouts at the gymnasium or on the running track strengthen the heart.

CORRECT More and more people are discovering the benefits

of exercise. **D**aily workouts at the gymnasium or on the running track strengthen the heart.

The first word of a sentence that is a direct quotation is capitalized even if the quotation begins within a sentence.

EXAMPLE *Elinor shouted, "**W**e did it!"*

For a fuller explanation of this rule, see the section on writing quotations, pages 555–61.

> ☞ NOTE Traditionally, the first word in a line of poetry is capitalized, whether or not the word begins a sentence:
>
> *W*hen I am dead, my dearest,
> *S*ing no sad songs for me

Some modern poets do not follow this style. When copying a poem, be sure to follow the capitalization the poet used.

22b. Capitalize the pronoun *I*.

EXAMPLE Recently **I** have begun to enjoy classical music.

22c. Capitalize the interjection *O*.

The interjection *O* is most often used on solemn or formal occasions. Notice that it is most often used with a word in direct address and that no mark of punctuation follows it.

EXAMPLES Hear our prayer, **O** Lord.
Protect us in the battle, **O** great Athena!

The interjection *oh* requires a capital letter only at the beginning of a sentence. It is usually followed by a comma.

EXAMPLES **Oh,** wait till you see tomorrow's assignment.
We haven't seen her for some time—**oh,** perhaps two or three months.

22d. Capitalize proper nouns.

The proper noun, which you studied on page 293, names a particular person, place, or thing. It is always capitalized. The common noun is capitalized only when it begins a sentence or is part of a title.

PROPER NOUNS	COMMON NOUNS
Cicely Tyson	actress
February	month
Tennessee	state

(1) Capitalize the names of persons.

EXAMPLES **J**ames **B**aldwin is my favorite writer.
Is **A**lice coming, too?
According to **M**rs. **S**andoz, **A**nnie **S**ullivan is a good subject for a biography.

(2) Capitalize geographical names.

Cities, Towns: **J**amestown, **S**an **D**iego, **A**kron
States: **G**eorgia, **I**daho, **H**awaii
Countries: **G**hana, **N**icaragua, **T**hailand
Sections of the Country: the **M**idwest, the **N**orth

> ☞ **NOTE** Do *not* capitalize *east, west, north, south,* or any combination like *southwest* when these words indicate direction; do capitalize them when they name a region: *If you fly west across the Pacific Ocean, you will arrive in the Far East.*

Islands: **I**sle of **W**ight, **M**olokai, **W**ake **I**sland, **A**ttu
Bodies of Water: **D**anville **R**eservoir, **T**ennessee **R**iver, **L**ake **E**rie, **N**iagara **F**alls, **T**ampa **B**ay, **I**ndian **O**cean, **P**uget **S**ound, **B**ering **S**ea, **S**traits of **G**ibraltar
Streets, Highways: **C**herry **L**ane, **T**aconic **A**venue, **C**rescent **C**ircle,**W**est **N**inety-fourth **S**treet, **R**oute 44, **S**kyline **D**rive

> ☞ **NOTE** In a hyphenated street number, the second word begins with a small letter: *East Seventy-eighth Street, South Forty-third Place.*

Parks: Estes Park, White Mountain National Forest
Mountains: Big Horn Mountains, Mount Washington, Sawtooth Range, Pikes Peak
Continents: North America, Europe, Africa, Asia

(3) Capitalize names of organizations, business firms, institutions, and government bodies.

Organizations: Debating Club, Future Farmers of America
Business Firms: Garcia's Hardware Store, United Tool and Die Corporation
Institutions: Cary Memorial Hospital, Hillcrest School, Antioch College
Government Bodies: Air National Guard, Department of Agriculture, Governor's Council on Indian Affairs

> ☞ **NOTE** Do *not* capitalize words like *school, circus, restaurant, club* unless they are part of a proper name: *an elementary school—Irving Elementary School; a circus —Ringling Brothers' Circus.*

(4) Capitalize special events and calendar items.

EXAMPLES	World Series	Fourth of July
	National Chess Tournament	Friday
	Rockland Lobster Festival	October

> ☞ **NOTE** Do *not* capitalize the names of seasons: *We go on fishing trips in the spring and the fall.*

MECHANICS

(5) Capitalize the names of historical events and periods.

EXAMPLES **I**ce **A**ge, **R**evolutionary **W**ar, **B**attle of **B**unker **H**ill, **M**iddle **A**ges, **R**enaissance, **C**rusades

(6) Capitalize the names of nationalities, races, and religions.

EXAMPLES **S**panish, **E**gyptian, **C**aucasian, **E**skimo, **L**utheran

(7) Capitalize the brand names of business products.

EXAMPLES **C**annon towels, **B**uick sedan, **I**vory soap [Notice that only the brand name is capitalized; the common noun following it begins with a small letter.]

(8) Capitalize the names of ships, planets, monuments, awards, and any other particular places, things, or events.

Monuments, Memorials: **W**ashington **M**onument, **V**ietnam **V**eterans **M**emorial
Awards: **P**ulitzer **P**rize, **N**ewbery **M**edal
Ships, Trains: U.S.S. ***M**aine, **Q**ueen **E**lizabeth, **S**ilver **R**ocket*
Planets, Stars: **V**enus, **S**aturn, the **M**ilky **W**ay, the **B**ig **D**ipper

> ☞ NOTE Planets, constellations, stars, and groups of stars are capitalized; *sun, moon,* and *earth* are not capitalized unless they are listed with other heavenly bodies.

MECHANICS

EXERCISE 1. Writing Common Nouns and Proper Nouns. Number your paper 1–10. For each proper noun, write a corresponding common noun. For each common noun, write a proper noun.

EXAMPLES 1. Chien Shiung Wu
1. *physicist*
2. city
2. *San Francisco*

1. mountain range
2. Geraldine Ferraro
3. historical event
4. river
5. North Dakota
6. Ethiopia
7. Washington Monument
8. poem
9. cereal
10. Environmental Protection Agency

EXERCISE 2. Using Capital Letters Correctly. After the proper number, rewrite each of the following expressions, using capital letters where they are needed.

EXAMPLE 1. a member of the peace corps
1. *a member of the Peace Corps*

1. veterans day ceremony
2. decisions of the united states supreme court
3. eastern half of iowa
4. eleanor roosevelt park
5. cree indians of north america
6. boulder dam
7. graduate of bryn mawr college
8. the statue of liberty
9. enid bagnold
10. saint patrick's day parade
11. general foods corporation
12. one street east of north fairview drive
13. 512 west twenty-fourth street
14. pictures of saturn sent by *voyager II*
15. the hawaiian island called maui
16. the great lakes
17. a catholic
18. sealtest cottage cheese
19. monday, april 29
20. the stone age

MECHANICS

EXERCISE 3. Correcting Sentences by Capitalizing Words. Number your paper 1–10. After the proper number, rewrite all words that need capital letters in the sentence. Treat a compound word as one word.

EXAMPLE 1. our class visited abraham lincoln's home in springfield, illinois.
1. *Our, Abraham Lincoln's, Springfield, Illinois*

1. according to the federal aviation administration, united states airlines are the safest in the world.
2. ethel waters lived in chester, pennsylvania, as a child.
3. the sacred muslim city of mecca is in saudi arabia.
4. in chicago, the sears tower and the museum of science and industry attract many tourists.
5. the detroit tigers won the world series in 1984.
6. the valentine's day dance is always the highlight of the winter.
7. several of my friends bought new adidas shoes at the big sporting goods sale in the mall.
8. the city-wide food pantry is sponsored and operated by protestants, catholics, and jews.
9. the second-place winners will receive polaroid cameras.
10. jane bryant quinn writes a magazine column on money management.

22e. Capitalize proper adjectives.

A proper adjective, which is formed from a proper noun, is always capitalized.

PROPER NOUN	PROPER ADJECTIVE
China	Chinese doctor
Egypt	Egyptian cotton
Ireland	Irish wolfhound
Middle East	Middle Eastern tour

EXERCISE 4. Correcting Sentences by Capitalizing Proper Nouns and Proper Adjectives. Number your paper 1–10. After the appropriate number, write and capitalize all proper nouns and proper adjectives in the sentence.

EXAMPLE 1. A finnish architect, eliel saarinen, designed a number of buildings in the detroit area.
1. *Finnish, Eliel Saarinen, Detroit*

1. Have you seen the exhibit of african art at the library?
2. The egyptian and israeli leaders met in jerusalem.
3. The european cities I plan to visit are paris and vienna.
4. Our english literature book includes hopi poems and cheyenne legends.
5. The south american rain forests contain many different kinds of plants and animals.
6. Maria has watched two shakespearean plays on television.
7. The alaskan wilderness is noted for its majestic beauty.
8. Our program will feature irish and scottish folk songs.
9. The language most widely spoken in brazil is portuguese.
10. The baptist leader heard the ruling of the supreme court.

22f. Do *not* capitalize the names of school subjects, except languages and course names followed by a number.

EXAMPLES I have tests in **E**nglish, **L**atin, and **m**ath.
You must pass **H**istory II before taking **H**istory III.

EXERCISE 5. Correcting Phrases by Capitalizing Words. Number your paper 1–5. After the proper number, write each phrase, inserting capitals where they are needed.

1. a lesson in spanish
2. report for english II
3. a program on chinese customs
4. problems in geometry
5. studying latin, history, chemistry, and government II

22g. Capitalize titles.

(1) Capitalize the title of a person when it comes before a name.

EXAMPLES There will be a short address by **G**overnor Halsey.
Report to **L**ieutenant Engstrom, please.
Dr. Politi has a new associate, a **M**s. Tam.
Is **M**s. Tam the new associate of **D**r. Politi?

This is the church in which the **R**everend Henry Ward Beecher preached.
How many terms did **P**resident Cleveland serve?

(2) Capitalize a title used alone or following a person's name only if it refers to a high official or to someone to whom you wish to show special respect.

EXAMPLES The **S**ecretary of **L**abor will hold a news conference this afternoon. [*Secretary of Labor* is a high office.]

The White House is the official residence of the **P**resident. [The word *President* is usually capitalized when it refers to the President of the United States.]

The **t**reasurer of our scout troop has the measles. [The title is not that of a high office.]

Ellen Rafferty, **c**hairperson of the program committee, reported on plans for the Winter Carnival. [The office is not a high one.]

> ☞ **NOTE** When a title is used instead of a name in direct address, it is usually capitalized: *Could you tell me how my sister is feeling, Nurse?*

MECHANICS

(3) Capitalize words showing family relationships when used with a person's name but *not* when preceded by a possessive.

EXAMPLES **A**unt Christine, **G**randfather Smith
Maria's **m**other, our **b**rother, her **a**unt

Exception: When family-relationship words are *usually* used before a name, so that they are considered part of the name, they are capitalized even when preceded by a possessive.

EXAMPLE Kim's **A**unt **B**etty

When family-relationship words are used in place of a person's name, they may or may not be capitalized.

EXAMPLE Ask **M**other, *or* Ask **m**other. [Either is correct.]

(4) Capitalize the first word and all important words in titles of books, magazines, newspapers, poems, stories, movies, paintings, and other works of art.

Unimportant words in a title are *a, an, the,* and prepositions and conjunctions of fewer than five letters. Such words should be capitalized only if they come first or last in the title.

EXAMPLES My sister asked me to read Denise Levertov's poem, "**W**ith **E**yes **at** **t**he **B**ack **o**f **O**ur **H**eads."

Katharine Hepburn and Humphrey Bogart starred in *The African Queen.*

Curtain Going Up! is a biography of Katharine Cornell.

Exception: When you write the names of newspapers and magazines within a sentence, do not capitalize the word *the* before the name.

EXAMPLES Is that the late edition of **t**he *New York Times*?

(5) Capitalize words referring to the Deity.

EXAMPLES **L**ord, **J**ehovah, the **C**reator, **S**on of **G**od, **A**llah

☞ NOTE The word *god* is not capitalized when referring to the gods in mythology: *The Roman god of war was Mars.*

MECHANICS

EXERCISE 6. Correcting Sentences by Capitalizing Words. Number your paper 1–10. After the proper number, write and capitalize the words requiring capitals. If a sentence is correct, write *C.*

1. During Woodrow Wilson's term as president of the united states, sheep grazed on the front lawn of the White House.
2. When aunt Jo visits, she shows slides of her most recent trip.

3. All of these pronunciations are taken from *the american heritage dictionary*.
4. Some of the gods in greek mythology were also worshiped in ancient asian and egyptian cultures.
5. Did you hear commissioner of education smathers' speech recommending a longer school day?
6. Was Carrie Fisher in *return of the jedi*?
7. After the secretary read the minutes, the treasurer reported on the club's budget.
8. Lillian Hellman wrote *watch on the rhine*.
9. My older brother subscribes to *field and stream*.
10. The first politician to make a shuttle flight was senator Jake Garn of Utah.

REVIEW EXERCISE A. Correcting Sentences by Capitalizing Words. Number your paper 1–10. After the proper number, write and capitalize the words requiring capitals.

1. The browns hosted an exchange student from argentina.
2. The king ranch in texas is as large as rhode island.
3. Ms. epstein is taking courses in computer programming I, french, and english at rand community college.
4. The sixth day of the week, friday, is named for the norse goddess of love, freya.
5. Both the christian holiday of christmas and the jewish holiday of chanukah are celebrated in december.
6. My uncle ron was stationed in the south pacific.
7. The liberty bell, on display in independence hall in philadelphia, was rung to proclaim the boston tea party and to announce the reading of the declaration of independence.
8. Is your mother still teaching an art appreciation class at the swen parson gallery?
9. Emily dickinson and robert frost, both new england poets, are among the best-loved american poets.
10. I walk to the eagle supermarket each sunday for the *miami herald* and a quart of tropicana orange juice.

WRITING APPLICATION: Using Capital Letters Correctly

Using capital letters correctly helps you make your writing clear. A capital letter signals your readers that you mean a specific person, place, or thing. Compare the following pairs of sentences:

EXAMPLES Exit at the third street ramp.
Exit at the Third Street ramp.

This new Mexican bracelet was a gift.
This New Mexican bracelet was a gift.

She perched on the back of the mustang to have her picture taken.
She perched on the back of the Mustang to have her picture taken.

To make your meaning clear, always proofread your writing carefully to make sure that you have used capital letters correctly.

Writing Assignment

Write ten sentences, using one of the items in the following list in each sentence. Proofread carefully to make sure that you have used capital letters correctly to make your meaning clear.

1. The name of a magazine
2. A business
3. A mountain range
4. The title of a person
5. The title of a book
6. A geographical section of the country
7. The name of a street
8. A language and two other school subjects
9. A historical event
10. A continent

REVIEW EXERCISE B. Correcting Sentences by Correcting Capitalization Errors. Number your paper 1–20. For each sentence, write in order the words that should be capitalized and capitalize them. Also write the words that are incorrectly capitalized, omitting the capitals.

1. Blind and deaf, Helen Keller met Presidents and Kings from all over the world.
2. In History class, we learned about women suffragettes elizabeth cady stanton, susan b. anthony, and lucretia c. mott.
3. A great many words came into the english language from greek and latin.
4. At elgin larkin high school, students must complete three years of Math, three of Science, and four of English.
5. Each summer a group from the methodist youth fellowship travels to appalachia to help poor people in the area.
6. The empire state building is taller than the eiffel tower.
7. In April, the cherry blossom festival will be celebrated by a Parade in the heart of the City.
8. The 1984 summer olympics were held in los angeles.
9. The rio grande flows along the Southern border of Texas; it is one of the most famous rivers in north america.
10. jane addams, an American Social Reformer who founded hull house in chicago, was awarded the 1931 nobel peace prize.
11. Many of the countries of europe are smaller than some states in our country.
12. The President of the local volunteer society received the outstanding volunteer award two years in a row.
13. My parents subscribe to *national geographic* and *time.*
14. William Least Heat Moon began his journey around America in the southeast.
15. Seeing the Redwood forests was a highlight of our trip to California.
16. Bonds were sold to raise money for the construction of a new

Junior High School in Sycamore.

17. Can we have a surprise Birthday party for grandpa, mom?
18. The University was the site of a convention of african and south american scientists.
19. The panama canal connects the atlantic ocean and the pacific ocean; the new york state barge canal connects the hudson river and lake erie.
20. Edna Ferber's *so big, cimarron,* and *giant* give a colorful picture of american life during times of rapid growth.

CHAPTER 22 REVIEW: POSTTEST

Correcting Sentences by Using Capitalization Correctly. Number your paper 1–25. Each of the following sentences contains an error in capitalization. After the proper number, write the word or words correctly, supplying capitals where they are necessary and omitting capitals where they are unnecessary.

EXAMPLE 1. The shubert Theater is located at 225 West Forty-fourth Street in New York.
1. *Shubert*

1. Several planets in our solar system were named for Roman Gods.
2. In history class we memorized the Capitals of all the states.
3. Uncle Ron owns one of the first honda motorcycles that were sold in America.
4. My cousin gave me a terrific book, *Rules of the game,* which illustrates the rules of all sorts of games.
5. My grandmother makes delicious boston brown bread.
6. Rajiv Gandhi, the prime minister of India, visited Washington, D.C., in June of 1985.
7. The Indus river flows from the Himalaya Mountains to the Arabian Sea.

8. Appearing on television and writing popular books, dr. Carl Sagan has done much to increase public interest in science.
9. In the afternoons i used to help Mrs. Parkhurst deliver the *Evening Independent,* a local Newspaper.
10. Stavros and his friend belong to the Civil air Patrol.
11. As economic conditions changed, people began leaving Northern states and moving to the South and West.
12. Ernest Hemingway and Robert Service are famous writers who served in the red cross during the Spanish Civil War.
13. My brother owns an olivetti typewriter.
14. Next year my sister will graduate from mayfair high school and go to the university in the state capital, where she intends to study mathematics and english.
15. When we found the injured german shepherd, we took it to our veterinarian, dr. Rita Molina.
16. Could you please tell me how to get to the chrysler Factory on highway 21 and riverside road?
17. The woman in the bait shop said to steer the boat North across the lake to the mouth of Fish-eating creek.
18. For father's day, we bought Dad a new power saw.
19. The Ohio department of education provided buses to help evacuate the victims of the tornado in June.
20. Anwar Sadat was one of the most famous egyptian leaders in Modern Times.
21. In the south, the civil war is sometimes called the war between the States.
22. When We read "fire and ice" by Robert Frost, I understood what the Poem meant.
23. At the beginning of their long journey, the Pioneer families knelt beside their wagons and prayed to god for guidance.
24. When I ate Supper at Cam's house, I tried *nuoc mam,* a vietnamese fish sauce.
25. To get to woodside mall, turn left at the deep pit barbecue palace; then turn right at park street, and you'll see the Mall on the Left.

SUMMARY STYLE SHEET

This list gives examples of the rules of capitalization in this chapter. Use it as a review by studying each item and explaining the use of each capital or small letter. The list will also be convenient for quick reference.

Johnson **C**ity
Aztec **M**otel
Second **S**treet
Milton **P**ond
the **N**ortheast
North Dakota
the Music **C**lub
Slater **W**oolen **C**ompany
Topeka **H**igh **S**chool
the Korean **W**ar
the John Hancock **B**uilding
Washington's **B**irthday
the Industrial **R**evolution
God, our **F**ather
the **W**inter **P**rom
the **S**ophomore **C**lass
French, **E**nglish, **R**ussian
Science II
Principal Harris
the **P**resident of the United States
Will you call **M**other (*or* **m**other)?
Aunt Marie
the ***A**merican **G**irl*
the ***D**allas **T**imes **H**erald*
***T**he **W**ar of the **W**orlds*
customs of the **J**apanese
an **E**piscopalian
Ford truck

a **c**ity in Tennessee
a **m**otel in Miami
a **s**treet in Pasadena
a **p**ond in Milton
a **n**ortheasterly gale
north of South Dakota
a **c**lub for musicians
a **w**oolen **c**ompany
a **h**igh **s**chool in Topeka
a **w**ar in Korea
an insurance **b**uilding
Christine's **b**irthday
a **r**evolution in manufacturing
the **g**ods of Greek mythology
a **p**rom in the **w**inter
a **c**lass of **s**ophomores
mathematics, **m**usic, **g**eography
a lesson in **s**cience
Ms. Harris, the **p**rincipal
the **p**resident of the company
My **m**other is here.
her **a**unt
a monthly **m**agazine
a **n**ewspaper
an exciting **b**ook
national customs
a sermon in **c**hurch
a **p**ickup truck

CHAPTER 23

Punctuation

END MARKS, COMMAS, SEMICOLONS, COLONS

In spoken language the voice indicates pauses and full stops, but in written language punctuation does this work. Although it might seem as if writing would be easier without using periods or commas or other marks of punctuation, the result would be very difficult to read. In this chapter and the next one, you will learn to master punctuation so that your writing will be clear.

MECHANICS

DIAGNOSTIC TEST

Correcting Sentences by Adding End Marks, Commas, Semicolons, and Colons. Write the following sentences, inserting end marks, commas, semicolons, and colons where they are needed.

EXAMPLE 1. Have you seen our teacher Ms. O'Donnell today
1. *Have you seen our teacher, Ms. O'Donnell, today?*

1. My neighbor the lady with red hair used to be my baby sitter when I was younger and I still visit her sometimes
2. We made a salad with the following vegetables from our garden lettuce cucumbers carrots and cherry tomatoes
3. Running after the bus Melody tripped and fell in a puddle

4. My first pet which I got when I was six was a beagle I named it Bagel
5. Sit in the back row Randy and don't disturb the class
6. The award was given for the best-written most interesting report about air pollution
7. My mother said that we could go to the lake however it looks as if it's going to rain
8. Does anyone know where the crank that we use to open the top windows is
9. The chickens clucked the dogs barked and the ducks squawked
10. Over the weekend I saw Charlie's twin brother who used to work at the grocery store at the motocross bike course
11. Wow That's the longest homer I've ever hit
12. After the rain stopped falling the blue jays hopped around the lawn in search of worms
13. Wasn't President John F. Kennedy assassinated on November 22 1963
14. Why wasn't Sid's last letter which was mailed May 5 delivered until June 5
15. Everybody had told her of course that it was useless to try
16. Preparing for takeoff the jetliner rolled slowly toward the runway
17. Hand in your test your answer sheet and your scratch paper
18. What shall we do after 3 00 when school lets out Yolanda
19. Her address is 142 Oak Hollow Court Mendota CA 93640
20. My cousins will stay here tonight or they will drive on to Aunt Cindy's house

---

END MARKS

23a. A statement is followed by a period.

EXAMPLES The lens is the most important part of a camera**.**
One of the figure skaters was Sonja Henie**.**

23b. A question is followed by a question mark.

EXAMPLES Have you watched Barbara Walters?
Is photography a science or an art?

23c. An exclamation is followed by an exclamation point.

EXAMPLES What a good time we had!
Wow! What a view!

23d. An imperative sentence is followed by either a period or an exclamation point.

EXAMPLES Please give me the scissors. [making a request]
Give me the scissors! [showing strong feeling]

EXERCISE 1. Correcting Paragraphs by Adding End Marks. Number your paper 1–10. In the following paragraphs, sentences have been run together without end marks. Write the last word of every sentence and the first word of the next sentence, inserting the proper end mark. There are ten end marks to supply. Use one line of your paper for each end mark.

In New Salem Park, Illinois, you will find a reproduction of the little village of New Salem, just as it was when Abraham Lincoln lived there If you visit this village, you will find that life in Lincoln's time was much harder than it is today

The cabin of the Onstats is not a reproduction but the original cabin where Lincoln spent many hours In that living room, on that very floor, young Abe Lincoln studied with Isaac Onstat It was the cabin's only room

Across the way hangs a big kettle once used by Mr. Waddell for boiling wool Mr. Waddell, the hatter of the village, made hats of wool and fur

Do any of you feel you would like to go back to those days What endurance those people must have had Could we manage to live as they did

MECHANICS

23e. An abbreviation is followed by a period.

EXAMPLES	min.	minute	Dr.	Doctor	Mr.	Mister
	St.	Street	Aug.	August	Co.	Company
	in.	inch	Neb.	Nebraska		

COMMAS

A *comma* does not indicate a full stop, as a period does. Instead, it divides a sentence into readable parts by indicating pauses. If you master the use of the comma, your written work will improve in clarity. One word of warning: Have a reason for every comma you put into a sentence.

Items in a Series

23f. Use commas to separate items in a series.

Words, phrases, and clauses in a series should be separated by commas so that the reader can tell where one item in the series ends and the next item begins.

(1) Use commas to separate words in a series.

EXAMPLES We have read poems by Longfellow, Teasdale, and Dickinson this week.

Tobacco, *hammock*, *canoe*, and *moccasin* are three of the words that English-speaking people owe to American Indians.

In the early morning, the lake looked cold, gray, and uninviting.

Get into the habit of using a comma before the *and* joining the last two items in a series. Although many writers omit this comma, it is sometimes necessary to make your meaning clear.

UNCLEAR Susie, Zack and I are going riding.
CLEAR Susie, Zack, and I are going riding.

The first sentence is perfectly clear if you are addressing Susie and informing her that Zack and you are going riding; but not if you mean to tell some other person that all three of you—Susie, Zack, and you—are going riding.

(2) Use commas to separate phrases in a series.

EXAMPLES We found seaweed in the water, on the sand, under the rocks, and even in our shoes.

It makes no difference whether that hamster is in a cage, on a string, or under a net—it always escapes.

(3) Use commas to separate subordinate clauses and short independent clauses in a series.

EXAMPLES Everyone wondered when he had been in the house, what he had wanted, and where he had gone.

We worked, we played, and we rested.

(4) If all items in a series are joined by *and* or *or,* do not use commas to separate them.

EXAMPLE Have you read *Huckleberry Finn* or *Tom Sawyer* or *A Connecticut Yankee in King Arthur's Court*?

EXERCISE 2. Correcting Sentences by Adding Commas. Number your paper 1–10. After the proper number, show where commas are needed in each sentence by writing the word before a necessary comma and adding the comma.

EXAMPLE 1. I read that each American eats an average of 117 pounds of potatoes 116 pounds of beef and 100 pounds of fresh vegetables each year.

1. *potatoes, beef,*

MECHANICS

1. Carlos and Anna and Francie ran across the park climbed over the fence and hurried to the bus stop.
2. The three states that have produced the most U.S. Presidents are Virginia Ohio and New York.
3. The school band includes clarinets saxophones trumpets trombones tubas flutes piccolos and drums.

4. Most flutes used by professional musicians are made of sterling silver 14-carat gold or platinum.
5. We discussed what we would write about where we would find sources and how we would organize our reports.
6. No one knew what had started the argument when the two had begun to fight or why they were now both laughing.
7. Financial writer Sylvia Porter has written a book explaining how to earn money and how to spend it borrow it and save it.
8. Last summer I read *The Red Badge of Courage The Wizard of Earthsea The Virginian* and *A Wrinkle in Time.*
9. The San Joaquin kit fox the ocelot the Florida panther and the red wolf are all endangered mammals in North America.
10. I would like to visit Thailand Nepal China and Japan, the Land of the Rising Sun.

23g. Use a comma to separate two or more adjectives preceding a noun.

EXAMPLES An Arabian horse is a fast**,** beautiful animal.
The rancher of old often depended on the small**,** tough**,** sure-footed mustang.

When the final adjective is so closely connected to the noun that the words seem to form one expression, do not use a comma before the final adjective.

EXAMPLE Training a frisky colt to become a gentle, dependable riding horse takes great patience.

In the above example, no comma is used between *dependable* and *riding* because the words *riding horse* are closely connected in meaning and may be taken as one term.

A comma should never be used between an adjective and the noun immediately following it.

INCORRECT Mary O'Hara wrote a tender, suspenseful, story about a young boy and his colt.
CORRECT Mary O'Hara wrote a tender, suspenseful story about a young boy and his colt.

EXERCISE 3. Correcting Sentences by Adding Commas. Write the following sentences, inserting commas where needed.

EXAMPLE 1. A squat dark cooking stove stood in one corner.
1. *A squat, dark cooking stove stood in one corner.*

1. They made a clubhouse in the empty unused storage shed.
2. This book describes the harsh isolated lives of pioneer women in Kansas.
3. What a lovely haunting melody that tune has!
4. A group of proud smiling parents watched the nervous young musicians take their places on the stage.
5. The delicate colorful wings of the hummingbird vibrate up to two hundred times each second.

Compound Sentences

23h. Use a comma before *and, but, or, nor, for,* and *yet* when they join independent clauses.

EXAMPLES The musical comedy originated in America**,** and it has retained a distinctly American flavor.

Grand opera is a popular form of entertainment in Europe**,** but few Americans take the opportunity to see live productions of operas.

If the clauses in a compound sentence are very short, the comma before the conjunction may be omitted.

EXAMPLE Hart wrote the words and Rodgers wrote the music.

To follow rule 23h, you must be able to tell a compound sentence from a simple sentence that has a compound verb.

COMPOUND SENTENCE Margo likes golf**,** but she doesn't enjoy archery. [comma between independent clauses joined by a conjunction]

SIMPLE SENTENCE WITH COMPOUND VERB Margo likes golf but doesn't enjoy archery. [no comma between parts of compound verb joined by a conjunction]

MECHANICS

EXERCISE 4. Correcting Compound Sentences by Adding Commas. After the proper number, write the words in the sentence that should be followed by commas according to rule 23h. Add the commas.

EXAMPLE 1. Have you read this article in *Nature* or do you want me to tell you about it?
1. *Nature,*

1. Human beings must study to become architects yet some animals build amazing structures by instinct.
2. One kind of male gardener bird builds a complex structure and he decorates it carefully to attract a mate.
3. This bird constructs a dome-shaped garden in a small tree and underneath the tree he lays a carpet of moss covered with brilliant tropical flowers.
4. As a finishing touch, the bird gathers twigs and he arranges them in a three-foot-wide circle around the display.
5. Prairie dogs might be called the city planners of the plains for they create huge networks of underground burrows.
6. These burrows may stretch hundreds of miles and they may house millions of prairie dogs.
7. The prairie dogs do not often leave their own small territories within the complex but they can somehow tell their neighbors from strangers.
8. The female European water spider builds a waterproof nest underwater and she stocks the nest with air bubbles.
9. This air supply is very important for it allows the spider to hunt underwater.
10. The water spider also lays its eggs in the waterproof nest and they hatch there.

Phrases and Clauses

Participial phrases, as you learned on page 363, act as adjectives to modify nouns or pronouns. Subordinate clauses may also act as adjectives (see pages 386–87).

In some sentences, the participial phrase or adjective clause is essential to the thought. It cannot be removed without destroying the meaning of the sentence.

EXAMPLE All farmers **growing hybrid corn** owe a debt to an Austrian monk named Gregor Mendel.

In the preceding example, the participial phrase in boldfaced type tells *which* farmers. It is essential to the meaning of the sentence.

EXAMPLE Mendel made the discoveries **that have become the basis of modern genetics.**

The adjective clause in the example above modifies *discoveries.* It cannot be removed without destroying the meaning of the sentence.

In other sentences, the participial phrase or adjective clause is *not* essential to the thought. Such a phrase or clause can be removed without changing the basic meaning.

EXAMPLE Sometimes seeds and nuts**, forgotten by the squirrels that hid them,** germinate far away from their parent plants.

Here the participial phrase can be removed without changing the basic meaning of the sentence: *Sometimes seeds and nuts germinate far away from their parent plants.*

EXAMPLE Migrating birds**, which often fly hundreds or thousands of miles,** are one of the main carriers of seeds.

Here the adjective clause can be removed without changing the basic meaning of the sentence: *Migrating birds are one of the main carriers of seeds.*

MECHANICS

23i. Use commas to set off participial phrases and adjective clauses that are not essential to the basic meaning of the sentence. Do not use commas with phrases or clauses that are essential to the meaning.

EXAMPLES A new spider web**, shining in the morning light,** is an impressive example of engineering. [nonessential participial phrase; commas needed]

Anyone **who finishes early** may start on tomorrow's assignment. [essential adjective clause; no commas needed]

To set off with commas means to separate from the rest of the sentence. If the nonessential phrase or clause comes in the middle of the sentence, a comma is needed before and after it. If the phrase or clause comes at the end, a comma is needed before it; if the phrase or clause comes at the beginning of the sentence, a comma is needed after it.

EXERCISE 5. Using Commas Correctly in Sentences with Participial Phrases and Adjective Clauses. Number your paper 1–10. Write the words that should be followed by commas and add the commas.

1. Ynes Mexia hoping to find new kinds of plants explored the dense jungles of Brazil.
2. The plants that she gathered carefully dried and preserved became the basis for a collection.
3. Traveling and working alone for many months she found a tremendous variety of new and unusual plants.
4. Mrs. Nina Floy who was an assistant to Ynes Mexia kept detailed records of Mexia's jungle discoveries.
5. Ynes Mexia who spent a year in search of unknown plants on the South American continent collected nearly one thousand new varieties of plants on her expedition.
6. President Carter whose full name is James Earl Carter prefers to be known as Jimmy.
7. Jimmy Carter was born in Plains which is a small town in Georgia.
8. Carter who graduated from the U.S. Naval Academy studied nuclear physics.
9. After his Navy service he returned to Georgia serving first as a state senator and later as Governor.
10. Winning the Democratic Party's nomination for the Presidency Carter defeated President Ford in the 1976 election.

23j. Use a comma after a participial phrase or an adverb clause that begins a sentence.

EXAMPLES **Forced onto the sidelines by a torn ligament,** Harris was restless and unhappy. [introductory participial phrase]

When March came, the huge ice pack began to melt and break up. [introductory adverb clause]

An adverb clause that comes at the end of a sentence does not usually need a comma.

EXAMPLE The huge ice pack began to melt and break up **when March came.**

EXERCISE 6. Using Commas Correctly in Sentences with Participial Phrases and Introductory Clauses. Number your paper 1–10. After the proper number, if a comma is needed in a sentence, write the word before it and add the comma. If no comma is needed, write *C* after the number.

EXAMPLE 1. Stopping at the post office I mailed the letters.
1. *office,*

1. Although mail delivery is as old as recorded history the first postage stamps were not used until the nineteenth century.
2. The idea of using prepaid postage stamps was adopted after it had been suggested by a British educator.
3. Originally picturing government officials or national symbols stamps soon began to feature a wide variety of other items.
4. Stamp collecting became a popular hobby when stamps became more varied.
5. Because stamps provide a colorful record of many areas of life they are fascinating.
6. Although most stamps are issued to pay for the delivery of mail special issues are produced for sale to collectors.
7. Enjoyed by more than twenty million people in the United States alone stamp collecting is a favorite pastime of both young and old.

8. Collectors can always look forward to adding new stamps because new designs are issued often.
9. Since a collection of every type of stamp ever issued would be too bulky many collectors concentrate on a single topic.
10. Filling albums with their treasures collectors enjoy examining their first stamps as well as their latest ones.

Interrupters

When an expression such as *of course* or *well* or a person's name interrupts a sentence, commas are needed to set off the interrupter. If the interrupting expression comes first or last in the sentence, only one comma is needed. If it comes in the middle of the sentence, two commas are needed—one before the interrupter, and one after.

23k. Use a comma after a word such as *well, yes, no, why* when it begins a sentence.

EXAMPLES Why, you really should know that!
Well, I don't.

> ☞ **NOTE** Words such as *well, yes, no* and *why* are not followed by a comma if they do not interrupt the sentence; that is, if no pause follows them: *Why is Rebecca early?*

23l. Use commas to set off an expression that interrupts a sentence.

(1) Appositives and appositive phrases are usually set off by commas.

An appositive is a word that means the same thing as the noun it follows; usually it explains or identifies the noun. It is set off by commas to show that it is not essential to the meaning of the sentence.

EXAMPLES My best friend, **Nancy,** is studying ballet. [*Nancy* is an appositive with exactly the same meaning as *My best friend.*]

We're out of our most popular flavor, **vanilla.**

Often an appositive is modified by other words, taking the form of an appositive phrase. The entire phrase is set off by commas.

EXAMPLES Nancy, **my best friend,** has won a dance scholarship. [In this sequence, *my best friend* is the appositive phrase.]

The Rio Grande, **one of the major rivers of North America,** forms part of the border between Texas and Mexico.

When the appositive is short, closely related to the noun it follows, and essential to the meaning of the sentence, no comma should be used.

EXAMPLES My ancestor **Alberto Pazienza** emigrated to America on the ship *Marianna.*

White House spokesman **Larry Speakes** issued a statement.

EXERCISE 7. Using Commas Correctly in Sentences with Introductory Words and Appositives. After the proper number, write the sentences that require commas. Insert the commas. If a sentence is correct, write *C.*

EXAMPLE 1. The dog a boxer is named Brindle.
1. *The dog, a boxer, is named Brindle.*

1. The composer Mozart wrote five short piano pieces when he was only six years old.
2. Katy Jurado the actress has appeared in many fine films.
3. Harper Lee author of *To Kill a Mockingbird* is from Alabama.
4. Did you know that the card game canasta is descended from mah-jongg an ancient Chinese game?
5. Jupiter the fifth planet from the sun is so large that all the other planets in our solar system would fit inside it.

6. No I do not enjoy murder mysteries.
7. The writing of Elizabeth Bowen an Irish novelist shows her keen, witty observations of life.
8. Charlemagne the king of the Franks in the eighth and ninth centuries became Emperor of the Holy Roman Empire.
9. Why those soldiers are only children!
10. Sarah Winnemucca a Paiute Indian opened a school in Nevada.

(2) Words used in direct address are set off by commas.

When someone speaks directly to another person, using that person's name, commas precede and follow the name.[1]

EXAMPLES **Mrs. Clarkson,** I just want to get to the beach.
Can you tell me**,** **Hazel,** when the next bus is due?

EXERCISE 8. Correcting Sentences by Adding Commas to Set Off Words in Direct Address. Number your paper 1–5. After the proper number, write the words in the sentence that should be followed by a comma, and add the comma.

EXAMPLE 1. Are you hungry Jan or have you had lunch?
1. *hungry, Jan,*

1. Ms. Wu will you schedule me for the computer lab tomorrow?
2. Have you signed up for a baseball team yet Aaron?
3. Your time was good in the hurdles Juanita but I know you can do better.
4. Wear sturdy shoes girls; those hills are hard on the feet!
5. Run Susan; the bus is pulling out!

MECHANICS

(3) Parenthetical expressions are set off by commas.

Occasionally a sentence is interrupted by an expression such as *to tell the truth, in my opinion, in fact.* Such expressions are called *parenthetical* because, like words enclosed in parentheses, they

[1] For rules governing the use of commas in dialogue, see page 559.

are not grammatically related to the rest of the sentence. These expressions are set off by commas.

EXAMPLES The President said**, off the record,** that he was deeply disappointed.

To be honest, I thought the movie was fairly good.
It wasn't very good**, in my opinion.**

The following expressions are often used parenthetically.

in fact	however	as I was saying
for example	mind you	to tell the truth
of course	nevertheless	on the contrary
I suppose	I know	I believe
I hope	in my opinion	if you ask me

Such expressions are not always parenthetical. Be careful to use commas only if they are needed.

EXAMPLES What**, in her opinion,** is the best closing hour? [a parenthetical expression set off by commas]

I have no faith **in her opinion.** [not a parenthetical expression; no commas needed]

Traveling by boat may take longer**, however.** [a parenthetical expression, preceded by a comma]

However you go, it will be a delightful trip. [*However* not used parenthetically; no commas needed]

EXERCISE 9. Correcting Sentences by Adding Commas to Set Off Parenthetical Expressions. Number your paper 1–5. After the proper number, write the words in the sentence that should be followed by commas, and add the commas.

EXAMPLE 1. Mathematics I'm afraid is my hardest subject.
1. *Mathematics, afraid,*

1. The situation is if you ask me very unfortunate.
2. Your subject I think should be limited further.
3. I'm not saying mind you that I agree with their methods.

4. Flying however will be more expensive.
5. Nevertheless his honesty pleased his parents.

23m. Use a comma in certain conventional situations.

English usage requires that commas be used in dates, in addresses, and after the salutations and closings of letters.

(1) Use a comma to separate items in dates and addresses.

EXAMPLES The delegates to the Constitutional Convention signed the Constitution on September 17, 1787, in Philadelphia, Pennsylvania.

Passover begins on Wednesday, April 14, this year.

My friend has just moved to 6448 Higgins Road, Chicago, Illinois.

In an address, you should leave some space between the ZIP code and the state (unless you are writing it in a sentence). No comma should come before it.

EXAMPLE Jackson Heights, New York 11372

> ☞ **NOTE** If a preposition is used between items of an address, a comma is not necessary: *He lives at 144 Smith Street in Moline, Illinois.*

(2) Use a comma after the salutation of a friendly letter and after the closing of any letter.

EXAMPLES Dear Aunt Margaret,
Sincerely yours,
Yours truly,

EXERCISE 10. Correcting Dates, Addresses, and Letter Parts by Adding Commas. After the proper number, write the following items on your paper, inserting necessary commas.

1. 11687 Montana Avenue Los Angeles CA 90049
2. 1615 West Touhy Avenue Chicago IL 60626
3. Monday December 2 1985
4. after January 1 1986
5. Dresser Road at North First Street in Lynchburg Virginia
6. Memorial Day 1985
7. from December 1 1985 to March 15 1986
8. either Thursday April 18 or Monday April 22
9. Dear Joanne
10. Sincerely yours

WRITING APPLICATION A:
Using Commas to Separate Items

Using commas between words, phrases, and short independent clauses tells your reader that each item is a separate one. Compare the following examples:

EXAMPLES We invited Mary Beth Hardy and Bill.
We invited Mary Beth, Hardy, and Bill.
We invited Mary, Beth, Hardy, and Bill.

The first sentence indicates that two persons were invited. The second sentence shows that three were invited, while the third sentence increases the guest list to four. As you can see, using commas to separate items can make a big difference in the meaning of a sentence.

Writing Assignment

Write a paragraph describing a busy scene, using words that appeal to the senses—sight, sound, touch, taste, and smell. After you revise your paragraph, proofread it carefully to be sure that you have used commas correctly to make your meaning clear. Then prepare a clean copy of your paragraph.

MECHANICS

REVIEW EXERCISE A. Correcting Sentences by Adding Commas and End Marks. Number your paper 1–20. After the proper number, supply commas and end marks in the following sentences by writing the word before a mark of punctuation and adding the comma or end mark.

1. If we include New York City in our vacation plans we will certainly go to the Statue of Liberty
2. The famous statue was dedicated on October 18 1886
3. Few people know its full name *Liberty Enlightening the World*
4. The statue which was given to the United States by France has become a symbol of freedom
5. Have you ever made the long tiring trip up the stairs to the head of the statue Alan
6. When you travel in Canada Joe you will know you are no longer in the United States
7. Notice for example the signs that allow speeds up to 100 kilometers per hour
8. How fast is that in miles per hour
9. Well it converts to about 62 miles per hour I think
10. Brenda and Beverly the twins next door have given their old bikes to Goodwill
11. If a piece of a supernova the size of a baseball were brought to earth it would weigh more than the Empire State Building
12. The blue whale weighs as much as thirty elephants grows as long as three buses and has an upper jawbone three feet long
13. Turtles crocodiles alligators frogs and dolphins must breathe air in order to survive
14. Lanolin a smelly fatty substance taken from the wool of sheep is used in many cosmetics
15. Although they were much bigger than other animals dinosaurs had very small brains
16. On May 29 1953 Sir Edmund Hillary a New Zealand explorer became the first person to climb Mount Everest the highest point on the earth's surface
17. Junko Tabei one of a team of Japanese women reached the summit in 1975

18. Many people who love climbing have been inspired by these feats
19. Will the first day of the twenty-first century begin officially on January 1 2000 or on January 1 2001 Sarah
20. What a great fireworks display that was

SEMICOLONS

The *semicolon* signals a pause stronger than a comma but not as strong as a period.

23n. Use a semicolon between independent clauses in a sentence if they are not joined by *and, but, or, nor, for, yet.*

EXAMPLES On our first trip to Houston I wanted to see the Astrodome**;** my little brother wanted to visit the Johnson Space Center.

Our parents settled the argument for us**;** they took us to see a rodeo in a nearby town.

A period (and capital) between the independent clauses would change each of these examples into two sentences. Creating two sentences would be correct, but it would not show how closely related the ideas are.

> ☞ NOTE Very short independent clauses without conjunctions may be separated by commas: *The leaves whispered, the brook gurgled, the sun beamed benignly.*

23o. Use a semicolon between independent clauses joined by such words as *for example, for instance, that is, besides, accordingly, moreover, nevertheless, furthermore, otherwise, therefore, however, consequently, instead, hence.*

EXAMPLES Mary Ishikawa decided not to stay at home**;** instead, she went to the game.

The popular names of certain animals are misleading**;** for example, the koala bear is not a bear.

English was Louise's most difficult subject**;** accordingly, she gave it more time than any other subject.

23p. A semicolon (rather than a comma) may be needed to separate the independent clauses of a compound sentence if there are commas within the clauses.

Ordinarily, a comma is used to separate independent clauses that are joined by *and, but, or, nor, for,* or *yet.* However, if there are already commas *within* the independent clauses, an additional comma *between* the clauses might be confusing. In such a case, a stronger mark of punctuation—the semicolon—is needed.

EXAMPLE A tall, slender woman entered the large, drafty room**;** and a short, slight, blond woman followed her.

EXERCISE 11. Correcting Sentences by Using Semicolons Between Independent Clauses. Number your paper 1–10. If a sentence requires a semicolon, write the words before and after the semicolon and insert the mark of punctuation. If the sentence does not require a semicolon, write *C.*

EXAMPLE 1. The gym is on the ground floor the classrooms are above it.
1. *floor***;** *the*

1. Map-makers have explored almost all areas of the earth, they are now exploring the floors of the oceans.
2. Some scientists predict the development of undersea cities, but this prediction seems at least questionable.
3. In the future, perhaps, people will choose to live in a city in space, or they may prefer to live in an undersea city.
4. Roger Maris hit his sixty-first home run during the last game of the 1961 baseball season, until then Babe Ruth had held the record for the most home runs in a season.
5. Some reptiles like a dry climate, but others prefer a wet climate.

6. Many of today's office buildings look like glass boxes, they appear to be made entirely of windows.
7. In April 1912, a new "unsinkable" ocean liner, the *Titanic,* struck an iceberg in the North Atlantic, as a result, 1,493 persons lost their lives.
8. The *Titanic* carried nearly 2,200 passengers and crew, however, it had only enough lifeboats to accommodate 950.
9. The tragedy brought stricter safety regulations for ships, for example, the new laws required more lifeboats.
10. Today's shipwrecks can produce a different kind of tragedy, for instance, if a large oil tanker is wrecked, the spilled oil damages beaches and kills wildlife.

COLONS

The colon says, in effect, "Note what follows."

23q. Use a colon before a list of items, especially after expressions like *as follows* or *the following*.

EXAMPLES Minimum equipment for camping is as follows**:** bedroll, utensils for cooking and eating, warm clothing, sturdy shoes, jackknife, rope, and flashlight.

This is what I have to do**:** clean my room, shop for a birthday present, baby-sit for Mrs. Magill for two hours, and do my Spanish homework.

23r. Use a colon in certain conventional situations.

(1) Use a colon between the hour and the minute when you write the time.

EXAMPLES 11**:**30 P.M. 4**:**08 A.M.

(2) Use a colon after the salutation of a business letter.

EXAMPLES Gentlemen**:**
Dear Ms. Gonzalez**:**
Dear Sir**:**

MECHANICS

REVIEW EXERCISE B. Correcting Sentences by Adding Colons and Commas. Number your paper 1–5. Supply necessary colons and commas by writing the word before a mark of punctuation and adding the punctuation.

1. During the field trip our teacher pointed out the following trees sugarberry pawpaw silverbell and mountain laurel.
2. The first lunch period begins at 11 00 A.M.
3. This is my motto laugh and the world laughs with you.
4. These languages are offered Spanish French Russian and German.
5. The artist showed me how to obtain a flesh color simply mix white, yellow and a little red.

WRITING APPLICATION B: Using Semicolons to Join Closely Related Ideas

Using semicolons between independent clauses signals your reader that the ideas in the clauses are closely related. However, few ideas are so closely related that they are equal in importance. Thus, you will probably not use the semicolon often. Compare the following examples:

EXAMPLES The rain began before dawn; I went shopping.
The rain began before dawn; it lasted all day.

The connection between the two ideas in the first example is not at all clear to the reader. The second sentence correctly combines two closely related ideas with a semicolon. When you use a semicolon, always check to make sure that the ideas it combines are closely related.

Writing Assignment

Write a paragraph explaining how something you said or did brought about an unexpected event. As you revise your paragraph, make sure that you have used semicolons to connect only closely related ideas. Then make a clean copy of your paragraph.

CHAPTER 23 REVIEW: POSTTEST

Correcting Sentences by Adding End Marks, Commas, Semicolons, and Colons. Rewrite the following paragraphs, inserting punctuation as needed.

EXAMPLE 1. Did I ever tell you how our washing machine which usually behaves itself once turned into a foaming monster

1. *Did I ever tell you how our washing machine, which usually behaves itself, once turned into a foaming monster?*

(1) "Oh no The basement is full of soapsuds!" my younger sister Sheila yelled (2) When I heard her I could tell how upset she was (3) Her voice had that tense strained tone that I know so well (4) Running downstairs to the basement I immediately saw why she was excited (5) Imagine the following scene the washing machine was completely hidden in a thick foamy flow of bubbles (6) I ran across the slippery floor fought my way through the foam and turned off the machine

(7) This of course only stopped the flow (8) Sheila and I now had to clean up the mess for we didn't want Mom and Dad to see it when they got home (9) We mopped up soapsuds we sponged water off the floor and we dried the outside of the washing machine (10) After nearly an hour of exhausting effort we were satisfied with our work and decided to try the washer

(11) Everything would have been fine if the machine had still worked however it would not even start (12) Can you imagine how upset we both were then (13) Thinking things over we decided to call a repair shop

(14) We frantically telephoned Mr Hodges who runs the appliance-repair business nearest to our town (15) We told him the problem then we asked him to come to 21 Crestview Drive Ellenville as soon as possible

(16) When he arrived Mr Hodges inspected the machine asked us a few questions and said that we had no real problem (17) The

MECHANICS

wires had become damp and we were to let the machine sit for a day before we tried to use it again

(18) Surprised and relieved we thanked Mr Hodges and started toward the stairs to show him the way out (19) He stopped us however and asked if we knew what had caused the problem with the suds (20) We didn't want to admit our ignorance but our hesitation gave us away (21) Well Mr Hodges suggested that from now on we should measure the soap instead of just pouring it into the machine

(22) Looking at the empty box of laundry powder I realized what had happened (23) It was I believe the first time Sheila had used the washing machine by herself and no one had told her to read the instructions on the box

(24) This incident occurred on November 10 1983 and we have never forgotten it (25) Whenever we do the laundry now we remember the lesson we learned the day the washer overflowed

CHAPTER 24

Punctuation

ITALICS, QUOTATION MARKS, APOSTROPHES, HYPHENS

Just as you use different facial expressions, gestures, and intonations to convey meaning when you speak, you need a variety of different marks of punctuation to make the meaning of your writing clear. In this chapter you will study the use of four more marks of punctuation.

MECHANICS

DIAGNOSTIC TEST

A. Proofreading Sentences for the Correct Use of Apostrophes and Hyphens. Number your paper 1–10. Each of the following sentences contains one or two errors in the use of apostrophes or hyphens. After the proper number, write each sentence correctly.

EXAMPLE 1. Rays mother said that hed have to mow the lawn before he could play soccer.
1. *Ray's mother said that he'd have to mow the lawn before he could play soccer.*

1. Marsha is this years captain of the girls basketball team.
2. The plants leaves had wilted and its stem had shriveled.

3. At one time or another, Ive tried to play the piano, the guitar, and the clarinet.
4. We couldnt have done the job without you're help.
5. Shes strict about being on time.
6. On my older brothers last birthday, he turned twenty one.
7. Wed have forgotten to turn off the computer if Maggie hadnt reminded us.
8. The recipe said to add two eggs, a teaspoon of salt, and a three quarter cup of milk.
9. My fathers office is on the twenty second floor.
10. The soldiers supplies had run out, and its doubtful whether they could have survived without reinforcements.

B. Proofreading Sentences for the Correct Use of Quotation Marks and Underlining (Italics). Number your paper 11–20. Each of the following sentences contains one or two errors in the use of quotation marks or underlining (italics). After the proper number, rewrite each sentence correctly.

EXAMPLE 1. Mary asked, "Did you read Robert Frost's poem Nothing Gold Can Stay out loud in class?"
1. *Mary asked, "Did you read Robert Frost's poem 'Nothing Gold Can Stay' out loud in class?"*

11. Uncle Ned reads the Wall Street Journal every day.
12. Fill in all the information on both sides of the form, the secretary said.
13. How many times have you seen the movie of Margaret Mitchell's novel Gone with the Wind?
14. Many of the students enjoyed the humor and irony in O. Henry's short story The Ransom of Red Chief.
15. My little sister asked, Why can't I have a hamster?
16. Please don't sing I've Been Working on the Railroad.
17. Over the summer my older sister played in a band on a Caribbean cruise ship named Bright Coastal Star.
18. "Read E. B. White's essay The Decline of Sport, and answer the study questions," the teacher announced.

19. Dudley Randall's poem Ancestors questions why people always seem to believe that their ancestors were aristocrats.
20. "Wait here," the clerk said, while I go to check the price.

UNDERLINING (ITALICS)

Italics are printed letters that lean to the right, *like this.* In handwritten or typewritten work, italics are indicated by underlining. If your composition were to be printed in a book or some other publication, the typesetter would use italics for underlined words. For example, if you wrote

Born Free is the story of a lioness that became a pet.

the printed version would look like this:

Born Free is the story of a lioness that became a pet.

24a. Use underlining (italics) for titles of books, periodicals, works of art, plays, films, television programs, ships, and so on.

EXAMPLES *Big Red* is a book about an Irish setter.
Van Gogh's *Sunflowers* is a well-known painting.
The *Philadelphia Inquirer* has won many of the nation's top journalism awards.
Jacques-Yves Cousteau has outfitted the *Calypso* as a seagoing research lab.
Star Wars was one of the most popular movies ever made.

☞ NOTE When writing the title of a newspaper or a magazine within a sentence, underline the title. Do not underline or capitalize the word *the* with the name of a newspaper or magazine within a sentence. The name of a city in a newspaper title is usually underlined.

EXAMPLE My parents subscribe to two newspapers published in other cities: the *St. Louis Post-Dispatch* and the *San Francisco Chronicle.*

EXERCISE 1. Using Underlining to Indicate Titles. Number your paper 1–10. After the proper number, write and underline the words in the sentence that should be in italics.

EXAMPLE 1. Have you read The Call of the Wild?
1. *The Call of the Wild*

1. Popular Mechanics, Sports Illustrated, and Seventeen are all popular magazines in our library.
2. In Wednesday's edition of the Globe-Democrat, there is a section on baking bread.
3. The final number will be a medley of excerpts from George Gershwin's opera Porgy and Bess.
4. Elizabeth Speare won the Newbery Medal twice, for her books The Witch of Blackbird Pond and The Bronze Bow.
5. Picasso's painting Guernica is named for a Spanish town that was destroyed during the Spanish Civil War.
6. Katharine Graham, the publisher of the Washington Post, is one of this year's commencement speakers.
7. The first battle between ironclad ships took place between the Monitor and the Merrimac in 1862.
8. Have you seen both versions of the movie Close Encounters of the Third Kind?
9. Betty Comden and Adolph Green have written such Broadway shows as Bells Are Ringing and Fade Out, Fade In.
10. The magazine rack held issues of National Wildlife, Time, Popular Photography, Ladies Home Journal, and Runner's World.

WRITING QUOTATIONS

Quotations are words spoken or written by someone and reported directly. In your writing you will often find it necessary to tell what someone has said, whether you are describing a true happening or an imaginary one. This section explains how to write quotations in a standard form that can be easily read by others.

24b. Use quotation marks to enclose a direct quotation—a person's exact words.

Quotation marks before and after a person's words show exactly what was said.

EXAMPLES **"**Has anyone in the class swum in the Great Salt Lake?**"** asked Ms. Estrada. [Ms. Estrada's exact words]

"I swam there last summer,**"** said June. [June's exact words]

Do not confuse a person's exact words with a rewording of the person's speech. If you tell what someone said without repeating the exact words, you are using an *indirect* quotation. No quotation marks are needed for an indirect quotation.

INDIRECT Pauline asked for **my interpretation of the poem.** [not Pauline's exact words; no quotation marks needed]

DIRECT Pauline asked, **"What is your interpretation of the poem?"** [Pauline's exact words; quotation marks needed]

INDIRECT I told her that **I thought the poet was expressing awe at the power of nature.**

DIRECT **"I think the poet is expressing awe at the power of nature,"** I said.

MECHANICS

24c. A direct quotation begins with a capital letter.

EXAMPLES Jimmy shouted, "**A** parade will be held tomorrow!"

"**Is** it true?" asked Sandra.

24d. When a quotation is divided into two parts by an interrupting expression such as *he said* or *Mother asked,* the second part begins with a small letter.

EXAMPLES "What are some of the things," asked Mrs. Perkins, "**t**hat the astronauts discovered on the moon?"

"One thing they discovered," answered Gwen, "**w**as that the moon is covered by a layer of dust."

"Gee," George added, "**m**y room at home is a lot like the moon, I guess."

If the second part of an interrupted quotation starts a new sentence, it should start with a capital letter.

EXAMPLE "Any new means of travel is exciting," she remarked. "**S**pace travel is no exception." [The second part begins with a capital because it is a new sentence.]

EXERCISE 2. Correcting Sentences by Adding Capital Letters and Punctuation. Write the following sentences, supplying whatever capitals and marks of punctuation are needed. For the two sentences that require no changes, write *C*.

EXAMPLE 1. Now, said the teacher, you may go to the library.
1. *"Now," said the teacher, "you may go to the library."*

1. I hope, said Elizabeth, that we will reach Atlanta soon.
2. if the traffic does not get worse, the driver predicted, we should be there in half an hour.
3. Mrs. Yamasaki, our physical education teacher, told us we would begin the volleyball unit Monday.
4. We took the injured young owl into the house, said Dick, and we made a nest for it in a basket.
5. Mr. Howard said that we might have trouble persuading the owlet to eat.

24e. A direct quotation is set off from the rest of the sentence by commas or by a question mark or exclamation point.

EXAMPLES "I've just finished reading a book about Narcissa Whitman**,**" Ellen said.

"Was she one of the early settlers in the Northwest**?**" asked Janet.

"What an adventure!" exclaimed Carol.
Tom said, "I wish I had been there."

24f. A period or a comma following a quotation should be placed inside the closing quotation marks. A period is only used if the quotation comes at the end of the sentence that includes it.

EXAMPLES Ramon said, "Hank Aaron was better than Babe Ruth because he hit more home runs in his career."

"But Hank Aaron never hit sixty in one year," countered Paula.

24g. A question mark or an exclamation point should be placed inside the closing quotation marks if the quotation is a question or an exclamation. Otherwise, it should be placed outside.

EXAMPLES "What is the time difference between Los Angeles and Chicago?" asked Ken. [The quotation is a question.]

Linda exclaimed, "I thought everyone knew that!" [The quotation is an exclamation.]

Is the right answer "two hours"? [The quotation is not a question, but the sentence as a whole is.]

If the sentence and the quotation are both questions, you still use only one question mark.

EXAMPLE Who said, "What's in a name?"

MECHANICS

EXERCISE 3. Correcting Sentences by Adding Capital Letters and Punctuation. Revise the following sentences, supplying capitals and marks of punctuation as needed.

EXAMPLE 1. Why she asked can't we leave now
1. *"Why," she asked, "can't we leave now?"*

1. Mother, will you take us to the soccer field asked Libby
2. Please hold my viola case for a minute, Dave Josh said I need to tie my shoelace
3. Cary asked What is pita bread

4. Did Therese answer It's a round, flat Middle Eastern bread
5. Run Run cried the boys a tornado is headed this way

24h. When you write dialogue (conversation), begin a new paragraph each time you change speakers.

EXAMPLE "What did you think of that movie about Japan?" Sara asked Ron as they left the school building.

"I was surprised at the scenes in Tokyo. I didn't know it was so much like Chicago or New York."

"I guess a lot of the young people don't wear traditional Japanese clothes nowadays," Sara said.

24i. When a quotation consists of several sentences, put quotation marks only at the beginning and at the end of the whole quotation, not around each sentence in the quotation.

INCORRECT "Memorize all your lines for Monday." "Have someone at home give you your cues." "Enjoy your weekend!" said Ms. Goodwin.

CORRECT **"**Memorize all your lines for Monday. Have someone at home give you your cues. Enjoy your weekend!**"** said Ms. Goodwin.

EXERCISE 4. Punctuating and Paragraphing Dialogue. Revise the following dialogue, punctuating and paragraphing it correctly.

Lynette, did you enjoy reading *The Yearling* Miss Bishop asked I think it's the best book I have ever read, Miss Bishop Can you tell us why you liked it The characters seemed so real Lynette replied and their struggles made me like them even more What were some of the struggles Jody and his family faced They struggled to raise crops and to gather food to get through the winter Jody was lonely until he found Flag What conflicts did keeping the deer as a pet cause Flag ate some of the crops, and Jody pleaded with his father to keep the deer Jody loved his pet and had trouble admitting it couldn't live with the family Good, Lynette

24j. Use single quotation marks to enclose a quotation within a quotation.

EXAMPLES "I said, 'The quiz will cover Unit 2 and your special reports,'" repeated Mr. Allyn.

"What poem begins with the line, 'I'm going out to clean the pasture spring'?" Carol asked.

24k. Use quotation marks to enclose titles of short works such as poems, short stories, articles, songs and individual episodes of television programs; and of chapters and other parts of books.[1]

EXAMPLES Irwin Shaw's "Strawberry Ice-Cream Soda" is a story of an older and a younger brother.

Our assignment for tomorrow is the first part of Chapter 11, "Americans Create New States out of the Wilderness."

The poetry of Elizabeth Madox Roberts is the subject of an article called "A Tent of Green" in the *Horn Book Magazine.*

EXERCISE 5. **Using Punctuation Marks, Quotation Marks, and Underlining (Italics).** Write the following sentences, inserting punctuation marks and quotation marks where needed. Underline words that should be in italics.

EXAMPLE 1. We sang Greensleeves for the assembly.
1. *We sang "Greensleeves" for the assembly.*

1. Has anyone read the story To Build a Fire asked the teacher.
2. I have said Eileen. It was written by Jack London.
3. Do you know the poem To Make a Prairie?
4. The New Yorker magazine features excellent short stories.
5. Did you read asked Ms. Carlson the article Animal Architects in the St. Louis Post-Dispatch?

MECHANICS

[1] For the use of italics for titles, see rule 24a on page 554.

REVIEW EXERCISE A. Correcting Sentences by Adding Punctuation and Capital Letters. If a sentence is correct, write *C* after its number on your paper. Revise the incorrect sentences, making all necessary corrections.

1. "Won't you stay," pleaded Wynnie, "there will be refreshments and music later."
2. "Why, Jason," said Irv, "you play the drums like an expert!"
3. The girls asked if we needed help finding our campsite.
4. "Elise, do you know who said a chicken in every pot" asked the teacher.
5. "What a wonderful day for a picnic!" exclaimed Susan.
6. Dear me whispered Connie doesn't this speaker know when to say In conclusion. . .
7. When President Lincoln heard of the South's defeat, he requested that the band play Dixie.
8. The latest issue of National Geographic has an article on rain forests.
9. What can have happened to Linda this time, Tina Didn't she say I'll be home long before you are ready to leave?
10. Langston Hughes's Dream Deferred is a moving poem.

WRITING APPLICATION A:
Using Dialogue in Narration

Using dialogue helps make your readers feel as though they are hearing an actual conversation. When you write narration, using dialogue that is natural and realistic can help show the personalities of your characters.

Writing Assignment

Write a one-page narrative using dialogue between two characters that reveals their personalities. After you revise what you have written, proofread it carefully. Make sure that you have used quotation marks and paragraphing correctly so that your readers will know which character is speaking. Then make a clean copy of your paper.

APOSTROPHES

The *apostrophe* has two uses: to show ownership or relationship, and to show where letters have been omitted in a contraction.

The Possessive Case

The possessive case of a noun or pronoun shows ownership or relationship.

OWNERSHIP	RELATIONSHIP
Sandra's boat	an hour's time
Mother's job	Julio's father
a book's title	person's responsibility

> ☞ **NOTE** Personal pronouns in the possessive case require no apostrophe: Is this bat *ours, yours,* or *theirs*?

24l. To form the possessive case of a singular noun, add an apostrophe and an *s*.

EXAMPLES a dog's collar
a moment's thought
one cent's worth
Charles's typewriter

Exception: A proper name ending in *s* may take only an apostrophe to form the possessive case under these conditions:

1. The name consists of two or more syllables.
2. Adding *'s* would make the name awkward to pronounce.

EXAMPLES Mr. and Mrs. Rogers' house
Marjorie Kinnan Rawlings' novels
Hercules' feats

EXERCISE 6. Supplying Apostrophes for Possessive Nouns. Number your paper 1–5. After the proper number, write the noun or nouns that are in the possessive case and supply the necessary apostrophes.

MECHANICS

EXAMPLE 1. The dogs leash is too short.
1. *dog's*

1. That trucks taillights are broken.
2. The judges were impressed with Veronicas project.
3. Last weeks meals were meatless ones.
4. Matthias dream is to have a horse like his sisters palomino.
5. Please pack your mothers books and Joans toys.

24m. To form the possessive case of a plural noun ending in *s*, add only the apostrophe.

EXAMPLES	friends' invitations	doctors' opinions
	citizens' committee	pupils' records

The few plural nouns that do not end in *s* form the possessive just as singular nouns do, by adding an apostrophe and an *s*.

EXAMPLES	men's suits	geese's noise
	mice's tracks	children's voices

> **NOTE** Do not use an apostrophe to form the *plural* of a noun. The apostrophe shows ownership or relationship, not number.

INCORRECT The new car's are sporty this year.
CORRECT The new cars are sporty this year. [plural]
CORRECT The new car's styling is sporty. [possessive]

A noun in the possessive case (shown by an apostrophe) is usually followed by a noun.

EXAMPLES	car's styling	women's group
	book's cover	Jean's friends

EXERCISE 7. Forming Plural Possessives. Number your paper 1–10. After the proper number, write the possessive for each of the following plural expressions.

EXAMPLE 1. artists paintings
1. *artists' paintings*

1. boys boots
2. women careers
3. friends comments
4. three days home
5. girls parents
6. Joneses cabin
7. men shoes
8. children games
9. cities mayors
10. oxen yokes

EXERCISE 8. Writing Singular Possessives, Plurals, and Plural Possessives. Number your paper 1–10. Divide your paper into three columns. Label the columns *Singular Possessive, Plural,* and *Plural Possessive.* In each column, write the form of the following nouns that the column label calls for.

1. stove
2. puppy
3. donkey
4. mouse
5. calf
6. potato
7. elephant
8. tooth
9. school
10. valley

Contractions

24n. Use an apostrophe to show where letters have been omitted in a contraction.

A *contraction* is a word made by combining two (or more) words to make one shorter word. An apostrophe takes the place of the letters that are omitted.

EXAMPLES **Where is** the exit?
Where's the exit?

We will have gone by then.
We'll have gone by then.

The word *not* is contracted *n't,* and is often added to a verb to form a contraction. Usually the spelling of the verb is unchanged.

is not	isn't	has not	hasn't
are not	aren't	have not	haven't
does not	doesn't	had not	hadn't
do not	don't	should not	shouldn't
was not	wasn't	would not	wouldn't
were not	weren't	could not	couldn't

MECHANICS

However, in some cases the spelling does change, as in the following contraction: *won't* for *will not.*

Contractions may also be formed with nouns or pronouns and verbs:

I am	I'm	you will	you'll
you are	you're	they are	they're
she would	she'd	Ann is	Ann's

Its and *It's*

The word *its* is a pronoun in the possessive case. It does not have an apostrophe.

The word *it's* is a contraction of *it is* or *it has* and requires an apostrophe.

EXAMPLES **Its** front tire is flat. [*Its* is a possessive pronoun.]
It's wet paint. [*It's* means *it is*.]
It's been a long time. [*It's* means *it has.*]

Whose and *Who's*

The word *whose* is a pronoun in the possessive case. It does not have an apostrophe.

The word *who's* means *who is* or *who has.* Since it is a contraction, it requires an apostrophe.

EXAMPLES **Whose** idea was it? [*Whose* is possessive.]
Who's next in line? [*Who's* means *who is.*]
Who's been in my room? [*Who's* means *who has.*]

Your and *You're*

The word *your* is a possessive pronoun. It does not have an apostrophe.

You're is a contraction of *you are.* It requires an apostrophe to show where the letter *a* is omitted.

EXAMPLES **Your** paper shows great improvement, Leon. [*Your* is a pronoun in the possessive case.]
You're going to get a better mark this term. [*You're* means *you are.*]

WRITING APPLICATION B:
Using Underlining, Quotation Marks, and Apostrophes to Make Your Writing Clear

Using underlining, quotation marks, and apostrophes correctly helps make your writing clear. Compare the following sets of sentences.

EXAMPLES Have you seen the sun today?
Have you seen the *Sun* today?

He said he cannot go with us.
He said, "He cannot go with us."

Well, take care of it right away.
We'll take care of it right away.

As you can see, the punctuation makes a great deal of difference. Always proofread your writing carefully to make sure that you have used punctuation marks correctly to make your meaning clear.

Writing Assignment

Write six sentences, using one of the following words in each sentence: *its, it's, whose, who's, your, you're.* Proofread your sentences to make sure that you have used the words correctly.

MECHANICS

Plurals

24o. Use an apostrophe and *s* to form the plurals of letters, numbers, and signs, and of words referred to as words.

EXAMPLES Doesn't he know the *ABC*'s?
Your *2*'s look like *5*'s.
Don't use *&*'s in place of *and*'s.
I hope to make all A's.

EXERCISE 9. Correcting Sentences by Adding Apostrophes. Number your paper 1–10. Rewrite the items that require apostrophes in the following sentences, and insert the apostrophes where they belong.

EXAMPLE 1. Do you know what youre doing?
1. *you're*

1. The girls didnt say when theyd be back.
2. Lets find out when the next game is.
3. Dorothy usually gets all *A*s and *B*s on her report card.
4. It isnt correct to use *&*s in your compositions.
5. Many of the scores were in the 80s and 90s.
6. They cant come with us; theyre studying.
7. Theyll meet us later, if its all right to tell them where were going.
8. Whos signed up for the talent show?
9. Dont those *2*s look like *z*s to you?
10. Your capital *L*s and *F*s are hard to tell apart.

HYPHENS

24p. Use a hyphen to divide a word at the end of a line.

Sometimes you will find that there is not enough space for a whole word at the end of the line. When this happens, you may divide the word, using a *hyphen* to indicate the division.

EXAMPLES How long has the building been under construction?
If you want to know, look it up in the almanac.

Be careful to divide words only between syllables. For the rules on dividing words, see page 42.

24q. Use a hyphen with compound numbers from twenty-one to ninety-nine and with fractions used as adjectives.

EXAMPLES There were twenty-one ducks in that flock.

A two-thirds majority will decide the issue, and the other one third will have to abide by the decision.

In the first use, *two-thirds* is a compound adjective modifying *majority;* in the second use, *third* is a noun modified by the single adjective *one.*

EXERCISE 10. Hyphenating Numbers and Fractions. Number your paper 1–5. After the proper number, write the words from the following expressions that require hyphens. Supply hyphens. If an expression is correct, write *C.*

1. a three fourths majority
2. one half of the money
3. one hundred twenty five contestants
4. Twenty third Street
5. forty eight decorated eggs

REVIEW EXERCISE B. Forming Contractions. Number your paper 1–20. Form contractions from the following groups of words.

1. will not	6. are not	11. you are	16. I am
2. there is	7. it is	12. does not	17. had not
3. who will	8. should not	13. he would	18. she is
4. they are	9. let us	14. has not	19. you will
5. who is	10. can not	15. we are	20. could not

MECHANICS

REVIEW EXERCISE C. Inserting Apostrophes and Hyphens. Number your paper 1–10. After the proper number, write the words in the following sentences that require apostrophes or hyphens. Supply the apostrophes and hyphens.

1. Theres where they live.
2. Wholl volunteer to participate in next weeks campaign?
3. The Lockwood sisters golden retriever is named Storm.
4. One third of Hollys allowance goes into the bank.

5. From Fifty third Street down to Forty fifth, there are ninety seven businesses.
6. Twenty six student council members voted to change the school song that theyd selected.
7. Shelly signed up for the writing class because shed heard how helpful it was.
8. If two thirds of the class has a score below seventy five, well all have to retake the test.
9. Lets see whats happening at the park today.
10. Ninety seven years ago my great-grandparents left Scotland for the United States.

REVIEW EXERCISE D. Correcting Sentences by Adding Punctuation. Rewrite the following sentences, supplying the needed punctuation marks, including quotation marks.

1. Ill see you at the sale tomorrow at Sport World said Vera Its on the corner of Thirty ninth and Vine.
2. Today's Geneva Gazeteer has a story about the fire at the Pattersons home; its roof was destroyed.
3. Belinda, Bill, Don, and Vickie have each read at least twenty one books since last years book fair.
4. I cant imagine remarked Judy a more terrifying short story than The Most Dangerous Game.
5. Seventy three percent of the legislators voted to extend the school day.
6. Lisa reported that one third of the students interviewed said they usually had no homework, while a two thirds majority said that they had too much.
7. Although I offered to help with the cleanup, Renee explained, Brian said that he could manage alone.
8. Augusta Savages Lift Every Voice and Sing is the sculpture Id most like to see for myself.
9. Larues eyes twinkled as he replied Why, Ive no idea what youre talking about nobodys planning a party.
10. Shell ride to todays meeting with us.

CHAPTER 24 REVIEW: POSTTEST

A. Proofreading Sentences for the Correct Use of Apostrophes and Hyphens. Number your paper 1–10. Each of the following sentences contains one or two errors in the use of apostrophes or hyphens. After the proper number, write each sentence correctly. Some words will require respelling.

EXAMPLE 1. Our ad appeared in todays paper, but our phone number wasnt included.
1. *Our ad appeared in today's paper, but our phone number wasn't included.*

1. The dog's havent been fed yet.
2. Its a two thirds mixture.
3. The decoration committees purchases included crepe paper, confetti, and seventy two balloons.
4. The car wouldn't start; its battery was dead.
5. Alinas sister looked at all the greeting cards and finally took the one shed selected to the cashier.
6. You're tour of Chicago should include a drive along Lake Michigan to see the citys skyline.
7. This work cant wait any longer; well have to do it now.
8. There was a big party at the Rogers house when Mr. Rogers was forty seven years old.
9. My great-grandfather often tells us to mind our *p*s and *q*s.
10. My aunt, who's job takes her all over the world, sends me postcards from the places she visits.

MECHANICS

B. Proofreading Sentences for the Correct Use of Quotation Marks and Underlining (Italics). Number your paper 11–20. Each of the following sentences requires underlining (italics), quotation marks, or both. After the proper number, write each sentence correctly.

EXAMPLE 1. Ted, can you answer the first question? Ms. Simmons asked.
1. *"Ted, can you answer the first question?" Ms. Simmons asked.*

11. The best chapter in our vocabulary book is the last one, More Word Games.
12. "I answered all the questions, Todd said, but I think that some of my answers were wrong."
13. There is a legend that the band on the Titanic played the hymn Nearer My God to Thee as the ship sank into the icy sea.
14. Mr. Washington asked Connie, "Which flag included the slogan Don't Tread on Me?"
15. Star Wars was more exciting on the big movie screen than it was on our small television set.
16. Play the Gene Autry tape again, Mom, Jonathan said, grinning at his mother.
17. Wendy wrote an article called Students, Where Are You? for our local newspaper, the Morning Beacon.
18. In the short story The Tell-Tale Heart, Edgar Allan Poe explores the theme of guilt.
19. "Can I read Treasure Island for my book report? Carmine asked.
20. Every Christmas Eve my uncle recites The Night Before Christmas for the children in the hospital.

CHAPTER 25

Spelling

IMPROVING YOUR SPELLING

English is a language that is not consistent in its representation of sounds. For this reason, learning to spell in English is a challenging task. You have learned to spell many thousands of words, but there are probably others that give you trouble. You can improve your ability to spell provided you approach the task slowly and easily—and provided you have the will and patience to learn.

MECHANICS

GOOD SPELLING HABITS

1. *Keep a list of your own errors.* As your ability to spell improves, you will notice that some words seem to be especially difficult for you. But don't be discouraged; make your own spelling book. The best way to master words that you find troublesome is to list them and review them frequently.

2. *Use the dictionary as a spelling aid.* Develop the habit of consulting a dictionary whenever you have a spelling problem.

3. *Spell by syllables.* If you have trouble spelling long words, break them up into syllables. A syllable is a part of a word that can be pronounced by itself. The word *remember* has three syllables: *re·mem·ber.* A long word then becomes a group of short parts, and you can learn it syllable by syllable.

4. *Avoid mispronunciations that lead to spelling errors.* If you listen and speak carefully, you will be less likely to misspell words because you are not pronouncing them correctly. Be sure that you are saying *chimney*, not *chimbly; library*, not *liberry; modern*, not *modren.*

5. *Proofread your papers to avoid careless spelling errors.* Half the trouble in spelling comes from careless haste. Whenever you do any writing, proofread your paper for errors in the spelling not only of difficult words but also of the ordinary, easy words that you may have misspelled through carelessness.

SPELLING RULES

The following rules are helpful, even though there are exceptions to them. If you learn them thoroughly, you will find it easier to spell correctly.

ie and *ei*

25a. Except after *c*, write *ie* when the sound is long *e*.

EXAMPLES bel**ie**ve, rel**ie**f, f**ie**ld, dec**ei**ve, c**ei**ling
EXCEPTIONS n**ei**ther, l**ei**sure, s**ei**ze, w**ei**rd

Write *ei* when the sound is not long *e,* especially when the sound is long *a.*

EXAMPLES r**ei**gn, w**ei**ght, **ei**ght, fr**ei**ght, h**ei**ght, sl**ei**ght
EXCEPTIONS fr**ie**nd, misch**ie**f

EXERCISE 1. Writing Words with *ie* and *ei*. Write the following words, supplying the missing letters (*e* and *i*) in the correct order. Be able to explain how the rules apply to each word.

1. fr...nd
2. p...ce
3. rec...ve
4. w...ght
5. bel...ve
6. c...ling
7. br...f
8. h...ght
9. n...ghbor
10. fr...ght

-cede, -ceed, -sede

25b. Only one word in English ends in *-sede—supersede;* only three words end in *-ceed—exceed, proceed,* and *succeed;* all other words of similar sound end in *-cede.*

EXAMPLES con**cede,** re**cede,** pre**cede**

EXERCISE 2. Writing Words with *-ceed, -cede,* and *-sede.* Write the following words, supplying *-ceed, -cede,* or *-sede.*

1. pre...
2. pro...
3. con...
4. super...
5. ex...

Adding Prefixes

A prefix is one or more letters added to the beginning of a word to change its meaning.

EXAMPLES un + able = **un**able
pre + arrange = **pre**arrange

25c. When a prefix is added to a word, the spelling of the word itself remains the same.

EXAMPLES il + logical = **il**logical
in + elegant = **in**elegant
un + selfish = **un**selfish
mis + apply = **mis**apply
over + see = **over**see

EXERCISE 3. Writing Words with Prefixes. Number your paper 1–10. Write correctly the words formed.

1. im + migrant
2. mis + inform
3. re + enter
4. over + rule
5. un + natural
6. dis + similar
7. il + legible
8. semi + annual
9. in + numerable
10. un + necessary

Adding Suffixes

A suffix is one or more letters added to the end of a word to change its meaning.

EXAMPLES care + less = care**less**
walk + ed = walk**ed**
comfort + able = comfort**able**

25d. When the suffixes *-ness* and *-ly* are added to a word, the spelling of the word itself is not changed.

EXAMPLES mean + ness = mean**ness**
casual + ly = casual**ly**

EXCEPTIONS Words ending in *y* usually change the *y* to *i* before *-ness* and *-ly:* misty—mist**iness;** happy—happ**ily.** One-syllable adjectives ending in *y* generally follow rule 25d: shy—shy**ly.**

25e. Drop the final *e* before a suffix beginning with a vowel.

EXAMPLES line + ing = lin**ing**
approve + al = approv**al**
desire + able = desir**able**

EXCEPTIONS In some words, the final *e* must be kept to retain the soft sound of a *c* or *g:* notice + able = notic**eable;** courage + ous = courag**eous.**

25f. Keep the final *e* before a suffix beginning with a consonant.

EXAMPLES hope + less = hope**less**
care + ful = care**ful**

EXCEPTIONS true + ly = tru**ly**
argue + ment = argu**ment**
judge + ment = judg**ment**

EXERCISE 4. Writing Words with Suffixes. Number your paper 1–10. Write correctly the words formed.

1. final + ly
2. love + able
3. true + ly
4. one + ness
5. outrage + ous
6. pretty + ly
7. advantage + ous
8. change + able
9. please + ing
10. hope + ful

25g. With words ending in *y* preceded by a consonant, change the *y* to *i* before any suffix not beginning with *i*.

EXAMPLES cry + ed = cr**ied**
lovely + ness = lovel**iness**
but cry + ing = cr**ying**

Note that words ending in *y* preceded by a vowel generally do not change their spelling when a suffix is added.

EXAMPLES pray + ing = pray**ing**
pay + ment = pay**ment**
boy + hood = boy**hood**

25h. With words of one syllable ending in a single consonant preceded by a single vowel, double the consonant before adding *-ing, -ed,* or *-er*.

EXAMPLES sit + ing = si**tt**ing
swim + ing = swi**mm**ing
drop + ed = dro**pp**ed

MECHANICS

25i. With words of more than one syllable ending in a single consonant preceded by a single vowel, double the consonant before adding *-ing, -ed,* or *-er* if the word is accented on the last syllable.

EXAMPLES occur′+ ed = occu**rr**ed
begin′+ er = begi**nn**er
permit′+ ing = permi**tt**ing

If the word is *not* accented on the last syllable, the final consonant is not doubled before a suffix.

EXAMPLES trav′el + er = trave**l**er
can′cel + ed = cance**l**ed

EXERCISE 5. Writing Words with Suffixes. Number your paper 1–10. Write correctly the words formed.

1. study + ed
2. hurry + ing
3. quiz + ing
4. fit + ed
5. cry + ed
6. deploy + ing
7. prefer + ed
8. plan + ed
9. admit + ing
10. run + er

THE PLURAL OF NOUNS

Plurals are formed in several ways, most of them covered by rules. To learn irregular plurals, you should enter them in your private spelling list and memorize them.

25j. Observe the rules for spelling the plural of nouns.

(1) The regular way to form the plural of a noun is to add an *-s*.

EXAMPLES desk, desks
idea, ideas

(2) The plural of some nouns ending in *s, x, z, ch,* or *sh* is formed by adding *-es*.

EXAMPLES pass, passes
fox, foxes
buzz, buzzes
clutch, clutches
dish, dishes

EXERCISE 6. Writing the Plurals of Nouns. Number your paper 1–10. Write the plurals of the following words:

1. wish
2. pilot
3. machine
4. match
5. automobile
6. porch
7. dance
8. mechanic
9. reflex
10. box

(3) The plural of nouns ending in *y* preceded by a consonant is formed by changing the *y* to *i* and adding *-es*.

EXAMPLES army, armi**es** city, citi**es**
country, countri**es** pony, poni**es**

(4) The plural of nouns ending in *y* preceded by a vowel is formed by adding -*s*.

EXAMPLES journey, journeys
key, keys

(5) The plural of most nouns ending in *f* is formed by adding -*s*. Some nouns ending in *f* or *fe,* however, form plurals by changing the *f* to *v* and adding -*s* or -*es*.

EXAMPLES grief, griefs shelf, shel**ves**
belief, beliefs knife, kni**ves**

(6) The plural of nouns ending in *o* preceded by a vowel is formed by adding -*s;* the plural of nouns ending in *o* preceded by a consonant is formed by adding -*es*.

EXAMPLES *o* following a vowel:
radio, radios patio, patios
o following a consonant:
tomato, tomato**es** echo, echo**es**

EXCEPTIONS Eskimos, silos, pianos, sopranos, altos

Note that many nouns ending in *o* that pertain to music are exceptions to this rule.

(7) The plural of a few nouns is formed in irregular ways.

EXAMPLES child, child**ren** goose, g**ee**se
ox, ox**en** foot, f**ee**t
woman, wom**e**n mouse, m**ice**
tooth, t**ee**th

EXERCISE 7. Writing the Plurals of Nouns. Number your paper 1–10. Write the plurals of the following nouns:

MECHANICS

1. chimney
2. company
3. valley
4. library
5. leaf
6. roof
7. volcano
8. child
9. tooth
10. woman

(8) The plural of compound nouns consisting of a noun plus a modifier is formed by making the noun plural.

EXAMPLES passer-by, passers-by
maid of honor, maids of honor
brother-in-law, brothers-in-law
editor in chief, editors in chief

(9) The plural of a few compound nouns is formed in irregular ways.

EXAMPLES drive-in, drive-ins
fourteen-year-old, fourteen-year-olds

(10) Some nouns are the same in the singular and plural.

EXAMPLES trout, salmon, sheep, Sioux, deer, moose

(11) The plural of numbers, letters, signs, and words considered as words is formed by adding an apostrophe and *s*.

EXAMPLES	1900	1900's	+	+'s
	ABC	ABC's	*and*	*and*'s

EXERCISE 8. Writing the Plurals of Nouns. Number your paper 1–10. Write the plurals of the following nouns:

1. sheep
2. weekend
3. trout
4. daughter-in-law
5. *a*
6. teen-ager
7. guard of honor
8. deer
9. cupful
10. 1800

MECHANICS

WORDS OFTEN CONFUSED

The words grouped together in the following lists are frequently confused with each other. Some of the words are *homonyms*—that is, their pronunciation is the same but their meanings and spellings are different. Others have the same or similar spellings. Study them carefully, and learn to distinguish both their meanings and their spellings.

---

accept *to receive with consent; to give approval to*
Many of his contemporaries did not *accept* Copernicus' theory that the earth moves around the sun.

except *[verb] leave out from a number; [prep.] with the exclusion of; but*
We were *excepted* from the assignment.
Everyone will be there *except* Mark.

---

advice *a recommendation about a course of action*
Good *advice* may be easy to give but hard to follow.

advise *to recommend a course of action; to give advice*
I *advise* you to continue your music lessons if you possibly can.

---

affect *to influence; to produce an effect upon*
The explosion of Krakatoa *affected* the sunsets all over the world.

effect *the result of an action; consequence*
It has long been observed that the phases of the moon have an *effect* on the tides of the oceans.

---

all right *everything is right* or *satisfactory* [This must be written as two words. The spelling *alright* is never correct.]
Maria did *all right* in the track meet.
Was my answer *all right?*

all ready *all prepared* or *in readiness*
The players are *all ready* for the big game.

already *previously*
Our class has *already* taken two field trips.

EXERCISE 9. Selecting Spelling Words to Complete Sentences. Number your paper 1–10. After the proper number, write the word given in the parentheses that makes the sentence correct.

1. Everyone likes to give (advice, advise).
2. The (affect, effect) of the victory was startling.
3. Why did you (accept, except) Carla from the class rule?
4. The scientists were (all ready, already) to watch the launching of the rocket.
5. The coach (advices, advises) us to stick to the training rules.
6. Her weeks of practice finally (affected, effected) her game.
7. Most of the rebels were offered a pardon and (accepted, excepted) it, but the leaders were (accepted, excepted) from the offer.
8. Juan has (all ready, already) learned how to water-ski.
9. Do you think my work is (all right, alright)?
10. Whose (advice, advise) are you going to take?

altar *a table for a religious ceremony*
The *altar* was banked with lilies.

alter *to change*
The outcome of the election *altered* the mayor's plan.

all together *everyone in the same place*
The director called us *all together* for rehearsal.

altogether *entirely*
Your story is *altogether* too late for this issue.

---

brake *a device to stop a machine*
Can you fix the *brake* on my bicycle?

break *to fracture, to shatter*
The winner will be the one who *breaks* the tape.

---

capital *a city; the seat of a government*
Olympia is the *capital* of Washington.

capitol *building; statehouse*
Where is the *capitol* in Albany?

---

choose [present tense, rhymes with *lose*] *to select*
Will you *choose* speech or civics as your elective next year?

chose [past tense, rhymes with *grows*] *selected*
Janet *chose* to play in the band rather than in the orchestra.

EXERCISE 10. Selecting Spelling Words to Complete Sentences. Number your paper 1–10. After the proper number, write the word given in parentheses that makes the sentence correct.

1. The building with the dome is the (capital, capitol).
2. By working (all together, altogether) we can do the job easily.
3. Because she loved dramatics, Alice (choose, chose) a difficult part in the school play.
4. Be careful not to (brake, break) those dishes.
5. That book is (all together, altogether) too complicated for you to enjoy.
6. The candles on the (altar, alter) glowed beautifully.
7. We don't know whether to (choose, chose) band or chorus.
8. A car without a good emergency (brake, break) is a menace.
9. Will Joan's accident (altar, alter) her plans?
10. Tallahassee is the (capital, capitol) of Florida.

clothes	*wearing apparel* One can learn a lot about a historical period by studying its fashions in *clothes.*
cloths	*pieces of fabric* You'll find some cleaning *cloths* in the bottom desk drawer.
coarse	*rough, crude* The beach is covered with *coarse* brown sand.
course	*path of action; planned program or route* [also used in the expression *of course*] The wind blew the ship slightly off its *course.*
consul	*a representative of a government in a foreign country* Who is the American *consul* in Nigeria?
council	*a group of people who meet together*
councilor	*a member of a council* The king called a meeting of the *council* and informed the *councilors* that the royal treasury was nearly empty.
counsel	*advice; to give words of advice* When choosing a career, seek *counsel* from your teacher.
counselor	*one who advises* Who is your guidance *counselor*?
desert [des′ ert]	*a dry, sandy region* The Sahara is the largest *desert* in Africa.
desert [de sert′]	*to abandon; to leave* Most dogs will not *desert* a friend in trouble.
dessert [des sert′]	*the final course of a meal* Fruit salad is my favorite *dessert.*

EXERCISE 11. Selecting Spelling Words to Complete Sentences. Number your paper 1–10. After the proper number, write the word or words given in the parentheses that will make the sentence correct.

1. Each class has four representatives on the student (council, counsel).
2. The guide threatened to (desert, dessert) us as we crossed the (desert, dessert).
3. Most young people are interested in (clothes, cloths).
4. Your guidance (councilor, counselor) can help you.
5. The (coarse, course) for the cross-country race is rugged.
6. The cleaning (clothes, cloths) must be washed often.
7. Do we have a Canadian (consul, council) in this city?
8. (Coarse, Course) gravel lines the driveway of our house.
9. The meal didn't seem complete without (desert, dessert).
10. The members of the losing team looked to their coach for (council, counsel).

---

formally *with dignity; following strict rules or procedures*
The Governor delivered the speech *formally.*

formerly *previously; in the past*
Formerly, I knew the Zubalsky family very well.

---

hear *to perceive sounds by ear*
Dogs can *hear* some sounds that are inaudible to people.

here *in this place*
The campsite is right *here.*

---

its possessive [of the pronoun *it*]
Mount Fuji is noted for *its* beauty.

it's [a contraction of *it is* or *it has*]
It's an extinct volcano.
It's been a long time.

---

lead [lēd] — [present tense] *to go first, to be a leader*
A small town in New Hampshire often *leads* the nation in filing its election returns.

lead [lĕd] — *a heavy metal*
A *lead* pencil actually has no *lead* in it.

led — [past tense] *went first*
The Governor *led* the slate with an impressive majority.

loose — [rhymes with *noose*] *not securely attached; not fitting tightly*
If a tourniquet is too *loose,* it will not serve its purpose.

lose — [pronounced looz] *to suffer loss*
Vegetables *lose* some of their vitamins when they are cooked.

EXERCISE 12. Selecting Spelling Words to Complete Sentences. Number your paper 1–10. After the proper number, write the word or words given in parentheses that will make the sentence correct.

1. (Its, It's) a long way from (hear, here) to the park.
2. The plumber is removing the (lead, led) pipes and putting in brass ones.
3. We don't want to (loose, lose) you in the crowd.
4. Before the club takes up new business, the secretary (formally, formerly) reads the minutes of the previous meeting.
5. (Its, It's) too bad that the tree has lost (its, it's) leaves.
6. Do you (hear, here) me, Ann? Come (hear, here) now!
7. The Yankees were ten runs behind, and it seemed certain that they were going to (loose, lose).
8. The marshal (lead, led) the class into the chapel.
9. Had Pepita ever done any running (formally, formerly)?
10. That (loose, lose) bolt can cause trouble.

---

passed [past tense of *pass*] *went by*
Our airplane *passed* over the Grand Canyon.

past *that which has gone by; beyond*
Some people live in the *past.*
They moved *past* the dozing sentry.

---

peace *security and quiet order*
We are striving for *peace* and prosperity.

piece *a part of something*
Some people can catch fish with a pole, a *piece* of string, and a bent pin.

---

plain *simple, common, unadorned; a flat area of land*
A *plain* jackknife is often as useful as one with several blades.
What is the difference between a prairie and a *plain*?

plane *a tool; an airplane; a flat surface*
The *plane* is useful in the carpenter's trade.
Four single-engine *planes* are in the hangar.
Rhoda says she likes *plane* geometry.

MECHANICS

principal *the head of a school; main or most important*
The *principal* is the chief officer of a school.
What are the *principal* exports of Brazil?

principle *a rule of conduct; a main fact or law*
She listed some of the *principles* of economics.

---

quiet *still and peaceful; without noise*
A *quiet* room is needed for concentrated study and reflection.

quite *wholly or entirely; to a great extent*
Winters in New England can be *quite* severe.

EXERCISE 13. Selecting Spelling Words to Complete Sentences. Number your paper 1–10. After the proper number, write the word or words given in parentheses that make the sentence correct.

1. A bright smile often makes a (plain, plane) face attractive.
2. The summer was (quiet, quite) over before the beginning of school brought a (quiet, quite) household once more.
3. This is an important (principal, principle) in mathematics.
4. On July 20, 1963, the moon (passed, past) between the earth and the sun, causing a total eclipse.
5. A (plain, plane) is a useful tool.
6. Save me a (peace, piece) of that blueberry pie.
7. Our (principal, principle) is leaving the school this year.
8. We should try to learn from (passed, past) experience.
9. The nation was working hard to attain (peace, piece).
10. Cattle were grazing over the (plain, plane).

---

shone [past tense of *shine*] *gleamed, glowed*
They polished the silver until it *shone.*

shown [past participle of *show*] *revealed*
The statue will be *shown* to the public.

---

stationary *in a fixed position*
Most of the furnishings of a space capsule must be *stationary.*

stationery *writing paper*
I need a new box of *stationery.*

---

than [a conjunction used for comparisons]
The Amazon River is longer *than* the Mississippi River.

then *at that time*
If the baby is awake by four o'clock, we will leave *then.*

---

there *a place [also used to begin a sentence]*
Go *there* in the fall when the leaves are turning.
There were no objections.

their [a possessive pronoun]
Their team seems very skillful.

they're *they are*
They're taller than most of our players.

---

threw [past tense of *throw*] *hurled*
Our pitcher *threw* four balls in succession.

through [a preposition]
Have you ever seen a ship go *through* the locks of a canal?

EXERCISE 14. Selecting Spelling Words to Complete Sentences. Number your paper 1–10. After the proper number, write the word or words given in parentheses that make the sentence correct.

1. We go (there, their, they're) often, for the children can get (there, their, they're) instruction in swimming, and we can see how (their, there, they're) progressing.
2. She has more (stationary, stationery) than she'll ever use.
3. The stars (shown, shone) brilliantly.
4. The city was so much larger (then, than) I expected.
5. The desks in our art room are not (stationary, stationery).
6. We often hear the planes break (threw, through) the sound barrier.
7. Sue will have the first ride; (than, then) it will be your turn.
8. The goal posts on the football field have been made (stationary, stationery).
9. We were (shone, shown) all the points of interest in the downtown area.
10. The pitcher (threw, through) a wild ball that hit the batter.

to [a preposition, also used with the infinitive of a verb]
A visit *to* Chinatown is an exciting treat.
Many small nations throughout the world are eager *to* be independent.

too *also; more than enough*
We have lived in Iowa and in Alaska, *too.*
It is *too* cold for rain today.

two *one plus one*
Americans can visit *two* foreign countries without leaving the continent.

---

weak *not strong; feeble*
My mother likes to drink *weak* tea.

week *seven days*
Your pictures will be ready in about a *week.*

---

weather *condition of the air or atmosphere*
Weather prediction is an important branch of meteorology.

whether [a conjunction] *if*
Jane Gordon is wondering *whether* the bond issue for the new school will be approved.

---

whose [a possessive]
Whose report are we hearing today?

who's *who is* or *who has*
Who's read today's newspaper?
Who's representing the yearbook staff?

---

your [a possessive]
Your work in math is improving.

you're *you are*
You're right on time!

EXERCISE 15. Selecting Spelling Words to Complete Sentences. Number your paper 1–10. After the proper number, write the word or words given in parentheses that make the sentence correct.

1. Lack of exercise made the runner's legs (weak, week).
2. (Weather, Whether) we'll go or not depends on the (weather, whether).
3. (Whose, Who's) books are you carrying?
4. Find out (whose, who's) going if you can.
5. Allen thought algebra was (to, too, two) difficult for him (to, too, two) master.
6. (Your, You're) a long distance off your course, captain.
7. We took (to, too, two) (weaks, weeks) for our trip.
8. The (weather, whether) was cloudy in Orlando, Florida.
9. Would you enjoy a trip (to, too, two) Mars, Flo?
10. Aren't you using (your, you're) compass?

50 Spelling Demons

ache
again
always
answer
blue
built
busy
buy
can't
color

cough
could
country

doctor
does
don't
early
easy
every
friend

guess
half
hour
instead
knew
know

laid
meant
minute
often

once
ready
said
says
shoes
since
straight
sugar
sure

tear

though
through
tired
tonight
trouble
wear
where
which
whole
women

250 Spelling Words

In studying the following list, pay particular attention to the letters in italics.

aband*o*n
absolut*e*ly
a*c*cept*a*nce
accident*a*lly
a*c*co*mm*odate
a*c*company
a*c*complish
ach*ie*ve
a*c*quaintance
a*c*quire

ac*t*u*a*lly
adverti*se*ment
ag*ai*nst
*a*isl*e*
a*m*o*u*nt
anal*y*sis
anti*ci*pate
an*xie*ty
apol*o*gy
a*pp*ar*e*nt

a*pp*ear*a*nce
a*pp*lication
a*pp*re*ci*ation
a*pp*roach
arg*u*ing
arg*u*ment
artic*le*
assist*a*nce
a*u*thority
bas*i*s

begi*nn*ing
bel*ie*ve
ben*e*fit
bound*ar*y
bo*uquet*

bull*e*tin
bus*i*ness
cance*l*ed
capa*c*ity
car*e*less

carr*i*er
c*ei*ling
chall*e*nge
choi*ce*
c*h*oir
c*h*orus
circ*ui*t
co*lo*nel
colu*mn*
co*m*ing

commer*ci*al
co*mm*i*tt*e*e*s
comp*e*tition
complet*e*ly
conc*ei*ve
conde*mn*
congra*t*ulations
con*scie*nce
con*scio*us
contro*l*

conven*ie*nce
c*o*urt*e*ous
crit*i*cism
c*y*linder
de*a*lt
dec*ei*t
decis*i*on
def*i*n*i*te
def*i*nition
d*e*scribe

d*e*scription
desi*ra*ble
d*e*spair
develo*p*
dif*fi*culties
disa*pp*ointment
dis*ci*pline
d*i*scussion
dis*ea*sed
distin*c*tion

distr*i*bution
doctrin*e*
dupl*icate*
ec*o*nomic
el*igi*ble
emba*rrass*
engin*ee*ring
enthu*s*ia*sm*
equi*pp*ed
eventu*al*ly

exa*c*tly
e*x*a*gg*erate
exc*ell*ent
exist*e*nce
exp*e*r*ie*nce
exper*i*ment
expl*a*nation
fas*c*inating
favor*ite*
Feb*r*uary

fin*a*lly
fl*u*
f*o*rty
f*ou*rth
friendl*i*ness

gener*al*ly
govern*o*r
gramm*a*r
gra*ti*tude
gu*a*r*a*nt*ee*

gu*a*rdi*a*n
g*y*mnasium
hatr*e*d
h*eigh*t
heroin*e*
hes*i*tate
hum*o*r*ous*
h*y*pocrit*e*
ignor*a*nce
i*m*agi*n*ation

i*mm*edi*a*tely
incident*al*ly
ind*i*vi*du*al
inf*e*rior
ini*ti*al
insp*i*ration
intell*i*gence
interf*ere*
inte*rr*upt
*i*nvolve

judg*m*ent
knowle*dge*
lab*o*ratory
l*ei*sure
lengthen
l*ieu*tenant
lone*li*ness
lunch*e*on
major*i*ty
manufac*t*ure

marr*i*age
me*ch*ani*c*al
med*ie*val
mil*i*tary
m*ou*rn
mult*i*pl*i*cation
muscul*ar*
m*y*st*e*ry
natur*al*ly
ne*cess*ary

nick*el*
nonsen*se*
n*ui*sance
numer*ous*
o*b*vious
occ*as*ion*ally*
occ*urre*nce
*o*pinion
opp*o*rtunity
or*ch*estra

origin*al*ly
pa*id*
par*allel*
parl*ia*ment
pa*ti*ence
pe*r*formance
person*al*
personal*i*ty
pers*ua*de
philoso*ph*er

picnic*k*ing
pla*nn*ed
ple*a*s*a*nt
po*ssess*
prec*ede*

prefe*rr*ed
pre*judice*
priv*ilege*
prob*a*bly
proc*e*dure

pro*f*ess*o*r
p*u*rs*ui*t
qual*i*fied
re*a*lize
rece*ipt*
recog*n*ize
rec*omm*end
re*f*e*rr*ing
reg*ula*rly
rel*ie*ve

rep*e*tition
res*ea*rch
respon*s*e
r*hy*thm
sat*i*sfied
s*au*cer
s*ch*edule
sci*ss*ors
sen*s*e
sent*i*ment

sep*arate*
ser*gea*nt
shep*he*rd
sim*ila*r
sim*ply*
sole*mn*
so*ur*ce
spon*sor*
stra*igh*ten
subscrip*t*ion

su*c*ceed
su*c*cess
suffici*e*nt
su*g*gest
s*upp*ress
su*r*pri*s*e
su*rr*ound
suspen*s*e
s*u*spicion
tail*o*r

temper*a*ment
tend*e*ncy
th*eo*ry
ther*e*for*e*

th*o*ro*ugh*
to*b*a*cc*o
ton*si*ls
tr*a*dition
trag*e*dy
transfe*rr*ed

tr*ie*s
tr*uly*
unan*i*m*ous*
u*nn*ece*ss*ary
unsat*is*factory
unti*l*
us*e*fu*l*
u*si*ng

ut*i*lized
va*cuu*m

var*iety*
vari*ous*
v*e*in
v*ie*w
vill*a*in
vi*o*lence
warr*a*nt
we*i*rd
*w*ho*ll*y
*w*ri*t*ing

MECHANICS

PART FOUR

RESOURCES FOR WRITING AND STUDYING

CHAPTER 26

Using the Dictionary

ARRANGEMENT OF A DICTIONARY, INFORMATION IN A DICTIONARY

Early Phoenician (late 2nd millenium B.C.)

Phoenician (8th century B.C.)

Early Greek (9th–7th centuries B.C.)

Western Greek (6th century B.C.)

Classical Greek (403 B.C.onward)

Early Etruscan (8th century B.C.)

Monumental Latin (4th century B.C.)

Classical Latin

Uncial

Half Uncial

Caroline miniscule

A good dictionary tells you what meanings a word has, how it is usually spelled and pronounced, what its history is, and, often, the kind of situations in which it is appropriate or inappropriate. Since dictionaries differ from one another in their methods of presenting information, the best guide to the use of your dictionary is the introductory section that explains the arrangement of entries, the system of showing pronunciations, and special features of that particular book. This chapter will show you how to use the general features that you will find in all dictionaries.

ARRANGEMENT

26a. Learn how to find a word in the dictionary.

The words in a dictionary are listed in alphabetical order. This does not mean simply that all words beginning with a particular letter are found in one section. It means that words having *a* as a second letter come before those that have *b* as a second letter, and so on through all the other letters in the word.

Two special problems should be kept in mind: abbreviations and entries of more than one word.

Some dictionaries explain abbreviations in a special section, but most dictionaries define them in the main part of the book. In such dictionaries, abbreviations are entered according to the letters in them, *not* according to the complete words that they stand for. The abbreviation *pt.* (meaning *pint* or *part*) comes after *psychology,* even though both words that the abbreviation can stand for would come before *psychology.* In a dictionary, the abbreviation *St.* (for *saint*) comes after *squirt* and before *stab.* A name like *St. Denis,* however, would appear under the full spelling—*saint.*

Two or more words used together as a single word (*open season, prime minister*) are treated as though they were a single word. Thus *open shop* appears after *openly.*

EXERCISE 1. Arranging Words, Phrases, and Abbreviations in Alphabetical Order. Arrange the following words, phrases, and abbreviations in alphabetical order.

watermelon	dept.	Mrs.	munificence
department	st.	departmental	munificent
curtain	curvature	curtail	water moccasin
stateside	static	mudguard	water wheel
municipal	muddy	mt.	department store

Guide Words

Guide words are printed in boldfaced type at the top of each dictionary page. The one on the left is the same as the first word defined on that page; the one on the right is the same as the last word on that page. Words that fall between guide words in the alphabet will appear on that page.

EXERCISE 2. Using Guide Words. Number your paper 1–10. Suppose that the guide words *needy* and *neither* appear on a particular dictionary page. After the proper number, make a plus sign if the corresponding word would appear on that page. Write *before* if it would appear on an earlier page and *after* if it would appear on a later page.

EXAMPLES 1. nefarious
1. +
2. navy
2. *before*

1. negative
2. needle
3. neophyte
4. ne'er-do-well
5. newcomer
6. necktie
7. negligent
8. Neanderthal
9. New Zealander
10. negotiate

FINDING THE RIGHT MEANING

26b. Learn to find the meaning you want.

Most English words have a number of different meanings. When you go to the dictionary, you are usually interested in a particular meaning of a word—one that will fit into the particular sentence or situation in which you heard or read the word. Nevertheless, it is a good idea to scan all of the meanings given. By doing so you will form a general impression of the range of meanings that word may have.

Each separate meaning of a word is explained in a numbered definition. Some dictionaries use letters within numbered definitions to distinguish between closely related meanings. To see how this works, examine the following dictionary entry for the word *offensive:*

[1]**of•fen•sive** \ə-'fen-siv\ *adj* **1 a** : of, relating to, or designed for attack ⟨*offensive* weapons⟩ **b** : being on the offense ⟨the *offensive* team⟩ **2** : giving unpleasant sensations ⟨*offensive* smells⟩ **3** : causing displeasure or resentment : INSULTING ⟨an *offensive* remark⟩ — **of•fen•sive•ly** *adv* — **of•fen•sive•ness** *n*

[2]**offensive** *n* **1** : the act of an attacking party ⟨on the *offensive*⟩ **2** : ATTACK ⟨launch an *offensive*⟩

Suppose you want to find the meaning of *offensive* in the sentence "The child was scolded for making such an offensive remark." By recognizing that the word is used as an adjective in this sentence, you can concentrate your search on the entry that gives definitions for the adjective (*adj.*) *offensive.* Definitions 1 and 2 do not fit the context, but definition 3 does. What is more, the illustrative example for 3 provides a context very similar to the one you have in mind.

Now look back at the sample entry and notice that *offensive* is listed again, this time as a noun (*n.*). This particular dictionary gives separate entries for each part of speech. The small numeral 2 before the entry word shows that it is the second entry for the same word. Other dictionaries may not list parts of speech in this way. They may have all the definitions of a word in one entry, with each part of speech in its own subgroup. The following definition, taken from a different dictionary, illustrates the latter method. Notice that the definitions for the noun subgroup, marked by *—n* for *noun*, begin with the numeral 1.

of•fen•sive |ə fĕn'sĭv| *adj.* **1.** Offending the senses; unpleasant: *an offensive smell.* **2.** Causing anger, displeasure, resentment, etc.: *offensive language.* **3.** |ô'fĕn'sĭv| *or* |ŏf'ĕn'-|. Of an attack; aggressive; attacking: *an offensive play in football.* *—n.* **1.** An aggressive action; an attack: *their third major offensive of the war.* **2.** An attitude of attack: *take the offensive.* **—of•fen'sive•ly** *adv.* **—of•fen'sive•ness** *n.*

EXERCISE 3. Finding the Correct Meaning in the Dictionary. Below are two groups of sentences, each group followed by a dictionary definition. Number your paper 1–5. After the appropriate number, write the number (3) or the number and letter

(2b) of the definition that gives the correct meaning of the word as it is used in the sentence.

1. This morning we had a *rough* exam in science.
2. Mrs. Logan made a *rough* sketch of the model.
3. Joan's coat is made of *rough* material.

[1]**rough** \'rəf\ *adj* **1 a** : having an uneven surface : not smooth **b** : covered with or made up of coarse and often shaggy hair or bristles ⟨a *rough*-coated terrier⟩ **c** : difficult to travel over or penetrate : WILD ⟨*rough* country⟩ **2 a** : characterized by harshness, violence, or force **b** : DIFFICULT, TRYING ⟨a *rough* day at the office⟩ **3** : coarse or rugged in character or appearance: as **a** : harsh to the ear **b** : crude in style or expression **c** : marked by a lack of refinement or grace : UNCOUTH **4** : marked by incompleteness or inexactness ⟨a *rough* draft⟩ ⟨*rough* estimates⟩ [Old English *rūh*] — **rough•ly** *adv* — **rough•ness** *n*

4. Astronomers will *train* their telescopes on Halley's comet.
5. Ms. McConnell *trains* every morning for the marathon race.

[2]**train** *vb* **1** : to direct the growth of (a plant) usually by bending, pruning, and tying **2 a** : to teach something (as a skill, profession, or trade) to ⟨was *trained* in the law⟩ **b** : to teach (an animal) to obey **3** : to make ready (as by exercise) for a test of skill **4** : to aim (as a gun) at a target **5** : to undergo instruction, discipline, or drill [Middle French *trainer* "to draw, drag"] **syn** see TEACH — **train•able** \'trā-nə-bəl\ *adj* — **train•ee** \trā-'nē\ *n*

CONTENT

26c. Learn what different kinds of information a dictionary gives you about words.

The typical dictionary definition contains a large amount of information. To take advantage of this information, you need to become familiar with the labels used in the dictionary. Examine the sample dictionary column on page 602. The explanations that follow correspond to the labels on this column. Consult the column as you study the notes.

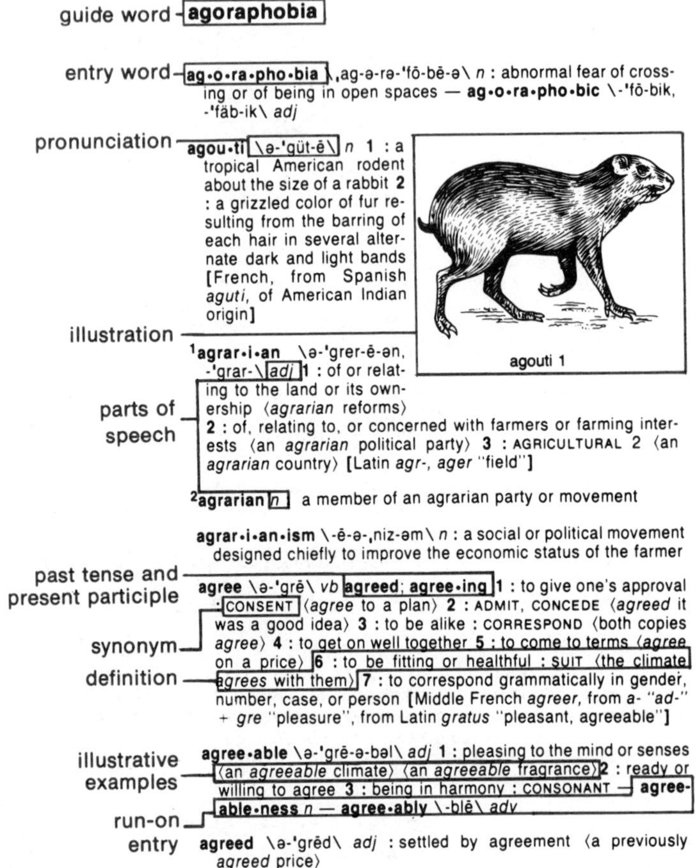

agoraphobia

ag·o·ra·pho·bia \ˌag-ə-rə-ˈfō-bē-ə\ *n* : abnormal fear of crossing or of being in open spaces — **ag·o·ra·pho·bic** \-ˈfō-bik, -ˈfäb-ik\ *adj*

agou·ti \ə-ˈgüt-ē\ *n* **1** : a tropical American rodent about the size of a rabbit **2** : a grizzled color of fur resulting from the barring of each hair in several alternate dark and light bands [French, from Spanish *aguti*, of American Indian origin]

[1]**agrar·i·an** \ə-ˈgrer-ē-ən, -ˈgrar-\ *adj* **1** : of or relating to the land or its ownership ⟨*agrarian* reforms⟩ **2** : of, relating to, or concerned with farmers or farming interests ⟨an *agrarian* political party⟩ **3** : AGRICULTURAL 2 ⟨an *agrarian* country⟩ [Latin *agr-, ager* "field"]

[2]**agrarian** *n* a member of an agrarian party or movement

agrar·i·an·ism \-ē-ə-ˌniz-əm\ *n* : a social or political movement designed chiefly to improve the economic status of the farmer

agree \ə-ˈgrē\ *vb* **agreed**; **agree·ing** **1** : to give one's approval : CONSENT ⟨*agree* to a plan⟩ **2** : ADMIT, CONCEDE ⟨*agreed* it was a good idea⟩ **3** : to be alike : CORRESPOND ⟨both copies *agree*⟩ **4** : to get on well together **5** : to come to terms ⟨*agree* on a price⟩ **6** : to be fitting or healthful : SUIT ⟨the climate *agrees* with them⟩ **7** : to correspond grammatically in gender, number, case, or person [Middle French *agreer*, from *a-* "ad-" + *gre* "pleasure", from Latin *gratus* "pleasant, agreeable"]

agree·able \ə-ˈgrē-ə-bəl\ *adj* **1** : pleasing to the mind or senses ⟨an *agreeable* climate⟩ ⟨an *agreeable* fragrance⟩ **2** : ready or willing to agree **3** : being in harmony : CONSONANT — **agree·able·ness** *n* — **agree·ably** \-blē\ *adv*

agreed \ə-ˈgrēd\ *adj* : settled by agreement ⟨a previously *agreed* price⟩

1. *Entry word.* The word to be defined is called the *entry word.* It appears in boldfaced type. You use the entry word to locate a definition, to get the correct spelling of a word, and to find out how it is divided into syllables, if it has more than one syllable. Most dictionaries also indicate words that are capitalized by beginning the entry word with a capital letter. However, capitalization may be indicated in other ways, especially in dictionaries not specially designed for high-school students. If there is more than one acceptable spelling of a word, the alternative is usually listed immediately after the entry word:

EXAMPLE **moustache** or **mustache**

In most cases the first spelling listed is the one that most people prefer to use.

2. *Illustration.* Sometimes the best way to indicate the meaning of a word is through an illustration. *Agouti* on page 602 is such a word.

3. *Pronunciation.* The pronunciation of a word is usually indicated immediately after the entry word by means of a special respelling, which is explained in detail on pages 610–11. The sounds represented by the symbols in the pronunciation respelling are explained in a key that usually appears inside the front cover of the dictionary. A shorter key may appear at the bottom of each page or of every other page. (For more about pronunciation, see pages 609–11.)

4. *Definition.* The definition gives the meaning or meanings of a word. When a word has more than one meaning, each meaning is defined separately in a numbered definition. (Some dictionaries use letters to distinguish between meanings so closely related that they are defined in a single numbered definition.)

5. *Illustrative example.* For many words, and for different meanings of the same word, sample contexts are provided to show how the word is used. Illustrative examples often provide the clues that will prevent you from making mistakes in usage.

6. *Synonyms.* Synonyms are words that have similar meanings. In the sample column on page 602, for example, *consent* is given as the synonym for *agree*. (The word *consent* is printed in block letters to indicate that it is a synonym.) Words that are synonyms can be used alike in some contexts but not in others. For example, the words *deep* and *profound* are synonyms when the subject is mystery.

7. *Run-on entry.* Many English words have companion forms that are closely related to them in meaning. Dictionaries include these words at the end of an entry as *run-on entries*. At the end of the adjective *bad,* for instance, you may find the notation "**—bad′ly** *adv.* **—bad′ness** *n.*" Although often no definitions are

given in a run-on entry, a part-of-speech label is provided for each companion form. Some dictionaries also give the pronunciation for the companion form. (For more about companion forms, see page 633.)

8. *Part of speech.* The part of speech is indicated by an italicized abbreviation:

n.	noun	*adv.*	adverb
pron.	pronoun	*prep.*	preposition
v. or *vb.*	verb[1]	*conj.*	conjunction
adj.	adjective	*interj.*	interjection

Many English words can be used as more than one part of speech. For such words, a dictionary will indicate how the definitions are related to the part-of-speech labels. In some dictionaries, all the definitions for one part of speech are grouped together after the label, as on page 602. Other dictionaries provide consecutively numbered definitions, with the part-of-speech label after each numeral. The most frequent usages are given first.

A dictionary also provides the following information:

Usage label. Not all words entered in a dictionary are equally acceptable in all situations. A usage label is a mild warning that people use a word (or use a particular meaning of a word) only in certain situations. For example, the label *slang* indicates a word that may be used in certain informal situations but is likely to call attention to itself when used in other situations. Another label, *archaic,* indicates that a word was once common but is now rarely used. A third label, *dialect,* indicates that a word is used in only one part of the country. The introduction to your dictionary explains the meaning of all the usage labels employed by your dictionary.

[1] Unabridged dictionaries and those designed for older students distinguish between verbs like *wonder* in the sentence "I wonder" and verbs that require another word to show who or what is receiving the action; for example, *hit* in "The batter hit a home run." Such dictionaries label verbs like *wonder,* in the first example, *v.i.,* and verbs like *hit,* in the second, *v.t.* The abbreviation *v.i.* stands for *intransitive verb; v.t.* stands for *transitive verb.* Transitive verbs always have to have an object—a word showing who or what was affected by the action expressed by the verb.

Origin. For some words, school dictionaries provide information about the history of a word, usually by indicating the language from which it was borrowed. Such information may appear near the beginning of the definition or at the end, as in the following example:

> **dex·ter·ous** [dek′strəs *or* dek′stər·əs] *adj.* **1** Skillful in using the hands or body; adroit: a *dexterous* billiard player. **2** Mentally quick; keen. **— dex′ter·ous·ly** *adv.* ◆ *Dexterous* comes from a Latin word meaning *skillful*, which in turn comes from a Latin root meaning *on the right* or *right-handed*.

Encyclopedia information. A small number of dictionary entries deal with people and places. There are better places, including encyclopedias, to find out about important people and places than in a dictionary—these are described in Chapter 27. However, if all you need is a general identification or location, the dictionary will usually provide it, as in the following entry:

> **Pierce** (pirs), **Franklin** 1804–69; 14th president of the U.S. (1853–57)

EXERCISE 4. Writing Synonyms of Words. Number your paper 1–5. Write a synonym for each of the following words. If necessary, use the dictionary.

1. coax
2. distinct
3. diversity
4. find
5. plain

EXERCISE 5. Understanding Usage Labels. Copy from your dictionary the usage labels for five of these words. Be prepared to explain what the labels tell you and how they would affect your use of the words.

1. afeared
2. corny
3. davenport
4. gabby
5. loco
6. lorry
7. ope
8. petrol
9. pone
10. raspberry

EXERCISE 6. Finding Run-on Entries for Specific Words. Copy from your dictionary a run-on entry for each of the following words.

1. celebrate
2. reform
3. fair
4. foolish
5. liquidate

EXERCISE 7. Writing Definitions According to Parts of Speech. Copy from your dictionary two definitions for each of the following words, each definition for a different part of speech. Following the definitions, indicate the parts of speech by using part-of-speech labels.

EXAMPLE 1. flower

1. *a. The part of a plant that normally bears the seed, n.*
   b. To blossom; to bloom, v.

1. back
2. Chinese
3. maneuver
4. net
5. tag

EXERCISE 8. Finding Information About Persons and Places in the Dictionary. Look up the following persons and places in your dictionary. Be able to tell what information the dictionary provides about them.

1. Ruth
2. Helen of Troy
3. Port Said
4. Orinoco
5. Sequoya

SPELLING

26d. Learn to use your dictionary for spelling and capitalization.

The dictionary is the authority on correct spelling. In English, the spelling of the initial sound of a word is much more regular than the spelling of sounds in the middle or at the end of words. To find how most words are spelled, simply follow the principles of alphabetical order and let the guide words help you.

Variant Spellings

A dictionary occasionally gives two spellings for a word: *abridgment* and *abridgement, coconut* and *cocoanut.* Both spellings are correct, but usually a dictionary indicates which spelling is preferred by listing it first.

EXERCISE 9. Finding Variant Spellings of Specific Words. Copy from your dictionary a variant spelling for the following words. Be able to tell whether one spelling is preferred.

1. demon
2. judgment
3. likeable
4. savior
5. sulfur

Unusual Plurals

If the plural of a noun is formed in an unusual way, a dictionary will give the plural form with the abbreviation *pl.* preceding it. For example, the plural of *datum* is given as *data.* Some dictionaries list plurals that are formed in the regular way if there is a chance that the plural will be misspelled. The plural of *valley* might be given (*valleys*) so that no one will make the mistake of ending the plural in *-ies*.

Unusual Verb Forms

If a verb forms its past tense, its past participle, or its present participle in an unusual way, a dictionary will list these irregular forms.

Comparatives and Superlatives

If the comparative and superlative forms of an adjective are spelled in an unusual way, a dictionary provides these forms either near the beginning or the end of an entry. Sometimes the abbreviations *compar.* and *superl.* are used.

love·ly [luv′lē] *adj.* **love·li·er, love·li·est** **1** Having qualities that make people love one: a *lovely* child. **2** Beautiful: a *lovely* rose. **3** *informal* Enjoyable; pleasant: to have a *lovely* time at a party. **—love′li·ness** *n.*

EXERCISE 10. Finding Unusual Spelling Forms for Specific Words. Copy from your dictionary the unusual spelling forms (if any) for the following words. After the forms, write (*1*) if they are unusual plurals, (*2*) if they are unusual verb forms, or (*3*) if they are unusual comparatives and superlatives.

EXAMPLE 1. swim
1. *swam, swum, swimming (2)*

1. choose
2. index
3. mad
4. needy
5. rise

CAPITALIZATION

If you are not sure about capitalizing a certain word, the dictionary will help you. Sometimes a word should be capitalized in one sense but not capitalized in another. In such a case, the dictionary indicates which meaning requires a capital. For example, some dictionaries print *Mass,* meaning "a religious ceremony," with a capital; but *mass,* meaning "a large amount or number," appears uncapitalized.

EXERCISE 11. Using the Dictionary for Capitalization. Look up the following words in a dictionary to see when they are capitalized. Be able to explain why they are or are not capitalized in each usage. Your dictionary may not give capitalized uses for all the words.

1. cupid
2. democrat
3. nativity
4. senate
5. west

SYLLABLE DIVISION

A dictionary divides all words into syllables. If your dictionary uses small dots or dashes between the syllables of a word, be careful not to confuse these marks with a hyphen. Look up a hyphenated word like *flip-flop* or *open-minded* to be sure you can tell the difference.

EXERCISE 12. Dividing Words into Syllables. Copy the following words, dividing them into syllables. Use the same method to indicate syllable division that your dictionary uses.

1. endurance	3. junior	5. underdog
2. flexible	4. socialize	

PRONUNCIATION

26e. Learn to use your dictionary for pronunciation.

One of the most important pieces of information given in a dictionary is the pronunciation of a word. This information usually comes immediately after the entry word and is enclosed within slant bars or within parentheses.

The Accent Mark

In words of two or more syllables, one syllable is always pronounced with greater force than the others. A dictionary indicates which syllable needs emphasis by using an *accent mark*. Most dictionaries use one of two kinds of accent marks: either the mark (ˈ) appearing before the syllable or the mark (′) placed after the syllable.

In a word of three or more syllables, a dictionary usually indicates two accent marks, one primary, the other secondary. The word *elevator* has a primary accent on the syllable *el* and a weaker accent on *vat*. Dictionaries generally show the secondary accent in one of three ways. When the mark (**′**) is used to indicate primary accent, the secondary accent is indicated by a weaker mark (′) or by two marks (″). When the primary accent (ˈ) is used, the secondary accent is a similar mark placed at the bottom of a syllable (ˌ).

EXERCISE 13. Dividing Words into Syllables and Indicating Accented Syllables. Copy the following words, dividing them into syllables, and indicate the accented syllables. Use the kinds of accent marks that are used in your dictionary.

1. detrimental
2. distribution
3. frugal
4. masquerade
5. Olympian

Pronunciation Symbols

A dictionary uses pronunciation symbols to indicate the pronunciation of a word. Most symbols are regular letters of the alphabet, but they are used more strictly than in ordinary writing. For example, the letter *c* can have several different pronunciations, as in the words *city, control,* and *cello.* A dictionary would indicate the beginning sounds of these words as *s, k,* and *ch.* To show the pronunciation of vowels, which is harder to indicate than the pronunciation of consonants, a dictionary uses *diacritical marks*—special symbols placed above the letters.

Dictionaries vary in their use of symbols. A key to these symbols usually appears inside the front cover and sometimes on each page as well.

In this chapter you will study several diacritical marks that are used by most dictionaries.

Long Vowels

To indicate a long vowel, a dictionary generally uses a diacritical mark called a *macron*—a long straight mark over the vowel. When a macron is used, the long vowel is said to have the sound of its own name.

EXAMPLES	main	/mān/
	mean	/mēn/
	mine	/mīn/
	moan	/mōn/
	immune	/imūn/

Short Vowels

The vowels in the words *mat, head, bid, dot,* and *cut* are called short vowels. Dictionaries differ in their methods of showing the sound of short vowels.

One method uses a symbol called a *breve* (pronounced *brĕv* or *brēv*) over the vowel. Another method is to leave short vowels unmarked.

EXAMPLES	mat	(măt)	or	/mat/
	head	(hĕd)	or	/hed/
	bid	(bĭd)	or	/bid/

Sometimes, when all that we pronounce in an unaccented syllable is the sound of the consonant, the pronunciation indication in certain dictionaries may omit the short vowel altogether.

The Schwa

Most recent dictionaries use an upside-down *e*, called a *schwa,* to represent the neutral vowel sound "uh." This sound occurs in the phrase *the pen* (thə pen) and in the following words:

minute (min′ ət), permit (pər mit′), police (pə lēs′).

Most dictionaries use the schwa for the "uh" sound only when it occurs in unaccented syllables, but several dictionaries also use this symbol when the sound occurs in accented syllables and in one-syllable words.

EXERCISE 14. Finding the Pronunciations of Specific Words. Copy from your dictionary the pronunciation of each of the following words. Follow the practice of your dictionary in using parentheses or slant lines to enclose the pronunciation. Be able to explain all the diacritical marks used.

1. diet
2. erase
3. bumblebee
4. matriarchy
5. nation
6. poverty
7. puny
8. revolve
9. seldom
10. sidesaddle

REVIEW EXERCISE. Understanding the Arrangement and Content of Dictionaries. Use complete sentences in writing the answers to the following questions. If necessary, look the information up in the chapter.

1. Define
   a. synonym c. guide word
   b. macron d. schwa
2. Name three kinds of information about spelling that a dictionary provides.
3. After which of the following words would *mother-in-law* occur in a dictionary?
   a. motherly c. motherhood
   b. mother d. motherland
4. What kind of information is given by the following terms: *slang, informal, archaic*?
5. List the types of information—other than spelling and pronunciation—that a dictionary entry gives about a word.

CHAPTER 27

Using the Library

ARRANGEMENT OF A LIBRARY, REFERENCE MATERIALS

The best place to look for information is a library or media center. To use a library efficiently, you must understand its system of arranging the books, magazines, pamphlets, and other materials it contains so that you can find what you want easily and quickly.

THE ARRANGEMENT OF A LIBRARY

Fiction

27a. Learn to locate books of fiction.

In most libraries all books of fiction are located in one section. The books are arranged in alphabetical order according to authors' last names. If you were looking for *The Good Earth* by Pearl S. Buck, you would go to the fiction section and find the books by authors whose last names begin with *B*. There you would find several books by Buck. Books by the same author are arranged in alphabetical order according to the first word in the title, unless that word is *a, an,* or *the.* In that case, the second word of the title is used. *The Good Earth* would then come in the *G* position.

> ☞ **NOTE** Books by authors whose names begin with *Mc* are arranged as though the name were spelled *Mac; St.* is arranged as though it were spelled out, *Saint.*

EXERCISE 1. Arranging Books of Fiction. Write the authors and titles of the following fiction books in the order in which the books would be arranged in the library.

1. *The Light in the Forest* by Conrad Richter
2. *Curtain* by Agatha Christie
3. *Jane Eyre* by Charlotte Brontë
4. *Dirt Track Summer* by William Campbell Gault
5. *Crooked House* by Agatha Christie
6. *The Incredible Journey* by Sheila Burnford
7. *The Friendly Persuasion* by Jessamyn West
8. *Wuthering Heights* by Emily Brontë
9. *The Tamarack Tree* by Betty Underwood
10. *The Martian Chronicles* by Ray Bradbury

Nonfiction

27b. Learn the Dewey decimal system of arranging nonfiction.

The Dewey decimal system is named for Melvil Dewey, the American librarian who developed it. Under this system, books are classified under ten headings, and each heading has a number. The numbers and headings are as follows:

000–099 General Works (encyclopedias, reference materials)
100–199 Philosophy
200–299 Religion
300–399 Social Sciences (economics, government, etc.)
400–499 Language
500–599 Science
600–699 Technology (engineering, aviation, inventions, etc.)
700–799 The Arts (architecture, music, sports, etc.)

800–899 Literature
900–999 History (including geography, travel, and biography)

The number given to a book is known as the book's call number. To see how the Dewey system works, take as an example Arthur Zaidenberg's *How to Draw Cartoons.* Since the book is about art, its number will be in the 700's. Within this broad category, the numbers 740–749 are used for books on drawing and decorative arts. Books on freehand drawing are given the number 741. By means of a decimal, the classification is narrowed further. The number 741.5 is given to books about drawing cartoons, and 741.5-Z is the call number for the book *How to Draw Cartoons.*

Biographies are arranged in alphabetical order according to the names of the persons written about, not according to the names of the persons who wrote the biographies. For example, *The Helen Keller Story* by Catherine Owens Peare will appear among the K's. The call number may consist of **B** (for biography) with **K** (for Keller) under it: $\frac{\mathbf{B}}{\mathbf{K}}$. Or it may consist of 92 with **K** under it: $\frac{92}{\mathbf{K}}$. Some librarians use the **B;** others use the 92, which is a short form of the Dewey number (920) for biography. Still others use 921.

EXERCISE 2. Classifying Nonfiction According to the Dewey Decimal System. Within which number range in the Dewey decimal system would you find each of the following?

EXAMPLE 1. A book on modeling in clay
1. *700-799*

1. A book about travels in Africa
2. A book about the Presidency
3. A book about baseball
4. A book about poetry
5. A collection of biographies of pioneer men and women

THE CARD CATALOG

You can find out the call number of any book in the library by looking the book up in the card catalog.

27c. Learn to use the card catalog.

The card catalog is a cabinet with small drawers that contain file cards arranged in alphabetical order for all the books in the library. For each book of fiction there are at least two cards, an *author card* and a *title card.* For each book of nonfiction, there are usually three cards, an *author card,* a *title card,* and a *subject card.* If the book is by two or more authors, there is an author card for each name.

Each card provides a different means of finding a book. If you are looking for a book by a particular author, you would look for the *author card.* If you know the title of the book but not the name of the author, you would look for the *title card.* If you need information about a particular subject (rockets and rocketry, for instance), look for a *subject card* with the word *ROCKETS* at the top.

Study the following sample cards and explanations:

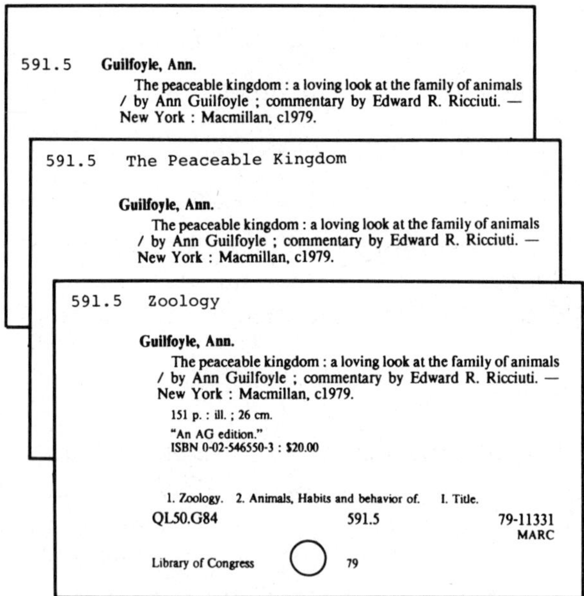

591.5 **Guilfoyle, Ann.**
The peaceable kingdom : a loving look at the family of animals / by Ann Guilfoyle ; commentary by Edward R. Ricciuti. — New York : Macmillan, c1979.

591.5 The Peaceable Kingdom

Guilfoyle, Ann.
The peaceable kingdom : a loving look at the family of animals / by Ann Guilfoyle ; commentary by Edward R. Ricciuti. — New York : Macmillan, c1979.

591.5 Zoology

Guilfoyle, Ann.
The peaceable kingdom : a loving look at the family of animals / by Ann Guilfoyle ; commentary by Edward R. Ricciuti. — New York : Macmillan, c1979.
151 p. : ill. ; 26 cm.
"An AG edition."
ISBN 0-02-546550-3 : $20.00

1. Zoology. 2. Animals, Habits and behavior of. I. Title.
QL50.G84 591.5 79-11331
MARC
Library of Congress 79

Principal Items of Information on a Card

1. *Name of author.* This information appears first on author

cards, which are filed alphabetically under the author's last name. All books by one author are then arranged in alphabetical order by titles.

2. *Call number.* This Dewey decimal number tells you where to find the book in the nonfiction section of the library.

3. *Title of book.* On title cards this information appears first. Title cards are filed alphabetically in the card catalog according to the first word of the title, not counting the words *a, an,* or *the.*

4. *Subject.* The subject of a book appears first on subject cards. Like author cards and title cards, they are arranged alphabetically in the card catalog.

5. *Publisher and date of publication.* The date of publication is an important guide if you want recent information on a subject. Always check each source's date of publication to make sure that you are using the most current edition. The place of publication is often given before the publisher's name.

6. *Number of pages.* Occasionally this fact will be useful. Obviously, a book about the history of the Supreme Court that is only seventy pages long cannot give much detailed information on the subject.

7. *"See" and "see also" references.* Sometimes a subject card has a "see" reference or a "see also" reference sending you to another card in the catalog. For example, if you looked up *Revolutionary War,* you might find a card saying, "See United States—History—Revolutionary War." If you looked up *Diving,* you might find, "See also Skin Diving."

EXERCISE 3. Using the Card Catalog. Using the card catalog, list the call number, title, author, and date of publication of one book on each of five of the following topics.

1. French Impressionist painters
2. Lasers
3. Birds of Europe
4. Baseball
5. Florence Nightingale
6. South America
7. American poets and poetry
8. Computer games
9. Japanese Americans
10. Scientists

REFERENCE BOOKS

27d. Learn to use the reference books available in the library.

The section devoted to reference books is one of the most important parts of a library. These books contain information on a great many subjects or tell where such information can be found. Once you become familiar with the reference books in your library, they will prove a valuable aid to your studies.

Encyclopedias

An encyclopedia contains articles by experts on a wide range of subjects. Many articles contain pictures, charts, maps, lists of facts, and tables of figures. An encyclopedia article will give you a good overall view of the subject and may also suggest more detailed sources of information.

You will likely find the following three encyclopedias handy for most reports:

Compton's Encyclopedia
World Book Encyclopedia
Collier's Encyclopedia

All these encyclopedias consist of many volumes and arrange their articles alphabetically by subject. The guide letter or letters on the spine of each volume will help you to find information about a particular subject. Guide words at the top of each page will help you to find a specific article. Use them as you would use guide words in a dictionary. (See page 598.) If you cannot find an article under a particular subject, look for a larger subject that includes yours. For example, information on *supersonic flight* can probably be found in an article on *aviation.*

You can also find information in an encyclopedia by using the index. Most encyclopedias have indexes, but the indexes are not always located in the same place. For example, the index of *Collier's Encyclopedia* is the last volume, while the index in *Compton's Encyclopedia* is at the end of each volume. You can use the index to locate maps, charts, tables, and illustrations, as well as articles about a particular subject. Usually there is a guide to using the index at the beginning of the index itself.

The index in the last volume of the *World Book Encyclopedia* is in somewhat different form. It is a "Reading and Study Guide," which is arranged by subjects. Each subject is divided into a series of smaller subjects for which a list of articles available in the encyclopedia is given.

EXERCISE 4. Using an Encyclopedia. Look up two of the topics below in an encyclopedia and take half a page of notes on each of them. Below each group of notes, write the title of the article, the name of the encyclopedia, the volume number, and the number of the page on which you found the information.

EXAMPLE 1. The tourist industry in Hawaii

1. *Each year, several million tourists enjoy vacations in Hawaii. They spend about 3 billion dollars. The busiest months are July, August, and December. In 1903, business people on the islands established an agency that later became the Hawaii Visitors Bureau. The bureau, with state assistance, conducts advertising campaigns to attract tourists.*
"Hawaii," World Book Encyclopedia, *volume 9, page 102*

1. Soft-coal mining in the United States
2. The paintings of Mary Cassatt
3. Famous volcanoes
4. Dinosaurs
5. The Battle of Hastings
6. The origin of bowling
7. Penguins
8. The native tribes of Australia
9. The rules and strategy of backgammon
10. The invention of the Diesel engine

Atlases

Atlases are reference books made up mainly of maps. Often they contain much other information, such as the population figures for cities, states, and countries; principal crops; natural resources; and major industries.

Some atlases contain maps for all the countries of the world. Others contain maps for a particular country only. Historical atlases show how countries have changed through the years, while economic atlases show such things as trade routes and natural resources. Some of the common atlases are

The Encyclopaedia Britannica Atlas
Hammond Contemporary World Atlas
National Geographic World Atlas
Rand McNally Popular World Atlas

Atlases will prove valuable in your history and geography courses. You should learn about the different kinds of information that atlases provide and become thoroughly familiar with at least one atlas.

EXERCISE 5. Using a World Atlas. Consult a world atlas and write answers to two of the following questions.

1. Name three national parks in California.
2. List the countries that border on each of the following:
   a. Switzerland b. Venezuela c. Turkey
3. List four major products of each of the following:
   a. Bolivia b. Ethiopia c. Pakistan d. Iraq
4. In which country is each of the following cities situated?
   a. Volgograd b. Riyadh c. Jena d. Sapporo
5. List the following states in order of population, beginning with the most populous:
   a. Illinois b. Virginia c. Maine d. Florida

Almanacs

An almanac contains lists of miscellaneous information, including sports statistics, names of government officials, population figures, and birth and death rates. In addition, an almanac is a good source of recent information since almanacs are published annually. For instance, if you want a review of the important events of last year, you should consult this year's almanac.

Three useful almanacs are *The World Almanac and Book of Facts, Information Please Almanac,* and *The CBS News Almanac.* The various kinds of information in an almanac are not always organized alphabetically or even systematically. The best way to find information in an almanac is to use the index.

EXERCISE 6. Using an Almanac. Consult one of the almanacs mentioned above and answer two of the following questions:

1. Give the birth dates and birthplaces of the following persons (look up "Personalities, noted" or "Celebrated persons"):
   a. Eudora Welty
   b. Stephen Spielberg
   c. Chris Evert Lloyd
   d. Robert Redford
   e. Jesse Jackson
2. Give the names of the Secretaries of State during the administration of the following Presidents:
   a. John Quincy Adams
   b. William Harrison
   c. Abraham Lincoln
   d. William Taft
   e. Warren Harding
3. Who won the Nobel Prize for physics in 1923? 1938? 1946? 1970? 1976?
4. Give the name of the author and title of the novel that won the Pulitzer Prize for fiction in each of the following years: 1926, 1928, 1947, 1955, 1959, 1980.

Biographical Reference Books

A biographical reference book contains short biographies of famous persons. The following are among the most useful:

Who's Who and *Who's Who in America*—useful for principal biographical facts about living persons only.

Webster's Biographical Dictionary—very short biographies of famous persons, modern and historical.

Contemporary Authors and *Contemporary Authors: First Revision*—interesting profiles of modern writers.

Current Biography—lives of persons currently prominent in the news. Published monthly.

The *Readers' Guide*

27e. To find a magazine article, use the *Readers' Guide.*

To find a magazine article on any subject, you use a reference book called the *Readers' Guide to Periodical Literature.* Published eighteen times a year, the *Readers' Guide* indexes articles in more than one hundred magazines. Every year the issues are collected and published in a large volume. You can look up an article by its subject or by its author. To save space, the listings use the abbreviations listed in the keys in the front of the *Readers' Guide.*

Suppose you are writing an article about ancient Egypt and wish to include some information about King Tut's tomb. You could begin by looking up the subject *Tutenkhamun.* Scanning the listings under *Tutenkhamun,* you would come to the subdivision *Tomb.*

author entry — **TUSHINSKY, Joseph S.**
Funny thing happened on the way to the office. il por Forbes 122:33-4 D 11 '78 •
title of article — Superscope: can a new product overcome losses from hi-fi? il por Bus W p 130+ D 11 '78 •
TUSKEGEE Institute, Tuskegee, Ala.
Tuskegee Institute in the 1920's. M. Marable. bibl f il Negro Hist Bull 40:764-8 N '77

subject entry — **TUTENKHAMUN, King of Egypt**
King Tut's tomb: the untold story; condensation. T. Hoving. il pors map Read Digest 114:176-80+ Ja '79 • — name of magazine
Tutmania finds relief in a spate of books and sidelines. D. Maryles. il Pub W 214:41-2+ N 20 '78 •

Anecdotes, facetiae, satire, etc.
date of magazine — King Tut book of etiquette. M. Stevenson. Harpers 258:97 Ja '79
King Tut live from the cradle of rock. D. Marsh. il Roll Stone p37 N 30 '78
Notes and comment. New Yorker 54:21 D 25 '78

division of main subject — **Tomb**
Dummies for mummies. Vasari. Art News 77:6+ N '78
volume number — Egyptomania in New York. S. Hochfield. il Art News 77:44-9 D '78
King Tut's revenge. J. Randi. il Humanist 38:44-7 Mr '78
Perils of guarding King Tut's treasures. W. H. Honan. il N Y Times Mag p40-1+ D 17 '78
Pharaoh's wine cellar; work of Leonard H. Lesko. Sci Am 238:74 Mr '78
author's name — There's much more in Cairo; at the Egyptian Museum. R. Ahrens. il Horizon 21:64-5 O '78
This little Pharaoh came to market. R. Christopher. il Macleans 91:44-6 D 18 '78
Tut tickets. New Yorker 54:28 O 2 '78
Tutglut. il Time 112:79 D 11 '78
page number — What Tut hath wrought. S. R. Weisman. il Horizon 21:61-3 O '78

An article about King Tut's tomb titled "Perils of Guarding King Tut's Treasures" by W. H. Honan can be found in the *New York Times Magazine.* The article, which is illustrated (il), begins on page 40 and is continued on later pages (p40–1+) of the December 17, 1978, issue (D 17 '78).

EXERCISE 7. Using the *Readers' Guide.* In the *Readers' Guide,* find an article listed under any four of the following subjects. Copy the entry for the article. Be ready to explain the information for the entry.

1. Scandinavia
2. Lakes
3. Colleges and universities
4. Space probes
5. Elephants
6. Submarines, atomic-powered

THE VERTICAL FILE

27f. To find a pamphlet, use the vertical file.

In addition to books and magazines, pamphlets can be a valuable resource when you are studying a topic. The U.S. Government publishes hundreds of pamphlets each year. In addition, state and local governments, businesses, colleges and universities, and health and other organizations publish pamphlets regularly. These pamphlets are found in a special filing cabinet called a vertical file. Sometimes newspaper clippings of special interest will also be included. Each pamphlet or clipping is placed in a folder and filed in alphabetical order by subject. For current information, you will find the vertical file very helpful.

MICROFILM AND MICROFICHE

27g. Use microfilm and microfiche to find information.

To save space, many libraries store some magazines, newspapers, and documents on microfilm or microfiche. *Microfilm* is a roll or reel of film containing photographically reduced pages. *Microfiche* is a small sheet of film containing photographically reduced pages. Both microfiche and microfilm can contain hundreds of pages. To use the microfilm and microfiche, you use special projectors which enlarge the microscopic images to a readable size. Your librarian can help you to use microfilm and microfiche.

COMPUTERS

27h. Use computers to find information.

Some libraries have computerized their book lists, periodical lists, and catalogs. In using a computerized system, type the information you need into the computer—for example, "subject: plant collecting." The computer will search for the titles and locations of books and periodicals on your subject and will print the information onto its screen. The computer might even be able to give a printed list. Your librarian can help you to use the computers.

REVIEW EXERCISE. Using Library Reference Tools. Number your paper 1–10. Write the reference tool from the list on page 625 to which you would turn first to get information on the corresponding subject in the list below.

1. Latest developments in cancer research
2. History of the Nobel Prize
3. Antarctica—climate, terrain, etc.
4. Title and author of a library book on outer space
5. Origins of jazz music
6. A list of magazine articles on a recent international crisis
7. Winners of the World Series since 1977
8. Height of Mount Everest
9. Facts about Ralph Ellison, the American author
10. The biography of a person who has only recently become prominent in the news

SUMMARY LIST OF LIBRARY REFERENCE TOOLS

The card catalog
Computers
Microfilm or microfiche
Reference books
- Encyclopedias
- Atlases
- Almanacs
- Biographical reference books
    - *Who's Who*
    - *Who's Who in America*
    - *Webster's Biographical Dictionary*
    - *Contemporary Authors*
    - *Contemporary Authors: First Revision*
    - *Current Biography*
- *Readers' Guide to Periodical Literature*
    - The vertical file

CHAPTER 28

Vocabulary

LEARNING AND USING NEW WORDS

Although there is no simple way to acquire a large vocabulary, there are ways in which you can learn and remember more of the words you encounter every day. This chapter will give you practice in using these methods. It will also introduce you to a number of words that are widely used in the books you will be reading this year and in the future.

An effective way to develop a wide vocabulary is to set aside a section of your notebook in which to enter the new words you learn. Along with this list of words, write a definition and a sentence or phrase illustrating how each word is used. You can begin your vocabulary notebook with any unfamiliar words that you encounter in the following diagnostic test.

DIAGNOSTIC TEST

A. Number your paper 1–10. After the proper number, write the letter of the word or phrase that is closest in meaning to the numbered word.

EXAMPLE 1. hamper a. build c. hinder
b. revise d. search

1. *c*

1. abashed
 a. beaten
 b. ashamed
 c. lowered
 d. fallen
2. belligerent
 a. dull
 b. warlike
 c. swift
 d. gentle
3. dexterity
 a. sugar
 b. duplicate
 c. handiness
 d. kindness
4. fatigue
 a. war
 b. weariness
 c. fatalist
 d. explosion
5. haughty
 a. moderate
 b. smiling
 c. proud
 d. slow
6. humdrum
 a. melodious
 b. loud
 c. aggressive
 d. dull
7. menace
 a. army
 b. threat
 c. song
 d. rival
8. primitive
 a. undeveloped
 b. prominent
 c. violent
 d. religious
9. remorse
 a. repetition
 b. guilt
 c. justice
 d. reason
10. revile
 a. abuse
 b. correct
 c. rebuild
 d. bury

B. Number your paper 11–20. After each number, write the letter of the word or phrase that best defines the italicized word in each sentence. Look for clues in the context to help you find the best meaning. You will not need to use all the definitions on the list.

a. pale
b. friendship
c. face
d. lukewarm
e. skillful
f. buried
g. lack of seriousness
h. torn down
i. flooded; overwhelmed
j. religious
k. energetic or of great intensity
l. a hearty burst of laughter

11. Julio should get a good grade in art because he's very *adept* at drawing.
12. The United States and Canada, its northern neighbor, have shared years of *amity*.

13. The radio station was *deluged* with telephone calls from people who wanted to win the car.
14. His loud *guffaw* during the play embarrassed the entire class.
15. The night before a test is not the time for *levity.*
16. Her *pallid* complexion warned us that she was still ill.
17. The historic hotel had to be *razed* for the new expressway.
18. Bathing in *tepid* water, not hot water, is now recommended by doctors.
19. We thought that Robert was the culprit until we heard his *vehement* denial.
20. The snow-covered *visage* at the window frightened us.

LEARNING NEW WORDS

Occasionally we see or hear a word used alone, but most of the time we encounter words used in combination with other words. If the word is unfamiliar, these surrounding words often supply valuable clues to meaning.

28a. Learn new words from context.

The *context* of a word means the words that surround it in a sentence and the whole situation in which the word is used. The context of the word supplies the main clue to the meaning of *inedible* in this sentence:

> The cook was told not to use toadstools in the stew because they are inedible.

Since the cook was warned against using the toadstools in a stew, it stands to reason that something *inedible* is something "not fit to eat." If you know that much about toadstools already, you can be even surer about your guess.

Many common English words have several meanings. The context often provides clues to their meanings. For example, *pound* means one thing in a grocery store, another in a story about a dogcatcher, and still another in a British movie. Context clues will aid you in understanding these words when you encounter them in your reading.

EXERCISE 1. Using Context Clues to Define Words. Number your paper 1–10. For each italicized word in the sentences that follow, write the letter of the definition that is closest in meaning. You will not need all the definitions in the list. Check your answers in the dictionary.

a. calm	e. pronounced	i. fearful
b. peak	f. honesty	j. avoid
c. guidance	g. reduce	k. ambition
d. respect	h. swung to hit	l. without success

1. Mrs. Tompkins has been the treasurer for twenty-seven years, and no one doubts her *integrity*.
2. At thirty, Lisa Chin is at the *summit* of her tennis career.
3. He is so *timorous* that he cannot sleep in the dark.
4. Unhappy, the baby *flailed* angrily at the bars of her playpen.
5. The doctor spoke comforting words to *allay* the patient's fears.
6. The speaker *articulated* her words with care.
7. The soldiers bowed to the emperor as a sign of *deference*.
8. With a roar, the crowd expressed its *jubilation* at the victory.
9. People should not attempt to *evade* their duties as citizens.
10. José's *aspiration* is to win the lead in the school play.

Using the Dictionary

28b. Learn to find the meaning you want in your dictionary.

If you cannot guess the meaning of a word from context, you should go to your dictionary. Context is still important, however. Most words have a number of different meanings, and the best way of finding the one you want is to look for the definition that fits the context in which you originally encountered the word. Consider the following sentence.

> Your jokes are in poor taste, Harold, and we can dispense with any more of them.

Dispense has the following meanings: (1) to give; (2) to distribute; (3) to get rid of; (4) to get along without. By trying each of these meanings in place of the word *dispense* in the example, you can easily eliminate all of the choices except the last one—the meaning you want.

Which of these numbered meanings for *dispense* fits the following sentence?

> The Red Cross dispensed clothing to the flood victims.

Dictionaries often supply sample contexts to help you distinguish between the various meanings of a word (see pages 599–600). Such phrases can be very helpful in showing you how to use the new word in your own speech and writing.

EXERCISE 2. Finding the Correct Meaning of a Word. The italicized words in the following sentences have a number of different meanings. Using your dictionary, select the meaning that best fits each sentence, and write it after the proper number.

EXAMPLE 1. A candidate for the presidency is likely to be an *eminent* political figure.
1. *prominent*

1. The doctor said that there was nothing to be feared from the *benign* swelling.
2. The old man gave us a *benign* smile.
3. The professor's lecture *illuminated* the subject for us.
4. With the flick of a switch, he can *illuminate* the garden.
5. As we drove into the valley, a beautiful *pastoral* scene unrolled before us.
6. The minister attended to his *pastoral* duties.
7. Your argument seems *valid* and has convinced us all.
8. Since this is a *valid* contract, you will have to live up to it.
9. The manager's *bland* words calmed the angry customer.
10. I don't like this cereal because it is too *bland*.

PREFIXES, ROOTS, AND SUFFIXES

Some words can be divided into parts, and some cannot. Those that can be divided, like *workbook* and *unhappy*, often consist of parts that mean something separately. By learning how to divide words into their parts, you can sometimes discover additional clues to meaning.

The basic part of a word is called a *root.* A part added before the root is called a *prefix;* a part added after the root is called a *suffix.* Becoming familiar with the common prefixes and suffixes discussed here will provide you with helpful leads to finding the meaning of a large number of new words.

Prefixes

28c. Learn how common prefixes change the meaning of words.

The following common prefixes occur in thousands of English words.

PREFIX	MEANING	EXAMPLE
auto-	self	automobile
bi-	two	bimonthly
circum-	around	circumference
con-	together	concord
de-	down or from	degrade
dis-	away or apart	disagree
ex-	out	expel
im-	not	impractical
mis-	wrong	misjudge
multi-	many	multiply
pre-	before	preview
semi-	half or partly	semiprecious

EXERCISE 3. Using Prefixes to Define Words. Number your paper 1–10. After the proper number, give the meaning of the italicized word in each of the sentences. Be prepared to tell how the prefix of the word helps determine its meaning. Use the dictionary if necessary.

1. The assistant principal *convened* the student council to draft a new student code of conduct.
2. An artillery shell completely *demolished* the hut.
3. Our newspaper is published *biweekly.*
4. Some of the czars of Russia were cruel *autocrats* who were feared by the people.
5. To call Alvin a worker is a *misnomer* because he is always asleep with a broom in his hands.
6. Ferdinand Magellan, the Portuguese sailor and explorer, *circumnavigated* the globe.
7. The girl held a large, *multicolored* ball in her hands.
8. The mechanic had to *dismantle* the motor to find the faulty part.
9. The theft of the jewels showed careful planning and must have been a *premeditated* crime.
10. We finally *dissuaded* Tom from writing a letter to the author.

EXERCISE 4. Using Prefixes to Define Words. Follow the directions for Exercise 3.

1. Frank has become so efficient at packaging toys that he moves like an *automaton.*
2. The people, angry over years of misrule, *deposed* the unjust king.
3. Remember Shakespeare's *immortal* words: "This above all, to thine own self be true."
4. The Smiths own *extensive* lands in this valley.
5. Mrs. Slocum showed how to *bisect* an angle.
6. Is the prisoner truly sorry for his *misdeeds,* or is he only sorry he was caught?
7. Ms. Feinstein stayed in a *semiprivate* hospital room.
8. The prisoner was allowed to move freely within a *circumscribed* area.
9. Next year our city will hold its *bicentennial* celebration.
10. Melba MacHenry Gardner, who donated the money for our new Civic Center, is a *multimillionaire.*

Suffixes

28d. Learn to recognize common suffixes when they occur in *companion forms.*

There are many English words to which suffixes can be added. The new words formed by adding suffixes are *companion forms* of the basic word. Adding suffixes to the root *free* results in the companion forms *freedom* and *freely.* If you are on the alert for companion forms and learn some common suffixes, you will often be able to guess the correct meanings of new words. One fact to keep in mind is that the spelling of the root may change when a suffix is added. For example, when *-ly* is added to *day,* the resulting word is not *dayly* but *daily.* When *-ition* is added to *repeat,* the resulting word is spelled *repetition.*

Sometimes adding a suffix will result in a word that is a different part of speech from the original word. For example, the suffix *-ly* added to the adjective *free* results in *freely,* an adverb. The suffix *-ly* occurs at the end of an adjective or an adverb but never at the end of a noun. Therefore, words ending in this suffix are never nouns. (When the letters *-ly* occur at the end of a noun such as *lily,* they are not a suffix but part of the basic word.)

Learn the following suffixes that occur in nouns.

SUFFIX	MEANING	EXAMPLE
-hood	condition	childhood
-ness	quality	goodness
-ance, -ence	state, act, fact	independence
-ation, -ition, -tion	action or state	celebration
-ity, -ty	quality	ability
-ment	result or action	employment

EXERCISE 5. Using Noun-forming Suffixes. Number your paper 1–10. Form nouns from the following words by using the suffixes just listed; then give the meanings of the new words. In some cases it will be necessary to change the spelling of the root. Check your answers in the dictionary.

EXAMPLES 1. kind
1. *kindness—the quality of being kind*
2. create
2. *creation—the act of creating*

1. replace
2. likely
3. articulate
4. accept
5. intense
6. man
7. fragile
8. aspire
9. improvise
10. friendly

The following suffixes occur in adjectives.

SUFFIX	MEANING	EXAMPLE
-ish	like or suggesting	foolish
-able, -ible	able	tolerable
-ous	having the quality of	religious
-esque	like	statuesque
-some	like or tending to	tiresome

EXERCISE 6. Using Adjective-forming Suffixes. Number your paper 1–10. Form adjectives from the following words by using the suffixes just listed; then give the meanings of the new words. Check your answers in the dictionary.

1. lone
2. picture
3. harmony
4. devil
5. grace
6. baby
7. luxury
8. depend
9. meddle
10. riot

The following suffixes occur in verbs.

SUFFIX	MEANING	EXAMPLE
-ate	cause to become	animate
-en	make or become	deepen
-fy	make or cause	fortify
-ize	cause to be	motorize

EXERCISE 7. Using Verb-forming Suffixes. Number your paper 1–10. Form verbs from the following words by using the suffixes just listed; then give the meanings of the new words. Check your answers in the dictionary.

1. captive
2. system
3. strength
4. nausea
5. glory
6. active
7. civil
8. sweet
9. illumine
10. beauty

USING EXACT WORDS

28e. Use the exact word in your speaking and writing.

In English, many thousands of words are available to help you express exactly what you mean. If you use the same few words to describe many different people or things or actions or situations, you are not taking advantage of the variety of your language. Avoid overworked words that are used in so many different contexts that they lose precise meaning. *Good* is one such word. If you were to refer to someone as "a good person," would you mean that he is capable, kind, or dependable? If you were to say, "I had a good day," would you mean an enjoyable, a productive, or a tranquil day? *Good* might be the first word that occurs to you to describe a person or a day, but a moment's thought will usually supply a better word to express your meaning.

Using Precise Adjectives to Describe

The English language is rich in adjectives. You should learn to use adjectives to express your meaning exactly. In talking about a book you enjoyed, for example, you might say it was *interesting,* but you would be more expressive if you called it *exciting* or *engrossing* or *stimulating*. Build your vocabulary by taking time to find the exact adjective to express your thought.

EXERCISE 8. Selecting Precise Adjectives. Each of the following sentences contains a vague or overworked adjective, in italics, which should be replaced by a more precise word. Number your paper 1–10. After the proper number, write the more precise adjective from the list preceding the sentences. You will not need all the words in the list. Use the dictionary, if necessary, to check your answers and make corrections.

eccentric	decrepit	devout	tangible
casual	customary	insipid	eligible
titanic	burly	appalling	boisterous
fragrant	sallow	fluent	

1. That rice pudding had a rather *flat* taste.
2. The *old* car drove slowly down the road.
3. The damage done by the hurricane was *shocking*.
4. The *muscular* sailor pushed against the door.
5. Paul is regarded as *odd* because he puts mustard on ice cream.
6. When we began to sing and shout, our counselor warned us that we were being too *lively*.
7. With a *great* effort, Samson tore down the pillars of the Philistine temple.
8. The foreman of the jury said that no *real* evidence of guilt had been produced.
9. No student who is failing one or more subjects is *qualified* for a student council position.
10. The roses were *sweet-smelling*.

Using Interesting Verbs to Express Action

Your ability to express yourself is directly dependent on your verb vocabulary. Verbs give action and color to your sentences. The following exercise includes a number of verbs that will add variety to your speaking and writing.

EXERCISE 9. Selecting Verbs to Complete Sentences. Number your paper 1–10. After the proper number, copy the verb whose meaning best completes the sentence. Change the tense if necessary to fit the sentence, and use your dictionary. You will not need all the verbs in the list.

soar	restrain	capitulate	browbeat
saturate	liberate	stray	wheedle
diverge	carouse	restore	elapse
confiscate	pollute	obliterate	

1. Because they could not pay their taxes, the government —— their property.
2. The fighter was badly beaten but refused to —— to his opponent.
3. Realizing that the bird would die in captivity, the girl took it to the woods and —— it.
4. As the plane —— above the clouds, the earth disappeared from view.
5. Several hours —— before the weary hikers returned home.
6. She is extremely timid and allows people to —— her.
7. Skillful detective work —— the stolen painting to its rightful owners.
8. The two hunters parted company when their paths —— .
9. Two centuries of wind and weather have almost —— the words carved on the stone.
10. Although we may be tempted to overeat, we should —— ourselves.

Using Vivid Adverbs to Modify Verbs

Because adverbs answer such questions as *How? When?* and *Where?* in connection with verbs, they are a very important part of your vocabulary. The exactness and vividness of your writing and speaking depend a great deal on your using adverbs well. In the exercise that follows, there are a number of adverbs for you to learn. Many of these adverbs are formed from words in the list beginning on page 644.

EXERCISE 10. Using Vivid Adverbs to Modify Verbs. Number your paper 1–10. After the proper number, write an adverb from the list that answers the question. You will not need all the adverbs in the list. Use the dictionary, if necessary.

immensely	resonantly	superficially
covertly	scrupulously	rigidly
abruptly	urgently	cautiously
excessively	anonymously	ostentatiously

1. How did the conscientious bookkeeper keep the company's records?
2. How did the woman who found there were burglars in her house call for the police?
3. How did the opera star sing the low notes in his aria?
4. How did the audience like the actor's superb performance?
5. How did the newly engaged girl display her engagement ring?
6. How did the tired student check her homework?
7. How did the little boy try to get a cookie from the cookie jar when his mother was in the next room?
8. How would a person stand if imitating a statue?
9. How does a doctor leave a dinner party upon receiving an emergency call?
10. How does a person cross a busy city street during rush hour?

Synonyms and Antonyms

A *synonym* is a word that means nearly the same thing as another word. Although words that are synonyms are close in meaning, they rarely have *exactly* the same meaning. At times you will be able to use one of several words in a sentence, but at other times only the exact word will do.

Pleasure, delight, and *joy* all have roughly the same meaning, yet each expresses a different shade of meaning. *Pleasure* is the most general of the three words; it covers a variety of situations, none of them very specifically. *Delight* indicates a sharp feeling of pleasure that lasts only a short time. *Joy* may indicate a deep and long-lasting happiness. In the following sentence, which of the three words fits most exactly?

I receive great —— from my study of mathematics.

Pleasure fits, of course, but is not very specific. *Delight* does not fit very well because the feeling indicated in this sentence would seem to last for some time. The synonym that most exactly expresses the desired meaning is *joy.*

When you look up a word in a dictionary, you will often find several synonyms listed. To help you to distinguish between synonyms, some dictionaries give *synonym articles*—brief explanations of a word's synonyms and how they differ in meaning. The more often you encounter a word in different contexts, the better you will be able to determine its meaning.

EXERCISE 11. Selecting Synonyms to Complete Sentences. Number your paper 1–10. After the proper number, write the synonym you have selected that best fits the sentence. Use the dictionary to learn the exact meaning of each synonym.

1. My jacket is made of a new (fabricated, imitation, synthetic) material.
2. Our (invincible, victorious, triumphant) army never has been and never should be defeated in battle.
3. The monks in several medieval monasteries kept (histories, annals, records) summarizing the important events of each year.
4. Medieval artists had a special (fashion, technique, system) for making stained-glass windows.
5. The young couple fondly (fed, nourished, sustained) their baby daughter.
6. You can imagine how (ridiculous, shaming, humiliating) it was to be spanked in front of all my relatives.
7. Her (guess, conjecture, estimate) that there would be a test the next day was based on the fact that Mrs. Brown had assigned no homework that night.
8. Although the lawyer stayed within the law, he relied on (guile, cunning, fraud) to win his case.
9. Under the new government, many citizens were (dispossessed, deprived, divested) of their rights.
10. After studying the problem I formed a working (theory, hypothesis, supposition), which I tested by experiment.

The *antonym* of a word is a word with the opposite meaning. *Bad* is the antonym of *good,* and *happy* is the antonym of *sad.* Sometimes an antonym of a word is formed by adding a prefix meaning *not:* an antonym of *wise* is *unwise.* Knowing the antonym of a word will often help you to understand the word's exact meaning (or at least one exact meaning). For example, knowing that *dexterity* is the antonym of *clumsiness* will lead you to a correct meaning for this word. A dictionary sometimes lists antonyms at the end of an entry for a word.

EXERCISE 12. Selecting Antonyms for Specific Words. Antonyms for words in the first column may be found in the second column. Number your paper 1–10. After the proper number, write the letter of the correct antonym. You will not need all the words in the second column. Use the dictionary, if necessary.

1. frustrate	a. tiny
2. contemptible	b. dawn
3. colossal	c. ornamental
4. impertinent	d. spiteful
5. upbraid	e. satisfy
6. twilight	f. wordiness
7. brevity	g. biased
8. neutral	h. probity
9. functional	i. courteous
10. random	j. eventual
	k. admirable
	l. orderly
	m. praise

SPECIAL VOCABULARIES

Each of your school subjects has special words that you must learn if you are to understand the concepts. Some of the words are new, while others, which are used in everyday speech, have special meanings in a particular subject.

A textbook often calls attention to these new words by printing them in italics or in boldfaced type. Printing a word in a special way shows that it is important. Often a definition immediately follows the word. If not, turn to the back of the book to see if there is a glossary—a short dictionary of special words. There, you will usually find a definition for the word. Always use a glossary when a textbook provides one. It is one of the most valuable features of a book.

EXERCISE 13. Defining Mathematics Words. The words in this exercise are used in mathematics books designed for students in your grade. Write each word on your paper, and follow it by a short definition. Then write a sentence using each word correctly. Use a dictionary or the glossary in your mathematics book.

acute	diameter	intersection	obtuse	radical
bisect	exponent	numeral	quotient	radius

EXERCISE 14. Defining Social Studies Words. The following words are likely to appear in your social studies assignments. Follow the directions for Exercise 13.

History: blockade, capitalism, depression, filibuster, gerrymander, initiative, recall, referendum, totalitarian, vassal

Geography: arid, fiord, fissure, meridian, monsoon, plateau, peninsula, precipitation, topography, tributary

EXERCISE 15. Defining Science Words. The following words are likely to appear in your science assignments. Follow the directions for Exercise 13.

antibody	electron	friction	nebula	satellite
condensation	embryo	fulcrum	radiation	spectrum

28f. Use the words from specialized vocabularies in your everyday speaking and writing.

Many words in a special field are often used outside the field. *Condensation* and *inertia* are often found in nonscientific books, while *exponent* and *radical* can be used by a political speaker as well as a mathematician. Learn the meanings of these words as used outside their fields. Use them in your own speaking and writing when they help to express your ideas exactly.

EXERCISE 16. Using Special Words in Everyday Writing. The following words used in mathematics, science, and social studies have meanings outside these fields. Use these words appropriately in the blanks in the sentences. You will not use all the words.

blockade	embryo	initiative	radical
condensation	fulcrum	intersection	spectrum
depression	inertia	obtuse	vassal

1. Harriet displayed great —— in forming a drama club and recruiting members for it.
2. When you have trouble getting started on your work, you are suffering from —— .
3. The newspapers have called Mayor Tompkins "a —— of special-interest groups."
4. George is so —— that he didn't get the joke even after she explained it.
5. The department store has been completely reorganized; you will discover some pretty —— changes when you go there.
6. To save space, the magazine published a —— of Madeleine L'Engle's new book.
7. The fugitive ran up the stairs to the attic and —— d the entry by pushing a heavy table against the wooden door.
8. Ann met us at the —— of Vernon Street and Third Avenue.
9. The student council was responsible for the entire —— of homecoming activities.
10. After receiving his test grade, Juan couldn't shake his mood of —— .

REVIEW EXERCISE. Defining Words. The words in this exercise have been chosen from all those you have studied in this chapter. Number your paper 1–20. After the proper number, write the letter of the word or phrase that is closest in meaning to the numbered word.

1. appalling	a. revealing	c. shocking
	b. annoying	d. rewarding
2. boisterous	a. lively	c. treacherous
	b. supporting	d. weak

3. concord
   a. sympathy
   b. conformity
   c. agreement
   d. boredom
4. covertly
   a. swiftly
   b. gaily
   c. badly
   d. secretly
5. decrepit
   a. decoyed
   b. feeble
   c. wise
   d. proud
6. deference
   a. pressure
   b. deceit
   c. respect
   d. loyalty
7. divest
   a. clothe
   b. deprive
   c. retreat
   d. amble
8. flail
   a. shrink
   b. beat
   c. reveal
   d. forget
9. jubilation
   a. anniversary
   b. ceremony
   c. terror
   d. rejoicing
10. nourish
    a. hate
    b. regret
    c. love
    d. feed
11. premeditated
    a. deliberate
    b. fiendish
    c. foolish
    d. great
12. random
    a. close
    b. emotional
    c. aimless
    d. knowing
13. restrain
    a. hold back
    b. teach
    c. dress up
    d. remember
14. rigidly
    a. stiffly
    b. stubbornly
    c. cleverly
    d. rudely
15. saturate
    a. wring out
    b. imitate
    c. treat badly
    d. fill completely
16. stray
    a. wander
    b. direct
    c. lonely
    d. puzzled
17. synthetic
    a. tiring
    b. expensive
    c. careless
    d. artificial
18. technique
    a. detail
    b. method
    c. instruction
    d. reason
19. titanic
    a. metallic
    b. huge
    c. backward
    d. alive
20. wheedle
    a. grow
    b. correct
    c. coax
    d. crawl

Word List

The following list of 300 words should form the basis of your vocabulary study for the year. You have already encountered some of them (or related forms) in this chapter. When you encounter a new word, add it to your vocabulary notebook. Write a definition of the word, and use the word in a sentence.

abuse
acceptance
access
accessory
accommodations
activate
adapt
adept
adequate
adjacent

advantageous
advent
aeronautics
affliction
aggressive
alliance
anonymous
antibiotics
anxiety
appalling

aristocrat
aroma
articulate
aspiration
assumption
attain
automaton
badger
baffle
bankrupt

barbarism
basis
baste
bewilder
blockade
boisterous
boycott
burly
calamity
calculation

capital
casual
catastrophe
category
censorship
charitable
childlike
circulate
circumnavigate
clarify

climax
colossal
commute
complement
condemn
confederation
confide
confiscate
congest
consecutive

considerate
contagious
contemporary
controversy
convert
creative
customary
decade
deceased
deceive

dedicate
deduction
defy
delegate
demolish
denial
depose
derive
descend
despise

detach
dictate
dilapidated
dilute
diminish
dingy
diplomat
disagreeable
discord
disintegrate

dismantle
dispatch
dispense
dissect
distraction
durable
eccentric
ecology
elegant
eligible

embarrass
emigrate
eminent
emphasize
endorse
enhance
epidemic
erosion
essay
evacuate

exaggeration
exertion
extensive
falter
famine
famished
feasible
feline
ferocious
fictitious

folklore
foresight
foreword
fortnight
fragile

fragment
fraudulent
frequency
gallery
generate

glorify
gnarled
gracious
grieve
hamper
harmonious
haughty
haven
hilarious
homicide

hospitable
humidity
humiliate
hydraulic
hypothesis
illuminate
immense
immigrate
impel
imperative

imply
impose
improvise
impulsive
incite
inclination
incomparable
inconsiderate
indelible
inevitable

inflexible
ingenious
inherit
inquisitive
insoluble
integrity
intelligible
intensity
intentional
intercept

intervene
intrigue
invariable
isolation
jeopardize
jubilation
knoll
latent
liable
liberate

literal
malfunction
malnutrition
manageable
maroon
massage
meddlesome
memento
menace
menagerie

miscellaneous
misdeed
modify
monopoly
morale

multicolored
multitude
mutual
myriad
nationality

negligent
neutral
notify
nourish
novelty
obituary
obscure
occupant
occurrence
omission

optimism
pacify
pamphlet
parasitic
persistent
petition
petty
pewter
phenomenon
photogenic

picturesque
pious
planetarium
pleasantry
pollute
populate
posterity
potential
prearrange
predicament

premier
premiere
presume
primitive
privilege
probable
probation
propaganda
proposal
provision

pulverize
pun
punctual
quaint
quench
rebate
recuperate
refuge
regime
remorse

remote
resolute
respiration
restore
restrain
revelation
rigid
riotous
romantic
ruthless

sable
salutation
sanctuary
sarcasm
satire

saturate
secluded
sedate
sincerity
sinew

spacious
sphere
sterile
strategy
successor
summit
superficial
sustain
synthetic
tangible

tariff
tarnish
technology
temperament
testify
therapy
thrifty
thrive
titanic
transit

tumult
unique
upbraid
urban
urgent
valid
valor
verify
vitality
warranty

CHAPTER 29

Studying and Test Taking

SKILLS AND STRATEGIES

In many of your classes, you are expected to study textbook materials, complete oral and written assignments, and take tests. This chapter provides strategies for making your studying more effective and your test taking more successful than before.

STUDY SKILLS

You study to gain information about a topic and to understand and evaluate knowledge that you have acquired. The following strategies and skills can help you improve your study skills.

Following the SQ3R Study Method

29a. Use the SQ3R Study Method.

The *SQ3R Method* was developed by Francis Robinson, an educational psychologist. The method consists of five steps.

1. *Survey*. Survey your selection by glancing quickly at the title, the subheadings, important terms in **boldface** and *italics,* and all charts, diagrams, illustrations, summaries, and questions.

In addition, read the introduction and the summary paragraph quickly to find the main ideas.

2. ***Question.*** Make a list of questions that you want to answer after you have read the selection. One way to do this is to use the subheadings. For example, if a subheading is *The Industrial Revolution,* you might write *What was the Industrial Revolution?* Sometimes such questions are included in the text. At other times, your teacher may provide them.

3. ***Read.*** Read your selection *carefully* to find answers to your questions. Look for main ideas and supporting details. Look up any unfamiliar words. Take notes as you read.

4. ***Recite.*** Read the questions that you have written down. Think carefully about the answers, and recite them in your own words. (Refer to your notes to make sure your answers are correct.) Write down the answers to the questions.

5. ***Review.*** Review the selection by asking yourself the questions and answering them without looking at your notes. Check your answers by consulting the selection and your notes. Then immediately review the selection to reinforce your knowledge.

EXERCISE 1. Applying the SQ3R Method to a Homework Assignment. Select a homework assignment in your science or social studies textbook. Follow the steps of the SQ3R Method to complete the assignment. Answer each question as you work.

1. *Survey.* What is the title? What are the subheadings? What are the new terms in boldface or italics? What charts, illustrations, diagrams, or summaries are there? What do the introductory and summary paragraphs say?
2. *Question.* Make a list of questions to be answered after you have read the selection. (If your teacher has assigned specific questions, use those instead.)
3. *Read.* Take notes on the main ideas and important details.
4. *Recite.* Recite the answers in your own words. Then write the answers to your questions.
5. *Review.* Use your questions to review the selection.

Adjusting Your Reading Rate to Your Purpose

29b. Adjust your reading rate according to your purpose.

Depending on what you are reading, you may need to read quickly, at a moderate rate, or very slowly. You should learn to adjust your reading rate to your reading purpose.

(1) Scan to find information quickly.

Scanning means to read quickly to find *specific* information, such as facts, dates, or names. For example, you scan a dictionary to find a particular word by moving your eyes quickly down the page until you find the word you seek. Materials that you scan include telephone directories, indexes, and tables of contents.

(2) Skim to get a general idea of what the selection covers.

Skimming means to read at a fast rate to get the *general* idea of a selection. In the Survey step of the SQ3R Method, you skim when you quickly read the title, subheadings, charts, diagrams, key terms, introductory and summary paragraphs, and questions.

(3) Read closely to understand the main ideas and details.

Reading closely means to read slowly and thoughtfully. You read closely to identify not only the main ideas but also the supporting details. You read closely to find answers to study questions. In the Read step of the SQ3R Method, you read closely.

(4) Read recreational materials lightly.

Reading lightly means to read at a fast rate. Light novels and some magazines are examples of materials that you read lightly.

EXERCISE 2. Determining Reading Approaches for Particular Situations. Determine the appropriate reading approach (scanning, skimming, reading closely, or reading lightly) for each situation. Be prepared to explain your answers.

EXAMPLE 1. You need to find the term *comma* in an index.
1. *scanning*

1. You need to find rule 29c in this chapter.
2. You want to get a general idea of what the next chapter in this textbook will cover.
3. You completed the Survey and Question parts of the SQ3R Method for your social studies assignment. Now you need to read the selection.
4. You want to read a novel for entertainment.

Recognizing Main Ideas

29c. Find the main ideas of the material being studied.

The main idea of a piece of writing is the most important point that the author wants to make. Sometimes the main idea is stated. Sometimes it is implied, or suggested.

(1) Main ideas may be stated.

The main idea of a piece of writing is usually stated as a complete sentence. For example, the main idea of a paragraph about cats may be *Cats are easier to care for than dogs*.

The following paragraph is from "Bears," by Ben East. The topic is "a bear track." The main idea is *A bear track is calculated to send shivers up the human spine.*

> A bear track is calculated to send shivers up the human spine. You stare at the footprints, printed big and deep in the sand of a woods road or the mud along a stream bank, and you say to yourself, "A bear walked here, in the black of night, cloaked in darkness, furtive and silent. On what bloody errand was he bent? What prey did he finally find? Did he surprise and brain a young deer? Sniff out a wild turkey on her nest? Raid a pigpen on some settler's brush-bordered farm? Or did he only tear a log apart for ants? What would have happened if I had met him face to face?"
>
> BEN EAST

Note that the main idea in this paragraph is stated in the first sentence. The main idea may also be stated in the middle or at the end of a paragraph.

(2) Main ideas may be implied.

When a main idea is implied, you will need to read closely, examine details, and state the main idea in your own words. As you read the following paragraph from "Nature's Medicines: Spearmint," think about the main idea that the writer implies.

> Ancient Greeks used to perfume their arms with spearmint so they could smell its refreshing scent wherever they went. Romans placed fresh sprigs of spearmint on their dining tables and in their sleeping chambers. Today many gardeners simply go out to their spearmint patches and breathe deeply. The smell is said to help them if they are nervous or have a headache.
>
> LOIS WICKSTROM

The subject of this paragraph is "spearmint." What does this paragraph tell us about spearmint? It tells us that ancient Greeks used spearmint as a perfume, that Romans used spearmint to scent their homes, and that today many gardeners grow spearmint and use its scent to relieve nervousness or headaches. These details support the main idea of the paragraph: For thousands of years people have valued the spearmint plant for its fragrant odor and beneficial effects.

EXERCISE 3. Finding the Main Idea. Write the stated or implied main idea for each of the following paragraphs.

1

> The January wind has a hundred voices. It can scream, it can bellow, it can whisper, and it can sing a lullaby. It can roar through the leafless oaks and shout down the hillside, and it can murmur in the white pines rooted among the granite ledges where lichen makes strange hieroglyphics. It can whistle down a chimney and set the hearth-flames to dancing. On a sunny day it can pause in a sheltered spot and breathe a

promise of spring and violets. In the cold of a lonely night it can rattle the sash and stay there muttering of ice and snowbanks and deep-frozen ponds.

HAL BORLAND

2

Imagine waiting all your life for a dream to come true! Some people achieve greatness during their lifetime. Others are recognized only after their deaths. John James Audubon was labeled a failure for most of his life. He knew a small measure of success before he died. Years later, organizations were named for him, and his monumental work was finally recognized for the magnificent achievement that it is.

ELEANOR P. ANDERSON

Finding Details That Support Main Ideas

29d. Find details that support main ideas.

In addition to identifying main ideas, you will need to identify their supporting details. Such details may include reasons, examples, or descriptions.

In the following paragraph, the main idea is expressed in the topic sentence (the first sentence). The other sentences contain details that explain the main idea.

Are you prepared to give your pet lifetime care? Even a fully grown pet is totally dependent on you for all of its needs. Every day, you must provide it with food and water, change its litter box or walk it and make sure that it gets sufficient exercise. You're also responsible for keeping it clean, watching over its health and taking it to the vet if necessary. What's more, you'll have to train and discipline your pet so that it doesn't become a nuisance, and give it attention and affection so that it remains loving and companionable. When your pet becomes a senior citizen, he will probably need even more affection and care.

ALICE HERRINGTON

The main idea of the paragraph above is *You must be prepared to care for a pet throughout its life.* To support this main idea, the writer uses the following details: (1) You must feed the pet, care for its needs, and make sure that it gets exercise. (2) You must keep it clean and healthy. (3) You need to train your pet and give it attention and affection. (4) When your pet ages, you will have to give it additional love and care.

EXERCISE 4. Using Supporting Details to Answer Questions. Read the following paragraphs, noting the main ideas and the supporting details. Then complete each activity.

1

That first winter in St. Catharines was a terrible one. Canada was a strange, frozen land, snow everywhere, ice everywhere, and a bone-biting cold the like of which none of them had ever experienced before. Harriet rented a small frame house in the town and set to work to make a home. The fugitives boarded with her. They worked in the forests, felling trees, and so did she. Sometimes she took other jobs, cooking or cleaning house for people in the town. She cheered on these newly arrived fugitives, working herself, finding work for them, finding food for them, praying for them, sometimes begging for them.

ANN PETRY

1. The details in the paragraph above explain why the first winter in St. Catharines was hard for Harriet Tubman. List at least four of these details.

2

In ancient times an elephant was as powerful and feared a weapon as a missile with a nuclear warhead is today. Generals depended on these animals, and it isn't hard to understand why. A group of elephants could trample an army or batter down the walls of a city. When sent into battle carrying a tower full of armed men, an elephant was the equivalent of a modern armed tank. Warrior elephants could inflict tremendous physical damage on the enemy, but that wasn't the most important reason for using them. When soldiers saw elephants for the first time, they were often so frightened that they forgot to fight; they simply dropped their weapons and ran. Horses panicked and refused to charge, and the elephants won easy victories. In the ancient world, elephants were such valuable weapons that every king wanted to have some, and a few rulers, like Queen Semiramis of Assyria, went to incredible lengths just to get hold of a few of these remarkable animals.

SUZANNE JURMAIN

2. Write four sentences explaining why the elephant, in ancient times, was powerful and feared. Use your own words.

Distinguishing Between Fact and Opinion

29e. Distinguish between fact and opinion.

Most of what you read and hear contains both facts and opinions. It is important to be able to distinguish between these two types of information.

(1) A statement of fact contains information that can be proved true.

A statement of fact contains information about things that have happened in the past or are happening in the present. For example, here are three statements of fact.

Amelia Earhart was born in 1898.
Oranges are a source of vitamin C.
Edgar Allan Poe wrote "The Raven."

(2) A statement of opinion contains information that cannot be proved.

A statement of opinion expresses a personal belief or attitude. The following examples state two different opinions.

Birthday parties are fun.
Soccer is a more exciting game than baseball.

Sometimes a statement of opinion contains expressions such as "Everyone knows that. . . " or "The truth is that. . . " or "It's a fact that. . . ." Do not let these expressions mislead you into thinking that a statement of opinion is a statement of fact.

Remember also that not everything presented as a fact is true or accurate. Be prepared to use a reliable source to prove that a given statement is true. Among the sources you might use are direct experience, an expert, an encyclopedia, a dictionary, an almanac, or any other authoritative reference.

EXERCISE 5. Distinguishing Between Facts and Opinions. Number your paper 1–5. After the proper number, write whether each of the following items is a fact or an opinion. If it is a fact, write some kind of evidence or a source (such as direct experience, an encyclopedia, a textbook, or an almanac) that you could use to determine that it is truly a fact.

EXAMPLES 1. The Bill of Rights was ratified in 1791.
1. *fact—social studies textbook*
2. Oranges are more delicious than apples.
2. *opinion*

1. Twenty-six times two equals fifty-two.
2. The United Nation's Children's Fund (UNICEF) aids children and teen-agers in developing countries.
3. Blue jeans are the most comfortable of all clothing.
4. Denver is the capital of Colorado.
5. Everyone knows that Denver is the best place for skiing.

Taking Effective Study Notes

29f. Take effective study notes.

Notes that you take while reading your textbooks will help you remember what you have read.[1] Your notes should be brief, but you need to be able to understand them. The following strategies will help you take effective study notes.

[1] See pages 691–96 for strategies in taking notes from class lessons.

1. Make sure that you have read your selection once closely.
2. Take notes on paper instead of on note cards.
3. Use the section title and subheadings in your textbook as the subject and topics in your notes. Leave room for main ideas and details under the topics.
4. As you read, look for statements that introduce main ideas. Be aware of transitional words or phrases, such as *first, next, therefore, however, more importantly,* and *on the other hand,* which often introduce main ideas.
5. Write the main ideas and details under the topics.
6. Use your own words.
7. Use words, phrases, or short sentences.
8. Use abbreviations when possible. Omit articles (*a, an, the*).
9. Review your notes soon after you have taken them.

Now read the following passage about how to make an artificial ant colony. Then read the sample study notes for the passage.

> The simplest way to have an artificial ant colony to study in your home is to take a large jar and fill it with soft black earth. Then find a colony of small black or brown ants. You must dig this colony out with a *trowel,*[1] keeping a sharp eye out for the queen, who is much larger and fatter than the small workers. When you find her, put her into the jar along with a couple of hundred workers. They will quickly get busy making passageways down into the earth, and if you feed them a little sugar, honey, meat, and bread crumbs each day, they will make their ant town right in your jar. To see their passageways under the earth, cover the jar up to the level of the dirt with black cloth or paper, and take this off only at rare intervals. When you do take it off, you will see passageways running next to the glass and will be able to watch the ants going about their work underground.
>
> VINSON BROWN

Study Notes: How to Make an Artificial Ant Colony
—Fill large jar with soft black dirt.
—Find colony of small black or brown ants.

[1] *trowel:* a tool with a scoop, used for digging up plants in gardens.

—Look for queen—fatter, larger.
—Put her and about two hundred others into jar with dirt.
—Feed each day—sugar, honey, meat, bread crumbs.
—Cover jar up to level of earth with black paper.
—Seldom take paper off.
—Will be passageways running down sides of jar.
—Can watch ants working.

EXERCISE 6. Taking Study Notes. Select a homework assignment in your science, social studies, or English textbook. Take study notes, using the strategies on pages 655–56. Be prepared to share your notes.

Writing a Summary of Study Material

29g. Write a summary to help you understand your study material.

A *summary* is a brief composition that covers the main ideas and important supporting details of a piece of writing. It should be approximately one-third the length of the original writing and should be written in your own words. Study the following steps for writing a summary.

1. Skim the selection.
2. Read the selection closely, looking for the author's main ideas.
3. Read the selection again to identify not only the main ideas but also the supporting details. Look up any unfamiliar words. Take notes as you read.
4. Identify the author's main ideas and important supporting details. (You might put a check mark [✔] next to those ideas in your notes.)
5. Write a summary in your own words. Include only the author's main ideas and *important* supporting details.
6. Revise your summary to make sure that you have covered the main ideas and important supporting details.
7. Revise your summary until it is approximately one-third the length of the original piece of writing.

Now read the passage on page 656 again. Then read the following example summary for that passage. Note that it is about one-third the length of the original.

Summary

To make an artificial ant colony, fill a jar with earth. Then find an ant colony and put the queen (the largest ant) and about two hundred other ants into the jar. Feed them every day. Cover the jar to the top of the earth with black paper. Remove the paper when you want to see the ants working.

EXERCISE 7. Writing a Summary. Select a homework assignment in your science or social studies textbook. Write a summary of one passage, using the strategies on page 657.

Writing in Other Courses

29h. Use writing to learn about ideas in social studies or history.

You can better understand a content-area subject, such as social studies or history, if you write about its important ideas. Most often you will write factual reports in these subjects (see pages 178–94). You can also explore ideas in social studies or history with other forms of writing.

One way to use writing in history or social studies is to write dialogues and narratives about historical figures. For example, you might write an imaginary dialogue between Thomas Jefferson and Meriwether Lewis, the explorer, about the Lewis and Clark expedition. Or, you might write an interview (using dialogue form) between Susan B. Anthony, the suffragette, and a television reporter. You might even want to be the reporter or a participant in the situation. (For more on writing dialogue, see pages 116–18.)

You might also write a narrative in which you are a person telling about an important historical event. For example, you might be Charles Lindbergh describing his historic flight across the Atlantic Ocean in 1927. Or, you might be Amelia Earhart describing her attempt to fly around the world in 1937. No matter which person you write about, use the same process you follow to write any other personal experience narrative (see pages 79–83).

For each of these activities, you will use your knowledge of writing and your understanding of history. You will have to write from the point of view of the historical figure. (See pages 81–82 on point of view.) You will also have to use what you know about that time in history. This kind of writing might help you to see history from a new angle.

Another way to use writing in social studies or history is to keep a journal. In this journal, you can write about the ideas and people you are studying. In this way, your journal is like the writer's notebook you might keep in English class (see page 14).

You can use your journal in two ways. First, you can record what you think about the events, ideas, and people you are studying. This will help you understand the course material from your own point of view. Second, you can use your journal to answer specific questions or discussion items your teacher gives you. For example, your history or social studies teacher might ask you to write about one of the following items:

1. Summarize the main ideas in the Bill of Rights.
2. Discuss how a country's geography and agriculture are related.
3. What were some of the major changes in the United States in the years between the Civil War and 1900?
4. Describe three of George Washington Carver's most important discoveries.

Items like these will also help you to understand the ideas, people, and events you are studying. When you write in your journal, be sure to apply your knowledge of writing sentences and paragraphs.

You can also use writing in social studies or history by writing book reports. You may already write book reports in your English class (see pages 195–200). In history or social studies class, your book report should be on a book that discusses an historical person or event, such as *The Battle of the Alamo,* by Keith Murphy. This also includes biographies and autobiographies, such as *Osceola: Seminole Warrior* by Joanne Oppenheim, or *The Story of My Life,* by Helen Keller.

In your book report, you should summarize the book's main events, without including every detail. You should also explain why you did or did not like the book. This means that you should include reasons for your opinion. These reasons should be specific details from the book. You might also want to read an encyclopedia article about the book's subject. This will help you to understand more about the subject.

Prepare for your book report by carefully reading the book. Jot down notes about important ideas or details as you read. Then, write your book report. Explain what the book is about and give your opinion of the book. You might also want to answer one of the following questions in your book report: How does this book help you to understand history or social studies? Does the book present the person or the event accurately? How do you know it does (or does not)? After you write a first draft of your book report, evaluate, revise, and proofread it—just as you would do for any other piece of writing.

No matter what kind of writing you do in history or social studies, or in your other classes, apply what you know about narration, description, and exposition (Chapters 4 and 5) and about writing paragraphs and compositions (Chapters 2, 3, and 5). Also remember to use what you know about the writing process (Chapter 1) to improve all the writing you do in school.

EXERCISE 8. Writing in Social Studies or History. Use the writing process to complete one of the following activities.

1. Write a dialogue, an interview, or a narrative about a person you are studying now.
2. Write a journal entry about an idea, person, or event you are studying now. Use the discussion items on page 659, or use questions your teacher gives you.
3. Write a book report on a book that discusses an important person or event in history. In your report, answer one of the questions above.

PREPARING FOR AND TAKING TESTS

Tests are designed to measure different things. Some tests measure how well you remember specific information; others determine how well you understand ideas. Some questions call for brief answers; others ask you to write a paragraph or more. The following skills and strategies will prepare you for different kinds of tests.

Preparing for Objective Tests

Objective tests measure how well you remember specific information, such as dates, names, terms, and definitions. Objective tests include multiple-choice, true-or-false, and fill-in-the blank questions as well as short-answer identifications and matching questions.

29i. Prepare for objective tests by studying the specific information that will be included on the test.

Follow these steps to prepare for objective tests.

1. Know what will be included on the test.
2. Gather the materials you will need, such as your textbook, study notes, and homework assignments.
3. Review your notes and assignments. Pay attention to names, dates, terms, and definitions. If your notes are not clear, reread the appropriate section in your textbook.
4. Make up questions that might be on the test. Then answer these questions. (Use your notes to check your answers.)

Taking Objective Tests

Follow these steps to take objective tests.

1. Read the directions closely. Note *exactly* what the directions ask you to do; for example, "Answer *three* of the following five questions."
2. Skim the rest of the test. Note how many questions there are, which ones are difficult, and which ones are easy. Complete

the easy ones first; then work through the more difficult ones.

3. Note how much time you have for the test and figure out how much time you can spend on each question. (Plan less time for easy questions and more time for difficult ones.)

4. If you do not understand something on the test, ask your teacher for help.

In addition, keep in mind these points about the specific kinds of objective tests.

Multiple-choice Questions

Multiple-choice questions ask you to choose the correct answer from three or more options. Follow these steps.

1. Read the question carefully.
2. Read *all* of the choices *before* you answer the question.
3. Eliminate choices that you know are incorrect. (Usually there will be one or two.)
4. Think carefully about the remaining choices. Based on what you know, determine which choice makes the most sense.

Now read the following multiple-choice question and its solution.

EXAMPLE A single entry word in the dictionary appears divided into two parts to show (a) that it is sometimes written as two words (b) the origin of the word (c) that the word consists of two syllables. [Having studied the dictionary, you would be able to eliminate choice *b*—information about origin follows the entry word. Of the two remaining choices, choice *c* makes more sense—the single word is divided into two syllables, not spelled as two words. The correct choice is *c*.]

True-or-false Questions

True-or-false questions ask you to determine whether a given statement is true or false. Follow these steps.

1. Read the entire statement carefully.
2. Look to see if *any* part of the statement is false. If this is the case, mark the statement false.

3. If all the parts of the statement are true, mark the statement true.

Now read the following true-or-false questions and solutions.

EXAMPLES
1. In 1875 Edison invented the phonograph. [This statement is false. Though Edison invented the phonograph, he invented it in 1877, not in 1875.]
2. The sun is the center of the solar system. [All parts of this statement are true; therefore, the statement is true.]

Fill-in-the-blank Questions

Fill-in-the-blank questions ask you to fill in the missing word or words that correctly complete the sentence. Follow these steps.

1. Read the question carefully.
2. Write a specific answer, using the terminology found in your notes or textbook.
3. Try to fill in all the blanks.

Now read the following fill-in-the-blank questions and solutions.

EXAMPLES
1. A —— gives inventors exclusive rights to make and sell their inventions. [patent]
2. Jimmy Carter was elected President in —— . [1976]
3. Sandra Day O'Connor was the first woman ever appointed to —— . [the United States Supreme Court]

Note that the first item asks you to fill in a term, the second asks you to fill in a figure, and the third asks you to fill in a name. Note also that all answers are appropriate to the subject.

Short-answer Identifications

Short-answer identifications usually ask you to answer a question with a word or a phrase or with one or two sentences. Follow these steps.

1. Read the question carefully.

2. Write a specific answer, using the terminology found in your notes or textbook.
3. Try to answer all questions.

Now read the following short-answer identifications and solutions.

EXAMPLES
1. In American politics, what does ERA stand for? [the Equal Rights Amendment]
2. Who was Nelson A. Rockefeller? [a former New York State governor who was chosen by President Ford as Vice-President]

Notice that each of the answers is specific and that the terminology is appropriate to the subject matter.

Matching Questions

Matching questions ask you to match the items in one list with the items in another list. Follow these steps.

1. Read the directions carefully. Some directions may explain that you do not have to use all the items. Other directions will inform you that you may use some items twice.
2. Read both lists and note how they are related. For example, one list may contain the names of famous people, and the other may include their accomplishments.
3. Skim through the items. Identify the easy ones and the difficult ones. Do the easy ones first.
4. Complete the rest of the test by making informed guesses, that is, by using clues to help you.

Now read the following matching questions and solutions for a test on the Constitution of the United States.

EXAMPLE

1. To accuse an official in the executive branch or a judge in a federal court of wrong doing	a. impeach b. bill c. amendment
2. Proposal for a law	
3. Set number of members required to conduct the business of Congress	d. quorum e. elastic clause

4. A change or an addition to a constitution
5. Provision that allows Congress to stretch its powers to meet new situations

Note that the list on the left contains definitions and the list on the right contains the corresponding terms. First, you might identify items 1, 2, and 4 as easy items and match item 1 with *a,* item 2 with *b,* and item 4 with *c.* Then, of the two remaining choices, you could examine the words in item 5 and determine that the word *stretch* is a clue: something that can be stretched is said to be elastic. Thus you would match item 5 with choice *e.* Last, you would correctly match item 3 with choice *d.*

EXERCISE 9. Applying Test-taking Skills. Write the answers to the following questions:

1. Identify ten key terms that might appear in an objective test on this chapter.
2. Using the terms you chose, prepare for a test on this chapter by writing sample questions. Include at least two of each of the following types of test questions:
   a. multiple-choice
   b. true-or-false
   c. fill-in-the-blank
   d. short-answer identifications

Preparing for Essay Tests

Essay tests are intended to measure your understanding of what you have learned. You express your understanding by writing an essay of one paragraph or more.

To prepare for essay tests, reread the appropriate parts of your textbook and your notes to identify main ideas and important supporting details. Study this information until you understand it. Try answering any questions in your textbook that ask you to write a paragraph or more. Then try making up your own essay questions.

Although there is no *right* answer on an essay test, your teacher will expect specific details in your essay answer. Therefore, be prepared to use your main ideas and important details to write complete, well-supported answers.

Taking Essay Tests

29j. Plan your time and your answer for an essay question.

Follow these steps when taking an essay test.

1. Read the directions closely. Note whether you have a choice of questions to answer.
2. Skim the rest of the test. Note how many questions there are, which ones are easy, and which ones are difficult.
3. If you have a choice of essay questions, decide which one(s) you will answer.
4. Figure out how much time you can spend on each question. (Be sure to leave enough time to plan and write your essay.)
5. Begin by reading the directions carefully. Note *what* task you are being asked to do, for example, to *compare* (point out likenesses *or* differences between) two characters or to *explain* (give reasons for) the causes of a war. In addition, note *how many* tasks are involved. For example, the following directions ask you to do two tasks: *Briefly describe the character traits and activities of Paul Bunyan and Pecos Bill. Then contrast* (*discuss the differences between*) *these two legendary folk heroes.*
6. Work through the stages of the writing process.
   a. *Prewriting.* Gather ideas for your answer. Write a sentence that expresses your main point. Be sure your sentence uses the key words of the question.
   b. *Writing.* Use your prewriting notes to help you write your answer. Begin by writing either the topic sentence of a paragraph or the thesis statement of a composition. Be sure that your supporting sentences develop this main idea.
   c. *Revising.* In most cases you will not have much time for revising. Reread the question and your answer to make sure that you have answered the question.

d. *Proofreading.* Proofread your paragraph for errors in grammar, usage, spelling, and mechanics.

Answering the Different Kinds of Essay Questions

29k. Know the different kinds of essay questions and what is expected in the answer for each type.

Essay questions generally ask you to complete one of several tasks. Each of these tasks is expressed by a verb. The following list shows some key verbs and the tasks each verb signals.

Essay Test Questions

KEY VERB(S)	TASK
analyze	Take something apart to show how each part works.
compare	Point out likenesses *or* differences.
contrast	Point out differences.
compare and contrast	Point out similarities *and* differences.
describe	Give a picture in words or an account of.
list, outline, trace	List events, show development.
discuss	Examine in detail.
explain	Give reasons for something's being the way it is.
demonstrate, illustrate, show	Provide examples to support a point.
interpret	Give the meaning or significance of something.

Now read the following example of an essay question:

EXAMPLE Contrast the Pilgrims' reasons for coming to North America with those of the Jamestown settlers.

This essay question asks you to point out the differences between the Pilgrims' reasons for coming to North America and those of the Jamestown settlers. The sentence that expresses your main idea might be *The Pilgrims' reasons for coming to North America were different from those of the Jamestown settlers.* Your details would include the Pilgrims' main reason for coming to North America (religious persecution in England) and the Jamestown settlers' reasons (lack of jobs in England, conflict with the government). You would provide details to support these reasons. You might arrange your essay test answer by first expressing your main idea, next discussing the Pilgrims' reasons, and then discussing the Jamestown settlers' reasons.

EXERCISE 10. Analyzing Essay Questions. For each of the following sample essay questions, identify the key word or words that state the specific task in the question. State briefly what task you must do to answer the question.

EXAMPLE 1. Explain why the United States replaced the spoils system with the merit system for hiring federal employees during the late 1800's.
1. *Explain—give reasons for the replacement of the spoils system with the merit system.*

1. Compare the Treaty of Versailles with President Wilson's Fourteen Points.
2. Interpret Robert Frost's poem "The Road Not Taken." Be sure to give reasons to support your point of view.
3. The conflict of the myth of Antigone involves two strong wills. In a single paragraph, explain the struggle between Antigone and Creon.
4. Describe the geography and climate of Costa Rica.
5. Several selections presented in this unit focus on beliefs that are part of America's heritage, particularly belief in independence, tolerance, and personal freedom. Choose two selections you have read, and in a brief essay show how they demonstrate characteristic American beliefs. Identify the selections by title and author.

PART FIVE

SPEAKING AND LISTENING

CHAPTER 30

Speaking

FORMAL AND INFORMAL SPEAKING SITUATIONS

Learning how to speak well and comfortably before groups or in unfamiliar situations is an important part of everyone's education. This chapter will help you to improve your speaking skills.

MAKING ANNOUNCEMENTS

To announce information about an event to other students, you do not need to make elaborate notes. Nevertheless, you should write down the information you are to give and check it over to be sure it includes all the essential facts. You have already used the *5 W-How?* questions to gather information for your writing. These same questions can help you organize information for your announcement.

30a. In making an announcement, be sure to include all the necessary facts.

Most announcements should include the following information: (1) the kind of event, (2) the time, (3) the place, (4) the admission fee, if any, and (5) special features. The following example includes four of these items, omitting only the admission fee.

EXAMPLE The Microcomputer Club will meet Tuesday, January 15, at 3:05 P.M. in Room 27. All members and any other interested students are invited for a program called "Using Computers to Create Sound Effects."

Go over the facts of an announcement several times in your mind before you speak. If you are not sure that you will remember them all while you are speaking, carry a note card with the information on it. You can glance at this card as you speak.

Use a normal rate of speaking, and make sure that you give your audience time to take in what you are saying. Speak loudly enough so that everyone will hear.

EXERCISE 1. Correcting Announcements. The following announcements omit essential items of information. What are these items? Rewrite each announcement so that it includes all the necessary information.

1. Students in Ms. Robertson's class who are going to the art museum tomorrow should be ready to leave at 11:15. The only expense will be for lunch in the museum cafeteria.
2. The Junior Philharmonic needs more members. Even if you are not sure of your musical talent, why not come to a rehearsal and join the preparation for the next concert?

EXERCISE 2. Preparing and Delivering Announcements. Prepare and deliver an announcement for one of the following events or for an actual event at your school. Give all the necessary information, using the *5 W-How?* questions as a guide.

1. A five-mile bicycle race to benefit handicapped children
2. The annual Spring Talent Show
3. The eighth-grade class trip to Washington, D.C.
4. Teacher Recognition Day
5. A science fair

PREPARING AN ORAL REPORT

30b. Learn how to prepare an oral report.

There are several similarities between planning an oral report and planning a piece of writing. In fact, you use the same skills to organize each form of communication: choosing a suitable subject, limiting the subject to a topic, and gathering and arranging information. These skills are the same as the prewriting steps in the writing process. For a review of these prewriting steps, refer to pages 5–28 in Chapter 1.

Oral reports and written reports, which are discussed in Chapter 6, are planned in much the same way. Also, both oral and written reports have the same purpose: to present information, to explain something about a subject, or to express and support an opinion. Still, there is one important difference: Oral reports are not written out word for word. Instead, you make some notes to help you remember your material as you speak. Be sure to use the following steps to prepare oral reports for any of your school subjects.

(1) Choose a suitable subject for your oral report.

If you are given a subject to report on, you have no problem of selection. If you are asked to choose your own subject, however, you can find subjects to talk about just as you find subjects to write about. You can use the methods discussed in Chapters 1 and 5 to find subjects for your talk: observation, brainstorming, clustering, and a writer's journal.

Choose a suitable subject, that is, one that is right for your report. Two ideas can guide your choice. First, focus on your interests and experiences. By discussing a subject you know about or are interested in, you will be able to speak confidently and enthusiastically. Your confidence and enthusiasm should also make your report more interesting to your audience.

Second, select a subject that will interest your audience. A report on how to identify types of clouds might bore some people, and a report on how to hang up your clothes would bore everybody. But a report on ways to earn money after school or on a new probe of a distant planet would be likely to interest many of your listeners.

EXERCISE 3. Choosing Suitable Subjects. Suppose that you must give an oral report that explains a subject to your classmates or supports an opinion. Using your interests and experiences and your audience's interests as guides, list at least five subjects that would be suitable for your report.

(2) Limit your subject to a narrow topic.

Once you have chosen a subject, you should limit it. That is, you should narrow your subject to a topic that can be covered reasonably well in the time you have for your report. Remember that the purpose of an oral report is to give information or an opinion about or to explain a particular subject to an audience. If the subject is too large, you will not be able to achieve this purpose.

To limit a subject to a narrow topic, divide it into smaller parts. Suppose you chose the subject "dinosaurs" for an oral report in science class. This subject is very broad—there is a great deal of information about dinosaurs that you could discuss.

To limit this broad subject, divide it into smaller parts: "how scientists identify dinosaur bones," "the climate when dinosaurs roamed the earth," and "places to see dinosaur exhibits in the United States." Notice how each topic focuses on a small part of the broad subject "dinosaurs." You could easily develop an oral report on any one of these limited topics. Depending on the time you have to present your report, sometimes you may need to continue narrowing your subject to even more limited topics. For more help on limiting subjects, see pages 17–19 in Chapter 1.

EXERCISE 4. Limiting Subjects. Each of the following subjects is too broad for an oral report. Limit each one to at least two narrow topics by dividing it into smaller parts. If your teacher prefers, you may instead limit the broad subjects you selected in Exercise 3. Keep the report's explanatory, informative, or persuasive purpose in mind.

1. Modern transportation
2. Great cities
3. Clothing
4. Community recreation
5. Women writers and artists

(3) Gather information for your report.

Your next step is to gather information for your report. There are at least three sources of information: (1) your own ideas and experiences, (2) other people who know something about your topic, and (3) books and periodicals. Consult all of these sources, and get as much information as you can.

The methods you use to gather information for your writing can also be used to gather information for your oral report. These methods include using a writer's journal, brainstorming, clustering, changing your point of view, and asking the *5 W-How?* questions. Refer to the information-gathering sections of Chapters 1 and 5 for more help. Be sure to write notes or brief summaries of the information you are gathering. You will use these notes to prepare your oral report.

EXERCISE 5. Gathering Information. Gather information for an oral report. Use any one of the narrow topics you developed in Exercise 4 on page 674, or use another narrow topic of your own. Be sure to write notes or brief summaries of the information you gather.

(4) Prepare an outline of your oral report.

From your notes, prepare an outline for your oral report. (Look at pages 151–53 in Chapter 5 to refresh your memory on how to prepare an outline.)

Suppose that you have decided to give a report in your science class on shooting stars. Having discovered that shooting stars are meteors, go to the library (see pages 613–25) and read articles on meteors in various reference works. Take notes and study them until the material is familiar to you. Prepare an outline from the notes. The outline might have four main headings:

I. Time: when meteors are seen
II. Nature: what the characteristics of meteors are
III. Place: where and why meteors are seen
IV. Fate: how speed, size, and course determine the final end of meteors

Under each heading, arrange your material in logical order. For some topics, you will give the major ideas first, with the details following them. For other topics—such as how to conduct an experiment—you will arrange ideas in chronological, or time, order. The logical order you use depends on your topic.

EXERCISE 6. Preparing an Outline. Using the information you have gathered on your topic, prepare an outline of your oral report.

(5) Write note cards to use as reminders when delivering your report.

It is not necessary to write out a speech word for word and memorize it. Instead, read and reread your material and your outline until they are so familiar that you need only an occasional reminder to help you talk freely about your topic.

Write these reminders on 3 × 5-inch note cards. Arrange the cards to correspond to the order of your outline. These cards make up the body of your oral report.

Reminder cards do not have to contain complete sentences; key words or phrases will do. Include the subheadings under the main idea on the card. Remember: These cards are not to be read aloud. They are meant to aid your memory.

A reminder card for a talk on shooting stars might look like this:

I. Time
  A. More after midnight than before
  B. More in the fall than in any other season
  C. Five per hour - 500 per minute

When giving your speech, you would start with this card. The items on the card are reminders. The main point tells what this part of the speech is about; the subheadings identify details to discuss. You might start your speech by saying:

> We are all familiar with shooting stars, or meteors. Often, on summer evenings, we have seen them streak across the dark sky. Most of us, however, are unaware that we can see more shooting stars after midnight than before and that we can see more in the fall of the year than in other seasons. Usually, about five shooting stars per hour can be sighted. However, when meteor showers occur, sometimes as many as five hundred meteors fall each minute. . . .

In some cases write full and exact details on a note card. If, for example, you want to give the ingredients of a recipe or the measurements of material needed to make a greenhouse, write out the full details on a note card.

You may want to use direct quotations from people whom you've interviewed. (Direct quotations will make your talk livelier and give it the weight of authority.) Write out quotations exactly, to avoid misquoting the person you interviewed.

If you are explaining a process to your audience, you may use charts and pictures. You may also want to use the chalkboard to write figures and dates or draw illustrations. A reminder card can tell you when to use these visual aids.

You may need only a few reminder cards if you know the material well—perhaps one for each main heading, plus one or two additional cards with details. Prepare as many cards as you think necessary.

As you speak, hold the cards in your hand. Glance at the top card, and talk about the subject on it. Then move this top card to the bottom, uncovering the next topic of your speech. Continue until you have spoken on every topic listed on your cards.

As you practice your speech, practice using your note cards also. You should be able to use them smoothly so that they do not distract your audience.

(6) Plan an interest-arousing introduction and a strong conclusion.

Write out an exciting first sentence, one that will arouse your audience's interest. Memorize this sentence so that you can look at your audience and speak the sentence naturally.

Similarly, work out a strong ending statement for your talk—a sentence or paragraph that ties your main ideas together. You may write this statement on a card. However, try not to spoil the effect of a good speech by reading the last part of it. (For more help in writing introductions and conclusions, see pages 155 and 157 in Chapter 5.)

EXERCISE 7. Completing an Oral Report. Prepare note cards and plan an introduction and a conclusion for a topic of your own. You may use the topic and information you have developed in previous exercises.

REVIEW EXERCISE A. Planning an Oral Report. Plan a short oral report on one of the following topics or on a topic of your own. Follow each of the steps explained in this chapter.

1. UFO's: reality or illusion?
2. Progress made to save the whales
3. What makes an airplane fly?
4. The monster called Sasquatch
5. Why —— is the best career
6. Family birthday customs in China
7. Can cars run on solar energy?
8. My choice for a personal hero
9. Programs I'd like to see on television
10. A hobby that earns money

DELIVERING AN ORAL REPORT

By planning your oral report, you have focused on the content of your speech: *what* you will explain to your audience about your topic. It is also important for you to consider *how* you will communicate this content to your audience. As you deliver your report, you need to think about nonverbal communication, pronunciation and enunciation, and expression.

Nonverbal Communication

People often communicate with unspoken, or nonverbal, signals. For example, someone who cannot talk may use sign language to converse. An umpire at a baseball game raises one thumb in the air to say, "You're out!"

Nonverbal communication—also called body language—is an important part of giving a speech. An audience will read, or interpret, a speaker's gestures and body movements in the same way that they will listen to words. Nonverbal signals should communicate exactly what a speaker wants to say.

30c. Learn how to use nonverbal signals as you speak.

You can improve your speech by using good posture and natural gestures.

Stand straight. Keep your weight on both feet. If you are sitting, place both feet squarely on the floor, and keep your back straight in the chair. Good posture communicates confidence.

Look at your audience as you speak. Glance around the room, and focus on the faces of your listeners. Eye contact is an effective way to hold the audience's attention. If you are using note cards, glance—but do not stare—at them as you speak. While speaking, try to smile occasionally. Smiling usually helps to relax the audience.

Keep gestures under control. Although it is natural to feel nervous about giving a talk, avoid nervous, random gestures, such as fidgeting with your hair or your note cards.

Think about what gestures may mean. Choose gestures that help rather than hinder your spoken words. Keeping your hands in your pockets, for example, suggests you are not well prepared to give the speech. Scratching your head suggests that you are not sure of what to say next. Avoid any gestures that detract from your message.

Pause for transition. A short pause between parts of your speech can be a nonverbal signal to your audience that you are about to introduce another topic. A pause can also give you a chance to take a deep breath and relax.

EXERCISE 8. Thinking About Nonverbal Communication. Write down at least five different forms of nonverbal communication that you notice at school, at home, and on television. Next to each form, write what you think it means. Prepare to discuss your list with your classmates.

Pronunciation and Enunciation

30d. Pronounce words correctly, and enunciate carefully.

Your audience must hear your speech plainly. An audience that must strain to hear becomes restless, and a talk that is not heard is wasted.

Take care to speak correctly and distinctly. In many cases the meaning of a word varies with the way it is pronounced. Remember that if your words are mispronounced or if you mumble or run words together, your audience will have difficulty in following you.

Vowel Sounds

Each vowel in our language may be pronounced in different ways. In some words vowels or combinations of vowels have sounds that you might not expect from the spelling. Make sure you use standard pronunciation for the following words:

despite	fertile	opaque	thorough
despot	genuine	suite	through
drought	mischievous	superfluous	vitamins

Consonant Sounds

Enunciation, the careful sounding of every syllable, is as important as pronunciation. Be especially careful with words that end in *-ing* and words that contain similar consonants—*p* and *b, m* and *n, t* and *th.*

For practice, say the following groups of words aloud, taking care to make the consonant sounds clearly distinguishable so that no one in the room mistakes the word you used.

d—t		*t—th*	
dent	tent	tank	thank
dare	tear	taught	thought
send	sent	tinker	thinker
bed	bet	ten	then
madder	matter	wetter	weather

b—p		*v—f*	
blank	plank	vendor	fender
bin	pin	veil	fail
bowl	pool	viewer	fewer
robe	rope	vault	fault
bunk	punk	veal	feel

EXERCISE 9. Practicing Vowel and Consonant Sounds. Practice reading aloud the following tongue twisters.

1. She said severely, "Son, shun the hot sun."
2. The tinker muttered thanks in a thin, throttled tone.
3. Jane's chuckles and antics jarred her ailing aunt and uncle.
4. The tank of thin tin was dank and dented.
5. His mother muttered that wetter weather would wash his wrath away.

Omitting Sounds

Take care not to omit sounds that belong in words. Here is a list of words frequently subject to nonstandard pronunciation.

arctic (not "artic")
asked (not "ask" or "ast")
exactly (not "zactly" or "exackly")
finally (not "finelly")
library (not "liberary" or "liberry")
mystery (not "mystry")
probably (not "probly" or "proely")

EXERCISE 10. Including Frequently Omitted Sounds. Use five of the words in the preceding list in sentences to be spoken aloud in class. Include all the sounds in each word.

Adding Sounds

Take care not to add sounds to a word—either inside a word or at the end. Do you add sounds to any of these words?

arithmetic (not "arith*uh*metic")
athlete (not "ath*uh*lete")
barbarous (not "barbar*i*ous")
chimney (not "chim*bl*ey" or "chim*uh*ney")
column (not "col*y*um")
corps (the *p* and *s* are silent)
height (ends in *t*, not *th*)
subtle (the *b* is silent)
umbrella (not "umbrell*er*" or "umb*e*rella")
vehicle (the *h* is silent)

EXERCISE 11. Practicing Frequently Mispronounced Words. Practice each of the preceding frequently mispronounced words. Choose a partner and take turns pronouncing each word twice. Do not add sounds to the words.

Changing Position of Sounds

Be careful not to change the position of a sound within a word. Sometimes such nonstandard pronunciation is based on the similarity of a word to another word that is almost like it in spelling. *Perspire* and *prescribe*, for example, have first syllables that are almost alike. *Perspire* is often mispronounced *prespire*, and *prescribe* is often mispronounced *perscribe*.

Here are some words whose sounds are often transposed.

apron (not "apern")
cavalry (not "calvary")
children (not "childern")
contradict (not "conterdict")
modern (not "modren")

EXERCISE 12. Pronouncing Words Correctly. Review all of the preceding lists. Be prepared to write words on the board and to pronounce them.

REVIEW EXERCISE B. Practicing Mispronounced Words. Here is a list of frequently mispronounced words. Be prepared to read them aloud to the class. Use the dictionary if you are not sure of the correct pronunciation.

admirable	hearth	partner
architect	hurtle	remembrance
champion	incomparable	scythe
favorite	infamous	superfluous
film	jubilant	theater
finale	mischievous	toward
gesture	museum	tremendous
handkerchief	ogre	yacht

Running Words Together

Another form of mispronouncing words is running them together when speaking. Telescoping words makes a wreckage of sense. Too often, for example, we run together the words of such a sentence as *I'm glad to meet you* into *Gladdameecha.*

EXERCISE 13. Pronouncing Words Distinctly. Translate the following mangled words into understandable language.

didja	gonna	woncha
thankslot	whereya	didjaseer
gimeyahan	lemmetry	wassamaddawichoo
wachasay	begyaparn	wyncha

Expression

30e. Learn to speak with expression and meaning.

We give meaning to language not only by our choice of words but also by the *feelings* we put into them—the tone of voice, the grouping of words, the emphasis, and the variety of tone. The tone and emphasis we use can greatly influence the meaning our words convey. Differing emphases on certain words or syllables can convey different meanings and emotions.

You can increase the effectiveness of your speech by giving attention to your tone of voice and to the amount and kind of expression you use.

EXERCISE 14. Speaking with Expression. Study these sentences before reading them aloud. The class will discuss how well each person expresses the different feelings.

1. You are taking care of a six-year-old. Tell her, "Susan, put that puppy down!"
   a. Say it as if the mother dog, growling furiously, is getting out of her box to leap at Susan.
   b. Say it as if you know Susan is going to plead with you to buy the puppy and you don't have the money.
2. Someone has just walked through your room with muddy feet, leaving tracks on the rug. You ask, "Kyle, did you just walk through my room?"
   a. Say it as if you have told him before to stay out of your room.
   b. Say it as if you have just cleaned your room.
3. You have started on a long walk when you discover that your small brother is walking behind you. You tell him, "Andy, go home and go to bed."
   a. Say it as if he is feverish with a bad cold, and you are very worried about him.
   b. Say it as if you've told him before that he could not come along.

EXERCISE 15. Changing Tone and Emphasis. See how many meanings you can put into the following remarks by varying your tone and the words you emphasize.

1. I'll go now, if you don't mind.
2. Bring all your money tomorrow.
3. I told you not to play with him.
4. You earned all that money yourself?
5. Did you say yes?

EVALUATING A SPEECH

30f. Learn to evaluate another person's report politely and constructively.

Often, after a student has given a report, the class is asked to evaluate the talk. The purpose of such an evaluation is to help the speaker improve by getting reactions. Another purpose is for the group to give recognition to the fine qualities as well as the weak points of the talk.

Be clear and definite. Always give reasons for your evaluation. Be generous with praise. If you find serious faults in a talk, begin by discussing strong points; then show how the talk might have been even stronger if certain faults had been corrected.

WEAK "I thought it was very interesting."
BETTER "His description of Mount Rainier was very interesting because his details were so sharp that I could almost see the mountain trail."

WEAK "I just couldn't follow the talk."
BETTER "Her explanation was clear and easy to follow except in a couple places. I wonder if she left out some steps."

Do your part in helping the class to establish an atmosphere of kind and constructive evaluation. When you evaluate a classmate's oral report, use the following guidelines.

1. Give praise when it is merited.
2. Avoid discussing points of little importance.
3. Point out strengths as well as weaknesses.
4. Be definite and constructive.

Your class may decide to use an evaluation sheet like the one on page 686 for evaluating speakers. After a talk each listener rates the speech, and the sheets are given to the speaker.

Knowing how to accept an evaluation is as important as knowing how to evaluate a speech. When your classmates evaluate your speech, keep the following points in mind:

1. Do not take the remarks personally. They are made to help you improve.
2. Study your weaknesses and take steps to improve them. Think about ways to make your strengths even stronger!
3. If evaluations are given orally, thank your classmates for their help.

EXERCISE 16. Delivering an Oral Report. Deliver the talk that you prepared in Exercise 7 or in Review Exercise A. Remember the importance of nonverbal communication, pronunciation and enunciation, and expression.

EXERCISE 17. Evaluating an Oral Report. Write a paragraph evaluating a talk someone has given in class. Use the following evaluation sheet as a basis for your evaluation, but also give your opinion of the talk as a whole.

EVALUATION SHEET

Speaker ______________________

Topic ______________________

Critic ______________________

	Very good	Good	Fair	Weak
Introduction				
Organization				
Conclusion				
Use of notes				
Posture				
Gestures				
Voice				
Pronunciation				
Other comments				

PARTICIPATING IN GROUP DISCUSSIONS

Another situation in which you can use your speaking skills is the group discussion. Throughout your schooling and later in adult life, you might often join with other people to discuss important issues or to explore solutions to problems. To discuss an issue or problem intelligently and fairly, you need to learn how to participate in a group discussion.

You already have some experience with participating in group discussions. You often converse with friends, teachers, and family members. These conversations are an informal, or unplanned, form of group discussion.

You may have already participated in group discussions that are more focused or planned than informal conversations. In school your teachers may have asked you to meet with classmates to discuss school-related topics, for example, ways to involve parents in tutoring or reasons for allowing students to help plan lunch menus.

Think about the group discussions you have participated in. Some may have had a discussion leader and an audience, but others may not. Some discussions may have gone very smoothly: the group discussed an issue or problem and came up with creative or useful ideas. In other cases, the group may have argued constantly and accomplished very little, so that the time spent together was wasted. To make a group discussion worthwhile and satisfying, you should learn several simple rules based on courtesy and common sense. By following these rules, you and your fellow group members should be able to express your ideas in an atmosphere of consideration and respect.

30g. Learn to participate in a group discussion.

(1) Be sure the discussion topic is manageable.

A discussion topic should be narrow, or limited, enough for the time you have available. Suppose your group wants to discuss ways to expand your school's extracurricular activities. If you only have thirty minutes for your discussion, you should divide this broad subject into smaller parts and discuss each one separately at a different time. For example, your group could instead discuss ways to expand after-school musical activities. This topic is more manageable for the time you have.

(2) Learn the duties of each participant in a group discussion.

A group discussion can have three different participants: a discussion leader, speakers or discussion members, and an audience. The *discussion leader* organizes and guides the discussion. He or she introduces the topic and the speakers, asks questions, keeps the speakers on the topic, and summarizes the discussion's main points. The *speakers* actively participate in the discussion. They should listen carefully and courteously to the other speakers, speak clearly, and stay on the topic. The *audience* should also listen quietly and carefully, and audience members can ask questions when the discussion leader invites them to do so.

(3) Prepare thoroughly for a discussion.

Whenever possible, prepare for the discussion beforehand. Gather information about the discussion topic by reading magazines, books, and encyclopedias and by discussing the topic with people who know about it. If each group member has spent some time studying and thinking about the topic, the discussion should proceed smoothly and intelligently.

(4) Be sure all group members have a chance to participate in the discussion.

Because some people feel more comfortable expressing their ideas in a group, it is always possible that one or two group members will dominate, or take over, the discussion. A group discussion should have *all* group members participating equally. Be sure that all members have a chance to express their ideas on the topic. Listening respectfully to each other should make group members feel comfortable sharing their ideas.

(5) Listen with an open mind.

Members of a group discussion who have different interests and experiences often express ideas and opinions that may be very different from your own. As you hear these different ideas, listen with an open mind. Remember that a group discussion should be a learning experience that allows an exchange of ideas.

(6) Focus on the discussion topic only.

With several people meeting together, it is easy to get off the subject and discuss ideas that are not related to the topic. Remember that your group is talking together for a specific purpose. Stay on the topic yourself, and politely remind your fellow group members to stay on the topic if the discussion begins to wander.

(7) Listen attentively to every speaker in the group.

Every speaker in your discussion group should have your full attention. Listen carefully to others as they express their ideas about the discussion topic, and do not chat with other members of the group while a speaker is talking. Rules of courtesy that apply to informal conversations apply to group discussions as well. Allow one speaker to talk at a time, and avoid shouting when group members disagree. Instead, calmly discuss your different ideas, and allow each person to contribute his or her views on the point of disagreement.

(8) Continue to improve your participation in group discussions.

It is likely that you will participate in group discussions throughout your schooling and your adult life. Learning to be a better participant in a group discussion is an important skill to work on. One way to improve is to focus on the preceding seven rules of courtesy and common sense for a group discussion.

Another way to improve is to ask yourself several questions after a group discussion. These questions will focus your attention on how well the discussion went and whether the group accomplished its purpose:

a. Did group members prepare beforehand? Did they study and think about the topic before the group met?
b. Did all group members contribute in some way to the discussion?
c. Did all group members understand and fulfill their role in the discussion?
d. Did the group stay on the discussion topic?

e. Did group members show respect and courtesy toward one another?

You and the group members should ask these questions after your discussion. Try to answer *yes* to each one, and improve how you participate in group discussions in the future.

EXERCISE 18. Participating in a Group Discussion. Join a discussion group assigned by your teacher, or form a discussion group with three or four classmates. Select one of the following topics or a topic of your own, and discuss it in the time period your teacher assigns. Remember that your group has a specific purpose to accomplish during this time. Your teacher may ask you to select a discussion leader.

1. Three reasons for allowing students to help establish school rules
2. Our class's most memorable contributions to school life
3. How to raise money for school projects without having bake sales or carwashes
4. A famous man and a famous woman that young people can respect
5. Three things you can do to contribute to a happy family life

EXERCISE 19. Evaluating a Group Discussion. After your group completes its discussion in Exercise 18, evaluate your group's work. Use the five questions on pages 689–90 to evaluate your discussion, and be prepared to discuss your evaluation in class.

EXERCISE 20. Evaluating a Group Discussion You Observe. Observe a group discussion—one your classmates are having or one on a television news program. Use the five questions on pages 689–90 to evaluate what you observe. Be prepared to explain whether the group accomplished its purpose and to discuss how the group could have improved its work together.

CHAPTER 31

Listening

IMPROVING YOUR LISTENING

Listening well is important. In school, at home, and among friends, you can learn more by listening well to others.

LISTENING TO MEDIA

You may spend many hours each week watching television, going to the movies, and listening to the radio. It is good to enjoy such entertainment, but you owe it to yourself to develop a critical appreciation of what you see and hear.

31a. Choose radio programs, television programs, and movies intelligently.

You can learn a great deal from radio, television, and movies if you plan ahead and decide what you want to see and hear. Newspaper reviews, suggestions from friends, and your own interests should guide your choice of these media.

EXERCISE 1. Identifying Preferences for Particular Movies and Radio and Television Programs. Look at the television, radio, and movie schedules for the next week. Make a list of the shows you want to see or hear. Next to each show, give the reason for your interest. In class, compare your list with others. Did you list the same shows? Do you have the same reasons?

LISTENING TO INSTRUCTIONS

A large part of what we listen to is informative. As students, much of your listening is done for the purpose of gaining information.

31b. Listen alertly to directions and class assignments.

You can save time and avoid errors by listening carefully to directions. If the directions are lengthy, jot down each step on a piece of paper. Do not interrupt with questions while the directions are being given. Wait, and ask your questions when the speaker has finished. Be sure that you have noted *all* the instructions and have understood them.

EXERCISE 2. Following Oral Directions. Someone in the class will read the following directions aloud. See if you can follow the directions after hearing them.

> Take out a piece of paper and write your name in the upper left-hand corner. Beneath your name write the day you were born.
>
> Draw a line down the middle of the page. Mark the left column with the letter *A* and the right column with the letter *B*. In column A, write the months of the year that begin with the letter *J*. In column B, write the days of the week that begin with the letter *T*. Compare the lists. If column B has more words, fold your paper in half.

LISTENING TO OTHERS

31c. Listen to talks and oral reports with an open mind.

The basis of good listening is *interest* and *purpose*. You listen very attentively to something that interests you. You also listen attentively to, and remember vividly, information that will serve a purpose that you consider important.

When listening to a talk, ask, *How can this information be of real help to me?* If you determine ways in which the content is important to you, listening and remembering will be easier.

Suppose you are listening to a talk on how a particular club serves the community. You may not be very interested. The club has staged a benefit dance to buy a record player and records for a local hospital. To you, this is of no immediate concern. If you pay attention, however, you may discover that the club sponsors trips for students or that it compiles job opportunities for summer employment.

Sometimes you know what you are listening for—as when you listen to directions or assignments. At other times you should keep an alert, open mind—you may learn something unexpectedly useful.

EXERCISE 3. Determining Purposes for Listening. Suppose the following people spoke in assembly programs at your school. What would be your purpose in listening to each?

1. The manager of a local department store talks on "How to Tell a Bargain from a Rip-off."
2. A graduate of your school gives a talk on two years spent with the Peace Corps in South America.
3. A professional guitarist speaks on "What to Listen for in Music," illustrating points on the guitar.
4. The head of a research laboratory gives a talk on new ways of using solar energy.

31d. Listen actively.

If you intend to use the information you are hearing, you must be alert to select the ideas that you can use and retain them so clearly that you will remember them later when you need them.

(1) Listen for the speaker's purpose.

Sometimes, while listening to a talk, you want to know the speaker's intention. Is the speaker trying to persuade you to do something? Are you expected to agree or disagree with the speaker? In such situations, concentrate on grasping the speaker's point of view. Ask yourself why the speaker wants you to do something or why the speaker holds certain opinions.

(2) Listen for a few main ideas.

Listen to understand the *main points* of the speech: the reasons the speaker gives for taking action or the ideas with which the speaker supports one side of an issue. Try to understand and remember each main idea presented.

When you are listening for the main ideas of a speech, pay special attention to the start and finish of the talk. A speaker's introduction often presents the main points that will be developed, and the conclusion often sums them up. An able speaker emphasizes important ideas so that you can easily recognize them.

EXERCISE 4. Listening for Main Ideas. Select six short news stories in a newspaper. Read each story aloud. Listeners will write down, in their own words, the main idea of each story. Compare the answers.

(3) Listen for specific details.

On some occasions your purpose in listening to a talk will be to get specific details. Suppose, for example, that you are listening to a talk on how to start a model airplane engine or how to tell edible mushrooms from poisonous ones. A general idea of the method will not be sufficient; you will want exact details.

EXERCISE 5. Listening for Specific Details. Your teacher will read aloud a set of instructions or directions. When the teacher has finished, write the details of the instructions or directions from memory. Then the teacher will reread the instructions and ask you to check the accuracy of what you remembered.

(4) Evaluate nonverbal signals such as gestures.

A speaker may use gestures for emphasis. Some of these gestures may be appropriate; for example, a comedian will often rely on gestures to draw laughs. Other gestures may be inappropriate; for example, nervous speakers will often wave one or both hands in the air as they speak. The best gestures add to a speech and communicate nonverbally what the speaker is trying to say.

EXERCISE 6. Evaluating Nonverbal Signals. Watch a popular comedian or other personality speaking. Notice how gestures are used. Describe these gestures to your classmates and indicate what they mean to you.

31e. Listen critically. Distinguish fact from opinion. Judge whether statements are backed up by evidence from dependable sources.

When you listen to a speaker, you do not wish to be fooled by trickery or unreliable sources of information. Ask yourself questions as you listen: Is this statement a fact or an opinion? If the speaker is presenting it as a fact, is it backed up with proof from a dependable source or a trustworthy expert? Is the speaker talking from experience?

Know the difference between fact and opinion. A *fact* is a statement that can be proved true or false, such as, "Winter temperatures averaged 12° Celsius this year." An *opinion* is a statement that cannot be proved true or false, such as, "It feels colder this winter than last."

Study the following examples. Can you see why two are opinions and two are facts?

OPINION The library facilities in this school are inadequate.
FACT There are 10 library books available for the assignment, but 50 students must do the assignment at once.

OPINION The referee is being unfair to our players!
FACT The referee has given our players three penalties in the last five minutes.

EXERCISE 7. Distinquishing Between Fact and Opinion. If you heard the following statements, would you accept them as fact or interpret them as opinion? After each number on your paper, write *fact* if you think the statement would be a fact or *opinion* if you think it would be an opinion. Be prepared to explain each choice.

1. We ought to irrigate our desert lands with fresh water made from sea water.
2. A tornado in Kansas today wrecked fifty homes.
3. Sunbathing is harmful.
4. Stanford beat Oregon at football today, 28 to 14.
5. There's no place like home.
6. TV comedies are all alike.
7. Mrs. Currier gives too much homework.
8. American cars give the best value among low-priced compacts.
9. The orchestra has improved greatly this year.
10. Mrs. Townsend has never been introduced to my family.

INDEX

Index

A

B

INDEX

C

INDEX

INDEX

D

F

G

H

I

N

O

P

INDEX

S

INDEX

T

U

V

W

Z

3
L 4
M 5
N 6
O 7
P 8
Q 9